Contents

THE JOURNAL OF INDUSTRIAL ECONOMICS

VOLUME XXXVI
1987–88

ISSN 0022–1821

BASIL BLACKWELL
OXFORD

CONTENTS

VOLUME XXXVI

Number 1, September 1987

STANLEY I. ORNSTEIN and DOMINIQUE M. HANSSENS
Resale Price Maintenance: Output Increasing or Restricting? The Case of Distilled Spirits in the United States 1

STEVEN C. SALOP and DAVID T. SCHEFFMAN
Cost-Raising Strategies 19

LOUIS MAKOWSKI
Are 'Rational Conjectures' Rational? 35

JOHN R. SCHROETER, SCOTT L. SMITH and STEVEN R. COX
Advertising and Competition in Routine Legal Service Markets: An Empirical Investigation 49

ANDREW J. CHALK
Market Forces and Commercial Aircraft Safety 61

ELIZABETH J. JENSEN
Research Expenditures and the Discovery of New Drugs 83

Short Articles and Notes

FRANK R. LICHTENBERG
The Effect of Government Funding on Private Industrial Research and Development: A Re-assessment 97

GEOFFREY S. ROTHWELL and KELLY A. EASTMAN
A Note on Allowed and Realized Rates of Return of the US Electric Utility Industry 105

Number 2, December 1987

J. A. KAY and C. N. MORRIS
The Economic Efficiency of Sunday Trading Restrictions 113

AVNER SHAKED and JOHN SUTTON
Product Differentiation and Industrial Structure 131

DAVID J. RAVENSCRAFT and F. M. SCHERER
Life After Takeover 147

STEVEN G. LANNING
Costs of Maintaining a Cartel 157

MARVIN B. LIEBERMAN
Market Growth, Economies of Scale, and Capacity Expansion in the Chemical Processing Industries 175

JOHN T. SCOTT and GEORGE PASCOE
Purposive Diversification of R & D in Manufacturing 193

SWATI BHATT
Strategic Product Choice in Differentiated Markets 207
MARCEL BOYER and MICHEL MOREAUX
On Stackelberg Equilibria with Differentiated Products: The Critical Role of the Strategy Space 217
JONG SEOK KIM
Optimal Price-Quality Schedules and Sustainability 231

Short Articles and Notes
ANDRÉ DE PALMA, VICTOR GINSBURGH and JACQUES-FRANÇOIS THISSE
On Existence of Location Equilibria in the 3-Firm Hotelling Problem 245
ALFRED KLEINKNECHT
Measuring R&D in Small Firms: How Much Are We Missing? 253

Number 3, March 1988

GIACOMO BONANNO and JOHN VICKERS
Vertical Separation 257
FREDERICK HARRIS
Testable Competing Hypotheses from Structure-Performance Theory: Efficient Structure Versus Market Power 267
ERIC RASMUSEN
Entry for Buyout 281
THOMAS W. ROSS
Brand Information and Price 301
MASAHIRO ABIRU
Vertical Integration, Variable Proportions and Successive Oligopolies 315
RALPH D. SANDLER
Market Share Instability in Commercial Airline Markets and the Impact of Deregulation 327
ANNE E. PRESTON
The Effects of Property Rights on Labor Costs of Nonprofit Firms: an Application to the Day Care Industry 337

Short Notes and Articles
THOMAS VON UNGERN-STERNBERG
Cartel Stability in Sealed Bid Second Price Auctions 351
THOMAS G. PARRY
The Multinational Enterprise and Restrictive Conditions in International Technology Transfer: Some New Australian Evidence 359

Number 4, June 1988

CHRISTOPHER BLISS
A Theory of Retail Pricing 375

RONALD BEWLEY and DENZIL G. FIEBIG
Estimation of Price Elasticities for an International Telephone Demand Model 393

DAVID BESANKO, SHABTAI DONNENFELD and LAWRENCE J. WHITE
The Multiproduct Firm, Quality Choice, and Regulation 411

X. MARTINEZ-GIRALT and D. J. NEVEN
Can Price Competition Dominate Market Segmentation? 431

J. C. H. JONES and D. G. FERGUSON
Location and Survival in the National Hockey League 443

ARAKEL BEDROSSIAN and DEMETRIOS MOSCHOS
Industrial Structure, Concentration and the Speed of Price Adjustment 459

Short Articles and Notes

VICTOR GINSBURGH and PHILIPPE MICHEL
Adjustment Costs, Concentration and Price Behaviour 477

Set in Monophoto Times by Advanced Filmsetters (Glasgow) Ltd
Printed and Bound in Great Britain by Whitstable Litho, Kent

THE JOURNAL OF INDUSTRIAL ECONOMICS

Volume XXXVI SEPTEMBER 1987 No. 1

STANLEY I. ORNSTEIN and DOMINIQUE M. HANSSENS
Resale Price Maintenance: Output Increasing or Restricting? The Case of Distilled Spirits in the United States 1
STEVEN C. SALOP and DAVID T. SCHEFFMAN
Cost-Raising Strategies 19
LOUIS MAKOWSKI
Are 'Rational Conjectures' Rational? 35
JOHN R. SCHROETER, SCOTT L. SMITH and STEVEN R. COX
Advertising and Competition in Routine Legal Service Markets: An Empirical Investigation 49
ANDREW J. CHALK
Market Forces and Commercial Aircraft Safety 61
ELIZABETH J. JENSEN
Research Expenditures and the Discovery of New Drugs 83

Short Articles and Notes
FRANK R. LICHTENBERG
The Effect of Government Funding on Private Industrial Research and Development: A Re-assessment 97
GEOFFREY S. ROTHWELL and KELLY A. EASTMAN
A Note on Allowed and Realized Rates of Return of the US Electric Utility Industry 105

ISSN 0022-1821
BASIL BLACKWELL OXFORD ENGLAND

THE JOURNAL OF INDUSTRIAL ECONOMICS 0022-1821 $2.00
Volume XXXVI September 1987 No. 1

RESALE PRICE MAINTENANCE: OUTPUT INCREASING OR RESTRICTING? THE CASE OF DISTILLED SPIRITS IN THE UNITED STATES*

STANLEY I. ORNSTEIN AND DOMINIQUE M. HANSSENS

Theories of resale price maintenance (RPM) differ strongly on the pro- and anticompetitive effects of RPM. There are few tests of the welfare gains or losses from RPM in industry case studies. This paper tests RPM's welfare effects in the retail sale of distilled spirits in the US. Using regression analysis to estimate demand, comparing liquor store license values over time, and analyzing political contributions, the study finds that efficiency arguments for RPM are unsupported, with RPM leading to a reduction in distilled spirits consumption. Evidence shows substantial wealth transfers from consumers to retail liquor store owners due to RPM.

I. INTRODUCTION

PROPONENTS OF resale price maintenance (RPM) argue that it promotes efficiency by protecting against free riding on both product specific and storewide retailer services. Opponents of RPM argue that it fosters manufacturer and retailer cartels, induces wasteful expenditures on marketing, and inhibits the adoption of more efficient distribution networks.[1] The debate ranges widely over such issues as the welfare effects of RPM, alternative theories of RPM, the likelihood of cartelization, and whether the many efficiency explanations of RPM are credibly supported.

Largely missing in the debate are empirical tests of alternative theories of RPM, such as tests of efficiency gains versus monopoly welfare losses. This paper offers some empirical tests of RPM, focusing on a major area of conflict: whether RPM serves to protect retailer special services or to effect a retailer cartel. These theories are tested in a study of distilled spirits at the retail level in the US. The findings show that the more prominently mentioned efficiency arguments lack logical plausibility in the retail sale of distilled spirits and, more importantly, lack empirical support. Contrary to efficiency arguments, we find that RPM led to a reduction in consumption and thus to a potential monopoly welfare loss. Evidence shows that rent

* This study was supported by the California Department of Alcohol and Drug Abuse and the Research Program in Competition and Business Policy, Graduate School of Management, UCLA. The authors are grateful to Kenneth Heyer, Clement Krouse, Alfred Nicols, Larry White, and two referees for helpful comments.

[1] The vast literature on RPM is exhaustively reviewed in Overstreet [1983]. Recent versions of the debate are in Comanor and Kirkwood [1985], Marvel [1985], Overstreet and Fisher [1985], Sharp [1985], and White [1985].

seeking motivated the continuation of RPM in the case of liquor stores and resulted in a substantial wealth transfer from consumers to retail store owners.

II. RPM: OUTPUT INCREASING OR RESTRICTING?

II(i). *Efficiency theories of RPM*

The product-specific special service theory of Telser [1960] has been found wanting in recent years. For many recent examples of products using RPM, such as underwear, raincoats, automobile parts, and shoes, no special service requirements can be readily identified (Overstreet [1983]). Attempting to remedy this, recent papers expand the special service theory from product-specific to storewide services. Marvel and McCafferty [1984] argue that dealers with established reputations act as agents for consumers, screening out low quality goods and selecting high style goods. RPM, coupled with sellers' refusal to sell to low quality stores, blocks free riding on dealer reputation and ensures product adoption by the optimal distribution network. Klein and Murphy [1986] posit that RPM provides an income premium to dealers that ensures compliance with manufacturer wishes owing to the threat of dealer termination. Any behavior that affects product quality or detracts from maximizing manufacturer sales is said to be controllable by RPM. Similar arguments are offered by Goldberg [1984], who adds buying shelf space to RPM's purposes.

II(ii). *Testing for efficiency effects*

Once service theories become storewide and not product-specific, they are far more difficult to test as sources of efficiency gains. Given the multitude of services offered by retailers, RPM under storewide theories can always be rationalized as pro-competitive. However, a simple enumeration of potential services offered by retailers is not convincing, since by themselves they indicate neither changes in demand nor in consumer welfare.

Estimating RPM's effects on output is a possible test of efficiencies. RPM-induced consumer benefits should shift demand outward or reduce price elasticity at existing output levels. Our test will be output changes. Such changes are at the heart of all efficiency theories of RPM and can be clearly contrasted with rent seeking output restrictions.[2]

[2] The welfare implications of an output increase for a single producer with RPM is in dispute. It is theoretically possible for RPM to induce an increase in output but nevertheless decrease welfare. See Comanor [1985], Marvel [1985], Scherer [1983], Mathewson and Winter [1983], and White [1985]. But an RPM-induced decrease in output should imply a decrease in welfare in most cases.

II(iii). *RPM and rent seeking*

Two conditions signal potential competitive problems: industrywide RPM and government mandated RPM. If RPM fails to increase a manufacturer's output, that is largely his problem. When output fails to increase under industrywide RPM, it suggests possible anticompetitive behavior: either a manufacturer or retailer cartel (Ornstein [1985]). Industrywide RPM instituted by manufacturers is, however, also consistent with the attainment of efficiencies by all manufacturers, who may share a common distribution technology. Examples of common firm efficiencies include guarding against product quality degradation (e.g., ethical drugs and fast food franchisees), seeking specialized outlets or an optimal number of outlets (e.g., designer label products), or gaining economies of scale in distribution (e.g., soft drinks and beer). In contrast, when there are broad differences in market segments, product quality, channels of distribution, and outlet types, industrywide RPM to effect efficiencies is suspect.

The use of government by private interests to administer mandatory, industrywide RPM raises further suspicions. Government imposed market restrictions are an invitation to rent seeking. They provide retailers and politicians with potential wealth gains if (along with increased price) entry and various forms of nonprice competition, such as advertising and promotions, tie-in sales, and hours of sale, are controlled.

The special interest group behind industrywide, government administered RPM is important in assessing its anticompetitive potential. As just noted, industrywide RPM generated by manufacturers may be due to efficiencies common to all firms in an industry. But to make RPM effective, it must be mandatory on all retailers. Further, government enforcement may minimize overall enforcement costs. But, in turn, this may provide the opportunity for retailer rent seeking. Hence, while the origin of RPM may be efficiency based, its government administration may subsequently be captured by rent seekers. Thus, in practice, the distinction between voluntary and mandatory RPM instituted by manufacturers can become blurred. Mandatory RPM sought by retailers is less ambiguous: it is almost always for anticompetitive purposes. Identifying the origins of RPM or who controls it in a state is, however, a difficult task.

III. EFFICIENCIES AND THE SALE OF DISTILLED SPIRITS

III(i). *Analyzing efficiencies*

Where RPM exists in the sale of distilled spirits, it is mandatory and industrywide (Distilled Spirits Council of the United States [1974]). However, the commonly mentioned RPM efficiencies for distilled spirits—product specific and store wide services, product quality preservation, and ensuring an optimal distribution network—are not plausible explanations. Product specific information, such as taste and quality, is available through low cost direct experience. Product information and brand image through advertising comes primarily from manufacturers (*Liquor Handbook* [1979]). Retail distilled spirits advertising consists almost exclusively of price advertising.

Retail liquor stores compete on numerous nonprice grounds, such as hours of sale, brands available, shopping convenience, and so forth. Storewide services of this nature are not subject to free riding, nor do they require RPM to assure their provision. Stores seeking repeat purchase customers have sufficient incentives to provide courtesy, cleanliness, etc. All stores have an incentive to carry the leading brands, with or without RPM, and to carry minor brands according to customer tastes.

Product quality is assured without RPM. Products are sold under Federal seal with high penalties for tampering. Degrading a product entails loss of a license to sell, which is a prohibitive cost. Product quality is further assured before products reach retailers by manufacturer brand name capital, federal bottle labeling laws, and pure food and beverage laws.

A more plausible RPM efficiency explanation in this case is to establish an optimal distribution network (Gould and Preston [1965]; Gallini and Winter [1983]). By restricting price discounting, RPM results in a relatively large number of small outlets, restrained in number by retail economies of scale and state limitations on number of licenses. Over time, however, economies of scale in distribution and retailing, and lower consumer shopping costs will favor larger, more efficient stores, or chain operations. Economies of scale in retailing can come from quantity discounts, chain store advertising, and, with higher sales volume, more efficient use of buildings and fixtures. As economies grow, RPM will block such gains, to the detriment of manufacturers. However, eliminating RPM will lower the value of retail liquor licenses, so retail trade associations will fight its repeal.

Although we are skeptical of efficiency claims for RPM in the sale of distilled spirits,[3] we recognize that the importance of services, such as brand coverage (analogous to book sales, where RPM was long used), store image, and so forth is arguable. This highlights the need for empirical testing.

III(ii). *Testing for efficiencies*

Four tests of RPM's efficiency effects are presented: a consumption test on whether RPM increases or decreases consumption; a distribution network test of RPM's relationship to retail economies of scale; a license value test of the effect of RPM on liquor store license values; and a political contribution test of whether contributions by special alcohol interests are consistent with rent seeking or efficiency promotion.

[3] Our arguments apply only to distilled spirits. Beer and wine may require services for maintaining product quality or providing information.

Consumption test. If RPM has demand-increasing effects, it should be reflected in higher *per capita* consumption in RPM states. Conversely, if RPM is part of rent seeking via alcohol control laws, it should be associated with lower *per capita* consumption.

We estimated a demand equation to test the impact of RPM on distilled spirits consumption across all license states for the period 1974–1978 (Ornstein and Hanssens [1985]).[4] The demand equation includes economic, socio-demographic, and legal control variables identified in prior demand estimation studies on distilled spirits (Ornstein [1980]). The model estimated did not include a supply equation since costs, absent transportation costs, are relatively constant across states. Spirits are produced in a few states and shipped nationwide, or they are imported. More importantly, roughly three-quarters of all states have most-favored-nation laws for spirits, requiring spirits manufacturers to sell to wholesalers at the lowest price sold in any other state. Excise taxes do differ across states, but they are included in the price variable.

Using a pooled time-series, cross-section sample of 185 observations, regression results (with t-values in parentheses) for RPM and other key explanatory variables of *per capita* consumption are:[5]

$$\underset{\textit{consumption}}{\textit{Per capita}} = \underset{(0.70)}{0.627} - \underset{(2.45)}{0.081}\,\text{RPM} - \underset{(3.94)}{0.614}\,\textit{Price of spirits}$$

$$+\underset{(4.67)}{0.042}\,\textit{Lowest adjacent state price} + \underset{(3.92)}{0.576}\,\textit{Income per capita}$$

$$+\underset{(13.0)}{0.273}\,\textit{Tourism} \qquad R^2 = 0.89$$

The results show that the presence of RPM is related to a *decrease* in *per capita* consumption of about 8 percent. This is diametrically opposite to efficiency explanations for RPM in spirits.

Distribution network test. The optimal distribution network theory is weakened if RPM forecloses economies of scale. A crude indicator of scale effects comes from comparing the population served by off-sale liquor outlets

[4] In the US distilled spirits are sold under either private license or state monopoly ownership.

[5] The variables are measured as follows: state consumption in gallons per 14 years of age and older; RPM is a dummy variable equal to one if present and zero otherwise; price is a weighted average of eight leading brands in each state; adjacent state price is the ratio of lowest adjacent state price to own state price, divided by own state size; income is real *per capita* state income; and tourism is annual state payroll in hotels, motels, and tourist courts divided by total state payroll. The full model is not reported to save space but it included variables for urbanization; age distribution of the population; Christian religious affiliation; mean temperature; minimum legal drinking age; number of outlets; bans on billboard advertising, price advertising, and novelty-give aways; and the legality of Sunday sales, sales in drug stores and sales in grocery stores. The measure of consumption is debatable. If RPM improves the quality mix of consumption, then quality-adjusted consumption may be higher in RPM states. Unfortunately, the data do not allow adjustments for quality changes.

in RPM and non-RPM states. Using our sample, the average number of people per off-premise outlet in ten non-RPM states in 1978 was 3309, while in seven RPM states it was 2422. RPM appears to have blocked the attainment of scale economies in liquor retailing.[6] This finding is also consistent with evidence on drug stores, where RPM was widely used. The average size of drug stores in RPM states in 1963 was significantly smaller than drug stores in non-RPM states (Marvel and McCafferty [1984]).

License value test. If RPM exists because of retailer rent seeking, an end to RPM would result in declining liquor store license values. Of course, if RPM exists for efficiency reasons its loss would also lower license values as industry sales decline. However, the loss should be less in the latter case since retailers would be affected more or less equally. More importantly, substitute distribution practices to protect services, such as selective dealer termination, would arise, preserving license values. If retailer rent seeking is the goal, there are no good substitutes for RPM. The average license values would fall as more efficient retailers captured sales from less efficient outlets.

We tested RPM's effect in a regression explaining license values by county in California before and after RPM was repealed in 1978. Average license values by county are available from 1970–1977, but were not collected annually after 1977. Fortunately, a special survey was conducted in 1984. Hence, the test is based on continuous annual data from 1970 to 1977, plus data for 1984. All counties with 100 000 population or above were used in order to minimize outliers due to only a few license exchanges, resulting in a sample of 31 counties.

License values in real terms are explained by the number of persons per license, real *per capita* income, a time trend variable, and a dummy variable for 1984 equal to one and representing the absence of RPM.[7] A proxy for urbanization was also tried, but the results were unstable due to collinearity and are not reported.

License values should be positively related to persons per license and to *per capita* income. The trend variable is included to account for shifts in consumer tastes toward distilled spirits. *Per capita* consumption of distilled spirits in California increased 9 percent from 1970 to 1979 but declined by 17 percent from 1980 to 1985. License values likely fell as a result. The dummy variable should be negative owing to the absence of RPM.

A logarithmic model provided the best fit on the pooled cross-section time-series data base. A Chow test for parameter homogeneity failed, resulting in

[6] These figures are only suggestive since the number of outlets in a state is influenced by factors besides economies of scale, many of which do not lend themselves to more formal regression analysis (Kiholm-Smith [1982]). The full population of license states could not be used since in many cases a single license provides for both on- and off-premises sales.

[7] License values and number of licenses by county were provided by the California Department of Alcoholic Beverage Control. Population, income, and the CPI for California came from the *California Statistical Abstract, 1984*.

TABLE I
REGRESSIONS EXPLAINING OFF-SALE GENERAL LICENSE VALUES IN CALIFORNIA COUNTIES

	Equations	
	VC	*OLSDV*
Intercept	13.43	
	(6.13)	
Persons per License	1.42	1.78
	(10.13)	(7.15)
Real Per Capita Income	0.44	0.62
	(2.07)	(2.33)
Time	−2.02	−2.61
	(−3.52)	(−3.94)
Year 1984	−0.29	−0.26
	(−3.74)	(−3.21)
R^2	n.a.	0.85
N	279	279

t-value in parentheses.

the use of variance components (VC) and, alternatively, OLS with dummy variables for each county (OLSDV).

The results, seen in Table I, are consistent with expectations. Persons per license and *per capita* income are positively related to license values. The trend variable is negative, reflecting the decline in distilled spirits consumption. Most importantly, the repeal of RPM had a significant negative impact on license values. The reduction in license values due to the absence of RPM is estimated to be between 23 and 25 percent (Halvorsen and Palmquist [1980]). This finding is consistent with RPM being used to establish supra-competitive retail prices.

Political contributions test. If the decline in license values represents a monopoly rent loss to retailers and not a demand reduction owing to a loss of services, it should be reflected in contrasting lobbying efforts of manufacturers and retailers. Indeed, the history of state alcohol regulation presents a classic example of the interest group theory of regulation. Rents are created by legislation, and politicians allocate these rents across groups to maximize voter support (Becker [1983]). The nature of alcohol regulations in each state, such as the level of taxes, bans on advertising, and bans on price competition, reflect the political strength of opposing interests by retailers, wholesalers, manufacturers, and temperance groups (Kiholm-Smith [1982]). Anticompetitive restrictions sought by retailers conflict with manufacturer goals of sales increases and should be reflected in opposing lobbying efforts.

Lobbying expenditures and campaign contributions in primary and general elections in California are given in Table II. These figures understate total contributions since they do not include all alcohol interests, such as

TABLE II
CAMPAIGN AND LOBBYING EXPENDITURES (US $) BY ALCOHOL INDUSTRY GROUPS IN CALIFORNIA

	1975–76	*1977–78*	*1979–80*	*1983–84*
Anheuser–Busch	0	5 150	24 456	238 765
California Beer Wholesalers Association	52 995	94 312	134 937	214 790
California Retail Liquor Dealers Association	154 029	133 665	65 945	55 484
California Association of Winegrape Growers	0	9 739	26 756	62 264
Coors Brewing Co.	0	17 000	21 968	0
Distilled Spirits Council of the US	12 090	12 195	21 275	79 024
E & J Gallo Wine Co.	63 143	54 637	98 949	0
Malt Beverage Industry Welfare Fund	32 880	61 998	51 950	0
Miller Brewing Co.	0	11 100	0	109 213
Wine & Spirits Wholesalers of California	75 050	114 440	146 163	233 235
Wine Institute	81 133	124 318	133 074	300 860
Total Expenditures	471 320	638 554	723 473	1 293 635

Sources: Derived from State of California, Fair Political Practices Commission, *A Report on Lobbying*, 1976, 1978, and 1980; State of California, Fair Political Practices Commission, *Campaign Contribution and Spending Report*, Primary and General Elections for 1976, 1978, and 1980; and, State of California, Fair Political Practices Commission, *Report on Lobbying 1983–1984*.

restaurants, hotels, and affiliated labor unions. They also exclude other often sizeable expenditures, such as paying politicians for speeches or hiring a politician's law firm. The figures are consistent with RPM's support coming from retailers and not from manufacturers. Expenditures increased during the period covered for almost all special interests. The contributions of wine and spirits wholesalers rose sharply, as did those of spirits manufacturers through their trade arm, the Distilled Spirits Council of the US. But expenditures of the Retail Liquor Dealers Association, which clearly had the greatest stake in RPM, were quite different. Retail liquor dealers' expenditures declined over the period and dramatically so after 1978 when RPM on distilled spirits was repealed by the California Supreme Court. In real terms, retail liquor dealers contributions fell more than five-fold, from $154 029 in 1975–76 to $29 517 in 1983–84. Hence, it appears quite likely that the bulk of the dealers' contributions in the 1970s were to support the continuance of RPM. These findings support the view that the fall in license values reflects a loss in monopoly rents, not in services to consumers.

IV. MONOPOLY WELFARE LOSSES

Given the finding of output restriction, it is instructive to estimate the size of the potential monopoly welfare loss. All estimates of monopoly welfare losses are controversial because of difficulties in measuring price elasticity and monopoly price increases and because of their static nature (Scherer [1980]; Rice and Ulen [1981]). Nonetheless, some welfare loss estimates are offered, rough as they may be, since informed public policy requires evidence when analyzing the costs and benefits of regulations.

IV(i). *A simple welfare model of control laws*

Estimating welfare changes from restricted consumption requires examining the trade-off between reduced social costs from lower drinking and monopoly welfare losses generated by anticompetitive control laws. A model is presented in Figure 1. Assume demand D for a hypothetical alcoholic beverage industry, along with marginal private costs, MC_p, and marginal private plus social costs, MC_{ps}. Under competitive conditions price is P_1 and output is Q_1, resulting in a social loss of P_2UVP_1. The socially optimal price P_2 assumes that each drinker contributes to the negative externalities of drinking in direct proportion to the amount purchased and enforcement costs are zero. However, internalizing social costs at P_2 is unlikely. Drinker contribution to

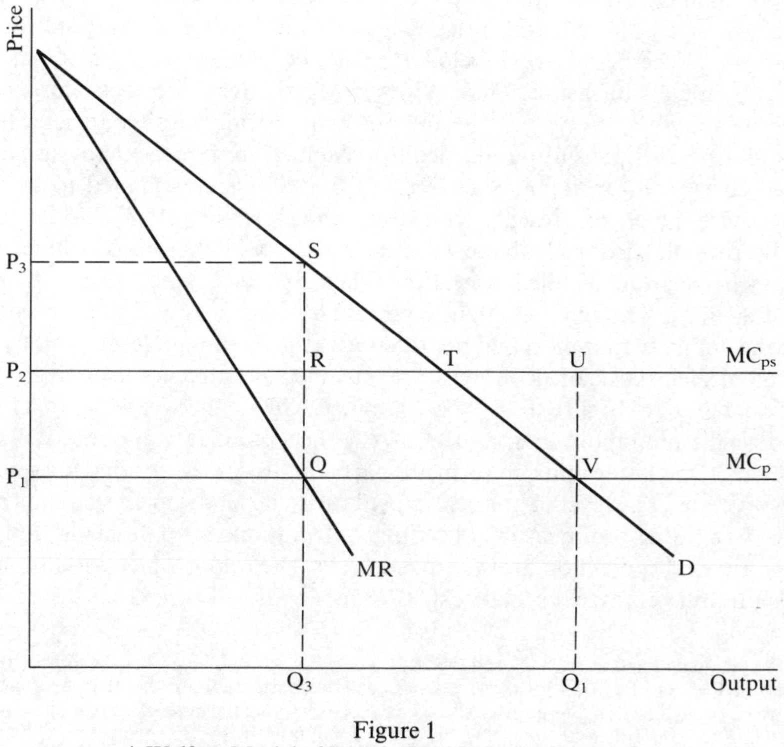

Figure 1
A Welfare Model of Restrictive Alcohol Consumption

negative externalities is not necessarily in direct proportion to purchases. Alcohol purchases are sometimes shared and often used as gifts. In addition, drinking distribution is highly skewed; 10 percent of drinkers account for 40 to 50 percent of all consumption (Cook [1981]). Under the plausible condition of increasing returns in externalities, a uniform price will not efficiently internalize the social costs of drinking. It will understate the externalities produced by some drinkers and overstate the externalities produced by the vast majority of drinkers. For drinkers who create no externalities, deadweight losses from state regulations come in many forms, including higher nominal prices, higher transaction costs from reduced hours of sale, and a suboptimal number of stores. Using a public interest theory of regulation, the vast majority of non-problem drinkers are unlikely to allow the price to be set at the socially optimal level.

Both state monopoly control and private licensing are compatible with monopoly pricing P_3. If $P_2 < P_3$, a welfare trade-off exists between the deadweight monopoly loss, *SRT*, and the social cost savings, *TUV*, from pricing at P_3. Unfortunately, measuring these areas is not feasible with present knowledge. If $P_2 \geqslant P_3$ there is no trade-off, but (as was just argued) a state is unlikely to set $P_2 \geqslant P_3$.

To summarize, there are two unknowns on pricing: whether P_2 is greater or less than P_3 and whether price is actually at P_2 or P_3? We hold that a uniform P_2, whether above or below P_3, will not fully internalize externalities and is politically infeasible. The theoretical P_2 to internalize social costs may be at or above P_3, but, again, it may not be politically feasible to set a high enough price. At present public alcohol revenues are far less than estimated social costs from drinking. Social costs for 1975 were estimated to be \$43 billion (US Dept. of Health, Education, and Welfare [1978]), while total public revenues from alcoholic beverages were \$9.7 billion, of which \$6.3 billion came from distilled spirits (Distilled Spirits Council of the United States [1977]). Though these figures pertain to total costs and total revenues, it seems unlikely that marginal tax rates are at high enough levels so that the marginal social costs of alcohol use are fully incorporated in the price.

Two areas in Figure 1 can be estimated: *SQV*, an overestimate of the deadweight monopoly loss, and P_3SQP_1, the potential monopoly rents to retailers.[8] The latter rents, in turn, are partially dissipated through payments to politicians. The level of political expenditures depends on expected retailer rents, free riding problems in collecting contributions for politicians, and the magnitude of opposition group expenditures. The opportunity costs of these expenditures represents social costs (Posner [1975]). These latter losses may

[8] We are assuming that $P_2 > P_3$ and that P_2 is not being set. Politicians are choosing between P_1 (non-RPM) and P_3 (RPM). Taxes are determined on considerations other than internalizing negative externalities. An alternative welfare analysis, examining the imposition of an externality correcting tax on either a monopoly or under conditions of perfect competition, but not comparing competition with monopoly as in Figure 1, is in Buchanan [1969].

be the most significant when rent seeking underlies various alcohol control laws, such as RPM.

The traditional deadweight monopoly welfare loss, DWL, can be measured by:

$$(1) \qquad DWL = \tfrac{1}{2}(e_p)(Q_m/P_m)(P_m - P_c)^2$$

where e_p is industry price elasticity, Q_m is monopoly output, P_m is monopoly price, and P_c is competitive price. The estimated loss, SQV, is an overstatement of the true DWL because of the social cost savings from reduced drinking. As stated, area $RTVQ$ cannot be estimated. Measures of e_p, Q_m, and P_m for distilled spirits are available, but P_c is unknown. By specifying an equation explaining prices across states, regression analysis can be used to estimate the price differential $P_m - P_c$ due to RPM.

IV(ii). *Price differences across states*

The price of distilled spirits is postulated to differ across states due to the presence or absence of RPM, the presence or absence of price advertising, state excise taxes, the level of income, the extent of tourist travel, and the degree of urbanization. We focus on estimating price differentials due to RPM and the absence of price advertising: the other variables are used as controls. With the exception of taxes, these are all demand variables. As noted earlier, supply side variables, other than taxes, are essentially constant across states, so a single, reduced form equation is used to explain price. The hypothesized relationships are as follows.

In the absence of price advertising, the mean level of price and price variance are higher. Consumer search costs are raised, leading to increased local monopoly power. Hence, price will be higher where price advertising is banned.[9] Examining the effects of advertising restrictions is more than academic. In 1983 legislative proposals to ban advertising of alcoholic beverages were debated in a number of states and existing advertising bans were upheld or extended in others.[10] In 1984 Congressional hearings were held on banning wine and beer commercials on television, and alcohol advertising was investigated by the Federal Trade Commission.

Another variable affecting price is state excise taxes. Under similar conditions of demand and supply across states, adjacent state prices differ largely by differences in state excise tax levels. Taxes are also included in the regression to separate monopoly welfare effects from tax welfare effects. By holding taxes constant, increases in the gross retail price facing consumers

[9] Tests of bans on price advertising have found this proposition to be true in the cases of prescription eyeglasses (Benham [1972]), prescription drugs (Cady [1976]), and gasoline (Maurizi and Kelly [1978]).

[10] Capital Cities Cable Inc., *et al.* v. CRISP, 699 F. 2d 490 (10th Cir.) 1983, 104 S. Ct. 2694 (1984); Queensgate Investment Co. v. Liquor Control Commission 69 Ohio St. 2d 361, 433 N.E. 2d 138 (1982).

due solely to RPM and bans on price advertising are captured. This is important, since we have no interest in measuring tax welfare losses, only monopoly losses for price gross of taxes.

The remaining explanatory variables are *per capita* income in real terms, a proxy for tourist travel, and urbanization. The higher is income, *ceteris paribus*, the higher is price.[11] Tourism's effect on price is ambiguous. States with large tourist travel centers, such as Nevada, may attempt to compete for travelers by offering lower prices on liquor and other products. However, if travel is primarily a function of other factors, such as scenic beauty or the location of financial or political centers, then the demand for alcoholic beverages may be relatively inelastic, leading to higher prices. Urbanization is used as a proxy for competition, with greater urbanization leading to lower prices.

Real price is a weighted (by sales) average of manufacturer suggested retail prices for eight leading brands in each state.[12] The independent variables are:

INCOME	*Per capita* real income.
TOURISM	Annual state payroll in hotels, motels, and tourist courts as a percentage of total state payroll.
URBANIZATION	State metropolitan population as a percentage of total state population.
RPM	Dummy variable equal to one if there is RPM, mandatory markups, or price posting from retailers to consumers (the latter two policies assumed equivalent to RPM); zero otherwise.
PRICEBAN	Dummy variable equal to one if print price advertising is allowed; zero if prohibited.
DSTAX	State excise taxes in real terms for distilled spirits.[13]

The sample covers 32 license states (two semi-license states, Mississippi and Wyoming, are missing owing to lack of tax data) plus Washington, DC for the period 1974 to 1978. Chow tests for poolability found sample homogeneity over time could not be rejected at the 0.01 level, but homogeneity cross-sectionally, tested by randomizing the states and splitting them into two subsamples, was rejected at the 0.01 level. Accordingly, regressions were estimated by variance-components analysis (VC) and OLS with dummy variables (OLSDV). The results are given in Table III.

[11] This expectation is based on the view that high income consumers prefer high quality, high priced brands, so that brand mix varies across states.

[12] The brands are: Seagram's 7-Crown, Old Crow. Old Grand-Dad, Dewar's, Smirnoff, Bacardi, Canadian Club, and Beefeater. Distilled Spirits Council of the US, 1978, 'Price per Fifth for Selected Types and Brands in License and Control States, 1973–1978', and *Liquor Handbook* [1979].

[13] Data were derived from the following sources: *INCOME*, *Survey of Current Business*; *TOURISM*, US Bureau of the Census, *County Business Patterns*; *URBANIZATION*, US Department of Commerce, *Current Population Reports*; *RPM* and *PRICEBAN*, Distilled Spirits Council of the US [1974, 1977]; *DSTAX*, Distilled Spirits Council of the US, *Distilled Spirits Industry 1978 Annual Statistical Review*.

TABLE III
REGRESSIONS IN LOGS EXPLAINING PRICE DIFFERENCES IN DISTILLED SPIRITS ACROSS LICENSE STATES, 1974–1978

	Equation	
	1 *VC*	*2* *OLSDV*
Intercept	1.360	1.467
	(9.80)	(16.68)
INCOME	0.109	0.071
	(1.56)	(1.47)
TOURISM	−0.011	−0.008
	(−0.72)	(−1.21)
URBANIZATION	−0.054	−0.043
	(−1.98)	(−3.19)
PRICEBAN	0.007	−0.032
	(0.27)	(−2.22)
RPM	0.045	0.046
	(2.19)	(3.93)
DSTAX	0.045	0.094
	(3.20)	(5.59)
Alaska		0.119
		(3.17)
Oklahoma		−0.256
		(−8.58)
R^2	n.a.	0.55

t-values in parentheses.

The results using VC are generally as expected; higher price with higher income, with RPM, and with higher taxes, and lower price with greater urbanization. TOURISM is negative but insignificant. Unexpectedly, price advertising is insignificant. The justification for variance-components is, however, weak when a random sample of a larger population is not being used (Judge *et al.* [1980, p, 331]). An alternative is to identify the outlier states and include them as intercept dummy variables.

The diagnostics of Belsley, Kuh, and Welsch [1980] allowed identification of two states as outliers: Alaska and Oklahoma.[14] Exogenous cost factors

[14] The diagnostics showed that Alaska's strong influence derives from relatively high income. High supply costs, including high transportation costs, translates into high income for Alaska (no similar effect was found for Hawaii). Oklahoma was an anomaly during the period tested: it banned advertising, had one of the highest state excise taxes, and had one of the lowest retail price structures for leading brands. Its low prices derive from unique distribution laws, leading to one of the lowest cost wholesale distribution systems in the nation.

Oklahoma wholesalers are not agents or franchisees of any distiller and can carry any brand they desire. By concentrating on major brands, significant cost savings are achieved relative to an agent who must promote, stock, and distribute full lines of individual distillers. This allows free riding on the marketing efforts of distillers and wholesalers in other states. Cost advantages were sufficient to allow Oklahoma wholesalers to ship leading brands to independent wholesalers in California at lower prices than the wholesale price to franchised wholesalers. In 1981, about half the liquor sold to Oklahoma wholesalers was resold out of state (Los Angeles Times, Aug. 17, 1981, Nov. 16, 1981, and July 2, 1982).

influence price for both states; distance in the case of Alaska and unique distribution laws for Oklahoma. These exogenous factors are treated by separate dummy variables for Alaska and Oklahoma in equation 2. As a consequence, INCOME is no longer significant (because of Alaska), and PRICEBAN now has the correct sign and is significant (because of Oklahoma).[15] For purposes of estimating monopoly welfare losses we used the results in equation 2: a RPM price markup of 4.7 percent and a 3.15 percent markup for a ban on print price advertising.[16]

A final econometric problem to be dealt with is collinearity. For the RPM parameter to be useful it must be independent of other parameters, such as taxes. Using the collinearity diagnostics of Belsley, Kuh, and Welsch [1980] no evidence of collinearity with RPM was found.[17]

IV(iii). *Welfare estimation results*

Estimates for the price elasticity of demand for distilled spirits for the US range from zero to −2.0, with more recent estimates falling in the −1.0 to −2.0 range (Ornstein [1980]; Ornstein and Hanssens [1985]). These are averages over all drinkers. Price elasticity for those who create the bulk of social costs, the 10 to 15 percent of all drinkers, is unknown. Estimates are therefore provided over a reasonable range of elasticities: −0.5, −1.0, and −1.5. Values for Q_m and P_m in equation (1) are taken from data on existing output and price for individual states subject to RPM or a ban on print price advertising.

On the assumption of linear demand in the relevant range of output, the estimates for *DWL* and wealth transfers for 1978 are shown in Table IV.[18] There were ten states with RPM that, if we assume an elasticity of −1.0, incurred an aggregate *DWL* of approximately $5 million. There were six states that banned price advertising, resulting in an aggregate *DWL* of $500 000 if a price elasticity of −1.0 is used. To put these figures in the perspective of industry sales, the *DWL* for RPM represents 0.1 percent of total estimated retail sales of distilled spirits in 1978, while for a ban on price

[15] Oklahoma's impact on PRICEBAN is indicated in another equation (not shown) where the dummy variable for Alaska is deleted. Oklahoma's dummy variable shows that its price is approximately 23 percent lower due to exogenous cost factors. Hence, the insignificance of PRICEBAN in equation 1 stems from Oklahoma's low price and ban on advertising.

[16] Since actual transaction prices are likely lower than suggested retail prices in non-RPM states, the RPM coefficient is probably biased downward.

[17] The tolerance value for RPM and PRICEBAN, which is measured as one minus R^2 resulting from regressing each on the other variables in the model was 0.69 for RPM and 0.64 for PRICEBAN, indicating no serious problem with collinearity. As a further test, ridge regression was run: as the ridge constant increased, the parameter estimates of all variables remained quite stable.

[18] The equation for *DWL* assumes linear demand while we estimated a constant-elasticity demand function. Because of the small price effects due to regulation, around 5 percent, it is safe to assume that demand is approximately linear in the relevant range of output.

TABLE IV
WELFARE ESTIMATES OF PRICE AND ADVERTISING RESTRICTIONS ON DISTILLED SPIRITS IN 1978

Welfare Effect	*Price Elasticity*	*RPM*	*Price Advertising Prohibition*
	−0.5	$2 489 969	$267 852
Deadweight Losses	−1.0	4 979 937	535 703
	−1.5	7 469 906	803 555
Wealth Transfers		$226 584 050	$34 869 300

advertising the *DWL* is 0.05 percent of total estimated sales.[19] For small states with low levels of consumption, such losses are trivially small. Moreover, the *DWL* figures overestimate true *DWL* since there are offsetting social gains from reduced drinking that may be as large or even larger. Therefore, *DWL* for many states can be virtually ignored.

In contrast, wealth transfers are substantial. The total wealth transfer due to RPM was $226.6 million in 1978, which was 4.5 percent of estimated retail sales in the affected states. The comparable figure for banning print price advertising is $34.9 million, or 3.1 percent of sales in the relevant states. These are not trivial amounts or percentages since the average profit margin before taxes in 1978–79 in retail liquor stores in the United States was 2.2 percent (Robert Morris Associates [1979]).

The proportion of this wealth transfer that was pure social loss—dissipated in seeking government protection from competition and preserving government granted monopoly—is unknown. In principle, the investments in obtaining protection should continue until, at the margin, the expected gains from obtaining protection are just equal to the costs. In practice, problems arise. When group benefits are sought, serious free rider problems among sellers reduce political expenditures. Moreover, the probability that the rent seeking effort may fail reduces the expected gain and thus the initial investment in seeking protection. In addition, since perfect foresight is unavailable, no one can know *a priori* what future rents will be. Nevertheless, part of the wealth transfer will be competed away in rent seeking and in preserving such rents by subsequent campaign contributions and other payments to politicians. These payments are not completely transfers since they entail opportunity costs, induce competition to become a politician, and provoke expenditures by opposition groups. There are also the costs of state bureaucracies administering control laws. Thus, it is clear that control laws can lead to social costs.

Given the problems inherent in such welfare estimates, the results are suggestive at best. They indicate that the most significant source of welfare

[19] Sales were estimated by multiplying quantity sold in fifths by mean retail price per fifth in each state.

loss may be in resources used in political competition. An indication of the magnitude of social costs relative to wealth transfers is reflected in a comparison of Tables II and IV. Though California accounted for $71 million of the estimated $226.6 million in wealth transfers due to RPM found in Table IV, the annual contributions of California liquor store owners (shown in Table II) were less than $155 000. Even if contributions by all alcohol interests in 1977–78 are counted, they amount to less than 1.0 percent of the $71 million in transfers. This wide disparity may reflect a number of factors: the main rent seeking expenditures may occur in the periods before protective legislation passes and before the full extent of future rents is known; free riding by retailers reduces total expenditures; and rents may be obtained and preserved at far less than their total value to acquiring firms (Fisher, [1985]). Nevertheless, the figures in Tables II and IV indicate that, contrary to our speculations, the bulk of potential welfare losses were in fact wealth transfers to retailers. The pure monopoly social costs due to control laws appear to be minimal.

V. SUMMARY AND CONCLUSIONS

With deeper insights into the relationships between manufacturers and retailers, special service theories of RPM are becoming more widespread. Tests of service theories, however, have been lacking. This paper examined one case of RPM, that of distilled spirits at the retail level. No compelling evidence of RPM efficiencies was found. Evidence of output restriction, which is inconsistent with demand-increasing special services and efficiency gains, was discovered. Further estimates indicated substantial wealth transfers from consumers to retail liquor store owners as a result of RPM.

The findings indicate that in the debate over RPM and efficiency, the position expressed by some, that all historical examples of retail RPM cartels were instances of RPM used for efficiency reasons, is an overstatement. The results offer ample evidence that efficiency gains do not explain all cases of RPM. When RPM is industrywide and administered via the government, the opportunities for retailer rent seeking are ever present. Under these conditions RPM is suspect as a source of efficiency gains.

STANLEY I. ORNSTEIN AND DOMINIQUE M. HANSSENS,
Graduate School of Management,
University of California,
Los Angeles, California 90024,
USA.

ACCEPTED JULY 1986

REFERENCES

Becker, G. S., 1983, 'A Theory of Competition Among Pressure Groups for Political Influence', *Quarterly Journal of Economics*, 98 (August), pp. 371–400.

BELSLEY, P.A., KUH, E. and WELSCH, R. E., 1980, *Regression Diagnostics* (John Wiley & Sons, New York).

BENHAM, L., 1972, 'The Effect of Advertising on the Price of Eyeglasses', *Journal of Law and Economics*, 15 (April), pp. 337–352.

BUCHANAN, J. M., 1969, 'External Diseconomies, Corrective Taxes, and Market Structure', *American Economic Review*, 59 (March), pp. 174–177.

CADY, J. F., 1976, 'An Estimation of the Price Effects of Restrictions on Drug Price Advertising', *Economic Inquiry*, 14 (December), pp. 493–511.

COMANOR, W. S., 1985, 'Vertical Price-Fixing, Vertical Market Restrictions, and the New Antitrust Policy', *Harvard Law Review*, 98 (March), pp. 983–1002.

COMANOR, W. S. and KIRKWOOD, J. B., 1985, 'Resale Price Maintenance and Antitrust Policy', *Contemporary Policy Issues*, 3 (1985), pp. 9–16.

COOK, P. J., 1981, 'The Effects of Liquor Taxes on Drinking, Cirrhosis, and Auto Fatalities', in M. H. MOORE and D. R. GERSTEIN, eds., *Alcohol and Public Policy: Beyond the Shadow of Prohibition* pp. 255–285 (National Academy Press, Washington, DC).

DISTILLED SPIRITS COUNCIL OF THE UNITED STATES, 1974, 1977, *Summary of State Laws and Regulations Relating to Distilled Spirits* (Washington, DC).

DISTILLED SPIRITS COUNCIL OF THE UNITED STATES, 1977, *1975 Public Revenues From Alcohol Beverages* (Washington, DC).

FISHER, F., 1985, 'The Social Costs of Monopoly and Regulation: Posner Reconsidered', *Journal of Political Economy*, 93 (April), pp. 410–416.

GALLINI, N. T. and WINTER, R. A., 1983, 'On Vertical Control in Monopolistic Competition', *International Journal of Industrial Organization*, 1 (September), pp. 275–286.

GOLDBERG, V., 1984, 'The Free Rider Problem, Imperfect Pricing, and the Economics of Retailing Services', *Northwestern University Law Review*, 79 (November), pp. 736–757.

GOULD, J. R. and PRESTON, L. E., 1965, 'Resale Price Maintenance and Retail Outlets', *Economica*, 32 (August), pp. 302–312.

HALVORSEN, R. and PALMQUIST, R., 1980, 'The Interpretation of Dummy Variables in Semilogarithmic Equations', *American Economic Review*, 70 (June), pp. 474–475.

JUDGE, G. G., GRIFFITHS, W. E., HILL, R. C. and LEE, T. C., 1980, *The Theory and Practice of Econometrics* (John Wiley & Sons, New York).

KIHOLM-SMITH, J., 1982, 'An Analysis of State Regulations Governing Liquor Store Licensees', *Journal of Law and Economics*, 25 (October), pp. 301–320.

KLEIN, B. and MURPHY, K. M., 1986, 'Vertical Restraints as Contract Enforcement Mechanisms: The Coors Case', University of California, Los Angeles, Department of Economics, Working Paper (July).

Liquor Handbook, 1979 (Gavin-Johnson Inc., New York).

MARVEL, H. P. and MCCAFFERTY, S., 1984, 'Resale Price Maintenance and Quality Certification', *Rand Journal of Economics*, 15 (Autumn), pp. 346–359.

MARVEL, H. P., 1985, 'How Fair is Fair Trade?' *Contemporary Policy Issues*, 3 (Spring), pp. 23–36.

MATHEWSON, G. F. and WINTER, R. A., 1983, 'The Incentives for Resale Price Maintenance Under Imperfect Information', *Economic Inquiry*, 21 (July), pp. 337–348.

MAURIZI, A. and KELLY, T., 1978, *Price and Consumer Information* (American Enterprise Institute, Washington, DC).

ORNSTEIN, S. I., 1985, 'Resale Price Maintenance and Cartels', *Antitrust Bulletin*, 30 (Summer), pp. 401–432.

ORNSTEIN, S. I. and HANSSENS, D. M., 1985, 'Alcohol Control Laws and the Consumption of Distilled Spirits and Beer', *Journal of Consumer Research*, 12 (September), pp. 200–213.

ORNSTEIN, S. I., 1980, 'Control of Alcohol Consumption Through Price Increases', *Journal of Studies on Alcohol*, 41 (September), pp. 807–818.

OVERSTREET, T. R., 1983, *Resale Price Maintenance: Economic Theories and Empirical Evidence* (Federal Trade Commission, Washington, DC).

OVERSTREET, T. R. and FISHER, A. A., 1985, 'Resale Price Maintenance and Distribution Efficiencies: Some Lessons from the Past', *Contemporary Policy Issues*, 3 (Spring), pp. 43–58.

POSNER, R., 1975, 'The Social Loss of Monopoly and Regulation', *Journal of Political Economy*, 83 (August), pp. 807–828.

RICE, E. and ULEN, T. S., 1981, 'Rent-Seeking and Welfare Loss', *Research in Law and Economics*, 3, pp. 53–65.

ROBERT MORRIS ASSOCIATES, 1979, *79 Annual Statement Studies* (Philadelphia, PA).

SCHERER, F. M., 1983, 'The Economics of Vertical Restraints', *Antitrust Law Journal*, 52, pp. 687–707.

SCHERER, F. M., 1980, *Industrial Market Structure and Economic Performance* (Rand McNally, New York).

SHARP, B. S., 1985, 'Comments on Marvel: How Fair is Fair Trade?', *Contemporary Policy Issues*, 3 (Spring), pp. 37–42.

TELSER, L., 1960, 'Why Should Manufacturers Want Fair Trade?', *Journal of Law and Economics*, 3 (October), pp. 86–105.

US DEPARTMENT OF HEALTH, EDUCATION, AND WELFARE, 1978, *Third Special Report to the U.S. Congress on Alcohol and Health*, E. P. NOBLE, ed. (Washington, DC).

WHITE, L. J., 1985, 'Resale Price Maintenance and the Problem of Marginal and Inframarginal Customers', *Contemporary Policy Issues*, 3 (Spring), pp. 17–22.

THE JOURNAL OF INDUSTRIAL ECONOMICS 0022-1821 $2.00
Volume XXXVI September 1987 No. 1

COST-RAISING STRATEGIES

STEVEN C. SALOP AND DAVID T. SCHEFFMAN*

This paper studies a variety of strategies by which firms could disadvantage rivals by raising their costs. In this paper, we show that strategies designed to raise rivals' costs have a number of advantages over predatory pricing: They are credible, do not necessarily require the victim to exit, and do not necessarily require the existence of classical market power. The paper sets up a general model, proves a number of general results, and then applies the model to specific strategies involving "overbuying" inputs and vertical integration.

I. INTRODUCTION

ECONOMISTS AND courts have long been concerned with conduct that creates or enhances market power by disadvantaging rivals. A variety of cost-raising strategies can be used to disadvantage rivals or drive them out of the market without the need to set low prices. For example, while AT&T was not found liable for predatory pricing, it did not escape liability for denying rivals equal access. In another classic antitrust case, the *Lorain Journal* newspaper conditioned sales of advertising space on advertisers' promises not to purchase additional advertising from a competing radio station.[1] Other possible cost-raising strategies include a variety of exclusive dealing arrangements, inducing input suppliers to discriminate against rivals, lobbying legislatures or regulatory agencies to create regulations that disadvantage rivals, commencing R & D and advertising wars, and adopting incompatible technologies. Because these strategies are predatory, but do not involve classic predatory pricing, they are sometimes referred to as "non-price predation".[2]

In this paper, we show that strategies designed to raise rivals' costs have a number of advantages over predatory pricing. First, cost-raising strategies do not have an inherent problem of credibility. Such strategies may be profitable whether or not the rivals exit, since higher cost rivals have an incentive to cut back output and raise prices immediately, which may make it possible for the predator to reap gains even in the short run.[3] Secondly, unlike predatory pricing, classical, single firm market power (i.e., downward sloping demand

* Professor of Economics at Georgetown University Law Center and Director, Bureau of Economics, Federal Trade Commission, respectively. This paper is a revised version of Salop and Scheffman [1984].

[1] 342 U.S. 143 (1951).

[2] Since these strategies sometimes involve prices (e.g., raising the price of an input), perhaps a better term is "cost-predation".

[3] See Salop and Scheffman [1983].

curve) in the relevant output market is not essential for the success of cost-raising strategies, since even perfect competitors can benefit if rivals have higher costs.[4]

This paper is organized as follows. In sections II and III, we set out the general model for analyzing cost-raising strategies. These sections generalize and extend the results reported in Salop and Scheffman [1983]. The specific model analyzed in section III assumes the predator can fully control a parameter that affects its costs and those of its rivals, for example, where the parameter is a regulatory instrument.[5] In section IV, we define and analyze strategies based on "overbuying" inputs, such as the conduct alleged in *Alcoa*. Finally, section V develops a theory of raising rivals' costs through vertical integration and shows that vertical integration can be anticompetitive, even for technologies in which an input is used in fixed proportions.

II. THE GENERAL MODEL

We begin with a general model of competition between the predator and a competitive (price-taking) fringe, where the predator may be either a price taker or a dominant firm.[6] Let $D(p)$ be market demand, and let the predator's and fringe's cost functions be given, respectively, by the functions $C(x, \alpha)$ and $G(y, \alpha)$, where outputs are given by x and y, and where a cost-raising parameter, α, influences the costs of all firms, perhaps symmetrically.[7] For example, α could be interpreted as a regulatory parameter, the price of an input, or expenditures on advertising or research and development.[8] We adopt the convention that increases in α raise the average and marginal costs of the fringe and the average costs of the predator—i.e., the partial derivatives C_α, G_α, and $G_{y\alpha}$ all are non-negative.[9] We assume that the predator has the power to control the level of α, subject to a general market constraint formalized by the equation $F(\alpha, p, x, y) \geqslant 0$. In subsequent sections, we consider particular forms for this constraint corresponding to specific institutional settings.

The fringe supply curve is denoted $S(p, \alpha)$, which can be derived from the

[4] Inframarginal rents increase with price, and higher cost rivals may shift up the industry supply curve, thereby increasing price.

[5] See Salop, Scheffman, and Schwartz [1984].

[6] See Salinger [1985] for the case of an oligopolistic fringe.

[7] The fringe cost function and resulting supply curve may be treated as long run functions encompassing potential entry by additional price-taking firms. Lack of entry barriers is signalled by constant marginal costs and a perfectly elastic supply curve. Thus, in principle, dynamic elements can be taken into account in the analysis. We treat p and α as scalars, although the results are generalized easily to vector-valued variables.

[8] We will not treat the case where market demand also depends on α (for example, when α represents advertising expenditures), but many of our results are easily generalized to that case.

[9] If increases in α reduce the predator's costs (i.e., if $C_\alpha < 0$), then increases in α would have an independent "efficiency" benefit to the "predator" beyond any exclusionary benefits.

fringe cost function in the usual manner:[10]

(1) $$S(p, \alpha) = \underset{y}{\operatorname{argmax}}\,[py - G(y, \alpha)]$$

Thus, the predator faces the general profit-maximizing problem:

(2) $$\max_{\{p, x, \alpha\}} \; [px - C(x, \alpha)],^{11}$$

subject to

$$x + y = D(p)$$

$$y = S(p, \alpha)$$

$$F(\alpha, p, x, y) \geqslant 0$$

Without placing more structure on the market constraint function $F(\alpha, p, x, y)$, the first order conditions for equations (2) do not yield interesting interpretations.

III. DIRECT CONTROL OVER α

In this section we assume that the market constraint has a very simple form: the predator has direct and complete control over α, subject only to the constraint $\alpha \geqslant \bar{\alpha}$. The *ex ante* value $\bar{\alpha}$ may correspond to the predator's choosing α solely on the basis of cost-minimization (that is, $C_{\alpha} = 0$), an exogenous *status quo*, or an alternative proposed by a rival. Thus, we assume that the predator has a type of market power in an "input market", in the sense that α corresponds to a variable in a relevant input market, such as price.[12] We assume here that the predator's choice of output level has no direct effect on the value of α.[13]

Several institutional settings are suggested by this formal structure. In the *Pennington* case studied by Williamson [1968], it was alleged that a large coal producer induced the labor union to drive up the wage rate. Under this interpretation, $\alpha > \bar{\alpha}$ would correspond to a wage increase.[14] In another

[10] Assuming $y > 0$, fringe supply satisfies the usual first-order condition relating price to marginal cost, $p = G_y(y, \alpha)$. The properties of the supply curve are as follows: $S_p = 1/G_{yy} \geqslant 0$ and $S_{\alpha} = -G_{y\alpha}/G_{yy} \leqslant 0$. If $G_{yy} > 0$, the fringe supply curve is upward sloping. If $G_{yy} = 0$, then $S_y = \infty$, and the predator has no classical market power in the downstream market, but instead faces a perfectly elastic residual demand curve. Of course, even in that case the predator may benefit from shifts in his residual demand curve.

[11] If the predator does not have classical market power in the output market, price is not a choice variable. Instead, output x is determined by the relationship $p = C_x(x, \alpha)$. See Salop, Scheffman and Schwartz (1984) for a detailed analysis of this case.

[12] In this formulation, regulations can be analyzed as inputs that are forced on the firms, rather than being purchased.

[13] This would not always be the case, for example, if α was the price of an input purchased by both the predator and the fringe in a competitive market. A model of this type is taken up in the following sections.

[14] In this formulation it is assumed that the union rations labor to clear the market at the higher wage.

interpretation, α and $\bar{\alpha}$ can be treated as alternative regulations that could be adopted by an agency the predator is trying to "capture".[15] One also could view α as a level of advertising or research and development expenditures chosen by the predator to which the fringe reacts by raising its own advertising or research levels.[16]

Formally, rewriting the maximization problem in (2), we have

$$(2') \qquad \max_{\{p,\alpha\}} p(D(p)-S(p,\alpha))-C(D(p,\alpha)-S((p,\alpha),\alpha)),$$

subject to

$$\alpha \geqslant \bar{\alpha}$$

The first order conditions for an interior maximum ($x, y > 0, \alpha > \bar{\alpha}$) are given as follows:

$$(3a) \qquad (p-C_x)/p = 1/\varepsilon^R$$

$$(3b) \qquad (p-C_x) = -C_\alpha/S_\alpha$$

where ε^R is the elasticity of residual demand faced by the predator.[17]

Equation (3a) is the usual Lerner markup equation for a dominant firm. At an interior equilibrium ($\alpha > \bar{\alpha}$), combining (3a) and (3b) yields[18]

$$(4) \qquad S_\alpha/(D_p-S_p) = C_\alpha/x$$

The interpretation of (4) is straightforward. The left-hand side of (4) equals $\partial p/\partial\alpha\,|_x$, where this derivative represents the change in price arising from the reduction in fringe output resulting from the increase in α, holding the output of the predator fixed. In other words, the left-hand side of (4) is the derivative representing the *vertical* shift in the residual demand curve facing the dominant firm. The right-hand side of (4) is the derivative of *average cost* (AC^D) of the predator with respect to α, holding its output fixed. Therefore, an interior solution must satisfy the condition $\partial p/\partial\alpha = \partial AC^D/\partial\alpha$, where these derivatives are evaluated at the profit-maximizing point (x^*, α^*).

We now state the following *sufficient* condition for a cost-raising strategy to be profitable, that is, for $\alpha^* > \bar{\alpha}$.

[15] Elsewhere, we have presented a model in which we examine the determinants of who controls the regulatory process (Salop, Scheffman and Schwartz [1984]). In that case, the "market power" may simply involve partial control over the regulatory process. For a summary of the literature on the use of regulation as a cost-raising strategy, see McCormick [1984].

[16] The fringe's profit-maximizing reaction function is implicit in the cost derivative G_α. However, under this interpretation, any effects of advertising or R & D on market demand are ignored.

[17] $\varepsilon^R = -(\partial(D-S)/\partial p)(p/(D-S)) = \varepsilon/\sigma + (1-\sigma)\zeta^F/\sigma$, where ε is the price-elasticity of market demand, ζ^F is the price-elasticity of fringe supply, and σ is the market share of the predator.

[18] It can easily be shown that the condition corresponding to (4), if the fringe has constant returns-to-scale technology, is: $[1-(p-C_x)\varepsilon/p]/(C_\alpha/D) = 1/AC^{F'}(\alpha)$, with ε the price elasticity of market demand and $AC^{F'}(\alpha)$ is the derivative of the fringe's average cost with respect to α. The first order conditions for y require $p-C_x \geqslant 0$ and $(p-C_x)y = 0$.

Proposition 1. Let $\bar{x}$ be the profit maximizing output for the predator when $\alpha = \bar{\alpha}$ (that is, $\bar{x}$ is the solution of (3a) for $\alpha = \bar{\alpha}$). $\alpha > \bar{\alpha}$ is profitable if

$$(5) \qquad \partial p/\partial\alpha > \partial AC^D/\partial\alpha$$

where the derivatives are evaluated at $(\bar{x}, \bar{\alpha})$.

This sufficient condition requires that the vertical shift in the predator's residual demand curve must exceed the vertical shift in its average cost curve, evaluated at the non-strategic equilibrium ($\alpha = \bar{\alpha}$). This result follows directly from the fact that the predator's profits at $\bar{x}$ equal $(p - AC^D)\bar{x}$, where AC^D is the predator's average costs.[19]

The sufficient condition (5) is more likely to hold: (i) the larger is the vertical shift in the fringe supply curve resulting from an increase in α (S_α large); (ii) the smaller is the impact of an increase in α on the predator's average costs (C_α/x small); and (iii) the less elastic are the market demand curve and the fringe supply curve ($-(D_p - S_p)p/x$ small).

(i). *Effect on price*

Consider now the effect of increasing α on price. If we denote the predator's profit by π^D, $dp/d\alpha$ can be determined by totally differentiating the predator's first order condition for price, $\pi_p^D = 0$. Since the second order conditions require $\pi_{pp}^D < 0$, sign $dp/d\alpha$ = sign $\pi_{p\alpha}^D$, or

$$(6) \qquad \text{sign}\, dp/d\alpha = \text{sign}\,[-S_\alpha - C_{x\alpha}(D_p - S_p) - (p - C_x)S_{p\alpha}]$$

The first term on the right hand side of equation (6) is positive. The sign of the second term is ambiguous because of the ambiguity of the sign of $C_{x\alpha}$; that is, the effect of an increase in α on the predator's *marginal* cost is ambiguous.[20] The sign of the third term depends on the sign of $(D_{p\alpha} - S_{p\alpha})$, the effect of an increase in α on the *slope* of the residual demand curve, which is also ambiguous. Thus, it is possible for $dp/d\alpha$ to be negative.[21]

This is a straightforward result, analogous to the well-known ambiguity of the effect of an increase in demand on a monopolist's profit-maximizing price. However, this result alerts us to the fact that if the predator has market power in the output market, both the shift in the fringe supply curve and its slope are critical in determining the effect of an increase in α on price. In summary, we have the following proposition.

[19] The interpretation of (5) is provided in Salop and Scheffman (1983).
[20] We have only assumed that C_α is negative.
[21] An example in which $dp/d\alpha < 0$ is as follows. Suppose market demand is $Q = (1-p)$, and that initially fringe supply is inelastic at one unit. Suppose further that the predator's costs are zero and that an increase in α changes fringe supply to the function: $y = p^2/100, p \leqslant 10$; $y = 1$, for $p > 10$. It is easy to see $S_\alpha \leqslant 0$. The initial equilibrium price is $p^* = 5$, while the equilibrium price after the increase in α is $p^* = 4.7$, so that the price falls with an increase in α. The key to this example is that although $S_\alpha \leqslant 0$, the fringe supply curve becomes much more elastic with an increase in α, making the predator's residual demand curve more elastic.

Proposition 2. Profitable cost-raising strategies may result in a *decrease* in price if the predator has market power in the output market. A sufficient condition for price to increase is $C_{x\alpha} \geqslant 0$ and $S_{p\alpha} \leqslant 0$.[22] If the predator does not have market power in the output market, profitability of cost-predation requires that price increase.

(ii). *Effect on fringe output and profits*

We now examine the effect of an increase in α on fringe output. From the fringe supply function, we have

$$dy/d\alpha = S_p dp/d\alpha + S_\alpha \tag{7}$$

Because, by assumption, $S_\alpha < 0$, then if $dp/d\alpha < 0$, it follows that fringe output necessarily falls ($dy/d\alpha < 0$). However, in some cases it may be profitable for the predator to increase price sufficiently to permit the fringe output even to expand ($dy/d\alpha > 0$), although in such a case the predator must restrict his own output enough so that total output falls in order to effect an increase in price.[23] As with the ambiguous price effect, the result depends on the effect of an increase in α on the elasticity of the predator's residual demand curve. Summarizing, we have the following result.

Proposition 3. An increase in α has an ambiguous effect on fringe output. However, if price falls ($dp/d\alpha < 0$), then fringe output also must fall ($dy/d\alpha < 0$).

Because an increase in α has an ambiguous effect on price and fringe output, it is probably not surprising that the effect of an increase in α on fringe "profits" (inframarginal rents) is also ambiguous.[24] Suppose that fringe supply is upward sloping and that further entry is blocked so that the fringe earns inframarginal rents. Fringe profits are given by $\pi^F = py - G(y, \alpha)$. Differentiating π^F and recalling that $p = G_y$, we have

$$d\pi^F/d\alpha = y(G_{yy} dy/d\alpha + G_{y\alpha} - G_{y\alpha}/y) \tag{8}$$

In the standard case in which fringe output falls ($dy/d\alpha < 0$), fringe profits necessarily fall, unless fringe marginal costs rise sufficiently relative to fringe average costs.[25] Summarizing, we have the following proposition.

[22] This should be clear since the critical issue is how C_x and ε^D change with α (see (3a)), and $-S_{\alpha p} \geqslant 0$ is a sufficient condition for $\partial\varepsilon^D/\partial\alpha \leqslant 0$.

[23] An example in which $dy/d\alpha > 0$ is as follows: Suppose market demand is $Q = (11-p)$ and the predator's costs are zero. Suppose further that for $\alpha = 0$, fringe supply curve is perfectly elastic at a price of one, but for $\alpha > 0$ the fringe supply curve becomes $y = (p-1)/\alpha$ for $0 < \alpha < 1$, $y = (p-1)$ for $\alpha \geqslant 1$. Then, for $\alpha = 0$, the equilibrium price $p^* = 1$ and output of the fringe is zero. However, if the predator can set α, it will set $\alpha^* = 1$, leading to a new price of $p^* = 5/2$ with fringe output rising to 3/2. Of course the key to this example is that the increase in α makes the fringe supply curve much less elastic.

[24] Thus, characterizing the conduct as necessarily "predatory" in this case would be in error. The conduct could sometimes be characterized as "collusive". Indeed, in the example discussed in footnote 27, fringe profits actually increase with α.

[25] It is easy to see that if fringe marginal costs increase much more than fringe average costs, the fringe's inframarginal rents (the area behind the fringe supply curve) may increase.

Proposition 4. Sufficient conditions for fringe profits to fall are: either (i) $dp/d\alpha < 0$, or (ii) $dy/d\alpha < 0$ and $(G_{y\alpha} - G_\alpha/y) < 0$. A sufficient condition for fringe profits to rise is $dy/d\alpha > 0$ (which itself requires $dp/d\alpha > 0$), and $(G_{y\alpha} - G_\alpha/y) > 0$.

These two conditions are of particular interest because they depend only on price or on the output of the fringe and its technology.

(iii). *Effect on welfare*

In this section, we analyze the welfare effects of these strategies. Let the conventional welfare indicator (the sum of consumer plus producer surplus) be denoted by W. Then, we have[26]

$$(9) \qquad dW/d\alpha = [D(p) - S(p, \alpha)]dp/d\alpha - (p - C_x)S_\alpha(p, \alpha) - C_\alpha - G_\alpha + \Omega'(\alpha)$$

where $\Omega(\alpha)$ is a measure of welfare in other markets affected by α.

Without placing more structure on the problem, the properties of $\Omega(\alpha)$ are undefined. If α is a regulatory parameter affecting only the relevant output market, the effects of increased regulation ($\alpha > \bar{\alpha}$) on welfare outside that market are likely to be unimportant, unless there are substantial resources used up (rather than simply transferred) to influence the regulatory authority. If α is the price of an input, then some of the increases in costs arising from an increase in α represent only a transfer to the input owners.[27] Until later sections, where we have sufficient structure to determine the properties of Ω, we will concentrate on partial equilibrium welfare effects. We will denote partial equilibrium welfare by $\hat{W}$, where

$$(10) \qquad \hat{W} = W - \Omega$$

From equation (9) it should be clear that the sign of $d\hat{W}/d\alpha$ is ambiguous.[28] For example, if $dp/d\alpha < 0$, it would not be surprising that $d\hat{W}/d\alpha > 0$. Furthermore, even if $dp/d\alpha \geqslant 0$, welfare could rise because the strategy may reduce the output of a higher cost rival, increasing producer surplus more than any decrease in consumer surplus.[29] This result only can occur if the

[26] $W(\bar{p}, \bar{\alpha}) = \int_p^\infty D(p)dp + \bar{p}\bar{x} - C(\bar{x}, \bar{\alpha}) + \bar{p}S(\bar{p}, \bar{\alpha}) - G(S(\bar{p}, \bar{\alpha}), \bar{\alpha}) + \Omega(\alpha)$. We normalize by setting $\Omega(\bar{\alpha}) = 0$.

[27] For example, in the case considered by Williamson [1968], the cost-raising strategy took the form of an increase in the union wage, which resulted in a transfer to union members. However, rent-seeking conduct may transform such transfers into welfare losses.

[28] This follows because if the predator has market power in the output market, fringe and predator marginal costs will not be equalized, leading to a typical second best welfare calculus.

[29] Suppose demand is $Q = (a - bp)$ and the predator's costs are zero. Suppose further that for $\alpha = 0$, fringe supply is $y = [(a - 4b) + bp]$ and for $\alpha = 1$, fringe supply is $y = (a - 6b) + 2bp$. It can easily be shown that the equilibrium price is $p = 2$ for $\alpha = 0$ or $\alpha = 1$, so that consumer surplus is the same in each equilibrium. However, producer surplus is larger in the case of $\alpha = 1$ because a greater proportion of the output is produced by the lower cost predator (which has zero costs). What is driving this example is that the marginal costs of the fringe and the predator are not equalized because of market power exercised in the output market by the predator.

predator has market power that results in $p > MC$. If price equals marginal cost, then the diversion of output to the predator must raise total costs.

Of course, a sufficient increase in price will cause enough reduction in consumer surplus to result in $d\hat{W}/d\alpha < 0$. Substituting (3b) into (9), we have:

(11) $$d\hat{W}/d\alpha < 0 \text{ if } dp/d\alpha > S_\alpha/(D_p - S_p) - (C_\alpha + G_\alpha)/(D - S)$$

The term $(S_\alpha/(D_p - S_p))$ is the price rise due to an increase in α, assuming the predator holds its output fixed. Therefore, equation (11) holds if the predator does not increase its output when α is increased. Summarizing, we have the following result:

Proposition 5. In general, increasing α has an ambiguous effect on partial equilibrium welfare, even if price rises, when the predator has classical market power. However, if the predator does not increase its output, welfare necessarily is reduced. If price rises, *consumer* welfare is reduced by an increase in α. If the predator is a price taker and price does not fall, total equilibrium welfare must fall.

(iv). *α as an input price*

We now place additional structure on the previous model by specifying the way in which α affects costs. We assume in this section that α is the price of an input A that is used by both the predator and the fringe. Denoting $\bar{\alpha}$ as the competitive price of A, we assume that the predator can raise the input price above the competitive level without increasing its purchases of A.[30] Although the first order conditions for the predator are still given by (3), when α is an input price additional results can be derived because of the properties of C_α and S_α.

By the usual duality properties of cost functions, we have $C_\alpha = A^D$ and $G_\alpha = A^F$, where A^D and A^F are the (cost minimizing) demands for A by the predator and fringe, respectively. On the assumption that fringe supply is given by (1), the fringe's (cost minimizing) demand for A satisfies $\partial A^F/\partial y = G_{y\alpha}$. Therefore, from (4) and (5), a sufficient condition for $\alpha > \bar{\alpha}$ to be profitable is

(12) $$(-\partial A^F/\partial y)/G_{yy}(D_p - S_p) > A^D/x, \text{ evaluated at } (\bar{x}, \bar{\alpha})$$

As with (5), the left hand side of (12) is $\partial p/\partial\alpha\,|_x$, and the right hand side of (12) is the derivative of average cost of the predator with respect to α for output of the predator kept fixed. Notice that a necessary condition for a cost-raising strategy to be profitable is that A not be an inferior factor for the

[30] Our specification of this model is similar to that of Williamson [1968]. Thus, we are assuming that some actor in the input market, e.g., a union, rations the sales of the input at a higher price. Williamson makes some restrictive assumptions (fixed coefficients, constant-returns-to-scale technology for the predator and the fringe), which, we will see, greatly limit the range of possible equilibrium outcomes.

fringe ($\partial A^F/\partial y \geqslant 0$), since otherwise an increase in α would increase fringe output.

Sufficient condition (12) can be rewritten to facilitate its interpretation. Let $\rho = (\partial A^F/\partial y)(y/A^F)$, the elasticity of fringe demand for input A with respect to fringe output. Then from (12), at $(\bar{x}, \bar{\alpha})$ we have

$$(13) \qquad -S_p/(D_p - S_p) > (A^D/x)/\rho(A^F/y)$$

Since the left hand side of (13) is less than one, (13) requires that $(A^D/x) < \rho(A^F/y)$. Hence, the greater is the fringe's use of input A per unit of output *relative to* the predator's use of that input per unit of output, the more likely that cost-predation will be profitable.[31] The results contained in (12) and (13) are summarized in the following proposition.

Proposition 6. If α is the price of input A, for the predator to raise α profitably, A must not be an inferior factor for the fringe. The profitability of a cost-raising strategy is more likely:

(i) the more elastic is the fringe input-expansion path for A;
(ii) the less elastic is the fringe supply curve;
(iii) the less elastic is the market demand curve; and
(iv) the greater is fringe use of input A per unit of output relative to the predator's.

Welfare effects. In assessing the welfare effects of an increase in the input price, we must recognize that some of the cost increase borne by the predator and the fringe is a transfer to input suppliers. In terms of the notation used above,

$$(14) \qquad \Omega'(\bar{\alpha}) = d[\alpha(A^D + A^F)]/d\alpha$$

i.e., the change in payments to owners of the input, which can be positive. Since $C_\alpha = A^D$ and $G_\alpha = A^F$, the welfare effect summarized in equation (9) can be written:

$$(9a) \qquad dW/d\alpha = [D(p) - S(p,\alpha)]dp/d\alpha - (p - C_x)S_\alpha(p,\alpha) - A^D - A^F + \Omega'(\alpha)$$

Since $dW/d\alpha = d\hat{W}/d\alpha + \Omega'(\bar{\alpha})$ and $\bar{\alpha}(d(A^D + A^F)/d\alpha) < 0$, it is easily seen from (11) that Proposition 5 now holds for *total* welfare W.

IV. OVERBUYING STRATEGIES

In this section we assume that α is the price of an input A that is supplied by a competitive industry according to the supply curve $A(\alpha)$. Now, in order to raise the input price, the predator must purchase additional quantities of the

[31] Since $\rho > 1$ is possible, this input use asymmetry is not necessary for the profitability of cost-predation.

input.[32] As a result, its marginal factor cost of increasing α exceeds C_α (where, as before, $C(x, \alpha)$ is the minimized cost of buying inputs to produce x at input price α).

The equilibrium condition in the input market corresponding to the market constraint $F(\alpha, p, x, y) \geqslant 0$ in (1) now is given by

$$(15) \qquad A(\alpha) - A^F(\alpha, p) - A^D = 0$$

where $A^F(\alpha, p)$ is the fringe demand function for input A and A^D is the quantity of A purchased by the predator. We make the standard assumptions that $A' > 0$, $A^F_\alpha < 0$, $A^F_p > 0$. From (15), we can derive the function $A^D(\alpha, p)$ that gives the level of purchases of A required for the predator in order to raise the price of A to α, given p (i.e., the residual supply function for A).

Let $z = (z^1, \ldots, z^m)$ denote the quantities of other inputs, $r = (r^1, \ldots, r^m)$ denote their prices, and let $f(z^D, A^D)$ denote the predator's production function. The predator's cost function, $\tilde{C}(x, \alpha, r, p)$, can be defined as follows:

$$(16) \qquad \tilde{C}(x, \alpha, r, p) = \min_{\{z_i^D\}} [\textstyle\sum r_i z^D + \alpha A^D(\alpha, p)],$$

subject to

$$f(z^D, A^D) = x$$

By the "Envelope Theorem", we have

$$(17a) \qquad \tilde{C}_\alpha = A^D + (\alpha - \chi f_A) A^D_\alpha,$$ [33] and

$$(17b) \qquad \tilde{C}_p = (\alpha - \chi f_A) A^D_p,$$ [34]

where $\chi = \tilde{C}_x$, is the predator's marginal cost.

The first order conditions for profit-maximization for the predator can be derived as in (4), yielding

$$(18a) \qquad (p - \tilde{C}_x)/p = (1 - \tilde{C}_p/x)/\varepsilon^D, \text{ and}$$

$$(18b) \qquad (p - \tilde{C}_x) = -\tilde{C}_\alpha / S_\alpha$$

Following equation (5), these equations can be combined to yield

$$(19) \qquad S_\alpha/(D_p - S_p) = (\tilde{C}_\alpha/x)/(1 - \tilde{C}_p/x)$$

As before, the left hand side of (19) is the vertical shift in the residual demand curve facing the predator and the right hand side is the vertical shift in its average costs.[35]

[32] This overpurchasing may be carried out by excessive open market purchases of inputs or by excessive purchases of productive capacity to produce inputs, i.e., by excessive vertical integration. We will discuss vertical integration explicitly in the next section.

[33] Notice that if the predator was a perfect competitor in the A-market, then $\tilde{C}_\alpha = A^D$ (the usual duality relationship). If the predator was a simple monopsonist in the A-market, the first order conditions for α would require $\tilde{C}_\alpha = 0$.

[34] $\tilde{C}_p$ is the change in the dominant firm costs arising from a change in p, resulting from the fact that a change in p changes the fringe demand for A and therefore the net supply of A available to the dominant firm.

[35] $\partial AC^D/\partial\alpha = [\tilde{C}_p(\partial p/\partial\alpha)]/x$.

In the model of the preceding section, it was straightforward to determine whether a cost-raising strategy was being pursued; a necessary and sufficient condition was $\alpha > \bar{\alpha}$. In the present model, however, all purchases of A automatically increase α, so that as long as the predator actually uses its purchases of A to produce output, we do not have a simple benchmark.

There are two potential benchmarks we may consider. One useful benchmark is classical (dominant firm) monopoly/monopsony conduct. By this we mean the level of input purchases that would arise if the predator behaved as a dominant firm facing a residual demand curve $R(p, \alpha)$ and a residual supply curve $A^D(\alpha, p)$, but ignored the strategic effects of α on its rivals' input costs and the resulting effects on price.[36] A second benchmark is the cost-minimizing (efficient) level of input purchases.

We take up the simple monopoly/monopsony (MM) benchmark first. In that model, the MM's optimal choice of A would imply $\tilde{C}_\alpha = 0$; that is,

$$A^D(\alpha - \chi f_A)A^D_\alpha = 0 \tag{20}$$

In this case, the MM's marginal revenue product for A equals the marginal factor cost (MFC) of A.[37] In contrast, if a strategically-minded MM also realizes and acts on the knowledge that α affects R and that p affects A^D, the first order conditions for α (17b) require

$$(\alpha - \chi f_A)A^D_\alpha + A^D > 0 \tag{21}$$

Thus, for strategic behavior, the marginal revenue product of A for the predator is below its marginal factor cost.[38] The intuition is straightforward. The predator, recognizing the effect of an increase in α on fringe supply, finds it in its interest to purchase relatively more A than if it were a simple monopsonist. It is in this sense that the predator "over-purchases" the input.[39] The results of this section are summarized in the following proposition.

Proposition 8. A necessary and sufficient condition for increasing α to be profitable is $MFC^D_A - \chi f_A > 0$; that is, the marginal factor cost of A exceeds the predator's marginal revenue product of A.

In principle, MFC^D_A and χf_A could be quantified, in which case an empirical test for overbuying could be carried out.

[36] Formally, this assumes that the dominant firm ignores the effect of α on the predator's residual demand function and the effect of p on A^D.

[37] The marginal revenue product of A is χf_A and the marginal factor cost of A is $\alpha + A^D/A^D_\alpha$.

[38] For a diagrammatic explanation of this result see Salop and Scheffman [1984].

[39] It is not possible to state a general result summarizing the relationship between the strategic and non-strategic equilibria. However, simple examples bear out the intuition about the effects of strategic overbuying. For example, let market demand be $a - bp$. Suppose both the fringe and the predator use one unit of A to produce one unit of output, and that $A^F(\alpha, p) = (p - \alpha)$. Suppose further that A is supplied according to the supply function $A(\alpha) = k\alpha$. Finally, assume that the predator's only cost of production is the cost of A. Then it can be shown that the cost-predation equilibrium has a lower p and higher α than the equilibrium in which the predator acts as a simple monopolist-monopsonist.

Using the simple monopoly/monopsony model as a benchmark has two shortcomings for policy purposes. First, the condition given in Proposition 8 may be difficult to measure in practice. Second, although buying more inputs than would a non-strategic MM indicates an *intent* to raise rivals' cost to gain power over price, the strategy may not reduce economic efficiency. This is because a monopsonist under-purchases the input, relative to the efficient level, so that purchasing more than a monopsonist may improve welfare.

These two considerations suggest a second possible benchmark: the input purchase level that would be chosen if the predator were a perfect competitor in both input and output markets. If the predator so overpurchases the input that the value of the input price α exceeds the value of the input's marginal product (pf_A), then it must be true that the purchaser both intended to raise rivals' costs and also bought so much extra input that economic welfare must have declined, even ignoring the additional inefficiencies induced by the increase in competitors' costs. This benchmark clearly is far more permissive than the classical monopoly/monopsony purchase level. However, it can be profitable to raise rivals' costs sufficiently to exceed this benchmark.[40]

This more permissive benchmark is analogous to Areeda and Turner's [1975] marginal cost pricing rule for judging allegations of predatory pricing. Although a price below the short run profit-maximizing level may indicate an intent to drive rivals from the market and may reduce economic welfare even if the entrant is less efficient,[41] Areeda and Turner chose the more permissive static, non-strategic pricing standard. Their arguments in favor of the Areeda-Turner rule can be applied to our competitive benchmark.

Moreover, it is interesting to note that our competitive benchmark also involves a comparison of marginal cost and price. If a perfectly competitive firm purchases inputs beyond the efficient level to a point where the price of the input exceeds its marginal value product, that firm will be in a position where its marginal cost (of increasing its output with an input) exceeds the price it receives for its output. This is easy to show. For a perfect competitor with no monopsony power, the marginal cost of increasing output by expanding use of a particular input equals the price of that input α divided by its marginal product f_A. Formally, if the predator was a perfect competitor, we would have $MC = \alpha/f_A$. It follows that the competitor's marginal cost

[40] Suppose that the fringe requires one unit of A to produce one unit of output. Then, assuming that the fringe has increasing costs in other inputs, a plausible fringe supply function is $S(p, \alpha)$, and fringe demand for A is $A^F(\alpha, p) = (p-\alpha) \geqslant 0$. Suppose that A is supplied inelastically at A^*, but that the predator does not use A in production. Thus, an equilibrium with $\alpha > 0$, $A^D > 0$ proves the result. Assume that the predator has constant average cost of production of c. Finally, assume that industry demand is linear, $D(p) = a-bp$. It is easily shown that the equilibrium in this model is $p^* = (a+bc-A^*)/2b$, $\alpha^* = [a-(b+1)A^*]/2b$, $A^D = (A^*-c)/2$, if $[a-(b+1)A^*] > 0$. If this condition holds $\alpha^* > 0$, then $A^{D*} > 0$, even though the marginal productivity of A for the predator is zero. Thus, the predator purchases A at a price above its marginal revenue product and above the value of the marginal product of A (which in this case are both zero).

[41] See Hay [1981].

exceeds the price of output p if the input price α exceeds the marginal value product pf_A (i.e., if $\alpha > pf_A$, then $MC = \alpha/f_A > p$). Thus, if the predator violates our competitive benchmark, his marginal cost *measured by treating him as a competitor* would exceed price.

V. VERTICAL INTEGRATION

Consider now the case in which the predator is partially vertically integrated; that is, it self-manufactures a portion of its overall input requirements. The model of section IV is easily extended to incorporate this possibility. We will now show that the firm may (over-) purchase inputs on the outside "merchant" market even when it is more efficient to produce the input internally, in order to increase the costs of competitors. This can occur even if the production technology exhibits fixed proportions.

Interpreting $A^D(\alpha, p)$ as *net* purchases of input A by the predator (where $A^D(\alpha, p) < 0$ means that predator is a net seller of A), let A^{*D} be the quantity of input A *produced* by the predator and let $c(A^{*D})$ be its cost of production. Then the predator's cost function is given by

$$(22) \qquad \tilde{C}(x, \alpha, p) = \min_{\{z_i^D, A^{*D}\}} \left[\sum r_i z_i^D + \alpha A^D(\alpha, p) + c(A^{*D})\right],$$

$$\text{subject to } f(z^D, A^{*D} + A^D(\alpha, p)) = x$$

It is easily seen that the minimization of (22) with respect to A^{*D} requires

$$(23) \qquad c'(A^{*D}) - \chi f_A = 0$$

This condition implies that the predator always *produces* input A efficiently, i.e., at the level at which its marginal cost of production is equal to its marginal revenue product.

The other equilibrium conditions are the same as (17). Therefore, since as shown above, $(\alpha - \chi f_A) > 0$ may be characteristic of an equilibrium, it follows from (23) that $(\alpha - c'(A^{*D})) > 0$ may also obtain.[42] In short, it may be profitable for the predator to purchase the input on the market at a price exceeding its own marginal cost of producing the input internally. This is because purchases of the input raise the costs of the fringe and the reduction in fringe supply may more than compensate for the predator's increased input cost.

Asymmetry in the extent of vertical integration enhances the likelihood

[42] An example in which $(\alpha - c'(A^{*D})) > 0$ can be easily constructed along the lines of the example of footnote 40. Assume now that the predator must also use one unit of A to produce one unit of output and that it can produce A at a constant average cost of c. If we assume the demand curve and technology of the fringe is the same as in footnote 40, the equilibrium in this model is also $p^* = (a + bc - A^*)/2b$, $\alpha^* = [a - (b+1)A^*]/2b$, $A^D = (A - c)/2$, $x^* = [a + bc - A^*]/2$, and $A^{*D} = [a + (2-b)c - A]/2$, where A^{*D} is the amount of A produced by the predator (assuming $(a + (2-b)c - A) > 0$). Since α^* does not depend on c, it is clearly possible to have $(\alpha^* - c) > 0$.

that this strategy will be profitable. This can be illustrated with the following simple example. Suppose the predator and the fringe each have a fixed proportion technology that requires one unit of the input to produce one unit of output. Assume that only the predator is vertically integrated into input production and it produces a fraction β of its input needs internally. In this case, an increase in α by an amount $\Delta\alpha$ increases the predator's average costs by $(1-\beta)\Delta\alpha$. This increase is smaller than the increase in fringe marginal cost of $\Delta\alpha$. Because market prices depend on fringe marginal costs, the asymmetry in vertical integration may be the basis of a profitable exclusionary strategy.

Of course, there is also an indirect effect on the predator's average cost equal to $\Delta\alpha A(\alpha)\varepsilon_A$ arising from the increased purchases required to increase α by $\Delta\alpha$, where ε_A is the price elasticity of supply of A. Nonetheless, the asymmetry between the vertically integrated predator and the unintegrated fringe is more likely to make cost-predation profitable, even if there is no input substitutability.[43] This is summarized in the following result.

Proposition 9. Vertical integration can be anticompetitive, even with a technology that permits no input substitution.

Proposition 9 shows that a fixed coefficient technology is *not* a sufficient condition for the absence of anticompetitive impact of a vertical merger (cf. Bork [1978]).

VI. SUMMARY AND CONCLUSIONS

In this paper, we have developed a general model in which a predator can use cost-raising strategies to increase its profits by disadvantaging its rivals. Our results suggest that cost-raising strategies can be an important anticompetitive instrument even if the "predator" is a price-taker in the output market. Such strategies can include pre-emption in upstream input markets and vertical integration, abuse of the regulatory process, advertising, and product differentiation. In addition, the effects of some cost-raising strategies can sometimes be collusive, in that the fringe's profits sometimes increase.

There is more work needed in this area. First, the models in this paper do not incorporate the possibility of fringe counterstrategies against the predator's conduct. Although we have shown elsewhere (Salop, Scheffman and Schwartz [1984]) that the scope of such counterstrategies is limited, they can provide a constraint on potential cost-raising strategies in some cases. Second, we have focused on the case of a competitive fringe. Some work has been carried out for oligopoly markets (see, e.g., Salinger (1985)), but additional structure could be added to that model and counterstrategies could be studied productively. Third, more detailed analysis of efficiency could allow the welfare results to be made more precise. Finally, models of

[43] The example in the preceding footnote provides proof of this proposition.

optimal antitrust policy in a regime of limited market information for the enforcement authorities could be constructed using the structure set out here.[44]

STEVEN C. SALOP,
Georgetown University Law Centre,
600 New Jersey Avenue, N.W.,
Washington, DC 20001,
USA.

ACCEPTED NOVEMBER 1986

DAVID T. SCHEFFMAN,
Bureau of Economics,
Federal Trade Commission,
Washington, DC 20580,
USA.

REFERENCES

AREEDA, P. and TURNER, D., 1975, 'Predatory Pricing and Related Practices Under Section 2 of the Sherman Act', *Harvard Law Review*, 88.

BORK, ROBERT, 1978, *The Antitrust Paradox* (Basic Books, New York).

EASTERBROOK, F., 1981, 'Predatory Strategies and Counterstrategies', *University of Chicago Law Review*, 48, pp. 263–337.

GILBERT, RICHARD, 1981, 'Patents, Sleeping Patents and Entry Deterrence', in S. SALOP (ed.), *Strategy, Predation and Antitrust Analysis*, pp. 205–270.

HAY, G., 1981, 'A Confused Lawyer's Guide to Predatory Pricing', in S. SALOP (ed.), *Strategy Predation and Antitrust Analysis*, pp. 155–202.

KRATTENMAKER, T. and SALOP, S., 1986, 'Anticompetitive Exclusion: Raising Rivals' Costs to Achieve Power Over Price', *Yale Law Journal*, 96 (November), pp. 209–295.

MALONEY, M. and MCCORMICK, R., 1982, 'A Positive Theory of Environmental Quality Regulation', *Journal of Law and Economics*, 25 (April), pp. 99–124.

MALONEY, M. and TOLLISON, R., 1979, 'Achieving Cartel Profits Through Unionization', *Southern Economic Journal*, 42 (October), pp. 628–634.

MCCORMICK, R., 1984, 'The Strategic Use of Regulation: A Review of the Literature', in ROGOWSKY and YANDLE [1984].

ORDOVER, J. and WILLIG, R., 1981, 'An Economic Definition of Predation: Pricing and Product Innovation', *Yale Law Review*, 91 (November), pp. 8–53.

PLOTT, C., 1981, 'Theories of Industrial Organization as Explanations of Experimental Market Behavior', in S. SALOP (ed.), *Strategy, Predation and the Antitrust Analysis*, pp. 523–578.

ROGOWSKY, R. and YANDLE, B., 1984, *The Political Economy of Regulation: Private Interests in the Regulatory Process* (Federal Trade Commission, Washington, DC).

SALLINGER, M., 1975, 'Vertical Mergers and Market Foreclosure', Columbia Business School, unpublished manuscript.

SALOP, S. C., 1979, 'Strategic Entry Deterrence', *American Economic Review*, 69 (May), pp. 335–338.

[44] For an explicit treatment of the concept of cost-raising strategies in an antitrust context with full market information see Krattenmaker and Salop (1986).

SALOP, S. C., 1981, 'Introduction', in S. C. SALOP (ed.), *Strategy, Predation and Antitrust Analysis* (Federal Trade Commission, Washington, DC), pp. 1–42.

SALOP, S. C. and SCHEFFMAN, D. T., 1983, 'Raising Rivals' Costs', *American Economic Review*, (May), pp. 267–271.

SALOP, S. C. and SCHEFFMAN, D. T., 1984, 'Multi-Market Strategies in a Dominant Firm Industry', (Federal Trade Commission Bureau of Economics Working Paper No. 100, Washington, DC).

SALOP, S. C., SCHEFFMAN, David T. and SCHWARTZ, W., 1984, 'A Bidding Analysis of Special Interest Regulation: Raising Rivals' Cost in Rent-Seeking Society', in ROGOWSKY and YANDLE [1984].

SALOP, S. C. and SHAPIRO, C., 1980, 'A Guide to Test Market Predation', Unpublished Manuscript.

SCHARFSTEIN, D., 1984, 'A Policy to Prevent Rational Test Market Predation', *Rand Journal of Economics*, 2 (Summer), pp. 229–243.

WILLIAMSON, O., 1968, 'Wage Rates as a Barrier to Entry: The Pennington Case', *Quarterly Journal of Economics*, (February), pp. 85–116.

THE JOURNAL OF INDUSTRIAL ECONOMICS 0022-1821 $2.00
Volume XXXVI September 1987 No. 1

ARE 'RATIONAL CONJECTURES' RATIONAL?

LOUIS MAKOWSKI*

The concepts of 'rational conjectures' and 'reasonable conjectures' are critically reviewed. It is shown that their operation depends crucially on an invisible, non-optimizing 'deus ex machina'. Hence, these concepts are not really suitable for understanding competition among *optimizing* firms. In addition, the widely claimed "fact" that Bertrand conjectures are locally rational conjectural variations is shown to be erroneous.

I. INTRODUCTION

THE MESSAGE of this paper should be plain from the title. It reflects a disillusionment with the concepts of 'rational conjectures' and 'reasonable conjectures', for helping us understand economic interactions under imperfect competition.

On the face of it, these concepts seem to offer the economic modeller some useful tools. Hence this paper is in some sense intended as a friendly warning to other economic modellers. There are inherent conceptual weaknesses in these concepts, that do not become apparent until one begins to penetrate their inner logic.

To make plain the weaknesses of 'rational conjectures' and 'reasonable conjectures', we shall concentrate on the simplest application of the ideas—to duopoly. And, we shall illustrate our points using the classical Cournot example of duopolists facing a common linear demand curve and having the same, constant marginal cost.

The reader may know that this example figures prominently in the rational conjectures literature, it being "shown" that Bertrand conjectures are locally rational conjectural variations. We shall see in section VI that this claim is not really valid, although widely asserted. But our real message is on a different plane, and pertains to the usefulness of the concepts in general.

II. THE SET-UP (FOR DUOPOLY)

There are two firms indexed by i, and also by j, where $j \neq i$. The A_i represents the set of possible actions for firm i. The function π_i from A to R_+ is firm i's

* This paper has grown out of many enjoyable conversations with Hamid Sabourian and Adam Brandenburger. (This is not to suggest that either necessarily agrees or disagrees with the punchline.) There were also some very nice conversations with Oliver Hart.

profit function, where $A \equiv \{\{a_i, a_j\}: a_i \in A_i \text{ and } a_j \in A_j\}$.[1] The function C_{ij} from $A_i \times A$ to A_j represents i's conjecture about j's response to any action $a_i' \in A_i$, when the 'status quo' is some joint action $a \in A$.

III. RATIONAL CONJECTURES (GLOBAL)

Consider the following problem for firm i, with the 'status quo' $a \in A$ being a parameter for i:

$$(1) \qquad \max_{a_i' \in A_i} \pi_i(a_i', C_{ij}(a_i', a))$$

Let $S_i(a)$ be the set of all a_i' that solve this problem for i. If the solution is unique, we write it as $s_i(a)$.

Definition I. α^* is a conjectural equilibrium ($a^* \in CE$) if, for all i,

$$(2) \qquad a_i^* \in S_i(a^*)$$

Definition II. a^* is a rational conjectural equilibrium ($a^* \in RCE$) if $a^* \in CE$ and, for all i,

$$(3) \qquad a_j \equiv C_{ij}(a_i, a^*) \in S_j(a) \quad \text{for all} \quad a_i \in A_i$$

where

$$a \equiv (a_i, a_j)$$

Condition (3) is usually interpreted as the test to see whether i's conjectures are 'rational', rather than merely arbitrary.[2] This is motivated by the observation that almost anything can be supported as a CE given that firms have sufficiently strange and capricious conjectures. For example, it is pointed out that Cournot conjectures are not rational since firm i would see that any deviation by it from the Cournot conjectural equilibrium would induce an active response by j, contradicting the no-response Cournot conjecture.

Does (3) do what it purports to do? Does it really test the rationality of i's conjectures about j, C_{ij}? In particular, if the status quo is a^* and i deviates to a_i, will j want to go to a_j? This is not what (3) requires! Instead, it requires that if j *finds* himself at the new status quo a, he will want to *stay* there given his conjectures about i. The *move* to a_j is not required to be an optimizing

[1] This set theoretic way of defining the set of possible joint actions is more general and flexible than the alternative of defining the set as $A_i \times A_j$. In particular, our definition allows us to treat i and j symmetrically, avoiding the need for annoying double definitions. Usually, we will take the liberty of writing (a_i, a_j) instead of $\{a_i, a_j\}$ for an element of A; no confusion should result, and it's simpler.

[2] This version of 'rational conjectures' appears for example in Ulph [1983], Hart [1982], and also in Sabourian [1983] (under the name of "*ex post* rationality").

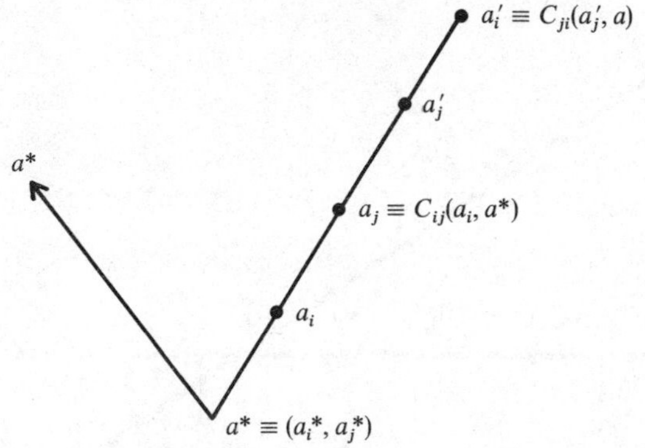

Figure 1
The Meaning of (3)

decision by j! The meaning of (3) is illustrated in Figure 1. Referring to the figure, notice that i is testing the profit potential of a deviation a_i from a^*. It is assumed that j will respond with an a_j such that

$$\pi_j(a) \geqslant \pi_j(a'), \quad \text{for all } a_j' \in A_j$$

where

$$a \equiv (a_i, a_j)$$

$$a' \equiv (a_i', a_j')$$

and

$$a_i' \equiv C_{ji}(a_j', a)$$

We have now stated our basic criticism of the RCE concept, that we shall amplify below: the first response by j to a deviation by i from the status quo is *imposed* on j, *not* on optimizing choice by j. We shall refer to this below by saying RCE imposes a deus ex machina (DEM) assumption on the first response to any deviation from the status quo.

Example (Bertrand conjectures are global RCE conjectures, but...). Following the literature, let actions be quantities. And, take Bertrand to mean $r_{ij} \equiv \partial C_{ij}(a_i', a)/\partial a_i' = -1$ for all $a_i' \in A_i$ and all $a \in A$. Also assume outputs must be non-negative, that is, $A_i = R_+$ for all i.

Let the inverse demand curve, $p(q)$, that the duopolists face be linear and downward sloping, as pictured in Figure 2. And let each firm i have constant marginal costs $c \geqslant 0$ (where $MC = AC$). The reader can easily verify for himself that a^* is an RCE under Bertrand conjectures, when a^* satisfies $p(a_1^* + a_2^*) = c$; for example, if $a_i = a_i^* + \Delta a_i$ then $a_j \equiv C_{ij}(a_i, a^*) = a_j^* - \Delta a_i$ maximizes $\pi_j(\cdot, C_{ji}(\cdot, a))$ over all outputs in A_j. Note that $\pi_j(a) = \pi_i(a^*) = 0$; that is, Bertrand yields the price $= MC$ solution. (In the literature this is sometimes called the 'competitive solution'.)

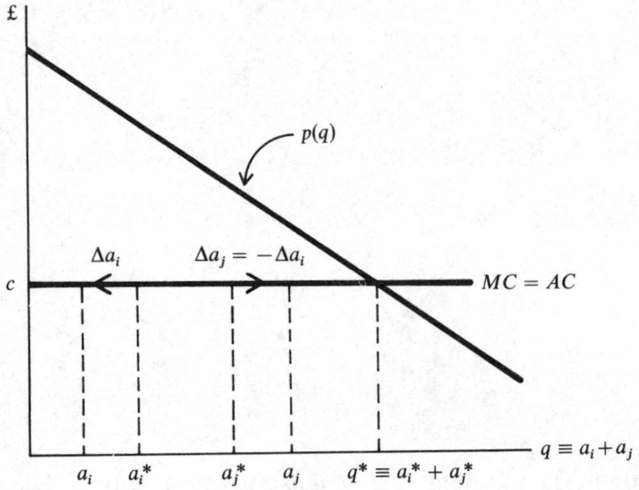

Figure 2
The Bertrand 'equilibrium'

Perhaps the reader already sees the deus ex machina (DEM) in this 'rational' solution? Why should j go to $a_j \equiv C_{ij}(a_i, a^*)$ when i deviated to a_i? It is simply *assumed* by i that j goes to a_j and *then* i checks to see if j will want to *stay* there (once he has found himself there). One way to see that in general j will not want to *go* to a_j is to see that Bertrand is not an "only slightly more rational"-RCE (next section). Another way to see this is as follows.

It is usually also assumed in RCE models that no deviation induces no response, i.e.

(4) $\quad C_{ji}(a_j, a) = a_i, \quad$ for all $a \in A$

If this were so and j could *choose* his first response to the deviation a_i, j could do better than $a_j \equiv a_j^* - \Delta a_i$ by simply sticking at a_j^* whenever i's output decreases from a_i^* (i.e. whenever $\Delta a_i < 0$; see Figure 2). By sticking at a_j^*, j could expect to make a positive profit given his conjectures satisfy (4).

Proof. $C_{ji}(a_j^*, (a_i, a_j^*)) = a_i$ (given (4)) so

$$\pi_j(a_j^*, C_{ji}(a_j^*, (a_i, a_j^*))) = \pi_j(a_j^*, a_i) > \pi_j(a) = 0, \quad \text{for all } a_i < a_i^*.$$

So, it is only "rational" for j to *stay* at a_j; not for j to *go* to a_j. This is another way to see that the conjectural response a_j must be *imposed* on j by a DEM in a RCE. It is not an optimizing choice by j.

IV. ONLY SLIGHTLY MORE RATIONAL, RATIONAL CONJECTURES (GLOBAL)

Before realizing there was a DEM in RCE's, I thought that a "rational conjectural equilibrium" was a CE in which the response that i anticipates

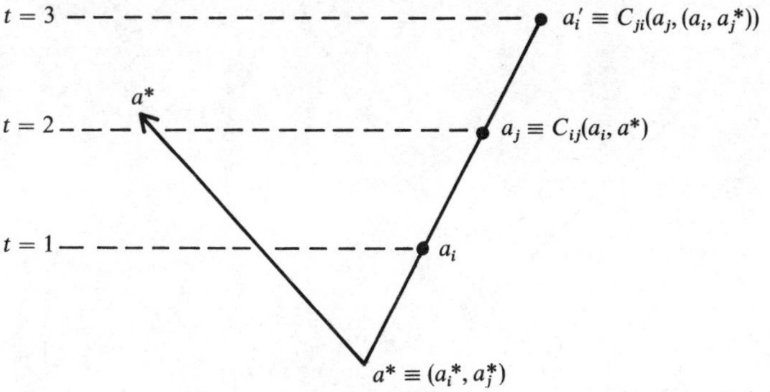

Figure 3
The Meaning of (5)

from j when he deviates to a_i is the response j perceives to be desirable when j finds himself at the new status quo (a_i, a_j^*)—*before* any DEM intervenes (see Figure 3).[3] This is sometimes how RCE's are explained, even by authors using Definition II! I shall call the above equilibrium concept an "only slightly more rational, rational conjectural equilibrium" (SMR-RCE).

Definition III. a^* is an SMR-RCE if $a^* \in CE$ and, for all i,

$$(5) \qquad a_j \equiv C_{ij}(a_i, a^*) \in S_j(a_i, a_j^*), \quad \text{for all } a_i \in A_i$$

The meaning of (5) is illustrated in Figure 3. Referring to the figure, notice that i is testing the profit potential of a deviation a_i from a^*. It is assumed that j will respond with an a_j such that

$$\pi_j(a_j, C_{ji}(a_j, (a_i, a_j^*))) \geqslant \pi_j(a_j', C_{ji}(a_j', (a_i, a_j^*))), \quad \text{for all } a_j' \in A_j$$

Example continued (Bertrand conjectures are *not* SMR-RCE conjectures). To see this observe that if i goes to $a_i \equiv a_i^* + \Delta a_i < a_i^*$, j will *not* generally want to go to $a_j^* - \Delta a_i$—as i conjectures under Bertrand—if j regards the new status quo as (a_i, a_j^*) and also has Bertrand conjectures. Rather, once at (a_i, a_j^*), j will want to take over the entire market (!) since $a_i + a_j^* < q^*$ implies $p(a_i + a_j^*) > c$, and $r_{ji} = -1$ implies j believes any increase in output by himself beyond a_j^* will be matched by a decrease in output by i, leaving total output and hence price unaffected. In particular, maximizing $p(\bar{a}_j)\bar{a}_j - c\bar{a}_j$ by choice of $\bar{a}_j$, subject to $\bar{a}_j \geqslant a_j^* + a_i$ (the driving i out of the market condition), shows:

$$(6a) \qquad s_j(a_i, a_j^*) = \begin{Bmatrix} q_m \\ a_j^* + a_i \end{Bmatrix} \text{ as } a_j^* + a_i \begin{Bmatrix} \leqslant \\ > \end{Bmatrix} q_m, \quad \text{for all } a_i < a_i^*$$

where $q_m = \text{argmax } p(q)q - cq \equiv$ the monopoly output level. Using similar

[3] I am grateful to Hamid Sabourian for finally disillusioning me on this point.

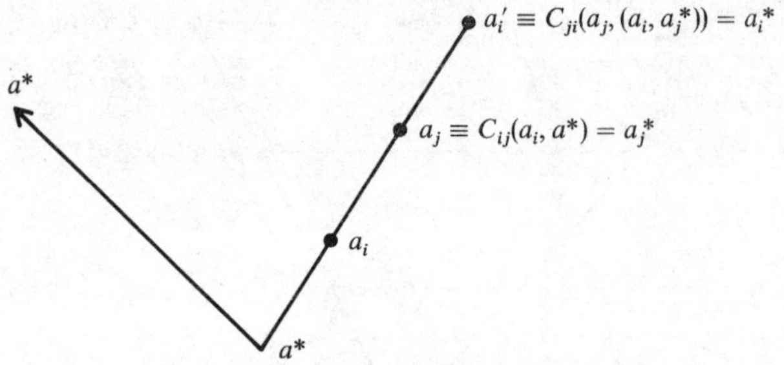

Figure 4
Cournot Outputs as an SMR-RCE

reasoning, it is also easy to verify that:

(6b) $s_j(a_i, a_j^*) = 0$, for all $a_i > a_i^*$

So Bertrand conjectures fail to satisfy test (5).

Remark (SMR-RCE's criticized). An SMR-RCE is only slightly more sensible than an RCE. It's not really "rational" either. But at least there is no DEM. We now state our basic criticism of this alternative concept.

Note that in a SMR-RCE i expects profits $\pi_i(a_i, C_{ij}(a_i, a^*))$ when he deviates: that is why he tries to solve (1). And j expects profits $\pi_j(a_j, C_{ji}(a_j, (a_i, a_j^*)))$ when he responds to a_i with a_j; that is why he tries to maximize $\pi_j(\cdot, C_{ji}(\cdot, (a_i, a_j^*)))$. So, i expects the "game" to end at "time" $t = 2$ (see Figure 3) after his deviation to a_i; and i expects j to respond with a_j. But j responds with a_j because j expects the game to end at time $t = 3$ (again see Figure 3) after i has responded with $a_i' \equiv C_{ji}(a_j, (a_i, a_j^*))$ to j's response of a_j. Since generally in an SMR-RCE $a_i' \neq a_i$, the agents' conjectures about one another's responses rest on inconsistent expectations. And so, they are not "rational" conjectures.

Example continued (Cournot outputs as an SMR-RCE, but...). Let a^* be output levels for i and j that would result from their having Cournot conjectures. Then a^* may be supported as an SMR-RCE if each firm i conjectures

(7) $C_{ij}(a_i', a) = a_j^*$, for all $a_i' \in A_i$ and all $a \in A$

To check that a^* is an SMR-RCE, observe that if j expects i to return to his Cournot output level after any deviation from it, then j's best response to any deviation by i is to play Cournot (see Figure 4). Also observe that $C_{ji}(a_j, (a_i, a_j^*)) = a_i^* \neq a_i$, illustrating the inconsistency of expectations under SMR-RCE (recall the Remark above).[4]

[4] Note that (7) violates the 'consistency assumption' (4), that is often imposed on RCE's. But, we do not need (4). Indeed Sabourian convincingly argues that (4) is not sensible away from "equilibrium" (see Sabourian [1983] or the citation in Hart's survey [1983]).

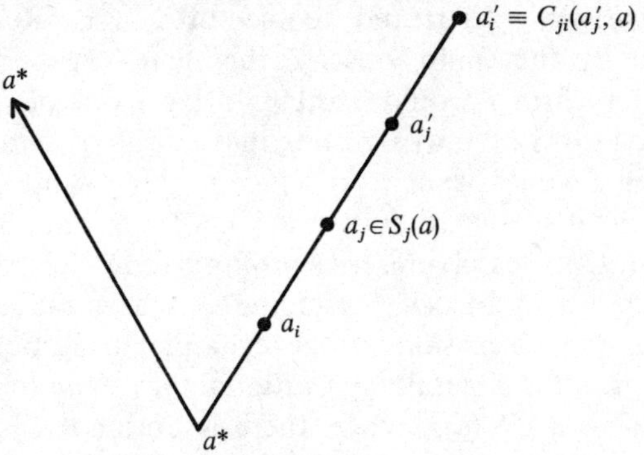

Figure 5
The Meaning of (8)

V. REASONABLE CONJECTURES (GLOBAL)

An alternative to RCE's introduced into the literature by Frank Hahn [1978], and more recently developed by Oliver Hart [1982], is that of "Reasonable Conjectures".

Definition IV. a^* is a reasonable conjectural equilibrium ($a^* \in ReCE$) if $a^* \in CE$ and for all i

$$(8) \qquad \pi_i(a^*) \geqslant \pi_i(a) \quad \text{for all } a \in A \quad \text{such that } a_j \in S_j(a)$$

The meaning of (8) is illustrated in Figure 5. In the figure, i is testing the profit potential of a deviation a_i from a^*. It is assumed that j will respond with the $a_j \in A_j$ that i likes the best (!), subject only to $a_j \in S_j(a)$; so, as in Figure 1,

$$\pi_j(a) \geqslant \pi_j(a') \quad \text{for all } a_j' \in A_j, \quad \text{where } a_i' \equiv C_{ji}(a_j', a)$$

As Hart notes, an ReCE is in the same spirit as an RCE (compare Figure 5 with Figure 1). Thus our basic criticism of the latter concept also applies to this alternative incarnation: ReCE also imposes a deus ex machina (DEM) assumption on j's initial response to any deviation a_i by i. Again, generally a_j is not where j *wants to go* (if he could choose, given his conjectures about i), but only where j wants to *stay* (once he finds himself at a_j).

But in at least one respect ReCE is a "stronger" concept than RCE. If more than one a_j satisfies $a_j \in S_j(a)$ then i supposes he can get the best of the bunch (see Figure 5). It is as if i can direct the DEM to put j at the $a_j \in S_j(a)$ that i likes the best. So the DEM operates with a vengeance! In this respect "reasonable conjectures" seem even less reasonable than "rational conjectures". (By now it is perhaps suspected that the 'DEM' of RCE's and ReCE's is an incarnation of the notorious Walrasian auctioneer?)

Example continued (Bertrand conjectures are ReCE conjectures, but...). To verify the claim, observe that if $a_i + a_j < q^*$ then, as in the derivation of (6a), firm j would want to drive i out of the market. So if $a_i + a_j < q^*$, then $a_j \in S_j(a)$ only if $a_i = 0$; that is, only if $\pi_i(a) = 0$. Similarly, if $a_i + a_j > q^*$ then j would want to produce nothing. And so, if $a_i + a_j > q^*$, then $a_j \in S_j(a)$ only if $a_i > q^*$; that is, only if $\pi_i(a) < 0$. Thus, any status quo a^* such that $p(a_i^* + a_j^*) = c$ maximizes i's profits given j's Bertrand conjectures.

But what is the significance of this finding? Just as in the case of Bertrand as an RCE (recall the discussion of the example in section III), given his conjectures about i it is generally not rational for j to *go* to an $a_j \in S_j(a)$; only for j to *stay* at an $a_j \in S_j(a)$. Hence, there is nothing reasonable about i's presumption that j *will* go to an $a_j \in S_j(a)$ when i deviates to a_i. And if i does not presume this, there is nothing reasonable about an economic optimizing model whose operation depends on an invisible, *but crucial* deus ex machina.

Remark (Hart's static interpretation of ReCE's). Hart [1982] gives an appealing static interpretation to Hahn's ReCE's. He shows that ReCE's can be interpreted as Nash equilibria in which firms take each other's supply correspondences as given. Thus, in this interpretation $S_j(\cdot)$ is viewed as j's supply response (a function of the status quo); and it is observed that in a ReCE no firm i can increase its profits taking as given j's supply response (and making the "optimistic assumption" that any status quo is feasible for i). Hart's motivation for such an interpretation seems to be as follows. We know if agents have Cournot conjectures then generally any one firm i can increase its profits given the other firm's conjectures. This is commonly expressed by observing that if firm i knows j believes Cournot, i can increase his profits by acting as a Stackelberg leader. By contrast, in a ReCE no firm i can increase its profits taking as given the other firm's conjectures. So, in an ReCE, firms are more sophisticated; no firm i has an incentive to act as a Stackelberg leader (even given the "optimistic assumption" that i can somehow manipulate—"lead"—j into any status quo). This is indeed an attractive interpretation, that fits ReCE's into a long line of economic theorizing. Note that RCE's apparently cannot be given an analogous, static "Nash in supply correspondences" interpretation. But how far does the interpretation go in terms of increasing our economic understanding of imperfect competition?

Under Hart's interpretation, there is no effort made to *derive* firm j's supply correspondence (or the conjectures about i that underly it) from *optimizing* considerations. Firm j may have completely crazy conjectures about i and consequently, a completely crazy supply correspondence; there could still be a ReCE *given* firms' crazy beliefs. This can be illustrated using our example: For any status quo, a, such that $a_i + a_j < q^*$ recall that $S_j(a)$ is based on j's conjecture that whenever j increases his output he will increase his profits because i will cooperate by decreasing his output and hence by decreasing his profits! Firm i takes this crazy belief by j as *given*; so a_i^* is the best i can do if j

blindly follows his Bertrand conjectures. As the illustration should make plain, under Hart's interpretation of ReCE's, we are no longer addressing the question of the reasonableness of firms' conjectures; the term "reasonable conjectures" becomes just a misnomer. "Reasonable conjectures" become basically just arbitrary conjectures in a larger space. My own belief is that the economics of imperfect competition requires addressing the question: what "supply correspondences" will *optimizing* imperfectly competitive firms *choose*?—a question that this interpretation does not even try to address. The interpretation thus only reinforces from another perspective the lesson that *I* would emphasize: the ReCE concept is not flexible enough to be a useful tool for guiding serious economic inquiry into imperfect competition.

A last, more far-reaching remark may be helpful, although anticipating somewhat our positive suggestion in section VII below. The Marshallian–Walrasian supply-and-demand apparatus that is being invoked in Hart's interpretation seems out of place. Duopolists are after all in a rivalrous, *price-making* situation; but the supply correspondence was designed to describe the output decisions of optimizing, *price-taking* firms. I do not believe this apparatus can be altered to gracefully dance to price-making music. A similar remark applies to the Negishi idea of polists facing exogenous "perceived demand curves". While it is undoubtedly useful to work with perceived demands when the number of polists is large or there is pure monopoly, so any one polist can safely ignore the reactions of other polists to his actions; when the number of polists is small but greater than one, such reactions cannot be ignored. In the latter circumstance, to work with exogenous, perceived demands is to beg the real economic question: what optimizing decisions by the competing polists generates any one polist's "perceived demand".

VI. LOCAL VARIATIONS ON A THEME

The literature also contains local versions of "rational conjectures". For example, Laitner [1980] studies local RCE's (definition II except (3) need only hold for all $a_i \in A_i \cap N_\varepsilon(a_i^*)$ (that is, in some ε-neighborhood of a_i^*, where $\varepsilon > 0$)). Of course, the DEM critique again applies, plus the obvious caveats about local conditions.

More popular are the calculus-using "conjectural variation" (CV) versions. For example, letting the ε of above go to zero and *assuming* the *differentiability* of C_{ij} and S_j at a^* (hence the uniqueness of S_j around a^*) we find:

Definition II-CV. a^* is a CV-RCE if $a^* \in CE$ and for all i

$$(9) \qquad r_{ij} \equiv \frac{\partial C_{ij}(a_i^*, a^*)}{\partial a_i} = \frac{ds_j(a^*)}{da_i}$$

where, if s_j is differentiable in both its arguments then $ds_j(a^*)/da_i = (\partial s_j(a^*)/\partial a_i) + (\partial s_j(a^*)/\partial a_j)r_{ij}$. Note that the CV version of Definition II involves the *total* derivative of s_j with respect to a_i. This is not always explicitly observed in the CV literature. There is also a CV version of Definition III possible:

Definition III-CV. a^* is a CV version of SMR-RCE if $a^* \in CE$ and for all i

$$(10) \qquad r_{ij} \equiv \frac{\partial C_{ij}(a_i^*, a^*)}{\partial a_i} = \frac{\partial s_j(a^*)}{\partial a_i}$$

Note that (10) only involves the partial derivative of s_j with respect to a_i. It is hard to tell if the CV literature means (9) or (10) by "rational conjectures" since the reader is often not told where derivatives are being evaluated. Note that (9) and (10) are equivalent if s_j is differentiable in both its arguments *and* $\partial s_j(a^*)/\partial a_j = 0$. Sometimes this appears to be implicitly assumed, e.g. in Perry [1982].[5]

Example continued. It is usual in the CV literature to "prove" Bertrand is a rational CV, e.g. see Bresnahan [1981] or Perry [1982]. The "proof" unfortunately is wrong since it *presumes* j's solution set under Bertrand conjectures, $S_j(a)$, is unique and differentiable at a^*, neither of which is true. In particular, we will see below that $S_j(a)$ is not even a continuous correspondence, much less a differentiable function at $a = a^* =$ the 'competitive solution' (see Figure 6). But even now, from our above work, we know that the limit $\partial s_j(a^*)/\partial a_i$ does not exist under Bertrand conjectures: we have already seen in deriving (6a) that any deviation $a_i < a_i^*$ leads to a large *jump* in j's desired output under Bertrand. Hence the calculus-based CV approach has been misapplied in Bresnahan [1981] and Perry [1982]: the calculus cannot be used in the example since S_j is not differentiable at a^*.

We can find j's solution set $S_j(a)$ under his Bertrand conjectures by solving:

$$\max_{a_j' \in A_j} \pi_j(a_j', C_{ji}(a_j', a)) = p(a_j' + C_{ji}(a_j', a))a_j' - ca_j'$$

$$\text{subject to } C_{ji}(a_j', a) = \begin{cases} a_i + r_{ji}(a_j' - a_j) = a_i - 1(a_j' - a_j) & \text{if } a_i - 1(a_j' - a_j) \geqslant 0 \\ 0 & \text{otherwise.} \end{cases}$$

Notice we have j assuming in Bertrand fashion that i's reaction $r_{ji} = -1$ (subject only to the fact that negative outputs are impossible for i). The reader can easily check that the solution set for this problem, as a function of the status quo a, is given by:

$$S_j(a) = [0, q^*] \qquad \text{if } p(a_i + a_j) = c$$

$$S_j(a) = \{0\} \qquad \text{if } p(a_i + a_j) < c$$

[5] This observation comes from Hamid Sabourian.

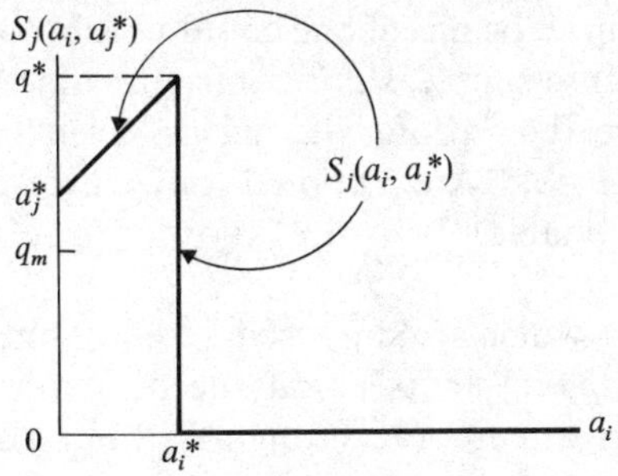

Figure 6
The non-existence of $\partial s_j(a_i^*, a_j^*)/\partial a_i$ and $ds_j(a_i^*, a_j^*)/da_i$ under Bertrand Conjectures

$$S_j(a) = \{\max\{a_i + a_j, q_m\}\} \text{ if } p(a_i + a_j) > c$$

where q^* satisfies $p(q^*) = c$ (it's the competitive market output). Thus, if the status quo a involves zero profits then $S_j(a)$ is an entire interval up to q^*. But if it involves non-zero profits then $S_j(a)$ consists of a unique point, as we already noted in (6). In particular, as asserted above and illustrated in Figure 6 for the case $a_j^* > q_m$, at $a = a^* =$ the 'competitive solution' $S_j(a)$ is not even a continuous *correspondence*, much less a differentiable *function*. Thus under Bertrand conjectures it is not meaningful to speak about the limits $\partial s_j(a^*)/\partial a_i$ or $ds_j(a^*)/da_i$. More forcefully expressed, under Bertrand these limits just do not exist, contrary to the *presumption* in Bresnahan [1981] and Perry [1982]. Thus, for example, when Perry claims to have shown that with a linear demand curve and constant costs (as in our example) Bertrand is the only CV-RCE, he has really shown there exists *no* CV-RCE. (He shows that Bertrand is the only CV satisfying the calculus, necessary first-order conditions for an RCE; the correct conclusion: the only possible candidate can be dismissed because it leads to a non-differentiable S_j.)

Of course, we have already verified in section III that Bertrand conjectures are global (non-calculus) RCE conjectures. All that we have shown here is that Bertrand conjectures are not (calculus-type) CV-RCE conjectures. But, not to lose sight of the bigger conceptual problems noted in section III, that Bertrand conjectures are RCE conjectures does not legitimize the undiscriminating use of either Bertrand conjectures or the RCE concept.

VII. 'CONJECTURES' AS GAME THEORY WITHOUT GAME THEORY: A POSITIVE SUGGESTION

The idea of conjectures was intended to help us model firms' decision making in an oligopolistic setting. In other words, to help us model imperfect competition. But I do not think it has really helped our understanding of imperfect competition.

It would, of course, be nice if one could sensibly encapsulate a complicated dynamic process into simple, *static* conjecture functions; and, if rational firms seek to maximize their profits taking as given these functions. But what conjectures are sensible? Are "rational conjectures" sensible? Are "reasonable conjectures" reasonable? I do not know of any good temporal story for rationalizing either.

But conjectures, which are supposed to reflect one firm's beliefs about other firms' strategic *responses* to its actions, need a temporal story to be legitimate. (*Responses* require a temporal setting.) Without a story, conjectures are just Cheshire cats: strategic responses devoid of a strategic situation. Without fully knowing the situation, how can we evaluate the rationality or irrationality of *any* proposed response?

Where do we go from here? My experience has been that one who tries to rationalize "rational" or "reasonable" conjectures finds himself just getting more and more confused. If firms are in an interaction situation (i.e. a game) that involves strategic responses, let's model that. The tools of game theory seem to be the right ones to use, with the possible actions of each player at each point in time modelled explicitly—not just as a smile without a body. Then we can hopefully use game theoretic solution concepts; not equilibrium concepts like 'CE', which we cannot really interpret or evaluate sensibly.

Of course, game theoretic solution concepts (e.g. perfect equilibria) have interpretative problems of their own. But turning to conjectures for help is like leaving a dimly lit room for a dark cave, in order to find some light.

In the spirit of this suggestion, there is by now emerging a considerable literature on intertemporal (dynamic) games. Notable in the current context is Kalai and Stanford [1985], which tries to rationalize some sorts of conjectural variations in a repeated duopoly game. They interpret conjectural variations in terms of the "slope" of tit-for-tat-type supergame strategies, and they show that such strategies can support some outcomes as Nash equilibria. But once the requirement of subgame perfection is added, they also show that their tit-for-tat-type strategies are no longer equilibrium strategies: these strategies apparently involve non-credible threats. It seems that more complicated punishment strategies than tit-for-tat (interpreted as conjectural variations) are needed to rationalize credible dynamic interactions; e.g., see the punishment strategies in Abreu [1983] or Fudenberg and Maskin [1986].

VIII. SUMMARY

Under "rational conjectures" or "reasonable conjectures", when a firm i deviates from a_i^* to a_i, the response i anticipates from j, a_j, will generally *not* be the response that j perceives to be desirable when j finds himself at the new status quo (a_i, a_j^*). It will only be desirable for j, given his conjectures about i, *after* j finds himself *at* a_j (as a result of some deus ex machina, 'DEM', moving him from a_j^* to a_j).

This 'DEM' is *a-rational*. So "rational" or "reasonable" conjectures are built upon an *ad hoc* foundation. To restrict the set of admissible CE's by simply imposing any, arbitrary extra constraint seems hardly less sensible than the thinning out of CE's achieved by imposing "rationality" conditions coupled with an *a-rational* DEM.

The admittedly 'irrational' Cournot conjectures seem at least as rational as RCE conjectures, at least as reasonable as ReCE conjectures, and a lot simpler than either of these fancy conjectures.

Finally, while the SMR-RCE concept does not require a DEM, it *arbitrarily* cuts off the (implicitly temporal) chain of strategic responses to any initial deviation by firm i, at time $t = 2$ for firm i and at time $t = 3$ for firm j (see Figure 3). This means the firms' conjectures are based on inconsistent temporal expectations. So, SMR-RCE's do not involve really "rational" conjectures either.

ACCEPTED SEPTEMBER 1986

LOUIS MAKOWSKI,
Department of Economics,
University of California, Davis,
Davis, California 95616,
USA

REFERENCES

ABREU, D., 1983, 'Repeated Games with Discounting', Ph.D. dissertation, Department of Economics, Princeton University.

BRESNAHAN, T. F., 1981, 'Duopoly Models with Consistent Conjectures', *American Economic Review*, 71 (December), pp. 934–945.

FUDENBERG, D. and MASKIN, E., 1986, 'The Folk Theorem in Repeated Games with Discounting and with Incomplete Information', *Econometrica*, 54 (May), pp. 533–554.

HAHN, F., 1978, 'On Non-Walrasian Equilibria', *Review of Economic Studies*, 45 (February), pp. 1–18.

HART, O. D., 1982, 'Reasonable Conjectures', mimeo, London School of Economics.

HART, O. D., 1983, 'Imperfect Competition in General Equilibrium: An Overview of Recent Work', mimeo, London School of Economics.

KALAI, E. and STANFORD, W., 1985, 'Conjectural Variations Strategies in Accelerated Cournot Games', *International Journal of Industrial Organization*, 3 (June), pp. 133–152.

LAITNER, J., 1980, '"Rational" Duopoly Equilibrium', *Quarterly Journal of Economics*, 95 (December), pp. 641–662.

PERRY, M. K., 1982, 'Oligopoly and Consistent Conjectural Variations', *Bell Journal of Economics*, 13 (Spring), pp. 197–205.

SABOURIAN, H., 1983, 'Rational Conjectural Equilibria from a Game Theoretic Perspective', mimeo, Cambridge University.

ULPH, D., 1983, 'Rational Conjectures in the Theory of Oligopoly', *International Journal of Industrial Organization*, 1 (June), pp. 131–154.

THE JOURNAL OF INDUSTRIAL ECONOMICS 0022-1821 $2.00
September XXXVI September 1987 No. 1

ADVERTISING AND COMPETITION IN ROUTINE LEGAL SERVICE MARKETS: AN EMPIRICAL INVESTIGATION

JOHN R. SCHROETER, SCOTT L. SMITH AND STEVEN R. COX*

This study's findings, together with the results of earlier studies of the relationship between advertising and market prices, provide considerable empirical support for the pro-competitive view of seller advertising. Data on attorney fees and advertising practices in seventeen metropolitan areas across the US were used to estimate the effect of market advertising intensity on firm demand elasticities, holding other possible influencing factors constant. The results obtained for all three routine legal services examined are consistent with the hypothesis that advertising increases competition among sellers in a market.

I. INTRODUCTION

THE RELATIONSHIP between advertising and competition, in one manifestation or another, has been explored in dozens of empirical studies.[1] A subset of these studies has concentrated on advertising's effects on price in professional service markets (see Benham [1972], Cady [1976], and Kwoka [1984]), and one (Jacobs *et al.* [1984]) has dealt specifically with routine legal service markets, which is the subject of our study.[2] The bulk of empirical evidence from this subset of studies supports the hypothesis that prices in professional service markets in which sellers advertise are lower, relative to costs, than they would be if such advertising were banned. One important mechanism through which this relationship can arise is the connection between advertising and sellers' individual demand elasticities.[3]

* The authors are, respectively: Assistant Professor of Economics, Iowa State University; Economist, General Accounting Office, U.S. Government; and, Associate Professor of Economics, Arizona State University. Financial support for this study was partially provided by National Science Foundation grant SES 79–17625. While retaining sole responsibility for the views expressed in this paper, the authors wish to thank two anonymous referees and the editor for their helpful comments.

[1] For a review of these, see the excellent survey article by Comanor and Wilson [1979].

[2] The work done by Jacobs *et al.* [1984] was conducted independently of our own. While it uses the same data set (to be described in note 13), it implements different modeling and estimation procedures. A routine legal service may be defined as one for which the time needed to complete it, while random, has small variance. See Cox *et al.* [1982, pp. 306–7].

[3] The observed inverse relationship between advertising intensity and price may also be due to the fact that advertising is the only means whereby a seller can attract enough patrons to realize production economies of scale (see Benham [1972]). We disregard this possibility in the case of legal services since we believe that their personalized nature would render scale economies relatively unimportant. Indeed, according to Comanor and Wilson ([1979, p. 458]) advertising's effect on price elasticities is the essential issue in the advertising/competition controversy.

One view of this nexus, the "information/search theoretic" view, traces its origins to the important works of Stigler [1961] and Nelson [1970]. Stigler considers the role of advertising in the low-price search process. Consumers confronting a distribution of prices for a homogeneous commodity will engage in costly search for a low price as long as the marginal benefits of continued search exceed the marginal cost. Advertising conveys information that reduces the cost of searching for low prices and, thus, stimulates search activity.[4] Since an increase in search activity will lead to a greater reduction in demand for any seller who raises price, the effect of advertising is to render sellers' demand curves more elastic.

Nelson's work, on the other hand, emphasizes the importance of information in markets for non-homogeneous commodities. His contention is that demand elasticity depends primarily upon the range of substitute brands for which quality information is available. Here, the information conveyed by advertising serves to familiarize the representative consumer with a wider variety of options. Thus, in Nelson's model of quality search under imperfect information, as in Stigler's low-price search scenario, advertising serves to make sellers' demand curves more elastic and, consequently, price-cost margins lower than they otherwise would be.[5]

If advertising is to occur, however, individual sellers must have incentives to engage in it. To the extent that a given firm's advertising effort is effective, it serves to insulate the firm from competition with rivals. Specifically, the advertising firm's product is differentiated from those of its competitors. As a result, its demand curve becomes somewhat less elastic. Hence, the "product differentiation" view of advertising's effects suggests that advertising firms enjoy lower demand elasticity (in absolute value) and correspondingly higher price-cost margins than non-advertising firms.[6]

According to economic theory, then, there are two hypotheses concerning the relationship between advertising and demand elasticities. The informa-

[4] In extending first amendment protection to attorneys' right to advertise their fees for routine legal services, the U.S. Supreme Court in *Bates v. State Bar of Arizona* [1977] assumed that certain benefits to consumers, like the increased ability to shop for prices, would follow from such advertising.

[5] As long as low price is among the criteria used by customers in selecting a seller, greater search activity will also tend to reduce the average *paid* price for any given distribution of *quoted* prices.

[6] Two caveats to this product differentiation view deserve mention. First, as Dorfman and Steiner [1954] and others have shown, the optimal level of advertising is characterized by equality between the marginal revenue product of advertising and the absolute value of the firm's price elasticity of demand. If, as is plausible, returns to advertising are eventually diminishing, optimality requires high levels of advertising in markets where firms face quite inelastic demand curves. Thus, the direction of causality between the level of a firm's advertising intensity and the price elasticity of its demand is not clear. Second, if a representative firm can obtain greater market power and higher profit margins through advertising, one would expect that all firms would advertise in the long run, and the inevitable result would be a profitless Chamberlinian equilibrium. If long-run benefits are to be derived, therefore, advertising must also involve entry barrier effects. See Scherer [1980] and Comanor and Wilson [1974] for further discussion of these points.

tion/search theoretic view predicts that individual demand curves will be more elastic the greater is the general level of advertising in a market. The product differentiation view implies that firms which advertise will have less elastic demand curves than those that do not. The purpose of this paper is to test these two hypotheses using data from routine legal service markets. The methodology we employ assumes that profit maximizing attorneys set prices optimally in view of individual demand elasticities, which in turn depend on the attorney's own advertising effort and the level of advertising intensity in the relevant market area. Our estimation technique enables us to infer at least the qualitative effects of these two advertising variables on price-cost margins and, indirectly, price elasticities of demand.[7]

II. BASIC MODEL

The focus of this inquiry is the relationship between routine legal service demand elasticities and advertising practice. Each routine legal service market examined is assumed to conform to the familiar Chamberlinian model of monopolistic competition. Caves and Williamson [1985] outline the two theoretical models that provide sufficient conditions for the existence of downward sloping demand curves for individual producers. One relies upon the inherent complexity of the commodity and the diversity of buyers' preferences for product attributes. The other is founded upon the imperfection of consumer information and implies that, in equilibrium, consumers will make choices based on different information sets. Important features of both of these models are obviously present in routine legal service markets.

The arguments presented in the introduction to this paper suggest that the price elasticity of demand for a specific legal service performed by the ith attorney in the jth market, ε_{ij}, should be taken to be a function of variables representing the attorney's own advertising effort, $\textit{OWNAD}_{ij}$, and the general level of advertising intensity in the jth market, $\textit{MARAD}_j$. Allowing that individual demand elasticities may also depend on additional characteristics of the seller or market, we write

$$(1) \qquad \varepsilon_{ij} = \varepsilon(\textit{OWNAD}_{ij}, \textit{MARAD}_j, Z_{ij})$$

where Z_{ij} is a vector of variables reflecting these additional characteristics. The product differentiation view of advertising's effects can be identified with the hypothesis that $\partial\varepsilon/\partial\textit{OWNAD}$ is positive, while the information/search theoretic view maintains that $\partial\varepsilon/\partial\textit{MARAD}$ is negative.

We assume that legal services are produced using the fixed factor, capital,

[7] Due to data deficiencies, few empirical studies have explored directly the relationship between advertising and demand elasticities. The careful and comprehensive work of J. J. Lambin [1976] is one exception. Also, not many econometric investigations of advertising's effects consider firm and industry advertising variables separately. One exception is a paper by Vernon and Nourse [1973].

and the variable factors of attorney, paralegal, and clerical worker time.[8] For a given capital stock, the attorney is assumed to combine the variable factors in a manner that minimizes the total cost of achieving any given output level. Moreover, marginal cost is assumed to be constant in a neighborhood about the profit maximizing output level. This constant unit cost is taken to be a translog function of the opportunity costs of the variable factors.[9] Specifically, if $C(w^a, w^p, w^c)$ is the unit cost of a legal service where w^a, w^p, and w^c are the opportunity costs of attorney, paralegal, and clerical work time, respectively, we have

$$\text{(2)} \qquad \ln C(w^a, w^p, w^c) = \alpha_0 + \sum_{k=a,p,c} \alpha_k \ln w^k + \frac{1}{2} \sum_{k=a,p,c} \sum_{l=a,p,c} \gamma_{kl} \ln w^k \ln w^l$$

Sufficient conditions for the linear homogeneity of $C(.,.,.)$ defined by equation (2) are

$$\sum_{k=a,p,c} \alpha_k = 1, \gamma_{kl} = \gamma_{lk} \text{ for } k, l = a, p, c \quad \text{and}$$

$$\sum_{l=a,p,c} \gamma_{kl} = 0 \text{ for } k = a, p, c$$

When these are imposed, equation (2) becomes

$$\text{(3)} \qquad \ln C(w^a, w^p, w^c) = \ln w^c + \alpha_0 + \alpha_a \ln (w^a/w^c) + \alpha_p \gamma_{kl} \ln w^k \ln w^l + \tfrac{1}{2}\gamma_{aa}[\ln (w^a/w^c)]^2 + \tfrac{1}{2}\gamma_{pp}[\ln (w^p/w^c)]^2 + \gamma_{ap}[\ln(w^a/w^c)]\,[\ln (w^p/w^c)]$$

Assume that P_{ij}, the price charged for a specific legal service by the ith attorney in the jth market, is set so as to maximize the profits associated with the provision of the service. Invoking the profit maximization condition, marginal revenue equals marginal costs and solving for P_{ij}, one obtains

$$\text{(4)} \qquad P_{ij} = \frac{C(w_{ij}^a, w_{ij}^p, w_{ij}^c)}{1 + 1/\varepsilon_{ij}}$$

Equation (4) will be the basis for econometric estimation.

III. ECONOMETRIC IMPLEMENTATION AND DATA

To estimate equation (4), it is first necessary to specify a functional form for equation (1). A particularly convenient choice, as we shall see, is to take

[8] This is essentially the approach taken by Feinberg [1984] in his study of substitutability among law firm labor inputs. We assume that the contribution to cost of the variable factor "materials" is negligible.

[9] The translog cost function can be shown to provide a second order approximation to any unit cost function which is everywhere positive for factor price vectors in the positive orthant, concave, and homogeneous of degree one. See Diewert [1974].

$\varepsilon(.,.,.)$ to be implicitly defined by

$$-\ln(1+1/\varepsilon_{ij}) = \beta_0 + \beta_1 \cdot \textit{OWNAD}_{ij} + \beta_2 \cdot \textit{MARAD}_j + B \cdot Z_{ij} \tag{5}$$

where β_0, β_1, and β_2 are unknown scalar parameters and B is an unknown parameter vector conformable with Z_{ij}.[10] For the other attorney or market characteristics affecting elasticities, the components of Z_{ij}, we make the relatively conventional choices of a firm size variable, $\textit{SIZE}_{ij}$, and a variable reflecting market concentration, the number of attorneys *per capita* in the market, $\textit{ATPC}_j$. Thus, we have

$$B \cdot Z_{ij} = \beta_3 \cdot \textit{SIZE}_{ij} + \beta_4 \cdot \textit{ATPC}_j \tag{6}$$

where β_3 and β_4 are unknown scalar parameters.

Taking logs of both sides of equation (4), substituting from equations (3), (5), and (6), and rearranging, one obtains

$$\begin{aligned} \ln(P_{ij}/w^c_{ij}) = {} & \alpha_0 + \beta_0 + \alpha_a \ln(w^a_{ij}/w^c_{ij}) + \alpha_p \ln(w^p_{ij}/w^c_{ij}) \\ & + \tfrac{1}{2}\gamma_{aa}[\ln(w^a_{ij}/w^c_{ij})]^2 + \tfrac{1}{2}\gamma_{pp}[\ln(w^p_{ij}/w^c_{ij})]^2 \\ & + \gamma_{ap}[\ln(w^a_{ij}/w^c_{ij})]\,[\ln(w^p_{ij}/w^c_{ij})] \\ & + \beta_1 \cdot \textit{OWNAD}_{ij} + \beta_2 \cdot \textit{MARAD}_j + \beta_3 \cdot \textit{SIZE}_{ij} + \beta_4 \cdot \textit{ATPC}_j \end{aligned} \tag{7}$$

As can be seen from equation (7), the advantage of the functional form in equation (5) is that it allows transformation of the model to a version that is linear in the parameters of interest. This feature will facilitate estimation. Of course, equation (7) is best viewed as one within a larger system of equations that simultaneously determines individual prices and other endogenous variables such as individual and area-wide advertising activity and attorneys' opportunity cost of time.[11]

Using equation (5), it is easy to show that the derivatives of $\varepsilon(.,.,.)$ with respect to each of the determinants of price elasticity of demand are given by

$$\partial\varepsilon/\partial X = \beta_k \cdot \varepsilon_{ij}(\varepsilon_{ij}+1) \tag{8}$$

where $k = 1$ when $X = \textit{OWNAD}$, $k = 2$ when $X = \textit{MARAD}$, $k = 3$ when $X = \textit{SIZE}$, and $k = 4$ when $X = \textit{ATPC}$. Since ε_{ij} will always be less than -1 at an optimum for a profit maximizing firm, equation (8) reveals that each derivative has the same sign as the corresponding β_k parameter. The information/search theoretic view of advertising's effects is, therefore, consistent with the hypothesis that $\beta_2 < 0$, while the product differentiation view predicts that $\beta_1 > 0$.

[10] Equation (5) amounts to the assumption that the log of the ratio of price to marginal cost is a linear function of the variables appearing on the right hand side of (5). The economically meaningful range of values for ε, $(-\infty, -1)$, corresponds to values for the expression on the right hand side of (5) between 0 and $+\infty$.

[11] Specification of such a system of equations would involve an ambitious modeling effort that we will not attempt here. The fact that equation (7) involves jointly determined variables will, of course, have implications for the estimation strategy.

In general, one would expect that large firm size would, if anything, confer market power, thereby rendering demand curves less elastic for attorneys in the firm. In this case, one would expect $\beta_3 > 0$. It is less clear what sign should be expected for β_4. The conventional wisdom regarding market structure and firm performance suggests that an increase in the number of sellers *per capita* would cause all sellers' demand curves to become more elastic. In this event, β_4 would be negative. Satterthwaite [1979], however, has presented a model of a market for "reputation goods", such as personal legal services, which admits the seemingly perverse result that an increase in the number of suppliers can render individual demand curves less elastic.[12] Hence, we have no confident *a priori* expectation regarding the sign of β_4.

Most of the data used for empirical analysis were collected via surveys of random samples of attorneys in private practice, in 1981 and 1982, in seventeen metropolitan areas across the US.[13] Attorney advertising regulations, and consequently advertising practices, differed widely among the seventeen sampled markets.[14] The survey questionnaire solicited responses to numerous questions about the nature of the attorney's practice, and price quotations for each of three routine legal services: a simple will, an uncon-

[12] In Satterthwaite's model, the efficiency of consumer search diminishes as the number of sellers increases. This is because, with a large number of sellers in a market, consumers will typically have accurate information on the reputations of only a few. Consequently, an individual's inquiries regarding the qualifications of a particular seller will tend to be unproductive.

[13] In 1980, the National Science Foundation funded a study, entitled "The Market Effects of Attorney Advertising". The major purpose of that study was to compare attorneys' fees and advertising practices across a sample of areas with widely different attorney advertising regulations. Sufficient funding was granted to a team of researchers at Arizona State University, headed by the senior author of this paper, to survey attorneys in six different cities across the US. Those surveys were conducted in early 1981 in: (1) Birmingham, Alabama; (2) Phoenix, Arizona; (3) Fresno, California; (4) Indianapolis, Indiana; (5) Jackson, Mississippi; and (6) Milwaukee, Wisconsin. One year later in early 1982, Louis Harris and Associates on behalf of the Federal Trade Commission conducted similar attorney surveys, using the research design developed by the Arizona State University researchers, in eleven additional cities. These cities included: (1) Hartford, Connecticut; (2) Wichita, Kansas; (3) Baltimore, Maryland; (4) Boston, Massachusetts; (5) Detroit, Michigan; (6) Springfield, Missouri; (7) Albuquerque, New Mexico; (8) Columbus, Ohio; (9) Oklahoma City, Oklahoma; (10) Nashville, Tennessee; and (11) Seattle, Washington.

[14] The US Supreme Court's decision in *Bates v. State Bar of Arizona* not only gave attorneys the right to advertise but it also left to the states the right to regulate attorney advertising practices (subject only to the requirement that some attorney advertising be permitted in every US jurisdiction). Following that decision, then, states adopted widely different attorney advertising regulations. In a few states, highly restrictive regulations were adopted that virtually limited the *Bates* ruling to its own facts, or nearly so. In a few others, highly permissive regulations were adopted which prohibited only that attorney advertising which is false or misleading. In most states, however, attorney advertising regulations were adopted that fell somewhere between these two extremes in terms of their relative restrictiveness (or, permissiveness) but that differed from state to state with respect to: (1) the specific legal services attorneys were allowed to advertise, (2) the information attorney advertisements could or must contain, and (3) the media attorneys were permitted to use in the promotion of their services and fees. The seventeen metropolitan areas in which attorneys were surveyed were purposely selected to provide a sample representative of the entire regulatory spectrum which developed in the early years after *Bates*.

tested personal bankruptcy, and an uncontested dissolution of marriage. The survey questionnaire presented detailed descriptions of each of these stylized services.[15] In each case, the hypothetical circumstances of the client's situation and the nature of the client's intentions were designed to be such that attorney skill, beyond minimum competence, would be a relatively insignificant factor in the performance of the service.

The design of the survey instrument used together with the routine nature of the legal services priced provide considerable assurance of actual service homogeneity across attorneys. To provide additional assurance, however, we restricted our samples for each service to areas in which pertinent state laws were comparable at the time the attorney surveys were conducted. For the simple will service, for example, we distinguished geographic areas on the basis of their community property status. Four of the seventeen states represented in our study's area sample had a community property law, while the other thirteen did not. The cities located in the former states, therefore, were eliminated from our analysis of the simple will case.[16] Six of the study's seventeen states prohibited the application of federal bankruptcy exemptions at the time the attorney surveys were conducted, while eleven permitted the application of either state or federal bankruptcy exemptions. Again, the cities located in the former states were eliminated from our sample in order to maximize sample size.[17] Finally, only one state in our area sample did not permit no-fault divorces when the study's attorney surveys were conducted, and so the city located in that state was omitted from our analysis of the uncontested divorce service.[18]

In the analysis of each of the three routine services, P_{ij} was taken to be the price that the ith responding attorney in the jth area said that he or she would charge for the service.[19] Obviously, no direct measurement of the attorney's own opportunity cost of time was available. Indeed, even data on attorney earnings is relatively sparse. However, annual survey data collected by Altman and Weil, Inc. did provide us with 1981 and 1982 median income figures for law firm associates and partners for several geographic areas of the

[15] The factual circumstances of, and the work to be performed for, each case were spelled out in substantial detail in the survey instrument used in order to ensure that all attorney respondents priced equivalent services. A copy of that questionnaire may be obtained by writing to Professor Steven R. Cox at the Department of Economics, Arizona State University, Tempe, Arizona 85287.

[16] Albuquerque, Fresno, Phoenix, and Seattle are the areas which were eliminated from our analysis of the simple will case.

[17] The six cities eliminated are Birmingham, Columbus, Indianapolis, Nashville, Phoenix, and Wichita.

[18] The one city is Baltimore.

[19] The percentage of attorney respondents who said they personally would perform the legal service priced and who quoted some flat fee for doing so ranged from a low of about 65 for the uncontested divorce case to a high of about 90 for the uncontested bankruptcy. The remaining attorneys who said they, too, would perform the service quoted an hourly rate for doing so. For these attorneys, a "price quotation" was calculated by multiplying their hourly rate quotation by the time each estimated it would take them to perform the service.

United States.[20] These figures were used to construct an index for our w^a variable.[21] The same surveys also produced median income figures for paralegals which allowed construction of an index for w^p. The variable w^c was taken to be an index of clerical wages in non-manufacturing industries based on US Census Bureau Area Wage Surveys. The three labor input cost variables were then scaled by their sample mean values.

The variable ATPC, as previously noted, was measured as the number of attorneys *per capita* in area j. SIZE_{ij} was taken to be the number of attorneys in the firm of which attorney i in area j is a member. MARAD, our index of area-wide advertising intensity, was taken to be the proportion of survey respondents, within an area, who responded that their firm had advertised in some medium sometime during the six months prior to the survey.[22] OWNAD, our variable reflecting the attorney's own advertising effort, was simply taken to be a dummy variable equal to one if the attorney's own firm had advertised within the previous six months and zero otherwise.

TABLE I

NONLINEAR TWO-STAGE LEAST-SQUARES ESTIMATES OF THE ELASTICITY COEFFICIENTS[a]

Coefficient	*Simple Will*	*Uncontested Bankruptcy*	*Uncontested Divorce*
β_1	0.246	−0.089	0.933
	(0.659)	(0.490)	(2.479)
β_2	−1.673	−0.471	−1.602
	(3.075)	(1.359)	(2.886)
β_3	0.011	0.012	0.015
	(4.748)	(5.332)	(4.331)
β_4	−0.092	−0.010	−0.005
	(1.769)	(0.232)	(0.086)
Number of Observations (n)	1297	458	1368
$F^b_{9,n-9}$	14.21	5.86	3.92

[a] Asymptotic t-statistics in parentheses.

[b] Asymptotically relevant to a test of the hypothesis that the model reduces to a constant term.

[20] The management consulting firm, Altman and Weil, Inc., conducts an annual Survey of Law Firm Economics. The major purpose of their survey is to measure law firm gross receipts, expenses, and income per lawyer. A few highlights of each year's survey appears in the annual edition of *The Lawyer's Almanac*. The data used in this study were generously provided by Altman and Weil, Inc.

[21] Attorneys in individual practice were treated as "partners" if they had six or more years of experience and "associates" otherwise.

[22] Each survey respondent was asked a set of questions about his/her firm's advertising practices. From the answers provided to two questions, it was possible to determine whether a particular law firm had done any advertising in the six months prior to the survey and in what media (e.g., Yellow Pages of a local telephone directory, local newspaper, TV, radio, etc.). As long as a respondent indicated that his/her law firm had done any advertising in any media, he/she was counted as an advertising attorney. The measure of area advertising intensity used for this study, then, was the ratio of the number of advertising attorney respondents to the number of total attorney respondents in each city examined.

IV. ESTIMATION RESULTS

As mentioned earlier, equation (7) contains jointly determined variables. For this reason, versions of equation (7) for each of the three routine legal services were estimated by nonlinear, two-stage least squares.[23] Table I reports estimates and asymptotic t-statistics for the elasticity parameters for each service.[24] The reported F statistics are asymptotically relevant to tests of the hypotheses that the models reduce to constant terms. Each of these is significant at the 1% level.

In each of the three cases, the estimates of β_3, the coefficient of SIZE, are significantly positive. Apparently attorneys who are members of large firms have, other things equal, less elastic demand curves than do their counterparts in small firms or in individual practices. Firm size appears to confer market power. All three point estimates of β_4, the coefficient of ATPC, are negative, but only one approaches significance at conventional levels. Given lower marginal significance levels, these negative estimates would support the conventional wisdom relating to market structure and competitiveness and are not consistent with Satterthwaite's hypothesis.

The estimates of β_1 and β_2 reveal advertising's effects on individual demand elasticities. In two of the three cases, simple will and uncontested divorce, β_2, the coefficient of MARAD, is negative and significant at the 1%

[23] Consistency and asymptotic normality of the nonlinear two-stage least-squares estimator are established by Amemiya [1974]. Since the model is linear in the parameters to be estimated, the estimator reduces to Kelejian's estimator [1971]. The estimation was conducted using instruments reflecting the respondent's status in the firm (partner or associate), number of years of experience, sex and race. Also included were the number of attorneys in the respondent's firm, the logarithm of the clerical wage index, the population and income *per capita* of the market area. Finally, dummy variables reflecting the degree of restrictiveness of the area's advertising regulations and a selection of area specific dummy variables were included.

[24] Estimates and asymptotic t-statistics (in parentheses) for the cost function parameters are as follows:

	SW	*UB*	*UD*
$\alpha_0+\beta_0$	−0.776	−0.179	−0.284
	(6.284)	(1.519)	(2.134)
α_a	4.391	0.853	1.091
	(7.079)	(2.850)	(2.356)
α_p	−4.937	−0.393	−1.779
	(6.631)	(0.953)	(2.377)
$1/2\gamma_{aa}$	7.154	1.512	1.706
	(7.128)	(2.774)	(2.158)
$1/2\gamma_{pp}$	11.703	3.625	13.810
	(1.199)	(1.045)	(2.625)
γ_{ap}	−15.413	−6.611	−18.690
	(2.451)	(3.289)	(4.100)

The translog unit cost function is linearly homogeneous by construction. There is no simple set of conditions on the parameters that guarantee that it is increasing in each factor price and concave. In fact, at the sample means of factor costs ($w^a = w^p = w^c = 1$), the three estimated cost functions are not increasing in the cost of paralegal time nor are they concave. Due to data limitations, the cost function parameters could not be estimated subject to the restrictions implied by factor demand functions. Nonetheless, the estimated cost functions may still provide reasonably good second-order approximations to the actual cost functions in a neighborhood about representative values for factor prices.

level. In the third case, uncontested bankruptcy, β_2 is negative with a marginal significance level of 9%.[25] These results are consistent with the hypothesis that advertising conveys information that facilitates buyer search, for quality or low-price, and thus renders individual demand curves more elastic. Only in the uncontested divorce case is the estimate of β_1, the coefficient of OWNAD, significant and here the point estimate is positive. Again, a positive value for this parameter is consistent with the product differentiation view of advertising's impact: namely, an attorney's own advertising effort serves to differentiate his or her product and, thus, makes demand less elastic. Of course, a failure to find a significantly positive value for β_1 in a particular market does not imply that attorneys' use of advertising is unproductive and therefore irrational. Since the nature of the advertising is not necessarily service specific, it may pay dividends in terms of increased market power in markets for other than simple will and uncontested bankruptcy services.

In order to quantify the impact of advertising on the general level of competitiveness in these markets, it would be useful to estimate the magnitudes of the elasticities or, equivalently, price-cost ratios. Regrettably, neither of these indexes of competitiveness is identified given our model because, as can be seen from equation (8), the assumed functional forms do not allow separate estimation of α_0 and β_0. This is a manifestation of a problem discussed by Sumner (1981).[26] Something can be said, however, about the relative effect of market-wide advertising intensity on, for example, the price-cost ratio. From equation (4), it is clear that the ratio of price to marginal cost for a profit maximizing monopolistic competitor is given by $(1+1/\varepsilon)^{-1}$, which, given equation (5), can be seen to equal $\exp(\beta_0+\beta_1 \cdot \text{OWNAD}+\beta_2 \cdot \text{MARAD}+\beta_3 \cdot \text{SIZE}+\beta_4 \cdot \text{ATPC})$. Thus, the elasticity of the price-cost ratio, with respect to advertising intensity, is $\beta_2 \cdot \text{MARAD}$. The seventeen surveyed cities had a mean value of MARAD of 0.14 with a standard deviation of 0.087. The estimation results suggest that a representative value for β_2 for the simple will and uncontested divorce services is -1.6. Hence, advertising elasticities of price-cost ratios, evaluated at the mean value of market-wide advertising intensity, might be approximately -0.224.

Collins and Preston [1968] have used accounting data to estimate price-cost ratios for 288 4-digit SIC manufacturing industries.[27] The median of this

[25] One possible reason for the weak statistical significance in this case is that low-price search, and hence advertising's effect on the search process, may be relatively unimportant in this market. A bankruptcy client may have no incentive to search for a low price since acceptance of a high price may serve only to reduce the amount that the client's creditors are able to recover.

[26] Sumner [1981] points out that a fundamental identification problem plagues attempts to use data on price and variables affecting marginal cost to infer the price-cost ratio. Identification of this ratio could be achieved, of course, but it would be contingent upon a maintained hypothesis of a specific, nonlinear functional form.

[27] The Collins and Preston estimates are not entirely satisfactory for purposes of comparison since their sample was comprised of manufacturing rather than service industries. The Sumner study, referred to in note 26, estimated price-cost ratios for cigarette manufacturers in the range of 1.03 to 1.08. We intend these estimates to serve only as rough benchmarks of competitiveness of markets.

distribution is 1.172, with a range of 1.030 to 1.513. If market-wide advertising intensity were increased from its mean value by one half of one standard deviation (a change of about 31%), then, assuming an elasticity of −0.224, the price cost ratio would fall by about 7%. Taking the median value of 1.172 as a representative starting point, the resulting value for the price-cost ratio would be about 1.09, which is less than the first decile point of the distribution of Collins and Preston's estimates (about 1.11). Thus, a relatively modest change in advertising intensity would appear to have the potential of bringing about an appreciable reduction in price-cost ratios.[28]

V. SUMMARY AND CONCLUSIONS

Theoretically, there are two views of the competitive effects of advertising. The information/search theoretic view asserts that advertising increases competition among sellers in a market in that it renders the representative firm's demand curve more elastic. The product differentiation view, on the other hand, maintains that advertising firms face less elastic demand curves than non-advertising firms. Empirically, this study's findings, together with the results of earlier studies of the relationship between advertising and market prices, provide considerable support for the former view. Thus, the trend over the past decade toward fewer restrictions on seller advertising in professional service markets would appear to be a very favorable one, at least as far as consumers are concerned.

ACCEPTED JULY 1986

JOHN R. SCHROETER,
Iowa State University,
Ames,
USA.

SCOTT L. SMITH,
General Accounting Office, US Government,
Washington, DC,
USA.

STEVEN R. COX,
Department of Economics,
Arizona State University,
Tempe, Arizona 85287,
USA.

[28] This calculation is meant to provide only a rough idea of the impact of area-wide advertising intensity in these markets. Obviously, if a change in advertising intensity were induced, perhaps as the result of an exogenous change in regulatory policy, its effects could be predicted only within the context of the complete model of which equation (7) is a part.

REFERENCES

ALTMAN and WEIL, INC., 1982 and 1983, *Survey of Law Firm Economics.*

AMEMIYA, T., 1974, 'The Nonlinear Two-Stage Least-Squares Estimator', *Journal of Econometrics*, 2 (July), pp. 105–110.

Bates v. State Bar of Arizona, 1977, 433 U.S. 350.

BENHAM, L., 1972, 'The Effects of Advertising on the Price of Eyeglasses', *Journal of Law and Economics*, 15 (October), pp. 337–351.

CADY, J. F., 1976, 'An Estimate of the Price Effects of Restrictions on Drug Price Advertising', *Economic Inquiry*, 14 (December), pp. 493–510.

CAVES, R. E. and WILLIAMSON, P. J., 1985, 'What is Product Differentiation, Really?', *Journal of Industrial Economics*, 34 (December), pp. 113–132.

COLLINS, N. R. and PRESTON, L. E., 1968, *Concentration and Price-Cost Margins in Manufacturing Industries* (University of California Press, Berkeley).

COMANOR, W. S. and WILSON, T. A., 1974, *Advertising and Market Power* (Harvard University Press, Cambridge).

COMANOR, W. S. and WILSON, T. A., 1979, 'The Effect of Advertising on Competition: A Survey', *Journal of Economic Literature*, 17 (June), pp. 453–476.

COX, S. R., DESERPA, A. C. and CANBY, W. C., JR., 1982, 'Consumer Information and the Pricing of Legal Services', *Journal of Industrial Economics*, 30 (March), pp. 305–318.

DIEWERT, W. E., 1974, 'Applications of Duality Theory', in M. D. INTRILLIGATOR and D. A. KENDRICK, eds., *Frontiers of Quantitative Economics*, vol. II (North-Holland Publishing Company, Amsterdam).

DORFMAN, R. and STEINER, P. O., 1954, 'Optimal Advertising and Optimal Quality', *American Economic Review*, 44 (December), pp. 826–836.

FEINBERG, R. M., 1984, 'Paralegals and Substitution Among Labor Inputs in the Law Firm', *Journal of Industrial Economics*, 33 (September), pp. 99–104.

JACOBS, W. W., *et al.*, 1984, *Improving Consumer Access to Legal Services: The Case for Removing Restrictions on Truthful Advertising* (Federal Trade Commission Staff Report).

KELEJIAN, H. H., 1971, 'Two-Stage Least Squares and Econometric Systems Linear in Parameters but Nonlinear in the Endogenous Variables', *Journal of the American Statistical Association*, 66 (June), pp. 373–374.

KWOKA, J. E., JR., 1984, 'Advertising and the Price and Quality of Optometric Services', *American Economic Review*, 74 (March), pp. 211–216.

LAMBIN, J. J., 1976, *Advertising, Competition and Market Conduct in Oligopoly Over Time* (North-Holland Publishing Company, Amsterdam).

NELSON, P., 1970, 'Information and Consumer Behavior', *Journal of Political Economy*, 78 (March/April), pp. 311–329.

SATTERTHWAITE, M. A., 1979, 'Consumer Information, Equilibrium Industry Price, and the Number of Sellers', *Bell Journal of Economics*, 10 (Autumn), pp. 483–502.

SCHERER. F. M., 1980, *Industrial Market Structure and Economic Performance*, second edition (Houghton Mifflin Company, Boston).

STIGLER, G. J., 1961, 'The Economics of Information', *Journal of Political Economy*, 69 (June), 213–225.

SUMNER, D. A., 1981, 'Measurement of Monopoly Behavior: An Application to the Cigarette Industry', *Journal of Political Economy*, 89 (October), pp. 1010–1019.

VERNON, J. M. and NOURSE, R. E. M., 1973, 'Profit Rates and Market Structure of Advertising Intensive Firms', *Journal of Industrial Economics*, 22 (September), pp. 1–20.

THE JOURNAL OF INDUSTRIAL ECONOMICS 0022-1821 $2.00
Volume XXXVI September 1987 No. 1

MARKET FORCES AND COMMERCIAL AIRCRAFT SAFETY*

ANDREW J. CHALK

This paper investigates the wealth impact on aircraft manufacturers of crashes involving their aircraft. We attempt to separate out the regulatory, tort law, and endogenous market components of these costs using stock market data. The results indicate that on average the manufacturer suffers a wealth loss of $21.3 million as the result of a fatal crash in which the structural integrity of the aircraft is at issue. The analysis suggests that not all of this amount can be attributed to regulatory or tort law mechanisms, and that market forces play a role in providing air travel safety.

I. INTRODUCTION

IN THE economic theory of consumer behavior it is recognized that the state of information about product hazards has a major effect on market provision of the desired level of consumer safety. The literature discusses mechanisms through which consumers can become informed such as search and pre-purchase inspection (Wilde and Schwartz [1979]), producer disclosure (Viscusi [1978]), private information gathering by consumer organizations, information provision by government agencies (Cornell, Noll and Weingast [1976]), the judicial process, repeat purchase mechanisms (Heal [1976]; Klein and Leffler [1981]) and, often, some combination of these. Little research in economics has addressed the question of how these mechanisms jointly work or what the producer response is in practice.

This paper is intended to provide evidence on the issue of how these safety forces come to bear in the marketplace, using commercial air travel safety as an example. Aircraft safety is an appropriate choice to test for market adjustment to new safety information for a number of reasons. First, modern commercial aviation is widely regarded as an area where the technological complexity of the product makes the consumer information problem

* I wish to acknowledge the comments of John Binder, Steven J. Brown, Michael Giliberto and participants in workshops at Washington University and Southern Methodist University. The extensive comments of the referee and the North American Editor of this *Journal* substantially improved the paper. I am especially indebted to my thesis supervisor, Barry R. Weingast for comments and encouragement. Financial support for this paper through a dissertation fellowship from the Center for the Study of American Business at Washington University is gratefully acknowledged.

especially severe.[1] Second, aircraft accidents can frequently involve fatalities and, if so, receive widespread publicity. Third, commercial aircraft accidents are rare, and it is therefore relatively easy to obtain records of those accidents that are likely to precipitate large market adjustments to new information contained in the accident.

Although market adjustment to new safety information takes place in the immediate product market, involving differing levels of safety provision by producers and adjustments in consumption patterns by consumers, this paper tests for these adjustments and attempts to measure their magnitude in terms of their effect on the expected future profitability of aircraft manufacturers. Thus, we look at the capital market effects of aircraft accidents under the maintained hypothesis that capital markets efficiently capitalize new public information into the value of the manufacturer's equity. This basic principle is explained fully and developed into a set of empirical tests in section III. First, section II summarizes the legal and regulatory framework that applies to commercial air travel. Results are reported in section IV, section V deals with some further implications, and section VI contains the conclusions.

II. REGULATION, TORT LAW AND MARKET INCENTIVES FOR AIR SAFETY

Federal regulation of air safety in the United States is extensive. The Federal Aviation Administration administers air traffic control, certifies aircraft and crew, and conducts extensive basic research on air safety problems. In the area of enforcement, its method of operation is not unlike that of the Occupational Health and Safety Administration (OSHA).[2] The Agency can punish offenders with a warning, impose fines and, by withdrawal of certification, effectively ground an aircraft type or an airline. The most severe penalty normally used against carriers is fines. These are limited to $1000 per offense, the same dollar value established in the 1930s. Although the Agency has found some creative ways to circumvent the statutory limit, the level of fines it imposes is still low. Chalk [1983] finds that average total fine revenue against all US scheduled air carriers over the period 1971–81 was less than

[1] E.g., Marcy [1979] states:

"The potential influence [of consumers on air safety], however, is not great because passengers lack both the opportunity and the knowledge to provide effective input into the design of a commercial airliner."... Even if passengers had an opportunity to express a preference for more crashworthy aircraft, most of them lack the knowledge to do so. Many would not perceive the possibility of the plane's design causing deaths and injuries after the crash had occurred. And if a passenger did recognize a potential problem, it is unlikely that he would have the engineering knowledge that would be necessary to determine whether the plane's design did, in fact, create an unreasonable risk of second collision deaths and injuries." (p. 1609) [*Text in brackets added.*]

[2] For a detailed account of OSHA enforcement procedures, see Cornell, Noll and Weingast [1976].

$100 000 per year. The average fine per offense was $1258. Furthermore, it is not likely that FAA enforcement establishes a very high probability of detection if a safety violation occurs since the Agency only had approximately 210 inspectors assigned to scheduled air carriers. Enforcement against manufacturers largely consists of airworthiness directives (ADs) mandating design alterations, manufacturing changes, or new tests. After a commercial aircraft's receipt of a type certificate, ADs relating to it are typically minor in scope. Only on one occasion in the jet era has the Agency exercised its power to decertify an aircraft—the DC-10, temporarily, in 1979. This unusual episode establishes, insofar as modern experience is concerned, the demonstrated upper limit of the Agency's power.

Under prevailing tort law, air carriers and manufacturers are liable under a negligence standard for wrongful death and personal injury claims following a crash.[3] Wrongful death judgments depend on the victim's age and earnings but the average figure was around $100 000 per fatality in 1966, increasing to $500 000 per fatality in 1979. In addition, manufacturers are strictly liable under products liability law in virtually all states. Clearly, the tort system can impose substantial costs in the event of an air crash. All, or virtually all, of the cost of damage awards is insured, implying that the immediate costs of a crash to a carrier or manufacturer are limited to the present value of all future *increases* in liability insurance premiums plus any direct litigation and "cleanup" costs.

The type of market equilibrium that prevails in the presence of incomplete consumer information and no efficiently functioning tort law or regulatory system is sometimes described as a market for "lemons" [Akerlof, 1970]. Akerlof concluded that the absence of specific product information leads to the use of market (or average quality) indices to judge quality, depriving potential high-quality producers of the gains they could appropriate and, hence, their incentive to produce.[4] This early exposition of the information externality problem has spawned a literature on endogenous market responses to costly information. This research focuses on institutions spontaneously generated by markets that eliminate information externalities and act to correct potential market failures—e.g., producer reputation (or brand names), guarantees, the use of agents, and learning from experience. Few empirical tests of these theories have been conducted;[5] hence the case for endogenous market responses in markets with complex products is unresolved.

[3] Firms may not insure against punitive damages in most states. However, none of the firms in this study has ever been subject to a successful punitive damages suit, suggesting the possibility of such uninsurable costs is remote.

[4] Akerlof's result (in the continuous quality case) can be looked upon as the polar case in which imperfect information completely eliminates the market. The models of Salop and Stiglitz [1977], Wilde and Schwartz [1979] and the earlier one of Scitovsky [1950] suggest the perfectly competitive market only partially degenerates into an imperfectly competitive market.

[5] An exception is Bond [1982].

III. TESTING FOR PRODUCT MARKET EFFECTS USING STOCK MARKET DATA

In an efficient capital market, at any given point in time the stock price of a firm represents the discounted present value of its expected future profits. If the firm supplies lower than desired product quality, and this is made known to consumers, the stock price will decrease by the stock market's assessment of the loss of firm value. The magnitude of the loss in firm value reflects the combined effects of regulation, litigation, and reduced demand for products in the future due to consumer learning and reputation effects. In the empirical work below, we attempt to establish whether regulatory and litigation costs can account for the whole dollar magnitude of the stock price effects we document in aircraft accidents or if there appears to be some additional endogenous market response as well.

III(i) *Experimental design and methodology*

To test for the stock market response to air crashes, we obtained a sample of 76 US airline accidents involving at least one fatality for the period 1966–1981.[6] The sample consists of all the crashes involving Boeing (32 crashes), McDonnell Douglas (34 crashes) and Lockheed (10 crashes).[7] To establish whether planes produced by a given manufacturer had a higher accident rate than any other is difficult due to the absence of data on the number of departures by each make of plane.[8]

Most air carrier accidents are not caused by the design of the plane, nor does it usually appear at the time of the crash that this was the cause. Our interest is in the effect on the manufacturer's stock in that subset of accidents in which it appears the aircraft design may be the cause. To isolate these cases, crash reports in *The New York Times* were examined to see if the crash was attributed to weather, pilot error, air traffic control, or some other non

[6] We used the *Annual Review of Aircraft Accident Data, US Air Carrier Operations*, which documents all those crashes involving US certified air carriers. Hence, major crashes involving foreign carriers flying US built planes are excluded, but this omission should not bias the results.

[7] The total number of fatal crashes over the period was 104. Hence our sample includes 69% of the total. The reasons for excluding the remainder were: (i) some involved foreign firms not listed on US stock exchanges, (ii) some involved firms that have since ceased production or merged. Inclusion of the three majors who annually held between 65–85% of the market over the period should be adequate to establish any effects. Only fatal crashes were included since non-fatal crashes are rarely reported, which makes inferences as to their causes difficult. Ideally, we would also perform tests on airline stocks, but because airlines insure their aircraft the size of insurance awards following a crash is not known. Unlike passenger liability the loss of an aircraft may not be fully insured and, indeed, the aircraft may be leased.

[8] Miles traveled per fatality is a biased measure of aircraft safety because the probability of an accident is not uniform over different phases of flight. There is a 50% probability that an accident will happen during takeoff and landing, given that it occurs (see, *National Transportation Safety Board*). Hence, departures per fatality is usually used as the measure of the accident rate.

aircraft-related cause.[9] We designated those crashes not attributed to these other causes as *suspect crashes*, i.e., those in which the cause may have been the manufacturer's fault. Frequently, news reports of suspect crashes speculated that this was the case. This procedure produced a group of 23 crashes. Of these 23, 19 were crashes of aircraft types that were still in production at the time of the crash. We designated this group of 19 the *current model suspect group*. The remaining four suspect crashes represent types of aircraft not in production when the crash occurred. We designate this group *past model suspect crashes*. Manufacturers still sustain tort awards if an aircraft in this fleet crashes, but may not sustain loss of reputation or otherwise reduced demand for aircraft they are currently producing. In principle, observing no abnormal stock price performance for this group, but a negative abnormal stock market impact for the current model suspect group, is consistent with tort awards having no effect (because they are insured, and problems can be corrected to prevent increased future insurance premiums) but endogenous market responses (such as diminished reputation) having a large effect. Also, the sample size of crashes of aircraft no longer in production (four crashes) makes any inference very tentative.

To show the stock price effect of crashes in which the aircraft is not suspect, the remaining 53 of the 76 crashes were classified as a *control group*, and the same tests were performed on them as on the past model suspect group (4) and the current model suspect group (19).[10] This enables us to separate safety effects relating to the structural integrity of the aircraft from other factors systematically affecting manufacturer stock price after a crash.[11]

The daily stock market returns data was obtained from the CRSP tapes.

[9] Among the cases excluded were missed landings in fog (mainly in the early part of the sample) where the article commented extensively on the relevant airport's lack of technical aids; mid-air collisions (8 in total); persons hit while walking down the runway (2 cases); persons walking into propellers or hit by planes in terminal areas (2 cases); a passenger opening an airplane door while the plane was in flight (1 case); a pilot trying to land on a runway closed for repairs that had construction vehicles parked on it (1 case) and terrorism (1 case). The bulk of the other cases were weather related.

[10] The nature of the problem (the frequency of airline accidents) constrains these sample sizes to be rather small but the situation is not as bad as it might seem. In their analysis of security price performance measures, Brown and Warner [1980, p. 243] found that the ability of these models to correctly reject the null hypothesis of no abnormal performance when it was false bore remarkably little dependence on sample size. For example, with 1% (4%) induced abnormal performance a sample size of 12 securities rejected H_0 9.6% (72.4%) of the time in repeated simulations. Increasing the sample size to 25 changed these rejection frequencies to 13.6% and 91.6% respectively.

What *is* critical, according to Brown and Warner [p. 249], is correctly identifying the *timing* of the 'event' that is postulated to induce abnormal performance. While this problem has plagued tests of such events as tender offers and proxy fights, this is a less serious problem with airline crashes.

[11] Examples of such costs are the expenses entailed in complying with the National Transportation Safety Board inspection, legal costs, etc.

The market index used is the CRSP equally weighted index of all NYSE and AMEX stocks.[12]

III(ii) *Empirical procedures*

Two methodologies are used to conduct the empirical tests. The first methodology is that pioneered by Fama, Fisher, Jensen and Roll [1969], frequently termed 'event-time' analysis. The general procedure, and a review of its use in the literature, are described in Schwert [1981]. The second methodology is seemingly unrelated regression (SUR) (Zellner [1962]) which permits us to test whether a crash involving one aircraft manufacturer was associated with stock market effects on other aircraft manufacturers. If such contemporaneous interfirm correlations exist, then they enable us to obtain more efficient parameter estimates using SUR than using ordinary least-squares (OLS). This technique is employed by Schipper and Thompson [1983] and its usefulness in financial economics assessed in Malatesta [1986].

We start from the premise that stock markets are 'efficient' in the semi-strong sense that prevailing prices reflect all public information (Copeland and Weston [1983]). Denote the stock price of firm i at time t as $\tilde{P}_{it}$, where the tilde denotes a random variable. Then, the return $\tilde{R}_{it}$ on any given stock i in time period t is defined as

$$(1) \qquad \tilde{R}_{it} = \frac{\tilde{P}_{it} - P_{it-1}}{P_{it-1}}$$

Define Φ_{t-1} as the set of public information available to investors in period $t-1$. The expected return on stock i in period t, conditional on this information set, is denoted $E(\tilde{R}_{it} \mid \Phi_{t-1})$. The assumption of semistrong-form market efficiency amounts to the proposition that the difference between the actual return and the expected return on stock i in period t, $\tilde{\varepsilon}_{it}$, has mean zero, i.e.,

$$(2) \qquad \tilde{\varepsilon}_{it} = \tilde{R}_{it} - E(R_{it} \mid \Phi_{t-1})$$
$$\tilde{E}(\varepsilon_{it}) = 0$$

III(iii) *Modeling equilibrium stock market prices—event-time methodology*

Equilibrium returns are modeled with the "market model" (Markowitz [1959], Sharp [1963]), which asserts that the return to a given stock i in period t, $\tilde{R}_{it}$, has a bivariate normal distribution with the returns on a portfolio of all securities, referred to as the market portfolio and denoted $\tilde{R}_{mt}$. An implication of these assumptions is that the expected return to stock

[12] The tests were also performed with the value-weighted index with no change in results. An exhaustive study of the relative merits of the two is contained in Brown and Warner [1980, pp. 239–243]. Their simulation technique found that t-tests (like those employed below) are more powerful using the equally-weighted index.

i in period t is a linear function of the return to the market portfolio. This function is written as

$$(3) \qquad E(\tilde{R}_{it} \mid R_{mt}) = \alpha_i + \beta_i R_{mt}$$

Hence, from (2) and (3), the model of actual stock returns is

$$(4) \qquad \tilde{R}_{it} = \alpha_i + \beta_i \tilde{R}_{mt} + \tilde{\varepsilon}_{it}$$

where $\tilde{\varepsilon}_{it} \sim N(0, \sigma_i^2)$, and $\tilde{\varepsilon}_{it}$ is independent of $\tilde{R}_{mt}$. The β term is sometimes referred to as "systematic risk" since it refers to how the return to a given stock varies in relation to the return to the market. Since all marketwide influences are reflected in beta, the forecast error from the stock return predicted by (4) in period t, $\hat{R}_{it}$, defined as

$$(5) \qquad e_{it} = R_{it} - \hat{R}_{it}$$

is a measure of effects on the present value of firm i that are uncorrelated with general market factors.

Two practical problems arise immediately in the implementation of the empirical tests. First, since we do not know the exact time that information on each crash reached the market, it is possible that some initial crash information is reflected in market prices the following day. Further, an examination of press reports established that additional information concerning the causes of a crash arrives subsequent to the initial information over a period of days as the National Transportation Safety Board (NTSB) investigation team makes its reports. Thus, we may observe the impact of information over a period of several days following a crash.

The market model of firm stock returns (equation (4)) is estimated over $N = 150$ trading days[13] around the crash period, 75 immediately prior to the crash and 75 from 30 days after the crash to 104 days after the crash. An unconditional forecast of firm returns is made over the crash date, day T, and the 29-day period subsequent to the crash. Summary statistics on these regressions are given in Table I.

The regressions generate a set of forecast errors for each crash i over the time period $T+s\,(s = 0, \ldots, 29)$. Each forecast error, e_{iT+s}, is standardized by its estimated standard error of forecast to give a standardized forecast error SFE_{iT+s} which is t-distributed, given the normality of e_{iT+s}, with N-2 degrees of freedom.[14] Since N is large, SFE_{iT+s} is assumed to be distributed $N(0, 1)$ under the null hypothesis of no stock market impact.

[13] Similar tests over estimation periods of 150 days, 120, 250 and 350 days did not substantially change the nature of the results.

[14] The estimated standard error of forecast is defined as:

$$S_f = \left\{ S^2 \left(1 + \frac{1}{N} + \frac{(R_{mt} - \bar{R}_m)^2}{\sum_{t=1}^{t=N} (R_{mt} - \bar{R}_m)^2} \right) \right\}^{1/2}$$

where S^2 is the sample residual variance and N is the length of the estimation period.

TABLE I
SUMMARY STATISTICS FOR ESTIMATED MARKET MODELS

Panel A: Control Group

	Number of Observations	$\hat{\alpha}$	$\hat{\beta}$	R^2	σ
Maximum	150	0.0031	2.1697	0.3774	0.0430
75th Percentile	150	0.0007	1.6959	0.2292	0.0272
Median	147	−0.0001	1.3199	0.1711	0.0232
25th Percentile	145	−0.0015	0.9589	0.1149	0.0180
Minimum	135	−0.0036	0.6770	0.0396	0.0132
Mean	146	−0.0003	1.3292	0.1769	0.0234

Panel B: Current Model Suspect Group

	Number of Observations	$\hat{\alpha}$	$\hat{\beta}$	R^2	σ
Maximum	150	0.0032	2.2223	0.3480	0.0321
75th Percentile	150	0.0009	1.5790	0.2224	0.0258
Median	150	0.0003	1.1410	0.1801	0.0232
25th Percentile	145	−0.0014	0.8035	0.1155	0.0170
Minimum	135	−0.0025	0.5056	0.0393	0.0152
Mean	147	0.0001	1.2205	0.1708	0.0223

Panel C: Past Model Suspect Group

	Number of Observations	$\hat{\alpha}$	$\hat{\beta}$	R^2	σ
Maximum	150	0.0020	1.9267	0.2648	0.0276
Second	150	0.0000	1.7602	0.2115	0.0247
Third	145	−0.0014	1.0552	0.1904	0.0206
Fourth	143	−0.0031	0.8280	0.0896	0.0192
Mean	147	−0.0006	1.3924	0.1891	0.0230

The statistics $\bar{Z}$ on day $T+s$ for a *sample* of n crashes is defined

$$\bar{Z}_{T+s} = \sqrt{n} \cdot \overline{SFE}_{T+s} = \sqrt{n}\frac{\sum_{i=1}^{n} SFE_{iT+s}}{n} \tag{6}$$

where $\bar{Z}_{T+s}$ is distributed $N(0,1)$.

The cumulative abnormal return from day s_1 to day s_2 is tested for significance using

$$\bar{Z}(s_1, s_2) = \frac{\sum_{s=s_1}^{s_2} \bar{Z}_{T+s}}{\sqrt{s_2 - s_1 + 1}} \tag{7}$$

which is distributed $N(0,1)$ under the assumption that SFE_{iT+s} is $N(0,1)$.

As a precaution against our results being dependent on the normality assumption about the daily forecast error, we perform a Wilcoxon sign-rank test. This nonparametric test has an advantage over the simple sign test in that it uses sample information about the magnitude as well as the sign of forecast errors.[15]

III(iv) *Seemingly unrelated regression estimation*

It is possible that the crash of manufacturer *i*'s aircraft influences the return to manufacturer *j*'s stock. The market model tests do not account for such potential interdependence across firms. A framework for analyzing such effects is the seemingly unrelated regression procedure (SUR) of Zellner [1962]. Seemingly unrelated regression estimates a system of equations with different explanatory variables in which there is contemporaneous correlation of disturbances between equations, but serial independence. Although OLS estimation of each equation produces unbiased parameter estimates under this situation, the estimates are not efficient since they ignore information contained in the residual covariance matrix. The SUR technique also permits a richer set of hypothesis tests to be accommodated easily within the empirical framework.

In the SUR system the following equation is specified for each firm *i*:

$$\tilde{R}_i = \alpha_{i0} + \beta_{i0}\tilde{R}_m + C_j\gamma_{ij} + D_k\alpha_{ik} + D_k\beta_{ik}\tilde{R}_m + \tilde{\varepsilon}_i \qquad i = 1,\ldots,3 \tag{8}$$

where

$\tilde{R}_i$ = a $T \times 1$ vector of the return on firm *i* on day *t*;
$\tilde{R}_m$ = a $T \times 1$ vector of the return on the market on day *t*;
C_j = a $T \times J$ matrix taking the value 1 on dates when there was a crash involving an aircraft manufactured by firm *j*, 0 otherwise ($j = 1,\ldots,3$).
D_k = a $T \times K$ matrix taking the value 1 on dates at least as great as the date

[15] On each day after the accident, $T+s$, the forecast errors are ranked in order of ascending absolute value. The sign of each forecast error is then assigned to its rank (the forecast error closest to zero on the real line would have the rank 1 assigned to it and its signed-rank be -1 or $+1$, etc.). We obtain a table of ranks, each with the sign of its corresponding forecast error. Denote all ranks with negative signs as $S_1, \cdot, S_i, \cdot, S_k$. The Wilcoxon signed-rank test then forms the statistic

$$V_s = \sum_{i=1}^{k} S_i$$

and the null hypothesis of no abnormal performance is rejected if $V_s \geqslant c$ where c is a constant. This occurs only if those forecast errors with high ranks also had negative signs and/or *k*, the number of negatives signs, was large. In terms of the stated hypothesis, this translates into the condition that those accidents with negative forecast errors have larger absolute values and/or occur frequently. Lehmann [1975, p. 123] shows that the distribution of V_s is asymptomatically normal as $n \to \infty$.

For examples of the use of the Wilcoxon sign-rank test in event studies see Kaplan and Roll [1972] or Collins and Dent [1979]. Brown and Warner [1980, pp. 217–222] show nonparametric tests have shortcomings of their own, finding they are likely to result in too high a probability of a Type II error.

of the kth crash but preceding the $k+1$st crash involving an aircraft manufactured by firm i, 0 otherwise ($k = 1, \ldots, K$);

ε_i = a $T \times 1$ vector of error terms distributed $N(0, \sigma^2)$, serially independent and independent of all right-hand side variables;

α_{i_0} = an intercept coefficient (implicitly multiplied by a $T \times 1$ vector of 1's);

β_{i_0} = a slope coefficient;

α_{ik} = a $K \times 1$ vector of intercept-shift coefficients;

β_{ik} = a $K \times 1$ vector of slope-shift coefficients;

γ_{ij} = a $J \times 1$ vector of coefficients representing the mean effect on the return of firm i of a crash involving an aircraft manufactured by firm j.

System (8) captures the direct effect of a crash on the stock price of the manufacturer through the coefficient γ_{ij} when $i = j$, and the cross-effects of a crash involving the aircraft of one manufacturer on another manufacturer through the coefficient γ_{ij} when $i \neq j$. The coefficients α_{ik} and β_{ik} permit intertemporal variation in the intercept and slope of the estimated equation (Gibbons [1980]).

IV. RESULTS

IV(i) *Market model results*

Summary statistics on the market model regressions are presented in Table I.

TABLE II
MARKET MODEL RESULTS

	Control Group (n = 53)					
	Mean Daily Forecast Error	*Cumulative Mean Daily Forecast Error*	$\bar{Z}$	$Z(T, T+s)$	V_s^a	$\bar{T}^b$
Column Number:	(1)	(2)	(3)	(4)	(5)	(6)
Days Relative to Crash						
0	−0.0013	−0.0013	−0.596	−0.596	−0.49	−0.296
1	0.0019	0.0007	0.688	0.066	−0.66	0.239
2	0.0017	0.0024	0.638	0.421	0.05	−0.010
3	−0.0005	0.0019	0.156	0.443	−0.07	−0.268
4	−0.0012	0.0007	−0.772	0.051	−0.94	0.197
5	−0.0046	−0.0038	−1.680	−0.639	−1.24	−1.230
6	0.0028	−0.0010	0.920	−0.244	−0.05	0.448
7	−0.0030	−0.0041	−0.999	−0.582	−1.31	−0.742
8	−0.0015	−0.0056	−0.780	−0.808	−0.51	−0.560
9	0.0007	−0.0049	0.124	−0.727	−0.03	0.260
10	0.0020	−0.0029	1.100	−0.362	1.09	0.941
20	0.0048	0.0052	1.951	0.520	0.39	1.389
29	0.0001	0.0093	−0.105	0.864	−1.09	−0.353

Current Model Suspect Group
(n = 19)

	Mean Daily Forecast Error	*Cumulative Mean Daily Forecast Error*	$\bar{Z}$	$Z(T, T+s)$	V_s^a	$\bar{T}^b$
Column Number:	*(1)*	*(2)*	*(3)*	*(4)*	*(5)*	*(6)*
Days Relative To Crash						
0	−0.0097	−0.0097	−1.657	−1.657	−2.27	−2.392
1	−0.0044	−0.0141	−0.911	−1.816	−0.46	−0.556
2	−0.0118	−0.0258	−1.802	−2.524	−1.83	−1.930
3	−0.0022	−0.0280	−0.124	−2.248	−1.19	−0.434
4	−0.0098	−0.0377	−2.291	−3.035	−1.72	−2.065
5	−0.0002	−0.0379	−0.176	−2.843	0.11	−0.028
6	0.0001	−0.0378	0.506	−2.440	0.34	0.023
7	−0.0020	−0.0398	−0.635	−2.507	0.54	−0.266
8	−0.0086	−0.0484	−1.613	−2.901	−1.55	−1.658
9	0.0110	−0.0374	2.421	−1.987	1.23	1.442
10	0.0007	−0.0367	0.453	−1.758	−0.39	0.102
20	0.0022	−0.0189	0.404	−0.390	0.30	0.511
29	0.0060	−0.0396	1.642	−0.810	0.87	1.098

Past Model Suspect Group
(n = 4)

	Mean Daily Forecast Error	*Cumulative Mean Daily Forecast Error*	$\bar{Z}$	$Z(T, T+s)$	V_s^a	$\bar{T}^b$
Column Number:	*(1)*	*(2)*	*(3)*	*(4)*	*(5)*	*(6)*
Days Relative To Crash						
0	−0.0046	−0.0046	−0.438	−0.438		−0.691
1	0.0123	0.0077	1.114	0.478		1.036
2	0.0232	0.0309	2.343	1.743		1.610
3	0.0054	0.0363	0.277	1.648		0.422
4	−0.0242	0.0121	−1.760	0.687		−1.241
5	−0.0187	−0.0066	−1.641	−0.043		−3.048
6	0.0175	0.0109	1.282	0.445		1.069
7	−0.0037	0.0072	−0.405	0.273		−0.220
8	0.0030	0.0102	0.330	0.367		0.929
9	−0.0008	0.0095	−0.029	0.339		−0.096
10	0.0109	0.0014	−1.013	0.018		−3.123
20	−0.0040	−0.0110	−0.709	−0.137		−0.479
29	0.0158	−0.0123	1.085	−0.275		0.859

[a] The statistic V_s is distributed approximately $N(0, 1)$ under the null hypothesis of no information.
[b] The statistic $\bar{T}$ is t distributed with $n-1$ degrees of freedom under the null hypothesis of no information effect.

The parameter estimates α and $\hat{\beta}$ seem reasonable and the mean R^2 of 0.1708 is respectably high for the market model. Table II exhibits mean daily forecast errors, cumulative mean daily forecast errors, and associated parametric and non-parametric statistical tests for each sample. There are marked differences between the various groups. For the control group, the mean daily forecast errors are generally insignificant and the cumulative mean forecast errors exhibit no trend. For the current model suspect group, however, the mean daily forecast error on the day of the crash is -0.967 percent, which is statistically less than zero at the five percent level ($\bar{Z}_T = -1.657$). However, not all relevant information appears to reach the market on the day of the crash. The mean forecast error on day $+2$ and day $+4$ is also significantly negative at the five-percent level ($\bar{Z}_{T+2} = -1.802$ and $\bar{Z}_{T+4} = -2.291$). The non-parametric test results are shown in Column (5) by the statistic V_s. This statistic is based on the cross-section of abnormal returns each day and is strictly valid only if the abnormal returns for that day are a simple random sample. Daily values of V_s confirm the results of the parametric tests. In particular, days T, $T+2$ and $T+4$ for the model-specific suspect group are significantly less than zero at the five-percent level, and other days are not. By contrast, control group daily forecast errors are insignificant.

Over the five-day interval from day 0 until day $+4$ the statistic $\bar{Z}(0,4)$ is -3.035 for the model-specific suspect group, which is statistically significant at the 0.0012 level. The cumulative mean abnormal return over this period is -3.774 percent. Multiplying this by each firm's market value of equity on the day preceding the crash (the number of outstanding common shares on the day before the crash, multiplied by the market price on that day) amounts to an average decrease of $21.319 million to shareholders of firms involved in suspect crashes over the five day crash period. This is far greater than the level of FAA fines, which amount to only a few thousand dollars. It also appears to be greater than the "cleanup" and investigation costs of crashes to the manufacturer, given the insignificant abnormal returns of the control group. Most of the decrease would appear to be related to the potentially far larger costs of tort law damages (reflected in future carrier liability insurance premiums) and market forces that lead to reduced demand for aircraft (e.g., passenger aversion to flying a certain type of aircraft, or reputation effects). The past model suspect group indicates that the negative stock performance may be the result of endogenous market mechanisms rather than tort awards. Since the manufacturer of a model of aircraft no longer in production faces court awards but no reduced future demand for that aircraft, any tort law effect is compounded in the stock price but product market effects are not. However, abnormal performance for the past model suspect group is insignificant (or positive). The small sample size of the past model suspect group makes this conclusion only tentative.

The statistic $\bar{Z}_{T+s}$ tests the statistical significance of the forecast error on day t relative to the time-series estimate of σ_f, the standard error of the regression over the market model estimation period. Strictly speaking, it tests the hypothesis that there was information on day t. If $\bar{Z}_{T+s}$ is significant, the effect on the sample should be tested for significance, conditional on there being information. We do this in column 6 of Table II which shows $\bar{T}$, the t-statistic for the daily cross-sectional mean abnormal return.[16] These t-statistics are generally consistent with the time-series estimates ($\bar{Z}_{T+s}$).

IV(ii) *Seemingly unrelated regression results*

Estimation of the SUR system (8) poses a number of dilemmas. Although the D_k variables can account for shifts in model parameters associated with crashes, they cannot account for shifts due to other factors. The effect of including them may lead one to erroneously attribute parameter shifts to crashes, when they are in fact due to factors not accounted for in the model. Estimating (8) over the full sample period 1966–1981 may lead to a mis-specified model if there is temporal fluctuation in alpha or beta. On the other hand, if some form of system (8) is estimated separately for each crash, one loses the ability easily to make cross-crash comparisons, while reducing the problem of parameter non-stationarity.

Given this situation, several specifications and a variety of statistical tests were employed in order to increase confidence in the results. In the first specification reported, we estimate (8) over the full sample period with α_i and β_i set equal to zero. This implies that the estimates are identical to OLS estimates, since the regressors are identical across equations. The interesting parameters reported in Table III, panel A, indicate that crashes of McDonnell Douglas aircraft have a statistically significant, negative impact on McDonnell Douglas, but that crashes of Boeing and Lockheed aircraft, although leading to negative average coefficients, do not have a statistically significant effect. This may be the result of the small sample sizes involved, especially with Lockheed, which has only one suspect crash. The F-test of the joint hypothesis that the coefficients on manufacturers whose aircraft crashed are all equal to zero is rejected at the 0.0166 level. However, the opposite conclusion emerges for firms whose aircraft are not involved on a day that a crash occurs. The F-statistic for a test that the sum of coefficients is equal to zero is 0.0277 (probability value 0.8677) and 0.0585 (probability value 0.9992) in a test that the coefficients are jointly equal to zero. Thus, in this specification, there is no evidence of a cross-manufacturer effect.

[16] The statistic $\bar{T}$ is calculated as:

$$\bar{T} = \frac{\overline{FE}}{\sigma_{\bar{\varepsilon}}}$$

where $\overline{FE} = \dfrac{\sum_{i=1}^{n} FE_i}{n}$ and n is the number of crashes in the sample,

and

$$\sigma_{\bar{\varepsilon}} = \left(\frac{\sum_{i=1}^{n} (FE_i - \overline{FE})^2}{n-1} \right)^{1/2}$$

TABLE III
SUR SYSTEM RESULTS[a]
ESTIMATION PERIOD: 1/1/66–12/31/81

Panel A: Specification without slope or intercept dummies.

Parameter[b]	Regressand: Boeing	Regressand: Lockheed	Regressand: McDonnell
$\hat{\alpha}_0$	−0.0003	−0.0005	−0.0003
	(−0.775)	(−0.974)	(−0.720)
$\hat{\beta}_0$	1.2661	1.4503	1.2443
	(31.246)	(25.632)	(30.192)
$\hat{\lambda}_{i \cdot boe}$	−0.0034	0.0014	0.0011
	(−1.072)	(0.308)	(0.344)
$\hat{\lambda}_{i \cdot loc}$	−0.0029	−0.0097	−0.0015
	(−0.299)	(−0.721)	(−0.156)
$\hat{\lambda}_{i \cdot mcd}$	−0.0007	0.0005	−0.0094
	(−0.215)	(0.111)	(−2.878)

Panel B: Specification with slope and intercept shift dummy variables.

Parameter	Regressand: Daily Returns to Boeing Corp. Parameter Estimate	t	Regressand: Daily Returns to McDonnell Douglas Corp. Parameter Estimate	t
$\hat{\alpha}_0$	−0.0004	−0.880	−0.0004	−0.826
$\hat{\beta}_0$	1.3547	24.686	1.1316	20.373
BCrash	−0.0045	−1.275	0.0009	0.283
LCrash	−0.0036	−0.371	−0.0003	−0.033
MCrash	−0.0005	−0.166	−0.0070	−2.043
$\hat{\alpha}_1$	0.9918	0.417	−0.0001	−0.036
$\hat{\alpha}_2$	−0.0011	−1.013	−0.0004	−0.301
$\hat{\alpha}_3$	0.0064	0.569	0.0010	0.920
$\hat{\alpha}_4$	−0.0019	−0.814	−0.0014	−0.531
$\hat{\alpha}_5$	0.0059	2.612	−0.0014	−0.374
$\hat{\alpha}_6$	0.0020	0.716	0.0004	0.248
$\hat{\alpha}_7$	−0.0002	−0.107	0.0009	0.558
$\hat{\alpha}_8$	−0.0013	−0.831	−0.0030	−1.297
$\hat{\alpha}_9$	0.0012	0.812	−0.0002	−0.228
$\hat{\beta}_1$	−0.7342	−1.376	1.0673	3.399

Parameter	Regressand: Daily Returns to Boeing Corp. Parameter Estimate	t	Regressand: Daily Returns to McDonnell Douglas Corp. Parameter Estimate	t
$\hat{\beta}_2$	−0.2322	−2.158	0.3175	1.877
$\hat{\beta}_3$	−0.7465	−0.601	0.2168	1.465
$\hat{\beta}_4$	−0.3196	−1.878	0.3453	0.934
$\hat{\beta}_5$	−0.2613	−1.202	−0.7657	−1.293
$\hat{\beta}_6$	0.0406	0.179	−0.0511	−0.169
$\hat{\beta}_7$	−0.2692	−1.544	−0.0008	−0.004
$\hat{\beta}_8$	0.0033	0.018	0.6019	1.714
$\hat{\beta}_9$	0.4665	1.622	0.2644	2.320

TABLE III (CONTINUED)

Parameter	*Regressand: Daily Returns to Lockheed Corp.* Parameter Estimate	t
$\hat{\alpha}_0$	−0.0005	−0.989
$\hat{\beta}_0$	1.4350	24.847
BCrash	0.0013	0.300
LCrash	−0.0148	−0.061
MCrash	0.0005	0.112
$\hat{\alpha}_1$	0.0015	0.578
$\hat{\beta}_1$	0.4235	1.456

[a] Estimation is based on the full covariance matrix of residuals from the first pass OLS regressions of equation (8).
[b] boe = Boeing Corp.; loc = Lockheed Corp.; mcd = McDonnell Douglas Corp.

Panel B of Table III shows the relevant parameters when the dummy variables D_k are included in regressions over the whole sample period. In this specification, slope and intercept shift dummies are included only for crashes of the firm whose stock returns are the regressand. Hence, SUR estimates are not identical to OLS estimates.[17] It appears that some of the slope dummies are significant at the 5 percent level. However, an F-test of the joint hypothesis that all the slope dummies are equal to zero is only rejected at the 0.0861 level for McDonnell Douglas (F-statistic 1.7302) and at far lower levels for the other two firms. As with the simpler specifications in Table III, panel A, McDonnell Douglas crashes have a statistically significant effect on McDonnell Douglas stock, but the other two manufacturers' crashes do not significantly affect them.

The evidence from OLS and SUR estimation over the whole sample period appears to be consistent with the hypothesis that suspect crashes have a negative effect on the manufacturer involved, although the results differ across firms. The less significant effect on Boeing than on McDonnell Douglas may reflect differences other than the identity of the manufacturer (such as the number of fatalities involved); these differences are explored in section V. The results consistently reject the hypothesis of a cross-firm effect following a crash.[18]

[17] An alternative specification, with slope and intercept dummies included for *all* crashes produced virtually identical results.

[18] For an application of SUR in this fashion, see Gilligan [1985]. As a check against non-stationarity in α and β, the system (8) was estimated over a period of 150 days surrounding each crash. The date of the crash was chosen to be day 76 of the estimation period. If another crash occurred during the estimation period, the five day period beginning on the date of that other crash was excluded from the estimation period. Thus, nineteen models, each a three-equation SUR system, were estimated in total. The average estimate of the effect of a crash on the firm involved is −0.0068, remarkably close to the mean of the firm crash dummies of −0.0089 obtained in the first SUR procedure. The cross-sectional mean of crash effects has a t-statistic of −3.294, corresponding to a significance level of 0.005 percent. An alternative way to make

V. FURTHER IMPLICATIONS

The above tests raise the question of what underlying variables determine the magnitude of the negative forecast error following a suspect crash. Theory suggests several causal variables. First, if information is costly, the amount of media coverage of an accident can alter the extent of public knowledge. There is a positive relationship between the number of fatalities and the amount of media coverage of a crash. If media coverage is a proxy for information, the extent of the effect on manufacturer's stock price will be positively correlated with the number of fatalities in the accident.

Second, we found in section IV that a crash only affects the manufacturer's stock price if the plane is still in production. Given this result, even if it is only approximately true, the size of the product market response will be negatively correlated with the size of the production run completed.

Finally, if a particular model has a second or subsequent crash, this is additional data for consumers to use when evaluating the plane. *A priori*, it seems that the number of prior accidents could have a positive or negative effect on the manufacturer.

To examine these three possibilities, we perform a cross-sectional regression of the effect of a crash i on the aircraft producer regressed on variables designed to capture the forces described above. The market model results reported in section IV(i) indicate that, for the model-specific suspect crashes, there are significant abnormal returns up to and including the fourth day following the crash. Thus, one measure of crash effects, for each crash i, is the cumulative abnormal return over the five-day period beginning on the date of the crash,[19] i.e.:

$$(9) \qquad CFE(0,4) = \sum_{t=T}^{T+4} FE_{iT+s}$$

$CFE(0,4)$ is interpreted as the total forecast error attributable to crash i. Since

cross-equation comparisons is with Pearson's p_λ test (Rao [1952, p. 44]). If $p_1, \ldots p_n$ are the coefficient significance levels n from n independent tests then it can be shown that $\lambda = -2\sum_{i=1}^{n} \log_e p_i$ is distributed i χ^2 with $2n$ degrees of freedom. For the hypothesis $\gamma_{ij} < 0$, $\lambda = 57.424$ (probability value 0.022 percent) for firms involved in suspect crashes ($i = j$) and $\lambda = 68.307$ (probability value 0.723 percent) for firms not involved in crashes ($i \neq j$) on the date that a crash occurred. These significance levels support the results from the previous set of tests. It should be recognized that the cross-sectional and Pearson p_λ tests are strictly valid only if crashes are independent. However, in an adaptive learning model, consumers may react to crashes differently, depending on the aircraft's total crash history. A test for such temporal crash dependence is performed in the next section and indicates that independence is, in fact, a reasonable assumption. Thus, the inference from the Pearson p_λ test is reasonable in this context.

[19] The statistic $CFE(0,4)$ may understate the relationship between crash firm effects and the independent variables. For some crashes the full effect is compounded sooner than day +4 and including subsequent days as in (9) introduces noise into the variable. An alternative measure (reported in an earlier draft) is to cumulate forecast errors that are significant. However, this variable may artificially bias results in favor of a large effect when there is none.

aircraft producers had different numbers of shares outstanding at different times we multiply (9) by the market value of firm i in order to obtain the total effect on the market value of equity due to crash i. The change in the market value of equity ΔMV_i is defined as

$$(10) \qquad \Delta MV_i = CFE(0,4) \cdot MV_{T-1}$$

We hypothesize the following relationship:

$$(11) \qquad \Delta MV_i = \beta_1 + \beta_2 \, RUN_i + \beta_3 \, FATAL_i + \beta_4 \, PRIORACC_i + \varepsilon_i$$

where

RUN_i = percentage of the production run completed up to crash i;
$FATAL_i$ = number of fatalities in accident i;
$PRIORACC_i$ = number of suspect accidents for that model of aircraft prior to i;
ε_i = an error term.[20]

The expected sign of the coefficient of RUN_i is positive, since expected ΔMV_i is negative. The coefficient of $FATAL_i$ (β_3) is hypothesized to be negative if a larger number of fatalities leads to a larger (negative) effect on the manufacturer. The *a priori* expected sign of β_4 (variable $PRIORACC_i$) is ambiguous, for the reasons stated above.

Estimation of (11) must account for the fact that ΔMV_i is an estimate constructed from the first-stage market model regressions. A likelihood ratio test for homoskedasticity of the standard errors of regression of the nineteen first-stage regressions (Hoel [1962, pp. 225–227]) was rejected with a test statistic of 285.9 (five-percent critical value 28.9). Consequently (11) is estimated using weighted least-squares, where the weights are the standard errors of the cumulative forecast errors from the first-stage regressions. Table IV reports results, with OLS estimates for comparison, for the aircraft manufacturers involved in suspect crashes.

The coefficient estimates in the table reflect many of the econometric problems of a small sample size and collinearity between regressors. Although FATAL is negative and significant at almost the 0.001 level, both RUN and

[20] The variable MV_{T-1} is obtained from the CRSP tapes. The number of fatalities, $FATAL_i$, is taken from the *Annual Review of Aircraft Accident Data: US Air Carrier Operations*. $PRIORACC_i$ is constructed from the data. The number of each aircraft model used to construct RUN_i was the number ordered by end 1981, the latest available data. This is a far from perfect measure of expectations made nearer the beginning of the data period, but it seems a reasonable proxy. Attempts to obtain planned production runs at all points in the data period proved fruitless. Boeing and McDonnell Douglas did nonetheless provide quarterly order/sales data for their models—Lockheed had to be estimated. The actual measure of RUN is

$$RUN_t = \frac{\text{number of planes ordered at end ofmost recent quarter preceding date } t}{\text{number of planes ordered at end of 1981}}$$

To estimate Lockheed (whose only model was the L-1011) we used McDonnell Douglas DC-10 order figures since the two planes emerged around the same time and directly competed with each other.

TABLE IV
RESULTS OF THE CROSS-SECTIONAL REGRESSIONS TO EXPLAIN THE CHANGE IN MARKET VALUE (IN $ MILLIONS) OF AIRCRAFT PRODUCERS IN SUSPECT CRASHES

	WLS		*OLS*	
Regressor	*Parameter Estimate*	*t*	*Parameter Estimate*	*t*
Intercept	34.7928	1.315	41.4333	1.515
RUN	−0.3541	−1.038	−0.3934	−1.090
FATAL	−0.2999	−3.878	−0.3440	−4.196
PRIORACC	−3.9465	−0.749	−3.7572	−0.700
$\bar{R}^2$	0.4227		0.4713	
F	5.393		6.348	
Prob. > *F*	0.0102		0.0054	

PRIORACC are insignificant and RUN has the wrong sign.[21] For this reason, it would be unwise to place too much weight on the results of these regressions. A literal interpretation of the coefficient of FATAL is that a marginal fatality reduced stockholder wealth by $299 900. Given that the mean of FATAL is 85 fatalities, the average marginal effect of FATAL is to reduce the manufacturer's market value of equity by $25.5 million. Since manufacturers are fully, or almost fully, insured against tort judgments, this magnitude is difficult to explain as a reaction to potential litigation. It suggests that the stock market considers a suspect crash to have more serious consequences, possibly product market effects due to consumer aversion to flying the aircraft. The significant effect of FATAL throws light on the differential magnitude of the stock price impact across manufacturers. The mean value of FATAL for McDonnell Douglas is 100, which is somewhat larger than the mean value of 68 for Boeing.

VI. CONCLUSION

This paper examined the effect of commercial aircraft accidents on the manufacturer of the aircraft involved. Several empirical techniques were employed to do this. The results of the market model regressions indicate that accidents in which the manufacturer is implicated and the aircraft is still in production result in a decrease in the market value of equity of −3.774 percent, equivalent to a reduction in the market value of equity of $21.32 million. In contrast, crashes that did not implicate the manufacturer did not

[21] One possible explanation for a negative sign on RUN is that manufacturers' accident costs increase with the number of planes in service due to mandated design alterations and inspections. In this case RUN is a proxy for the total number of aircraft of a given type in service. To see if there was any evidence for this proposition we included the number of planes produced as an independent variable in a regression like equation (8). As in the reported results for RUN, the variable was insignificant and unstable.

result in any stock price effect. Suspect crashes of aircraft no longer in production also exhibit no negative effect on the manufacturer (although the sample size for this group is small). These results suggest that endogenous responses in the product market are responsible for the negative effect on manufacturers. Seemingly unrelated regressions bear out the results from the market model and indicate that any anticipated cross-effect on manufacturers is non-existent.

The size of the negative effect in the current model suspect group is (negatively) correlated with the number of fatalities, consistent with fatalities as a proxy for information or the size of tort judgments. We must repeat the caveat stated in the introduction, that even if abnormal performance reflects the influence of market forces, we cannot show that the extent of market adjustment is optimal. Hence, regulatory and tort law mechanisms may not be superfluous. If anything, the results indicate the importance of information-based strategies for regulatory agencies.[22]

The methodology used here has validity elsewhere for the analysis of markets when an exogenous event is posited to have an impact on the stock value of the firms in the industry. In the safety area alone, examples such as product recalls, new scientific discoveries of potential harmful effects from a certain product, regulatory bans, and serious accidents are all potentially analyzable.

ANDREW J. CHALK,
Edwin L. Cox School of Business,
Southern Methodist University,
Dallas, Texas 75275,
USA.

ACCEPTED JULY 1986

REFERENCES

AKERLOF, G. A., 1970, 'The Market for "Lemons": Quality Uncertainty and the Market Mechanism', *Quarterly Journal of Economics*, 84 (August), pp. 488–500.

ARROW, K. J., 1962, 'Economic Welfare and the Allocation of Resources for Invention', in *The Rate and Direction of Inventive Activity: Economic and Social Factors* (National Bureau of Economic Research).

BROWN, S. J. and WARNER, J. B., 1980, 'Measuring Security Price Performance', *Journal of Financial Economics*, 8 (September), pp. 205–258.

BOND, E. W., 1982, 'A Direct Test of the "Lemons" Model: The Market for Used Pickup Trucks', *American Economic Review*, 72 (September), pp. 836–840.

CHALK, A. J., 1983, 'The Role of Brand Names in the Provision of Safety: An Empirical Test on the US Passenger Aircraft Market', mimeo, Washington University, (June).

[22] In practice, with the exception of one administrator (Langhorne Bond), the FAA has refused to publicize the serious safety infractions it uncovers. This papers suggests that if a deliberate effort were made to publish accurate information about these violations, consumers could make informed choices about various airlines' safety precautions and establish incentives for levels of producer care closer to the optimal level.

CHALK, A. J., 1983, *The Economics of Airline Safety*. Unpublished Ph.D. dissertation, Washington University.

COLLINS, D. W. and DENT, W. T., 1979, 'The Proposed Elimination of Full Cost Accounting in the Extractive Petroleum Industry', *Journal of Accounting and Economics*, 1 (March), pp. 3–44.

COPELAND, T. E. and WESTON, J. F., 1983, *Financial Theory and Corporate Policy*, 2nd ed. (Addison-Wesley Publishing Co. Reading, Mass.).

CORNELL, N., NOLL, R. and WEINGAST, B., 1976, 'Safety Regulation' in H. OWEN and C. L. SCHULTZ, eds., *Setting National Priorities: The Next Decade* (Brookings Institution, Washington, D.C.).

DODD, P. and RUBACK, R. S., 1977, 'Tender Offers and Stockholder Returns', *Journal of Financial Economics*, 5 (November), pp. 351–373.

FAMA, E. F., FISHER, L., JENSEN, J. and ROLL, R., 1969, 'The Adjustment of Stock Prices to New Information', *International Economic Review*, 10 (February), pp. 1–21.

GIBBONS, M., 1980, 'Econometric Models for Testing a Class of Financial Models: An Application of the Nonlinear Multivariate Regression Model'. Ph.D. dissertation, University of Chicago, School of Business Administration.

GILLIGAN, T. W., 1985, 'The Competitive Effects of Resale Price Maintenance', mimeo, California Institute of Technology.

HEAL, G., 1976, 'Do Bad Products Drive Out Good?', *Quarterly Journal of Economics*, 90 (August), pp. 499–503.

HOEL, P., 1962, *Introduction to Mathematical Statistics*, 3rd ed. (John Wiley and Sons, New York).

KAPLAN, R. S. and ROLL, R., 1972, 'Investor Evaluation of Accounting Information: Some Empirical Evidence', *Journal of Business*, 45 (April), pp. 225–257.

KLEIN, B. and LEFFLER, K. B., 1981, 'The Role of Market Forces in Assessing Contractual Performance', *Journal of Political Economy*, 89 (August), pp. 615–641.

LEHMANN, E. L., 1975, *Nonparametrics: Statistical Methods Based on Ranks* (Holden Day, San Francisco).

MALATESTA, P., 1986, 'Measuring Abnormal Performance: The Event Parameter Approach Using Joint Generalized Least Squares', *Journal of Financial and Quantitative Analysis* (forthcoming).

MARCY, D. E., 1979, 'The Crashworthiness Doctrine and the Allocation of Risks in Commercial Aviation', *Southern California Law Review*, 52 (July), pp. 1581–1626.

MARKOWITZ, H., 1959, *Portfolio Selection: Efficient Diversification of Investment* (John Wiley and Sons, New York).

NATIONAL TRANSPORTATION SAFETY BOARD, *Annual Review of Aircraft Accident Data: U.S. Air Carrier Operations*, U.S. Government, Washington, D.C. (annually).

RAO, C. R., 1952, *Advanced Statistical Methods in Biometric Research*, 3rd ed. (Wiley, New York).

SALOP, S. and STIGLITZ, J., 1977, 'Bargains and Ripoffs: A Model of Monopolistically Competitive Price Dispersion', *Review of Economic Studies*, 44 (October), pp. 494–510.

SCHIPPER, K. and THOMPSON, R., 1983, 'The Impact of Merger-Related Regulations on the Shareholders of Acquiring Firms', *Journal of Accounting Research*, 21 (Spring), pp. 184–221.

SCHWERT, G. W., 1981, 'Using Financial Data to Measure Effects of Regulation', *Journal of Law and Economics*, 24 (April), pp. 121–158.

SCITOVSKY, T., 1950, 'Ignorance as a Source of Monopoly Power', *American Economic Review*, 4 (May), pp. 48–53.

SHARPE, W. F., 1963, 'A Simplified Model for Portfolio Analysis', *Management Science*, 9 (January), pp. 277–293.

U.S. CONGRESS, HOUSE, COMMITTEE ON GOVERNMENT OPERATIONS, *FAA Aviation Safety Issues, Hearings before a Subcommittee of the Committee on Government Operations*. 95th Cong., 1st Sess., 1979.

U.S. CONGRESS, SENATE COMMITTEE ON COMMERCE, SCIENCE AND TRANSPORTATION, *Aviation Safety, Hearings before the Subcommittee on Aviation*. 95th Cong., 2nd Sess., 1980.

VISCUSI, W. K., 1978, 'A Note on "Lemons" Markets with Quality Certification', *Bell Journal of Economics*, 9 (Spring), pp. 277–279.

WILDE, L. L. and SCHWARTZ, A., 1979, 'Equilibrium Comparison Shopping', *Review of Economic Studies*, 46 (July), pp. 543–553.

ZELLNER, A., 1962, 'An Efficient Method of Estimating Seemingly Unrelated Regressions and Tests for Aggregation Bias', *Journal of the American Statistical Association*, 57 (June), pp. 348–368.

THE JOURNAL OF INDUSTRIAL ECONOMICS 0022-1821 $2.00
Volume XXXVI September 1987 No. 1

RESEARCH EXPENDITURES AND THE DISCOVERY OF NEW DRUGS

ELIZABETH J. JENSEN*

This paper examines technical change in the ethical pharmaceutical industry. A Poisson specification is used to estimate a productivity relationship between research expenditures and drug discoveries, thus taking into account the integer nature of the data. The results of estimations using panel data indicate that there is a positive correlation between a firm's research and development intensity and its probability of discovering a new drug. Firm size, however, does not significantly affect the marginal productivity of research expenditures. Finally, the estimates show that an increase in regulatory stringency decreases the expected number of new drug discoveries.

I. INTRODUCTION

RESEARCHERS RECENTLY have realized that technological change is itself an economic variable influenced by the search for profits and have focused research upon this process. (See, for example, Griliches [1984], Scherer [1983], and Hausman, Hall and Griliches [1984].) However, both theoretical and empirical work on the determinants of technological change remain incomplete. This paper analyzes some aspects of technological change in the context of a specific industry, the US ethical pharmaceutical industry.[1]

The basic relationship under examination in this paper is that between research expenditures and the discovery of new drugs. The paper improves upon previous work by using a Poisson distribution in the estimation rather than assuming a normal probability distribution. The Poisson distribution is attractive because it is consistent with the integer nature of the data on discoveries of new drugs. The following section describes the model; section III discusses the sample and the variables used in the estimation. Results are presented and discussed in section IV, while section V contains a test of the Poisson specification. The final section summarizes the empirical results.

* This paper is a revision of work done for my dissertation; an earlier version of the paper was presented at the Econometric Society meetings in Dallas, Texas, December 28–30, 1984. I would like to thank Peter Temin, Paul Joskow, Bob Turner and two anonymous referees for their help. The Alfred P. Sloan Foundation provided financial support for the initial work.

[1] Ethical drugs are those advertised only to physicians and pharmacists while proprietary or over-the-counter drugs are advertised directly to the public. This research is concerned with the discovery of ethical and not proprietary drugs. However, I will frequently omit the qualifier "ethical".

II. THE MODEL

Almost all of the previous empirical work on innovation in the pharmaceutical industry has been based upon productivity relationships.[2] (See for example, Comanor [1965], Vernon and Gusen [1974], Baily [1972], Grabowski, Vernon and Thomas [1978] and Wiggins [1981].) These estimations take the form:

$$(1) \qquad NCE = f(Res, X)$$

where NCE is a count of new chemical entities introduced over some unit of observation (see the following discussion of the data); Res is a measure of research inputs; and X is a vector of other variables hypothesized to affect innovation.

Different variables have been included in X, depending on the questions being examined. Comanor [1965] and Vernon and Gusen [1974], for example, used cross-section data to examine the returns to R & D expenditures and the relationship between firm size and innovation. Other researchers, such as Baily [1972] and Grabowski, Vernon and Thomas [1978], analyzed the effects of regulation upon pharmaceutical industry innovation, including a measure of regulatory stringency in their time series estimations. This study utilizes panel data. As a consequence, both firm specific questions, such as the returns to R & D expenditures, and industry specific questions, such as the effect of increased regulatory stringency upon innovation, can be examined.

The major difference between this study and previous work concerns the assumption underlying the estimation of the productivity relationship. The dependent variable in previous studies has been a count of discoveries of NCE's over some unit of observation, such as per firm or per year. Because the dependent variable can take on only non-negative values, the equations were often estimated in logarithmic form by ordinary least squares or in linear form by Tobit. While these estimation techniques do take the truncation from below into account, both OLS and Tobit are based on the assumption that the errors are distributed normally. This assumption may be valid for integer dependent variables that take on large values; however, it does not seem appropriate for counts of NCE's, which are small integers. Also, the dependent variable in these regressions frequently is equal to zero, since many firms do not discover a new drug in any given year. No previous study of innovation in the pharmaceutical industry has taken account of the integer nature of the data.

In this study an approach pioneered by Hausman, Hall, and Griliches [1984] is used to estimate a productivity relationship. The specification used is

$$(2) \qquad \log m_{it} = X_{it}B$$

[2] Peltzman's research [1973] differs in that his estimation is based upon a demand-pull model of innovation.

where m_{it} is the expected number of discoveries of new drugs by firm i in year t; and X_{it} is a vector of firm characteristics.

Discoveries are assumed to arrive according to a Poisson process where m_{it} is the Poisson parameter. m_{it} thus represents the arrival rate of drug discoveries per firm per year and also the expected number of discoveries per firm per year. This specification is attractive because it is consistent with the integer nature of the data and particularly with the fact that in any given year many firms do not discover a new drug.[3, 4]

The idea underlying this approach is that pharmaceutical firm managers associate an expected economic return with each technical success.[5] If this expected return is greater than the expected cost of getting the new drug to the market, the firm will proceed with testing and development. Thus, measures of new drugs introduced to the market actually count the number of technically successful projects that have positive net expected returns. If the distribution of net expected returns to discovering new drugs remains stable, then the technique described above can be used to estimate the relationship between research expenditures and the probability that projects will be technically successful. In this case the variable(s) included in X, the vector of firm characteristics, would be measures of the firm's research efforts.

A crucial assumption of this approach is that the distribution of net expected returns remains stable. Modeling the formation of expectations is a difficult task not addressed at the current stage of this research. Still, this assumption will be modified by including in X two variables hypothesized to shift the distribution of net expected returns. These are a time trend and a measure of regulatory stringency. Reasons for this are given in the following discussion of the variables that affect the arrival rate of new drug discoveries.

III. THE DATA: SAMPLE AND VARIABLES

The sample

Marketing guides to the pharmaceutical industry were used to develop an initial list of ethical pharmaceutical firms. Data limitations then dictated the selection of the final sample from this initial list. The final sample contains data on twenty-eight firms over the years 1969 through 1979.

[3] See Hausman, Hall, and Griliches [1984] for details on the log likelihood function, the first order conditions, and the Hessian. Maddala also discusses Poisson regressions [1983, pp. 51–54].

[4] Modeling discovery as a stochastic process differs from the approach employed in much of the theoretical literature on potential rivalry, pre-emptive patenting, and innovative activity. See, for example, Kamien and Schwartz [1974] and [1978] and Gilbert and Newbery [1982]. However, some recent theoretical articles on innovation do model discovery as stochastic. The theoretical model developed in Loury [1979] and Dasgupta and Stiglitz [1980] is close to that used in this paper. Specifically, the R&D technology is modeled as Poisson, with the Poisson parameter depending on the present value of future research expenditures at the time the research is undertaken on the project.

[5] See Pakes and Griliches [1984, note 3].

The average worldwide ethical sales of the sample firms in 1980 were approximately $727 million (in current dollars) while the median firm had 1980 ethical sales of $690.8 million. The minimum of 1980 sales was $82.2 million, the maximum was $1894 million, and the standard deviation was $493 million. The 1980 worldwide sales of ethical drugs of the sample firms accounted for approximately eighty-nine percent of the total industry sales reported by the Pharmaceutical Manufacturers Association in their annual survey.

The variables

The focus of this research, technological change in the ethical pharmaceutical industry, is measured by a count of new chemical entities (*NCE*'s) per firm per year. *NCE*'s are single chemical compounds not previously known; they are the target of most of the R & D expenditures of pharmaceutical firms. Data on *NCE*'s were obtained from annual surveys of Paul de Haen, Inc.[6]

The first of the explanatory variables is research and development expenditures. These data were collected from 10**K** forms and annual reports of the sample firms. Reported information on the breakdown of R & D expenditures was used to derive an estimate of research expenditures on ethical products only.[7]

In order to deflate research and development expenditures, an index constructed along the lines suggested by Jaffe [NSF, 1972] was used. This index is simply a weighted average of the index of hourly labor compensation and the implicit deflator in the non-financial corporations sector, with relative weights of 0.49 and 0.51.

One question that will be examined is whether the relationship between R & D and the probability of drug discovery is linear. Economies of scale arising from fixed costs may exist in the discovery of new drugs. Some economists have emphasized the importance of employing a multidisciplinary research team: having such a team within an industrial laboratory permits the exchange of information across disciplines and the testing of numerous leads. The need to screen promising compounds in a number of therapeutic areas may constitute another source of scale economies. A minimum number of research projects may need to be undertaken in order to utilize the services of the specialists and the screens (the tests for both therapeutic effects and undesired side effects) efficiently. Thus it is possible that the number of drugs

[6] Vaccines, serums, immune globulins, and new salts and esters of previously marketed drugs were excluded from the analysis. Because a primary purpose of this research is analyzing the relationship between research and development inputs and innovative output, *NCE*'s were attributed to the discovering firm rather than the introducing firm if the two were not the same. Data from de Haen were used to distinguish between discovering firm and introducing firm. Vernon and Gusen [1974] also made this distinction; other researchers appear to have looked at introductions of *NCE*'s per firm.

[7] This procedure is described in detail in an appendix available on request from the author.

discovered increases more than proportionately with increases in research inputs, at least over some range. Previous empirical work has come to inconclusive results about the returns to research intensity in the ethical pharmaceutical industry.[8]

The marginal productivity of research expenditures may vary across firms of different sizes. However, the expected effect of firm size on the arrival rate of new discoveries is ambiguous. On the one hand, increases in size are sometimes argued to result in increases in managerial problems of coordination and control.[9] On the other hand, the 1962 Kefauver–Harris Amendments to the Federal Food, Drug, and Cosmetic Act of 1938 sharply increased the cost and time required to bring a new drug to the marketplace.[10] In addition, the regulatory changes led to a much higher attrition rate on new drug candidates. The increased risk means that pharmaceutical firms must pool larger numbers of more expensive research projects in order to diversify the risk. Small firms, because of their more limited resources, may be less able to adapt to this new environment.[11]

In order to measure the effect of firm size on research and development productivity, controlling for research expenditures, an interaction variable is included in the specification.[12] This interaction variable is the product of R & D expenditures and firm size, measured by worldwide sales of ethical drug products.[13] The CPI for prescription drugs was used to deflate the sales figures.

Two additional explanatory variables are a time trend, added to allow the distribution of expected returns to discovering a drug to shift for exogenous reasons over time[14] and a measure of regulatory stringency, since changes in regulatory stringency may change the number of technical successes that a

[8] Comanor [1965] found that returns to R & D vary with firm size, ranging from increasing returns for small firms to decreasing returns for large firms. Vernon and Gusen [1974] found diminishing returns to R & D for a firm of a given size, while Schwartzman [1976] found increasing returns to R & D intensity. None of these researchers, however, reported tests of significance of the results on the returns to research intensity.

[9] Comanor [1965] argues that this is true for the ethical pharmaceutical industry. However, his estimations are based on data from a period before the 1962 Amendments to the FDC Act and one effect of these amendments may have been to increase the advantages of being large.

[10] See Schwartzman [1976] and Hansen [1979].

[11] This argument is expressed by a number of economists. See, for example, Grabowski and Vernon [1979, pp. 46–47]. Of course, a large firm will have to do as well as a small one on average in order to remain profitable. However, because of a larger pool of internal resources, the risk that any specific failure will result in bankruptcy is less for the larger firm.

[12] The hypothesis underlying the interaction variable is that a change in firm size changes the marginal productivity of research expenditures. This is the approach taken by previous researchers studying pharmaceutical industry innovation (Comanor [1965] and Vernon and Gusen [1974]).

[13] Data on sales were collected from 10K forms and annual reports of the pharmaceutical firms. In a few cases a firm's sales for a missing year were calculated by interpolation of the percentage of total sales represented by sales of ethical drugs in the non-missing years.

[14] This possibility is suggested by empirical work on the relationship between patent and R & D expenditures (Hausman, Hall, and Griliches [1984]).

firm chooses to bring to the market. By raising the development costs per drug, increased regulatory stringency decreases the net expected return associated with each technical success.

The variable used to measure regulatory stringency is the average delay that an *NCE* faces in gaining FDA approval for marketing.[15] Wiggins' conversations with executives of pharmaceutical firms revealed that NDA approval times are regarded as good indicators of the expected stringency of regulation[16] (Wiggins [1979, p. 131]).

IV. RESULTS

Before arriving at a final specification, the question of what lags to employ on research expenditures and the measure of regulatory stringency was considered. Current innovation is the result of research expenditures over a number of previous years; therefore, the lag structure for past R & D effects on current innovation is a complicated set of weights. Moreover, these weights have changed over time as the average lag between synthesis of an *NCE* and its introduction to the market has increased. Directly estimating these weights is not possible with the existing data. Previous studies of the effects of regulation upon innovation in the pharmaceutical industry have typically employed a three to five year lag on research expenditures and a somewhat longer lag on the measure of regulatory stringency.[17] However, these studies grouped drugs according to their year of approval for marketing or of introduction to the market. Because discoveries have been grouped according to the year of NDA submission in this study, a shorter lag on both research expenditures and regulatory stringency is appropriate. (See note 19.)

A number of specifications were estimated with lags on research expenditures and average NDA approval time up through four years. The estimated coefficients on the research and sales variables are very close using different lagged values. None of the qualitative results in the following discussion is altered by choice of lag. However, once the research and sales data from one year have been included, no further information is provided by the data from the other years. This is not surprising since most of the

[15] This variable was used as a measure of regulatory stringency by Grabowski, Vernon and Thomas [1978] and by Wiggins [1981]. To calculate this variable, all *NCE*'s were grouped according to their year of introduction, excluding salts and esters, biologicals, and immune globulins. Then information on the number of months from submission of the NDA to its approval was obtained for each *NCE* and these approval times were averaged for all drugs introduced in a given year. I would like to thank Dale Hattis of MIT's Center for Policy Alternatives for sharing information on NDA approval times with me.

[16] It should be noted, however, that the average NDA approval time reflects not only the rules and procedures of the FDA but also the characteristics of the specific drugs that companies develop for testing. Thus, NDA approval time could increase even in the absence of tighter regulatory standards.

[17] See Baily [1972], Grabowski, Vernon and Thomas [1978], and Wiggins [1979] for discussions of the lag structure on research expenditures.

movement within these variables is in the cross-section data. There is not enough information in the sample to differentiate the effects of current and previous years' research expenditures. Because using only the current values of research and sales variables allows the largest sample to be used, this is the approach followed in the remainder of the paper.

In order to examine the question of the length of the lag on the regulatory delay variable, a series of nested tests was done. The unrestricted specification includes the NDA approval times from the four previous years; the restricted specifications constrain the coefficient(s) of one or more of the regulatory delay variables to equal zero. The results of likelihood ratio tests indicate that for this sample, the final specification should include the second and third lagged values of the NDA approval times.[18]

Comparison of OLS, Tobit, and Poisson estimations

This is the first use of a specification that recognizes the integer nature of the data on discoveries of *NCE*'s. Because of this, ordinary least squares and a Tobit estimation procedure were used in several initial estimations for purposes of comparison. Tobit improves upon OLS by taking account of the truncation at zero from below of the number of discoveries. However, normality is still assumed to hold in the Tobit estimation.

Table I shows OLS, Tobit, and Poisson results for the specification described above.[19] This specification includes a constant, the current value of research and development expenditures on ethical products (*RD*), this value squared and cubed, research expenditures interacted with current sales of ethical drugs (*RDS*), the second and third previous years' values of the average NDA approval time (*NDA*), and a time trend ($YEAR = 69$ in 1969, 70 in 1970, and so on).

The results of the three estimation procedures are broadly similar although the OLS results differ noticeably from the Tobit and Poisson results. This is

[18] The choice of the "final" specification—that is, which lags of the regulatory delay variables have estimated coefficients that are significantly different from zero—is somewhat sensitive to the sample period. However, the qualitative results on the effects of regulation are not sensitive to the sample, and the coefficients on the other included variables are robust to the sample period (Jensen [1984]).

[19] In a few instances, current R&D information was not available and these observations were excluded. This reduced the sample to 290 observations from a potential 308. In these estimations new drugs are grouped according to the year of NDA submission. This contrasts with the procedure used by previous researchers who grouped drugs according to either their year of approval by the FDA or their year of introduction to the United States market. Drugs approved or introduced in the same year have often been in the regulatory "pipeline" for widely varying amounts of time. The wide variance in regulatory approval times could potentially lead to problems in estimation because research will have been done on the drugs over a long period of time. Thus a three to five year lag on R&D expenditures might be appropriate for some drugs introduced in a given year while a longer lag might better measure research inputs for other drugs introduced in that year. Grouping drugs according to the year of NDA submission should reduce this aggregation bias.

TABLE I
COMPARISON OF OLS, TOBIT, and POISSON RESULTS

	OLS	*Tobit*	*Poisson*
Constant	5.354*	19.22*	17.02*
	(1.628)	(6.74)	(6.98)
RD	0.0103	0.1054*	0.1217*
	(0.0059)	(0.0292)	(0.0337)
RD^2	-0.7243×10^{-4}	-0.1151×10^{-2}*	-0.1419×10^{-2}*
	(0.1164×10^{-3})	(0.4747×10^{-3})	(0.5070×10^{-3})
RD^3	-0.1727×10^{-6}	0.3373×10^{-5}	$0.4620 - 10^{-5}$*
	(0.6006×10^{-6})	(0.2290×10^{-5})	(0.2342×10^{-5})
RDS	0.7174×10^{-5}*	0.1316×10^{-4}	0.1327×10^{-4}
	(0.3522×10^{-5})	(0.1132×10^{-4})	(0.9813×10^{-5})
NDA2	−0.0172*	−0.0749*	−0.0640*
	(0.0076)	(0.0301)	(0.0301)
NDA3	−0.0256*	−0.1053*	−0.0977*
	(0.0084)	(0.0343)	(0.0343)
YEAR	−0.0575*	−0.2408*	−0.2290*
	(0.0177)	(0.0747)	(0.0771)

* Indicates significance at the 5 percent level; the numbers in parentheses are standard errors or asymptotic standard errors.

Note: RD and sales are measured in millions of 1977 $.

not surprising considering that the values taken on by the dependent variable in the OLS and Tobit specifications, discoveries per firm per year, are clustered around zero. As expected, the truncation causes the OLS coefficients to be biased towards zero. The estimated coefficients and standard errors of the Tobit and Poisson results are quite similar. Because of the similarity of the Tobit and Poisson results and the theoretical superiority of the Poisson specification given the counting nature of the data, only Poisson results are considered in the remainder of the paper.

Discussion of the results

The results of the estimation indicate that research expenditures have a positive effect on the arrival rate or expected number of new drug discoveries. The elasticity of *m*, the expected number of discoveries, with respect to research expenditures is given by:

$$\frac{\partial m}{\partial RD} \times \frac{RD}{m} = \frac{\partial \log m}{\partial RD} \times RD$$

Because $\partial \log m / \partial RD$ from Table I depends on both research expenditures and sales, and because R & D to sales ratios vary across firms, this estimated elasticity can differ for two firms of the same size or for two firms with the same research expenditures. For the smallest five firms in the distribution of average annual research expenditures, the elasticity of the expected number of discoveries with respect to R & D is significantly less than one. With the exception of two of the remaining twenty-three firms, this estimated elasticity is not significantly different from one.[20]

No explicit model of the behavior of pharmaceutical firms is presented here. However, according to established models, there are only a few special cases in which we would expect to observe a firm in equilibrium operating in a range of decreasing returns. A possible reason for the estimated elasticities for the smallest firms being less than one is that these firms are not in long run equilibrium. The fact that most of these small firms have been involved in a period of transition lends some support to this hypothesis.[21] These firms may be in short run equilibrium but may not be of the optimal size. That they are all firms with small R & D budgets provides some evidence of a threshold in pharmaceutical research. Perhaps in order to perform research on new drugs at an efficient level, a minimum investment must be made. The estimated relationship between R & D expenditures and the probability of discovering a new drug indicates that this minimum level is somewhere between $6 and $10 million (1977 dollars).[22]

A second question of interest is whether the marginal productivity of research expenditures varies across firms of different sizes. As discussed above, the sign of the expected effect of firm size on the expected number of discoveries is ambiguous. Previous empirical evidence is also inconclusive; Comanor [1965] found that the marginal productivity of research personnel is inversely related to firm size while others such as Vernon and Gusen [1974] found that the marginal productivity of R & D increases with firm size. The estimated coefficient of the interaction variable, *RDS*, is not significantly different from zero. This indicates that, once the effect of firm size on R & D expenditures is controlled for, there are no advantages or disadvantages to locating a given R & D program in a larger firm. Size also had no significant effect on the expected number of drug discoveries when it was entered as a separate explanatory variable.

The estimated coefficient of the time trend (*YEAR*) is negative and significantly different from zero. This indicates that the probability of

[20] The two exceptions are two of the largest firms, for which the estimated elasticity is significantly less than one. The estimated elasticity depends upon the specification chosen. In an earlier version of the paper the cubic term was omitted. Using this specification, the elasticity of the expected number of discoveries with respect to R & D was significantly less than one for the smallest eight firms and for a few more of the larger firms. A referee suggested that the anomalous result of decreasing returns for the largest firms could be due to the functional form. Another alternative functional form uses log *RD* as an explanatory variable. Using this specification, the elasticity of discoveries with respect to R & D, which does not vary across firms, was not significantly different from one.

None of the other qualitative results discussed in the paper is dependent upon the choice of specification.

[21] Some firms left the industry. Others are recent entrants. A third type of transition is mergers and acquisitions.

[22] A *Business Week* article of February 20, 1982 reported that Pennwalt's 1983 investment in drug R & D of $10 million (about $6 million in 1977 dollars) was considered by industry analysts to be well below the minimum expenditures "necessary to survive in pharmaceuticals" (p. 76).

discovering a drug whose expected revenues exceed the expected costs of bringing it to the market has decreased over time, controlling for research expenditures.

The final variables to be considered are those measuring regulatory stringency. The coefficients on the lagged values of NDA approval times in Table I indicate that regulatory stringency does have a strong effect on the expected number of drug discoveries. The magnitude of this effect appears to be large: a one month decrease in each of the two regulatory delay variables would lead to an increase of approximately fifteen percent in the number of *NCE*'s discovered per year, *ceteris paribus*.

This result supports the evidence found in previous studies of the effects of the 1962 Amendments on pharmaceutical industry innovation, although the methodology differs in several ways from previous research. Firm specific data rather than industry wide data are used to address this question. Also, the specification employed to estimate these effects differs from that employed by previous researchers. Finally, the estimations presented here use data from the 1970s, avoiding both the early and mid 1960s. The early 1960s are a controversial period because there may have been a decrease in technological opportunities apart from the change in the regulatory environment, and the mid 1960s may have been a period of disequilibrium for both the pharmaceutical industry and the FDA.[23] My research indicates that regulatory stringency continues to be an important factor in pharmaceutical industry innovation.[24]

V. A TEST OF THE POISSON SPECIFICATION

Analyses of linear panel data have frequently found evidence of unobserved firm specific effects such as management ability that cause a particular firm to deviate in the same way from the "average" firm in each of the sample years. In the presence of such fixed effects, the residuals for a given firm would all tend to be of the same sign: the expected number of discoveries for the firms with the "better" managers would tend to be underpredicted.

To evaluate the adequacy of the Poisson specification, define u_{it} as the Poisson residual ($m_{it} - m_{(\text{predicted})it}$) and then form the standardized residual, e_{it}, by dividing u_{it} by its estimated standard deviation. The time independence assumption can then be tested by forming the covariance matrix of the

[23] The mid 1960s was a period of chronic shortages of medical reviewing personnel at the FDA often met by temporary loans of people from the Public Health Service. In addition, even though the Kefauver-Harris Amendments were enacted by Congress in 1962, formal regulations were not promulgated by the FDA for some years (Temin [1980]).

[24] Two cautionary notes should be mentioned. The magnitude of the estimated effect of regulation is sensitive to the inclusion of the time trend. Also, average NDA approval times depend on the decisions of pharmaceutical firm managers as well as on the actions of the FDA. Further research will consider different specifications of the time trend and more detailed classifications of the types of *NCE*'s being introduced.

standardized residuals for each firm, $\sum_i = e_i e_i'$, where e_i is a vector of residuals for firm i. Given the Poisson assumptions, the off-diagonal elements should be zero; there should be no correlation of the residuals for different time periods.[25]

This procedure was carried out using the predicted values of m_{it} from Table I. Then the off-diagonal elements were averaged across firms to form $\sum = \frac{1}{N} \sum_{i=1}^{N} e_i e_i'$. The largest absolute value of the off diagonal elements in this average covariance matrix was 0.43, and most of the elements were less than 0.2 in absolute value. The average of all off-diagonal elements was -0.01. Serial correlation thus does not appear to be a serious problem.[26]

VI. CONCLUSION

The basic relationship analyzed in this paper is that between research and development expenditures and the probability that research projects will be technically successful. A Poisson specification is used to estimate this relationship.[27]

The results of the final estimated equation provide evidence that increases in R & D expenditures increase the probability of discovering a new drug. For most of the firms the estimated elasticity of the arrival rate of new drug discoveries with respect to research expenditures is not significantly different from one. However, this estimated elasticity is significantly less than one for the smallest firms in the sample, perhaps because these firms are not in long run equilibrium.

The results show that the marginal productivity of research expenditures does not depend on firm size. Managerial problems of coordination and control do not appear to affect innovation in the ethical pharmaceutical industry. On the other hand, there is also no indication that there are advantages to locating a research budget of a given size in a larger firm.

Another question of interest, especially to policymakers, is the effect of regulatory changes upon innovation in the ethical pharmaceutical industry.

[25] This procedure was used by Hausman, Hall and Griliches [1984].

[26] Hausman, Hall and Griliches [1984] found strong evidence of unobserved firm specific effects in their sample with the off-diagonal elements in the estimated correlation matrix of the standardized residuals approximately equal to 0.8. A possible reason for the difference between their finding of serious serial correlation and the results of this research is the samples employed. Hausman, Hall, and Griliches analyzed the relationship between patenting and research expenditures for a sample of 121 firms across industries over eight years. It seems likely that there are indeed unobserved firm specific effects in the propensity to patent for a sample of firms from different industries because the importance of research and patenting varies across industries. However, the sample used in this research is much more homogeneous.

[27] A potential problem with the specifications estimated in this paper is that *NCE*'s were aggregated over therapeutic classes. Aggregating in this way may not be valid for several reasons (see Jensen [1984, pp. 105–107]). However, estimations using drugs disaggregated by therapeutic class support the conclusions of this research (Jensen [1984, Ch. 4]).

The results of this paper support the evidence of previous researchers that an increase in regulatory stringency decreases the expected number of new drug discoveries. The tradeoff between tighter regulatory standards and the number of new drug discoveries found to exist in the 1960s has persisted as pharmaceutical firms adapted to the new regulatory environment. Furthermore, this tradeoff is estimated to be quite steep. Finally, an exogenous decrease in the probability of discovering a new drug is found over the sample years.

ELIZABETH J. JENSEN,
Department of Economics,
Hamilton College,
Clinton, New York 13323,
USA.

ACCEPTED OCTOBER 1986

REFERENCES

BAILY, M. N., 1972, 'Research and Development Costs and Returns: The US Pharmaceutical Industry', *Journal of Political Economy*, 80, 1 (January/February), pp. 70–85.

COMANOR, W. S., 1965, 'Research and Technical Change in the Pharmaceutical Industry', *The Review of Economics and Statistics*, 47, 2 (May), pp. 182–190.

DASGUPTA, P. and STIGLITZ, J., 1980, 'Uncertainty, Industrial Structure, and the Speed of R&D', *The Bell Journal of Economics*, 11, 1 (Spring), pp. 1–28.

DE HAEN, P., 1961, *Review of Drugs, 1941–1961* (Paul de Haen, Inc., New York).

DE HAEN, P., 1966, *Compilation of New Drugs, 1940–1966* (Paul de Haen, Inc., New York).

DE HAEN, P., various years, *New Drug Analysis, USA* (Paul de Haen, Inc., New York).

DE HAEN, P., various years, *New Product Survey* (Paul de Haen, Inc. New York).

DE HAEN, P., 1982, *Nonproprietary Name Index, 1982* (Micromedex, Inc., Englewood, CO).

GILBERT, R. J. and NEWBERY, D. M. G., 1982, 'Preemptive Patenting and the Persistence of Monopoly', *The American Economic Review*, 72, 3 (June), pp. 514–526.

GRABOWSKI, H. and VERNON, J., 1979, 'New Studies on Market Definition, Concentration, Theory of Supply, Entry, and Promotion', in R. I. CHIEN (ed.), *Issues in Pharmaceutical Economics* (Lexington Books, Lexington, MA).

GRABOWSKI, H. G., VERNON, J. and THOMAS, L. G., 1978, 'Estimating the Effects of Regulation on Innovation: An International Comparative Analysis of the Drug Industry', *Journal of Law and Economics*, 21, 1 (April), pp. 133–163.

GRILICHES, Z., (ed.), 1984, *R&D, Patents, and Productivity* (The University of Chicago Press, Chicago).

HANSEN, R. W., 1979, 'The Pharmaceutical Development Process: Estimates of Development Costs and Times and the Effects of Proposed Regulatory Changes', in R. I. CHIEN (ed.), *Issues in Pharmaceutical Economics* (Lexington Books, Lexington, MA).

HAUSMAN, J., HALL, B. H. and GRILICHES, Z., 1984, 'Econometric Models for Count Data with an Application to the Patents—R&D Relationship', *Econometrica*, 52, 4 (July), pp. 909–938.

JENSEN, E. J., 1984, 'Research Expenditures, Regulation, and Innovation in the Ethical Pharmaceutical Industry', unpublished M.I.T. Ph.D. thesis, Cambridge, MA.

KAMIEN, M. I. and SCHWARTZ, N. L., 1974, 'Patent Life and R&D Rivalry', *The American Economic Review*, 64, 1 (March), pp. 183–187.

KAMIEN, M. I. and SCHWARTZ, N. L., 1978, 'Potential Rivalry, Monopoly Profits and the Pace of Innovative Activity', *The Review of Economic Studies*, 45, 141 (October), pp. 547–558.

LOURY, G. C., 1979, 'Market Structure and Innovation', *The Quarterly Journal of Economics*, 93 (August), pp. 395–410.

MADDALA, G. S., 1983, *Limited-Dependent and Qualitative Variables in Econometrics* (Cambridge University Press, Cambridge, England).

THE NATIONAL SCIENCE FOUNDATION, 1972, *A Price Index for Deflation of Academic R&D Expenditures* (NSF 72-310, Washington, DC).

PAKES, A. and GRILICHES, Z., 1984, 'Patents and R&D at the Firm Level: A First Look', in Z. GRILICHES (ed.), *R&D, Patents, and Productivity* (University of Chicago Press, Chicago).

PELTZMAN, S., 1973, 'An Evaluation of Consumer Protection Legislation: The 1962 Drug Amendments', *Journal of Political Economy*, 81, 5 (September/October), pp. 1049–1091.

PHARMACEUTICAL MANUFACTURERS ASSOCIATION, various years, *Annual Survey Report* (PMA, Washington, DC).

PHARMACEUTICAL MANUFACTURERS ASSOCIATION, various years, *Prescription Drug Industry Factbook* (PMA, Washington, DC).

SCHERER, F. M., 1983, 'The Propensity to Patent', *International Journal of Industrial Organization*, 1, 1 (March), pp. 107–128.

SCHWARTZMAN, D., 1976, *Innovation in the Pharmaceutical Industry* (The Johns Hopkins Press, Baltimore).

TEMIN, P., 1980, *Taking Your Medicine: Drug Regulation in the United States* (Harvard University Press, Cambridge, MA).

VERNON, J. M. and GUSEN, P., 1974, 'Technical Change and Firm Size: The Pharmaceutical Industry', *Review of Economics and Statistics*, 56, 3 (August), pp. 294–302.

WIGGINS, S. N., 1979, 'Product Quality and Innovation in the Pharmaceutical Industry', unpublished M.I.T. Ph.D. thesis, Cambridge, MA.

WIGGINS, S. N., 1981, 'Product Quality Regulation and New Drug Introductions: Some New Evidence from the 1970s', *Review of Economics and Statistics*, 63, 4 (November), pp. 615–619.

THE JOURNAL OF INDUSTRIAL ECONOMICS 0022-1821 $2.00
Volume XXXVI September 1987 No. 1

THE EFFECT OF GOVERNMENT FUNDING ON PRIVATE INDUSTRIAL RESEARCH AND DEVELOPMENT: A RE-ASSESSMENT

FRANK R. LICHTENBERG*

A number of previous studies have attempted to determine the effect of federal support of research and development (R & D) performed in industry on the rate of private investment in R & D, by estimating regressions of private R & D expenditure on federal industrial R & D expenditure, controlling for total demand (sales) and in some cases other variables. This paper presents arguments and econometric evidence in support of the hypothesis that, due to misspecification of the private R & D equation (i.e., failure to distinguish government sales from other sales), previous estimates of the effect of federal industrial R & D on private R & D funding are seriously upwardly biased.

I.

A LARGE number of studies have demonstrated that privately funded research and development (R & D) investment has a significant positive effect on productivity, profitability, and other measures of economic performance.[1] Because of this, economists and policymakers are interested in determining the effects of various kinds of government policies (e.g., preferential tax treatment) on the rate of private investment in R & D.[2]

One government policy that may influence privately funded investment in R & D is government support of R & D performed in industry. In 1983, about one-third of all R & D performed by industrial firms was funded by the US (federal) government. Although influencing private incentives to invest in R & D is not the primary motive of most federally funded industrial R & D, theoretical arguments can be made (these will be considered in the next section) that federal funding of R & D may either stimulate or decrease private R & D investment. Because the net effect of federal R & D on private R & D funding is essentially an empirical question, previous analysts have attempted to determine this effect by estimating regressions of private R & D expenditure on federal R & D funding and other variables (particularly sales or GNP, to

* Columbia University Graduate School of Business, and National Bureau of Economic Research.

[1] Federal R & D appears to have a significantly smaller impact on performance measures. See, for example, Griliches [1986].

[2] Mansfield [1983] concluded from his survey of several countries' experience with tax credits that their effects on private R & D investment are quite small.

capture the effects of demand shifts). These studies have often found a positive, significant partial relationship between federal and private R & D, from which one might conclude that federally funded R & D tends to stimulate privately funded investment in R & D.

The purpose of this note is to provide arguments and evidence that the models upon which this inference is based are misspecified and that the misspecification results in both a serious overstatement of, and possible misinterpretation of, the federal R & D coefficient. In particular, we shall argue that these models fail to control for shifts in the composition (federal vs. non-federal) of final demand that are both correlated with federal R & D funding and that determine equilibrium private R & D expenditure. Consequently, at least part of the partial correlation between federal and private R & D is statistically "spurious".

II.

A number of previous investigators have attempted to determine the effect of federally funded industrial R & D (*FRD*) expenditure on privately funded (company) R & D expenditure (*CRD*) by estimating regressions of private R & D on federal R & D, controlling for total sales or demand and perhaps other variables. Total sales (*SALES*) is controlled for either by including it as a separate regressor in the private R & D equation or by dividing both private and federal R & D by sales. Let us consider a specification of the first type, i.e. an equation of the form[3]

$$CRD = \beta_0 + \beta_1 FRD + \beta_2 SALES + u \tag{1}$$

Although an explicit theoretical foundation for equation (1) is not always provided, we believe that it is useful to interpret this equation as the reduced form of the following supply-and-demand model of private-R & D expenditure determination:

(2) (supply) $P_S = a_0 + a_1 CRD + a_2 FRD + \varepsilon_1$

(3) (demand) $P_D = b_0 + b_1 CRD + b_2 SALES + \varepsilon_2$

where P_S denotes the "supply price" (marginal cost), and P_D denotes the "demand price" (marginal returns) of privately-produced innovations. One might reasonably hypothesize that $a_1 > 0$ (increasing marginal costs of R & D investment), $b_1 < 0$ (diminishing marginal returns), and that $b_2 > 0$ (the returns to R & D increase with the size of the market). *FRD*, on the other hand, may be postulated to have two distinct, and opposite, effects on the marginal cost of R & D, so that the sign of a_2 is indeterminate, *a priori*. Increases in *FRD*

[3] We ignore for simplicitly other potential determinants of *CRD*. The second type of specification is essentially a restricted version of the first, in which the restriction $\beta_0 = 0$ is imposed.

may (at least in the short run) drive up the prices of R & D inputs such as scientists and engineers, hence raising marginal cost. On the other hand, *FRD* expenditure may generate "spillovers", i.e. knowledge that increases the *productivity* of privately-employed R & D inputs, thus lowering private costs of achieving given process and product improvements. If we append to equations (2) and (3) the equilibrium condition $P_S = P_D$, and solve the system for *CRD*, we obtain a reduced-form equation of the form (1), where $\text{sgn}(\beta_1) = -\text{sgn}(a_2)$. Hence under the assumptions of this model, one can make inferences about the sign and significance of a_2, which measures the net effect of *FRD* on private costs of innovation, from the reduced form coefficient β_1.

Levy and Terleckyj [1983] estimated equations similar to (1) on US aggregate time-series data. Levin and Reiss [1984] and Scott [1984] estimated the restricted version on cross-sectional industry-level data and on cross-sectional line-of-business ("below" firm-level) data, respectively. In all three studies, the estimated coefficient on the federal R & D variable was found to be positive and significant. Since the partial correlation between *CRD* and *FRD* (controlling for total sales) is evidently positive, one might infer from these three studies that the net effect of *FRD* is to reduce private R & D costs and hence that the "spillover" effect dominates the "crowding-out" effect.

We shall argue, however, that due to a misspecification of the R & D-demand equation, the reduced form coefficient β_1 is not a consistent estimate of $-a_2/(a_1 - b_1)$ (which it would be if the demand equation were correctly specified). Because of this misspecification, it is incorrect to interpret the positive partial correlation between *CRD* and *FRD* as reflecting (entirely or perhaps even in part) private R & D cost reduction attributable to *FRD*. We now explain the nature of the hypothesized misspecification and the consequences of it for the reduced-form coefficient of *FRD*.

As noted above, *SALES* is included in the demand equation (2), and therefore in the reduced-form *CRD* equation (1), in an attempt to control for the effect of the size of the market on the expected rewards to investing in R & D. The total sales of a firm or sector are obviously the sum of its sales to each of its customers. Equations (1) and (2) embody the implicit *a priori* restrictions that sales to each customer (or the size of each specific market) have the same effect on the marginal returns to, and hence equilibrium expenditure on, R & D. But this assumption is clearly false: In reality, the R & D intensity (R & D expenditure per dollar of sales) of products and services consumed varies considerably across customers (even those of a single firm). Although false, this assumption would probably be relatively innocuous if we were merely interested in estimating the "average" marginal effect of sales on R & D expenditure. We are primarily concerned, however, with consistent estimation of β_1, and estimates of this parameter are likely to be seriously (upwardly) biased by inappropriate imposition of the restriction of equality of the coefficients on sales classified by customer. In particular, bias is likely to result from the restriction that sales to the federal government and sales to all other customers have identical coefficients.

To remedy this possible misspecification, we propose the following generalization of equation (1):

$$(4) \qquad CRD = \beta_0^* + \beta_1^* FRD + \beta_2^* GOV + \beta_3^* OTH + u^*$$

where GOV denotes sales to the government and OTH denotes sales to all other customers. There are two reasons why the least-squares estimate of β_1^* from the unrestricted model (4) is more likely to be a consistent estimate of the partial effect of FRD on CRD than the estimate of β_1 from the restricted model (1). The first is that β_2^* is likely to be substantially larger than β_3^*: an increase in government purchases of goods and services will tend to stimulate more private R&D investment than an increase in other customers' demand. The second reason is that FRD and GOV are likely to be strongly positively correlated: if the government is a major R & D sponsor, it is also often an important customer. Together, these two propositions (which will be elaborated upon below) imply that at least part of what has previously been estimated as the "effect" of FRD on CRD may be due to unmeasured variation in the government's (relatively R & D-intensive) share in sales.

The notion that a considerable amount of private R & D investment is directed towards federal purchases of goods and services (which are largely for national defense in the US), let alone the notion that $\beta_2^* > \beta_3^*$, is perhaps not widely held. This may be due, in part, to the fact that official government statistics on the "mission-distribution" of US R & D investment are based on the *assumption* that all private R & D is "civilian". But several pieces of evidence provide strong support for the hypothesis, not only that $\beta_2^* > 0$, but that $\beta_2^* > \beta_3^* > 0$. "Linked" R & D and patent data developed by Scherer [1984] imply that about 11.3 percent of private industrial R & D expenditure in 1974 was directed primarily towards the government space and defense sector and that the average private R & D intensity of such government sales was 1.57 percent, compared to 0.46 percent in the case of personal consumption expenditures. A comparison of the average private R & D-intensity of "government-oriented" business segments (defined as segments for which $GOV/SALES \geqslant 0.10$) with that of other business segments, based on data from the Compustat Industry Segment File, also suggests that government sales is much more (over 3 times as) R & D intensive.

An important reason why a nonnegligible share of private R & D investment is devoted to government defense and space purchases is that the government awards some large contracts by a method of procurement known as "procurement by design and technical competition". Under this method of procurement, the government chooses suppliers on the basis of long and complex technical proposals submitted by rival firms. A firm's technical proposal is intended to show that the firm and its subcontractors constitute the most capable source of supply. The development of high-quality technical proposals requires substantial R & D investment, most of which is not performed under government contract.

The view that government support (contracting) for industrial R & D is highly correlated, across firms and industries and over time, with government purchases of (non-R & D) goods and services is probably uncontroversial. R & D contracting is in one sense merely the "front end" of the entire procurement process, accounting for roughly 15 to 20 percent of the value of all contracts. Firms that are awarded initial R & D contracts under a procurement program are very likely to be awarded subsequent "follow-on" contracts for production, maintenance, spare parts, and so forth. Authors of case studies of government influence on private innovation (see, e.g., Nelson [1982]) have noted that, because the government often plays both the role of R & D sponsor and that of major customer, it is very difficult to determine the independent effect of each role on private R & D behavior. By estimating equation (4), however, we should be able to identify these two effects separately.[4]

III.

In the previous section we presented theoretical arguments to support the claim that, to estimate the effect of *FRD* on *CRD* consistently, we should estimate equation (4) rather than equation (1). In this section we provide some empirical evidence, in the form of estimates of both restricted and unrestricted equations. If our argument is correct, our estimate of β_1^* should be significantly smaller than our estimate of β_1.

We have estimated both the restricted and the unrestricted models on two different data sets, one containing US aggregate time-series data, and the other, cross-sectional firm-level data. Estimates of equations (1) and (4) based on aggregate annual time-series data for 1956–1983 are reported in the first two columns of Table I.[5] Because there are questions about the *timing* of the

[4] A point about the specifications of equations (1) and (4) is in order. Revenue that the firm receives under federal R & D contracts is included in its reported values of government sales (and therefore total sales). Since *FRD* is included in both *SALES* and *GOV*, the coefficient on *FRD* should be interpreted as the *difference* between the effect of *FRD* on *CRD* and the effect of non-*FRD* sales on *CRD*. The *total* effect of *FRD* on *CRD* is the *sum* of the coefficients on *FRD* and either *SALES* (in the restricted version) or *GOV* (in the unrestricted version). An equivalent way of estimating equation (1), for example, would be to regress *CRD* on *FRD* and ($SALES - FRD$); in that case the *FRD* coefficient would measure the total, rather than the additional, effect of *FRD*. We choose the alternative formulation, both to be consistent with previous studies, and because we think hypothesis tests about the additional effect of *FRD* are of greater interest than tests about the total effect.

[5] *FRD* and *CRD* are defined, respectively, as "federal funds for R & D" and "company funds for R & D" reported by the National Science Foundation in *Research and Development in Industry*. *SALES* is defined as GNP; *GOV* is defined as Federal purchases of goods and services from the national income accounts; and $OTH \equiv SALES - GOV$. All variables are deflated by the GNP implicit price deflator. The equations in column (1) and (2) both included a time trend (which accounts for the small size and significance of *SALES* and *OTH*, which grew smoothly over period), and both were estimated with an adjustment for first-order serial correlation of residuals. Point estimates (t-statistics) of the serial correlation parameter were 0.404 (1.82) in column (1) and 0.173 (0.66) in column (2).

TABLE I
ESTIMATES OF RESTRICTED EQUATION (1) AND UNRESTRICTED EQUATION (4) ON AGGREGATE TIME-SERIES AND FIRM-LEVEL CROSS-SECTIONAL DATA (t-VALUES IN PARENTHESES)

Column	*1*	*2*	*3*	*4*
Data set	Aggregate Time-series	Aggregate Time-series	Firm-level Cross-section	Firm-level Cross-section
Model	Restricted	Unrestricted	Restricted	Unrestricted
Variable				
FRD	0.330	0.109	0.126	−0.003
	(2.45)	(0.60)	(4.91)	(0.06)
SALES	0.006		0.021	
	(1.19)		(34.9)	
GOV		0.052		0.067
		(2.09)		(5.98)
OTH		0.005		0.020
		(0.92)		(32.6)

effects of *FRD* and *SALES* (or its components) on *CRD*, we have included the next[6] and previous year's values, as well as the current value, of each RHS variable; the estimates shown in columns (1) and (2) of the table refer to the *sums* of the corresponding variable's coefficients.[7] The point estimate of the sum of the *FRD* coefficients from the restricted model is 0.33 and highly significant, an estimate similar to that obtained by Levy and Terleckyj using a similar data set and specification. Relaxing (in column (2)) the restriction that *GOV* and *OTH* have identical coefficients (which is rejected at the 5 percent level) reduces our point estimate of the total effect of *FRD* on *CRD* by about half (from 0.336 to 0.161) and of the additional effect by about two-thirds (from 0.330 to 0.109). The insignificance of *FRD* indicates that we cannot reject the hypothesis that federal purchases of R & D services have the same effect on private R & D expenditures as federal purchases of non-R & D services and products.

We obtain qualitatively similar results when we estimate a logarithmic version of the model. As Griliches [1986; p. 145] has shown, one can allow for differences in the effects of *GOV* and *OTH* on *CRD* in a logarithmic specification as follows:

$$(5)\qquad \log CRD = \alpha_0 + \alpha_1 \log FRD + \alpha_2 \log(OTH + (1+\theta)GOV) + u$$

[6] Private R & D expenditure decisions might be hypothesized to be influenced by *expected future* values of *FRD* and *SALES*; if forecasts are unbiased (which is plausible at least in the case of *FRD*, for which appropriations lead expenditures), actual future values are reasonable proxies for expected values.

[7] Qualitatively similar (albeit somewhat less dramatic) results are obtained when we constrain the equation to include only the contemporaneous value of *SALES* (or its components) and the lagged value of *FRD*. (*FRD* is most significant in the equation if we lag it one period; current *FRD* is not significant when lagged *FRD* is also included). In this version, going from the restricted to the unrestricted model reduces the coefficient (t-ratio) of lagged *FRD* from 0.267 (1.73) to 0.159 (0.97).

which may be approximated by

$$\log CRD = \alpha_0 + \alpha_1 \log FRD + \alpha_2 \log SALES + \alpha_2 \theta \frac{GOV}{SALES} + u \tag{6}$$

The hypothesis that GOV has a significantly larger effect than OTH on CRD implies that the ratio $GOV/SALES$ has a positive and significant coefficient in equation (6); excluding this ratio is equivalent to imposing equality of the GOV and OTH coefficients. When this ratio is included, its coefficient is positive and highly significant; the implied value of θ is slightly greater than 2, suggesting (consistent with the evidence cited above) that government sales are about three times as R & D intensive as non-government sales. The effect of including this ratio is to reduce the coefficient (t-ratio) on $\log FRD$ by about two-thirds, from 0.122 (1.65) to 0.045 (0.60).

Estimates based on firm-level cross-sectional data for 1979–1984 for 187 firms jointly accounting for about two-thirds of US private industrial R & D expenditure are shown in columns (3) and (4).[8] As in the case of the aggregate time-series-based estimates, in the restricted model the coefficient on FRD is positive and significant, but this is not the case in the unrestricted model. Once we control for the composition of $SALES$, FRD no longer appears to have any additional effect on private R & D investment.

In conclusion, empirical analyses of both macro and micro data appear to provide strong support for the claim that, due to misspecification of the equation determining private R & D expenditure, estimates of the effect of FRD on CRD obtained in previous investigations have been substantially upwardly biased. A large part of what had been interpreted as the "effect" of federal R & D funding on privately funded R & D expenditure is in fact attributable to variation in the government's share of output.

FRANK R. LICHTENBERG,
Graduate School of Business,
Columbia University,
New York, NY 10027,
USA.

ACCEPTED SEPTEMBER 1986

REFERENCES

GRILICHES, Z., 1986, 'Productivity, R & D, and Basic Research at the Firm Level in the 1970s', *American Economic Review*, 76 (March), pp. 141–154.

LEVIN, R. C. and REISS, P. C., 1984, 'Tests of a Schumpeterian Model of R&D and Market Structure', in Z. GRILICHES (ed.), *R&D, Patents, and Productivity* (University of Chicago Press, Chicago).

LEVY, D. M. and TERLECKYJ, N. E., 1983, 'Effects of Government R&D on Private R&D

[8] Data on CRD and $SALES$ are from the Compustat General Annual Industrial File. Data on FRD and GOV are from the Federal Procurement Data System. The equations were estimated on pooled annual data for the six years and included a set of year dummy variables.

Investment and Productivity: A Macroeconomic Analysis', *Bell Journal of Economics*, 14 (Autumn), pp. 551–561.

MANSFIELD, E., 1983, 'Commentary' on 'Capital Formation, Technology, and Economic Policy', in FEDERAL RESERVE BANK OF KANSAS CITY, *Industrial Change and Public Policy* (Federal Reserve Bank of Kansas City, Kansas City).

NELSON, R. (ed.), 1982, *Government and Technical Progress, a Cross-Industry Analysis* (Pergamon Press, New York).

SCHERER, F. M., 1984, 'Using Linked Patent and R&D Data to Measure Interindustry Technology Flows', in Z. GRILICHES (ed.), *R&D, Patents, and Productivity* (University of Chicago Press, Chicago).

SCOTT, J. T., 1984, 'Firm versus Industry Variability in R&D Intensity', in Z. GRILICHES (ed.), *R&D, Patents, and Productivity* (University of Chicago Press, Chicago).

THE JOURNAL OF INDUSTRIAL ECONOMICS 0022-1821 $2.00
Volume XXXVI September 1987 No. 1

A NOTE ON ALLOWED AND REALIZED RATES OF RETURN OF THE US ELECTRIC UTILITY INDUSTRY*

GEOFFREY S. ROTHWELL AND KELLY A. EASTMAN

For US electric utilities realized rates of return were less than allowed rates from 1977–82 and less than the market cost of capital from 1979–82. Also, allowed rates were less than the cost of capital in 1980 and 1981. Estimates of the influence of rate-of-return regulation on the behavior of electric utilities have assumed that the allowed and realized rates are equal in equilibrium and that the allowed rate is at least as great as the cost of capital. We test the validity of these assumptions by examining rates of return and costs of capital between 1973 and 1982.

IN RECENT years a number of economists have empirically estimated the influence of rate-of-return regulation on the behavior of electric utilities. Many of them tested the single-period form of the Averch–Johnson hypothesis: An allowed rate of return greater than the cost of capital leads to over-capitalization. These tests differ in model specification, econometric methods, sample size, and results. However, almost all the tests used the realized rate of return on the rate base as a proxy for the allowed rate of return under the assumption that the allowed and realized rates are equal in equilibrium. Also, the single-period forms of the Averch–Johnson model require the allowed rate of return to be at least as great as the cost of capital. While others have criticized this model for its myopic naïveté, we examine the validity of the assumptions made in the empirical tests of it. For electric utilities in the United States we find that (1) the realized rate of return was less than the allowed rate of return from 1977 to 1982, (2) the realized rate of return was less than the market cost of capital from 1979 to 1982, and (3) the allowed rate of return was less than the cost of capital in 1980 and 1981.

I. RATES OF RETURN AND THE COST OF CAPITAL

There are thirteen regimes defined by the relations between the allowed rate of return (s), the realized rate of return (z), and the cost of capital (r). One can distinguish the regimes by their satisfaction of two assumptions: (1) The firm earns no more than its allowed rate of return (the regulatory constraint), that

* We would like to thank Theodore Keeler, Jeffrey Dubin, Leland Johnson, Lawrence White, and two anonymous referees for their valuable comments. Research was funded by a grant from the Exxon Educational Foundation to the Environmental Quality Laboratory at the California Institute of Technology. However, this paper reflects our own views, and any errors are our sole responsibility.

is, $s \geqslant z$. (2) The firm must earn its cost of capital in the long run, or exit the market (the financial constraint), that is, $z \geqslant r$. These assumptions imply that the allowed rate of return is at least as great as the cost of capital, that is, $s \geqslant r$. Any regime consistent with all three assumptions must satisfy $s \geqslant z \geqslant r$.

Most empirical tests assume that $s_t = z_t > r_t$ holds for the average firm, where t indicates the period. As Smithson [1978, p. 569] states, the substitution of the realized rate for the allowed rate, where the allowed rate is greater than the realized rate, results in a biased estimate of over-capitalization.[1] In long-run equilibrium models, this assumption requires that $s = z$ in every period under consideration. A more appropriate approach would be the formulation and testing of a dynamic model. Some authors have addressed this issue. Spann [1974] controls his sample period to assure that firms are in equilibrium. On the other hand, Gollop and Karlson [1980, p. 303] note that the equality of allowed and realized rates is an important assumption, but their multi-period model is not restricted to regimes where $s_t \geqslant z_t \geqslant r_t$. They allow for violations of the financial and regulatory constraints in individual periods. While one should test the Averch–Johnson model with long-run expectations for s_t, z_t, and r_t, we examine electric utility experience in the US with these rates for each year between 1973 and 1982.

II. DIFFERENCES AMONG RATES

To conduct this inquiry, we must define the cost of capital. We use two measures, one based on regulatory practices and the other from financial theory. The first is the Allowance for Funds Used During Construction (AFUDC) rate, r_a, a weighted average of the cost of debt and realized rates of return on the book value of equity. It is the rate at which firms are allowed to capitalize plant construction expenditures. The second is r_m, derived from the capital asset pricing model's definition of the market price of equity.[2] We describe both measures in the Appendix. The market cost of capital was greater than the AFUDC rate after 1973, and significantly greater in 1974, 1975, and from 1978 to 1982. Hence, it will not be surprising to find that our results are sensitive to the measure of the cost of capital.

First, consider whether $s \geqslant z$; that is, was the allowed rate-of-return constraint binding? Let $u = s - z$. Given that our allowed rate-of-return data are confined to observations on regulatory jurisdictions, we average s and z

[1] Only Perrakis and Zerbinis [1981] used allowed rates of return. Their data were gathered by the National Association of Regulatory Utility Commissioners (NARUC) and were published jointly by the NARUC, the US Federal Power Commission, and the US Federal Communications Commission. See US Federal Power Commission [1973]. The following studies used the realized rate of return as a proxy for the allowed rate: Spann [1974], Petersen [1975], Cowing [1978], Gollop and Karlson [1980], and Nelson [1984]. For others, see Rothwell [1985, pp. 53–55].

[2] On the relationship of the capital asset pricing model to other measures of the cost of capital, see Kolbe, Read, and Hall [1984].

TABLE I
RESULTS

Year	s	z	r_m	r_a	$s-z$	$z-r_m$	$z-r_a$	$s-r_m$	$s-r_a$
1973	7.74	7.88	6.36	6.67	−0.14	1.53	1.21	1.38	1.07
					(−0.78)	(9.34)	(10.87)	(12.84)	(6.63)
1974	8.03	7.68	7.68	6.95	0.35	0.01	0.73	0.36	1.08
					(1.87)	(0.03)	(4.23)	(3.01)	(7.41)
1975	8.44	8.28	7.36	7.14	0.16	0.93	1.14	1.09	1.30
					(1.05)	(5.37)	(8.12)	(8.35)	(8.80)
1976	8.64	8.55	6.98	6.90	0.09	1.57	1.65	1.66	1.74
					(0.71)	(10.66)	(12.64)	(12.54)	(12.05)
1977	8.88	8.54	6.92	6.80	0.34	1.61	1.73	1.95	2.07
					(2.06)	(10.95)	(13.12)	(13.70)	(13.21)
1978	9.00	8.68	7.82	7.04	0.32	0.86	1.64	1.18	1.96
					(1.80)	(4.37)	(9.77)	(8.22)	(13.04)
1979	9.23	8.51	9.11	7.39	0.72	−0.60	1.12	0.12	1.84
					(3.65)	(−2.75)	(6.05)	(0.82)	(12.11)
1980	9.79	8.96	10.54	8.32	0.83	−1.59	0.64	−0.76	1.47
					(3.88)	(−8.40)	(3.83)	(−4.14)	(7.99)
1981	10.31	9.05	12.08	9.31	1.26	−3.03	−0.26	−1.77	1.01
					(5.82)	(−13.76)	(−1.34)	(−10.39)	(5.85)
1982	10.94	10.42	10.99	9.56	0.52	−0.57	0.86	−0.04	1.39
					(2.09)	(−2.35)	(3.86)	(−0.22)	(6.66)

where s is the average allowed rate of return,
z is the average realized rate of return,
r_m is the cost of capital from the market model,
r_a is the cost of capital equal to the AFUDC rate, and
t-statistics (in parentheses) apply to the paired differences.

for each state.[3] We calculate t-statistics for paired differences, assuming s and z are approximately normal. Table I presents the sample means and test statistics. Except for 1973, the realized rate was less than that allowed by regulators.[4] It was significantly less after 1977 (Table I, column 6). While firms were allowed to earn more than they did earn, other factors, such as AFUDC regulation, restricted returns.

Second, we test the null hypothesis that $z \geqslant r$, that is, whether the financial constraint was binding in each period. Let $w_m = z - r_m$ and $w_a = z - r_a$. The alternative hypothesis becomes $0 > w_m, w_a$. The AFUDC rate is less than z for 1973–1980 and 1982, and insignificantly greater in 1981 (Table I, column 8). But we find the market measure of the cost of capital less than or

[3] The lack of bond ratings on utilities in nine states reduced the sample size to 41. These are Alaska, Hawaii, Idaho, Nebraska, Rhode Island, South Dakota, Tennessee, Washington, and Wyoming. The District of Columbia brought the sample size to 42.

[4] Differences between the allowed and realized rates of return may result from (1) lags in reporting the allowed rate of return, or (2) problems in aggregating across different regulatory jurisdictions. We examined the relationship between allowed rates and regulatory characteristics, e.g., fair-value and original-cost accounting or the inclusion in the rate base of (1) construction work in progress, (2) the AFUDC account, (3) research and development expenditures, and (4) accumulated tax deferrals. None of these factors systematically explained differences across states in every year.

equal to z from 1973 to 1978, and greater than z from 1979 to 1982. (Averaging rates over a three-year period, as done in Spann [1974] and Gollop and Karlson [1980], gave less dramatic, but similar, results.) Rates of return less than the cost of capital weakened the health of the US electric utility industry in the short run, but no firm left the market during this period.

Finally, we test whether $s \geqslant r$, or alternatively, whether $s-r < 0$. Let $v_m = s-r_m$ and $v_a = s-r_a$. See Table I, columns 9 and 10. The allowed rate was always greater than the AFUDC rate. Also, between 1973 and 1978, s was significantly greater than r_m. However, in 1979 and 1982 the allowed rate and the market cost of capital were almost equal, and in 1980 and 1981 the allowed rate was less than the cost of capital. If we were to rely on the market cost of capital, we would conclude that regulators were not allowing adequate returns in 1980 and 1981.

III. CONCLUSIONS

Different measures of the cost of capital yield different conclusions about the appropriateness of using models assuming the same financial and regulatory constraints as in Averch and Johnson [1962]. The realized rate of return was greater than the AFUDC rate for all years except 1981. However, when we use a market price of the cost of capital, the realized rate of return was less than the cost of capital from 1979 to 1982. This finding violates the financial constraint of the single-period Averch–Johnson model, suggesting that the model is an inappropriate description of electric utility behavior in the late 1970s and early 1980s. (This does not imply that the model is necessarily appropriate before the late 1970s.) Also, we found that the allowed rate of return was greater than the realized rate after 1976. Using the realized rate as a proxy for the allowed rate in single-period models will bias estimates of overcapitalization toward accepting the Averch–Johnson thesis.

This note leaves many questions unanswered: Why were firms unable to earn their allowed rate of return? What were firms' long-run expectations regarding rates of return and costs of capital? How did the lack of an adequate rate of return influence capital investment decisions? We suggest that future research investigate these issues.

ACCEPTED DECEMBER 1986

GEOFFREY S. ROTHWELL,
Department of Economics,
Stanford University,
Stanford, CA 94305,
USA.

KELLY A. EASTMAN,
The Brookings Institute,
Washington DC,
USA.

APPENDIX: DATA

We derived a market-based, weighted average cost of capital, r_m, from the capital asset pricing model. Let

$$r_m = i \cdot (1-T) \cdot (1-EC) + [r_f + \beta \cdot (r_e - r_f)] \cdot EC$$

where i is the interest rate on debt, T is the corporate tax rate (set equal to 0.50), EC is the equity-to-total-capitalization ratio, r_f is the risk-free rate of return, β is the covariance of the rate of return on firm equity with the rate of return on a market portfolio, divided by the variance of the return on the portfolio, and $(r_e - r_f)$ is the expected difference between the market return and the risk-free rate. We determined interest rates by comparing bond ratings with average bond yields. Bond ratings for each firm were from "Securities Offered", *Moody's Public Utility Manual, 1973–1975*, or *Moody's Corporate Credit Report* (November 9, 1983). We compared these ratings to "Moody's Bond Yields by Rating Groups", *Moody's Public Utility Manual, 1983.* The equity-to-total-capitalization ratios were found in US Department of Energy (DOE) or US Federal Power Commission (FPC), "Capitalization Ratio of Common Equity", *Statistics of Privately Owned Utilities.* We assumed the risk-free rate to be equal to the rate on three-month US Treasury securities. See *Economic Report of the President* [1985, p. 310]. Calculated betas are available in *Value Line Investment Survey.* The expected difference on a market portfolio and the risk-free rate was taken from Ibbotson and Sinquefield [1977]. We assumed that the expected premium through 1976 holds after 1976.

In defining r_a, we follow the US FPC's 1977 definition of the Allowance for Funds Used During Construction (AFUDC) rate. It is a weighted average of the interest rate (as discussed above) and the cost of equity. The rates of return on common equity were taken from US DOE or US FPC, "Selected Financial Ratios", *Statistics of Privately Owned Utilities.*

Realized rates of return on the rate base, z, are available in US DOE or US FPC, "Selected Financial Ratios", *Statistics of Privately Owned Utilities.* They equal electric utility operating income divided by the rate base. The rate base equals net plant plus an allowance for working capital. We aggregated across utilities in each state, while making one change: We excluded 19 utilities with equity-to-total-capitalization ratios greater than 90% or less than 10%. These utilities tend to report realized rates that differ significantly from state norms. See Eastman [1985, p. 16] for a list of these.

The National Association of Regulatory Utility Commissioners (NARUC) publish rates of return allowed by state commissions, s, in their *Annual Report on Utility and Carrier Regulation* [1973–1982]: "Section F: Basis of Rate of Return". This source was supplemented by US FPC [1973]. Several adjustments were required. We assumed that the rate was in effect from the first day of the month of the date given and remained effective until a different rate was reported. Sometimes regulatory agencies did not furnish the allowed rate of return to NARUC. For missing values, we substituted a regional average, based on the ten federal regions as defined by the US DOE. At times more than one rate was reported. Where a range was given, we averaged the reported values. The procedure presented no problems where the specified range was small (less than 0.5%). This was true for every state except for Kansas from 1974 to 1978. There, the highest value of the allowed rate was most consistent with the values reported for 1979 through 1982. We made no attempt to distinguish between electric utilities and electric/gas combination firms. We calculated the geometric mean across months for a yearly average. Values for all variables are available from the authors.

REFERENCES

AVERCH, H. and JOHNSON, L., 1962, 'Behavior of the Firm under Regulatory Constraint', *American Economic Review*, 52, 5 (December), pp. 1052–1069.

COWING, T., 1978, 'The Effectiveness of Rate-of-Return Regulation: An Empirical Test Using Profit Functions', in M. FUSS and D. MCFADDEN (eds.), *Production Economics: A Dual Approach to Theory and Applications* (North-Holland Publishing Company, Amsterdam 1978), pp. 215–246.

EASTMAN, K. A., 1985, 'The Difference between Allowed and Actual Rates of Return and Its Effect on Empirical Tests of the Averch–Johnson Thesis', unpublished B.A. honors thesis, University of California, Berkeley.

GOLLOP, F. M. and KARLSON, S. J., 1980, 'The Electric Power Industry: An Econometric Model of Intertemporal Behavior', *Land Economics*, 56, 3 (August), pp. 299–314.

IBBOTSON, R. G. and SINQUEFIELD, R. A., 1977, *Stocks, Bonds, Bills, and Inflation: The Past (1926–1976) and the Future (1977–2000)* (Financial Analysts Research Foundation, Charlottesville, VI).

KOLBE, A. L. and READ, J. A. with HALL, G. R., 1984, *The Cost of Capital: Estimating the Rate of Return for Public Utilities* (MIT Press, Cambridge, MA).

MOODY'S INVESTORS SERVICE, INC., 1983, *Moody's Corporate Credit Report* (November 9).

MOODY'S INVESTORS SERVICE, INC., 1973–1982, *Moody's Public Utility Manual.*

NATIONAL ASSOCIATION OF REGULATORY UTILITY COMMISSIONERS, 1973–1982, *Annual Report on Utility and Carrier Regulation.*

NELSON, R. A., 1984, 'Regulation, Capital Vintage, and Technical Change in the Electric Utility Industry', *Review of Economics and Statistics*, 66, 1 (February), pp. 59–69.

PERRAKIS, S. and ZERBINIS, J., 1981, 'An Empirical Analysis of Monopoly Regulation under Uncertainty', *Applied Economics*, 13, 1 (March), pp. 109–125.

PETERSEN, H. C., 1975, 'An Empirical Test of Regulatory Effects', *The Bell Journal of Economics*, 6, 1 (Spring), pp. 111–126.

ROTHWELL, G. S., 1985, 'Electric Utility Power Plant Choice Under Investment Regulation', unpublished Ph.D. dissertation, University of California, Berkeley.

SMITHSON, C. W., 1978, 'The Degree of Regulation and the Monopoly Firm: Further Empirical Evidence', *Southern Economics Journal*, 44, 3 (January), pp. 568–580.

SPANN, R. M., 1974, 'Rate of Return Regulation and Efficiency in Production: An Empirical Test of the Averch–Johnson Thesis', *The Bell Journal of Economics*, 5, 1 (Spring), pp. 38–52.

US COUNCIL OF ECONOMIC ADVISORS, 1985, *Economic Report of the President.*

US DEPARTMENT OF ENERGY, 1976–1982, *Statistics of Privately Owned Utilities in the United States.*

US FEDERAL POWER COMMISSION, 1973, *Federal and State Commission Jurisdiction and Regulation of Electric, Gas and Telephone Utilities.*

US FEDERAL POWER COMMISSION, 1973–1975, *Statistics of Privately Owned Utilities in the United States.*

US FEDERAL POWER COMMISSION, 1977, 'Uniform System of Accounts for Public Utilities Funds Used During Construction and Revisions of Certain Schedule Pages of FPC Reports', Order No. 561, *Federal Register*, 42 (February 2), p. 9161.

P. W. S. ANDREWS MEMORIAL ESSAY PRIZE—£300

The PWSA Memorial Prize of £300 is awarded annually. Competitors for the prize are asked to submit an essay on a subject of their own choice within the general field of Industrial Economics and Theory of the Firm, broadly interpreted. Entry to the competition is open to anyone under 30 years of age (or over 30, if not more than eight years have elapsed since taking a first degree). The essay, written in English, and not exceeding 10 000 words in length, should be a work of original research by the candidate only, not previously published and not previously awarded any other prize.

The winning essay must be submitted to *The Journal of Industrial Economics*, though the decision whether or not to publish it rests with the Editors.

The closing date for entries is 31st December.

Further details are available from:

Miss B. Cox,
University House,
The University of Lancaster,
Bailrigg, Lancaster, LA1 4YX, UK.

The General Editor,
Journal of Industrial Economics,
The Institute of Economics and Statistics,
The University of Oxford,
St Cross Building, Manor Road,
Oxford, OX1 3UL, UK.

The North American Editor,
Journal of Industrial Economics,
Department of Public Policy and Management,
The Wharton School,
University of Pennsylvania,
Philadelphia, PA 19104-6372,
USA.

EDITORIAL DATA: UK AND NORTH AMERICAN OFFICES

The following table indicates the number of weeks that elapsed between receipt of a typescript in the editorial offices and the first letter of response to the author/s. The information is based on *all* submissions received between 1 July 1985 and 30 June 1986.

Number of weeks (*w*)	% *of typescripts*
$0 < w \leqslant 5$	17.4
$5 < w \leqslant 10$	32.9
$10 < w \leqslant 15$	27.7
$15 < w \leqslant 20$	16.4
$20 < w \leqslant 25$	4.6
$25 < w$	1.0

Median w = 11
Mean w = 11

The Editors hope to improve substantially on this performance in future years. However, much depends on a speedy response from our referees, many of whom are, of course, very hard pressed.

THE JOURNAL OF INDUSTRIAL ECONOMICS

Published first in October 1952, the *Journal* has a very wide international circulation, and has established itself as the leading journal in the field of industrial economics. It was founded to promote the analysis of modern industry, particularly the behaviour of firms, and the functioning of markets. More specifically it seeks to bring the tools of modern economic analysis to bear on the analysis of real problems of industrial economies.

Contributions are welcomed covering all the major areas of industrial economics. One such area is the relationship between market structure and market behaviour in the areas of pricing, product differentiation, advertising and the dissemination of information and R&D. Another area focuses more directly on the firm, its objectives, finance, investment and growth. A third area comprises the background environment within which industrial firms operate: the changing structure of industry, public policy on monopoly and restrictive trade practices, regulation, fiscal and monetary policies as they affect firms, and underlying changes in productivity and international competitiveness.

The *Journal* has a tradition of publishing a blend of theory and evidence. Theoretical discussion is welcomed provided that the more abstract theory includes sufficient introduction and other explanation to convey the significance of the material to the general reader who wants to decide whether to follow the analysis through. Empirical analysis, and especially econometric analysis, should include an explanation of the data sources used, of the methods applied and of the underlying theoretical basis of the study. The *Journal* has a particular tradition of case studies of firms and industries, which the Editors would wish to continue. However, contributors of such studies are asked to remember that a study will be of interest to the international readership of the *Journal* only if it makes a particular contribution to the methodology of such studies, or if the empirical results are exceptionally interesting.

Alongside articles of more normal length, the Editors are ready to publish shorter notes, especially where these give interim results of important research studies, or where they report significant new empirical results. Books are not reviewed, but substantial review articles will be considered for publication.

Information for Contributors

Submissions (*three* copies are required) should be well written, clearly typed and carefully prepared for the printer in accordance with the *Journal*'s 'Notes for Contributors' (*Journal of Industrial Economics*, 35 (March 1987), pp. 359–363), copies of which may be obtained from the General Editor. An Abstract, conforming to the requirements of *The Journal of Economic Literature* and not exceeding 100 words, must accompany each submission.

Typescripts from North America should be sent to the North American Editor, Journal of Industrial Economics, Department of Public Policy and Management, The Wharton School, University of Pennsylvania, Philadelphia 19104, USA.

Typescripts from *all* other countries should be sent to the General Editor, Journal of Industrial Economics, Institute of Economics and Statistics, University of Oxford, St Cross Building, Manor Road, Oxford OX1 3UL, UK.

Information for Subscribers

The *Journal* is published four times a year, in September, December, March and June, by Basil Blackwell Ltd., 108 Cowley Road, Oxford OX4 1JF, UK, *or* PO Box 1320, Murray Hill Station, NY 10156, USA.

	UK	Overseas	USA
Institutions	£34.00	£43.00	$76.00
Individuals	£17.00	£22.00	$35.00
Students	£8.00	£10.00	$15.00

The reduced rates will be allowed to any individual student for a maximum period of three years.

CONTRIBUTORS TO THE ISSUE

STANLEY I. ORNSTEIN: University of California, USA.
DOMINIQUE M. HANSSENS: University of California, USA.
STEVEN C. SALOP: Georgetown University Law Centre, USA, and Associate Editor of this *Journal*.
DAVID T. SCHEFFMAN: Federal Trade Commission, Washington, DC, USA.
LOUIS MAKOWSKI: University of California, Davis, USA.
JOHN R. SCHROETER: Iowa State University, USA.
SCOTT L. SMITH: General Accounting Office, US Government, Washington, DC, USA.
STEVEN R. COX: Arizona State University, USA.
ANDREW J. CHALK: Southern Methodist University, USA.
ELIZABETH J. JENSEN: Hamilton College, New York, USA.
FRANK R. LICHTENBERG: Columbia University, New York, USA.
GEOFFREY S. ROTHWELL: Stanford University, USA.
KELLY A. EASTMAN: The Brookings Institute, Washington, DC, USA.

US Mailing: Second class postage paid at New York. Postmaster: Send address corrections to: Journal of Industrial Economics, c/o Expediters of the Printed Word Ltd., 515 Madison Avenue, New York, NY 10022 (US Mailing Agent).

Reprints of Back Volumes: Volumes 1–28 of the *Journal* are available (in complete volumes only) from the Kraus Reprint Corporation, Route 100, Millwood, New York 10546, USA. More recent back issues are available from the publisher at the current single issue price.

Microfilm: An agreement for the supply of microfilm copies from Volume 1 onwards has been made with University Microfilms International, Department PR, 30–32 Mortimer Street, London W1N 7RA, England, or 300 North Zeeb Road, Ann Arbor, Michigan 48106, USA.

Set in Monophoto Times by Advanced Filmsetters (Glasgow) Ltd
Printed and Bound in Great Britain by Whitstable Litho, Kent

THE JOURNAL OF INDUSTRIAL ECONOMICS

Volume XXXVI DECEMBER 1987 No. 2

J. A. KAY and C. N. MORRIS
The Economic Efficiency of Sunday Trading Restrictions 113

AVNER SHAKED and JOHN SUTTON
Product Differentiation and Industrial Structure 131

DAVID J. RAVENSCRAFT and F. M. SCHERER
Life After Takeover 147

STEVEN G. LANNING
Costs of Maintaining a Cartel 157

MARVIN B. LIEBERMAN
Market Growth, Economies of Scale, and Capacity Expansion in the Chemical Processing Industries 175

JOHN T. SCOTT and GEORGE PASCOE
Purposive Diversification of R & D in Manufacturing 193

SWATI BHATT
Strategic Product Choice in Differentiated Markets 207

MARCEL BOYER and MICHEL MOREAUX
On Stackelberg Equilibria with Differentiated Products: The Critical Role of the Strategy Space 217

JONG SEOK KIM
Optimal Price-Quality Schedules and Sustainability 231

Short Articles and Notes

ANDRÉ DE PALMA, VICTOR GINSBURGH and JACQUES-FRANÇOIS THISSE
On Existence of Location Equilibria in the 3-Firm Hotelling Problem 245

ALFRED KLEINKNECHT
Measuring R & D in Small Firms: How Much Are We Missing? 253

ISSN 0022-1821
BASIL BLACKWELL OXFORD ENGLAND

THE JOURNAL OF INDUSTRIAL ECONOMICS 0022-1821 $2.00
Volume XXXVI December 1987 No. 2

THE ECONOMIC EFFICIENCY OF SUNDAY TRADING RESTRICTIONS*

J. A. Kay and C. N. Morris

Restriction of shop opening hours is current, but controversial, practice in Britain and most other European countries. The economic case commonly presented for such restrictions is that, given the constraint that individual shops may not vary their price by time of day, competitive pressures would induce excessive opening at times when high costs would be incurred, such as on Sundays. The paper shows that inefficient equilibria of this type are indeed a theoretical possibility. Empirical evidence on costs and demand in the UK shows, however, that this case does not in practice arise and that deregulation of opening hours would lead to lower costs and prices in the retail sector.

I. INTRODUCTION

Most Western European countries restrict the hours for which shops can open and many American states limit trading through 'blue laws'. These regulations are of considerable antiquity—those of England can be traced back to the Fairs and Markets Act of 1448: They were extended in the earlier part of the twentieth century as a result of pressure from a diverse collection of interest groups including retailers (especially small traders), shopworkers and religious bodies. More recently, both the enforcement and rationale of these restrictions have come into question. After a twelve year experimental period, and a series of enquiries, the Swedish government announced the permanent abandonment of regulation of trading hours in January 1984. The 'blue laws' of Massachusetts were repealed in 1983.

In the UK, there have been repeated attempts to introduce legislative reform. Private members have introduced bills in Parliament on thirteen occasions. In 1984 an official Committee of Inquiry recommended the removal of all restrictions on opening hours. A government sponsored bill to implement this recommendation was defeated in the House of Commons in 1986. Although the principal considerations involved are evidently social and libertarian rather than economic, the vast majority of the submissions made to the Committee dealt with alleged economic benefits or detriments from legal restrictions on trading hours. From an economic perspective, it is not immediately obvious what the issue is. If commodities can be perfectly differentiated by time and day of week, the usual fundamental theorems of

* This paper is based on work carried out for the UK Committee of Inquiry into Reform of the Shops Act 1950, published as Kay *et al.* [1984]. The authors are very grateful to Sue Jaffer and Shirley Meadowcroft for research assistance and referees for comments.

welfare economics apply and market outcomes would achieve an appropriate tradeoff between the higher costs, if any, of extended trading hours and the benefits of wider choice of shopping time given to consumers.

There are three principal groups of weaknesses in this assessment. First, there may be externalities associated with Sunday shopping—I may find the resulting noise and congestion distressing if I do not go shopping myself, or even if I do. Second, retailing may not be perfectly competitive. There is some evidence for slight scale economies in retailing (see, for example, Noteboom [1982]), and retailed goods are differentiated by location. The outcome is an imperfectly competitive spatial equilibrium, in which efficiency theorems cannot be assumed to apply. Some implications of this are pursued by de Meza [1984].

A final possibility is the existence of constraints which prevent the achievement of a first best equilibrium. One in particular stands out. Although the concept of temporally differentiated commodities is familiar to economists, retailers are almost unanimous in their view that it is not only not familiar to, but not acceptable to, consumers. Customers do not see why they should pay different amounts for the same commodity at different times, even if the store is more congested or the wages of the shop assistant are higher; and it is generally believed by retailers that the ill-will which they would incur by varying prices in this way would cost considerably more than the associated gains in economic efficiency. Curiously, consumers do seem prepared to accept that shops with extended opening hours should charge more than other shops, provided they charge more at all times, and not just when other shops are closed.

We do not enquire here whether this constraint is real or imaginary. We note only that it is believed to exist, and that this is reflected in retailing practice. Its consequence is that extra costs from Sunday opening could be recovered only by charging higher prices throughout the week, and this concern formed the basis of most of the arguments which retailers put against relaxation of the restrictions on Sunday opening.

In section II we consider the nature of the trading equilibrium reached under the constraint of a uniform price on all days of the week. Section III examines the efficiency of such equilibrium, and we show that under certain assumptions about the split between the fixed and variable costs of retailing, and about the pattern of Sunday demand, an inefficient equilibrium in which undesirable Sunday opening occurs is indeed possible. Section IV considers the effects of variation in retailing capacity on the arguments of section III. In V and VI we assemble evidence on the structure of retailing costs and attempt to determine whether an inefficient outcome is likely in practice.

II. TRADING EQUILIBRIA

Retailing is taken to be characterised by many firms and free entry, so that there are zero profits in any trading equilibrium. There are n shops, each with sales of Q. Each shop incurs fixed costs D and variable costs c per unit of sales. These fixed costs D reflect the capital costs of providing premises, fittings etc., and will in the long run vary with the level of sales. We consider in section IV how the zero profit constraint, combined with a profit maximisation condition, determines the number of shops and the aggregate capacity of the retailing sector. For each individual retailer contemplating Sunday opening, however, the size of his own store and the number of his competitors are given.

If all shops were to open on Sunday, a fraction λ of sales would occur on that day. Thus the maximum potential Sunday trade is λnQ. If only some shops open, a number of these potential Sunday shoppers will find that their preferred outlet is closed. Some of them will instead visit that shop on a day on which it is open, so that actual Sunday sales will be less than λnQ: others will visit a less preferred outlet which is open on Sundays.

If any particular shop is deciding whether or not to open on Sunday, it will be concerned, not with λ, but rather with the fraction of its own sales which it would lose by Sunday closing (μ). Note that μ is not normally equal to λ, and will in general be a function of the number of other shops which are open on Sunday. We can derive μ by supposing that a fraction $f(x)$ of customers who are frustrated by finding their preferred outlet closed will shop elsewhere instead, where x is the number of other shops that are open. We assume $f(0) = 0$, $f'(x) > 0$ and $f(n-1) = f_{\max} \leqslant 1$. With x shops open, there are $\lambda Q(n-x)$ customers who find their Sunday shopping frustrated, of whom $f(x)\lambda Q(n-x)$ will shop elsewhere on Sundays. Thus, by shutting, you will lose two groups of customers. One group, totalling $(1/x)f(x)\lambda Q(n-x)$, are the customers who have come to you on finding their preferred shop closed. The other group—totalling $f(x)\lambda Q$—comprises your own customers who, finding your shop closed, will go to other shops that are open. Hence

$$\text{(1)} \qquad \mu Q = -f(x)\lambda Q(n-x) + f(x)\lambda Q$$

Rearranging gives

$$\text{(2)} \qquad \frac{\mu}{\lambda} = f(x)\frac{n}{x}$$

Thus μ/x is an increasing function of $f(x)$—customer disloyalty—and a decreasing function of x/n, the extent of Sunday opening.

$$\text{(3)} \qquad \frac{\partial\left(\dfrac{\mu}{\lambda}\right)}{\partial x} = \frac{n}{x}\left(f' - \frac{f}{x}\right) < 0 \text{ if } \frac{f'x}{f} < 1$$

$f'x/f$ is the elasticity of customer defection with respect to opportunity. If shopping opportunities are, in some natural sense, evenly distributed, then we would expect the proportion of customers who abandon their preferred establishment to increase less rapidly than the availability of opportunities to do so. Suppose, for example, customers and shops are uniformly distributed across an infinite plane. Any prospective purchaser will go to the best alternative shop if it is less than a given distance away, but otherwise will return to his or her preferred shop on another day of the week. Then the number of acceptable alternatives for any customer will follow a Poisson distribution with mean cx where x is the number of shops open.

Then the probability of defection is the probability that at least one alternative shop is acceptable so that

$$f(x) = 1 - e^{-cx}$$

and hence

$$\text{(4)} \qquad \frac{f'_x}{f} = \frac{cxe^{-cx}}{1-e^{-cx}} = \frac{p\,(\text{one shop acceptable})}{p\,(\text{more than one acceptable})} < 1$$

Under this condition then

$$\mu_{\min} = f_{\max}$$

and

$$\text{(5)} \qquad \mu_{\max} = \frac{\lambda}{n} \lim_{x \to 0} \frac{f(x)}{x} = \frac{\lambda}{n} f'(0)$$

There are three possible types of equilibrium: no shops open on Sundays, all open, or some open. We consider each in turn. If no shops are open on Sundays, price will be $p = c + (D/Q)$. Any shop considering opening will balance the costs of Sunday opening, S, against the margin, D/Q, which it would earn on potential Sunday sales. It will decide against Sunday trading if

$$\text{(6)} \qquad S > \frac{D}{Q} \cdot \mu_{\max} Q = \mu_{\max} D$$

Thus a 'no Sunday trading' equilibrium will exist if $(S/D) > \mu_{\max}$.

Now consider a full trading equilibrium in which all shops open on Sundays. In this case the price will be $p = c + (D+S)/Q$. Any shop considering shutting will balance the costs of Sunday opening, S, against the margin $(D+S)/Q$, which it will lose on its Sunday sales of $\mu_{\min} Q$. Hence it will shut only if

$$\text{(7)} \qquad S > \mu_{\min} Q \frac{D+S}{Q} = \mu_{\min}(D+S)$$

and so a 'universal Sunday trading' equilibrium will exist if

$$\text{(8)} \qquad \frac{S}{D+S} < \mu_{\min}$$

We now examine the possibility of a limited trading equilibrium in which x out of n shops are open. If retailing is perfectly competitive, and shops cannot differentiate their prices by day of the week, then shops which trade on Sundays and those which do not will both charge the same price.

If x shops are open on Sundays the price will be

$$p = c + \frac{D}{Q} + \frac{x}{n} \cdot \frac{S}{Q} \tag{9}$$

Since in a competitive equilibrium it must be equally profitable to open on Sundays or on weekdays only, we have

$$\begin{aligned} S &= \mu Q\left(\frac{D}{Q} + \frac{x}{n} \cdot \frac{S}{Q}\right) \\ &= \lambda f(x)\left(S + \frac{n}{x} D\right) \end{aligned} \tag{10}$$

and rearranging gives

$$x = \frac{\lambda f(x) n D}{S - \lambda f(x) S} \tag{11}$$

This has a solution if

$$0 < \frac{\lambda f(x) n D}{S - \lambda f(x) S} < n \tag{12}$$

that is, if $f_{max} < \dfrac{S}{\lambda(D+S)}$

(13) or equivalently $S > \mu_{min}(D+S)$

Setting (8) and (13) together shows that however high the costs of Sunday trading, there always exists either a universal Sunday trading equilibrium or a limited trading equilibrium. The reason for this is that however high the costs of general Sunday opening, costs can be reduced below any finite amount by opening on a sufficiently limited scale. Condition (3) implies that any opening, however limited in extent, will attract at least some customers. Thus such opening is justified. If these costs of Sunday opening are sufficiently high, however, there may also be an equilibrium in which there is no Sunday trading (see relation (7)). If there is a limited trading equilibrium, there may be more than one (see (11)) or conceivably a universal opening equilibrium as well.

III. THE EFFICIENCY OF EQUILIBRIA

If there are potentially many equilibria, we should like to consider whether any or all of them are efficient. Suppose that each Sunday shopper would be willing to pay a premium π to shop on Sunday rather than at his next most preferred time. The less widespread is Sunday opening, the more likely it is that those who nevertheless shop on Sundays have a strong preference for Sunday over other days; thus we write π as a function of x with $\pi'(x) < 0$. First we consider the no trading equilibrium. If one shop were to open on Sundays, costs S would be incurred but its services would be of value $\pi(0)$ to its $\mu_{\max}Q$ customers. Hence it should open if

(14) $$S < \pi(0)\mu_{\max}Q$$

but will not open if $S > \mu_{\max}D$ (from relation (6)). Hence there will be an inefficient Sunday closing equilibrium if

(15) $$\pi(0)\mu_{\max}Q > S > \mu_{\max}D$$

or

(16) $$\frac{\pi(0)}{p} > \frac{S}{pQ}\cdot\frac{1}{\mu_{\max}} > \frac{D}{pQ}$$

which requires that the premium for Sunday shopping when no shops are open is larger in relation to the price of retailing than are fixed costs in relation to total costs.

Can there be an inefficient opening equilibrium? We approach this issue by considering a universal opening equilibrium and showing that it might be socially desirable if some shops were to shut. With x shops open, there are Qx customers who shop on Sundays but at shops which were not their first preference. Hence the net benefit from Sunday opening is

(17) $$B = \{\lambda Qx + f(x)(n-x)\lambda Q\}\pi(x) - Sx$$

We assume that as $x \to n$, $f'(x)$ and $(x) \to 0$; that is, if almost all shops are already open, the opening of additional shops has negligible effects either in inducing frustrated customers to shop on Sundays or on the inconvenience which they suffer. Hence, for $x \to n$,

(18) $$\frac{\partial B}{\partial x} = \lambda Q\pi(1-f(x)) - S$$

Hence $(\partial B/\partial x) < 0$ at $x = n$ if $S > \lambda Q\pi(1-f_{\max})$.

Rearranging (17), the condition for a general opening equilibrium to exist gives

(19) $$\lambda Q\pi(1-f_{\max}) < S < \frac{\lambda f D}{1-\lambda f}$$

which can be rewritten as

(20) $$\lambda\frac{\pi}{p}(1-f_{\max}) < \frac{S}{pQ} < \frac{\lambda f_{\max}}{1-\lambda f_{\max}}\frac{D}{pQ}$$

Note that if $f_{max} = 1$ (that is, customers have no loyalty to any particular shop), any universal Sunday opening is definitely inefficient; and also, from (21), more probable. The rationale of this is straightforward: if consumers have no particular preferences as to where they buy, and Sunday opening is more costly than weekday opening, it will be undesirable for as many shops to be open on Sundays as on other days. More generally, inefficient equilibria are likely if π/p is small—that is, consumers' preferences for Sunday trading are weak, even though possibly widespread; and if D/pQ is large—fixed costs are a substantial proportion of total costs.

We have shown that there will always be an equilibrium with some Sunday trading. From (15), we note that it is better to have no shops open on Sunday than to have one if

(21) $$S < \pi(0)\mu_{max}Q$$

The benefits of an additional shop opening if x are open will be

$$\pi(x)\mu(x)Q < \pi(0)\mu_{max}Q$$

Hence, if it is undesirable to have one shop open, it is also undesirable to have more than one shop open. Thus there may be Sunday trading equilibria, although no Sunday trading would be preferable.

We have shown above that there may be:

(i) equilibria in which no Sunday trade takes place although it is desirable;

(ii) universal Sunday trading equilibria although it would be preferable that some shops should shut on Sunday;

(iii) equilibria with limited Sunday trading in which no Sunday trade would be preferable;

and that there will commonly be different equilibria consistent with one particular level of the costs of Sunday trading. A view on the economic desirability or otherwise of Sunday opening cannot be founded on *a priori* considerations, and we turn in section V to consider the empirical information required for a resolution of the issues.

IV. CHANGES IN RETAILING CAPACITY

In section III we have considered the possibility that regulation might lead to gains in efficiency. We have done so by showing that requiring particular shops to open or close on Sunday might produce benefits in excess of costs. The general imposition of regulation would, however, be likely to lead to changes in overall retailing capacity. Indeed, the likelihood of changes in the structure of retailing was noted by many of those giving evidence to the Committee of Inquiry as a probable consequence of Sunday trading.

The trade attracted by any retailer depends on his capacity—in terms of number of outlets and size of store—and his price. Thus each individual retailer chooses capacity K and price p to maximise

$$P = (p-c)Q(p, K)-K$$

This generates two first order conditions on p and K respectively which, together with the zero profit condition implied by free entry, determine price and capacity. The structure of models of this kind, and the potential efficiency of competitive outcomes, is discussed in Kay [1979]. The outcome depends on the size of $(\partial p/\partial K)Q$—the consumers' trade off between price and capacity. They can face relatively high prices and extensive retailing capacity, allowing uncongested shopping and short travel times, or lower prices and more limited capacity.

To explore that tradeoff here would go beyond the scope of this paper. We assume instead that it has been, and continues to be, determined optimally, so that new equilibrium capacity is established when weekday trade per unit of capacity returns to its critical level. If x shops open on Sundays and in consequence the total number of shops falls to m, then weekday trade is now

$$Qn-\lambda Qx-f(x)\lambda Q(m-x) \tag{22}$$

With constant weekday sales per unit of capacity we have

$$Qn-\lambda Qx-f(x)\lambda Q(m-x) = Qm \tag{23}$$

Zero profits in equilibrium imply that

$$p = c+\frac{Dm+Sx}{Qn} \tag{24}$$

Thus the movement of prices as a result of Sunday trading depends on the change in total costs

$$\Delta C = Dm+Sx-Dn \tag{25}$$

From rearrangement of (23) we have

$$m = \frac{n-x(1-f)}{1+\lambda f} \tag{26}$$

Substituting in (25) gives

$$\Delta C = Sx(1+\lambda f)-D(\lambda x(1-f)+n(1+\lambda f)) \tag{27}$$

Let total retailing costs before regulation be Cn. Then rearranging (27) and using (3) to eliminate t gives

$$\frac{\Delta C}{Cn} = \frac{S}{c}\cdot\frac{x}{n}\left(1+\mu\frac{x}{n}\right)-\frac{D}{C}\left(\mu\cdot\frac{x}{n}\left(1-\frac{1}{\lambda}\cdot\mu\frac{x}{n}\right)+\left(1+\frac{x}{n}\right)\right) \tag{28}$$

If $f = 1$ and $x-n$, then $\Delta C \gtreqless 0$ as $S \gtreqless D$ and, since it is implausible that $S > D$, Sunday opening would seem advantageous. Even here, however, setting $f = 1$ and calculating

$$\frac{\partial \Delta C}{\partial x} = S(1 + \lambda f) \tag{29}$$

confirms that although full Sunday opening would be better than no Sunday opening, limited opening would be better still.

In general, however, if $\Delta C < 0$ then it is clear that the economic case for general restrictions on Sunday trading fails (although an argument for limited restriction might survive). If $\Delta C > 0$, then it is necessary to measure and assess the likelihood of inefficient Sunday trading equilibria of the kind described in section III arising, and to balance the economic costs and benefits of permitting Sunday opening.

V. THE EXTENT OF SUNDAY TRADING

Equation (28) indicates the information necessary for a first assessment of the likelihood of an inefficient Sunday trading outcome. On the side of costs, we need to measure S/C and D/C. These reflect the impact of Sunday opening on trading costs and the relationship between fixed costs and total costs. On the demand side, it is necessary to estimate μ—the proportion of any individual retailer's trade which would be lost if he were to shut on Sundays—and λ, the fraction of total trade which could, potentially, occur on that day. Together these factors determine x/n, the proportion of shops which would choose to open on Sundays. In this section, we explain how this data was assembled and used to estimate x/n.

We begin with costs. For this we assembled a database providing cost information for 150 types of retailer in the UK. This information was obtained from published accounts of companies principally engaged in retailing, from responses to a questionnaire sent to a number of retailers; from detailed case studies of a number of retailers, and from special analysis undertaken on our behalf. The assembly of the database is described in detail in Jaffer and Morris [1984]. Each 'model' retailer was distinguished by principal commodity group and by turnover, and weights attached to each based on tabulations from the 1982 Retailing Enquiry supplied by the Business Statistics Office.

Various adjustments were made to the disaggregated cost data assembled in this way, also described in detail in Jaffer and Morris [1984], [1986]. These were to make the data from different sources consistent and also to move from the accounting conventions used by retailers towards concepts more appropriate for economic analysis. In particular retailers discuss profit by reference to a concept called 'net margin'. This is (approximately) equal to sales revenue less all direct costs—rent, rates, labour, energy, services etc.—but deductions are not made to reflect the use value of owned or partly-owned premises and equipment. Net margin thus provides an upward-biased

TABLE I

	As % of Gross Margin				
Cost Element	*Food*	*Clothing*	*Drink, Confectionery and Tobacco*	*Household Goods and DIY*	*Mixed Retailer*
Labour	47.74	45.66	39.90	39.22	41.01
Premises	28.56	35.38	24.95	29.76	27.11
Energy	4.31	5.10	3.04	4.88	4.34
Services and Transport	20.33	20.39	22.80	19.64	16.33
Stockholding	0.68	1.27	0.81	1.42	0.85
Average Gross Margin	20.72	39.76	25.66	32.23	31.82

Source: IFS Retail Cost Model. (See Morris [1984].)

estimate of retailers' underlying profitability. In the database we have constructed, premises costs are imputed by reference to the (CCA) fixed assets of the concern. This cost analysis is summarised in Table I. Labour costs (mostly variable) account for between 40% and 50% of the total retailing costs: premises costs (mostly fixed) are in the range of 25%–35%. Other cost items such as energy and administration are partly fixed, partly related to trading hours and partly to sales volumes.

In discussion with retailers we assessed the additional variable costs likely to be incurred by a given number of hours additional trading. These variable costs mostly consist of increased labour costs, but also include increased charges for energy and services. Wages paid in retailing on Sundays are currently prescribed by rules laid down by wages councils, which broadly require payment at twice the rate applied to weekly working. There is some evidence that this is above the market rate, i.e. that Sunday working needs to be rationed among employees at this price. This evidence, and its implications, are discussed further in Kay *et al.* [1984]. In case studies of retailers with experience of Sunday trading, we were told of cost savings induced by the high cost of Sunday labour. Non-essential staff are not employed on Sundays and tasks like stock handling and clerical duties are postponed until slack weekday periods. Similarly, energy costs are not directly proportional to hours open, since many costs occur anyway—freezers for example.

Using these estimates, the addition to labour costs is around 20% and this is overwhelmingly the largest element increasing total retail costs, which rise by just under 10% for food and just over 10% for non-food. Total retail costs as a percentage of turnover (known as the gross retail margin) averaged 28% of net of tax retail sales in 1982. This figure covers a range from 20% for food to 41% for clothing. By this means, *S* and *D* were computed for each individual model type of retailer.

Our primary source of information on the demand for Sunday trading is a market research survey conducted on our behalf in May 1984 by Market and Opinion Research International (MORI). This survey asked respondents to estimate their expenditure on food and clothing and its current distribution over peak and non-peak shopping hours. Only for food and clothing did it seem likely that shoppers could make reasonable assessments of these figures. For other commodities, the questionnaire asked how likely consumers were to purchase each type of good if shops were open on Sundays. On the basis of these replies we prepared estimates of λ, the proportion of consumer expenditure which would occur on Sunday if all shops were open on that day. Our benchmark figures are 16% of total clothing expenditure and 9% of total food spending. Since Sunday opening would account for around one eighth of total trading hours, Sunday is potentially a more than averagely popular time to shop for clothes and a less than averagely popular time to shop for food.

Estimating $f(x)$, the likelihood that frustrated customers will seek to make their purchases elsewhere given that x shops are open, is a matter of particular difficulty. We can only be guided by our own intuition and retailer's assessments. For drink, confectionary and tobacco, we have assumed $f(x)$ close to one for all but very low levels of x. Customers have little loyalty to particular outlets in considering purchases of these commodities. In clothing, however, they do perceive substantial differences between retailers and it is likely that even if most other shops were open on Sunday, many people who find their preferred shop closed would make their purchase on a weekday instead. Food, household goods and mixed retailers lie somewhere in between.

The estimation of μ, the loss of sales to an individual retailer from Sunday trading, is given from (3) by $\mu = \lambda f(x)/n/x$. Since (n/x) is in turn a function of μ, this requires an iterative routine. We illustrate the estimation of μ for food and clothing in our central cases. Let $f(0.45) = 0.5$ for food, i.e. if about half of all food shops are open on Sundays then customers of these shops would, if these shops closed, divide roughly equally between other shops which are open on Sunday and the same shop on another day of the week. $\mu = 0.10$ could be an equilibrium solution if 45% of retailers opened on Sundays, since (3) could be fulfilled with $x/n = 0.45$, $f(x/n) = 0.5$ and $\lambda = 0.09$.

To see whether this is in fact a solution we assess the likely extent of Sunday opening at $\mu = 0.10$ (i.e. if Sunday traders would lose 10% of their trade if they closed on that day). We cannot apply relation (11) straightforwardly. The reason is that the costs of Sunday trading differ across retailers, and those with the lowest costs will be the first to choose to open. Hence application of (11) to sector averages would both underestimate the cost and overestimate the extent of Sunday opening. Instead we apply (5) directly to each individual retailer in turn, opening each retailing type in order of costs (starting from the lowest) until it no longer pays to open. At this point, retailers accounting for 46% of all turnover in food open, and hence we have identified an equilibrium with about half of the food sector open on Sundays.

TABLE II
ESTIMATING THE PATTERN OF SUNDAY OPENING

	Average Sunday Sales % for Break-even	*Assumed Sales Loss from Closing on Sunday*	*Estimated % Opening*	*Resulting % of Trade on Sunday*
Food	10.6	10	46	5
Clothing and Footwear	12.5	12	23	3
Drink, Confectionery and Tobacco	10.0	15	100	15
Household goods	13.0	20	100	20
Mixed retail	12.4	10	15	2
Other	13.3	10	0	0
All		12	48	7

Source: IFS Retail Cost Model.

Equilibria were calculated in a similar way for each other retailing sector. Thus for clothing we have $\lambda = 0.16$ from our consumer survey. Setting $f(0.23) = 0.17$ (i.e. assuming that with limited Sunday opening a high degree of customer loyalty persists) gives an equilibrium with 23% of shops open on Sunday and a loss of trade for those who shut of 12% of turnover. This implies that about 3% of all trade in clothing would occur on Sunday. Corresponding equilibria for other sectors are shown in Table II. In two sectors—drink, confectionery and tobacco and household goods—a full opening equilibrium is predicted.

VI. THE EFFICIENCY OF SUNDAY TRADING

In section V we assembled empirical evidence relevant to the issues posed in sections II and III in order to examine the likely structure of post-liberalisation equilibria. Section IV went on to examine consequential effects on the structure of the industry: we now develop the empirical analysis of this. Following the opening pattern described above, a substantial proportion of sales would occur on Sundays and, since it is improbable that total retail expenditure would increase by this amount, if at all, there would be a corresponding reduction in weekday sales. This would imply an increase in the effective capacity of the retailing sector. The extent of this increase would depend on the pattern of resulting weekday trade.

Our investigation of consumer intentions (the MORI poll) included an examination of the current pattern of weekday trading for food and clothing. Table III summarises information collected in this way and also provides additional information on the likely reduction in the rise of the peak following a shift to trading on Sunday based both on this poll and on the evidence of our case studies. The table shows that the peak is more pronounced for

TABLE III
DISTRIBUTION OF SHOPPING TIMES BY DAY OF WEEK

		Monday to Thursday	*Friday*	*Evenings*	*Saturday*	*Sunday*
Current						
	Food	43	21	19	17	—
	Clothing	35	8	1	57	—
If all shops open on Sunday						
	Food	41	19	16	14	9
	Clothing	30	7	1	44	16

Source: MORI Research study for IFS, 1984.

clothing, where a larger part of the week's trade occurs on Friday evenings and Saturdays, and that the existence of greater shopping opportunities on Sunday could be expected to reduce the peak to a disproportionate extent. For food, the existing pattern of weekday sales is more homogeneous and interest in Sunday shopping is smaller.

Retailing capacity is dependent on both peak and average levels of demand. Since Sunday trading would be drawn more from the peak than from the average, the reduction in capacity which could be accommodated would not be less than the reduction in average weekday demand. This loss of weekday sales would be experienced by all retailers, whether they opened on Sundays or not. Thus we apply conditions (23) and (24) to determine the new equilibrium. These imply that trade per shop returns to the pre-Sunday opening level and that the sector as a whole makes zero profits.

Again the heterogeneity of the retailing sector makes application more complex than the substitution of averages into (23) and (24) since it is retailers with above-average costs who are likely to exit from the industry. The procedure adopted was to rank retailers in order of profitability and contract the industry until these two conditions are met. We interpret zero profits as the restoration of profits to their existing level.

The profitability of the UK retailing sector as a whole is currently positive even after the full imputation of capital costs. We attribute this to the goodwill enjoyed by famous retailing names such as Harrods, Marks and Spencer and Sainsbury and assume that those rents would continue to be earned even after liberalisation.

The capacity reductions implied by this are shown in Table IV. These are marginal for most retail sectors, but very large for household goods, where the effect of Sunday trading is effectively to double the extent of peak trading hours. It should be noted, however, that the comparison made is between equilibria with no Sunday trading and with free Sunday trading. There is already extensive illegal opening in the household goods sector and hence the

TABLE IV
ESTIMATED EFFECTS ON WEEKDAY TRADE OF SUNDAY OPENING

	Expected Sunday Sales %	*Extent of Existing Sales Peak* %	*Estimated Reduction in Peak Sales*	*Medium Term Impact on Costs* (% of gross margin)	*Likely Reduction in Capacity* %
Food	10	20	30	2.03	5.8
Clothing and Footwear	12	40	60	3.04	3.4
Drink, Confectionery and Tobacco	15	15	20	1.18	17.6
Household goods	20	35	70	4.18	30.0
Mixed retail	10	30	50	0.50	2.0

Source: IFS Retail Cost Model.

extent of capacity reduction compared with the present position is likely to be somewhat less dramatic than this table suggests.

In Table V we provide estimates of the two elements of cost change shown in relation (28) for each retailing sector. In each case, the additional costs are offset by savings from lower retail capacity; and in all cases it is more than offset. The implication is that C is negative, and that, in the long run, Sunday trading should lead to a lower average cost per unit of sales.

Table VI considers the sensitivity of this estimate to the variety of assumptions required to reach it. First, we have reduced expected Sunday sales by one half. This reduces the benefits of Sunday trading substantially but, at the same time, it reduces the extent of Sunday opening and hence the extra costs implied. For food and clothing, our assumptions suggest that no shops would open on Sunday: as (16) shows, it is quite likely that this is an

TABLE V
OVERALL EFFECT OF SUNDAY TRADING

	Changes in Costs as a % of Gross Margin			
Industry	*Estimated % Reduction in Capacity*	*Cost Saving from Reduced Capacity*	*Increased Variable Cost of Trading*	*Overall Effects*
Food	5.8	2.56	2.03	−0.53
Drink, Confectionery and Tobacco	17.6	7.52	3.04	−4.48
Clothing and Footwear	3.4	1.79	1.18	−0.61
Household goods	30.0	13.75	4.18	−9.57

Source: IFS Retail Cost Model.

TABLE VI
SENSITIVITY ANALYSIS OF PRICE EFFECTS

	FOOD			*HOUSEHOLD (including DIY)*			*DRINK-CONF. TOBACCO*			*CLOTHING*		
	% Open	*% Reduction Capacity*	*Final Change in Price as % of Turnover*	*% Open*	*% Reduction Capacity*	*Final Change in Price as % of Turnover*	*% Open*	*% Reduction Capacity*	*Final Change in Price as % of Turnover*	*% Open*	*% Reduction Capacity*	*Final Change in Price as % of Turnover*
Base	46.2	5.8	−0.12	100.0	29.9	−3.24	100.0	17.6	−1.18	22.6	3.4	−0.23
Sunday Sales × 1/2	0.0	0.0	0.00	22.5	3.3	−0.28	26.2	2.3	−0.06	0.0	0.0	0.00
Sales Inc. 1%	46.2	5.4	−0.18	100.0	29.6	−3.30	100.0	17.0	−1.25	22.6	2.9	−0.36
Sales Inc. 5%	46.2	3.4	−0.40	100.0	28.0	−3.55	100.0	15.4	−1.46	22.6	1.0	−0.85
Labour premium 1.5	86.1	10.8	−0.37	100.0	30.0	−4.04	100.0	17.6	−1.18	94.4	14.2	−0.98
Labour premium 2.5	4.5	0.5	−0.01	83.2	25.0	−2.24	35.4	6.2	−0.40	17.8	2.7	−0.10

Source: IFS Retail Cost Model.

inefficient outcome. Much discussion on Sunday trading has regarded the issue of whether or not it is likely to increase sales as central to any assessment of its costs and benefits. This approach is mistaken since in the long run any general increase or reduction in overall sales levels is likely to be matched by a corresponding change in retailing capacity. We show that assuming 1% or 5% increases in aggregate retailing turnover has little effect on the average level of retailing costs (although it does substantially affect the size of the retail sector). We noted that the existing 'double time' payment for Sunday working may exceed the market rate required to attract the labour needed. We therefore consider the effect of a reduction to 1.5 in that premium. This reduces the cost of Sunday opening, but increases its extent. Hence there is surprisingly little change in the total effect on costs. If the premium were 2.5—we use this as a simple way of allowing for the possibility that we have underestimated the additional costs of Sunday opening—then there would be much less Sunday trade and again the effect on costs is small.

In general, the outcome is extremely robust to these changes. In no case do costs actually increase with Sunday opening, and it remains true even with substantial costs to Sunday opening that the cost reductions are largest where Sunday trading is most widespread.

VII. CONCLUSION

In the first part of this paper we showed that there was a possibility that inefficient Sunday trading equilibria could occur; that shops would open on Sundays although consumers as a whole would be better off if they were compelled to close. In the second part we have described a comprehensive exercise of collecting relevant data on costs and demand in UK retailing. From this, we can conclude that although these inefficient equilibria could occur, in fact they do not; and our sensitivity tests suggest that it is improbable that there are any reasonable assumptions under which this could be characteristic of the British retail sector as it is today. It follows that there is no economic case for general restrictions on Sunday trading, and that any argument about the subject should be conducted on other grounds. It does not, however, follow that the extent of Sunday opening in an unrestricted equilibrium would necessarily be optimal. This is an important conclusion but, given the difficulties of enforcing any intermediate position which are extensively discussed in the report of the Committee, one which has limited practical relevance.

J. A. KAY,
Centre for Business Strategy,
London Business School,
Sussex Place,
Regent's Park,
London NW1 4SA.

ACCEPTED DECEMBER 1986

C. N. MORRIS,
London Economics,
104–112 Marylebone Lane,
London W1M 5FU,
UK.

REFERENCES

BUSINESS STATISTICS OFFICE, Pre-publication estimates for *Business Monitor SDA 25* (HMSO, London).

JAFFER, S. M. and MORRIS, C. N., 1984, *A Simulation Model of Retailing Costs*, IFS Working Paper 53, London.

JAFFER, S. M. and MORRIS, C. N., 1986, 'The Economic Effects of Sunday Trading', in L. PELLEGRINI and S. K. REDDY (eds.), *The Distributive Trades: An International Perspective* (Franco Angeli, Milan).

KAY, J. A., 1979, 'Uncertainty, Congestion and Peak Load Pricing', *Review of Economic Studies*, 46, pp. 601–611.

KAY, J. A., MORRIS, C. N., JAFFER, S. M. and MEADOWCROFT, S. A., 1984, 'The Regulation of Retail Trading Hours', Appendix 6 to the Report of the Committee of Inquiry into Proposals to Amend the Shops Act, *The Shops Act: Late Night and Sunday Opening* (HMSO, London).

DE MEZA, D., 1984, 'The Fourth Commandment: is it Pareto Efficient', *Economic Journal*, 17, pp. 163–186.

NOTEBOOM, B., 1982, 'A New Theory of Retailing Costs', *European Economic Review*, 17, pp. 163–186.

THE JOURNAL OF INDUSTRIAL ECONOMICS 0022-1821 $2.00
Volume XXXVI December 1987 No. 2

PRODUCT DIFFERENTIATION AND INDUSTRIAL STRUCTURE

AVNER SHAKED AND JOHN SUTTON*

Some recent literature on "vertical product differentiation" has developed the idea that if the nature of technology and tastes in some industry take a certain form, then the industry must necessarily be "concentrated"; and must remain so, no matter how large the economy becomes. The present paper develops this idea further, and looks at some of its implications. This approach offers a simple unified framework within which to re-explore many issues which arise in considering the relationship between advertising, R & D, and market structure.

A NUMBER of recent papers have been concerned with models of vertical product differentiation (i.e. differentiation by quality). Such models permit a unified treatment of certain situations in which firms incur increased fixed costs with a view to enhancing consumers' willingness to pay for their respective products. These include, in particular, the case of R & D expenditures devoted to product development or improvement, and the case of advertising outlays aimed at increasing perceived quality. What such situations have in common is the fact that the level of fixed cost incurred by firms is endogenously determined, and its equilibrium level reflects the interplay of demand conditions and the underlying technology—the latter being expressed as a relationship between costs and product attributes. What the present paper is concerned with is the relationship between these exogenous parameters, and the equilibrium form of industry structure.

A useful point of departure is given by considering a different and more familiar setting, in which the level of fixed costs is treated as a constant. In this setting, the size of fixed costs, relative to the size of the economy, determines the number of firms, and therefore the degree of concentration. As the size of the economy increases, the level of concentration falls. Economies of scale thus become "less important" as a barrier to entry in "large economies".

This idea can be captured formally by reference to a number of familiar models, such as Hotelling's model of "horizontal" product differentiation. In such models, as the size of the economy increases, the market share of every firm present will become arbitrarily small.

Our aim in the present paper is to delineate some conditions which are sufficient to exclude this tendency towards "fragmentation". Now the recent

* The authors would like to acknowledge the financial support of the International Centre for Economics and Related Disciplines (LSE). John Sutton would also like to thank the ESRC for financial support.

literature on vertical product differentiation provides some models in which the property fails in a very extreme manner: the number of firms and the pattern of market shares may remain completely unaffected as the size of the economy increases (the "finiteness" property, Shaked and Sutton [1982]). This very extreme failure of the "fragmentation" property is particular to a quite special type of "pure vertical differentiation" model, however. In the present paper, we set out to develop conditions on technology and tastes which will lead to the *minimal* failure of the "fragmentation" property, i.e. at least one firm should continue to retain some particular level of market share no matter how large the economy becomes (though the total number of firms present may become arbitrarily large).

It is worth emphasizing at the outset that our aim is to set out very weak and general requirements, and so it is appropriate to begin from this extremely weak notion of "concentration", i.e. a failure of the fragmentation property.

In doing this, we seek to set out suitable conditions which will hold over a wide range of underlying models. One of the main complaints about the recent increase in the use of oligopoly models in industrial organization is that "with oligopoly, anything may happen". It is therefore of particular interest to draw out properties which are relatively robust in respect of alternative specifications of the model (for example: Cournot versus Bertrand equilibria; simultaneous or sequential patterns of entry and product choice; whether firms are single product or multiproduct). It is especially important in the present context to ensure that our results hold for cases where products are differentiated both in respect of vertical (quality) attributes, and in terms of "horizontal" attributes—since a striking feature of the existing literature is the fact that the results obtaining in the cases of the "pure vertical" and "pure horizontal" differentiation literatures are sharply different, but the—empirically relevant—case in which both types of attribute are present, has not been widely studied.[1]

The price which we pay, in trying to come to terms with the need to provide such a robust characterization result, is that we cannot provide a correspondingly wide treatment of existence problems. It is notorious in models of product differentiation that equilibria may fail to exist for many reasonable specifications of the standard models. *Here, we aim merely to point out some characteristics which equilibria must have, if they do exist.* We do not prove existence, though we offer some remarks as to particular specifications where existence problems may arise, and to some cases where existence is assured. The models discussed here are based on a two-stage process, where firms

[1] It is easily shown, for example that the "finiteness" property which is central to the "pure vertical differentiation" case, fails to hold once both horizontal and vertical attributes are present. Nonetheless, the conditions which we develop for the following general case are motivated by, and are precisely in the same spirit as, the conditions leading to the "finiteness" result in the "pure vertical differentiation" case.

incur sunk costs in choosing ("developing") their products at the first stage. Then, at the second stage, taking product specifications as fixed, they compete in prices. Existence problems may arise at both stages.

In the case of "pure horizontal" differentiation, a (pure strategy) price equilibrium may fail to exist at the second stage (d'Aspremont, Gabszewicz and Thisse [1979]). To ensure existence, suitable convexity assumptions need to be imposed on consumer preferences (Neven [1985]). The case of "pure vertical" differentiation is relatively "well behaved" in this respect (Gabszewicz, Shaked, Sutton and Thisse [1981]). Assuming that a price equilibrium exists for any set of products, existence problems may still arise at the first (product choice) stage, if firms choose their products simultaneously. If, on the other hand, (a finite number of) firms choose products sequentially, existence of a pure strategy equilibrium is assured (Börgers [1985], Harris [1985]).

The structure of the present paper is as follows. We first make clear precisely what we mean by the "fragmentation" property, by illustrating it in the context of the familiar Hotelling model (section I). In section II we set out our model, and we develop our main proposition. Section III sets out our conclusions.

I. PRELIMINARIES: A "FRAGMENTATION" RESULT

The simplest representation of "product differentiation" is provided by Hotelling's location model, in which sellers are positioned at various points along some line segment. Consumers are distributed along the line segment, and each purchases one unit from the lowest cost supplier; cost equals price plus transport cost.

It is standard in this context to employ a 2-stage equilibrium concept. In the first stage each firm either enters, by paying sunk cost $\sigma > 0$, and chooses its location, or else it decides not to enter. In the second stage, each firm may produce any volume of output at zero cost. Here, we seek a Nash equilibrium in prices (which will depend upon the entry and location choices made by all firms at the first stage). We then seek a Perfect Equilibrium in this two-stage game.[2]

What we mean by the size of the economy in what follows is the total number of consumers present. We increase the size of the economy by replication, i.e. the distribution of consumer tastes remains unchanged.

[2] i.e. Having solved the "price" game played at the second stage, to find the Nash equilibrium, we express the profits (payoffs) earned at this equilibrium as a function of the locations of the firms. (These locations are *fixed*, once the second stage is reached, and they appear as parameters in our solution). We then define a new game, in which we use the functions thus calculated (profit as a function of locations) as our payoff functions; and we seek a Nash equilibrium in that game. This is a "Perfect Equilibrium" in the 2-stage game.

For this model, the following proposition holds (the assumptions are stated, and the proof is set out, in the Appendix):

Proposition I. For any $\varepsilon > 0$, there exists an economy size S^* such that for any size $S > S^*$, every firm has an equilibrium market share less than ε.

What Proposition I ensures is that all firms have a "small" market share at equilibrium. Traditionally, such a market was described as being "atomistic". Currently the term appears to cause confusion, since in the technical literature the terms "atom" and "atomic" are used with precisely the opposite connotation—a usage borrowed from measure theory. To avoid ambiguity, we will refer to this form of market structure as "fragmented", a usage which is not uncommon.

The type of product differentiation which is represented by Hotelling's "location" framework, is labelled "horizontal differentiation". In this framework, given any number of sellers offering distinct products at equal prices each seller has a strictly positive market share.

We may contrast this with the case of "vertical differentiation", defined as follows: given any two distinct products, *if they were sold at the same price*, then *all* consumers would choose the same one (the "higher quality" product).[3] At the equilibrium, of course, higher quality products will sell at higher prices: we asssume that consumers differ in their willingness to pay for quality improvement. To motivate this, it is assumed that consumers differ in income, or in tastes (i.e. sensitivity to quality), or both.

Clearly, products will in practice be differentiated both in respect of attributes which correspond to the "horizontal" case, and also in respect of "vertical" attributes. "Horizontal" attributes might for instance include colour, or various "aesthetic" features (design). An example of a "vertical" attribute would be, say, the operating speed of a computer. Only in the latter case can we speak unambiguously of "product improvement"; and we shall simply refer to such attributes as corresponding to some level of "quality" henceforward.

A general theory of product differentiation, then, requires an analysis of situations in which products may be differentiated both "horizontally" and "vertically"; and it is to this case that we turn in the next section.

II. THE MODEL

The model is as follows: a *product* is described by two characteristics, u and h, where we identify the first as vertical, and the second as horizontal. A consumer is specified by two parameters; his income Y, and his "most

[3] On a point of terminology: it might seem natural to reserve the term "differentiation by quality" for this case. However, many authors use the word "quality" quite loosely in this literature, treating it as a synonym for "variety", within the context of "location" type models. Our present terminology, due to Lancaster, avoids ambiguity.

preferred" value of the horizontal attribute, α. (For simplicity, we confine ourselves to a set-up in which a consumer's willingness to pay for a higher quality is determined solely by his income; but the results can be extended trivially to allow consumers to differ in their tastes over the vertical attribute also.)

The utility score of the consumer, when he buys one unit of product (u, h) at price p, is given by

$$U(u, d, y)$$

where $d = |h - \alpha|$ and $y = Y - p$ denotes income spent on "outside goods". We assume that Y is distributed according to a density $f(Y, \alpha)$ on some compact set, where $\bar{f} \geqslant f(Y, \alpha) \geqslant \underline{f} > 0$.

We assume that $U_u > 0$, $U_d < 0$. We also assume $U_{uy} > 0$, which ensures that richer consumers are willing to pay more for a given quality increment.

To complete our description of the model, we need to specify the firms' choice of products, and the nature of price competition. Here, a number of alternative specifications appear reasonable. We note the following points in regard to which our results turn out to be robust:

(i) In respect of the "final" stage in which firms set prices, we use the standard "Bertrand" assumption (Nash equilibrium in prices). Our result remains true, however, for the alternative "Cournot" scheme (Nash equilibrium in quantities). Clearly, other possibilities might be considered, but this should suffice to reassure the reader that the result is fairly robust in this respect.

(ii) In respect of the preceding stage in which firms choose their product specifications, two standard formulations are used in the literature. The proof which follows refers to the "simultaneous entry" case, but we note below that it extends to the case of "sequential entry" also (i.e. where a finite number of potential entrants choose their products in a predetermined order, and thereafter compete in price. (For a full description of this approach see Lane [1980].)

(iii) Our characterization holds good both for single product firms and also for the more realistic—though relatively neglected—case of competition between multiproduct firms (with an appropriate definition of the cost structure).

Now, since we aim to formulate a result which is independent of these several choices, it should be clear that a sharp dividing line cannot be drawn between those combinations of technology and tastes which must lead to a fragmented structure, and those which must lead to a concentrated one. Clearly there will be some middle ground, over which the choices made in respect of (i)–(iii) will influence the result. We confine ourselves to the delineation of conditions *sufficient* to ensure a concentrated structure.

For the sake of concreteness, we will set out the analysis which follows in the context of the simplest possible model, and then we will note how the proof can be extended to cover the several additional possibilities just noted. To this end, we define the equilibrium concept as follows: We consider a 2-stage game. In stage 1, each firm either chooses a single product, of specification (u, h), at cost $F(u)$; or else it chooses not to enter. In the second stage, we seek a Nash equilibrium in prices (Bertrand equilibrium). We characterize a Perfect Equilibrium in the 2-stage game.

We now introduce two assumptions on technology which turn out to be sufficient to imply a concentrated structure. Let $F(u)$ denote the fixed cost incurred in developing a product with attributes (u, h), and let $c(u)$ denote the unit variable cost incurred in its production. Our first assumption relates to the form of $c(u)$, and it *embodies the basic idea which we carry over from the "pure vertical differentiation" literature* (Shaked and Sutton [1983]).

Assumption 1 may be described loosely as requiring that the costs of quality improvement involve at most only a modest rate of increase in unit variable cost. Specifically, what it says is that for any given improvement in quality, *the increase in unit variable cost is strictly less than the marginal valuation of the richest consumer*. Formally, we require:

Assumption 1: There exists some strictly positive triple (μ, p, Δ), such that, if each other firm offers a good with $u \leqslant \bar{u}$, and any h, at unit variable cost, then a firm offering a good of quality $\bar{u}+\Delta$, and any h, at a price $p+c(\bar{u}+\Delta)$ will capture at least fraction μ of consumers.

It may seem more attractive to restate directly in terms of utility and cost functions. Assumption 1 may, for example, be replaced by the (stronger) requirement that: U_u is bounded away from zero; U_y, $|U_d|$ are bounded above, and $c(u)$ is bounded above by some income level which is less than the maximum value of consumer income, which we will denote as $\bar{U}$.

In what sort of context, then, is Assumption 1 likely to be satisfied? The burden of quality improvement might fall primarily on fixed costs in some cases (R & D effort to improve computer speed, say), but on unit variable cost in others (the production of higher quality furniture, by the way of using more expensive raw materials, say). No *a priori* restriction can be placed on the relationship between product quality—measured in terms of consumers' willingness to pay—and the level of *unit variable costs*. Assumption 1 is more likely to be valid in those industries in which the main burden of product improvement falls on fixed cost, rather than variable costs.

Our second Assumption relates to the relationship between product quality and fixed cost $F(u)$. We assume that *quality improvement always involves an increase in fixed costs; and that the proportionate increase in fixed cost required to achieve a given quality increment is bounded.* Formally, we require:

Assumption 2: On $u \in (0, \infty)$, $F(u) > 0$, $F'(u) > 0$ and $F'(u)/F(u)$ is bounded above. (Denote an upper bound to F'/F as β.)

The role of Assumption 2 is as follows. As the size of the economy increases, we expect that, given our assumption on $c(u)$, there will be a tendency for the maximum quality offered to increase. This leads to the possibility that, as S increases, the fractional increase in cost required to achieve a given increment to quality might become arbitrarily large; Assumption 2 excludes this possibility.

We have chosen, for ease of exposition, to write our Assumptions in terms of the "quality index" u. The requirement of Assumption 2 is well defined in this representation. It is very important to emphasize, however, that all that matters here is the relationship between costs and consumers' willingness to pay. In fact, the combination of Assumptions 1 and 2 can be restated as follows: there is some factor k such that, by incurring k times more fixed cost than any other market participant, a firm can guarantee sales of μS at a mark-up p over unit variable cost, irrespective of the prices set by rival firms. (In fact, k is equal to $e^{\beta\Delta}$ in the terminology of Assumptions 1 and 2).[4] The role of Assumption 2 is illustrated by an example, below.

We now show how Assumptions 1 and 2 imply that in any equilibrium, industrial structure must remain "concentrated", in the sense that no "limit theorem" of the kind described in Proposition 1 above can hold good.

We assume throughout the presence of a "large" number of potential entrants.

Proposition II: Under Assumptions 1, 2, it follows that there exists some $\varepsilon > 0$, such that at equilibrium at least one firm has a market share greater than ε, irrespective of the size of the economy.

Remark: We first establish this for the case of a Nash equilibrium in prices, single product firms, and simultaneous entry. For the several extensions, see the following Remarks.

Proof: The proof follows immediately from A1 and A2.

Choose

$$\varepsilon < \frac{\mu p}{\bar{Y}(1+e^{\beta\Delta})}$$

where μ, p and Δ are given by Assumption 1, $\bar{Y}$ is the maximum level of consumer income, and β is an upper bound to F'/F. We now show that any configuration of products in which each firm has market share ε or less is not an equilibrium. We do this by showing that any firm can increase its profit by choosing a different, higher, quality. Note that if each firm has a market share $\leqslant \varepsilon$, then *all* firms earn revenue, and so profit, less than $\varepsilon \bar{Y} S$.

Let $\bar{u}$ denote the maximum quality on offer. Note that the firm producing $\bar{u}$ incurs fixed cost $F(\bar{u})$, and this cannot exceed its revenue, at equilibrium. But

[4] By writing $F'(u)/F(u) = \beta$ and integrating from u to $u+\Delta$. This observation makes it clear that the present analysis does not rest on the use of some unobservable "quality index". For the empirical use of "willingness to pay" measures, see Beggs, Cardell and Hausman (1981).

its revenue is at most $\varepsilon \bar{Y} S$, whence $F(\bar{u}) \leqslant \varepsilon \bar{Y} S$. Suppose some firm offers a product $(\bar{u}+\Delta, h)$, for some h (the product choices of other firms being held fixed). Now, this will affect the equilibrium vector of prices (in the "second stage"). We know, however, that no firm with positive sales can have price below unit variable cost, at a Nash equilibrium in prices. From Assumption 1, the entrant can capture a share μ at a price $p+c(\bar{u}+\Delta)$ independently of the prices set by rivals. Hence its revenue, net of variable cost, at equilibrium, exceeds $\mu p S$. But from Assumption 2, (by integrating),

$$F(\bar{u}+\Delta) \leqslant F(\bar{u}) \cdot e^{\beta\Delta}$$

Hence its profit $\pi \geqslant \mu p S - F(\bar{u}) e^{\beta\Delta} = (\mu p - \varepsilon \bar{Y} e^{\beta\Delta}) S > \varepsilon \bar{Y} S$ (by our choice of ε). Thus this change in product specification raises profits, and contradicts our assumption that the original configuration was an equilibrium.

This completes our proof.

Remark 1 (*Cournot Equilibrium*). The above proof holds good, with a trivial modification, if we replace the Bertrand equilibrium in the final stage, by Cournot equilibrium. To see this, note that all we require, concerning the final stage equilibrium, is the following: that the firm offering quality $\bar{u}+\Delta$ will enjoy profits at least equal to $\mu p S - F(\bar{u}+\Delta)$. In the proof, we used the fact that, under Bertrand competition, it can certainly achieve this level of profit by setting price $c(\bar{u}+\Delta)+p$, whatever the prices set by rival firms. To extend the result to Cournot competition, we note that it can certainly achieve this level of profit by setting quantity μ, whatever the quantities chosen by other firms. For, as we show in the Appendix, any vector of quantities X is mapped into a non-negative vector of prices $\bar{p}$, where either $p_i > 0$, $D_i(\bar{p}) = X_i$; or $p_i = 0$, $D_i(\bar{p}) \leqslant X_i$ where $D_i(p)$ denotes demand. But Assumption 1 ensures that, for price at or below $c(\bar{u}+\Delta)+p$, the firm offering quality $\bar{u}+\Delta$ has demand μ or greater. Hence the desired property follows.

Remark 2 (*Sequential Entry*). In the case in which, for any S, a finite number of firms choose their products in a predetermined sequence, the above argument may be applied directly to the last firm in the sequence. As noted above, the existence of an equilibrium configuration of products in this setting is ensured, so long as price equilibrium exists for any set of products in the ensuing subgame. (see p. 133). To permit the possibility of entry by an arbitrarily large number of firms, the number of potential entrants may be increased *pari passu* with the size of the economy. (We have not been able to extend the proof of Proposition II to the case where we have an infinite sequence of potential entrants; here, we cannot exclude the appearance of certain pathological equilibria).

Remark 3 (*Multiproduct Firms*). Suppose each firm can produce a number of products $(u_1, h_1), (u_2, h_2), \ldots, (u_n, h_n)$. Suppose that it incurs cost $F(\bar{u})+(n-1)\alpha$ where $\alpha > 0$ and $\bar{u} = \max(u_1, u_2, \ldots, u_n)$. This seems a natural way of extending our cost structure to the multiproduct firm. Then the preceding proof goes through as before (where the relevant market share is that of a *firm*, not a product).

It is of interest to note, incidentally, that the "fragmentation" result for horizontal product differentiation, which we stated as Proposition 1 above, *does* rely on the notion that each firm offers a single product. With multiproduct firms, and sequential entry, for example, it may be the case that the first mover would enter "many" products, and so the fragmentation property may fail. (On such "product proliferation" strategies, see Schmalensee [1978], Bonanno [1987]. For a full analysis, see Shaked and Sutton [1987].)

Remark 4. It is worth noting that in models of the present kind, free entry does not exclude the possibility that intramarginal firms earn positive profits (see Shaked and Sutton [1982]). All that can be said is that, given the strategy of entrants, any firm which at equilibrium chooses not to enter, would make negative profits by entering.

What Proposition II says, loosely, is that where the burden of quality improvement falls primarily on fixed cost (in the sense of Assumption 1), then we cannot obtain a fragmented market structure, even in the limit.

What, then, determines the *degree* of concentration in the present setting? This will depend upon the preferences of consumers, and the shape of the technology $(c(u), F(u))$. It is worth emphasizing that it is the *interplay* of these two factors which matters. As noted above, all that matters is the relationship between costs and consumers' willingness to pay. In order to specify the *degree* of concentration, then, we need to impose more structure on the model. In the present paper, we have confined our attention to the minimal departure from a "fragmented" structure—the failure of the "convergence" property.

If market shares do not converge to a fragmented structure, then, what is the impact of an increase in the size of the economy? This question, it is worth noting, is of particular interest in the context of trade theory, where the standard starting point for analyzing trade in differentiated products, produced under increasing returns, is to consider the impact of joining together a number of identical economies.

We are unable to give a general characterization of this. In what follows, we confine ourselves to the case of "simultaneous entry". Here we can readily establish the following, intuitively appealing, corollary to Proposition II.

Corollary. Under "simultaneous entry", the top quality on offer, $\bar{u}$, and the associated level of fixed costs $F(\bar{u})$, increase to infinity with the size of the economy S.

Proof. Note first that, since $F(0) > 0$, it follows that, for any S, only a finite number of firms enter. Hence we may define the maximum level of u over all firms; call this $\bar{u}$. Now consider any firm which chooses not to enter at equilibrium. Such a firm can earn revenue of at least μpS, by entering with a quality level $\bar{u}+\Delta$, whence its costs would be at most $e^{\beta\Delta}F(\bar{u})$. So at any equilibrium,

$$\mu pS < F(\bar{u})e^{\beta\Delta}$$

(since equilibrium requires that nonentrants, should they enter, make non-positive profits).

Hence: $\mu pSe^{-\beta\Delta} < F(\bar{u})$

from which it follows that $F(\bar{u})$, and so $\bar{u}$, tends to infinity with S.

This result implies that increases in the size of the economy (or the linking of similar economies via free trade) will lead not to a fragmented industry, but to a concentrated industry, operating at higher levels of fixed costs, and producing "better" products. In other words, the equilibrium level of expenditure on fixed costs (R & D and advertising, say) will increase with the size of the economy. Thus, in contrast to Proposition I, there is no tendency for fixed costs to become less important as a "barrier to entry", as the size of the economy increases. This is a theme which we have explored elsewhere, within the "pure vertical differentiation" model (Shaked and Sutton [1984]).

The role of Assumption 2 deserves further comment. This is seen most clearly by considering an extreme example, as follows: Consider the family of functions parameterized by n:

$$F_n(u) = \max(1, \exp n(u-\bar{u})^3)$$

each of which violates Assumption 2. Take the limiting function as $n \to \infty$, viz. the fixed cost schedule $F(u)$ is constant on $[0, \bar{u}]$ but is $+\infty$ for $u > \bar{u}$ (Figure 1). Suppose, for example, that unit variable cost $c(u) = 0$ for all u, so

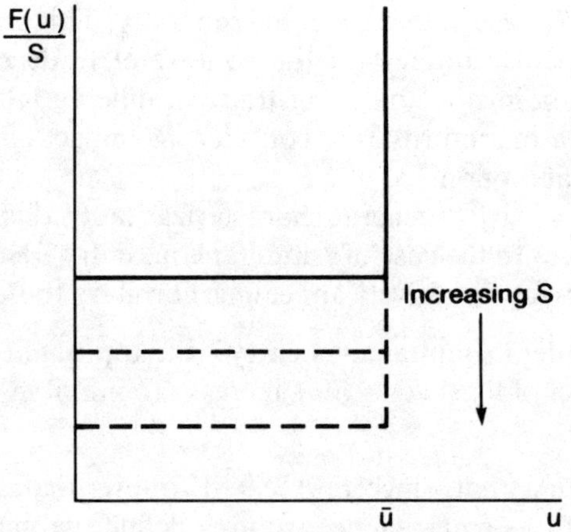

Figure 1

that Assumption 1 is satisfied. Let firms enter simultaneously, and then compete in prices *à la* Bertrand.

In this case, as $S \to \infty$, we converge to a fragmented structure in the manner of Proposition I. As S becomes large, a large number of products of quality $\bar{u}$, and various h, are offered; and each product has an arbitrarily small market share.

To see this, consider the horizontal differentiation case, following the proof of Proposition I (Appendix): in order to ensure that each firm has an arbitrarily small market share at equilibrium, it suffices to show that a δ-net of products of the form (u, h), for various h, will be offered in the limit $S \to \infty$.

Notice that this argument relies crucially on the fact that products are differentiated horizontally as well as vertically. In the special case of *pure vertical differentiation* the preceding assumption in regard to the cost function $F(u)$ leads to an equilibrium in which only a *finite* number of firms enter (see Shaked and Sutton [1982]).

We remark, finally, on one further assumption implicit in our analysis. This is the notion that the cost $F(u)$ incurred in product development is independent of the qualities offered by other firms. In the R & D context, we can think of this as embodying the notion of patent protection; clearly, any relaxation of this will alter our conclusions. This raises a number of familiar issues concerning R & D and patent protection, which lie beyond our present scope.

III. CONCLUDING REMARKS

The theory of product differentiation offers a useful framework within which to explore the relationship between the level of fixed costs (notably R & D and advertising expenditures) and industrial concentration.

Our present analysis focusses attention on the idea, that what matters in regard to the influence which any such fixed costs will have, is not the size of fixed costs per se (*the usual focus of attention*), *but rather the extent to which these fixed expenditures* (*can*) *substitute for higher variable cost, in product improvement* (*whether real or "perceived"*).

In the present model, given the size of the market, it is the interplay between consumers' tastes and the underlying technology (specified by a series of feasible cost-quality combination) which simultaneously determine the degree of concentration and the level of fixed costs.

Thus, for example, we are led to question the familiar argument that certain industries are highly concentrated because the level of fixed costs involved is high. Instead, we would argue that the manufacture of aircraft, or mainframe computers, say, is limited to a small number of firms, not *because* the fixed costs of product development are so high, relative to the size of the market—but rather because the possibility exists, primarily through incurring additional *fixed* costs, of shifting the technological frontier constantly forward towards more sophisticated products.[5] Indeed, we argue that, given such a technology as we posit here, fixed costs in these industries are high *because* the market is large. This is the point made by the Corollary to Proposition II above, and in our earlier work.[6]

Finally, some clarificatory remarks are in order, regarding the relationship between the present analysis and the traditional Bain paradigm, which states that the presence of various "Barriers to Entry" to an industry determines its level of concentration (structure); that high levels of concentration in turn facilitate cooperative price behaviour (conduct); and this collusive behaviour then leads to high profits (performance). This idea of a chain of causation running from Structure to Conduct to Performance has, of course, been increasingly questioned in the more recent literature. In the present paper, taking technology and tastes as our exogenous variables, we have chosen to proceed by exploring the implications of *non-cooperative* behaviour, in the context of a model in which structure and performance are simultaneously determined.

Our theme has been, that *even under competitive pricing*, a concentrated structure necessarily obtains if technology and tastes take a certain form. We wish to emphasize that we do not question the view that a concentrated structure may in turn facilitate collusion, as Bain's view emphasized. A richer dynamic structure might allow such collusive outcomes to be supported as noncooperative equilibria; but this lies outside our present scope.[7]

AVNER SHAKED AND JOHN SUTTON,
The London School of Economics and Political Science,
Houghton Street,
London WC2A 2AE.

ACCEPTED OCTOBER 1987

APPENDIX

I. STATEMENT AND PROOF OF PROPOSITION I

Assumptions

1. Consumers are distributed along $[0, 1]$ according to some atomless density function $S \cdot f(\alpha)$. We assume that f is bounded, and strictly positive, viz.

[5] It is helpful in some contexts to think of the curve $F(u)$ as the envelope of a series of curves pertaining to successive "technologies" in the manner of the familiar "overlapping technologies" diagram. What we then determine, within the model, is which of these technologies will be exploited.

[6] Insofar as the level of fixed costs and the degree of concentration are determined simultaneously within the model, we also question arguments which rely on the reverse direction of causation here: as in the idea that "high concentration induces innovation".

[7] What if behaviour is in fact collusive? Here, a familiar, if paradoxical, story suggests itself: more collusion, insofar as it raises profits, will tend to induce further entry, and so *reduce* measured concentration levels. This of course implies a *reversal* of the direction of causation between concentration and conduct suggested by Bain.

$0 < \underline{f} < f(\alpha) < \bar{f}$ on $0 \leqslant \alpha \leqslant 1$ and that $\int_0^1 f(\alpha)d\alpha = 1$. Thus S denotes the population of consumers in the market.

2. A consumer located at α patronizing a seller at location h, incurs a premium $H(|h-\alpha|)$, where $H(\cdot)$ is a strictly increasing convex function.

3. Firm are free to enter at any particular location by paying a sunk cost of entry σ, and may thereafter produce at zero marginal cost.

Remark 1. It is well known that a number of questions concerning existence of equilibrium in this model remain open. As noted earlier, we do not address these questions here.[8]

Remark 2. For any set of locations, and prices, the assumptions that $H(\cdot)$ is convex implies that the market share of each firm has the form of an *interval* of consumers. Note, however, that this interval need not include the consumers located in the neighbourhood of the firm itself.

Proposition I. For every $\varepsilon > 0$, there exists an economy size S^* such that in every equilibrium in a market of size $S > S^*$, each firm has a market share less than ε.

Proof. Our proof proceeds in two steps. We first show that:
(i) as $S \to \infty$, the spacing between firms becomes arbitrarily close, i.e. for any $\delta > 0$, there exists $\bar{S}$ such that in any equilibrium set of products in an economy of any size $S > \bar{S}$, the distance between any two neighbouring firms is less than δ (as is the distance from 0 to the left-most firm, and from the right-most firm to 1).

To show this, note that if two firms are a distance δ apart, a firm entering midway between them can certainly capture a market share corresponding to an interval of length $(\delta/2)$ by setting price zero, i.e. a share of at least $\underline{f} \cdot \delta/2$. Hence it can certainly capture a market share of $\underline{f} \cdot \delta/4$, say, at a strictly positive price *independently of the prices set by other firms, and the size of economy S.* (We here rely on the fact that $H(\cdot)$ is strictly increasing.)

Now if assertion (i) is false, we can find a sequence of market sizes $S^k \to \infty$, and an equilibrium for each k, such that in each of these equilibria, some pair of firms is more than distance δ apart (or, that one "end" firm is more than distance δ from the endpoint). But as $S^k \to \infty$, it follows that the profits of such a firm (which are proportional to S^k) must exceed entry cost σ, for k sufficiently large. *Thus entry is profitable, and so this is not an equilibrium.* This establishes (i).

(ii) We now establish Proposition I. Suppose it were false. Then for some market share $\varepsilon > 0$, there exists a sequence of market sizes $S^k \to \infty$, together with an equilibrium for every k such that some firm in each equilibrium has a share of at least ε. But from (i), it follows that by choosing k sufficiently large, we can ensure that the minimum distance between neighbouring firms is less than any $\delta > 0$.

Let

$$\delta = \frac{\varepsilon^2}{36(1-\varepsilon)\bar{f}} \frac{H(\varepsilon/6\bar{f})}{H(1)} \tag{1}$$

and choose a corresponding value of k (as prescribed in (i) above).

We now show that, at a Nash equilibrium in prices, it cannot be the case that one firm has a market share of ε or greater; thus obtaining a contradiction.

[8] See for instance d'Aspremont, Jaskold Gabszewicz and Thisse (1979), Neven (1985). It may be worth noting that a formulation in which firms choose price and location simultaneously is much more problematic. It is easily shown that no Nash equilibrium in (price, location) pairs exist (Novshek [1980]).

Take a firm whose market share is ε or greater. Label it firm 1. We can find an interval containing fraction $\varepsilon/2$ of all consumers, all served by firm 1, and lying wholly on one or other side of firm 1's location. (See Figure A1.) Divide that interval into three subintervals, each containing a fraction $\varepsilon/6$ of all consumers. Each subinterval is at least $\frac{\varepsilon}{6\bar{f}}$ in length. Take the middle subinterval. Note that any firm in this subinterval is a distance $\varepsilon/6\bar{f}$ or more from firm 1, and so it can capture the fraction $\frac{\varepsilon}{6}$ of consumers in the outer subinterval by setting any price below $p_1+H(\varepsilon/6\bar{f})$.

From (i), we know that this middle subinterval contains at least $\varepsilon/6\bar{f}\delta$ firms. At least one of these firms must therefore have a market share of at most r, where r satisfies

$$\varepsilon+r\cdot\varepsilon/6\bar{f}\delta = 1$$

i.e. we have $r=\frac{1-\varepsilon}{\varepsilon}\cdot 6\bar{f}\delta$. Label this firm as "2". Now if firm 2 sets a price at or above $p_1+H(1)$, it certainly has sales zero. Hence, since its revenue is necessarily positive at equilibrium,

$$p_2 < p_1+H(1)$$

and so its revenue is at most

$$S\cdot[p_1+H(1)]\cdot\frac{1-\varepsilon}{\varepsilon}6\bar{f}\delta \tag{2}$$

But by setting price

$$p_2' = p_1+H(\varepsilon/6\bar{f})$$

it can capture a market share of $\varepsilon/6$, and so will earn revenue

$$S\cdot[p_1+H(\varepsilon/6\bar{f})]\cdot\frac{\varepsilon}{6} \tag{3}$$

Our definition (1) of δ ensures that expression (3) exceeds expression (2) and therefore that p_2 is not an optimal choice of price for firm 2. (It is optimal for firm 2 to lower its

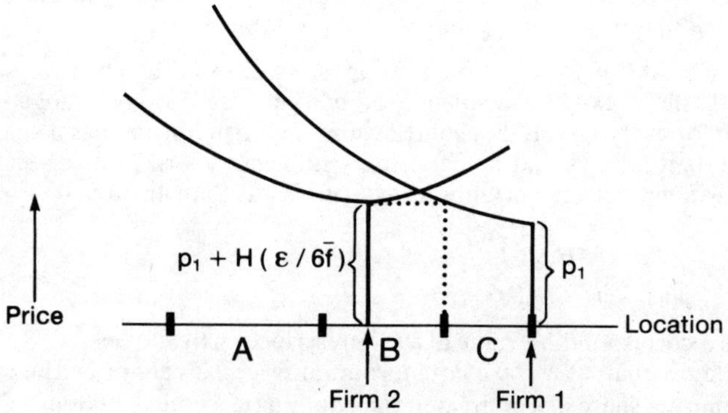

Figure AI: To illustrate proof of Proposition I, part (ii). Firm 1 has a market share exceeding ε. Each interval A, B, C corresponds to a market share of at least $\varepsilon/6$, and is of length $\varepsilon/6\bar{f}$, or greater. Any firm in interval B can capture all consumers in interval A by setting price $p_1+H(\varepsilon/6\bar{f})$

price, and so capture a larger market share.) This contradicts the supposed optimality of the prices.

This completes our proof.

II. COURNOT EQUILIBRIUM WITH DIFFERENTIATED PRODUCTS

Since it is standard in the product differentiation literature to employ a Bertrand equilibrium, it may be worth setting out the method of analysis appropriate to the Cournot case.

Given n goods, then for each vector of quantities $\bar{X} = (X_1, \ldots, X_n)$ we map this vector into a vector of prices $\bar{p}(\bar{X}) = (p_1, \ldots, p_n)$ and demand levels $(D_1, \ldots, D_n)$ satisfying

$$D_i(\bar{p}) = X_i, \qquad \text{if } p_i > 0$$

$$D_i(\bar{p}) \leqslant X_i, \qquad \text{if } p_i = 0$$

To establish the existence of such a price vector, we proceed as follows: define the function

$$M_i(\bar{p}) = \max(-p_i; D_i(\bar{p}) - X_i), \qquad i = 1, \ldots, n$$

This function clearly satisfies the condition:

(i) if $p_i > 0$ and $X_i < D_i(\bar{p})$, then $M_i(\bar{p}) > 0$

(ii) if $p_i = 0$ and $X_i \geqslant D_i(\bar{p})$, then $M_i(\bar{p}) = 0$

Within our setting, where each consumer buys 1 unit or none, $D_i(\bar{p})$, and so $M_i(\bar{p})$, is bounded by the total population of the economy, which we denote S.

Define the function $T(\bar{p}) = \bar{p} + M(\bar{p})$ on $\bar{p} \geqslant 0$. Clearly, $T(\bar{p}) \geqslant 0$. Define the domain, $0 \leqslant p_i \leqslant \bar{Y} + S$, where $\bar{Y}$ is the upper bound to the income of any individual consumer. The mapping $p \rightarrow T(p)$ is continuous, and maps the domain into itself, as is easily checked. Hence there exists a fixed point, and it satisfies conditions (i), (ii) above. It is necessary, within any specific model, to check that this price vector is uniquely defined. The vectors $\bar{X}$ and $\bar{p}(\bar{X})$ determine the payoff of each firm, and so we can solve for the Nash equilibrium, taking the quantities as strategies.

REFERENCES

BEGGS, S., CARDELL, S. and HAUSMAN, J., 1981, 'Assessing the Potential Demand for Electric Cars', *Journal of Econometrics*, 17, pp. 1–20.

BONANNO, G., 1987, 'Product Proliferation and Entry Deterrence Revisited', *Review of Economic Studies*, 54, pp. 37–46.

BORGERS, TILMAN, 1985, 'Existence of Sequential Entry Equilibrium in Product Differentiation Models', mimeo.

D'ASPREMONT, C., GABSZEWICZ, J. JASKOLD and THISSE, J. F., 1979, 'On Hotelling's "Stability in Competition"', *Econometrica*, 47, pp. 1145–1150.

GABSZEWICZ, J. JASKOLD, SHAKED, A., SUTTON, J. and THISSE, J. F., 1981, 'Price Competition among Differentiated Products: A Detailed Study of a Nash Equilibrium', ICERD working paper no. 37, LSE.

HARRIS, CHRISTOPHER, 1985, 'Existence and Characterization of Perfect Equilibrium in Games of Perfect Information', *Econometrica*, 53, pp. 613–616.

LANE, W., 1980, 'Product Differentiation in a Market with Endogenous Sequential Entry', *Bell Journal of Economics*, 11, pp. 237–260.

NEVEN, D., 1985, 'Two Stage (Perfect) Equilibrium in Hotelling's Model'; *Journal of Industrial Economics*, 33, pp. 317–326.

NOVSHEK, W., 1980, 'Equilibrium in Simple Spatial (or Differentiated Product) Models', *Journal of Economic Theory*, 22, pp. 313–326.

SCHMALENSEE, R., 1978, 'Entry Deterrence in the Ready-to-Eat Breakfast Cereal Industry', *Bell Journal of Economics*, 9, pp. 305–327.

SHAKED, AVNER and SUTTON, JOHN, 1982, 'Relaxing Price Competition Through Product Differentiation', *Review of Economic Studies*, 49, pp. 3–14.

SHAKED, AVNER and SUTTON, JOHN, 1983, 'Natural Oligopolies', *Econometrica*, 51, pp. 1469–1484.

SHAKED, AVNER and SUTTON, JOHN, 1984, 'Natural Oligopolies and International Trade' in H. KIERZKOWSKI (ed.), *Monopolistic Competition and International Trade* (Oxford: Oxford University Press).

SHAKED, AVNER and SUTTON, JOHN, 1987, 'Multiproduct Firms and Market Structure', ICERD Working Paper no. 154, LSE.

THE JOURNAL OF INDUSTRIAL ECONOMICS 0022-1821 $2.00
Volume XXXVI December 1987 No. 2

LIFE AFTER TAKEOVER

DAVID J. RAVENSCRAFT AND F. M. SCHERER*

Economic consequences of takeovers are investigated by analyzing profitability of enterprises acquired as a direct or indirect ("white knight") result of tender offers. Target companies' pre-tender profitability averaged 0.97 percentage points below peer industry norms. Nine years after takeover, acquired lines of business had operating income/assets percentages 3.10 points below those of non-tender lines with similar industry bases, market shares, and merger accounting methods. Most of the targets' post-takeover profit decline stemmed from asset value writeups. There is no indication that on average the acquirers raised their targets' operating profitability, net of merger-related accounting adjustments.

FOR THE fourth time in this century, the United States has experienced merger mania. A distinguishing characteristic of the 1980's merger wave has been the high incidence of tender offer takeovers—that is, mergers effected following an offer from a would-be acquirer directly to target company share-holders, bypassing management.

There is a substantial literature in economics, corporate finance, and law arguing that such tender offer takeovers play an important role in purging inefficient managers and forcing incumbents to hew to the profit maximization line or face displacement.[1] This implies two testable hypotheses. First, to the extent that a sizable fraction of takeovers are directed toward displacing inefficient managers, the pre-takeover profitability of targets should be lower than that of non-target peer firms, other things (such as industry business conditions) being held equal. Second, both the logic of inefficient management displacement and the possibility of gaining post-takeover "synergies" imply an improvement in post-takeover profitability relative to the pre-takeover situation. These are hypotheses that should be tested directly and not merely

* Federal Trade Commission Bureau of Economics and Swarthmore College respectively. Scherer's work was supported under National Science Foundation grant SES-8209766 and a Brookings Institution visiting fellowship. The authors are indebted to Nathaniel Levy for research assistance and to Larry White and Willard Carleton for helpful comments.

Use is made of Line of Business data collected by the Federal Trade Commission. A review by FTC staff has determined that individual company data are not disclosed. The conclusions are the authors' and not necessarily those of the FTC.

[1] See e.g. Marris [1963], Manne [1965], Easterbrook and Fischel [1981], Jensen and Ruback [1983], Yarrow [1985, p. 3], and US Council of Economic Advisers [1985, Chapter 6]. In his pioneering article on the subject, Marris [1963, pp. 189–190] proposed two further behavioral hypotheses we do not test here: that firms will retain too high a share of their earnings, and that they will maintain excessive liquidity.

offered as one of many possible explanations for the movement of stock prices at the time of a takeover "event".[2]

I. THE LINE OF BUSINESS DATA

An obstacle to evaluating post-merger performance is that the acquired entity normally ceases to publish income statement and balance sheet information once it is absorbed. To continue tracking the target's history, one needs financial performance data disaggregated to the level of individual operating units. Such data were systematically gathered under the Federal Trade Commission's (now discontinued) Line of Business program. For the years 1975–77, a panel of more than 450 large corporations broke down their domestic financial reports by individual "LBs" defined to conform with 261 possible manufacturing and 14 (broader) nonmanufacturing industry categories. The average sample member reported in 1977 on eight manufacturing LBs, with a range of one to approximately 53. The Line of Business companies were responsible for three-fourths of all manufacturing and minerals industry mergers, measured by volume of assets acquired, on the Federal Trade Commission's lists [1978] of acquisitions of companies with $10 million assets or more over the years 1950–76. The Line of Business data share the well-known limitations of accounting-based performance information and carry the added burdens associated with segmental reporting. However, diverse studies have shown that the data reflect underlying supply and demand conditions and have considerable power in explaining such phenomena as exit from an industry. (See Scherer *et al.* [1987].)

In addition to consummating approximately 6000 "normal" (i.e., bilaterally negotiated) mergers, the Line of Business respondents were involved in at least 96 manufacturing company tender offer acquisitions, according to lists compiled by Douglas V. Austin and Anand Desai.[3] Most were not opposed overtly by the target firms' managements, but in 25 cases, a "hostile" tender offer went through despite incumbent management opposition, and in 20 other cases the acquirer was a "white knight" favoured by target management over a "hostile" tender offer from some other company. The median time of consummation was 1968, if all of the acquisitions are included, or 1967, if a 1974 terminal date is imposed, as we shall do in most of what follows.

[2] See Jensen and Ruback [1983], and the studies surveyed therein.

[3] The Austin lists are published in Austin [1969, 1973, 1975, 1980]. The "Desai" list also includes data collected by Michael Bradley, Peter Dodd, and Richard Ruback. It was brought to our attention by Ellen Magenheim only after Scherer [1986] summarized results of an analysis using the Austin lists only. Twenty-two relevant tender offers were on the Desai list but not on the Austin lists; 15 verified tender offers were on the Austin lists but not on the Desai list. Cross-checking also permitted the elimination of certain borderline tender offers that were "arranged" by key controlling "inside" stockholders or that involved "mopping up" share purchases following a negotiated merger.

II. PRE-OFFER PERFORMANCE

For 95 of the 96 targets, it was possible to obtain information on profitability for two years prior to (or in some cases partially overlapping) the precipitating tender offer announcement. Consistent with the post-tender analysis that follows in section III, the profitability statistic used, OPINC:A, is the ratio of operating income (before deduction of interest charges, extraordinary items, and income taxes) to end-of-fiscal year assets. To control for industry membership and business cycle effects, each individual company's pre-tender operating income/assets percentage was "normalized" by subtracting the comparable percentage for the most closely corresponding industry covered by the FTC's *Quarterly Financial Report* series for the most closely coinciding fiscal year.[4] Before normalization, the simple average operating income/assets percentage was 11.15% in the last year before (or overlapping) takeover initiation and 11.01% in the preceding year. The inter-year differences between both non-normalized and normalized profit figures were minute and statistically insignificant ($F < 0.05$), and so the two years' data are pooled.

Over the two pre-tender offer years, the average normalized profitability percentages for the 95 targets and subsets thereof were as follows, with standard errors given in subscripted parentheses:

All 95 tender offer targets		−0.973%
		(0.513)
25 companies taken over by acquirers incumbent management opposed	−2.281%	
	(0.839)	
20 companies acquired by "white knights"	−0.558%	
	(0.718)	
50 companies acquired in other tender offers uncontested by management	−0.486%	
	(0.829)	

For all target companies together, pre-tender profitability was below industry norms by 0.97 points on average—a difference statistically significant at the 0.05 level in a one-tail test. If operating income/assets ratios for all manufacturing companies, rather than the targets' principal two-digit industries, are used as the standard, the average deviation is −0.403, which is not statistically significant. Thus the home base industries of the tender offer targets had profit returns 0.57 percentage points on average above the all-manufacturing norm (the mean of which was 11.49%). Although the companies taken over in "hostile" bids exhibited lower average returns than

[4] For 12 relatively diversified targets, two or more *QFR* industry category norms were averaged, and for two highly diversified targets, the all-manufacturing benchmarks were used. Even so, the "fit" between company activities and the (typically two-digit) *QFR* industry categories was sometimes imperfect—e.g., when a paint maker had to be compared to the entire chemicals industry, or a sporting goods producer to lumber, furniture, and miscellaneous durable goods.

other targets, the differences among the three classes are not statistically significant [$F(2,187) = 1.16$].

III. POST-TAKEOVER PERFORMANCE

Our post-takeover analysis covers a much broader sample encompassing 2732 manufacturing lines of business (LBs) for which data quality control criteria over all three years 1975–77 were satisfied. Among those lines, 153 had a tender offer acquisition history, including 46 LBs affected by "hostile" tenders unsuccessfully opposed by incumbent management and 44 LBs acquired by "white knights". The remaining 2579 non-tender lines serve as a control group. The 153 tender offer lines belonged to 62 target companies. Thirty-three tender offer acquisition companies for which pre-merger profitability data were available (plus one without pre-merger data) were excluded from the main analysis because the acquired lines were divested before 1975; because the tender offer acquisitions occurred only in 1975 or 1976, too late for the three-year sample analysis; or because other sample inclusion criteria were not satisfied.[5] The two-year average pre-acquisition normalized profit performance of the included and excluded company cohorts was as follows:

	Normalized Operating Income / Assets
62 companies included in the three-year analysis	−1.57%
11 companies acquired in 1975 or 1976	−1.93%
4 companies whose lines were sold off before 1975	−0.49%
18 companies failing to meet other sample inclusion criteria	+1.57%

The profitability differences among groups are not statistically significant; $F(3,186) = 2.02$, with the 5% point being 2.65. Nevertheless, the negative 1.57% average for the three-year analysis companies, which is significantly different from zero ($t = 2.35$), cautions that the tender offer companies began life after takeover with modestly sub-par performance records.

The principal dependent variable OPINC:A used in our analysis of post-acquisition performance is the operating income/assets percentage for an individual line of business (LB), averaged over the three reporting years 1975–77. Inter-industry differences are taken into account by means of a "fixed effects" regression analysis. That is, each of the 257 four-digit manu-

[5] All but four of the 18 "other" excluded companies' LBs had extensive acquisition or sell-off activity in one or more of the years 1975–77. The data for such years often contain significant biases, and must therefore be excluded. See Meeks and Meeks [1981]. In the other four cases, company merger histories were incomplete, precluding an accurate assignment of non-tender mergers to LBs. A sensitivity analysis adding those cases to the sample produced no noteworthy changes in results.

facturing industry categories with LB observations was allowed to have its own profitability regression intercept term. Also controlled for are the following variables, each measured at the individual LB level:

SHR Market share of LB in its four-digit industry category (scaled in ratio form).

POOL Fraction of end-of-period assets traced to acquisitions treated under pooling-of-interests accounting.

PURCH Fraction of end-of-period assets traced to acquisitions treated under purchase accounting.

EQUALS Dummy variable with value of 1 if the LB had a "merger of equals", defined as a pooling merger among firms whose pre-merger size differed by no more than a factor of two.

NEW Dummy variable with value of 1 if the line entered the parent's operations after 1950 and experienced no acquisitions.

The POOL and PURCH variables take into account not only the fraction of assets acquired, but also the type of accounting used in transferring acquired assets to the acquirer's books. Under pooling of interests accounting, assets are recorded at their pre-merger book value. Under purchase accounting, assets are recorded in effect at the price actually paid, which usually exceeded pre-merger book values because prevailing replacement costs and/or stock market values were above accounting values and because tender offers are almost always consummated at a stock price premium. Details on these measurements and other methodological matters are presented in Ravenscraft and Scherer [1987].

If we hold those other variables constant, the influence of a tender offer history is ascertained by means of a dummy variable TENDER, with unit value if the line was acquired in whole or in part as the consequence of a tender offer and zero otherwise. Alternatively, a more detailed breakdown is achieved by forming three distinct tender offer dummies:

HOSTILE Acquisition actively opposed by target management.

WHITE Acquirer was a white knight.

OTHER Tender offer acquisition meeting neither of the above conditions.

Averaging the data for all lines meeting quality control criteria for the years 1975–77, the following regressions, with t-ratios in subscripted brackets, resulted:

$$(1) \quad \text{OPINC:A} = [257 \text{ constants}] - \underset{[2.41]}{3.10}\ \text{TENDER} + \underset{[5.68]}{30.18}\ \text{SHR}$$

$$+ \underset{[0.58]}{0.66}\ \text{POOL} - \underset{[2.24]}{2.81}\ \text{PURCH} + \underset{[0.82]}{0.83}\ \text{NEW} + \underset{[1.48]}{1.43}\ \text{EQUALS};$$

$$R^2 = 0.1823,\ N = 2732;\ \text{mean OPINC:A} = 13.34.$$

$$\text{(2)} \quad \textit{OPINC}: A = [257 \text{ constants}] - \underset{[1.65]}{3.65}\,\textit{HOSTILE} - \underset{[1.69]}{3.77}\,\textit{WHITE}$$

$$- \underset{[1.18]}{2.23}\,\textit{OTHER} + \underset{[5.67]}{30.15}\,\textit{SHR} + \underset{[0.60]}{0.68}\,\textit{POOL} - \underset{[2.24]}{2.82}\,\textit{PURCH}$$

$$+ \underset{[0.83]}{0.84}\,\textit{NEW} + \underset{[1.51]}{1.46}\,\textit{EQUALS};\ R^2 = 0.1824,\ N = 2732.$$

With all tender offer types combined in regression (1), the coefficient on TENDER is negative and significant at the 0.02 level in a two-tail test. Breaking the tender offer set into three subsets, as in regression (2), contributes insignificant variance reduction [$F(2,2467) = 0.20$].

The TENDER coefficient value of regression (1) indicates that lines with a tender offer history were 3.10 percentage points less profitable on average than lines without such a history, but with similar industry membership, market shares, merger accounting methods, and levels of (non-tender) acquired assets.[6] Relative to the all-sample operating income/assets average of 13.34 percent, this is a substantial difference. In conjunction with our earlier finding that the 62 tender offer targets included in the three-year analysis had average pre-merger profitability 1.57 percentage points lower than that of their two-digit industry peers, the −3.10 TENDER coefficient is inconsistent with the hypothesis that post-tender acquisition profitability *improved*, all else equal. Indeed, the implication is in one sense more severe. Roughly two-thirds of the tender offer acquisitions were treated under purchase accounting or "dirty pooling" (a blend of purchase and pooling accounting). To find the full impact on reported profitability of an acquisition that stemmed from tender offer *and* that contributed 100 percent of a line's assets under purchase accounting (PURCH = 1.0), one must add the −3.10 TENDER coefficient and the −2.81 PURCH coefficient. Together, the coefficients imply a 5.91 percent degradation of returns relative to control values. For a line with an average market share in an industry of average profitability, this means an average return on assets of approximately 7.43 percent.[7] This is well below the median 12 percent after-tax "hurdle rate" applied by US corporations during the late 1960s in judging new capital investment proposals. See Williams [1970, p. 21].

[6] Other coefficients in regression (1) are interpreted as follows. Moving from having an infinitesimal market share to controlling the whole market (SHR = 1) raises the operating income/assets percentage by an impressive 30.2 points. Lines originating under pooling of interests mergers were slightly, but insignificantly, more profitable than their no-merger counterparts. Mergers of equals were 1.43 percentage points more profitable on average; new internal growth lines 0.83 points more profitable.

[7] The mean 1975–77 operating income/assets value for the 153 tender offer lines was 10.09 percent, which is well below the all-sample average of 13.34%. This average differs from the value predicted by regression analysis because only the latter controls for industry, market share, and accounting choice influences.

A major reason for the depressed post-acquisition returns of tender offer mergers must be the premiums paid to reflect prevailing stock market values and to induce target firm shareholder and/or management acquiescence. Under the purchase accounting adopted following most tender offer takeovers, acquired assets were written up to reflect the value of premiums paid over pre-acquisition book entries. Such writeups increase the denominator of OPINC:A and hence reduce the ratio. They may also affect the numerator by raising depreciation charges, but this is less certain, since asset writeups charged to a goodwill account were seldom amortized before 1970 and were subjected to long (e.g., 40 year) amortization periods thereafter.

To test for the role of asset writeups, equation (1) is re-estimated with a dependent variable measured as the ratio of operating income to sales. The result is:

$$\text{(3)} \quad \textit{OPINC:S} = [257 \text{ constants}] - \underset{[1.56]}{1.20}\, \textit{TENDER} + \underset{[6.88]}{21.91}\, \textit{SHR}$$

$$+ \underset{[0.73]}{0.50}\, \textit{POOL} - \underset{[1.03]}{0.78}\, \textit{PURCH} - \underset{[0.12]}{0.07}\, \textit{NEW} + \underset{[1.49]}{0.86}\, \textit{EQUALS};$$

$$R^2 = 0.2128, N = 2732, \text{mean } \textit{OPINC:S} = 7.54.$$

Here the tender offer effect is significant only at the 0.12 level. It indicates an average deviation in proportion to all-sample operating income/sales ratios of only 15.9 percent, compared to the 23.2 percent deviation in assets-denominated regression (1). Evidently, a substantial component of the post-takeover depression of tender offer LB profitability came from the asset writeups resulting from the premiums over book value paid in effectuating the takeovers.

To purge the effect of such writeups from the numerator of profitability measures, a third variable, the ratio of cash flow (i.e., operating income before deduction of depreciation) to sales, was computed. With it as dependent variable, the result is:

$$\text{(4)} \quad \textit{CASHFLO:S} = [257 \text{ constants}] - \underset{[1.43]}{1.09}\, \textit{TENDER} + \underset{[7.29]}{23.12}\, \textit{SHR}$$

$$+ \underset{[0.72]}{0.49}\, \textit{POOL} - \underset{[1.16]}{0.87}\, \textit{PURCH} + \underset{[0.27]}{0.16}\, \textit{NEW} + \underset{[1.26]}{0.73}\, \textit{EQUALS};$$

$$R^2 = 0.2393, N = 2732; \text{mean } \textit{CASHFLO:S} = 10.12.$$

The tender offer coefficient and its t-ratio fade a bit more, suggesting the presence of a modest depreciation effect in regression (3). At 10.8 percent of the all-sample cash flow/sales ratio, the negative tender offer coefficient approximates the 12.9 percent *pre-merger* operating income/assets deficit relative to industry norms recorded for the three-year sample tender offer targets. The closeness of the two deviations, one pre-merger and the other post-merger, compels an agnostic inference that takeover neither improved nor degraded the basic operating performance of target firms.[8]

It is widely believed that the Williams Act increased takeover premiums. If so, we might expect the negative effect of TENDER on OPINC:A to be greater for post-1968 takeovers than for those carried out before the Act took force. Eighty-nine of the 153 tender offer LBs came from acquisitions commenced (at least by the successful bidder) after most Williams Act provisions became effective July 29, 1968. When TENDER is multiplied by a dummy variable with a value of 1 for post-Williams Act cases, the resulting regression is:

$$\text{(5)} \quad OPINC{:}A = [257\ \text{constants}] \underset{[1.99]}{-3.72}\ TENDER \underset{[0.46]}{+1.09}\ WILLIAMS \underset{[5.67]}{+30.13}\ SHR \underset{[0.59]}{+0.67}\ POOL \underset{[2.26]}{-2.83}\ PURCH \underset{[0.82]}{+0.83}\ NEW \underset{[1.49]}{+1.43}\ EQUALS;\ R^2 = 0.1823,\ N = 2732.$$

There is a hint of less, not more, negative profitability for post-Williams Act acquisitions, but the WILLIAMS coefficient is not statistically significant, there are signs of multi-collinearity, and there is no increase in R^2 relative to equation (1).[9]

IV. CONCLUSION

Tender offer targets of the 1960s and early 1970s entered their acquirers' organizations with a profit record slightly inferior to that of their two-digit industry peers. Nine years later on average, they performed appreciably less well. An important reason for their deteriorated post-takeover returns was the writeup of asset values stemming from the payment of acquisition premiums. But those premiums were supposedly paid in anticipation of enhanced profitability, which is not evident in our post-takeover operating

[8] That the pre-merger deviation is statistically significant while the post-merger coefficient is not does not vitiate the conclusion that the two differ trivially. The significance difference stems from the fact that Line of Business profit data are more variable, with a standard deviation nearly three times that of comparably-defined company-level data.

[9] Two additional analyses were suggested by referees. A linear time-weighted version of TENDER implied that the significantly negative profits were *most* negative for the most recent tender offers. However, the regression had explanatory power inferior to that of equation (1). Relating operating income to mid-period assets rather than end-of-year assets moved the TENDER coefficient in the analogue of equation (1) to -3.31, with $t = 2.53$.

A further check added a dummy variable when a Line of Business company had been acquired in a tender offer made by a foreign company, and when the US corporate shell was retained after the acquisition. Asset revaluations are less likely in such cases. The dummy variable was positive but statistically insignificant ($t = 0.58$) in the operating income/assets regression, while the TENDER coefficient became slightly more negative. The foreign parent dummy was negative but statistically insignificant ($t = 0.18$) in the operating income/sales regression.

income and cash flow regressions. This is an anomaly for the theory of takeovers as an efficiency-increasing mechanism. If improvements did occur, their impact must have been concentrated not in operating returns, but below the "bottom line" of our operating income measures—e.g., in income taxes or interest costs. Tax savings are a zero-sum game against the Treasury. Since there are clear and persistent economies of scale in financing,[10] capital cost savings may have been overlooked by our analysis. Yet they could scarcely have been large enough to justify the low average pre-interest returns on assets revealed by regressions (1) and (2), nor was tender offer takeover the only way to secure them.

At the very least, these results suggest a need for direct and affirmative evidence on whence the purported economic benefits of takeovers originate and whether tenderers have in fact succeeded in managing their acquisitions better than the displaced managers. Absent such evidence, the hypothesis that tender offer takeovers are on average efficiency-increasing warrants much more skepticism than it has received thus far in the literatures of economics, corporate finance, and securities law.

ACCEPTED DECEMBER 1986

DAVID J. RAVENSCRAFT,
School of Business Administration,
University of North Carolina,
Chapel Hill, NC 27514,
USA.

F. M. SCHERER,
Department of Economics,
Swarthmore College,
Swarthmore, Pennsylvania 19081,
USA.

REFERENCES

AUSTIN, DOUGLAS V. and FISHMAN, JAY A., 1969, 'The Tender Takeover', *Mergers & Acquisitions*, 4 (May–June), pp. 4–23.

AUSTIN, DOUGLAS, V., 1973, 'Tender Offers Revisited: 1968–72', *Mergers & Acquisitions*, 8 (Fall), pp. 16–29.

AUSTIN, DOUGLAS V., 1975, 'Tender Offer Statistics: New Strategies Are Paying Off', *Mergers & Acquisitions*, 10 (Fall), pp. 9–18.

AUSTIN, DOUGLAS V., 1980, 'Tender Offer Update: 1978–1979', *Mergers & Acquisitions*, 15 (Summer), pp. 13–32.

EASTERBROOK, FRANK H. and FISCHEL, DANIEL R., 1981, 'The Proper Role of a Target's Management in Responding to a Tender Offer', *Harvard Law Review*, 94 (April), pp. 1161–1204.

JENSEN, MICHAEL C. and RUBACK, RICHARD S., 1983, 'The Market for Corporate Control', *Journal of Financial Economics*, 11 (No. 1), pp. 5–50.

[10] See Scherer *et al.* [1975, pp. 284–288], where a tenfold increase in company size was found to reduce interest rates paid by 0.46 percentage points during the mid-1960s.

MANNE, HENRY G., 1965, 'Mergers and the Market for Corporate Control', *Journal of Political Economy*, 73 (April), pp. 110–120.

MARRIS, ROBIN, 1963, 'A Model of the "Managerial" Enterprise', *Quarterly Journal of Economics*, 77 (May), pp. 185–209.

MEEKS, G. and MEEKS, J. G., 1981, 'Profitability Measures as Indicators of Post-Merger Efficiency', *The Journal of Industrial Economics*, 29 (June), pp. 335–344.

RAVENSCRAFT, DAVID J. and SCHERER, F. M., 1987, *Mergers, Sell-Offs, and Economic Efficiency* (Brookings: Washington).

SCHERER, F. M., BECKENSTEIN, ALAN, KAUFER, ERICH, and MURPHY, R. D., 1975, *The Economics of Multi-Plant Operation: An International Comparisons Study* (Harvard University Press, Cambridge, MA).

SCHERER, F. M., 1986, 'Takeovers: Present and Future Dangers', *The Brookings Review*, 4 (Winter/Spring), pp. 15–20.

SCHERER, F. M., LONG, W. F., MARTIN, STEPHEN, MUELLER, DENNIS C., PASCOE, GEORGE, RAVENSCRAFT, D. J., SCOTT, JOHN T. and WEISS, LEONARD W., 1987, 'The Validity of Studies with Line of Business Data: Comment', *American Economic Review*, 77 (March), pp. 205–217.

US COUNCIL OF ECONOMIC ADVISERS, 1985, *Annual Report*, in *Economic Report of the President* (Washington, DC).

US FEDERAL TRADE COMMISSION, *Quarterly Financial Report for Manufacturing and Mining Corporations* (various dates, Washington, DC).

US FEDERAL TRADE COMMISSION, 1978, *Statistical Report on Mergers and Acquisitions* (December, Washington, DC).

WILLIAMS, JR., R. B., 1970, 'Industry Practice in Allocating Capital Resources', *Managerial Planning*, 19 (May/June), pp. 15–22.

YARROW, G. K., 1985, 'Shareholder Protection, Compulsory Acquisition and the Efficiency of the Takeover Process', *The Journal of Industrial Economics*, 34 (September), pp. 3–16.

THE JOURNAL OF INDUSTRIAL ECONOMICS 0022-1821 $2.00
Volume XXXVI December 1987 No. 2

COSTS OF MAINTAINING A CARTEL

STEVEN G. LANNING*

The costs of operating a cartel are determined by the effort spent on policing member firms and errors in detection of cheaters. An output review is modeled that may be used with trigger pricing. In the presence of a Wiener process to describe disturbances in demand, the cartel uses trigger pricing first and then switches to an output review. Costs generated by cartel maintenance affect social welfare and provide a foundation for analyzing the impact of a cartel on society.

I. INTRODUCTION

THE LEADING methods of cartel maintenance that have been suggested in theoretical literature are based on trigger pricing and output review. Both models predict that no firm will ever cheat on the cartel assigned quota, but differ in that trigger pricing predicts reversions to penalty periods as requirements necessary to maintain credibility. Each strategy has been proven to work separately and may be considered a strategic corner solution. Friedman [1971] introduced a random output review used with credible retaliatory periods in a game theoretic setting, Radner [1985] generalized output review to include errors in monitoring, and Lanning [1985] considered the effect of costs generated by an output review program. Porter [1983] and Green and Porter [1984] revived the notion that trigger pricing may be a valid strategy by proving that trigger pricing satisfies a sufficient set of game theoretic properties. Abreu, Pearce and Stacchetti [1985] have generalized the set of conditions for which trigger pricing is a valid strategy.

The present paper goes beyond earlier work by modeling the cartel as choosing the optimal combination of trigger price and output verification strategies. The results suggest that a cartel would switch between corner solutions. The predicted cartel profit profiles are related to the number of firms in the cartel, but are more sensitive to the availability of information necessary to maintain the cartel and to the costs of obtaining the information. Consequently, two cartels with equal numbers of firms and identical price-cost ratios may adopt different strategies and generate different profit levels, which may range from noncollusive to continual joint-profit-maximization levels.

* This paper was written while I was an Assistant Professor at the University of Notre Dame and was improved by comments in seminars there and at Northwestern University. I thank Ronald Braeutigam for many helpful comments. I am most thankful for comments and suggestions from anonymous referees and the editor. Any remaining errors are my responsibility. Financial support from the Business Partners' Fund of the University of Notre Dame is gratefully acknowledged.

The method of the present paper is to consider the optimal choices of output verification and trigger pricing. When employing output verification exclusively, the cartel is paying for its information while ignoring the movement of the price level, which is freely available.[1] To take advantage of the information in price variations, the cartel is assumed to adopt a trigger price strategy. A trigger price represents a means by which the cartel uses price variation to test statistically for the existence of cheating with known levels of confidence and power. In the second section, the market is described and the assumptions of the model are made explicit. In the third section the choice to cheat is analyzed, and the requirements for feasibility are explored. In section four the costs of maintaining the cartel are derived from the feasibility requirement, and the length of a retaliatory period is derived from the credibility requirement. In the fifth section, the relation between cartel costs and welfare is developed, and welfare under the cartel is compared to welfare under a monopolist, so as to suggest when merger prevention may improve welfare, and when welfare may be diminished.

II. MODEL

The output of the cartel is a business environment that induces firms to restrict aggregate output and maximize profits. The cartel produces a collusive environment by imposing penalties when it detects sufficient evidence of cheating. Firms have an incentive to cheat on the cartel because it represents a departure from a noncooperative equilibrium, and any persistent departure from the prevailing noncooperative equilibrium represents a profit opportunity. If potential cheaters believe the cartel will penalize them upon detection (e.g., by the cartel deciding to revert to a noncollusive mode), then the cartel's threat is defined to be credible. If consideration of a credible threat leads the firm to collude rather than cheat, then the cartel will be referred to as feasible. The definition of feasibility does not allow cheating.[2] If the expected net return to collusion is greater than the expected return in a noncollusive equilibrium, then the cartel is sustainable. The definitions of credibility, feasibility, and sustainability are restated in the context of the model in section four.

The market in which the cartel operates has the following features:

1. Output characteristics are homogeneous and not subject to the control of

[1] Price information may not be free, but must be collected to allocate quotas correctly in an environment of changing demand under either scheme and is therefore free in the sense of opportunity costs.

[2] The allowance of cheating may be optimal where there are adjustment costs in the scale of production. With no adjustment costs, knowledge of a cheater prompts a competitive reaction, which in turn leads to a chain reaction with a noncooperative equilibrium as the immediate result.

the firm or the cartel. Further, the output produced at time t is sold at time t.

2. There is a single market price that is freely observed. Because output is uniform, demand may be described by the inverse demand function,

$$P(y, \theta(t)) = a + \theta(t) - y \tag{1}$$

where: $y = y_1 + \ldots + y_n$, is the sum of the outputs by each firm, a is a constant, and θ is stochastic and varies according to a Wiener process where $d\theta = \sigma dz$ and $\theta(0) = 0$.

The Wiener process captures unanticipated shifts in demand so that movements in price due to changes in output cannot be distinguished from changes in price due to stochastic variation.[3] Consequently, there is a problem in maintaining the cartel because one cannot be sure that a firm is cheating when price falls.[4]

3. The production cost for each firm is a constant, c, per unit, and there are no costs to adjusting the scale of production.

For the constant cost condition to be valid, there can be no technological change, or change must occur slowly and be diffused quickly enough that no firm gains a cost advantage. Whereas the constancy of cost is not so restrictive, identical costs are. Constant identical costs with no adjustment costs tend to occur in mature industries with excess capacity. Also, constant costs may be the most difficult condition in which the cartel may operate because firms are not committed to produce cartel output levels by investment in limited capital stock and sharply rising marginal costs.

4. There are n firms in the market. There is no entry or exit in the market. A model of entry would include issues of limit pricing, as are found in Gaskins [1971] or Kamien and Schwartz [1971].

5. The cartel considers two methods of detecting cheaters: Trigger pricing and random output verification. Detection of cheating causes the cartel to revert to a noncollusive mode.

With trigger pricing, if the price realized is less than the minimum previously agreed upon, then the cartel reacts as though a cheater exists. By contrast, when using random output verification the cartel knows that a cheater exists because overproduction of the assigned quotas is incontrovertible evidence. However, the identity of the cheater is of no additional

[3] The probability that the realized price is less than cost reflects the probability that the economic activity becomes noncompensatory, and the probability that demand exceeds capacity is the probability that the constant cost assumption is violated.

[4] Rotemberg and Saloner [1986] introduced a model where demand disturbances are observable at the beginning of a period, and the results of price or output choices by each firm are known at the end of the period. The difficulty in maintaining a cartel arises from the uncertainty concerning the penalties for cheating.

value to knowing that a cheater exists because exclusion from the cartel is equivalent to condoning the cheater. Thus, the cartel reaction to explicit output verification is the same as the reaction to a trigger price.[5] The probabilities of reversion with output verification, trigger pricing and both together, are developed below and given in equations (2), (3) and (4).

6. As Green and Porter [1984] note, it is necessary for all firms to observe a common variable in order to know the behavioral mode of the cartel, either collusive or penalty. With a pure trigger price, the common variable is price, and with output verification, the common variable is the announced quota.

Output verification is performed by sending an inspector to the plant(s) of a given firm at random times so it is not possible to make appropriate adjustments. The check is assumed to be accurate, and the cost of this accuracy is reflected in the price of a single check. Thus, it is assumed that the cartel may determine whether or not a firm is producing output consistent with its assigned quota. The time until a firm is detected cheating is represented by the exponential distribution,

$$F^{v} = 1 - \mathrm{EXP}[-(\eta + \phi)t] \tag{2}$$

where: η = the rate at which cheating is detected for free, $\eta \geqslant 0$,
ϕ = the rate at which the cartel randomly verifies the output of each member, and $\phi \geqslant 0$.

The alternative cartel control is a trigger price that is established by the allowed variation in the price level (hereafter allowed price variation). The trigger price represents a one-tailed test of whether or not realized price variation can be explained in terms of the stochastic disturbances known to affect demand. In particular, equation (1) implies that from the inception of the cartel at time $t = 0$ until the moment $t = s$, the variation in the stochastic element of demand is normally distributed, $N(0, s\sigma)$.[6] The effect of cheating on the assigned quota at time $t = s$ by the quantity $\Delta(s)$ is to shift the distribution of the price level downward by Δ so that unexplainable price variation is normally distributed, $N(\Delta, s\sigma)$. The probability of surpassing the allowed price variation at time t is directly related to the rate at which cheating is suspected at time t and is embedded in an exponential detection function that gives the probability that the allowed price variation is surpassed at time t:

$$F^{r}(t) = 1 - \mathrm{EXP}[-\lambda t] \tag{3}$$

[5] Alternative equilibria for penalties, such as Stackelberg price leadership designed to punish the known cheater, are not considered in the present paper. However, such an equilibrium would increase the severity of penalty and thus increase collusive profits because less effort would be necessary to establish feasibility.

[6] See Schuss [1980].

where

$$\lambda(t) = \frac{\alpha(t)}{1-\alpha(t)}$$

and

$$\alpha = \Phi\left(\frac{\delta+\Delta}{\sigma t}\right)$$

If a cheater deviates from quota ($\Delta > 0$) at the inception of the cartel, then immediate reversion to a noncooperative mode is assured because the probability of reversion, α, approaches one, and the rate of reversion, λ, approaches infinity.[7] If a cheater increases output gradually, then it is difficult to distinguish between stochastic price variation and excessive production. The cartel determines the risk of surpassing the allowed price variation by choosing the control $\delta(t)$, where δ is a real number. However, the effectiveness of the control is limited because the Wiener process dictates that the longer the cartel has been operating, the lower is the degree of confidence with which cheating can be distinguished from stochastic price movements. Eventually stochastic variation makes the distinction impossible.

The cartel chooses allowed price variations and the rate of output verification optimally. The choice of cartel policing methods affects the probability of detecting or suspecting a cheater and then reverting to a penalty mode in the following way: The probability of reversion, F, is expressed in terms of the hazard function,

$$dF/dt = (1-F)[I(\eta+\phi)+\lambda\{(\delta+\Delta)/(t\sigma)\}] \tag{4}$$

where $I = \begin{cases} 0 \text{ if } \Delta = 0 \\ 1 \text{ otherwise.} \end{cases}$

The hazard function (4) captures a number of features. Within a given finite period of time the probability of detection is higher when the rate at which the cartel checks the output of its members is higher and when the range of allowed price variations is smaller (greater δ or equivalently, the higher is the trigger price). Also the probability of reversion is higher, the faster a cheater adjusts output away from the collusive mode (greater Δ at fixed time). If the cartel is sensitive to price variations, then the probability of reversion is always positive, but if the cartel only verifies output, then the probability of reversion is positive only when there is a cheater.

The hazard function (4) is constructed as follows: Direct verification of cheating occurs with exponential probability given by (2), and the allowed price variation is surpassed at the exponential rate given in (3). The probability of reversion by output verification is independent of the probability of reversion by trigger price because the random checks of output verification

[7] To avoid immediate reversion the cartel may choose $\delta = 0$.

are independent of stochastic price movements. There is no reaction when no cheater is detected and the allowed price variation is not surpassed, which occurs with probability $1-F=(1-F^v)(1-F^r)$. The derivative of F with respect to t is the hazard function.

A firm cheats on the cartel by choosing to produce an output level, y^m, different from the quota, y^c, which leaves the remaining $n-1$ firms producing y^{c-1}. The cheating firm compares the expected returns to cheating with the expected returns to colluding and cheats only if the expected cheating returns are greater.

When firms collude there are no deviations from quota so that a share of collusive returns is

$$R^c = (a+\theta(t)-c-y^c)(y^c/n) \tag{5}$$

Following the Cournot model, the cheating firm takes the announced quota as given and does not conjecture quota adjustments in response to its output, y^m. The resulting profit is a function of deviations from quota, $\Delta = y^m - y^c/n$, given by

$$R^m = (a+\theta(t)-c-y^c-\Delta)[(y^c/n)+\Delta] \tag{6}$$

The Cournot profit at time t is defined by the realization of demand:

$$R^{nc}(t) = [(a+\theta(t)-c)/(n+1)]^2 \tag{7}$$

Noncooperative Cournot profits, R^{nc}, are earned when there is no collusion or when the cartel is in a penalty mode.[8] Because the Cournot equilibrium is assumed to depend on the realization of the stochastic demand element at each moment, output is also determined by these realizations. Consequently, price is a direct indicator of the stochastic realizations when the cartel is in the noncollusive mode. When the cartel reverts to a noncollusive equilibrium, it learns the exact realization of the stochastic element so that at the end of a reversionary period it is starting anew.

The gains to cheating may be naturally divided into episodes. Each episode of cheating is comprised of a period of stochastic length in which the cheater is not detected and a period of penalty after detection. The cheater affects the length of an episode by the degree of cheating, and the cartel affects the length by the strategy chosen to maintain itself. The objective function considered for a firm is the discounted gains to cheating (the difference between what is earned while cheating and the return to colluding) over a single episode because they are consistent with both a short-run and a long-run strategy of

[8] For an equilibrium more severe than the noncollusive equilibrium to be credible requires considerable proof, and a more severe credible penalty does not generally exist. See Friedman [1986] for a statement on limitations on the existence of penalties more severe than the noncollusive equilibrium.

cheating.[9] The objective function considered for the cartel is maximization of the infinite discounted feasible returns net of the cost of maintaining feasibility.

III. PROFIT MAXIMIZATION BY THE CHEATING FIRM

The firm chooses the output level that maximizes its expected stream of profits. An episode of cheating is taken as representative of the game played between the cartel and each member firm. The (maximum) expected return to the firm for an episode of cheating is

$$(8) \qquad J(F) = \max_{\Delta} E\left\{\int_0^{\infty}\left[e^{-rt}(R^m - R^c)(1-F) + [F - F(\Delta=0)]\int_t^{t+T} e^{-rs}(R^{nc} - R^c + w\phi)ds\right]dt\right\}$$

subject to (1) and (4), and where r is the discount rate.

The output choice of the cheater does not depend on cartel costs because they are determined by the cartel. Following Kamien and Schwartz [1981] we can write (8) in terms of the following optimality condition:

$$(9) \qquad -J = \max_{\Delta}[e^{-rt}(R^m - R^c)(1-F) + [F - F(\Delta=0)]Y + J_t + (1-F)[\eta + \phi(t) + \lambda(z)]J_F + (1/2)\sigma^2 J_{\theta\theta}]$$

where

$$Y = \int_t^{t+T} e^{-rs}(R^{nc} - R^c + w\phi)ds$$

and

$$z = \frac{\delta + \Delta/t}{\sigma}$$

Taking the partial derivative with respect to deviations from quota, Δ, implicitly defines the optimal deviation from quota at time t,

$$(10) \qquad e^{-rt}[a + \theta - c - y^{c+1} - 2\Delta] + \frac{[\partial\lambda(z)/\partial z]J_F}{\sigma t} = 0 \text{ where } y^{c+1} = \frac{n+1}{n}y^c$$

The first term in the sum is the discounted marginal gain to cheating, and the second term represents the marginal cost. The optimal deviation from quota

[9] The equivalence of maximizing (by choice of the cheater's output) the gain to cheating and the return to cheating is immediate because the collusive return does not depend on an output decision by the cheater. The equivalence between maximizing the gain to cheating over a representative episode and all episodes follows from the equivalence of the episodes: nothing is learned and no reputations are established, so the game starts as though the cartel were just initiated.

$\Delta(t)$, may be positive or negative depending on the allowed price variations, δ. If allowed price variations are too tolerant (δ is too small, meaning the trigger price is set too low), then the cheater will choose an approach path to $\Delta = [a+\theta-c-y^{c+1}]/2$. If allowed price variations are too intolerant (δ is too large), then the second term will dominate, and the cheater will partially offset the high rate of reversions by restricting output below quota. It should be understood that J_F depends on the rate of output verification. The greater is the rate of output verification, the greater is the probability of detection so that the cost of cheating may be greater than the gain.

The decision for the cheater to deviate from quota at time t is illustrated in Figure 1. The graph is drawn under the assumption that the cheater is on an optimal path and represents the immediate consequences of deviating from the path. Returns to cheating under three cartel strategies are depicted: a pure trigger price, a pure verification model, and a mixed strategy. The effect of each strategy on the cheater is illustrated by comparison to the optimal choice of deviating from quota when there is no cartel enforcement mechanism, as represented by the upper curve.

Figure 1
Optimal Deviation from Quota

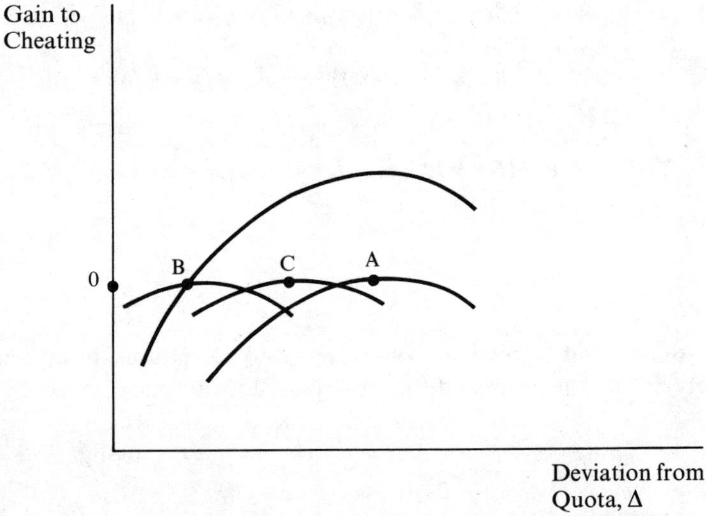

Note: The upper curve represents gains to cheating in the absence of cartel maintenance. The curve with a maximum at A occurs at the same deviation from quota as the upper curve and represents the gain to cheating when the cartel uses only output verification. The curve with a maximum at B represents the gain to cheating when the cartel uses trigger pricing exclusively. The curve with a maximum at C represents the gain to cheating when the cartel employs a combination of output verification and trigger pricing. All three of the lower curves are drawn to have a maximum gain of zero to be consistent with feasibility.

The effect of pure verification is to reduce the level of the curve for all points greater than quota. Verification sufficient for feasibility is shown in Figure 1 by point A. The decision to cheat depends on the level of demand and the current rate of output verification.

The effect of allowed price variations is to decrease the optimal deviation from quota at time t. As more is produced by a cheater, the current gains are offset by putting future gains at risk. Thus, the peak of the cheating returns occurs at a deviation from quota that is less than the optimal deviation under pure output verification. If the allowed price variation is chosen precisely, then the optimal deviation is zero, as illustrated by point B in Figure 1.

The effect of combining the strategies is to shift the gains downward and to decrease the optimal deviation. The reduction in the optimal deviation reduces gains to cheating, and verification shifts the function downward. As in the case of a pure verification strategy, the cheater checks to see if there is a positive gain relative to no deviation from quota. An optimal choice for a cheater that assures feasibility is shown in Figure 1 as point C.

IV. JOINT PROFIT MAXIMIZATION BY THE CARTEL

The cartel chooses the rate of output detection, allowed price variations, length of retaliatory period, and size of quotas to maximize profits. To circumvent agency problems, it is assumed that the cartel earns a percentage of the gains to collusion: the difference between net collusive profits (after cartel costs) and noncollusive profits. The cartel thus acts as a separate entity or trade association with the best interests of its member firms as its single objective. There are three conditions the optimal choice must satisfy:

1. *Feasibility*. The expected gains to cheating cannot exceed zero, which is true if the gain defined in (8), $J(F(t)) \leqslant 0$ for each firm.

2. *Credibility*. In the event that a firm has just been detected cheating or the allowed price variation has been exceeded, then the threatened action must be implemented to maintain credibility. The "perfect" way to establish credibility is to choose the length of the retaliatory period optimally in the event that a firm has just been detected cheating. Thus, credibility is assured when ϕ, δ, T and y^c satisfy

$$(11) \qquad \max_{\phi, \delta, T, y^c} E\left[\int_0^T e^{-rt} R^{nc} dt + \sum_{t > T} G(t) Q^t V\right]$$

subject to $J \leqslant 0$
where: Q is the discount term, V is the expected return to an episode of collusion,[10]

[10] The expectation of the value of an episode of cheating is time independent. See the appendix for more details.

$$V = E\left[\int_0^\infty e^{-rs}[(R^c - w\phi)(1-F) + F\int_t^{t+T} e^{-rv}R^{nc}dv]ds\right]$$

$G(t)$ is the probability that an episode begins at time t, given the episode of collusion following reversion begins at time T, and w is the price of verification.

The definition of credibility used in (11) is conditioned on the constraint that no cheating occurs and that reversions are only the result of stochastic price realizations exceeding allowed price variations. This definition of credibility relies on the feasibility of the cartel.

3. *Sustainability*. The expectation of returns to collusion must exceed the alternative noncollusive return,

$$\int_0^\infty G(t)V(t,\phi^*,\delta^*,y^{c*})dt \geqslant E\int_0^\infty e^{-rt}R^{nc}dt \tag{12}$$

Sustainability is not always possible with output verification, but is possible with a trigger price because the penalty is the noncollusive equilibrium. The expenditure on output verification sufficient to assure feasibility may be so excessive that the cartel is not sustainable.

IV(i). *Quota choice*

In this section, the quota is shown to have little strategic value in maintaining the feasibility of the cartel and is therefore chosen to maximize instantaneous profits. The quota may be considered by some to be a strategic variable because the optimal quota may incorporate a sticky downward adjustment in response to lower prices, or expanded quotas may be less costly to maintain because they represent smaller departures from the noncollusive equilibrium. However, it is argued that sticky adjustments are not optimal by proving that deviations from instantaneous profit maximization do not reduce the cost of maintaining feasibility.

A major difficulty for the cartel is that it cannot distinguish between movement in demand and the effect of deviations from its assigned quota. When the cartel interprets a deviation from quota as a movement in demand, its quota becomes

$$y^c = (a + \theta^0 - c)/2 \tag{13}$$

where $\theta^0 = \theta - \Delta$ is the demand realization imputed by the cartel that has not detected a cheater.

The cartel is fooled by the cheater, which has the effect of improving the returns of the cheater relative to the static model.

There are three cases to address: output verification, allowed price variation, and a mixed strategy.

Output verification. Consider deviations from the hypothesized quota, $y^{c*} = (a+\theta^0 - c)/2$. Increasing the quota has the effect of decreasing feasible collusive returns, R^c, decreasing cheating returns, R^m, and decreasing the gain $= R^m - R^c$.[11] Inspection of the feasibility constraint reveals that the effect of increasing the quota is to reduce the gain and to decrease the severity of the penalty, R^{nc}, by a greater degree. A greater probability of detection is then required for feasibility, which in turn requires a higher rate of output verification and greater cartel expense to maintain a quota that yields inferior gross returns. The alternative is to restrict output from y^{c*}, which has the effect of decreasing feasible collusive returns, increasing cheating returns, increasing the gain to cheating, and decreasing the severity of penalty. A higher probability of detection is then required for feasibility, which requires a higher rate of output detection. Thus, deviation from the hypothesized optimal quota, y^{c*}, reduces gross profit and increases cartel expense so that deviations are not optimal.

Allowed price variation. Again, consider deviations from the hypothesized quota, $y^{c*} = (a+\theta^0 - c)/2$. Any deviation has the effect of reducing the feasible collusive return, R^c, and thus reduces the return to an episode of collusion if the hazard rate of reversion is unaffected. However, if lower quotas allowed the feasible cartel to lower its allowed price variation (lower δ means that more downward price variation is allowed), then the hazard rate of reversion will decrease and the length of time between reversions will increase, which implies a reduction in the cost of cartel maintenance. By showing that a deviation from the hypothesized quota does not allow a reduction in the allowed price variation, the optimality of the hypothesized quota is proven. The effect of increasing the quota relative to the hypothesized quota is to reduce the gain to cheating and reduce the degree by which a cheater will deviate from quota. Consequently, the effect on price is smaller so that distinguishing between cheating and stochastic price movement is more difficult. Feasibility then requires less tolerance of downward price variation. By contrast, the effect of restricting quotas is to increase the gain to cheating, increase the degree by which a cheater will ultimately deviate from quota, and decrease the severity of the penalty. By inspection of (8) it follows that a greater probability of reversion is necessary to maintain feasibility. Again, any deviation from the hypothesized quota increases the cost of the cartel (in reversions) and reduces collusive returns so that deviations cannot be optimal.

Combined strategies. The proofs that deviations from the hypothesized quota under output verification and allowed price variations were really the same: Consider a deviation from the hypothesized quota and show that

[11] The feasible collusive return is the return when no cheating occurs. The feasible return is the relevant comparison for calculating the gains to cheating because it is the alternative opportunity. To calculate R^c substitute $y^c = (a+\theta-c)/2$ into (5) and to calculate R^m substitute y^{c*} into (6).

greater cartel costs are implied by the feasibility constraint. It follows that deviation from the hypothesized quota under a mixed strategy would also not be optimal.

IV(ii). *Price-insensitive cartel*

The cartel that uses output verification ($\eta, \phi > 0$ and $\delta = -\infty$) is considered. The relation between output verification and the other cartel choice variables is derived from the feasibility constraint, $J \leqslant 0$ where J is defined in (8):[12]

$$(14) \qquad \left\{ w\phi + (\eta w + R^{nc} - R^{c})\phi + \left[\frac{R^{m} - R^{c}}{1 - e^{-rT}} + \eta(R^{nc} - R^{c}) \right] \right\} \Bigg|_{\theta = 0} \leqslant 0$$

In the case that inequality is satisfied by a sufficiently large rate of free detection, η, there are never any reversions, and trigger pricing is never employed. (Such a case could arise if public government information is made available to a trade association with sufficient speed.) In the alternative case, the rate of detection may be solved for as a positive real root of the equality $J = 0$:

$$(15) \qquad \phi^* = -\frac{A}{2w} - \frac{1}{2w}[A^2 - 4wB]^{1/2}$$

where

$$A = \eta w + R^{nc} - R^{c}$$

and

$$B = \left[\frac{R^{m} - R^{c}}{1 - e^{-rT}} + \eta(R^{nc} - R^{c}) \right]$$

The optimal rate of detection is real if $A^2 - 4wB \geqslant 0$. It is worth noting that the output detection rate is negatively related to the length of the retaliatory period in (15), and the optimal rate of output verification in (15) is greater than the rate of free verification sufficient for feasibility because expenditures on verification reduce the real penalty. Also, the pure output verification strategy may not be sustainable because the expenditures on output checks may exceed the gain to collusion, as suggested in (12).[13]

The remaining choice variable for the cartel is the length of a retaliatory period. Cartel costs are directly related to the length of the period because a longer retaliatory period allows the use of a lower rate of output verification.[14]

[12] See the appendix for details on method of integration.

[13] The pure verification strategy fails when the price of verification is sufficiently high or when demand is sufficiently low. See Lanning [1985] for numeric examples.

[14] The expression in brackets in (15) is increased as T increases because $R^m - R^c > 0$ and $\partial[\mathrm{EXP}(-rT) - 1]^{-1}/\partial T < 0$.

Figure 2
Set of Feasible Combinations of Output Verification and Allowed Price Variation

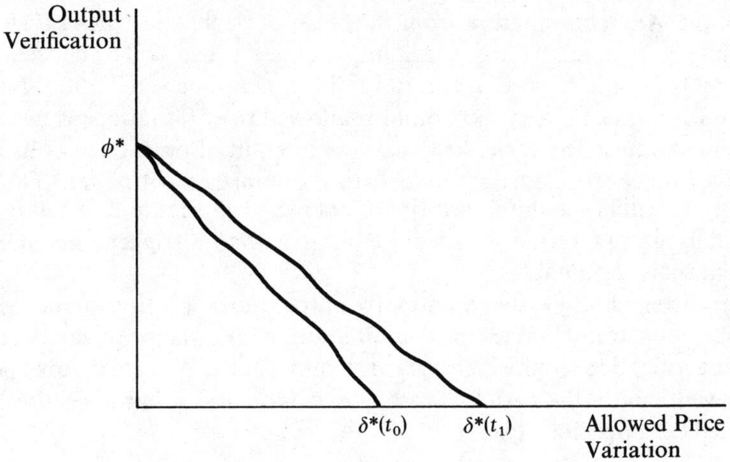

Note: time $t_0 < t_1$, and the demand curve is held constant. The scales are exponential to allow representation of no trigger pricing ($\delta = -\infty$) as 0.

Longer retaliation obviously costs the cartel foregone profits, but it reduces future costs, so the cartel will balance profits foregone in the immediate retaliatory period with higher future costs. The optimal balance is determined by the discount rate.

IV(iii). *Allowed price variations and output verification*

The cartel may use a pure trigger price strategy, a pure output verification strategy when it is sustainable, or the two simultaneously. The optimal solution may be a persistent trigger price strategy if the price of verification is sufficiently high that pure verification is not sustainable. However, a persistent pure output verification strategy (that requires $\phi > 0$) is not optimal because initially a trigger price strategy costs less. Allowed price variations are used exclusively at the initiation of the cartel because stochastic variation is negligible, so that allowance of very little price variation insures feasibility at no cost.

In Figure 2 the combination of controls that ensure feasibility are illustrated. The possible combinations of strategies have the pure strategies as end points. The curve is drawn under the assumption that before and after time t, the cartel is on an optimal path. For a threatened reversion of length T, the cartel may use output verification exclusively, which is represented along the vertical axis by ϕ^*, or it may use allowed price variation exclusively which is represented along the horizontal axis by δ^*, or any combination of the two.[15] The curve is downward sloping because there is a tradeoff between the two that is apparent directly from the hazard function (4) and the feasibility constraint. Any combination from the set of feasible strategies satisfies the feasibility constraint so the one that implies lowest costs will be chosen. For a given realization of demand, the end point for output verification does not change with time, but the end point for allowed price variations is increasing with time because the cartel becomes less tolerant of price deviations as the power of the one-tailed test for cheating diminishes with time. Thus, the strategy set shifts outward with time as depicted in Figure 2. It follows that eventually output verification will be cheaper than a trigger price if output verification is sustainable.

The cartel chooses the monopoly output level for its quotas, so the feasibility constraint defines the combinations of allowed price variations and output verification from which the cartel may choose. For retaliatory periods of a given length, the cartel chooses the combination that gives the lowest expected cost. Specifically,

$$(16) \qquad C(\phi, \delta) = \min_{\phi,\delta} E \int_0^\infty \left[e^{-rt}(1-F(\delta))w\phi + F(\delta) \int_t^{t+T} e^{-rs}(R^c - R^{nc} - w\phi)ds \right] dt$$

$$\text{subject to } J \leqslant 0$$

The cost of verification is subtracted from the penalty in the second integral in (16) because there are no verification costs while in a reversionary mode. The foregone profit is the real penalty or cost of a reversion and is the difference between the return earned in a collusive mode and the return while in a reversion minus the expenditure on verification. The optimal combination depends on the length of the retaliatory period, which is defined by the credibility constraint.

The cartel chooses the combination of output verification and allowed price variation to minimize the cost of feasibility at every instant. Let the function $\phi^*(\delta)$ define the rate of output verification that satisfies the feasibility constraint for a given allowed price variation. The instantaneous expenditure on feasibility, $c(\phi, \delta, t)$ is the integrand of (16). Taking the derivative with respect to the allowed price variation along the feasible set of strategies yields

$$(17) \qquad \partial c/\partial\delta = e^{-rt}\left[w\frac{\partial\phi^*}{\partial\delta}e^{-\lambda t} - w\phi t\frac{\partial\lambda}{\partial\delta}e^{-\lambda t}\right.$$

[15] Green and Porter [1984] and Abreu, Pearce and Stacchetti [1985] have established the existence of trigger prices that ensure feasibility in the context of models more general than the present model.

$$+t\frac{\partial\lambda}{\partial\delta}e^{-\lambda t}(1-e^{-rt})(R^c-R^{nc}-w\phi)/r$$

$$\left.-(1-e^{-\lambda t})(1-e^{-rT})\frac{w}{r}\frac{\partial\phi^*}{\partial\delta}\right]$$

To establish that the cartel uses trigger pricing exclusively at its inception, evaluate (17) at the inception of a collusive mode ($t = 0$), and note that the derivative is negative for all values of allowed price variations that support feasibility:

$$\partial c/\partial\delta\,|_{t=0} = w(\partial\phi^*/\partial\delta) < 0$$

The derivative $\partial\phi^*/\partial\delta$ is negative because there is a negative tradeoff between output verification and allowed price variations. This implies a corner solution of trigger pricing alone.

Eventually, the cartel switches away from trigger pricing to output verification. The optimality of such a switch is evident from the limit of the undiscounted instantaneous cost, which is the expression inside the square braces in (17):

$$\lim_{t\to\infty} e^{rt}\partial c/\partial\delta = -(w/r)(\partial\phi^*/\partial\delta) > 0$$

Expenditures on feasibility are increasing over all feasible combinations as the allowed price variation is increased. Consequently, a corner solution of pure output verification must eventually prevail.

The cartel switches between its two strategies rather than making a transition that uses them simultaneously. The strategies are perfect complements in the sense that a trigger price exists so that the rate of reversion, λ, has an additive effect with output verification on the rate of reversion given in (4). Thus, intuition suggests that the cartel should choose the cheapest strategy. However, the costs generated from each have different effects on feasibility. Output verification reduces the real penalty and increases the information requirement necessary for feasibility. In this way, the deterrent effect of trigger pricing is eroded. As noted in section IV(ii) above, the same is true of output verification. Consequently, the intuition is correct, and the cartel should choose the least expensive strategy. To prove that the cartel switches, it is sufficient to show that $\partial c/\partial\delta$ is monotonically increasing in time ($\partial^2 c/\partial\delta\partial t > 0$), which follows directly from the positive sign on $\partial\lambda/\partial\delta$ and the negative sign on $\partial\phi^*/\partial\delta$. The cartel first employs trigger pricing and, if it lasts long enough, it switches to output verification.

Thus, cartel behavior first appears as a Markov chain as described by Green and Porter [1984], and Abreu, Pearce and Stacchetti [1985] with the modification that there is an absorbing state that is attained if the time between reversions equals the switching time. A young cartel may be characterized as one that uses trigger pricing and a mature cartel as one that uses output verification. An empirical test of cartels confronted with stationary demand curves are presented by Green and Porter [1984]. The test is predicated on the Markov prices, collusive and penalty, that result from optimal cartel behavior. The test may be generalized by adding to the Markov model the "absorbing" state that results from output verification.[16]

V. IMPLICATIONS OF CARTEL COSTS AND CONCLUSION

In the event that firms cannot agree to a merger or merger is blocked by antitrust authorities, the second best solution is collusion whenever it is sustainable. Collusion is a second best solution to cost free mergers because it involves unavoidable costs to maintain the feasibility of a cartel. When demand is nonstationary, the costs of maintaining a cartel are increasing because the effectiveness of a given trigger price decays with time until the cost equals that of output verification, and a switch is optimal. The implications for welfare are necessarily mixed. While the cartel is young and alternating between collusive and noncollusive modes, welfare is improved relative to a monopoly. However, welfare is decreased relative to a monopoly once the cartel is mature because it produces the monopoly output at greater cost. Thus, welfare relative to a monopolist depends on the discount rate and the probability that a cartel will attain maturity by a given date. An implication for policy is also mixed. Increasing the costs of operating a cartel by imposing greater penalties may reduce the sustainability of some cartels and alter the optimal switching in a way that improves welfare. However, these deterrents may also make mergers more attractive and improve the likelihood that merger negotiations are successful. A result without a mixed conclusion is that if the government has decided to allow a long standing cartel, then it should supply the cartel with output verification because it can do so at less expense. This follows from the observation that less free output verification (to the cartel) is required to support feasibility than is required when the cartel is paying because the expense reduces real penalties.

The characterization of a cartel has been generalized. The cartel that uses a trigger price may eventually switch to output verification, and in the event that verification becomes nonsustainable, the cartel returns to trigger pricing at the end of a retaliatory period. The nature of the demand-disturbance term drives the model to an optimal switching time. If independently identically distributed (stationary) disturbances characterized demand variation instead of a Wiener process, then the cartel will choose the strategy that generates the

[16] The degree of absorption will depend on the price level at the time of the switch. A lower price level implies a greater probability that demand will fall below the level at which verification is sustainable and trigger a reversion. Thus, the higher is the price level, the greater is the degree of absorption. The Markov properties of a trigger price model with Wiener demand disturbances have been investigated by Abreu, Pearce and Stacchetti [1985].

lowest maintenance costs and never switch. Cartels that choose a trigger price strategy will exhibit occasional reversions, whereas cartels that choose output verification will have no reversions to penalty or noncollusive equilibria. The prediction supported by these results is that when demand is stationary, cartels may choose a strategy of pure trigger pricing or pure output review, and when demand is nonstationary, they switch from trigger pricing to an output review.

STEVEN G. LANNING,
Bell Laboratories,
600 Mountain Avenue,
Murray Hill,
New Jersey 07974,
USA

ACCEPTED DECEMBER 1986

APPENDIX

Derivation of (11): The expectation of $e^{-rt}(R^c - w\phi)$ is finite for finite t and the limit of $E_\theta[e^{-rt}(R^c - w\phi)] = \lim_{t\to\infty} [\sigma t e^{-rt} + R^c(0) - w\phi] = 0 + R^c(0) - w\phi$, so the expectation, $E_\theta \int_0^\infty e^{-rt}(R^c(\theta(t)) - w\phi)dt = 0 + [R^c(0) - w\phi]/r$. See Schuss [1980, p. 64] for proof that the expectation of a definite stochastic integral is zero if the expectation of the integrand is finite.

Derivation of (14): When the cartel is not sensitive to price variation, allowed price variation, $\delta = -\infty$, so $\lambda = 0$ and the second term in (10) is zero. It follows that the optimal degree of deviation from quota is given by $\Delta = (a + \theta - c - y^{c+1})/2$ and may be substituted directly into (8) and evaluated like a Riemann integral with $\theta = 0$ because the expectation of $\theta(t)e^{-rt}$ and $\theta^2(t)e^{-rt}$ are zero for finite t and the limit of the expectation of both terms is zero as $t \to \infty$. See Schuss [1980, p. 64] for details on definite stochastic integrals.

REFERENCES

ABREU, D., PEARCE, D. and STACCHETTI, E., 1985, 'Optimal Cartel Equilibria with Imperfect Monitoring', mimeo, Harvard University.

FRIEDMAN, J. W., 1971, 'A Noncooperative Equilibrium for Supergames', *Review of Economic Studies*, 28, pp. 1–12.

FRIEDMAN, J. W., 1986, *Game Theory with Applications to Economics* (Oxford University Press).

GASKINS, D. W., 1971, 'Dynamic Limit Pricing: Optimal Pricing Under Threat of New Entry', *Journal of Economic Theory*, 3, 306–322.

GREEN, E. J. and PORTER, R. H., 1984, 'Noncooperative Collusion under Imperfect Price Information', *Econometrica*, 52, pp. 87–100.

KAMIEN, M. I. and SCHWARTZ, N. L., 1971, 'Limit Pricing and Uncertain Entry', *Econometrica*, 39, pp. 441–454.

KAMIEN, M. I. and SCHWARTZ, N. L., 1981, *Dynamic Optimization: The Calculus of Variations and Optimal Control in Economics and Management* (North Holland).

Lanning, S. G., 1985, 'Cartel Costs, Quotas and Regulation', mimeo.

Porter, R. H., 1983, 'Optimal Cartel Trigger Price Strategies', *Journal of Economic Theory*, 29, pp. 313–338.

Radner, R., 1985, 'Repeated Principal-Agent Games with Discounting', *Econometrica*, 53, pp. 1173–1198.

Rotemberg, J. R. and Saloner, G., 1986, 'A Supergame-Theoretic Model of Price Wars during Booms', *American Economic Review*, 76, pp. 390–407.

Salant, S. W., Switzer, S. and Reynolds, R. J., 1983, 'Losses From Horizontal Merger: The Effects of an Exogenous Change in Industry Structure on Cournot-Nash Equilibrium', *Quarterly Journal of Economics*, 98, pp. 185–199.

Schuss, Z., 1980, *Theory and Applications of Stochastic Differential Equations* (Wiley & Sons).

THE JOURNAL OF INDUSTRIAL ECONOMICS 0022-1821 $2.00
Volume XXXVI December 1987 No. 2

MARKET GROWTH, ECONOMIES OF SCALE, AND PLANT SIZE IN THE CHEMICAL PROCESSING INDUSTRIES*

MARVIN B. LIEBERMAN

What factors determine the size of new industrial plants? This study uses data on 22 chemical products to test alternative models of capacity expansion, including the Manne model and a "scale frontier" model. The empirical results strongly support the scale frontier model: the size of new plants increased along a time trend that was unrelated to market concentration, market growth, or the magnitude of investment scale economies. Entrants typically built smaller plants than incumbents, but all firms built plants closer to the technological frontier when small plants carried a higher relative cost penalty.

INTRODUCTION

IN INDUSTRIES with plant-level economies of scale, do firms undertake larger capacity expansions when industry growth is more rapid? Do new entrants tend to build smaller plants than incumbents? More generally, what factors influence the size of new plants and shifts in optimal plant size over time? This paper explores these issues and tests alternative models of capacity expansion.[1]

The analysis is based on a data sample covering 22 chemical products over a period of roughly 25 years. The sample includes a total of 422 plants that were constructed during the coverage period. The chemical industry provides an excellent focus for the empirical analysis, given the availability of plant capacity and engineering data and the existence of well-documented economies of scale at the plant level.

Two alternative models of capacity expansion are tested. The first is the classic model of capacity expansion originally developed by Alan Manne [1967]. This model, based on a trade-off between scale economies and capacity holding costs, implies that the optimal policy is to expand with a fixed cycle time between investment dates, so that expansion sizes are directly proportional to market growth. The alternative model, which has never been clearly formalized in the literature, suggests that although economies of scale are in principle available up to very large plant sizes, at any given point in time the maximum feasible scale is limited by technological constraints. With

* Helpful comments of Raphael Amit, Robert Hayes, Alan Manne, Steven Wheelright, Larry White and two anonymous referees are gratefully acknowledged.

[1] This paper focuses on the *size* of new plants; related papers (Gilbert and Lieberman [1987], Lieberman [1987]) examine the *timing* of capacity expansion decisions.

technical progress over time, these constraints are gradually lifted, thereby allowing the construction of larger-scale plants.

The paper is organized as follows. Section I discusses the Manne model and its implications regarding the scale and timing of new plant capacity. Section II discusses the scale frontier model. Section III describes the data sample and the variables used in the empirical tests. Section IV tests the Manne and the scale frontier models. Section V considers a series of factors that might be expected to influence the movement of the scale frontier. A concluding section summarizes the empirical findings and appraises the models and the validity of their underlying assumptions.

I. MANNE MODEL

The classic model of capacity expansion with investment economies of scale is Manne [1967]. The model gives the cost minimizing investment policy for a single firm that must build new plants to service a growing demand. Given the assumptions of the model, the optimal policy is to allow a constant cycle time between investment dates. This implies that the capacity of each new plant equals the incremental demand growth between investment dates.

The assumptions of the basic model are as follows:

(1) Demand grows at a constant linear rate of G units per year.[2] Assuming a time interval of T years between successive expansions, plant size equals GT.

(2) The firm is required to service all demand—backlogs and deficits are not permitted.[3]

(3) The firm cannot adjust price to change the quantity demanded. Moreover, there is no price or quantity competition among producers.

(4) All expansions take the form of new plants—expansion of existing plants is not permitted.

(5) Capital investment costs are an exponential function of plant size, i.e.,

$$C(GT) = c_0(GT)^{\alpha}, \qquad \alpha < 1 \tag{1.1}$$

where $C(GT)$ represents the total plant investment cost, GT is the capacity of the plant, and α is the scale economy parameter. The model assumes that an infinite range of plant sizes are technically feasible, and scale economies are characterized by the parameter α over the entire range.[4]

(6) Plants have an infinite economic life (or equivalently, are replaced by an identical plant at the end of their life).

[2] The model yields similar results if demand growth is geometric (Srinivasan [1967]) or stochastic (Manne [1961]; Giglio [1970]).

[3] Allowing for backlogs and deficits leads to an increase in the optimal plant size and cycle time; however, the constant cycle time policy remains optimal. See Manne [1961] and Erlenkotter [1967].

[4] The exponential function provides a reasonably accurate representation of scale economies in many industries, at least within the range of existing plant sizes. See Haldi and Whitcomb [1967], and Chilton [1960].

(7) Operating costs (labor and materials) are constant per unit of output and independent of plant size. In other words, scale economies arise only in fixed investment costs. The average variable cost curve is horizontal up to the full production capacity of the plant.
(8) The opportunity cost of capital is constant at interest rate r.

Given the validity of these assumptions, choice of the optimal plant size involves trading off scale economies in capital investment against the cost of holding greater idle capacity during the early life of the plant. (In the absence of scale economies, expansion would take place in infinitely small increments.) The firm's optimal policy is to allow a constant cycle time between investment dates. If demand growth is arithmetic, this cycle time T, is given implicitly by the formula (Manne [1967]):

$$(1.2) \qquad \alpha = \frac{rT}{e^{rT}-1}$$

where α is the scale economy parameter and r is the interest rate. While this formula must be solved numerically, Freidenfelds [1981, p. 82] shows that:

$$(1.3) \qquad t = 2(1/r)(1/\alpha - 1)$$

provides a good approximation for the optimal cycle time between expansions.

A key result of the model is that this cycle time is independent of the growth rate of demand. This implies that the optimal plant size is proportional to the demand growth rate. The constant cycle time result is fairly robust to changes in the assumptions regarding demand growth or the nature of investment scale economies; it holds if demand grows at a constant geometric rate (Srinivasan [1967]), or if the investment cost function is characterized by an initial fixed cost plus a variable cost per unit of capacity (Freidenfelds [1981, pp. 73–81]).[5]

Optimal plant size equals optimal cycle time multiplied by G, the market growth rate faced by the firm. Unfortunately, data on output and output growth at the individual firm level are not publicly available. Thus, for the empirical work it is necessary to assume that the firm obtains some fraction of total industry output growth. If this fraction depends on the firm's pre-expansion share of industry capacity, the firm's output growth rate can be represented as:

$$(1.4) \qquad g = Q(\Delta Q/Q)S^{b_1}$$

where Q total is industry output and S is the capacity share of the firm.

New entrants have an initial capacity share of zero, so it is necessary to assign them some positive fraction of industry output growth. This is done by

[5] Although the model yields a unique optimum cycle time, the total discounted cost function is relatively flat over a wide range in the vicinity of the optimum. This means that deviations from the optimum cycle time (within a reasonable range) have only a small impact on total discounted costs.

arbitrarily setting S for new entrants equal to $1/(N+1)$, where N is the number of firms in the industry, and including an entry dummy to correct for the average bias introduced by this procedure. The firm's output growth thus becomes:

$$(1.5) \qquad g = Q(\Delta Q/Q)S^{b_1}E^{b_2}$$

where E is the entry dummy.

Combining equations (1.3) and (1.5), the optimal plant size, K', is approximately equal to:

$$(1.6) \qquad K' \approx gt$$
$$\approx 2Q(\Delta Q/Q)S^{b_1}E^{b_2}(1/r)(1/\alpha - 1)$$

Taking logs one obtains:

$$(1.7) \qquad \log K' \approx c + \log Q + \log(\Delta Q/Q) + b_1 \log S + b_2 \log E$$
$$- \log r + \log(1/\alpha - 1)$$

A regression conforming to this specification for the Manne model is tested empirically in section IV. The model predicts a negative regression coefficient for the interest rate ($\log r$), and positive, unitary coefficients for market size ($\log Q$), market growth ($\log \Delta Q/Q$), and the degree of investment scale economies ($\log(1/\alpha - 1)$).

II. SCALE FRONTIER MODEL

Several studies have noted that while scale economies are available in principle up to very large plant sizes, the construction of ever-larger plants typically requires the solution of numerous technical problems (Levin [1977]; Hughes [1971]; Cowing [1974]; Pearl and Enos [1975]; Hollander, [1965]; Sultan [1975]). In effect, there is a moving "scale frontier" that defines the largest economically feasible plant that can be constructed at any point in time. Technical progress in many capital intensive industries has taken the form of pushing out this scale frontier to exploit potential scale economies.

In a production function framework, movement in the scale frontier can be modeled as scale-augmenting technical change. Empirically, however, it is typically difficult to distinguish scale-augmenting change from other forms of non-neutral technical change (Lau and Tamura [1972]; Diamond, McFadden and Rodriguez [1978]; Sato [1970]). Consequently, the production function approach has not been particularly fruitful in this area, and the interpretation of results is often arbitrary.

There have been few attempts to model the scale frontier phenomenon theoretically. One notable exception is Levin [1978] who considers the effects of scale-augmenting technical change on barriers to entry and market structure. Levin assumes that the rate of advance depends solely on the research expenditures of each individual firm; different results would apply if the rate of advance is determined by the collective expenditures of all firms in the industry or by the research activities of outside firms. Levin's work thus raises an important (but empirically unresolved) question: is movement in the scale frontier exogenously determined, or is it influenced by endogenous factors such as R & D spending and market concentration?

While prior studies have documented the scale frontier phenomenon, they have failed to evaluate the mechanisms that advance the frontier. The rate of advance may be a function of time, or of investment in new capacity, or of resources devoted to process improvement. Given this lack of knowledge regarding the mechanisms that shift the scale frontier, we initially model the frontier as a simple geometric time trend. Let $K_{i,t}$ be the scale frontier at any time t, and b_0 be the rate of advance. The moving frontier can then be represented as:

$$K_{i,t} = ce^{b_0 t} K_{i,t_0} \tag{2.1}$$

$$\log K_{i,t} = c' + b_0 t + \log K_{i,t_0} \tag{2.2}$$

This formulation assumes that all firms will build their new plants at the prevailing scale frontier. Such behavior is consistent with cost minimization in a constrained version of the Manne model, where maximum feasible plant size is less than the optimal plant size given by the unconstrained model. However, even if the range of feasible plant sizes extends beyond the Manne optimum, competitive price adjustment may force all firms to build frontier-scale plants.

Furthermore, there are a number of reasons why firms may choose to build plants of less than frontier scale. New entrants may lack the construction and operating expertise needed to build and run frontier-scale plants and thus may opt for smaller, more proven designs. Entrants may build relatively small plants to avoid generating excess capacity that could trigger industry price cutting or retaliation by market incumbents. Entrants and vertically-integrated incumbents may simply lack outlets to market the entire output of large-scale plants.

Thus, one might expect plants of less than frontier size to be constructed by new entrants, or by incumbent firms facing marketing constraints. However, the extent of deviation from the frontier should depend upon the relative cost penalty associated with small scale plants. With a larger cost penalty, all plants would be built closer to the frontier.

These factors suggest the following more general formulation:

$$\log K_{i,t} = c' + b_0 t + b_1 \log K_{i,t_0} + b_2\, \text{ENTRY} + b_3 \log CDR_i + \varepsilon \tag{2.3}$$

where $K_{i,t}$ represents the size of plants actually constructed, K_{i,t_0} is a benchmark plant size for year t_0, ENTRY is a dummy variable defined for new entry, CDR represents the relative cost disadvantage of small scale plants,

TABLE I
LIST OF PRODUCTS INCLUDED IN DATA SAMPLE

Acrylonitrile (1959–82)
Aniline (1961–82)
Ammonia (1960–82)
Bisphenol A (1959–82)
Caprolactam (1962–82)
Cyclohexane (1956–82)
Ethylene (1964–82)
Ethylene Glycol (1960–82)
Formaldehyde (1962–82)
Isopropyl Alcohol (1964–82)
Maleic Anhydride (1959–82)
Methanol (1957–82)
Nylon Fibers (1954–82)
Phenol (1959–82)
Phthalic Anhydride (1955–82)
Polyester Fibers (1954–82)
Polyethylene-LD (1958–82)
Polyethylene-HD (1958–82)
Styrene (1958–82)
Urea (1962–82)
Vinyl Acetate (1960–82)
Vinyl Chloride (1962–82)

and ε is a random error term. This is the regression specification tested empirically in section IV. We expect $b_0 > 0$ if new plant sizes increased over time, $b_2 < 0$ if entrants built smaller plants than incumbents, and $b_3 > 0$ if firms built plants closer to the scale frontier when small plants carried a relatively greater cost penalty.

III. DATA SAMPLE AND COMPUTATION OF VARIABLES

The data sample used in this study covers the 22 chemical products listed in Table I. There are approximately 20 years of coverage for each product. The sample includes 422 chemical plants. The sample is limited to new "greenfield" plants; expansions of existing facilities are excluded.[6]

The data on new plant capacity were collected from annual issues of the *Directory of Chemical Producers* published by SRI International. Annual data on total industry output of each product were obtained from annual issues of *Synthetic Organic Chemicals.* Engineering estimates of investment scale economies and unit production costs over a range of plant sizes were obtained from the 1976 issue of the *SRI Process Economics Program Handbook.* Additional data on R&D expenditures were obtained from

[6] The sample is a subset of a larger dataset on the chemical industry collected by the author. The sample includes plants for all products in the larger dataset for which engineering data on plant-level scale economies could be obtained.

Compustat; and data on process patents were collected from *Chemical Abstracts*.[7]

The products in the sample are all homogeneous, commodity-type chemicals or related products. Production capacities of all products are well defined; chemicals with production processes involving significant joint products have been excluded, as have those where production capacity can be switched from one product to another in response to shifts in market demand. Unit variable costs for any given plant tend to be relatively constant up to the level defined by its full production capacity.

Output was often consumed captively in firms' downstream operations, but for all products at least 25 percent of industry output was sold through arms-length channels. All products in the sample demonstrated positive net output growth from the earliest year of coverage through at least 1975. Thus, the sample represents products with growing demand, although in a few cases output declined after 1975.

Dependent variable

The sample consists of one observation for each new plant built during the coverage period for each product in Table I. The dependent variable, K_{ijt}, equals the total announced initial capacity of a new plant to produce product i constructed by firm j during year t.[8] Capacity is measured in thousands of pounds per year. K_{ijt} was converted to logarithms.

Independent variables

The following independent variables were used in the regressions. All variables except the time trend and entry dummy were converted to logarithms.

Time trend ($TIME_t$). The last 2 digits of the observation year were used as a time trend.

Total industry output. Q_{it} is the total physical volume of output of product i (measured in thousands of pounds) produced by all firms in the industry during the observation year t in which expansion took place.

Growth rate of industry output. $GROW_{it}$ is the percentage increase in industry output over the three years prior to and including the expansion year, measured in thousands of pounds. ($GROW_{it} = (Q_{it} - Q_{it-3})/Q_{it-3}$). Since all variables were converted to logarithms, GROW is defined only for observations with positive market growth.

[7] A detailed appendix describing the data and sources is available from the author.

[8] The mean value of K_{ijt} obviously varies across industries. To control for industry effects, the regressions in Table II were also run with the dependent variable scaled to represent plant size as a fraction of total industry output (K_{ijt}/Q_{it}) and plant size relative to the SRI benchmark ($K_{ijt}/K76_i$), with the output and benchmark variables omitted from the right-hand-side of the regressions. The results for the remaining variables were very similar to those reported in Table II.

Capacity of "typical" new plant in 1976. $K76_i$ is the benchmark plant size used by SRI. SRI estimates the cost of plants constructed at both one-half and twice this benchmark size. According to SRI, "these (benchmark) capacities are representative of sizes for competitive U.S. plants which might be built today (1976)."

Extent of scale economies in capital investment costs. $SCALE_i$ equals $(1/\alpha_i - 1)$, where α_i is the scale economy exponent for the product, based on SRI estimates. A larger value of SCALE implies more extensive scale economies.

Cost disadvantage ratio of small scale plants. CDR_i equals the average total unit cost of a small scale plant (one-half benchmark scale) divided by the average total unit cost of a large scale plant (twice benchmark scale), based on SRI engineering estimates. *CDR* is based on *total* production costs rather than capital investment costs alone. *CDR* is distinct from SCALE primarily because of differences across products in the magnitude of capital costs as a percent of total production costs.

Entry dummy. $ENTRY_{ijt}$ was set equal to 1 if the plant was built by a firm that had not previously produced product *i*.

TABLE II
REGRESSION ANALYSIS OF NEW PLANT SIZE†
Dependent Variable: K_{ijt}

Model:	1 Manne	2 Scale Frontier	3 Combined
constant	−1.1	−5.49	−5.39
	(−3.1)	(−8.6)	(−7.3)
r_t	0.280		0.297
	(1.7)		(2.0)
$SCALE_i$	−1.41		−0.191
	(−10.1)		(−1.0)
Q_{it}	0.540		0.178
	(11.1)		(3.0)
$GROW_{it}$	−0.182		0.010
	(−3.0)		(0.2)
$SHARE_{ijt}$	0.089		0.231
	(1.3)		(3.6)
$ENTRY_{ijt}$	−0.459	−0.512	−0.498
	(−4.8)	(−5.7)	(−5.7)
$TIME_t$		0.087	0.073
		(10.4)	(6.6)
$K76_i$		0.767	0.698
		(16.8)	(8.4)
CDR_i		1.84	1.58
		(2.1)	(1.7)
R^2	0.531	0.594	0.619
No. of Obs.	392	392	392

† All variables except TIME and ENTRY are in logarithms. Plants built during periods of negative growth are excluded. Numbers in parenthesis are t-statistics.

Real interest rate. The real interest rate, r_t, was estimated as the BAA long-term corporate bond rate, minus the expected rate of inflation. The expected inflation rate was taken as a five-year moving average of changes in the GNP deflator, with linearly declining weights over the period.

Firm's share of total industry capacity. $SHARE_{ijt}$ is firm j's share of total industry capacity for product i, prior to construction of the new plant. For new entrants, SHARE is set equal to $1/(N+1)$, where N is the number of firms in the industry prior to entry.

Several additional explanatory variables are defined in section V.

IV. EMPIRICAL TEST OF MANNE AND SCALE FRONTIER MODELS

Table II reports regression results comparing the Manne and scale frontier models. The Manne model (in the form represented by equation (1.7)) is estimated in regression 1. The model performs quite poorly in describing the size of plants in the sample. The key parameters of the model—r, SCALE, and GROW—have signs opposite to those predicted. The regression coefficients imply (rather perversely) that lower interest rates, more rapid market growth, and more extensive scale economies led firms to build comparatively *smaller* plants.

Other coefficients in regression 1 are more consistent with expectations. Plant size was positively related to total market size. This is largely a scaling effect, reflecting the fact that low unit value chemicals (e.g., fertilizers) tend to have large tonnage markets and are also produced in large tonnage plants. The SHARE coefficient in regression 1 is positive but small—on average a doubling of market share induced only a 6% increase in new plant size.[9]

In the test of the scale frontier model (regression 2), the coefficients generally conform to predictions and are all highly significant. The TIME coefficients reveal that the size of new plants increased at an average rate of about 8% per year across all products in the sample. Thus, there is clear evidence of a shifting "scale frontier."

The benchmark plant size, $K76$, appears highly significant, although its coefficient is below unity. It is likely that this downward bias results from "errors" in the benchmark estimates.[10]

ENTRY appears uniformly negative and significant, confirming that new plants built by entrants were substantially smaller than those built by incumbents. The coefficients imply that, on average, entrants' plants were only about 60% as large as incumbents' plants.[11] Entrants were an important

[9] The coefficient in regression 3 is somewhat larger, implying a 17% increase in plant size for each doubling of share. A detailed analysis of the time intervals between capacity expansions by a given firm (including incremental expansions) revealed that larger firms tended to expand more frequently, rather than in larger absolute increments. The Manne model predicts identical inter-expansion cycle times for all firms.

[10] Deviations between the SRI estimates and the "true" scale frontier in 1976 biases the K76 coefficient downward.

[11] Entrants' relative plant size equals e^{b_2}, where b_2 is the coefficient of the ENTRY dummy.

source of new plants, accounting for about half of the new plants in the sample.

Although entrants built smaller plants than incumbents, their plant size decisions were sensitive to the cost penalty of small scale operation, as recorded by *CDR*. Entrants' plant scale was closer to that of incumbents (and in general, all new plants were built closer to the prevailing scale frontier) when *CDR* was large. As a rough guide, the *CDR* coefficients imply that each 1% differential in unit production cost between small and large scale plants led to about a 2% increase in the average size of new plants relative to the SRI benchmarks.

Regression 3 includes the variables from both models. The scale frontier parameters are highly significant and retain the expected signs. In contrast, the two key variables of the Manne model, *SCALE* and *GROW*, are statistically insignificant, and the interest rate, *r*, continues to carry the "wrong" sign. Thus, the empirical evidence strongly supports the *SCALE* frontier model. The size of new plants increased over time, remarkably independent of changes in market growth, interest rates, or the extent of static scale economies.[12]

The poor performance of the Manne model indicates that at least one of the model's underlying assumptions is invalid. One obvious candidate is the assumption that an infinite range of plant sizes is technically feasible. In their planning study, Erlenkotter and Manne [1968] found that technical limits on the size of fertilizer plants in the 1960s virtually determined the optimal plant size. This finding appears to have held more generally for a wide range of chemical products over a relatively long period of time.

V. FACTORS AFFECTING THE RATE OF SCALE ADVANCE

The results in Table II document significant increases in plant size over time. To supplement these results, a series of additional variables and interaction terms were tested to identify factors influencing the rate of advance of the scale frontier and the relative size differential between entrants' and incumbents' plants. The interaction terms were computed by multiplying *TIME* and *ENTRY* by various interaction variables described below.

[12] The Manne and scale frontier models ignore changes in factor prices that might influence firms' plant size decisions. In a capital-intensive industry such as chemicals, firms might be particularly sensitive to anticipated changes in plant construction costs. The commonly accepted index of construction costs in the chemical industry is the Plant Construction Cost Index published annually by *Chemical Engineering*. The percentage change in this index (over the 3-year period prior to the observation year) was tested as an explanatory variable in the regressions. This measure proved statistically insignificant. However, the percentage change in plant construction costs, divided by the percentage change in the price index for "chemicals and allied products," proved positive and significant (0.05 level), thus indicating some tendency for firms to build larger plants during periods when construction costs were escalating faster than product prices. However, this relative inflation term added little to the variance in plant sizes explained by the regression model.

TABLE III
SUPPLEMENTARY REGRESSION RESULTS FOR THE SCALE FRONTIER MODEL†
Dependent Variable: K_{ijt}

	4	5	6	7	8
constant	*a*	*a*	*a*	*a*	*a*
$TIME_t$	0.081	0.143	0.112	0.041	0.069
	(6.0)	(5.7)	(8.4)	(1.3)	(2.9)
$TIME_t \times SCALE_i$		−0.146			
		(−2.8)			
Q_{it}		−0.048	−0.070		
		(−0.4)	(−0.6)		
r_t	0.152	0.090			
	(1.2)	(0.7)			
$ENTRY_{ijt}$	−0.481	−0.806	−0.321	−0.174	
	(−5.9)	(−4.8)	(−2.5)	(−1.3)	
$SHARE_{ijt}$		0.109			
		(2.1)			
OIL_{ijt}		0.204			
		(2.0)			
$ICUMCAP_{it}$					0.021
					(0.1)
$FCUMCAP_{ijt}$					0.108
					(2.0)
$PATFOR_{it}$				0.669	
				(2.8)	
$PATUSA_{it}$				−0.233	
				(−0.8)	
$DPAT_{ijt}$				0.239	
				(1.8)	
R^2	0.659	0.671	0.684	0.716	0.630
No. of Obs.	422	422	140[b]	140[b]	201[c]

† All variables except TIME, ENTRY, OIL, and the patent measures are in logarithms. Numbers in parenthesis are t-statistics.
[a] Separate constant terms estimated for each product.
[b] Patent data cover only 13 products and are limited to years prior to 1975.
[c] Excludes observations for new entrants.

In these regressions, some of which are reported in Table III, separate constant terms were included for each of the products in the sample. These constant terms control for differences across products in mean plant size. Hence the other regression terms reported in Table III reflect changes in plant size over time.

Time trend

To examine the linearity of the time trend, annual time dummies were defined over the sample coverage period. The results, which are graphed in Figure 1, show a fairly steady increase in plant size over time. There is some indication that growth in plant size accelerated in the mid-1960s, slowed in the early 1970s, and accelerated again after 1975. There is no general evidence of a diminishing growth rate over the period.

Figure 1
Average Size of New Chemical Plants, 1957–82[1]

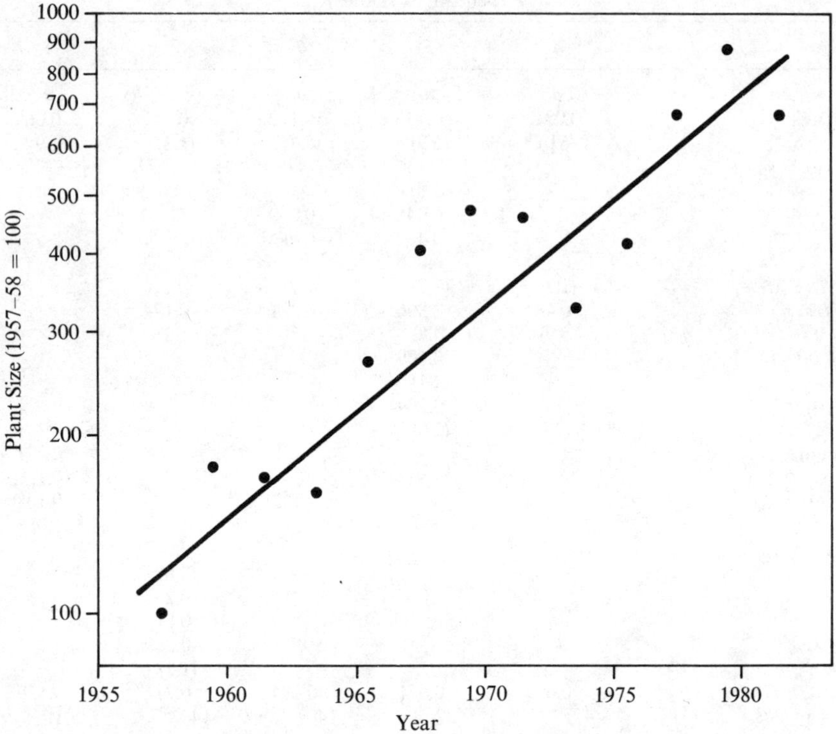

[1] Based on coefficients of dummy variables for each two-year period from 1957 to 1982.

Homogeneity of the time trend across products was tested by allowing each product to have a separate TIME coefficient in the regression. The results revealed statistically significant but relatively small differences across products in the rate of movement of the scale frontier.[13]

Conceivably, these small inter-product differences in the rate of plant size growth might be linked to the extent of scale economies. The more steeply unit investment costs decrease with plant size, the more resources firms might rationally invest to accelerate the rate of scale advance. To test this hypothesis, a multiplicative interaction between TIME and SCALE was included in the regressions. As shown in regression 5, this interaction term proves statistically significant but negative, implying that the rate of scale advance was actually slower for products with greater potential scale economies.

[13] The model was fit in constrained form (regression 4) and also with separate time trend coefficients for each product. Based on this test, the null hypothesis that all the time coefficients are identical was rejected. The F-statistic was 2.1, which exceeds the critical value 1.9[F(21, 375)] required to reject the null hypothesis at the 0.01 level. However, the increase in R^2 was relatively small, from 0.66 to 0.69.

The hypothesis that the rate of increase in plant size was influenced by market concentration was tested by interacting *TIME* with several alternative concentration measures, including (1) the Herfindahl index of producer concentration, (2) the logarithm of the number of firms, and (3) the logarithm of the number of plants. None of these interaction measures proved statistically significant. Thus, there appears to have been no connection between producer concentration and the rate of scale advance. This suggests that most technological improvements came from outside the firms that ultimately adopted them.

In general, the *TIME* interactions indicated a surprisingly strong regularity across products in the growth rate of new plant sizes. This suggests that shifts in the scale frontier were based on common underlying advances in chemical engineering technology. The uniformity of the time trend, and its persistence in the regressions despite the inclusion of alternative explanatory variables, is quite striking.

Base industry of firm

Oil companies, which entered the chemical industry in large numbers during the 1960s, are reputed to have built unusually large-scale plants. This scale orientation presumably reflects the importance of scale economies and high-volume operation in their base industry of petroleum refining. Dummy variables were defined for both oil companies (SIC 291) and major chemical companies (SIC 280) in order to determine whether such firms differed from others in their plant scale choices. The oil dummy (*OIL*) proved statistically significant (0.05 level); its coefficient in regression 5 implies that on average, oil companies built plants about 20% larger than other firms in the sample.

R & D expenditures

In Levin's [1978] model of scale advance, increases in plant scale arise from the R & D expenditures of individual firms. Compustat data on total corporate R & D expenditures are available for many firms in the sample. These data were used to compute company-level R & D to sales ratios which were tested for significance in the regression model. The results failed to show any connection between plant size and company R & D intensity.

Patent applications

Patents are another proxy for technological activity to which the shifting scale frontier might be linked. For thirteen products in the sample, data are available from *Chemical Abstracts* on the number of patent applications pertaining to new or improved production processes filed by US and foreign firms. (These data are described in detail in Lieberman [1987, forthcoming].) Three patent measures were tested in the regressions: (1) the cumulative number of patent applications by foreign firms (*PATFOR*), (2) the cumulative number of patent applications by US firms (PATUSA), and (3) a dummy variable which registers whether or not the specific firm had filed any process patents for the product in question (DPAT). The results in regression 7 suggest a connection between movements in the scale frontier and cumulative patents by foreign firms. (Patents by foreign firms outnumbered those by US companies by about two to one.) The drop in the time coefficient between regressions 6 and 7 suggests that more than half of the observed increase in plant size may be related to such patent activity. There is also some weak evidence that firms that filed process patents built relatively larger plants.

Cumulative investment experience

A further hypothesis is that growth in plant size is related to the cumulative experience of firms in building and operating new plants, as in a learning-type model. One proxy for experience is cumulative capacity constructed to date. For each product, the plant capacity data were cumulated at both the individual firm level (FCUMCAP), and the industry level (ICUMCAP). These measures were then tested in the regression model. Regression 8 shows the results, where the sample is limited to extant firms. Only the firm-level experience measure proves statistically significant, implying that firm-level learning is relevant. However, the time trend remains large in magnitude, indicating that most of the increase in plant scale must be attributed to factors other than firm-level experience. One interpretation is that more experienced firms simply built plants closer to the technological frontier; this explanation may also account for the size differential between entrants and incumbents. Unfortunately, collinearity between FCUMCAP and SHARE makes it impossible to determine conclusively whether the effect is truly related to cumulative experience or more simply to market share at the time of construction of the plant.

Relative size of entrants' plants

The size differential between entrants' and incumbents' plants was studied in detail by interacting the ENTRY dummy with *CDR*, GROW, TIME, and several market concentration measures, including the Herfindahl index and the logarithm of the number of firms. Of these interaction variables, only *CDR* proved statistically significant; i.e., entrants approached the plant sizes of incumbents only when there was a sizable cost penalty associated with small-scale operation. Rapid growth failed to stimulate entrants to build larger plants; and the size differential between entrants and incumbents failed to diminish over time.

The interaction tests revealed that the relative plant size of entrants was unrelated to market concentration. This casts doubt on the hypothesis (e.g. Scherer, *et al.* [1975, pp. 147–154]) that entrants opt for smaller plants in order to avoid generating overcapacity, which could trigger price cutting and potential retaliation by incumbents. If this were the case, one would observe smaller-scale plants built by entrants in concentrated industries, but not in competitive industries with a large number of firms. The results showed quite clearly that entrants tended to build smaller plants for all products, regardless of seller concentration.

What, then, explains the relative size differential of entrants' plants? One explanation consistent with the results is that without prior production experience, entrants are less capable than incumbents of solving the technical problems which frequently arise during start-up of a state-of-the-art plant. Thus, entrants are more conservative in their technological choices and less likely to take the risks inherent in building plants of frontier scale and beyond. Also, for many firms in the sample, the primary motivation for entry was backward or forward integration; in such cases, plant capacities were often chosen to achieve balance with the firm's other operations. The observed size differentials are consistent with vertical entry occurring as soon as firms' existing upstream or downstream operations reached a threshold size sufficient to permit vertical entry without too severe a cost penalty.

VI. SUMMARY AND CONCLUSIONS

The size of new chemical plants increased more than five-fold over the period from the late 1950s through the early 1980s. This increase in new plant size was unrelated to key parameters of the Manne model; plant sizes were not, in general, influenced by market growth, capital costs, or the magnitude of investment scale economies. Rather, growth in new plant size appears to have been driven by steady technological progress over time.

The rate of change in plant size was independent of market concentration and firm-level R & D expenditures, and only weakly linked to patent applications and firm-level cumulative investment. Plant size decisions were, however, influenced by the slope of the unit production cost curve and whether or not the firm was a new entrant. Entrants built smaller plants than incumbents, but all firms built plants closer to the technological frontier when small plants carried a higher relative cost penalty. The size differential between entrants' and incumbents' plants was not influenced by seller concentration or by the rate of market growth.

The poor performance of the Manne model can be attributed to the lack of validity of one or more of its underlying assumptions. In particular, the assumption that scale economies are available over an infinite range of plant sizes is refuted by the scale frontier results, as well as by engineering data. For most products in the sample, maximum feasible plant size remained below the optimal scale dictated by the Manne model.

These empirical results underscore the limited state of our knowledge regarding economies of scale. Clearly, in many industries, static economies of scale are less important than technological progress leading to shifts in the scale frontier. The standard economic distinction between "static" economies of scale and "dynamic" technical change ignores the fact that in many industries they are closely interrelated. This finding has important implications regarding the effect of scale economies on entry barriers and the process of industry evolution over time.

The empirical results presented here cover only one industrial sector over a relatively brief period. While similar results have been documented for a small number of other industries, the findings may be specific to capital-intensive industries with sizable economies of scale and investment lumpiness, such as materials processing, transportation equipment, and electric power. To understand the scale-frontier phenomenon more fully, it would be useful to have comparative results covering a broader set of industries.

MARVIN B. LIEBERMAN,
Graduate School of Business,
Stanford University,
Stanford, California 94305,
USA.

ACCEPTED SEPTEMBER 1986

REFERENCES

CHILTON, C. H., 1960, 'Six Tenths Factor Applies to Complete Plant Costs', in *Cost Engineering in the Process Industries* (McGraw-Hill, New York).

COWING, T. G., 1974, 'Technical Change and Scale Economics in an Engineering Production Function: The Case of Steam Electric Power', *Journal of Industrial Economics*, Vol. 23, pp. 135–152.

DIAMOND, P., MCFADDEN, D. and RODRIGUEZ, M., 1978, 'Measurement of the Elasticity of Factor Substitution and Bias of Technical Change', in M. FUSS and D. MCFADDEN (eds.), *Production Economics: A Dual Approach to Theory and Application, vol. 2* (Kluwer–Nijhoff Publishing, Boston).

ERLENKOTTER, D., 1967, 'Optimal Plant Size with Time-Phased Imports', in A. S. MANNE (ed.), *Investments for Capacity Expansion: Size, Location and Time-Phasing* (MIT Press, Cambridge, Mass.), pp. 157–177.

ERLENKOTTER, D. and MANNE, A. S., 1968, 'Capacity Expansion for India's Nitrogenous Fertilizer Industry', *Management Science*, Vol. 14, pp. B-553–B-572.

FREIDENFELDS, J., 1981, *Capacity Expansion, Analysis of Simple Models with Applications* (Elsevier, New York).

GIGLIO, R. J., 1970, 'Stochastic Capacity Models', *Management Science*, Vol. 17, no. 3, pp. 174–184.

GILBERT, R. and LIEBERMAN, M., 1987, 'Investment and Coordination in Oligopolistic Industries', *Rand Journal of Economics*, 18, pp. 17–33.

HALDI and WHITCOMB, 1967, 'Economies of Scale in Industrial Plants', *Journal of Political Economy*, Vol. 75, pp. 373–385.

HOLLANDER, S., 1965, *The Sources of Increased Efficiency: A Study of DuPont Rayon Plants* (MIT Press, Cambridge, Mass.).

HUGHES, W. R., 1971, 'Scale Frontiers in Electric Power', in WILLIAM M. CAPRON (ed.), *Technological Change in Regulated Industries* (Brookings Institution, Washington, DC).

LAU, L. J. and TAMURA, S., 1972, 'Economies of Scale, Technical Progress, and the

Nonhomothetic Leontief Production Function: An Application to the Japanese Petrochemical Processing Industry', *Journal of Political Economy*, Vol. 80, pp. 1167–1187.

LEVIN, R. C., 1977, 'Technical Change and Optimal Scale: Some Evidence and Implications', *Southern Economic Journal*, Vol. 44, pp. 208–221.

LEVIN, R. C., 1978, 'Technical Change, Barriers to Entry, and Market Structure', *Economica*, Vol. 45, pp. 347–361.

LIEBERMAN, M. B., 1987, forthcoming, 'Patents, Learning by Doing, and Market Structure in the Chemical Processing Industries', *International Journal of Industrial Organization.*

LIEBERMAN, M. B., 1987, Excess Capacity as a Barrier to Entry: An Empirical Appraisal, *Journal of Industrial Economics*, 35, pp. 607–627.

LUSS, H., 1982, 'Operations Research and Capacity Expansion Problems: A Survey', *Operations Research*, Vol. 30, No. 5, pp. 907–947.

MANNE, A. S., 1961, 'Capacity Expansion and Probabilistic Growth', *Econometrica*, Vol. 29, pp. 632–649.

MANNE, A. S., 1967, *Investments for Capacity Expansion: Size, Location and Time-Phasing* (MIT Press, Cambridge, Mass.).

PEARL, D. J. and ENOS, J. L., 1975, 'Engineering Production Functions and Technological Progress', *The Journal of Industrial Economics*, Vol. XXIV, pp. 55–72.

SATO, R., 1970, 'The Estimation of Biased Technical Progress and the Production Function', *International Economic Review*, Vol. 11, pp. 179–208.

SCHERER, F. M., *et al.*, 1975, *The Economics of Multi-Plant Operation* (Harvard University Press, Cambridge, Mass).

SRI INTERNATIONAL, 1976, 'Process Economics Program Yearbook', SRI International, Menlo Park, California.

SRI INTERNATIONAL, annual issues, 'Directory of Chemical Producers', Menlo Park, California.

SRINIVASAN, T. N., 1967, 'Geometric Rate of Growth of Demand', in A. S. MANNE (ed.), *Investments for Capacity Expansion: Size, Location and Time-Phasing* (MIT Press, Cambridge, Mass.).

SULTAN, R. G. M., 1975, *Pricing in the Electrical Oligopoly* (*Vol. 2*), Division of Research, Graduate School of Business Administration, Harvard University.

UNITED STATES INTERNATIONAL TRADE COMMISSION, annual issues, 'Synthetic Organic Chemicals, US Production and Sales', GPO, Washington.

THE JOURNAL OF INDUSTRIAL ECONOMICS 0022-1821 $2.00
Volume XXXVI December 1987 No. 2

PURPOSIVE DIVERSIFICATION OF R & D IN MANUFACTURING

JOHN T. SCOTT AND GEORGE PASCOE*

The R & D diversification in manufacturing of large US firms is found to be purposive, exploiting complementarities of various research activities and forming groups of related industry categories. Purposively diversified firms are seen to behave differently than randomly diversified or undiversified firms. Further, the behavioral differences between purposively diversified firms and others result because the former allocate relatively more R & D funds to industry categories where appropriability conditions are good and relatively fewer funds to those categories where appropriation of the returns from R&D is difficult. Finally, R&D expenditure and productivity are more closely linked at the group level than at the industry-category level, suggesting knowledge spills across industry categories are important.

I. PURPOSIVE DIVERSIFICATION

IN THIS paper, we explore the implications, for research and development (R & D) behavior and productivity, of purposive diversification of R & D activities in US manufacturing. In section II, we use the methodology developed in Scott [1982] to distinguish random diversification from any purposive diversification into a set of related, or close, R & D activities. We use the Federal Trade Commission's (FTC's) Line of Business (LB) data for the sample of 376 large publicly traded US manufacturing firms described and studied in Scott and Pascoe [1984, 1986]. Table I shows the diversification of manufacturing R & D activities for our sampled firms.

We study here the 352 firms in the sample that reported R & D throughout the sample period for one or more FTC 4-digit manufacturing categories. The procedure in section II finds the activities that are close and allows grouping of related R & D activities of one firm with those of other firms. Our

* Respectively, Associate Professor, Department of Economics, Dartmouth College, Hanover, N. H. 03755, and Economist, Bureau of Economics, US Federal Trade Commission. John Scott is responsible for the research design and writing. George Pascoe carried out the data processing and provided an insider's understanding of the Line of Business data.

We thank Zvi Griliches for the productivity data and Richard C. Levin for the appropriability data. Participants in the industrial organization seminar at Harvard University and in the corporate strategy seminar at Northwestern University provided valuable comments on earlier versions. We also thank Lawrence J. White and two anonymous referees for many useful comments.

The conclusions presented herein are those of the authors and have not been adopted by the Federal Trade Commission or any entity within the Commission. The FTC's Disclosure Avoidance Officer has certified that the data included in this paper do not identify individual company LB data.

TABLE I
DIVERSIFICATION OF THE SAMPLED FIRMS' MANUFACTURING R & D EFFORTS ACROSS FOUR-DIGIT FTC INDUSTRY CATEGORIES

The Number of Firms with n Non-sporadic Four-digit R & D Activities (i.e., R & D of each category was done in each of the sampled years)

n		*n*	
0	24	11	11
1	33	12	6
2	43	13	3
3	48	14	9
4	37	15	10
5	37	16–17*	5
6	30	18	4
7	18	19–20*	5
8	19	21–25*	4
9	16	30–42*	5
10	9		

Total 376

* These categories have been combined to comply with procedures to avoid the disclosure of individual company data.

investigation of the behavioral and performance implications of such groups complements the study of Jaffe [1984] who uses a clustering procedure to form groups of close firms. In contrast, we apply Scott's [1982] method to every possible combination of pairs of firms to discern multiple groups of activities within each given firm; and thus, firm A may be close to firms B and C, even though the activities of B and C do not overlap. In other words, our procedure allows a given firm to belong to numerous clusters of firms, as will be the case when the firm pursues different sets of related activities. For example, a firm might be part of a group of firms combining research in a food industry and in a chemicals industry, yet also be part of a group of firms combining research in an area of machinery and in a type of transportation equipment.

Given the groups distinguished in section II, section III demonstrates a significant group effect on R & D behavior. Firms are expected to diversify into related R & D activities to realize economies of multi-industry operation or better appropriability conditions.[1] Purposive diversification, then, offers a potentially important explanation for the firm effects on R & D behavior that have been found [Scott, 1984] to be large and significant. The reason that firms in the same industry category behave differently may be that some are

[1] Nelson [1959, p. 302], when discussing basic research, emphasizes that the firm more diversified into several product markets is more likely to be able to appropriate research benefits in a post-innovation market since it can more readily convert ideas into patentable innovations.

purposively diversified while others are not. Or, more generally, firms in a category may have different patterns of purposive multi-industry diversification. Firms in the same industry category, but differing in the extent or type of multi-category R & D, may behave differently in the category they have in common. For example, a firm combining research in chemicals and in food may behave differently in chemicals research than one having research activity in chemicals alone, or than one not combining chemicals research purposively with its other research activities, or than one combining research in chemicals and in petroleum refining. Section III demonstrates that some firm effects do result from such group effects. In the same industry category, purposively diversified firms are seen to behave differently than randomly diversified or undiversified firms. In the same industry category, firms purposively diversified in different ways have relatively similar behavior. Further, there is clear evidence that the behavioral differences between purposively diversified firms and others result because the former allocate relatively more R & D funds to industry categories where appropriability conditions are good and relatively fewer funds to those categories where appropriation of the returns from R & D is difficult.

Section IV provides a different view of the interindustry spillover effects pursued by Terleckyj [1977, 1980], Scherer [1982], Griliches and Lichtenberg [1984] and Jaffe [1984]. The total factor productivity data of Griliches are juxtaposed with our restructuring into groups of the FTC's LB R & D data. We demonstrate that R & D expenditure and productivity are more closely linked at the group level than at the industry-category level, suggesting knowledge spills across industry categories are important.

II. DISTINGUISHING PURPOSIVE DIVERSIFICATION OF R & D EFFORT

We designate as a line of business (LB) a firm's operations in an industry category. For a LB of a large US manufacturing firm, evidence suggests that once we have controlled for the industrial environment, the ratio of LB R & D expenditures to LB sales is constant through all levels of sales for those LB's with R & D activity.[2] This constant proportion of sales devoted to R & D expenditures is expected to vary across lines of business, even within the same industry category, because firm effects are quite significant (Scott [1984]). The issue here is whether changes in the degree and character of purposive diversification would change that R & D intensity.

If a firm diversifies its R & D effort purposively to take advantage of better appropriability or because of cost advantages of common facilities or complementarities of research across multiple industries, and if similar opportunities are available to other firms, we should find significant groupings of firms. That is, firms purposively combining multi-category R & D activities

[2] For example, after controlling for all FTC 4-digit industry effects, Scott [1984, Table 10.6, equation 3, p. 243] finds the elasticity of LB R & D expenditures with respect to LB sales to be 0.99.

will meet in the "group" of those activities more than would occur by chance given random diversification.

To find "the groups", every possible pair of firms in the sample was examined. Groups of multiple categories within which spillovers of knowledge are *a priori* likely are defined to be those sets of categories where "significant" meetings are found.

Let n (equal to 253 here) be the number of 4-digit FTC manufacturing categories in which our 352 firms have R & D expenditures. For each pair of firms, let s be the number of 4-digit categories in which one firm has R & D. Let t ($t \leqslant s$) be the number of 4-digit categories in which the other firm does R & D. Let g denote the number of categories in which the two firms meet. Let $C_{x,y}$ denote the combination of x things taken y at a time. Then for each pair of firms for which both firms have R & D activity, we compute

$$AP = 1 - \sum_{f=0}^{g-1} p(f) = 1 - \sum_{f=0}^{g-1} [(C_{t,f} \cdot C_{n-t,s-f})/C_{n,s}] \quad (1)$$

the probability that the firms would meet as much or more than they do if diversification were random. Both to reduce the computational burden and to be "certain" we are studying significant phenomena, we consider only the most significant groupings here. Namely, when AP is less than or equal to 0.00001, the null hypothesis of random diversification is rejected and the alternative, purposive diversification, is accepted.

The procedure finds (after elimination of duplicates) 127 groups of related categories, and an illustrative set of examples is given in Table II.[3] Note that a given firm can be a member of more than one group (with some of its LB's in one group and others of its LB's in other groups—but note that the same LB can be a member of more than one group), only one group (with some or all of the firm's LB's in that group), or none.[4]

Note that to form these groups, we have used the three years, 1974 through 1976, for which data were available. We use the total R & D expenditures

[3] The complete set of 127 groups is available on request. A meaningful reduction of the data into a smaller number of fairly typical patterns would be useful and is the focus of current research.

[4] Note, then, that if firm A performs R & D in industries 1 and 2, while firms B and C each do R & D in 1, 2, and 3, and if all meetings are significant, industries 1 and 2 form a group in which all three firms do R & D, while industries 1, 2, and 3 form a separate group in which B and C do R & D. In the estimations below, the construction could in principle allow results to be influenced by a few (outlier) firms that belong to many groups. However, the frequency distribution of the number of firms in one group, two groups, three groups, and so on, shows that most of the firms belonging to one or more groups belong to one or two, and only 5 percent of the R & D performing firms in our sample are members of more than four groups. Further, 69 percent of our R & D performing firms do not belong to any group. Thus, the density of significant cases in Table III, the balanced design of group versus nongroup firms in the individual tests, and the presence of a different set of firms in each test, all suggest that the independence assumption in the statistical tests is not a bad approximation and that the pattern of results is not simply because of the behavior of the most diversified firms.

TABLE II
SOME OF THE 127 GROUPS

Industry Categories in the Group
{2803, industrial inorganic chemicals, except industrial gases and inorganic pigments; 2804, plastics materials and resins; 2813, industrial organic chemicals, except gum and wood chemicals; 3006, misc. plastics products}
{2402, sawmills and planing mills; 2403, millwork, plywood and structural members; 2405, misc. wood products, including wood containers; 2602, paper mills, except building paper; 2610, paperboard containers and boxes}
{3420, valves and pipe fittings, except plumbers' brass goods; 3501, turbines and turbine generator sets; 3504, lawn and garden equipment; 3522, pumps and pumping equipment; 3524, air and gas compressors; 3602, switchgear and switchboard apparatus; 3603, motors and generators}
{2405, misc. wood products, including wood containers; 2611, building paper and board mills; 2902, paving and roofing materials; 3006, misc. plastics products; 3213, gypsum products; 3216, asbestos products; 3217, mineral wool; 3410, metal doors, sash, frames, molding, and trim}

in each line of business for a firm because the decision to combine R & D in various industry categories is expected to take account of the fact that government-financed R & D, and R & D performed under contract more generally, provide knowledge spillovers to the firm.[5] To lessen the importance of outliers that could result from startups or catastrophes destroying sales, in our subsequent analyses we use *RS*, the sales-weighted average of R & D expenditures to sales during the three years for each line of business.

III. PURPOSIVE DIVERSIFICATION AND BEHAVIOR

We focus on the difference within a given industry category between (1) the average behavior for the LB's of firms that are diversified into a particular group of related industry categories and (2) the average behavior for the LB's of firms not in any group. We shall be asking if purposively diversified firms behave differently in a particular industry category than the firms in that category that are not purposively diversified. The simple model used examines, industry category by industry category, the t-statistic on the difference in means of *RS* behavior of purposively diversified firms and those not purposively diversified. The sign and significance of this difference indicates the direction and significance of the differences between the behavior of purposively diversified firms and other firms in an industry category.

[5] Several studies have documented a complementary relationship between government-financed and company-financed R & D expenditures. Scott [1984], at the LB level, and Levin *et al.* [1985], at the industry level, report such effects using FTC LB data. Levy and Terleckyj [1983] find that government contract R & D performed in industry induced private R & D expenditure and that the stock of government contract R & D has a discernible effect on private sector productivity.

TABLE III
PERCENTAGE DISTRIBUTION OF t-STATISTICS ON 653 DIFFERENCES OF MEANS OF R & D INTENSITY (RS) FOR FIRMS WITHIN A GROUP AND A MATCHED SET OF FIRMS[a]

Significance Level of t-*statistics,* p *(two tails)*	*Percentage of Cases*	
	+[b]	−[c]
$p \leqslant 0.10$	8.88%	6.13%
$0.10 < p \leqslant 0.15$	2.60	1.84
$0.15 < p \leqslant 0.20$	2.30	1.68
$0.20 < p \leqslant 0.25$	2.76	1.84
$0.25 < p \leqslant 0.30$	3.68	1.68
"Insignificant"	34.92	31.70

[a] Based on 127 groups with comparisons at the 4-digit industry level. The "non-group" firms were randomly selected (i.e., each firm had an equal chance of being chosen) from those having R & D expenditures within the 4-digit category but not within any group. There were 653 cases for which the matched sample comparisons could be made. See the text for the definition of a group.
[b] Instances in which the difference was positive.
[c] Instances in which the difference was negative.

Table III reports the distribution of these t-statistics by significance ranges. The table indicates that purposively diversified firms differ from firms that have not purposively diversified. To see this point, imagine a random distribution of m items across n "boxes" of equal size. Let x_i be the random variable which is one if the ith item appears in a particular box and zero otherwise. Then a measure of the number of items appearing in a particular box is the random variable $X = \sum_{i=1}^{m} x_i$. Its expected value is

$$E(X) = \sum_{i=1}^{m} (1 \cdot 1/n + 0 \cdot (1 - 1/n)) = m/n$$

Its variance is

$$\begin{aligned} \operatorname{var}(X) &= \sum_{i=1}^{m} \operatorname{var}(x_i) = m \operatorname{var}(x_i) \\ &= m\{[1 - 1/n]^2 (1/n) + [0 - 1/n]^2 (1 - 1/n)\} \end{aligned}$$

If we consider each of the two top "boxes" of Table III, $n = 20$. This is true because a two-tailed test at the 10% level implies that there should be 5 percent of the cases in each tail; there thus are 100%/5% = 20 such equally likely categories or "boxes" into which cases can fall under the null hypothesis. Here $m = 653$, and for each 5% box $E(X) = 32.65$. The $\sqrt{\operatorname{var}(X)} = 5.57$. Now, since there are 58 items in the top left box, the number of items in the box exceeds the expected value by 4.55 standard deviations. And the number of items, 40, in the top right box exceeds the expected value by 1.32 standard deviations.

Thus, purposively diversified firms appear to behave differently than their competitors that have not undertaken such diversification. There is also a tendency for purposively diversified firms not only to behave differently, but specifically to do more R & D than their undiversified competitors. Considering the top 5 boxes on the left as a single box, or the top 5 boxes on the right as a single box, $n = \frac{1}{0.15} = 6\frac{2}{3}$. Then $E(X) = m/n = 653/(6\frac{2}{3}) = 97.95$, and $\sqrt{\text{var}(X)} = 9.12$. Now, in the top 5 boxes on the left, there are 132 items, or 3.73 standard deviations above the expected number if the behavior of purposively diversified firms is no different from that of others. But in the top 5 boxes on the right, there are 86 items, or 1.31 standard deviations below the expected number.

Purposively diversified firms are relatively homogeneous in their behavior, since if we reproduce Table III, but compare the purposively diversified firms of each of the 127 groups to all other firms (purposively diversified or not) in each particular industry category, the pattern of the behavioral differences remains, but its significance is greatly attenuated. We find that of 712 cases, 49 fall in the top left box. Given the null hypothesis, 35.6 are expected, and the standard deviation is 5.82. The number of cases exceeds the expected number by 2.3 standard deviations. But the top right box has 5.1% of the sample—not much more than what is expected, and the tendency for positive differences remains but is greatly lessened.

One interesting possible explanation for the different behavior of purposively diversified firms is that such firms are more sensitive to the differences in profitability of R & D across industry categories or are better able to exploit such differences. If so, the positive difference cases should occur in industry categories where appropriability conditions are good. The negative difference cases should occur in categories where appropriation of the returns from R & D is difficult.

To test this proposition we examined the 58 positive cases and 40 negative cases for $p \leqslant 0.10$ in Table III. These cases covered 39 different FTC 4-digit categories. Of those, 35 categories always had the same sign—19 positive and 16 negative. Those 35 cases are reported in Table IV.

The Levin *et al.* [1984] survey asked industries to report imitation time lags and costs for major and minor, process and product, and patented and unpatented innovations. As reported by Levin *et al.* [1985], these measures are typically highly correlated. Richard Levin has let us use *IMLAG*, the average time needed to duplicate a patented, major product innovation; this is the same variable used in Levin *et al.* [1985].

TABLE IV

INDUSTRY CATEGORIES WITH SIGNIFICANT DIFFERENCES IN MEANS BETWEEN GROUP AND NONGROUP FIRMS' R & D INTENSITY[a]

Positive Differences:

2212: Misc. textile goods, except tire cord and fabric
2602: Paper mills, except building paper
2603: Paperboard mills
2607: Sanitary paper products
2803: Industrial inorganic chemicals, except industrial gases and inorganic pigments
2804: Plastics materials and resins
2807: Drugs, ethical
2811: Paints and allied products
2814: Fertilizers
2815: Pesticides and agricultural chemicals, not classified elsewhere
2817: Misc. chemical products, except explosives
2901: Petroleum refining
3419: Ordnance and accessories, except vehicles and guided missiles
3522: Pumps and pumping equipment
3528: Mechanical power transmission equipment, not classified elsewhere
3537: Misc. machinery, except electrical
3601: Transformers
3624: Electronic capacitors, resistors, coils and transformers, connectors and components, not classified elsewhere
3705: Motor vehicle parts

Negative Differences:

2004: Dairy products except fluid milk
2009: Cereal breakfast foods
2029: Misc. foods and kindred products, except roasted coffee
2402: Sawmills and planing mills
2403: Millwork, plywood and structural members
2606: Bags, except textile bags
2610: Paperboard containers and boxes
2809: Perfumes, cosmetics, and other toilet preparations
3311: Nonferrous wire drawing and insulating
3312: Nonferrous foundries
3515: Metalworking, machinery, not classified elsewhere, including metal forming machine tools, special dies and tools, die sets, jigs and fixtures, industrial molds and rolling mill machinery and equipment
3604: Industrial controls
3620: Radio and TV communication equipment
3621: Electron tubes, receiving and transmitting types
3802: Measuring and controlling devices
3904: Dolls, games, toys, and children's vehicles

[a] Significance measured at the 0.10 level for a two-tailed test.

We have IMLAG for 156 of the 253 FTC 4-digit categories covered by our sample of firms. Because of the nature of the survey, IMLAG really gives ordinal rather than cardinal data. We therefore ranked the 156 industry categories for which the R & D activities of our firms overlap with the 4-digit categories sampled in the Levin *et al.* [1984] survey; the longest lag category was ranked number one, the next longest lag was ranked number two, etc. Our 156 categories of the

253 are distributed over 54 distinct time lag values (i.e., many categories have the same value for IMLAG) ranked from the highest value of IMLAG to the lowest value.

Of the 19 positive difference cases, we have IMLAG for 13. Of the 16 negative difference cases, we have IMLAG for 14. If our 13 positive difference cases were a random sample from all differences, the expected value of the average rank, *r*, would be

$$E(r) = E(1/13) \sum_{j=1}^{13} r_j = (1/13) \sum_{j=1}^{13} \mu = \mu \tag{2}$$

where $\mu = \sum_{i=1}^{54} ip(i)$, $p(i) = n_i/156$, and n_i is the number of cases in rank *i*. The variance of *r* is

$$\sigma^2(r) = (1/13) \sum_{i=1}^{54} (i-\mu)^2 p(i) \tag{3}$$

If we assume random selection for our 13 positive differences, $E(r)$ is 32.1026, and the standard deviation $\sigma(r)$ is 4.41009. For our 14 negative differences, $E(r)$ is of course again 32.1026, while the standard deviation $\sigma(r)$ is 4.24967. For the 13 positive differences, *r* is 21.7, which is 2.4 standard deviations below the mean, assuming no relation between appropriability conditions and the R & D behavior of purposively diversified firms *vis-à-vis* firms that have not pursued such diversification of their R & D activities. For the 14 negative differences, *r* is 41.0, which is 2.1 standard deviations above the mean.

Thus, the evidence implies that as compared with firms that have not purposively diversified, our purposively diversified firms allocate more R & D resources to industry categories where appropriability conditions are good (i.e., where imitation time lags are long) and fewer R & D resources to industry categories where appropriability is difficult (i.e., where imitation time lags are short).

IV. OBSERVING THE PERFORMANCE EFFECT OF PURPOSIVE R & D DIVERSIFICATION

Does R & D in an industry category affect productivity for that industry only, or does the R & D in a set of "technologically close" industry categories affect the productivity for the whole set? For example, we might find only a little R & D in category *i* but high productivity, and a lot of R & D in category *j* but low productivity. But if categories *i* and *j* are "close", the proper level of aggregation might indicate intermediate R & D and intermediate productivity.

Do such R & D spillover effects exist? They appear to be important. Griliches has provided us with his productivity data for 3-digit SIC industries. Except for random error, the aggregate growth rate in total factor productivity

TABLE V

THE IMPACT OF R & D INTENSITY[a] (RS) ON THE AVERAGE ANNUAL RATE OF GROWTH IN TOTAL FACTOR PRODUCTIVITY[b] ($T\dot{F}P/TFP$) IN US MANUFACTURING

Observations on 133 Industry Categories:

$$T\dot{F}P/TFP = \underset{(t\,=\,-4.7)^{**}}{-0.0089} + \underset{(t\,=\,3.8)^{**}}{0.14\,RS},$$

F-value = 15*, $R^2 = 0.10$, degrees of freedom = 131.

Observations on the 93 Sets of Industry Categories:

$$T\dot{F}P/TFP = \underset{(t\,=\,-12)^{**}}{-0.027} + \underset{(t\,=\,7.6)^{**}}{0.37\,RS},$$

F-value = 58**, $R^2 = 0.39$, degrees of freedom = 91.

[a] Measured as R & D expenditures divided by sales, using the FTC's LB data.

[b] Measured as proportions, using Griliches' average annual rates of total factor productivity growth for the 1969–73 to 1974–78 period for 3-digit SIC manufacturing industries. A dot denotes a time derivative, and the unit of time is one year. Griliches and Lichtenberg [1984, p. 327] explain the appropriateness of juxtaposing these mid-70s productivity data with the LB R & D data.

Note: Significance levels (one-tailed test): ** = 0.0001, * = 0.0002. Significance levels for the F-value and t-value for the slope coefficient in the first equation differ because a one-tailed test is appropriate here.

in each SIC 3-digit industry is assumed to be the same for our sample of 352 large manufacturing firms as it was for the entire population. The questions are (1) whether the variance in their R & D intensity across 3-digit industries explains the cross-sectional variance in the rate of growth in their total factor productivity, and (2) whether any additional explanatory power comes from considering the spillovers of knowledge from R & D done in technologically close industries. To answer this question, we first re-estimated the group probability model at the 3-digit level and found 93 groups of significantly close 3-digit industry categories.

If we use conventional industry categories and correlate Griliches' productivity growth measures with R & D intensity, we find the regression relation reported in the first equation of Table V. The regression is derived from a model in which $T\dot{F}P/TFP = \lambda + (\partial Q/\partial R)(\dot{R}/Q) + \varepsilon$, where λ is an exogenous rate of growth in TFP, R is R & D stock, Q is output, $\partial Q/\partial R$ is the marginal product of R & D, and ε is random error.[6] Thus, the regression suggests that for every one percent increase in R & D/Sales, the rate of growth in total factor productivity increased 0.14 of a percent. Or, interpreting the coefficient on R & D intensity as the marginal product of R & D, at the margin an increase in R & D stock by one dollar increases the value of annual output

[6] The estimation in Table V is based on the following conceptualization. Letting $Q = \Phi e^{\lambda t} R^{\delta} K^{\alpha} L^{\beta} M^{\gamma}$, where Q, R, K, L, and M denote respectively output, R & D capital, physical capital, labor, and materials, then $\dot{Q}/Q - \alpha(\dot{K}/K) - \beta(\dot{L}/L) - \gamma(\dot{M}/M) = \lambda + \delta(\dot{R}/R)$. As Terleckyj [1974] observed, since $\delta = (\partial Q/\partial R)(R/Q)$, then $\delta\dot{R}/R = (\partial Q/\partial R)(\dot{R}/Q)$. Letting TFP denote total factor productivity, we have $T\dot{F}P/TFP = \lambda + (\partial Q/\partial R)(\dot{R}/Q)$.

14 cents. For expositions of this interpretation, see Terleckyj [1974] and Scherer [1982, p. 628].

Suppose we then hypothesize that R & D is a public good in the sense that when an industry category is a member of more than one group, its productivity effect is felt in all groups. To test this proposition, we blend the productivity growth measures for each industry category within a group[7] to get appropriate productivity growth for the 93 sets of industry categories. If industry categories were combined randomly into a smaller number of groups, or if the population of such combinations were taken, the explanatory power and the coefficients of the productivity relation would be expected to be the same as obtained in the non-grouped data. The least squares line passes through the means of the variables $T\dot{F}P/TFP$ and $\dot{R}/Q$, and the expected means do not change whether grouped or ungrouped data are used. Both the sum of squared deviations of the observations from the mean and from the least squares line change in the same proportion. Thus both the coefficients and the explanatory power are expected to be the same before and after grouping.[8]

In fact, as seen in the second equation of Table V, both R^2 and slope coefficient increase markedly. The slope coefficient for the second equation exceeds that of the first equation by 4.7 standard errors. This result is consistent with our hypothesis of purposive exploitation of knowledge spillovers, since the relationship would be expected to be stronger when the grouped data are used.

Terleckyj [1977, 1980], Scherer [1982], and Griliches and Lichtenberg [1984] have pursued the possibility of spillovers of knowledge from R & D done in technologically close industries by exploring the possibility that knowledge is embodied in inputs. Our procedure is more general, incorporating that possibility but allowing for the possibility that knowledge spreads through other channels. As Griliches [1979, p. 104] observes, pure knowledge flows need not be linked to the pattern of purchase of inputs.

V. DISCUSSION

The evidence on appropriability and factor productivity growth supports the view that the activity of firms in our groups is purposive. But these implications raise a new question. What is the explanation for non-purposive activity? Note that even a firm that is purposively diversified into a set or sets of categories that "belong together" may have some R & D activities that "don't belong." This may reflect growth via diversification for reasons other

[7] The productivity growth measure for each group of industries is constructed by weighting the growth measure for each industry category in the group by the relative size (measured by sales) in our sample of the associated industry category (relative to the size of the group in our sample).

[8] Many readers will find it intuitively fairly obvious that a random consolidation of data points should yield unbiased coefficients, but a proof is available on request.

than the R & D complementarity of the acquired fields. And what are the "nonpurposive" firms up to? Are they not as smart about the spillovers? Do they find it harder to finance diversified R & D? Since all firms in the sample are among the largest 1000 US manufacturers, none are absolutely small; yet, 69 percent of the R & D performing firms in our sample do not "purposively diversify" their R & D. If we compare the "purposively diversified" firms with the others by industry category, we find that the purposively diversified firms are absolutely more diversified.[9] Why so many firms do not purposively diversify poses a mystery for future research.

ACCEPTED JANUARY 1987

JOHN T. SCOTT,
Department of Economics,
Dartmouth College,
Hanover, NH 03755,
USA.

GEORGE PASCOE,
Bureau of Economics,
US Federal Trade Commission,
Washington, DC,
USA.

REFERENCES

GRILICHES, Z., 1979, 'Issues in Assessing the Contribution of Research and Development to Productivity Growth', *The Bell Journal of Economics*, 10 (Spring), pp. 92–116.

GRILICHES, Z. and LICHTENBERG, F., 1984, 'Interindustry Technology Flows and Productivity Growth: A Reexamination', *The Review of Economics and Statistics*, 66 (May), pp. 324–329.

JAFFE, A. B., 1984, 'The Effects of Market Demand, Technological Opportunity and Research Spillovers on R&D Intensity and Productivity Growth', manuscript (March).

LEVIN, R. C., KLEVORICK, R. C., NELSON, R. R. and WINTER, S. G., 1984, 'Survey Research on R & D Appropriability and Technological Opportunity: Part 1', Working paper, Yale University (July).

LEVIN, R. C., COHEN, W. M. and MOWERY, D. C., 1985, 'R & D Appropriability,

[9] The difference, examined using Table III's method, is highly significant. Diversification was measured by the inverse Herfindahl index for R & D for each firm, *IHR*.

$$IHR = 1 \Big/ \sum_{i=1}^{253} s_i^2$$

where s_i is the share of the firm's R & D expenditures in industry category *i*. Thus the measure will increase with the number of industry categories in which the firm has R & D and will decrease as the variation in activity shares increases. When the firm has an equal share of its R & D expenditures in each industry category, the diversification index equals the number of categories in which the firm has R & D expenditures.

Opportunity, and Market Structure: New Evidence on Some Schumpeterian Hypotheses', *American Economic Review*, 75 (May), pp. 20–24.

LEVY, D. M. and TERLECKYJ, N. E., 1983, 'Effects of Government R&D on Private R&D Investment and Productivity: A Macroeconomic Analysis', *The Bell Journal of Economics*, 14 (Autumn), pp. 551–561.

NELSON, R. R., 1959, 'The Simple Economics of Basic Scientific Research', *Journal of Political Economy*, 67 (June), pp. 297–306.

SCHERER, F. M., 1982, 'Inter-industry Technology Flows and Productivity Growth', *The Review of Economics and Statistics*, 64 (November), pp. 627–634.

SCOTT, J. T., 1982, 'Multimarket Contact and Economic Performance', *The Review of Economics and Statistics*, 64 (August), pp. 368–375.

SCOTT, J. T., 1984, 'Firm Versus Industry Variability in R&D Intensity', in Z. GRILICHES, ed., *R&D, Patents, and Productivity* (University of Chicago Press for the National Bureau of Economic Research, Chicago).

SCOTT, J. T. and PASCOE, G., 1984, 'Capital Costs and Profitability', *International Journal of Industrial Organization*, 2 (September), pp. 217–233.

SCOTT, J. T. and PASCOE, G., 1986, 'Beyond Firm and Industry Effects on Profitability in Imperfect Markets', *The Review of Economics and Statistics*, 68 (May), pp. 284–292.

TERLECKYJ, N. E., 1974, *Effects of R&D on the Productivity Growth of Industries: An Exploratory Study* (National Planning Association, Washington, D.C.).

TERLECKYJ, N. E., 1977, 'Output of Industrial Research and Development Measured as Increments to Production of Economic Sectors'. Paper given at the 15th Conference of the International Association for Research in Income and Wealth, York, England.

TERLECKYJ, N. E., 1980, 'Direct and Indirect Effects of Industrial Research and Development on the Productivity Growth of Industries', in J. W. KENDRICK and B. N. VACCARA, eds., *New Developments in Productivity Measurement and Analysis* (University of Chicago Press for the National Bureau of Economic Research, Chicago).

THE JOURNAL OF INDUSTRIAL ECONOMICS 0022-1821 $2.00
Volume XXXVI December 1987 No. 2

STRATEGIC PRODUCT CHOICE IN DIFFERENTIATED MARKETS*

SWATI BHATT

Widespread diversification of firms compels viewing them as a portfolio of activities rather than as entities competing independently in separate markets. This paper posits that product specification or product choice is a distinct strategic variable. In particular, the optimal relationship between the new and existing products of an oligopolistic firm is examined. In the absence of market size inequalities, clustering or market invasion is shown to be the Nash solution to the product choice game when firms play strategically.

I. INTRODUCTION

THE PRODUCT choice decision in oligopolistic industries is, in effect, a three-step process. Step one, the scope decision, fixes the number of products; step two, the line decision, establishes the firm in a differentiated market. For single-product firms the process ends here. However, multi-product firms face a third stage, the line expansion decision, which is the subject of this paper.[1]

The central question is the following: what would be the optimal direction for expansion for firms extending their product line? Would segmentation (close substitutes to the existing products) be preferred to interlacing (more distant substitutes), when rival oligopolists have already established themselves in these distant markets?[2] Consider, for example, the high technology industry with numerous interrelated product lines (computers, printers, disk storage devices, software, etc). The product choice question facing a firm like IBM is one of proliferating within the original mainframe computer market versus expansion into more distant markets of, say, personal computers where rival firms have already formed a stronghold.[3] Firms in this industry

* This paper is based on Chapter 1 of my Ph.D. dissertation at Princeton University. I am grateful to my advisers, Avinash Dixit, Michael Katz and Robert Willig, for their guidance and help. Lawrence White and two anonymous referees provided useful comments. Responsibility for all errors remains mine.

[1] It is not imperative for growing firms to expand within the existing industry; conceivably there are other lucrative industries. However, it is more plausible to argue that the advantages of established firms ease their transit over the entry barriers. Intangible assets or excess capacity in tangible assets reduces the opportunity cost of entry.

[2] The terms "interlacing" and "segmentation" are due to Brander and Eaton [1984]. They are used here for uniformity, since the same phenomenon is referred to.

[3] Incidentally, IBM did face such a decision problem in 1979 and chose to produce over the next four years 14 different models of its 4300 series, each differing in price or performance, rather than enter the personal computer market. Subsequently, in 1981, IBM reversed its decision and entered the personal computer market.

tend to invade one another's markets rather than proliferating into markets closer to their own.

It is found, in the context of the model developed in subsequent sections, that under certain reasonable conditions cross-penetration or interlacing is the perfect Nash solution to the product choice game when firms play strategically and markets are replicas. However, this equilibrium is Pareto dominated by market segmentation, an outcome which could obtain when markets are unequal in size. Two important issues considered in this paper need to be emphasized: (i) Oligopolistic firms compete in *several* markets. (ii) Differentiated product markets are wide enough to accommodate line expansion by rival firms. Each market must be sufficiently heterogeneous in product characteristics and consumer preferences to allow for the entry of more than one product. This feature precludes the emergence of a deterrence equilibrium since incomplete pre-emption of the adjacent product space renders deterrence non-optimal.

Define an industry as consisting of a set of products linked by non-negligible cross-elasticities of demand. Then a differentiated product industry may consist of markets or sub-sets of products $X_k \subset I$, $k = 1, \ldots, N$, such that the cross-elasticities *within* each sub-set of products, X_k, exceeds that *between* different subsets.[4] Firms may then choose to operate in one or more segments of this industry depending upon the nature of demand and cost interactions. Each market permitting the entry of more than one product simply translates to allowing each set X_k to contain more than one product $x_i \in X_k$.

Schmalensee [1978] studied the problem in a model with single product markets and found that firms tend to introduce several similar products so as to pre-empt rivals or potential entrants from entering their niche of the industry.[5] The multi-product problem was first posed by Brander and Eaton [1984], henceforth B & E, in a differentiated product duopoly game with each firm producing two products. Amongst several possible Nash equilibria they emphasized segmentation and interlacing and found the former to be the preferred solution since the adverse impact of one sub-market on the other is internalized. However, allowing for more products in each market changes

[4] Caves and Porter [1977] have an interesting discussion of industry sub-groups arising from differing structural characteristics and imperfect substitutability.

[5] Schmalensee [1978], in his study of the RTE cereal industry, argues that a brand proliferation strategy deters costly entry to the extent that each brand will have relatively low market shares; the share that an imitator can hope to capture is correspondingly reduced. However, entry costs (e.g., advertising) need not be incurred by established firms who possess similar product processes, expertise specific to the industry and other potential advantages flowing from the closeness of markets. Thus a deterrence equilibrium is obtained in the RTE industry more as a result of the oligopolists' having achieved a relatively full consensus on price, advertising and other key variables than as a result of a pure proliferation strategy. If the consensus was incomplete with bouts of active rivalry present, then invasion by rival firms would be an effective surrogate for entry by outside firms. In the cereal industry, invasion was ruled out as being a mutually destructive strategy and firms proliferated into close substitutes instead.

the nature of rivalry in the industry so that strategic pre-emption is no longer found to be optimal.

There are two major differences between this paper and the B & E model. First, the line establishment decision is taken as an initial condition for the line expansion decision, whereas B & E consider the two simultaneously. Second, each market contains more than two products.

Judd [1985] finds, in a differentiated duopoly with small exit costs, that proliferating along the product spectrum does not credibly deter entry. An entrant may be successful if the incumbent has related products that would lose sales if the post-entry competition were intense. The incumbent is induced to exit so as to allow profits on related products to increase. A similar reason underlies firms' invasion of each other's markets here.

The paper is organized as follows. Section II outlines the model; section III solves for the equilibrium for replica markets, while section IV considers non-replica markets with linear demand. Conclusions are drawn in section V.

II. THE MODEL

Following B & E, product choice is viewed as a commitment. Once decided upon, it is not amenable to change. Then the problem can be modeled as a two-stage game where firms choose their products first and subsequently compete in a Cournot quantity game. The strategies are, therefore, the product choices and quantities, while the payoffs are the profit functions. The solution to this game is a Nash equilibrium, if each firm's equilibrium choices are optimal given the equilibrium decisions made by other firms. Assume that firms can correctly see through to the second stage equilibrium when making their first stage decisions. Therefore one can restrict attention to the set of sub-game perfect equilibria for this game. Assume also that the firms have perfect information about the nature of the game and the payoff function parameters.

To make the problem tractable I consider a simplified model consisting of two firms, A and B, selling in a differentiated product industry. Firms face identical and constant average costs. This cost assumption is made so as to focus attention on the demand side. Initially, let firm A produce $X_0 \in \mathbf{X}$ and firm B produce $Y_0 \in \mathbf{Y}$, where $\mathbf{X}$ and $\mathbf{Y}$ are markets containing three products each so that $\mathbf{X} = \{X_0, X_A, X_B\}$ and $\mathbf{Y} = \{Y_0, Y_A, Y_B\}$.

Modelling demand functions faced by firms in a differentiated product oligopoly is non-trivial. The inverse demand facing an individual firm is assumed to be a function of all products in the market. One must therefore specify the nature of oligopolistic interaction, which itself is derived from underlying preferences over the related products. Since this paper focuses on the consequences arising from the *existence* of significant cross-effects between products in a market rather than perturbations due to differential or asymmetric cross-effects, all cross-effects within a market are taken to be identical. This assumption implies a class of demand functions represented by:

$$p^i(X_0, X_A, X_B) = F_i(X_i) - G(X_0 + X_A + X_B), \quad i = 0, A, B \tag{1}$$

where $F' < 0$, $F'' < 0$, $G' > 0$, $G'' > 0$, to ensure concavity of the profit functions. $p^i(\cdot)$ is the inverse demand curve for product X_i, $i = 0, A, B$. The oligopolistic interdependence is captured by $G(\cdot)$ so that the inverse demand for product i shifts inward whenever total output in the industry increases. Note that linear demand functions are a special case of (1).

Assume that demand for Y_0, Y_A and Y_B is given by identical functions as in (1) with X_i replaced by the appropriate Y_i. If the sub-markets are replicas, $F_0 = F_A = F_B$ for all $\mathbf{X}$. This does not imply perfect substitutability between products because, for instance, $F(\cdot)$ could be non-linear.

Both firms are endowed with finite resources, R, that allow the production of exactly one additional product. Firm A can expand within its own market, $\mathbf{X}$, and produce X_A or enter B's market, $\mathbf{Y}$, and produce Y_A. Similarly, B could produce Y_B in its own market or X_B in the opposite market, $\mathbf{X}$. More importantly, assume that entry costs are large enough to deter further entry in both markets, i.e., entry is effectively blockaded, in Bain's [1956] terminology.

Thus firm A's profits are a continuous function of X_0, X_A and Y_A. We restrict attention to the sets (X_0, X_A) and (X_0, Y_A) that maximize the two constrained optimization problems, with the constraints $Y_A = 0$ and $X_A = 0$ respectively. Profits can be written as:

$$\begin{aligned} \pi^i(X, Y) = {} & p^0(X_0, X_A, X_B)X_0 + p^i(X_0, X_A, X_B)X_i \\ & + p^i(Y_0, Y_A, Y_B)Y_i - R, \quad i = A, B \end{aligned} \tag{2}$$

The constant average costs are absorbed into the inverse demand functions. The assumptions on p^i ensure strict concavity of the profit functions.

Figure 1 depicts the game tree when firms make their product choice decision sequentially. The four possible outcomes are:

(3) Outcome I where $\mathbf{X} = (X_0, X_B)$; $\mathbf{Y} = (Y_0, Y_A)$

Outcome C where $\mathbf{X} = (X_0, X_A)$; $\mathbf{Y} = (Y_0, Y_B)$

Outcome AM where $\mathbf{X} = (X_0)$; $\mathbf{Y} = (Y_0, Y_A, Y_B)$

Outcome BM where $\mathbf{X} = (X_0, X_A, X_B)$; $\mathbf{Y} = (Y_0)$

I is the invasion outcome where firm A produces X_0 and Y_A while B produces Y_0 and X_B. C refers to the collusive outcome (since one firm maximizes jointly over two products in the same sub-market) where A produces X_0 and X_A and B produces Y_0 and Y_B. AM is the outcome when both A and B introduce products in B's home market; consequently A remains a monopolist in its own market. BM is the converse of AM, with A and B switching roles. It is the

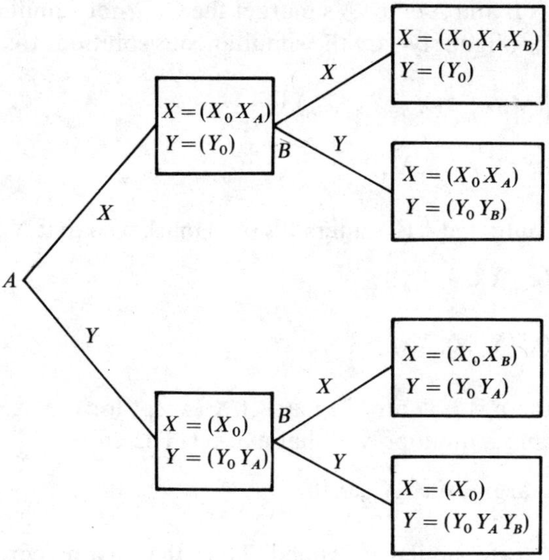

Figure 1

presence of these last two outcomes, *AM* and *BM*, that distinguishes this analysis from that of B & E. The next section examines the solution to this game.

III. EQUILIBRIUM IN REPLICA MARKETS

In this section I assume that $F_0 = F_A = F_B$ in (1). Thus markets are replicas. Firms can now play strategically by selecting at every possible move the strategy that leads to the maximum payoff associated with that move. By ranking the payoffs evaluating every outcome we can obtain the best reply of each firm to the strategy chosen by the other. The Nash solution is obtained by solving the game backwards. That is, holding the first stage choice fixed one solves for the second stage quantity game.

Before proceeding, some new notation is required to describe the reduced-form payoffs arising from the Cournot quantity game under each of the four possible outcomes. From (2), it is clear that $\pi^A(\cdot)$ and $\pi^B(\cdot)$ are each functions of six variables: X_0, X_A, X_B, Y_0, Y_A and Y_B. In defining Cournot equilibria in market **X** the output in market **Y** is suppressed since the cross-effects between the two are assumed to be zero. Hence, in the following discussion Y_0, Y_A and Y_B are suppressed. Market **Y** equilibria are similarly defined.

If firm A introduces a new product in its own market, **X**, it will maximize profits from X_0, X_A jointly. Thus X_0^C and X_A^C (for collusive output) solve

$$(4) \qquad \max_{X_0}\left(\max_{X_A} \pi^A(X_0, X_A; 0)\right)$$

When both firms B and A enter A's market the Cournot equilibrium outputs, X_0^o, X_A^o, X_B^o (o for oligopoly), are the simultaneous solutions to:

$$\text{(5)} \qquad \max_{X_0}\left(\max_{X_A} \pi^A(X_0, X_A; X_B)\right)$$
$$\max_{X_B}(\pi^B(X_B; X_0, X_A))$$

In the invasion outcome A (B) enters B's (A's) market so that X_0^I, X_B^I solve

$$\text{(6)} \qquad \max_{X_0}(\pi^A(X_0, 0; X_B))$$
$$\max_{X_B}(\pi^B(X_B; 0, X_0))$$

Finally, when there is no entry in market **X** except for the existing product, X_0, firm A remains a monopoly in that market. Therefore

$$\text{(7)} \qquad X_0^M = \operatorname*{argmax}_{X_0} \pi^A(X_0, 0, 0)$$

Y_0^M, Y_0^o, Y_0^I, etc., are similarly defined. Thus the payoffs corresponding to each of the outcomes in (3) can be written as:

$$\text{(8)} \qquad I\colon\ \pi^A(I) = p^0(X_0^I, 0, X_B^I)X_0^I + p^A(Y_0^I, Y_A^I, 0)\,Y_A^I - R$$
$$C\colon\ \pi^A(C) = p^0(X_0^C, X_A^C, 0)X_0^C + p^A(X_0^C, X_A^C, 0)X_A^C - R$$
$$AM\colon\ \pi^A(AM) = p^0(X_0^M, 0, 0)X_0^M + p^A(Y_0^o, Y_A^o, Y_B^o)Y_A^o - R$$
$$BM\colon\ \pi^A(BM) = p^0(X_0^o, X_A^o, X_B^o)X_0^o + p^A(X_0^o, X_A^o, X_B^o)X_A^o - R$$

and similarly for firm B, with the appropriate Y_i replacing X_i.

Having obtained the reduced-form payoffs arising from the second stage, we can now solve the game in product choice. This essentially involves ranking the payoffs in (8). By symmetry between the firms, it is only necessary to derive the rankings for one firm; the corresponding ranking will then hold for the other.

Both firms find C preferable to I: because of the symmetry between markets each firm can always "invade" its own market (i.e., firm A produces X_A^I instead of Y_A^I). However, by maximizing jointly over both products the firm can do better than invading, since it internalizes the adverse impact generated by the cross-effect between products. More formally[6]

Proposition 1. $\pi^A(C) > \pi^A(I)$ and $\pi^B(C) > \pi^B(I)$

i.e., outcome C is preferable to I.

However, I is preferred by A to the "oligopolistic" outcome BM, where B enters market **X** when A has already done so. Similarly, I is preferred to AM

[6] Proofs to Propositions 1 and 2 and other details are contained in Bhatt [1985].

by firm B. The reason is that the firm that already has a stake in the market has taken up the burden of restricting output for the whole market since it constrains output in one sub-market to mitigate the adverse effect on the adjacent sub-market. This is the idea behind Proposition 2.

Proposition 2. $\pi^A(I) > \pi^A(BM)$ and $\pi^B(I) > \pi^B(AM)$

One more comparison is required in order to solve for the product choice game. Does firm A(B) prefer C to $AM(BM)$, the case where one of the firms remains a monopoly in its own market? In case C, profits are jointly maximized with respect to X_0 and X_A. In case AM, although a monopoly position is achieved in market **X**, A competes against two products, Y_0 and Y_B, in market **Y**. Clearly there exists a trade-off between profits from the existing product, X_0, and profits from the newly introduced product which is either X_A *or* Y_A. The direction of the inequality between AM and C depends upon the underlying parameters of the demand functions. Therefore the two cases are considered as distinct possibilities.

Case I.

(9a) $\pi^A(AM) > \pi^A(C)$ and $\pi^B(BM) > \pi^B(C)$

Case II.

(9b) $\pi^A(AM) \leqslant \pi^A(C)$ and $\pi^B(BM) \leqslant \pi^B(C)$

Assume first that Case I holds. Let the firms choose products sequentially such that firm A moves first followed by B. Note that because of the symmetry between firms, it is irrelevant which particular firm has the first move. There is no strategic advantage derived from being the first mover.

Theorem 1. If Case I holds, and firms choose products simultaneously or sequentially, the unique equilibrium is mutual invasion.

Proof. Consider the game in extensive form in Figure 1. If A produces X_A, B obtains a payoff of $\pi^B(BM)$ if it produces X_B and $\pi^B(C)$ if it remains in its home market with Y_B. By (9a), $\pi^B(BM) > \pi^B(C)$. Therefore B is better off invading market **X**.

If A produces Y_A in market **Y**, B gets $\pi^B(I)$ if it invades market **X** and $\pi^B(AM)$ if it does not. By Proposition 2, $\pi^B(I) > \pi^B(AM)$. Therefore B invades.

Given that B invades in either case, A's best response is to invade because, by Proposition 2, $\pi^A(I) > \pi^A(BM)$. Hence, by symmetry, invasion is the unique equilibrium outcome.

If the product choice game is played simultaneously, invasion is a dominant strategy since regardless of the other player's strategy, each firm's best response is to invade.

In normal form this game is simply a Prisoners' Dilemma. Although both players are better off at the no-invasion outcome, they invade. Moreover no promise that either player makes can be credible. Suppose B promises not to invade if A does likewise. But at either node B's optimal strategy is to invade. Knowing that, A will not believe the promise.

The basic point that emerges is that firms' entry into one another's markets can be induced by strategic manoeuvres rather than market expansion incentives. Firms invade to avoid being caught in a situation where they share their market with their rivals after having entered their own markets with a new product. Knowing that the best outcome, $\pi^A(AM)$, will not be available, firm A would like the next best, $\pi^A(C)$. This choice, however, would induce invasion by B. Thus invasion is a defensive measure designed to avert the worst outcome, $\pi^A(BM)$. Such an issue would not arise in single-market models. Without the need for a defensive strategy, proliferation into close substitutes is optimal since it pre-empts rivals and potential entrants from slicing into one's own market. A deterrence equilibrium via pre-emption can arise only if pre-emption can be absolute. As in Judd [1985], firm A(B) finds it optimal to invade B's(A's) market when the latter has entered its own market, or, equivalently, if the incumbent has related products in the same market.

Case II leads to a different set of equilibria, as the relative rankings of the payoffs have been altered.

Theorem 2. If Case II holds and firms play the product-choice game sequentially, the unique equilibrium is the collusive outcome.

Proof. Suppose firm A invades market **Y** with Y_A. Then firm B obtains $\pi^B(AM)$ if it does not invade and $\pi^B(I)$ if it invades. By Proposition 2, $\pi^B(I) > \pi^B(AM)$. If A does not invade and produces X_A, B obtains $\pi^B(BM)$ if it invades and $\pi^B(C)$ if it remains in market **Y**. By (9b), $\pi^B(BM) \leqslant \pi^B(C)$. Hence B does not invade.

A obtains $\pi^A(I)$ if it invades and $\pi^A(C)$ if it does not. By Proposition 1, $\pi^A(C) > \pi^A(I)$. Hence, neither A nor B invade, and the unique outcome is collusion. Firms attain the Pareto optimal profit point.

Suppose, now, that firms play the product-choice game simultaneously and that Case II holds. Then we have two Nash equilibria in pure strategies arising from the existence of weakly dominated strategies. Each firm finds "invasion" to be the best response to "invasion" and "no invasion" the best response to "no invasion". In addition, there exists an equilibrium in mixed strategies, where each firm randomizes over the two pure strategies. However, by Proposition 1, the "no invasion" Nash equilibrium Pareto dominates the other two equilibria. By being mutually recognizable as the best strategy there is a focal point argument for firms to choose the pure strategy "no invasion". Thus, there is some reasonable convention which is intrinsic to the structure of the game that assists in selection of one of the equilibria, C, as the actual outcome.

IV. EQUILIBRIUM IN NON-REPLICA MARKETS: LINEAR DEMAND CASE

To investigate the effect of non-replica markets, I consider the tractable case of linear demand. Then the profit functions are given by:

$$\text{(10)}\qquad \begin{aligned} \pi^A(X_0, X_A, Y_A) &= (a - dX_0 - b(X_A + X_B))X_0 \\ &\quad + (\alpha - \delta X_A - b(X_0 + X_B))X_A \\ &\quad + (\alpha - \delta Y_A - b(Y_0 + Y_B))Y_A - R \\ \pi^B(Y_0, Y_B, X_B) &= (a - dY_0 - b(Y_A + Y_B))Y_0 \\ &\quad + (\tilde{\alpha} - \tilde{\delta} Y_B - b(Y_0 + Y_A))Y_B \\ &\quad + (\tilde{\alpha} - \tilde{\delta} X_B - b(X_0 + X_A))X_B - R \end{aligned}$$

First, assume that markets are replicas. Then $a = \alpha = \tilde{\alpha}$ and $d = \delta = \tilde{\delta}$. A straightforward calculation of the Cournot equilibrium quantities and the corresponding payoffs shows that under these assumptions Case I holds—that is, $\pi^A(AM) > \pi^A(C)$ for firm A and similarly for firm B. Hence, by Theorem 1, mutual invasion is the unique equilibrium.

There exist a number of ways in which one could allow for inter-market differences, each of which could lead to a possibly different set of equilibria. I shall consider the specific case where $a < \alpha = \tilde{\alpha}$ and $d = \delta = \tilde{\delta}$. This makes potential sub-markets symmetrically larger for both firms. With entry into home as well as foreign markets made equally attractive, the preferred product line of each firm is unclear. It can be shown that when occupied markets are not significantly smaller than potential markets (that is, $\alpha > a$), (9a) applies and we have mutual invasion as the outcome of the game. However, if initially occupied markets are *significantly* larger than potential markets (that is, $\alpha \gg a$), then (9b) holds. By Theorem 2, the collusive outcome obtains, and firms segment instead of interlacing. If new markets are sufficiently large, a monopoly in the old market combined with a shared rival's market is less attractive than expanding at home.

V. CONCLUDING REMARKS

Two principal results have been obtained in this paper. Firstly, using a simple differentiated product duopoly model, it has been shown that given an unserved market and sequential or simultaneous entry, monopolistic pre-emption is not an unqualified result. When pre-emption cannot be absolute, firms prefer to invade rather than proliferate in home markets since the latter strategy makes them vulnerable to invasion at a stage when aggressive behavior is least appealing. The point is that once firms have diversified in a given market they have "raised the stakes" in that market so that aggressive output strategies are particularly infelicitous. Entry by other firms into such a market creates an asymmetry between the entrant who plays as a simple duopolist and the incumbent who is a double duopolist in that the latter has to coordinate the strategies of all its products in that market in the post-entry Cournot game. This coordination leaves the incumbent with a disproportionate amount of the burden of restricting output for the whole market. This very disadvantage induces firms to invade precisely when rivals have diversified within their own markets.

This analysis may shed some light on the relative unprofitability of horizontal mergers. Firms may not have incentives for such mergers even in the absence of anti-trust legislation. On the contrary, there could be a greater move towards corporate mergers or mergers across markets related by low cross-elasticities. Applying this analysis to international trade across oligopolistic markets, one can argue that invading foreign markets may be preferable to developing new products within home markets, absent any trade restrictions. Correspondingly, if firms in an industry have diversified widely, there exists an incentive to install trade restrictions so as to impede invasion by foreign firms into a market where firms have "raised the stakes".

A second result obtained in this paper is that despite the fact that firms play strategically to improve their profit position (i.e., when the actions of other firms, particularly potential entrants, are taken into account), the Pareto-optimal outcome is not, in general, attained. Moreover, the incentive structure of the game makes it unprofitable for any one firm to ignore the possibility of strategic play while other firms do not.

SWATI BHATT,
Federal Reserve Bank of New York,
33 Liberty Street,
New York, NY 10045,
USA.

ACCEPTED OCTOBER 1986

REFERENCES

BAIN, J. S., 1956, *Barriers to New Competition* (Harvard University Press).

BHATT, S., 1985, 'Non-price Competition in Oligopolistic Industries', unpublished Ph.D. thesis, Princeton University.

BRANDER, A. J. and EATON, J., 1984, 'Product Line Rivalry', *American Economic Review*, Vol. 74, No. 3, pp. 323–334.

CAVES, R. E. and PORTER, M. E., 1977, 'From Entry Barriers to Mobility Barriers', *Quarterly Journal of Economics*, Vol. 91, No. 2, pp. 241–261.

JUDD, K., 1985, 'Credible Spatial Preemption', *Rand Journal of Economics*, Vol. 16, No. 2, pp. 153–167.

SCHMALENSEE, R., 1978, 'Entry Deterrence in the Ready-to-Eat Breakfast Cereal Industry', *Bell Journal of Economics*, Vol. 9, No. 2, pp. 305–327.

THE JOURNAL OF INDUSTRIAL ECONOMICS 0022-1821 $2.00
Volume XXXVI December 1987 No. 2

ON STACKELBERG EQUILIBRIA WITH DIFFERENTIATED PRODUCTS: THE CRITICAL ROLE OF THE STRATEGY SPACE

MARCEL BOYER AND MICHEL MOREAUX

Comparing the Nash and Stackelberg equilibria in a differentiated products model under price and for quantity strategy spaces, it is shown that, whatever the role (leader, follower, Nash competitor), it is always more profitable to be a quantity (price) setter if the goods are substitutes (complements). However for the consumers price competition is always the best. Concerning total surpluses the ranking is first the Bertrand equilibrium, then the price Stackelberg, followed by the mixed Nash, the quantity Stackelberg and the Cournot equilibria for both the complement and substitute cases.

I. INTRODUCTION

IN THIS paper we systematically explore the effects of the distribution of roles between duopolists (leader, follower, Nash competitor), the kind of cross-relations between goods (complements or substitutes) and the strategy spaces (prices and/or quantities) on first profits, second consumer surplus and third total surplus.

The surplus comparisons are evidently relevant for appraising the intensity of the non-competitive distortions raised by different market configurations. The profit comparisons may be of some interest if we wish to improve our understanding of the forces at work in the emergence of different market structures. We do not pretend to have an endogenous determination of such market structures. However, without a clear evaluation of the gains, we doubt that such a determination can ever be made.

The kind of inter-relation between products is a classical choice variable of the firms, via the characteristics of the goods. On the contrary the strategy spaces are often given exogenously in most models. As it was rightly pointed out by Singh and Vives [1984], firms can commit themselves to different binding contracts with customers, some of which are equivalent to a commitment on prices and other ones to a commitment on quantites.

It is a well known result in duopoly theory that the nature and efficiency characteristics of an equilibrium state of the market (or markets if products are differentiated) depend crucially on the kind of strategy space, prices or

* We would like to express our thanks to two anonymous referees and to the editor for helpful comments and advice on this paper. Needless to say, we remain solely responsible for any remaining imperfections.

quantities, used by the firms. It is a trivial result if firms sell a homogeneous product. But this is only a case of extreme substitutability, and perhaps not the most frequently experienced. However we know very little about this relationship when the goods are differentiated and in particular when they are complements rather than substitutes. Recently, such problems began to be systematically scrutinized for Nash equilibria (see for example Deneckere [1983], Singh and Vives [1984]). In Stackelberg equilibria the problem is even more crucial since the profitability of leadership or followership, consumers' surplus and social surplus can critically depend upon the kind of strategy, price or quantity, and the sort of cross-relation between the goods. For example, it is quite clear that in a case of perfect substitutability, if both the leader and the follower are quantity setters, the leader's position will be better than the follower's. But if the game is a price game, then it will be better to be the follower. Indeed, the follower (second mover) can always capture all the market by undercutting slightly the price quoted by the leader (first-mover) (see Ono [1978, 1982]; Boyer and Moreaux [1986(a), 1986(b)]; and Gal-Or [1985] for more on this subject). As for efficiency, it will be better, indeed optimal, if firms compete in prices rather than in quantities. What happens if the two goods are not perfect substitutes, or if the two goods are complements?

To switch from a Nash equilibrium to a Stackelberg one (within the same strategy space) implies that one of the duopolists will improve his gains and the other one will be made worse off. But the two moves do not necessarily balance. Moreover, the total welfare and the consumer welfare can change in the process. It will be shown that the two must be carefully distinguished and that their changes can take different directions.

In order to properly isolate the differences resulting only from the asymmetrical leadership or followership positions, it will be assumed that the demands for the two goods are the same, i.e. that the quantity sold of each good by either duopolist is the same function of its own price, and that the cross-effects are also the same. Furthermore, we will work with the simplest model allowing the detection of structural changes when passing from a system of substitutes to a system of complements. In other words, the possible changes coming from more or less intense substitutability alone, or from more or less intense complementarity alone, will not be investigated (that such alterations could be consequential has been made clear by Deneckere [1983]; see also Shubik [1980]). Only substitutability and complementarity in the neighborhood of independence will be studied here. This will allow us to provide a rather exhaustive characterization which could not be achieved otherwise.

The paper is organized as follows: the model is presented in section II. The Stackelberg equilibria are studied in section III, and Nash equilibria in section IV. In section V we compare the two sets of equilibria. In the conclusion, we summarize the results.

II. THE MODEL

We consider an economy with a continuum [0, 1] of identical consumers. Let the typical consumer's utility function be

$$(1)\qquad U(q_1, q_2, m) = \frac{1-\alpha}{1-\alpha^2}(q_1+q_2) - \frac{1}{2(1-\alpha^2)}(q_1^2 - 2\alpha q_1 q_2 + q_2^2) + m,$$

$-1 < \alpha < 1$, where $q_i, i = 1, 2$, is the amount of good i and m the amount of some numeraire good consumed by the individual. If $p_i, i = 1, 2$, is the price of good i, then the consumer's utility maximization leads to the following system of demand functions:

$$(2)\qquad q_i(p_1, p_2) = \max\{1 - p_i - \alpha p_j, 0\}, \qquad j, i = 1, 2 \quad j \neq i$$

Assuming that the measure of consumers over [0, 1] is equal to 1, the market demand functions are:

$$(3)\qquad q_i^M(p_1, p_2) = \max\{1 - p_i - \alpha p_j, 0\}, \qquad i, j = 1, 2 \quad j \neq i$$

For negative, zero or positive α values, the non-numeraire goods are respectively substitutes, independent or complements. It will be noticed that in such a model, perfect substitutability is excluded, since for whatever value of α, $\alpha \in (-1, 0)$, the market of good i cannot disappear whatever the quoted price of good $j \neq i$ is. But, as explained in the introduction, only α values in the neighborhood of zero will be taken into consideration since we are primarily interested in the qualitative changes when passing from one type of intermarket cross-effect to the other.

The inverse demand functions are:

$$(4)\qquad p_i = \frac{1-\alpha}{1-\alpha^2} - \frac{1}{1-\alpha^2} q_i + \frac{\alpha}{1-\alpha^2} q_j, \qquad j, i = 1, 2 \quad j \neq i$$

for $1 - \alpha + \alpha q_j \geqslant q_i \geqslant 0$, $j, i = 1, 2, j \neq i$. Any pair (q_1, q_2) which would not satisfy these inequalities imply that the free exchange market rules are violated since some consumers would then buy at least one of the goods in such a quantity that its marginal utility for that good would be negative.

We will assume that each good i is sold by a different firm i, working at zero cost. It would do equally well to assume that each one is working with some non-zero constant marginal cost lower than one, provided that profits above variable costs cover fixed costs.

In this simple framework, total welfare (surplus) is obtained by evaluating the utility function (1) at the equilibrium values (q_1^*, q_2^*), and the consumer surplus is obtained by substracting the profits of the two firms from the total surplus.

III. THE LEADER-FOLLOWER GAMES

Let us first examine the case where the leader, which we will index as #1, selects as a strategy space the price p_1 of good #1. Given the choice of p_1 by the leader, the follower (firm #2)'s profits, π_2, become:

(5) $$\pi_2 = \max\{p_2 - \alpha p_1 p_2 - p_2^2, 0\}, \qquad p_1, p_2 \geqslant 0$$

so that the follower best reply function $\hat{p}_2(p_1)$ is:

(6) $$\hat{p}_2(p_1) = \max\{\tfrac{1}{2}(1-\alpha p_1), 0\}, \qquad p_1 \geqslant 0$$

Taking into account the follower's reaction, the leader maximizes his own profit:

(7) $$\pi_1 = \max\{(1 - p_1 - \alpha \max\{\tfrac{1}{2}(1-\alpha p_1), 0\})p_1, 0\}$$

Direct calculations show that the equilibrium state is defined by the following values of the relevant variables where (LF/p) stands for "in a leader-follower game with prices as the strategy space":

(8) $$p_1^*(LF/p) = \frac{2-\alpha}{2(2-\alpha^2)}, \; q_1^*(LF/p) = \frac{2-\alpha}{4}, \; \pi_1^*(LF/p) = \frac{(2-\alpha)^2}{8(2-\alpha^2)}$$

$$p_2^*(LF/p) = \frac{4-2\alpha-\alpha^2}{4(2-\alpha^2)}, \; q_2^*(LF/p) = \frac{4-2\alpha-\alpha^2}{4(2-\alpha^2)},$$

$$\pi_2^*(LF/p) = \frac{(4-2\alpha-\alpha^2)^2}{16(2-\alpha^2)^2}$$

Before we compare the leader and follower positions, it must be stressed that what matters is the leader's choice of the price as a strategy space, and that the follower's choice of announcing prices rather than quantities is inconsequential. The follower's profit function could be expressed as:

(9) $$\pi_2 = \max\{(1-\alpha p_1)q_2 - q_2^2, 0\}, \qquad q_2 \geqslant 0, p_1 \geqslant 0$$

so that the quantity best reply function would take the form:

(10) $$\hat{q}_2(p_1) = \max\{\tfrac{1}{2}(1-\alpha p_1), 0\}, \qquad p_1 \geqslant 0$$

Given the inverse demand function (4) of good #1, q_1 can be expressed as a function of q_2 and p_1:

$$q_1 = 1 - \alpha + \alpha q_2 - (1-\alpha^2)p_1$$

so that, given the best-reply (10) of firm #2, the leader's profit becomes:

(11) $$\pi_1 = \max\{(1-(\alpha/2))p_1 - (1-(\alpha^2/2))p_1^2, 0\}, \qquad p_1 \geqslant 0$$

Maximization of π_1 implies $p_1^* = \dfrac{2-\alpha}{2(2-\alpha^2)}$, and the same values for p_2^*, q_1^* and q_2^*, and therefore π_1^* and π_2^*, as in (8).

Comparing now the prices, quantities and profits for the leader and the follower, we get

$$(12)\qquad \frac{p_1^*(LF/p)}{p_2^*(LF/p)} = \frac{K}{K-\alpha^2}, \frac{q_1^*(LF/p)}{q_2^*(LF/p)} = \frac{K-\alpha^2(1-\alpha)}{K},$$

$$\frac{\pi_1^*(LF/p)}{\pi_2^*(LF/p)} = \frac{K+\alpha^3(4-3\alpha)}{K}$$

where K is a polynomial in α whose value is positive for K in the neighborhood of zero. The value of K is the same in the numerator and denominator of any given ratio, but may be different in different ratios (the same convention on K will be used throughout this paper). Hence:

Proposition I.[1] In the price leader model:
(1) the price quoted by the leader is always higher than the price quoted by the follower, whether the goods are substitutes or complements,
(2) the quantity sold by the leader is always smaller than the quantity sold by the follower,
(3) the leader's profit is smaller (larger) than the follower's when the goods are substitutes (complements).

Suppose now that the leader selects quantity as a strategy space. For a given q_1 the profit function of duopolist #2 is:

$$(13)\qquad \pi_2 = \max\left\{\frac{1-\alpha}{1-\alpha^2} + \frac{\alpha}{1-\alpha^2}q_2q_1 - \frac{1}{1-\alpha^2}q_2^2, 0\right\}, \qquad q_1, q_2 \geqslant 0$$

so that the quantity best reply function $\hat{q}_2(q_1)$ will be

$$(14)\qquad \hat{q}_2(q_1) = \max\{\tfrac{1}{2}(1-\alpha+\alpha q_1), 0\}, \qquad q_1 \geqslant 0$$

Given the follower's reaction, the leader's profit as a function of his own production level q_1 can be written as:

$$(15)\qquad \pi_1 = \max\{\tfrac{1}{2}((2+\alpha)(1-\alpha)q_1 - (2-\alpha^2)q_1^2), 0\}, \qquad q_1 \geqslant 0$$

Maximization of the leader's profit determines the equilibrium state of the markets. Straightforward calculations lead to:

$$(16)\qquad p_1^*(LF/q) = \frac{2+\alpha}{4(1+\alpha)}, \; q_1^*(LF/q) = \frac{(1-\alpha)(2+\alpha)}{2(2-\alpha^2)},$$

$$\pi_1^*(LF/q) = \frac{(1-\alpha)(2+\alpha)^2}{8(1+\alpha)(2-\alpha^2)}, \; p_2^*(LF/q) = \frac{4+2\alpha-\alpha^2}{4(1+\alpha)(2-\alpha^2)},$$

$$q_2^*(LF/q) = \frac{(1+\alpha)(4+2\alpha-\alpha^2)}{4(2-\alpha^2)}, \; \pi_2^*(LF/q) = \frac{(1-\alpha)(4+2\alpha-\alpha^2)^2}{16(1+\alpha)(2-\alpha^2)^2}$$

As in the price leadership model, what matters here is the choice by the

[1] All the propositions must be read as meaning: "In some neighborhood of $\alpha = 0, \ldots$" even if some of them extend over the whole range $\alpha \in (-1, +1)$.

leader of the quantity as a strategy space, i.e. whatever the choice of a strategy space by the follower, either prices or quantities, the equilibrium values in the markets will remain the same. Given q_1, the profit function of the follower could be rewritten:

$$\pi_2 = \max\{(1-\alpha+\alpha q_1)p_2-(1-\alpha^2)p_2^2, 0\}, \qquad q_1, p_2 \geqslant 0 \tag{17}$$

from which one gets the price best reply function:

$$\hat{p}_2(q_1) = \max\left\{\frac{1}{2(1-\alpha^2)}(1-\alpha+\alpha q_1), 0\right\}, \qquad q_1 \geqslant 0 \tag{18}$$

From the demand function of good #1, the price of good #1 can be expressed as a function of its own price p_1 and the quantity sold q_2 of good #2:

$$p_1 = 1-\alpha p_2 - q_1$$

Hence, given the best-reply (18) of firm #2, the leader's profit is:

$$\pi_1 = \max\left\{\left(1-\frac{\alpha(1-\alpha)}{2(1-\alpha^2)}\right)q_1 - \left(1+\frac{\alpha^2}{2(1-\alpha^2)}\right)q_1^2, 0\right\} \tag{19}$$

and maximization of π_1 implies that $q_1^* = ((1-\alpha)(2+\alpha))/2(2-\alpha^2)$ giving the same values of $p_1^*, q_2^*, p_2^*, \pi_1^*$ and π_2^* as in (16).

In this quantity leadership model, comparison of the follower's and leader's prices, quantities and profits leads to:

$$\frac{p_1^*(LF/q)}{p_2^*(LF/q)} = \frac{K-\alpha^2(1-\alpha)}{K}, \quad \frac{q_1^*(LF/q)}{q_2^*(LF/q)} = \frac{K}{K-\alpha^2}, \tag{20}$$

$$\frac{\pi_1^*(LF/q)}{\pi_2^*(LF/q)} = \frac{K-\alpha^3(4+3\alpha)}{K}$$

hence, the following proposition:

Proposition II. In the quantity leader model:
(1) the price quoted by the leader is smaller than the price quoted by the follower,
(2) the quantity sold by the leader is larger than the quantity sold by the follower,
(3) the leader's profit is larger (smaller) than the follower's when the goods are substitutes (complements).

Part 3 of propositions I and II are special cases of the main result in Gal-Or [1985]. She showed that the first mover earns higher (lower) profits when reaction functions are downward-sloping (upward-sloping). In the price leader model, reaction functions are indeed downward-sloping when goods are complements, while in the quantity leader model they are downward-sloping when goods are substitutes.

It remains to be checked if the choice of the strategy space is more important, in some sense, than the "role" (leader or follower) actually played. Since:

$$(21)\qquad \frac{\pi_2^*(LF/q)}{\pi_2^*(LF/p)} = \frac{K}{K+2\alpha^5}$$

and given (12) and (20), profits can be ordered as follows:

$$(22)\qquad \alpha < 0: \pi_1^*(LF/q) > \pi_2^*(LF/q) > \pi_2^*(LF/p) > \pi_1^*(LF/p)$$

$$(23)\qquad \alpha > 0: \pi_1^*(LF/p) > \pi_2^*(LF/p) > \pi_2^*(LF/q) > \pi_1^*(LF/q)$$

Inequalities (22) and (23) imply

Proposition III. The choice of the strategy space "dominates" the role distribution in the following sense: if the goods are substitutes (complements) profits accruing to any duopolist in the quantity (price) game, whatever his role in this game, will be larger than in the price (quantity) game, whatever his role in this last game.

It will be noticed that this ranking of profits comes mainly via a price effect in the case of substitutes and a quantity effect in the case of complements. From (8) and (16), we get:

$$(24)\qquad \frac{p_2^*(LF/q)}{p_1^*(LF/p)} = \frac{K}{K-\alpha^2}, \frac{p_1^*(LF/p)}{p_1^*(LF/q)} = \frac{K}{K-\alpha^3}, \frac{p_1^*(LF/q)}{p_2^*(LF/p)} = \frac{K}{K-\alpha^2}$$

$$(25)\qquad \frac{q_2^*(LF/p)}{q_1^*(LF/q)} = \frac{K}{K-\alpha^2}, \frac{q_1^*(LF/q)}{q_1^*(LF/p)} = \frac{K}{K+\alpha^3}, \frac{q_1^*(LF/p)}{q_2^*(LF/q)} = \frac{K}{K-\alpha^2}$$

so that, taking into account (12) and (20), the prices and quantities rankings are the following:

$$(26)\qquad \alpha < 0: p_2^*(LF/q) > p_1^*(LF/q) > p_1^*(LF/p) > p_2^*(LF/p)$$
$$q_2^*(LF/p) > q_1^*(LF/q) > q_1^*(LF/p) > q_2^*(LF/q)$$

$$(27)\qquad \alpha > 0: p_2^*(LF/q) > p_1^*(LF/p) > p_1^*(LF/q) > p_2^*(LF/p)$$
$$q_2^*(LF/p) > q_1^*(LF/p) > q_1^*(LF/q) > q_2^*(LF/q)$$

Hence, when the goods are substitutes, the prices quoted by any duopolist are always higher in the quantity game than those quoted by any of the duopolists in the price game, but no simple quantity ranking arises. When the goods are complements, the quantity sold by any duopolist is always larger in the price game than that sold by any one in the quantity game, but no simple price ranking appears.

An immediate consequence of the ranking of profits (22)–(23) is that, as far as the strategy space is not pre-ordained outside the model, the leader will always choose to fight with quantities if the goods are substitutes and with prices if the goods are complements. Hence, since the kind of response, price or quantity, by the follower is unimportant, we get in the leader-follower model an endogenous determination of the strategy space. As will be shown in the following section, it is not the case with Nash models.

The last point to examine is the consumer and total welfares in the two kinds of competition. A look at (27) shows that in case of substitutes (complements), the price (quantity) game will provide more goods than the quantity (price) game, so that in this symmetrical model consumer and total surpluses would have to be larger in the price (quantity) leadership model than in the quantity (price) leadership model. Simple calculations reveal that consumer (*CS*) and total (*B*) surpluses are the following where "hot" stands for *h*igher *o*rder *t*erms, and $X = 32(1+\alpha)(1-\alpha^2)(2-\alpha^2)^2$:

$$(28)\qquad CS(LF/p)=\frac{32-32\alpha-48\alpha^2+hot}{X},\ CS(LF/q)=\frac{32-32\alpha-64\alpha^2+hot}{X}$$

$$(29)\qquad TS(LF/p)=\frac{96-32\alpha-192\alpha^2+hot}{X},$$

$$TS(LF/q)=\frac{96-32\alpha-208\alpha^2+hot}{X}$$

from which we conclude:

Proposition IV.[1] Consumer and total surpluses are larger in the price leader-follower competition than in the quantity leader-follower competition in both the substitutes and the complements cases.

IV. NASH GAMES

In a Nash setting, one can conceive of price competition, quantity competition and some kind of mixed competition. By mixed competition we do not refer to the usual meaning of the term in game theory (i.e. mixed strategies as probability distributions with pure strategies as support) but to the fact that the two duopolists do not move in the same strategy space, one of the duopolists being a price setter and the other one being a quantity setter. (These types of equilibria have been studied by Salant [1976] and Ulph [1980] in the context of exhaustible resource markets.) This possibility is excluded in the leader-follower model since, as shown in the preceding section, the kind of reply by the follower in terms of prices and quantities does not matter. Because the comparison between price and quantity competition has been dealt in detail by Singh and Vives [1984] we will concentrate our analysis on the mixed case.

—From Singh and Vives [1984] we know that, at the Bertrand equilibrium:

$$(30)\qquad p^*(B)=\frac{1}{2+\alpha},\ q^*(B)=\frac{1}{2+\alpha},\ \pi^*(B)=\frac{1}{(2+\alpha)^2}$$

and that at the Cournot equilibrium:

$$(31) \qquad p^*(C)=\frac{1}{(1+\alpha)(2-\alpha)},\ q^*(C)=\frac{1-\alpha}{2+\alpha},\ \pi^*(C)=\frac{1}{(1+\alpha)(2-\alpha)^2}$$

—Now from the reaction functions (10) and (18), the mixed equilibrium, with firm #1 announcing a price p_1 and firm #2 announcing a quantity q_2, is defined by the two following equations

$$(32) \qquad p_1=\frac{1}{2(1-\alpha^2)}(1-\alpha+q_2)$$

$$(33) \qquad q_2=\tfrac{1}{2}(1-\alpha p_1)$$

so that:

$$(34) \qquad p^*(M/p)=\frac{2-\alpha}{4-3\alpha^2},\ q^*(M/p)=\frac{(1-\alpha^2)(2-\alpha)}{4-3\alpha^2},$$

$$\pi^*(M/p)=\frac{(1-\alpha^2)(2-\alpha)^2}{(4-3\alpha^2)^2}$$

$$(35) \qquad p^*(M/q)=\frac{2-\alpha-\alpha^2}{4-3\alpha^2},\ q^*(M/q)=\frac{2-\alpha-\alpha^2}{4-3\alpha^2},$$

$$\pi^*(M/q)=\frac{(2-\alpha-\alpha^2)^2}{(4-3\alpha^2)^2}$$

where $x^*(M/q)$ and $x^*(M/p)$ are the equilibrium values of the variable x for the quantity setter and the price setter respectively.

—Elementary calculations show that the rankings of prices, quantities and profits are:

$$(36) \qquad \alpha<0: p^*(C)>p^*(M/p)>p^*(M/q)>p^*(B)$$

$$q^*(M/q)>q^*(B)>q^*(C)>q^*(M/p)$$

$$\pi^*(C)>\pi^*(M/q)>\pi^*(B)>\pi^*(M/p)$$

$$(37) \qquad \alpha>0: p^*(M/p)>p^*(C)>p^*(B)>p^*(M/q)$$

$$q^*(B)>q^*(M/q)>q^*(M/p)>q^*(C)$$

$$\pi^*(B)>\pi^*(M/p)>\pi^*(C)>\pi^*(M/q)$$

Whatever the strategy space of the rival, it is always better to be a quantity setter than a price setter if goods are substitutes, and to be a price setter rather than a quantity setter if goods are complements. As shown by the prices and quantities rankings, these results come from intricate price and quantity effects, mainly as far as the mixed equilibrium is concerned. However, it is worthwhile noticing the following points: *First*, concerning prices in the mixed equilibrium, it is always the price of the good sold by the price setter which is the highest, whatever the kind of relation between the two goods (contrary to what might have been guessed from the pure quantity and the pure price competition models) and, furthermore, if prices of the mixed equilibrium are between Cournot prices and Bertrand prices in case of substitutes, they switch to the extreme ends of the range in case of complements. Symmetrically, the quantity sold by the quantity setter is always larger than that sold by the price setter in both cases of substitutes and complements, and these quantities are between the Bertrand and Cournot ones in the case of complements, but switch to the extremities of the range in the case of substitutes. *Second*, with respect to profits, to be a quantity setter is a more comfortable position than to be a price setter if goods are substitutes, but to be a price setter is better if goods are complements. However, the best position in the mixed equilibrium is always worse than the best position in pure (quantity if substitutes, prices if complements) competition, and the worst position in that case is always the worst of all. Hence the mixed equilibrium does not appear as some sort of averaging of the Bertrand and Cournot equilibria as far as profits are concerned at the firm level. At the industry level, however, the aggregate profits of the two firms are between the Bertrand and Cournot profits in both cases of substitutes and complements.

It remains to assess which one of these equilibria is the most efficient. Since the quantities in the Bertrand equilibrium are always larger than in the Cournot equilibrium, total welfare (TS) is always greater in the Bertrand competition than in the Cournot one. But the total welfare in the mixed equilibrium cannot be assessed by a simple look at quantities because, in the case of substitutes, the Bertrand and Cournot quantities are between the mixed equilibrium quantities, and, in the case of complements, the mixed equilibrium quantities are between the Bertrand and Cournot ones. Also, the consumer surpluses (CS) cannot be immediately compared since the profit rankings sometimes depart from the quantities rankings. Calculations show the following, where

$$\gamma = 2(1-\alpha^2)(2-\alpha)^2(2+\alpha)^2(4-3\alpha^2)^2:$$

(38) $$CS(C)=\frac{128-256\alpha-160\alpha^2+hot}{Y}, \quad CS(B)=\frac{128-256\alpha-32\alpha^2+hot}{Y}$$

$$CS(M)=\frac{128-256\alpha-96\alpha^2+hot}{Y}$$

(39) $$TS(C)=\frac{384-512\alpha-736\alpha^2+hot}{Y},$$

$$TS(B)=\frac{384-512\alpha-608\alpha^2+hot}{Y}$$

$$TS(M)=\frac{384-512\alpha-672\alpha^2+hot}{Y}$$

(40) $$\forall\alpha: CS(B) > CS(M) > CS(C)$$
$$TS(B) > TS(M) > TS(C)$$

Pure price competition is always better than mixed competition, which is itself better than quantity competition both for consumer welfare and total welfare, whether the goods are substitutes or complements.

V. A COMPARISON OF STACKELBERG AND NASH EQUILIBRIA

In both main types of models, Stackelberg and Nash, a systematic relation can be made explicit between, first, the strategy spaces, and second, the type of intermarket cross-effects. In case of substitutes, quantity competition is more profitable than price competition, and in case of complements, price competition is more profitable than the quantity rivalry. This seems a very robust result since when profits for any role in any model are compared, the ranking persists. Indeed calculations show that:

(41) $$\frac{\pi_1^*(LF/q)}{\pi^*(C)} = \frac{K+\alpha^4}{K}, \quad \frac{\pi_2^*(LF/q)}{\pi^*(M/q)} = \frac{K+0\alpha^3+hot}{K-64\alpha^3+hot}$$
$$\frac{\pi_1^*(LF/p)}{\pi^*(B)} = \frac{K+\alpha^4}{K}, \quad \frac{\pi_2^*(LF/p)}{\pi^*(M/p)} = \frac{K+448\alpha^3+hot}{K+512\alpha^3+hot}$$

Hence, taking into account (22), (23), (41), we get:

(42) $$\alpha < 0: \pi_1^*(LF/q) > \pi^*(C) > \pi^*(M/q) > \pi_2^*(LF/q)$$
$$> \pi_2^*(LF/p) > \pi_1^*(LF/p) > \pi^*(B) > \pi^*(M/p)$$

(43) $$\alpha > 0: \pi_1^*(LF/p) > \pi^*(B) > \pi^*(M/p) > \pi_2^*(LF/p)$$
$$> \pi_2^*(LF/q) > \pi_1^*(LF/q) > \pi^*(C) > \pi^*(M/q)$$

Proposition V.[1] Whatever the role (leader, follower, Nash competitor) it is always more profitable to be a quantity setter if goods are substitutes, and to be a price setter if goods are complements.

It was also clearly apparent in the two preceding sections that price competition was always better than quantity competition for both total welfare and consumer welfare. For total welfare, prevailing price competition is always better since calculations show, with:

$$V = 24\,576 - 8192\alpha$$
$$Y = 32(1+\alpha)(1-\alpha^2)(4-\alpha^2)^2(2-\alpha^2)^2(4-3\alpha^2)^2$$

that:

(44) $$TS(C) = \frac{V - 104\,448\alpha^2 + hot}{Y}, \quad TS(B) = \frac{V - 96\,252\alpha^2 + hot}{Y}$$

$$TS(M) = \frac{V - 100\,352\alpha^2 + hot}{Y}, \quad TS(LF/q) = \frac{V - 102\,400\alpha^2 + hot}{Y}$$

$$TS(LF/p) = \frac{V - 98\,304\alpha^2 + hot}{Y}$$

so that

(45) $$\forall\alpha: TS(B) > TS(LF/p) > TS(M) > TS(LF/q) > TS(C)$$

But generally switching from a Nash equilibrium to a Stackelberg equilibrium (with the same strategy space) implies a loss of total industry profits. And the result is that a Stackelberg equilibrium will be generally better than a Nash equilibrium in terms of consumer surplus. Calculations show that:

(46) $$CS(C) = \frac{W - 43\,008\alpha^2 + hot}{Y}, \quad CS(B) = \frac{W - 26\,624\alpha^2 + hot}{Y}$$

$$CS(M) = \frac{W - 38\,912\alpha^2 + hot}{Y}, \quad CS(LF/q) = \frac{W - 32\,762\alpha^2 + hot}{Y}$$

$$CS(LF/p) = \frac{W - 28\,672\alpha^2 + hot}{Y}$$

and so:

(47) $$\forall\alpha: CS(B) > CS(LF/p) > CS(LF/q) > CS(M) > CS(C)$$

Proposition VI.[1] In both the substitutes and complements cases, the consumer and total surpluses are larger in the Bertrand Equilibrium than in the mixed Nash Equilibrium and larger in the latter than in the Cournot Equilibrium.

Proposition VII.[1] In both the substitutes and complements cases, the Bertrand Equilibrium dominates the two Stackelberg Equilibria (leader in price, leader in quantity) which dominate the *other two Nash Equilibria* (mixed, Cournot). However, when total surplus is considered, then the Bertrand Equilibrium comes on top followed in decreasing order by the Stackelberg-in-price, the mixed Nash, the Stackelberg-in-quantity and the Cournot Equilibria.

CONCLUSION

We have shown in this paper that in a differentiated product world, the relationship between those products (substitutes or complements) could be an important factor in the determination of the kind of strategic competition which duopolists would prefer to see emerging. We also identified which type of competition best serves the consumer's interests and which type maximizes social efficiency. Intransitivities arise between the different cases and criteria.

When the goods are substitutes [complements] it always better to fight in the quantity [price] space whatever the role.

But whether goods are substitutes or complements, the consumer's interest is always best served if the firms are involved in a Bertrand type competition through prices. Therefore, there is no strategic context which uniformly meets both the industry and the consumer's interests. We showed also that total surplus, and therefore social efficiency, is in fact maximized in a Bertrand framework, that is a context where firms compete in prices without anyone taking a leadership role.

Clearly there is a significant gap between showing that two agents would benefit by competing in terms of a certain set of variables rather than in terms of another set, and stating or predicting that the former set will be used. It remains however that identifying such sets do represent a preliminary step in building a theory of endogenous role distribution and of endogenous choice of strategy spaces. We have shown elsewhere (Boyer and Moreaux [1986(a), 1986(b)] that indeed, there exist situations where taking the role of leader (first mover) is a survival strategy for a firm. The results of this paper further suggest that a theory of the endogenous determination of roles and strategy spaces, that is a theory of endogenously determined industrial organization framework, may be developed through the formal analysis of price and/or quantity competition *and* implicit cooperation on roles and strategy spaces. This should be an important item on the agenda of economic theorists.

ACCEPTED FEBRUARY 1987

MARCEL BOYER,
Departement de Sciences Economiques,
Université de Montréal,
Montréal,
Canada.

MICHEL MOREAUX,
GREMAQ,
Université des Sciences Sociales de Toulouse,
Place Anatole-France,
31042 Toulouse Cedex,
France.

REFERENCES

Boyer, Marcel and Moreaux, Michel, 1986(a), 'Rationnement, anticipations rationnelles et équilibre de Stackelberg', *Annales d'Economie et de Statistique*, Vol. 1, pp. 55–73.

Boyer, Marcel and Moreaux, Michel, 1986(b), 'Being a Leader or a Follower: Reflections on von Stackelberg', *International Journal of Industrial Organization*, forthcoming.

Deneckere, Raymond, 1983, 'Duopoly Supergames with Product Differentiation', *Economic Letters*, Vol. 11, pp. 37–42.

GAL-OR, ESTHER, 1985, 'First Mover and Second Mover Advantages', *International Economic Review*, Vol. 26, pp. 649–653.

ONO, YOSHIYASU, 1978, 'The Equilibrium of Duopoly in a Market of Homogeneous Goods', *Economica*, Vol. 45, pp. 287–295.

ONO, YOSHIYASU, 1982, 'Price Leadership: A Theoretical Analysis', *Economica*, Vol. 49, pp. 11–30.

SALANT, STEVEN, 1976, 'Exhaustible Resources and Industrial Structure: A Nash-Cournot Approach to the World Oil Market', *Journal of Political Economy*, Vol. 84, pp. 1079–1093.

SHUBIK, MARTIN (with RICHARD LEVITAN), 1980, *Market Structure and Behavior* (Harvard UP, Cambridge).

SINGH, NIRVIKAR and VIVES, XAVIER, 1984, 'Price and Quantity Competition in a Differentiated Duopoly', *Rand Journal of Economics*, Vol. 15, pp. 546–554.

ULPH, ALISTAIR and FOLIE, G. M., 1980, 'Economic Implications of Stackelberg and Nash-Cournot Equilibria', *Zeitschrift für Nationalökonomie*, Vol. 40, pp. 343–354.

THE JOURNAL OF INDUSTRIAL ECONOMICS 0022-1821 $2.00
Volume XXXVI December 1987 No. 2

OPTIMAL PRICE-QUALITY SCHEDULES AND SUSTAINABILITY*

JONG SEOK KIM

This paper derives a general solution for optimal price-quality scheduling under imperfect information. The solution is general in the sense that it generates the first best, the second best, and the profit maximizing solutions depending on the weights in the objective function. The important assumption is that the fixed setup cost is related to the range of qualities produced by a firm. This paper also demonstrates a nonlinear version of the occasional incompatibility between the second best pricing and sustainability, and derives the conditions for sustainability of the second best price-quality schedule.

I. INTRODUCTION

IN MANY markets, firms can provide many different qualities for a generic type of product with relatively little cost disadvantage. If such markets are characterized by heterogeneous consumers who have different evaluations of product qualities, firms would find it optimal to offer a multitude of different qualities at different prices in order to discriminate among consumers. However, since a firm cannot normally determine each individual consumer's willingness to pay for quality, the firm would have to design a price-quality schedule that discriminates among consumers through self-selection, if the firm knows the overall distribution of consumer tastes.

Mussa and Rosen [1978] considered a monopolist's problem of selecting a price-quality schedule that maximizes profit, given the same information constraint mentioned above. Maskin and Riley [1984] considered a monopolist's profit maximizing quantity discount strategy under the same information constraint in a more general model, which can readily incorporate and extend Mussa and Rosen's results by interpreting quantity as quality. Both of the studies, however, assumed constant returns to scale technologies, and Mussa and Rosen did not assume the cost disadvantage that can arise from producing a wide range of qualities.

In this paper, we analyze a firm that can provide a continuum of different price and quality pairs for a certain range of qualities. We assume that the cost of production is related to the range of qualities produced as well as the quality level of each output. We assume an increasing returns to scale

* This article is a revised version of a chapter of my dissertation. I would like to thank Robert Willig, Michael Katz, and Carl Shapiro for their guidance. I am also very grateful to the editor and two anonymous referees of this journal for their helpful comments on an earlier draft of this paper. Of course, I am solely responsible for any remaining errors.

technology by assuming that a firm must incur a fixed setup cost when it begins operation and that the fixed setup cost is an increasing function of the measure of quality sets produced by the firm. Like the previous studies, we also assume that the firm knows the distribution of consumer tastes, but cannot distinguish individual consumers.

We define the firm's objective as a weighted sum of consumer surplus and profit. This characterization of the objective function is useful, since the solution would include the socially optimal solution, the profit maximizing solution, and the second best solution that maximizes consumer surplus subject to a profit constraint, depending on the weights assigned to consumer surplus and profit. We show that incomplete separation of consumers would occur not only within a quality spectrum depending on the consumer taste distribution as shown originally by Mussa and Rosen but would also always occur at both ends of the quality spectrum.

We then examine sustainability of the second best solution in the contestable market and derive the conditions for sustainability. Panzar and Postlewaite [1984] considered sustainability of quantity discount schedules in the contestable market. They show that nonlinearity of a price-quantity schedule is necessary for sustainability, and that there always exist second best schedules that are sustainable, if marginal costs are constant. We show in this paper, however, that their result is a consequence of the assumption that the fixed cost is constant and not related to the scope of production. We show that, once we assume a "variable" fixed cost that is related to the scope of production, sustainability of the second best scheduling is not necessarily guaranteed, and that subadditivity of the fixed cost function is necessary for sustainability. We then show that the second best scheduling is sustainable, if the fixed cost function exhibits set convexity and the consumer taste distribution satisfies certain conditions.

II. THE MODEL

Consider a market for a product that can be produced at a number of different quality levels. Let q denote a quality level. Larger values of q indicate higher quality levels. The unit cost of production for any particular quality is denoted as $C(q)$ and is assumed to be an increasing convex function of q, that is, $C'(q) > 0$, $C''(q) > 0$ for all $q \geqslant 0$. Also, $C(0) = 0$, and there is a fixed setup cost that the firm must incur if it begins production. The fixed setup cost to produce a set of qualities, Q, is given by a set function $K(Q)$.

Each consumer purchases one unit of the product per period and chooses the variety that gives him or her a maximum surplus. Assuming that each consumer spends a small fraction of total expenditure on the product in question, we denote the utility function of a consumer type θ as

$$u = \theta q - p \tag{1}$$

where θ is a parameter that measures a consumer's evaluation of quality, and p is the price the consumer pays for the product. θ is defined on the interval $[0, \infty]$, and the distribution of consumer taste is given by a continuously differentiable density function $f(\theta)$ and a distribution function $F(\theta) = \int f(\theta)\,d\theta$. The number of consumers in this market is normalized, so that $F(\infty) = 1$.

Given this specification of the model, the firm's problem is now to find an optimal price-quality schedule, $P(q)$ or, equivalently, assignment functions of price and quality to consumer type θ, $p(\theta)$ and $q(\theta)$,[1] respectively, subject to the self-selection constraint. The firm must also determine the marginal consumer type, θ^*, and the range of qualities to be produced, i.e., the highest and the lowest qualities to be produced, q_H and q_L, respectively.[2] Therefore, given $p(\theta)$ and $q(\theta)$, the consumer's utility function can be represented as a function of θ:

(2) $$u(\theta) = \theta \cdot q(\theta) - p(\theta), \quad \theta \geqslant \theta^*$$

The self-selection constraint requires specific conditions on $p(\theta)$, $q(\theta)$, and $u(\theta)$. This is discussed in the following section.

III. SELF-SELECTION CONSTRAINTS

First, as is well known, $q(\theta)$ must be nondecreasing in θ.[3] Second, there are marginal consumers, type θ^*, who are indifferent between buying and not buying. Since consumer surplus for any variant is increasing in θ, it follows that (i) consumers of type $\theta < \theta^*$ will not join the market; and (ii) all of the consumers type $\theta \geqslant \theta^*$ will join the market.

Third, determination of optimal $q(\theta)$ for $\theta \geqslant \theta^*$ uniquely determines $p(\theta)$ as

[1] As we will see later in section III, $\dot{q}(\theta) \geqslant 0$ and $\dot{p}(\theta) \geqslant 0$, and $\dot{p}(\theta) = 0$ if $\dot{q}(\theta) = 0$, where $\dot{q}(\theta) \equiv dq(\theta)/d\theta$, and $\dot{p}(\theta) \equiv dp(\theta)/d\theta$. Therefore, $p(\theta)$ is uniquely defined for each value of $q(\theta)$; that is, determination of $p(\theta)$ and $q(\theta)$ is equivalent to determination of $P(q)$.

[2] As we will see later, the optimal quality spectrum offered by the firm is connected and continuous between q_H and q_L, since optimal $q(\theta)$ is continuous when $f(\theta)$ is continuous. That is, optimal $P(q)$ is continuous.

[3] This can be demonstrated as follows: Suppose (q_i, p_i) and (q_j, p_j) are on a price-quality schedule offered by the firm and the optimal choices made by consumer θ_i and θ_j, respectively. Then, the following should be true:

(a) $\theta_i q_j - p_j \leqslant \theta_i q_i - p_i$, and

(b) $\theta_j q_i - p_i \leqslant \theta_j q_j - p_j$

(a) and (b) together imply that

$$\theta_j(q_i - q_j) \leqslant (p_i - p_j) \leqslant \theta_i(q_i - q_j), \text{ or}$$

(c) $(\theta_i - \theta_j)(q_i - q_j) \geqslant \theta$

which means that consumer type θ_i would not buy a lower quality item than a consumer type θ_j, if $\theta_i > \theta_j$. That is, $q(\theta)$ must be nondecreasing in θ.

well, since the self-selection constraint requires[4]

$$(3)\qquad p(\theta) = \theta \cdot q(\theta) - \int_{\theta^*}^{\theta} q(t)dt$$

Because of this simplifying result, the problem is now reduced to finding an optimal quality assignment function, $q(\theta)$, θ^*, and the quality range, $[q_L, q_H]$.

We now define the following:

Definition. A price-quality schedule, $(p(\theta), q(\theta))$, for $\theta \geqslant \theta^*$ is *admissible*, if

$$(4)\qquad \dot{q}(\theta) \geqslant 0, \text{ and}$$

$$(5)\qquad p(\theta) = \theta \cdot q(\theta) - \int_{\theta^*}^{\theta} q(t)dt$$

Definition. $\theta_H = \min\{\theta \mid q_H = q(\theta)\}$

$\theta_L = \max\{\theta \mid q_L = q(\theta)\}$

$\theta^* = \min\{\theta \mid q_L = q(\theta)\}$

IV. OPTIMAL SOLUTIONS

The objective function is defined as a weighted sum of total consumer surplus

[4] This is originally due to Mussa and Rosen, although there are differences in assumptions and derivations. Relationship (3) can be derived as follows:

Since $u(\theta+\Delta) = (\theta+\Delta)\cdot q(\theta+\Delta) - p(\theta+\Delta)$

$$u(\theta+\Delta) - u(\theta) = \theta[q(\theta+\Delta) - q(\theta)] + \Delta \cdot q(\theta+\Delta) - [p(\theta+\Delta) - p(\theta)]$$

Dividing both sides of the above by Δ, and taking the limit as $\Delta \to 0$, we get

$$\text{(a)}\qquad \dot{u}(\theta) = \theta \cdot \dot{q}(\theta) + q(\theta) - \dot{p}(\theta)$$

where $\dot{u}(\theta) \equiv du(\theta)/d\theta$, $\dot{q}(\theta) \equiv dq(\theta)/d\theta$, and $\dot{p}(\theta) \equiv dp(\theta)/d\theta$. Now, consumers' utility maximizing behavior requires

$$P'(q) = \theta$$

that is, $\dot{p}(\theta)/\dot{q}(\theta) = \theta$, or $\dot{p}(\theta) = \theta \cdot \dot{q}(\theta)$

if there is a complete separation of consumers near $q(\theta)$, that is, if $P(q)$ is differentiable at $q(\theta)$. If "bunching" of consumers occurs at $q(\theta)$—that is, if a sharp corner exists on $P(q)$ *at* $q(\theta)$—then $\dot{q}(\theta) = \dot{p}(\theta) = 0$. Therefore, in either case, (a) becomes

$$\text{(b)}\qquad \dot{u}(\theta) = q(\theta)$$

Integrating (b) over $t \in [\theta^*, \theta]$, we have

$$u(\theta) = \int_{\theta^*}^{\theta} q(t)\,dt$$

since $u(\theta^*) = 0$. Therefore, consumer surplus for consumers of type θ can be represented as a function only of $q(\theta)$, and thus characterization of optimal $q(\theta)$ also characterizes $p(\theta)$ simultaneously, as shown by (3).

and profit: i.e.

$$\begin{aligned}(6)\qquad SW &= \int_{\theta^*}^{\infty} u(\theta) f(\theta)\, d\theta + \lambda\Pi \\ &= \int_{\theta^*}^{\infty} [\theta \cdot q(\theta) - p(\theta)] f(\theta)\, d\theta + \lambda \int_{\theta^*}^{\infty} [p(\theta) - C(q(\theta))] f(\theta)\, d\theta \\ &\quad - \lambda K(q_L, q_H) \\ &= \int_{\theta^*}^{\theta_L} [(\theta \cdot q_L - p_L) + \lambda(p_L - C(q_L))] f(\theta)\, d\theta \\ &\quad + \int_{\theta_L}^{\theta_H} [(\theta q(\theta) - p(\theta)) + \lambda(p(\theta) - C(q(\theta)))] f(\theta)\, d\theta \\ &\quad + \int_{\theta_H}^{\infty} [(\theta \cdot q_H - p_H) + \lambda(p_H - C(q_H))] f(\theta)\, d\theta - \lambda K(q_L, q_H)\end{aligned}$$

where $\lambda \geqslant 1$, $p_H \equiv p(\theta_H)$, $p_L \equiv p(\theta_L)$, and $K(q_L, q_H)$ is the fixed cost to produce quality range $[q_L, q_H]$. The first and third integrals above represent the fact that all of the consumers of type $\theta > \theta_H$ would choose q_H and pay p_H, and all of the consumers of type $\theta \in [\theta^*, \theta_L]$ would choose q_L and pay p_L. Then, the optimal solutions are θ^*, θ_L, θ_H, and $q(\theta)$ that maximize SW.

The first order conditions are as follows: The condition $\partial SW/\partial q(\theta) = 0$ yields

$$(7)\qquad \theta - C'(q) = \alpha/\rho(\theta), \quad \text{for } \theta \in (\theta_L, \theta_H)$$

where $\alpha = (\lambda - 1)/\lambda$, and $\rho(\theta) = f(\theta)/[1 - F(\theta)]$, the hazard rate. See Appendix 1 for derivation. Since $f(\theta) > 0$, and $C'(q)$ and $f(\theta)$ are continuous, we can note that $q(\theta)$ defined by (7) is continuous. In fact, we can note that $q(\theta)$ will have an upward discontinuity (i.e. discontinuous quality spectrum) only if $f(\theta)$ has an upward discontinuity.[5]

The condition $\partial SW/\partial\theta^* = 0$ yields

$$(8)\qquad \theta^* - C(q_L)/q_L = \alpha/\rho(\theta^*)$$

The condition $\partial SW/\partial\theta_H = 0$ yields

$$(9)\qquad (1-\alpha)\int_{\theta_H}^{\infty} \theta f(\theta)\, d\theta + \alpha\theta_H(1 - F_H) = K'_H + C'(q_H)(1 - F_H)$$

where $F_H = F(\theta_H)$, and $K'_H = \partial K(q_L, q_H)/\partial q_H$.

[5] If $f(\theta)$ has a downward discontinuity, as we shall see later, bunching of consumers will happen.

The condition $\partial SW/\partial\theta_L = 0$ yields

$$(10)\qquad (1-\alpha)\int_{\theta^*}^{\theta_L}\theta f(\theta)d\theta+\alpha[\theta^*(1-F^*)-\theta_L(1-F_L)]=K_L'+C'(q_L)(F_L-F^*)$$

where $F_L = F(\theta_L)$, and $K_L' = \partial K(q_L, q_H)/\partial q_L$. Note that $K_L' < 0$.

The first order conditions (9) and (10) imply that q_H and q_L are determined at the levels where the weighted sums of the marginal social benefit (more accurately, the marginal increase in the sum of consumer surplus and producer revenue) and the marginal private benefit (i.e. the marginal increase in producer revenue) of changing q_H and q_L are equal to the marginal costs of changing q_H and q_L, respectively. The value of α could be adjusted to meet a specific profit requirement. Especially, the above conditions generate the profit maximizing solutions, if $\alpha\rightarrow 1$, and the socially optimal solutions, if $\alpha\rightarrow 0$. We can also note that, within the interior of $[\theta_L, \theta_H]$, the optimal quality assignment function, $q(\theta)$ defined by (7), is not necessarily compatible with the self-selection condition that $q(\theta)$ must be nondecreasing. Specifically, since $C''(q) > 0$, if $z'(\theta) < 0$ for some intervals of θ, where

$$(11)\qquad z(\theta) \equiv \theta-\alpha/\rho(\theta)$$

the quality assignment function defined by (7) would be decreasing in θ, violating the self-selection constraint.[6] $z'(\theta) < 0$ is likely to happen when the hazard rate declines sharply for some intervals of θ. Therefore, complete separation of consumers for $\theta\in[\theta_L, \theta_H]$ is optimal, if and only if

$$(12)\qquad z'(\theta) = 1+\alpha+[\alpha/\rho(\theta)]\,[f'(\theta)/f(\theta)] > 0, \quad \text{for all } \theta\in[\theta_L, \theta_H]$$

If $z'(\theta) < 0$ for some $\theta\in[\theta_L, \theta_H]$, incomplete separation of consumers should occur, as Mussa and Rosen originally showed for the profit maximizing case.[7] The characterization of the incomplete separation for the interval $[\theta_L, \theta_H]$ is discussed in Appendix 2.[8]

V. SUSTAINABILITY OF THE SECOND BEST SOLUTION

In this section, we examine sustainability of the second best solution, or the Ramsey scheduling, which maximizes consumer surplus subject to a zero profit constraint. The definition of sustainability in this paper is an extension of the original definition by Panzar and Willig [1977] in the sense that firms are now contemplating price-quality schedules instead of uniform prices.

[6] In technical terms, if $z'(\theta) < 0$, the first order condition characterized by (13) does not characterize a maximum, since the second order condition is not satisfied.

[7] For an intuitive graphic explanation why a profit maximizing firm would find incomplete separation optimal, refer to Maskin and Riley, Section 2.

[8] Since we have the general solutions as functions of α, we can analyze the direction of the "optimal departure" of each variable from the first best solution by performing comparative statics around $\alpha = 0$. For the results of this analysis, see Kim [1986].

Definition. An admissible price-quality schedule, $(p(\theta), q(\theta))$ for $\theta \in S \subseteq N$, is *sustainable*, if there exists no admissible $(\hat{p}(\theta), \hat{q}(\theta))$ for $\theta \in V \subseteq N$, such that $S \cap V \neq \emptyset$, and $\hat{u}(\theta) \geqslant u(\theta)$ for all $\theta \in S \cap V$ with

$$\hat{\pi} \equiv \pi(\hat{p}(\theta), \hat{q}(\theta)) \equiv \int_{\theta \in V} [\hat{p}(\theta) - C(\hat{q}(\theta))] f(\theta) d\theta - K(Q_V) > 0 \tag{13}$$

where Q_V is the set of qualities purchased by consumer group V.

Now, it is straightforward from the definition that the following conditions are necessary for an admissible price-quality schedule for $\theta \in M$ to be sustainable:

(C1) the firm's profit must be zero; i.e.,

$$\int_M [p(\theta) - C(q(\theta))] f(\theta) d\theta = K(Q_M), \text{ and}$$

(C2) no cross-subsidization exists between consumer groups; i.e.,

$$\int_S [p(\theta) - C(q(\theta))] f(\theta) d\theta \leqslant K(Q_S), \quad \text{for all } S \subseteq M$$

(C3) $K(Q)$ must be subadditive; i.e.,

$$K(Q) \leqslant \textstyle\sum_i K(Q_i), \text{ where } \cup_i Q_i = Q, \text{ and } Q_i \cap Q_j = \emptyset \text{ for } i \neq j.$$

Since the condition for no cross-subsidization, (C2), is affected by the structural conditions, we now analyze these conditions. In order to focus more sharply on the effect of the consumer taste distribution on sustainability, let us assume that the extra fixed costs over the quality range are constant; i.e.,

$$K(q_L, q_H) = k_0 + k_1(q_H - q_L) \tag{14}$$

Then, we can state the following.

Lemma. Under zero profit constraint, (C2) is true, if and only if

$$t(\theta) f(\theta) \geqslant k_1 \dot{q}(\theta), \quad \text{for } \dot{q}(\theta) > 0, \text{ and} \tag{15}$$

$$\int_\Omega t(\theta) f(\theta) d\theta \leqslant k_0 \tag{16}$$

where $\Omega = \{\theta \mid \dot{q}(\theta) = 0\}$, and

$$t(\theta) \equiv p(\theta) - C(q(\theta)) = \alpha(q_L/\rho(\theta^*)) + \alpha \int_{\theta^*}^{\theta} [\dot{q}(s)/\rho(s)] ds \tag{17}$$

$t(\theta)$ is the net contribution to the fixed cost by a single consumer of type θ. See Appendix 3 for derivation of (17).

Condition (15) implies that, for consumers who are completely sorted, the net revenue contribution made by consumers of type θ to the fixed cost should be no less than the additional fixed cost of the quality available to them, $k_1\dot{q}(\theta)$. Condition (16) implies that the constant portion of the fixed cost should be no less than the net revenue contribution made by the consumers who are bunched together. This condition is necessary because, if (16) is not met, a potential rival could profitably take away the consumers who are bunched together by offering a finite number of discrete qualities only for those consumers.

As we can see in (15) and (16), there is no inherent relationship between the subsidy free conditions and the second best optimality conditions specified in section IV. Therefore, for given values of k_0, k_1, and α, the second best solution may or may not imply the absence of cross-subsidization, depending on the specific properties of the consumer taste distribution. To illustrate this point, we use an example below.

Suppose that the consumer taste is exponentially distributed such that $f(\theta) = \mu e^{-\mu\theta}$, $\mu > 0$, and that the marginal cost of quality is given by $C'(q) = q$. Then, from (7), $q(\theta) = \theta - \alpha/\mu$ for $\theta \in [\theta_L, \theta_H]$. Therefore, the net revenue contribution to the fixed cost by consumers type θ_H is

(18) $$t(\theta_H)f(\theta_H) = \alpha q_H e^{-\mu\theta_H}$$

From the marginal condition (9), the incremental fixed cost necessary to serve θ_H is

(19) $$k_1 = (1/\mu)e^{-\mu\theta_H}$$

Then, the subsidy free condition (15) requires

$$\alpha q_H e^{-\mu\theta_H} \geqslant (1/\mu)e^{-\mu\theta_H}, \text{ or equivalently,}$$

(20) $$1 + \alpha^2 + \alpha \ln(k_1\mu) \leqslant 0$$

where $\ln(k_1\mu)$ is the natural logarithm of $k_1\mu$.

Since the zero profit constraint and the magnitude of k_1 and k_0 would determine the value of α, (20) may or may not hold depending on the value of μ, i.e. depending on the distribution of θ. If μ is sufficiently large, i.e., if the exponential distribution of consumer tastes has a sufficiently thin tail, then (20) will not hold. That is, the consumers in the neighborhood of θ_H are not contributing enough to the fixed cost, resulting in the cross-subsidization.

As we can see in the previous example, sustainability of the second best solution depends on the distribution of consumer tastes. Specifically, we can infer from the previous example that when $f(\theta)$ is sufficiently small for some θ, (15) is very likely to be violated for those θ. The economic reason behind this result is simple. When only a small number of consumers are present to support a quality level, it would be very likely that their net revenue contribution to the fixed cost is less than sufficient to cover the necessary additional fixed cost, resulting in cross-subsidization under the zero profit constraint.

Also, we can note from (15) that, for a sufficiently large value of $[f'(\theta)/f(\theta)]$, (15) could be violated, since

$$\dot{q}(\theta) = (1+\alpha+[\alpha/\rho(\theta)]\,[f'(\theta)/f(\theta)])/C''(q(\theta))$$

This can happen, because, if $[f'(\theta)/f(\theta)]$ is very large for some θ, the optimal behavior of the firm would result in a wider quality range available for those θ, resulting in a larger marginal fixed cost burden on those θ.

In sum, the economic reason why the cross-subsidization can happen in the second best schedule is that the firm's maximizing behavior depends on the marginal conditions, whereas the cross-subsidization is determined by the average conditions. In other words, the firm's decision to price a variety is based not only on $f(\theta)$—that is, how many consumers are buying the variety—but also on $[1-F(\theta)]$—that is, how many others are there to buy higher qualities—while the cross-subsidization solely depends on how many consumers are buying the variety at a given price.

Now, we can state the property of $K(\cdot)$ that is sufficient for sustainability.

Proposition. The second best (Ramsey) price-quality schedule is sustainable, if

(C2) $$\int_S [p(\theta)-C(q(\theta))]\,f(\theta)\,d\theta \leqslant K(Q_S), \quad \text{for all } S \subseteq M$$

where M is the set of consumers served by the firm, and

(C4) $K(\cdot)$ is a convex set function; i.e.,

$$K(Q_1 \cup Q_2)+K(Q_1 \cap Q_2) \leqslant K(Q_1)+K(Q_2)$$

(The proof is given in Appendix 4.)

The intuition behind this result is straightforward. If it is possible for a potential entrant to offer a schedule that allows it to cover its fixed costs, Q_V, with the consumers in $V \cap M$ preferring the entrant's schedule, then it would have been financially feasible for the incumbent firm to offer the superior combination of the two schedules initially to serve $V \cup M$. For the consumers who are in $M-V$ contribute to the fixed cost at least as large as the incremental fixed cost of serving them (no cross subsidization), and there exists an advantage in the fixed cost from a larger scope production (set convexity). Such a superior combination of the two schedules would generate a strictly greater level of welfare than the original schedule. Therefore, if there is no cross subsidization and the fixed cost function exhibits set convexity, the Ramsey schedule should be sustainable.

The set convexity of $K(\cdot)$ is equivalent to concavity of a fixed cost function that is defined on the length of quality spectrum, and is a stronger condition than subadditivity of $K(\cdot)$. Since subadditivity of $K(\cdot)$ makes the technology a natural monopoly, we can note that being a natural monopoly alone is not sufficient, although necessary, for sustainability in this model. Now, we can state the following corollary.

Corollary. If the fixed cost is not related to the range of qualities produced, then the Ramsey price-quality schedule is sustainable.

Proof. If $K(\cdot)$ is a costant, $K(\cdot)$ is clearly a convex set function, and (C2) is always true under the zero profit constraint. Q.E.D.

This corollary is basically what Panzár and Postlewaite showed in their paper, although their result was about quantity discounts under a discrete consumer taste distribution. This result implies that, under certain cost conditions, the Ramsey scheduling is sustainable regardless of the demand side conditions. As Panzar and Postlewaite claim, this result could be considered as a nonlinear version of the Weak Invisible Hand Theorems of Baumol, Bailey and Willig [1977] that the second best multiproduct pricing is sustainable under certain cost conditions.

VI. SUMMARY

In this paper we derived optimal solutions for price-quality scheduling under imperfect information, which maximize the weighted sum of consumer surplus and profit. The solutions are therefore general in the sense that they include the first best, the second best, and the profit maximizing solutions depending on the weights.

We then demonstrated a nonlinear version of the occasional incompatibility between the second best pricing and sustainability and derived the conditions for sustainability of the second best price-quality schedule. The critical assumption for the result is that the fixed setup cost is related to the range of qualities produced by a firm.

JONG SEOK KIM,
Department of Economics,
Dartmouth College,
Hanover, New Hampshire 03755,
USA.

ACCEPTED DECEMBER 1986

APPENDIX 1

Since $\dot{u}(\theta) = q(\theta)$, integrating by parts, we have the following relationship:

$$\text{(A1)} \quad \int_{\theta_L}^{\theta_H} u(\theta)f(\theta)d\theta = \int_{\theta_L}^{\theta_H} [1-F(\theta)]q(\theta)d\theta - [1-F(\theta_H)]u(\theta_H) + [1-F(\theta_L)]u(\theta_L)$$

Then, using the relationship (A1) and $p = \theta q - u$, we can establish the following:

$$\text{(A2)} \quad \int_{\theta_L}^{\theta_H} \{u\cdot f + \lambda[p - C(q)]f\}\,d\theta = \int_{\theta_L}^{\theta_H} \{uf + \lambda[\theta q - u - C(q)]f\}\,d\theta$$

$$= \int_{\theta_L}^{\theta_H} \{(1-\lambda)uf + \lambda[\theta q - C(q)]f\}\, d\theta$$

$$= \int_{\theta_L}^{\theta_H} \{(1-\lambda)(1-F)q + \lambda[\theta q - C(q)]f\}\, d\theta - (1-\lambda)[1-F(\theta_H)]u(\theta_H) + (1-\lambda)[1-F(\theta_L)]u(\theta_L)$$

Then, the first order condition,

$$\partial SW/\partial q(\theta) = 0$$

yields

(A3) $\quad (1-\lambda)(1-F) + \lambda[\theta - C'(q)]f = 0$

Rearranging the terms in (A3), we have

(A4) $\quad [\theta - C'(q)] = \alpha/\rho(\theta), \quad \text{for } \theta \in [\theta_L, \theta_H]$

where $\rho(\theta) \equiv f(\theta)/[1-F(\theta)]$, the hazard rate, and

$$\alpha \equiv (\lambda - 1)/\lambda, \alpha \in [0, 1]$$

APPENDIX 2

The problem here is one of the constrained maximization problems. If we add the inequality constraint,

(A5) $\quad \dot{q}(\theta) \geqslant 0, \quad \text{for } \theta \in [\theta_L, \theta_H]$

to the optimization problem, then we can form the Lagrange expression as follows:

(A6) $\quad I(q, \dot{q}, \theta, \theta^*, \theta_L, \theta_H, \lambda, \mu) \equiv SW(q, \theta, \theta^*, \theta_L, \theta_H, \lambda) + \mu \cdot \dot{q}(\theta)$

Then, the first order conditions lead to the Euler equation:

(A7) $\quad \partial I/\partial q = \partial(\partial I/\partial \dot{q})/\partial\theta$

Since (A7) is equivalent to

(A8) $\quad \partial SW/\partial q = \dot{\mu}(\theta)$

where $\dot{\mu}(\theta) \equiv d\mu(\theta)/d\theta$, the complete first order conditions are (A8) and the complementary slackness conditions:

(A9) $\quad \dot{q}(\theta) \geqslant 0, \mu(\theta) \leqslant 0, \text{ and } \mu(\theta) \cdot \dot{q}(\theta) = 0$

(A8) and (A9) therefore imply that, for some intervals of θ where the condition $\partial SW/\partial q = 0$ is compatible with the constraint $\dot{q}(\theta) \geqslant 0$, $q(\theta)$ should be increasing as defined by (7), since $\dot{\mu}(\theta) = \mu(\theta) = 0$.

If $z'(\theta) < 0$ for some θ, then $\partial SW/\partial q = \dot{\mu}(\theta) < 0$, and therefore $\mu(\theta) < 0$. If $\mu(\theta) < 0$, (A9) requires that $\dot{q}(\theta)$ should be equal to zero, i.e., $q(\theta)$ should be kept constant for some θ. That is, a single quality level should be offered to some consumers with different values of θ. Characterization of the intervals where $q(\theta)$ should be kept constant can be done as follows.

Suppose $\mu(\theta) < 0$ for $\theta \in (\theta^1, \theta^2) \subseteq [\theta_L, \theta_H]$ and thus consumers in $[\theta^1, \theta^2]$ are offered the same quality, $\bar{q} = q(\theta^1) = q(\theta^2)$. Since the neighboring intervals have

$\dot{q}(\theta) > 0$ and $q(\theta)$ is continuous,

(A10) $\mu(\theta^1) = \mu(\theta^2) = 0$

Since (A8) implies

(A11) $$\mu(\theta^2) - \mu(\theta^1) = \int_{\theta^1}^{\theta^2} (\partial SW/\partial q)\, d\theta$$

(A10) and (A11) together imply that

(A12) $$\tau(\bar{q}) \equiv \int_{\theta^1}^{\theta^2} (\partial SW/\partial q)\Big|_{\bar{q}} d\theta = \int_{\theta^1}^{\theta^2} \lambda[\theta - \alpha/\rho(\theta) - C'(\bar{q})] f\, d\theta = 0$$

Therefore, $\bar{q}$ must satisfy

(A13) $\tau(\bar{q}) = 0$, and $\bar{q} = q(\theta^1) = q(\theta^2)$

Since $\tau(q)$ is a monotone decreasing function of q, (A13) uniquely characterizes the values of $\bar{q}$, θ^1, and θ^2.

APPENDIX 3

Derivation of (17):

(A14) $$p(\theta) - C(q(\theta)) = \theta q(\theta) - u(\theta) - C(q(\theta)) = \theta q(\theta) - \int_{\theta^*}^{\theta} q(s)\, ds - \int_{\theta^*}^{\theta} C'(q(s))\dot{q}(s)\, ds - C(q_L)$$

since $u(\theta) = \int_{\theta^*}^{\theta} q(s)\, ds$

$C(q(\theta)) = C(q_L) + \int_{\theta^*}^{\theta} C'(q(s))\dot{q}(s)\, ds$, and

$\dot{q}(\theta) = 0$ for $\theta \in (\theta^*, \theta_L)$

Integrating by parts, we have

(A15) $$\theta q(\theta) - \theta^* q_L - \int_{\theta^*}^{\theta} q(s)\, ds = \int_{\theta^*}^{\theta} s\dot{q}(s)\, ds$$

since $q(\theta^*) = q_L$. From the first order condition (8)

(A16) $\theta^* q_L - C(q_L) = \alpha(q_L/\rho(\theta^*))$.

Then, using (A15) and (A16), we have

(A17) $$p(\theta) - C(q(\theta)) = \int_{\theta^*}^{\theta} [s - C'(q(s))]\dot{q}(s)\, ds + \alpha(q_L/\rho(\theta^*)) = \alpha \int_{\theta^*}^{\theta} [\dot{q}(s)/\rho(s)]\, ds + \alpha(q_L/\rho(\theta^*))$$

since $[s - C'(q(s))] = \alpha/\rho(s)$.

APPENDIX 4

Proof. Suppose to the contrary that there exists an admissible price-quality schedule, $(\hat{p}(\theta), \hat{q}(\theta))$, for $\theta \in V \subseteq N$, such that $V \cap M \neq \emptyset$, and $\hat{u} \geqslant u$ for all $\theta \in V \cap M$ with $\hat{\pi} > 0$. Consider a schedule $(\tilde{p}(\theta), \tilde{q}(\theta))$ for $\theta \in V \cup M$ defined by the "higher envelope" of $(\hat{p}, \hat{q})$ and (p, q); that is,

$$(\tilde{p}(\theta), \tilde{q}(\theta)) \equiv \arg\max\,[\hat{u} = \theta \cdot \hat{q} - \hat{p},\, u = \theta \cdot q - p], \quad \text{for all } \theta \in \mathrm{V} \cup \mathrm{M}$$

Clearly, $(\tilde{p}, \tilde{q})$ is an admissible price-quality schedule, and no consumer in $V \cup M$ would strictly prefer $(\hat{p}, \hat{q})$ or (p, q) to $(\tilde{p}, \tilde{q})$.[9] If $(\tilde{p}, \tilde{q})$ was offered by a firm,

$$\tilde{\pi} \equiv \pi(\tilde{p}, \tilde{q}) = \int_V [\hat{p} - C(\hat{q})] f\, d\theta + \int_{M-V} [p - C(q)] f\, d\theta - K(Q_M \cup Q_V)$$

$$= \hat{\pi} + \int_{M-V} [p - C(q)] f\, d\theta - K(Q_M \cup Q_V) + K(Q_V)$$

Now, to establish a contradiction, it remains to show that $\tilde{\pi} > 0$ by showing that

$$\int_{M-V} [p - C(q)] f\, d\theta - K(Q_M \cup Q_V) + K(Q_V) \geqslant 0$$

Since $-K(Q_M \cup Q_V) + K(Q_V) \geqslant -K(Q_M) + K(Q_M \cap Q_V)$ by set convexity of $K(\cdot)$,

$$\int_{M-V} [p - C(q)] f\, d\theta - K(Q_M \cup Q_V) + K(Q_V)$$

$$\geqslant \int_{M-V} [p - C(q)] f\, d\theta - K(Q_M) + K(Q_M \cap Q_V)$$

Now, the zero profit constraint and (C2) together imply that

$$K(Q_M) - K(Q_S) \leqslant \int_{M-S} [p - C(q)] f\, d\theta$$

By replacing S with $M \cap V$ above, we have

$$\int_{M-V} [p - C(q)] f\, d\theta - K(Q_M) + K(Q_M \cap Q_V) \geqslant 0$$

This establishes that $\tilde{\pi} > 0$, which contradicts the hypothesis that $(p(\theta), q(\theta))$ maximizes consumer surplus with a zero profit constraint. Q.E.D.

REFERENCES

Baumol, W. J. and Bradford, D. E., 1970, 'Optimal Departures from Marginal Cost Pricing', *American Economic Review*, 60, 2 (June), pp. 265–283.

Baumol, W. J., Bailey, E. E. and Willig, R. D., 1977, 'Weak Invisible Hand Theorems on the Sustainability of Prices in a Multiproduct Monopoly', *American Economic Review*, 67, 3 (June), pp. 350–365.

Kim, J. S., 1986, 'Price-Quality Schedules', Department of Economics, Working Paper 86-11, Dartmouth College.

[9] $(\tilde{p}, \tilde{q})$ satisfies the self-selection constraint, since $\hat{u}$ and u are nondecreasing in θ, and therefore $\tilde{u} \equiv \theta\tilde{q} - \tilde{p}$ is nondecreasing in θ.

MASKIN, E. and RILEY, J., 1984, 'Monopoly with Incomplete Information', *Rand Journal of Economics*, 15, 2 (Summer), pp. 171–196.

MUSSA, M. and ROSEN, S., 1978, 'Monopoly and Product Quality', *Journal of Economic Theory*, 18, pp. 301–317.

PANZAR, J. C. and WILLIG, R. D., 1977, 'Free Entry and the Sustainability of Monopoly', *Bell Journal of Economics*, 8, 1 (Spring), pp. 1–22.

PANZAR, J. C. and POSTLEWAITE, A. W., 1984, 'Sustainable Outlay Schedules', The Center for Mathematical Studies in Economics and Management Science, Discussion Paper #626S, Northwestern University.

THE JOURNAL OF INDUSTRIAL ECONOMICS 0022-1821 $2.00
Volume XXXVI December 1987 No. 2

ON EXISTENCE OF LOCATION EQUILIBRIA IN THE 3-FIRM HOTELLING PROBLEM*

ANDRÉ DE PALMA, VICTOR GINSBURGH AND JACQUES-FRANÇOIS THISSE

If consumers have a positive probability to purchase from each firm, then centrally agglomerated and/or symmetric dispersed location equilibria may exist in the 3-firm Hotelling problem.

I. INTRODUCTION

IT IS well known that the Hotelling model of spatial competition with three firms admits no equilibrium solution; see Chamberlin [1933] and Lerner and Singer [1937]. Apparently, this non-existence result is associated with the assumption that customers patronize the nearest firm. Now, empirical evidence supports the idea that consumers do not necessarily choose to buy from the closest firm, since they also take variables other than distance into account. As these variables are often unobservable, firms cease to be fully informed about consumers' motivations. Consequently, they can at best determine the shopping behavior of a particular customer *up to a probability distribution.*

The purpose of this note is to reconsider the 3-firm Hotelling problem within a probabilistic framework. It is shown that two different types of equilibria emerge: *centrally agglomerated* equilibria, in which the three firms are clustered, and *symmetric dispersed* equilibria, in which the three firms have distinct locations. These equilibria are compared to the socially optimal locations.

II. THE MODEL

The assumptions of the standard 3-firm Hotelling location model are as follows:

(i) Three firms $i = 1, 2, 3$ locate on a segment of unit length, at locations x_i ($i = 1, 2, 3$) and sell a homogeneous commodity.

(ii) The distribution of customers is uniform on the segment (with unit density), and each of them buys a single unit of the commodity per unit of time.

(iii) Firms produce at zero marginal cost and sell at the same given mill price p; transportation costs increase linearly with distance, so that a

* We thank the referees and the Editor for careful comments. The first two authors acknowledge support from Actions de Recherches Concertées, Contract no. 84/89-65.

customer located at x will pay $p+c|x-x_i|$ if he buys from firm i, where $c|x-x_i|$ stands for the transport cost between x and x_i.

(iv) As the mill price is the same, customers buy from the nearest firm. Accordingly, the demand addressed to firm i, denoted by $D_i(x_1, x_2, x_3)$, is given by the measure of the set of consumers closer to x_i than to x_j or x_k.

(v) Firm i chooses its location x_i in order to maximize its profits $\Pi_i(x_1, x_2, x_3) = pD_i(x_1, x_2, x_3)$.

(vi) The equilibrium corresponds to a non-cooperative Nash equilibrium in location, i.e., a triple x_1^*, x_2^*, and x_3^* such that $\Pi_i(x_i^*, x_j^*, x_k^*) \geqslant \Pi_i(x_i, x_j^*, x_k^*)$ for any $x_i \in [0, 1]$, $i = 1, 2, 3$ and $i \neq j \neq k$.

Discontinuities in the profit functions are fundamental for explaining the non-existence of equilibria in the above model. A natural idea is therefore to reformulate the model so as to generate continuous profit functions, like in de Palma *et al.* [1985], where it is assumed that *firms are not able to predict with certainty the decisions of customers.*[1] The reason is that, when they make their buying decisions, customers do take into account variables other than just the full delivered price. Under these circumstances, firms cannot do better but endowing customers with purchasing probabilities, which depend on the delivered prices. To determine these probabilities we assume that, before selecting their locations, firms are able to collect observations on the shopping behavior of customers who can choose between the three alternative firms. Denote by y_h a random variable which takes the value $i = 1$, 2 or 3 when customer h chooses to buy from firm 1, 2, or 3. The firms then estimate the vector of parameters β_i of the following econometric model (see, e.g., Amemiya [1981])

$$\Pr(y_h = i) = \beta_{0i} - \beta_{1i}|x_h - x_i|$$

where the first coefficient can be considered as an index of the "attractiveness" of firm i; $|x_h - x_i|$ is the distance between customer h and firm i, and $\beta_{1i}|x_h - x_i|$ measures the cost of the corresponding trip. Then, if the observations are distributed according to the logistic function we obtain

$$(1) \qquad \Pr(y_h = i) = \frac{\exp[(\beta_{0i} - \beta_{1i}|x_h - x_i|)/\delta]}{\sum_{j=1}^{3} \exp[(\beta_{0j} - \beta_{1j}|x_h - x_j|)/\delta]}$$

where $\delta > 0$ is a normalization constant.

[1] Kohlberg [1982] and Shaked [1982] have tackled the problem in other directions. Kohlberg suggests to add waiting time for service (which in turn depends on the number of customers visiting a firm) as argument of the utility function of each customer. As shown by Kohlberg, this restores continuity of the profit functions, but not existence of a Nash equilibrium. Shaked [1982] suggests to use mixed strategies instead of pure strategies. In spite of the discontinuities, Shaked was able to show that a Nash equilibrium in mixed strategies always exists in the 3-firm Hotelling problem. Though mathematically very elegant, it is hard to imagine that the model with mixed strategies still has sufficient predictive power to account for most locational decisions.

As is well known, a similar expression can also be derived from random utility maximization; see, e.g. McFadden [1974]. Assume indeed that firms choose to model the utility of a customer at x purchasing from firm i, as $-p-c|x-x_i|+\mu\varepsilon_i(x)$, instead of $-p-c|x-x_i|$ as in the standard model. Here, $\mu\varepsilon_i(x)$ is a random variable with zero mean and unit variance, which represents the utility associated with non-observable and/or non-measurable characteristics attributed by a consumer at x to the commodity sold by firm i. It is important to notice that $\varepsilon_i(x)$ is treated as a random variable to reflect the firms' lack of information about this consumer's tastes, and not (necessarily) to reflect inconsistencies in his/her behavior.

Given that consumers are utility-maximizers, and if the $\varepsilon_i(x)$ are identically, independently Gumbel distributed, the probability that the customer at x will purchase from firm i is given by

$$(2) \qquad P_i(x) = \frac{\exp[(-p-c|x-x_i|)/\mu]}{\sum_{j=1}^{3} \exp[(-p-c|x-x_j|)/\mu]}$$

In this model, μ is positive and can be interpreted as a measure of the degree of heterogeneity in customers' tastes.[2]

At this stage, it is clear that the two expressions (1) and (2) are identical provided that $p = -\beta_{0i}$, $c = \beta_{1i}$ and $\mu = \delta$.

In both cases, we are led to replace the above definition of the demand to firm i by

$$D_i(x_1, x_2, x_3) = \int_0^1 P_i(x; x_1, x_2, x_3)dx$$

i.e., the expected demand. Given the expressions of the probabilities (1) and (2), $D_i(\cdot)$ is now continuous in x_1, x_2 and x_3.

III. RESULTS

III(i). Let us first investigate the possible existence of an *agglomerated equilibrium*, i.e. a Nash equilibrium (x_1^*, x_2^*, x_3^*) which satisfies the additional property $x_1^* = x_2^* = x_3^* = x^*$.

The following results hold (see de Palma *et al.* [1985]):

Proposition 1

(a) If $0 < \mu/c < \infty$, then an agglomerated equilibrium can occur only at the center of the market segment, that is $x^* = 1/2$.

(b) If $\mu/c < 1/6$, then no agglomerated equilibrium exists.

(c) If $\mu/c \geqslant 1/3$, then an agglomerated equilibrium exists.

[2] Another interpretation of the model is obtained when consumers have a variety-seeking behavior which is modelled by means of an entropy-like utility function (see Anderson *et al.* [1986]). In this context, (2) represents the frequency of purchases from firm i over a certain period of time. A larger μ means that the customer at x chooses from a more dispersed shopping pattern.

As can be seen, the existence of an agglomerated equilibrium crucially depends on the value of μ/c, the ratio of the degree of variation in consumers' tastes and the transportation rate. This is so because the choices of consumers are more and more determined by their individual tastes, while the influence of the objective characteristic of firms (here the full price) gets weaker. The profit maximizing choice for firms is then central agglomeration.

The above results deal with the (non-) existence of an agglomerated equilibrium. Nothing is said, however, about the existence of a *dispersed equilibrium*, i.e., an equilibrium such that $x_1^* \neq x_2^* \neq x_3^*$. The issue is discussed now. More precisely, we want to answer the following questions.

(1) Does a dispersed equilibrium exist for some value of μ/c?
(2) Can an agglomerated equilibrium and a dispersed equilibrium simultaneously exist?

The complexity of the problem has made it impossible for us to find solutions analytically. We have therefore decided to resort to numerical computations. For simplicity, we focus on *symmetric equilibria*. The profits of the three firms have been computed for the following locations: $0 \leqslant x_1 < 1/2$, $x_2 = 1/2$ and $x_3 = 1-x_1$. More specifically, the values of $\pi_1(\pi_3)$ and π_2 have been computed with a grid size of 10^{-3} for integer values of $100\mu/c$ with $0 \leqslant \mu/c \leqslant 0.40$.

The following results have been obtained:

Proposition 2

(a) If $\mu/c < 0.157$, there exists no symmetric equilibrium.
(b) If $0.157 \leqslant \mu/c < 1/6$, then there exists no agglomerated equilibrium, but symmetric dispersed equilibria do exist.
(c) If $1/6 \leqslant \mu/c < 0.27$, then there exist both agglomerated and symmetric dispersed equilibria.
(d) If $\mu/c \geqslant 0.27$, then there exists an agglomerated equilibrium, but symmetric dispersed equilibria vanish.

Figure 1 depicts the four possible regions. In region 1, there is no equilibrium; in region 2, there exist only dispersed equilibria; in region 4, there exist only agglomerated equilibria while in region 3, both types of equilibria coexist. For μ positive but very small relative to c, the profit functions are continuous but no equilibrium occurs. This is because the shape of the profit functions is still very close to what it is for $\mu = 0$. A minimal amount of heterogeneity is therefore required to restore existence. When c is not too small relative to μ, that is transport costs still matter, each firm may enjoy a local monopoly in equilibrium. Otherwise, the agglomeration is the only possible outcome. It is interesting to point out that, in the dispersed equilibrium, the distance between the two peripheral firms decreases monotonically as μ/c increases from 1/6 to 0.27. It should be apparent, therefore, that μ/c *acts as an agglomerative factor* in the present revision of the 3-firm Hotelling problem.

Our results can be given a nice interpretation in terms of product specification by competitive firms. As is standard in the theory of product differentiation, c can be viewed as the loss parameter in the consumers' utility derived from the observable characteristic. For small values of c, consumers

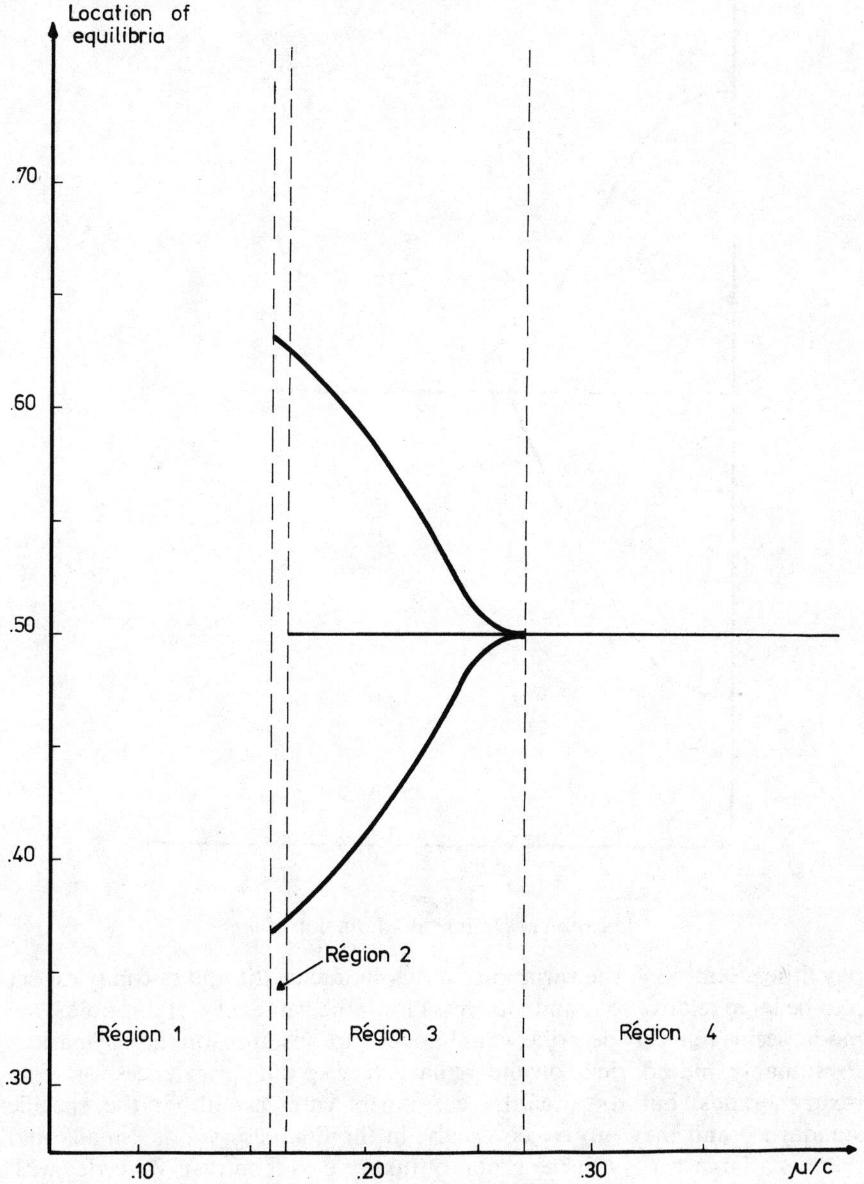

Figure 1
Location of Equilibria as a Function of μ/c

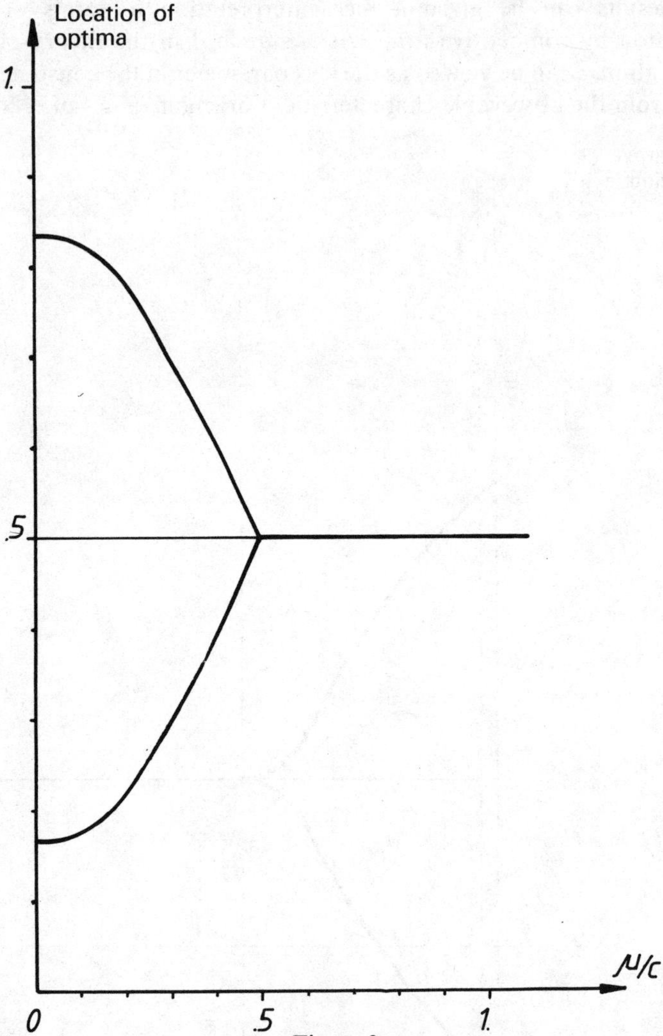

Figure 2
Location of Optima as a Function of μ/c

pay little attention to the variations in this characteristic and one may expect μ to be large relative to c; and vice versa for large values of c. If this holds, the model seems to nicely describe what happens, for instance, on the car market. Presumably, indeed, rich consumers have very specific preferences for some luxury brands, but less wealthy consumers care less about the specific standard brand they buy. Accordingly, in the first case, μ/c is "small" and there is a large variety in the group of luxury cars (contrast Mercedes with Rolls Royce and Ferrari) while, in the second, μ/c is "large" and popular cars look very much the same.

III(ii). We have also computed the socially optimal locations. Small and Rosen [1981] have derived the consumer surplus function associated with the logit. In the present context, this function can be written as $(\mu/c)\int_0^1 \sum_{j=1}^{3} \exp(-c\,|x-x_i|/\mu)dx$. Applying the FOC for symmetric locations gives rise to a transcendental equation that we have solved numerically, using the same grid size and the same values of μ/c as above. The results, depicted in Figure 2, are as follows:

Proposition 3
(a) When $\mu/c = 0$, the optimal locations are $x_1^0 = 1/6, x_2^0 = 1/2$ and $x_3^0 = 5/6$.
(b) As μ/c increases, the distance between the two peripheral firms decreases.
(c) For $\mu/c \geqslant 0.5$, the three firms are agglomerated.

A comparison of Figures 1 and 2 reveals that, for $\mu/c < 0.5$, the equilibrium locations (whenever they exist) are always *more concentrated* than the socially optimal locations. This is because the utility function underlying the above consumer surplus function embodies a dispersion effect (see Anderson *et al.* [1986]), whereas, in equilibrium, firms want to be close to the largest number of consumers, thus leading to less dispersion.[3]

ANDRÉ DE PALMA,
Université Libre de Bruxelles,
50 Avenue F. Roosevelt,
1050 Brussels,
Belgium.

ACCEPTED FEBRUARY 1987

VICTOR GINSBURGH,
Université Libre de Bruxelles and *CORE.*

JACQUES-FRANÇOIS THISSE,
CORE,
Université Catholique de Louvain,
34 voie du Roman Pays,
1348 Louvain-la-Neuve,
Belgium.

REFERENCES

AMEMIYA, T., 1981, 'Qualitative Response Models: a Survey', *Journal of Economic Literature*, 19, pp. 1483–1536.

ANDERSON, S., DE PALMA, A. and THISSE, J.-F., 1986, 'A Representative Consumer Theory of the Logit Model', Université Catholique de Louvain, CORE Discussion Paper.

[3] For μ/c sufficiently large, but smaller than 0.5, the optimal configuration can be sustained as an equilibrium by a tax on transport. On the other hand, for μ/c small, this is not possible because the optimal configuration does not correspond to any equilibrium.

CHAMBERLIN, E. H., 1933, *The Theory of Monopolistic Competition* (Harvard University Press, Cambridge, Mass.).

DE PALMA, A., GINSBURGH, V., PAPAGEORGIOU, Y. Y. and THISSE, J.-F., 1985, 'The Principle of Minimum Differentiation Holds under Sufficient Heterogeneity', *Econometrica*, 53, pp. 767–781.

KOHLBERG, E., 1982, 'Equilibrium Store Locations when Consumers Minimize Travel Time plus Waiting Time', Harvard Business School, Discussion Paper 82–02.

LERNER, A. and SINGER, H., 1937, 'Some Notes on Duopoly and Spatial Competition', *Journal of Political Economy*, 45, pp. 145–186.

MCFADDEN, D., 1974, 'Conditional Logit Analysis of Qualitative Choice Behavior', in P. ZAREMBKA (ed.), *Frontiers in Econometrics* (Academic Press, New York).

SHAKED, A., 1982, 'Existence and Computation of a Mixed Strategy Nash Equilibrium for 3-Firms Location Problems', *Journal of Industrial Economics*, 31, pp. 93–96.

SMALL, K. A. and ROSEN, H. S., 1981, 'Applied Welfare in Economics with Discrete Choice Models', *Econometrica*, 49, pp. 105–130.

THE JOURNAL OF INDUSTRIAL ECONOMICS 0000-1821 $2.00
Volume XXXVI December 1987 No. 2

MEASURING R & D IN SMALL FIRMS: HOW MUCH ARE WE MISSING?

ALFRED KLEINKNECHT*

The OECD surveys on R & D are considerably biased towards underestimating R & D in small firms. This conclusion is derived from the author's comparison between the official Dutch R & D survey and the findings of his own survey among 3000 firms. Although being based on Dutch observations only, the author's considerations have an impact on other OECD countries, since the official Dutch R & D survey is fully compatible with those in other countries. The findings call into question the results from a number of empirical studies, bearing on subjects such as market structure and R & D, firm size and R & D or R & D and growth.

THIS PAPER draws from the author's innovation survey in Dutch manufacturing industry which is based on a sample of some 3000 firms of which 1842 (= 63.1%) responded. The principal outcomes of our survey as compared with the official Dutch R & D survey are summarized in Table I. While, in the category of firms having 500 and more employees, man-years of R & D in both surveys are by and large compatible, there are differences in the categories of firms having less than 500 employees, and these differences increase as firm size diminishes. Similar differences exist in the numbers of firms performing any R & D, which are not documented here (see Kleinknecht [1987] for more complete information).

It should be mentioned that the differences in Table I show up in spite of an extremely cautious extrapolation of our data: Since we could not exclude the possibility that a positive correlation exists between the innovativeness of a firm and its readiness to respond to an innovation survey, we assumed that firms which did not respond (36.9% of the sample) have *no* R & D. Because of this extreme assumption, our extrapolation clearly involves a downward bias (see also footnote (b) in Table I).

It should be noted that in our survey we used exactly the same definition of R & D (according to the Frascati-Manual of the OECD) which is used in the official Dutch R & D survey. Our survey, however, does differ from the official survey in that it is restricted to the most simple R & D indicator possible, i.e.

*My research was sponsored by the Dutch Ministry of Economic Affairs. I am indebted to my student assistants, Hans Bieshaar, Aat Keet, Jos den Ronden and Bart Verspagen, for administrative support of the mailing survey and computer processing of the data. Moreover I wish to express my gratitude to J. T. Kolfoort, R. Luijendijk and J. van der Steen from the Department of R & D Statistics of the Dutch Central Statistical Office, whose comments very much facilitated comparison of my results with their data.

TABLE I
MAN-YEARS OF INTRAMURAL R & D BY SIZE OF FIRM (OUR RESULTS COMPARED WITH THE DATA FROM THE OFFICIAL SURVEY).

	R & D Man-years in 1981 and 1983				
	According to official survey in 1981([a])		*According to our most cautious extrapolation (with downward bias)*([b])		
Firm Sizes (employees)	*Man-years*	*Percentages*	*Man-years*	*Percentages*	
10 to 19	n.a.	n.a.	534	2.2%	—
20 to 49	n.a.	n.a.	967	4.0%	—
50 to 99	301	1.2%	903	3.7%	3.9%
100 to 199	650	2.7%	1386	5.7%	6.1%
200 to 499	1228	5.1%	1745	7.2%	7.6%
500 and more	21 992	91.0%	18 839	77.3%	82.4%
Total	24 171	±100%	24 374	±100%	±100%

Notes:
([a]) Source: telephone information from the Department of R & D Statistics of the Dutch Central Statistical Office (CBS).
([b]) The original data have only been extrapolated in order to adjust the difference between sample size and population. No extrapolation has been made to correct for non-responding firms, i.e. firms which did not respond (36.9% of the sample) are assumed to have *no* R & D activities.

R & D man-years. Moreover, we included the following question for firms which have no formal R & D department:

> "If your enterprise does *not* have an R & D department, R & D activities might be carried out by other departments within your enterprise. For example: the sales department might develop a new product, or the production department might introduce improvements to a production process.
>
> Have any R & D activities been carried out within your enterprise during 1983 even though you do not have a formal R & D department?
> —No.
> —Yes. If so, can you give an estimate of the number of man-years that were devoted to such activities in 1983 (if necessary, give a *rough* estimate)?
> Man-years devoted to R & D during 1983:...."

The above question was designed in order to avoid reactions such as: we have no R & D department, hence there is no R & D. Our attempt to capture the rather informal R & D work was encouraged by evidence from a growing number of field studies which suggest that in small firms, development work is often mixed with other activities and done without even having a formal R & D budget (R & D being paid for out of the cash-flow), frequently occurring outside regular working hours. It is conceivable that such R & D cannot be captured by means of the rather detailed questionnaires in the official surveys: some entrepreneurs, having small amounts of R & D, may fill in 'zero R & D', simply in order to get rid of the complicated questionnaire. Even those willing to respond correctly may have difficulties in doing so because of insufficient internal accounting of their R & D. The perfectionism of the official questionnaires is likely to be counter-productive.

To be fair, we should mention two possible causes of an upward bias in our estimates. First, the Ministry of Economic Affairs was mentioned in our survey questionnaire as having financially sponsored our survey, and a letter of recommendation by the Minister was included. Although firms were assured that no information concerning individual respondents would be given to the Ministry, we cannot exclude the possibility that there have been companies which have overestimated their innovation activities in order to make a good impression on the Ministry, which is a source of subsidies for innovation. Secondly, in doubtful cases, the Dutch Central Statistical Office sometimes phones up firms in order to check their interpretation of the definition of R & D. This occasionally leads them to disregard the R & D reported. No such control was built into our survey. However, these two considerations can explain only a small fraction of the discrepancies between the official survey and our data. Neither can the differences in Table I be wholly explained by the fact that our data refer to the year 1983, while the official survey covers 1981, although there has been a certain increase in R & D activities in recent years.

We believe the principal explanation for the differences between the two surveys lies in the previously quoted question which tries to take into account the often rather informal character of R & D work in small firms. This may have led many small firms to report even quite small-scale R & D work which they would (and often could) not have reported in the official surveys. And this small-scale R & D work appears to be quite important: for example, among the firms which report any R & D work, 71% of firms having 10 to 49 employees (and 39% of firms having 50 to 199 employees) report having one man-year or less of R & D (for more details see Kleinknecht [1987]). It is obvious that much (if not all) of this R & D refers to the "D" rather than to the "R" component of R & D.

Our attempt to capture such R & D work leads to a notable shift in the observed concentration of R & D in large firms. Table I shows that according to the official R & D survey, 91% of private R & D in Dutch manufacturing firms is done by large firms (having 500 and more employees). According to our estimate, this percentage would fall to 82.4% (when considering only firms having 50 and more employees). The percentage would fall even lower to 77.3% when adding the R & D done in firms having 10 to 49 employees which are not covered in the official survey.

From the above we can conclude that even the most cautious (and probably downward biased) extrapolation of our data gives a clear indication that the official Dutch R & D survey is missing a considerable amount of small-scale industrial R & D. Because of the aim of international comparability of

R & D data, the methods of accounting for R & D in the Netherlands are in principle compatible with those in other OECD countries. Therefore, our findings and conclusions are likely to apply to the other OECD surveys as well, although our investigation was restricted to the Netherlands. Judging from our survey experience, we can say that there is a real need to improve the present R & D surveys and that this can be achieved by altering the survey methods so that more account is taken of the specific organizational settings of R & D in small firms. This would imply first of all a radical simplification of the survey questionnaires.

If R & D in small firms was more adequately measured in the official surveys, this would not only have implications for innovation policy, but also for innovation research. A whole range of empirical studies in which the biased figures of the OECD have been used as an input indicator of the innovation process (e.g. studies on the relationship between firm size and R & D, market structure and R & D, or R & D and growth) would appear to be obsolete and will have to be repeated as soon as better figures are available.

ALFRED KLEINKNECHT,
Faculty of Economics,
Rijksuniversiteit Limburg,
PO Box 616,
NL-6200 MD Maastricht,
The Netherlands.

ACCEPTED MAY 1987

REFERENCES

KLEINKNECHT, A., 1987 (with the assistance of H. Bieshaar, A. Keet, J. den Ronden and B. Verspagen), *Industriële innovatie in Nederland. Een enquête-onderzoek* (Assen: Van Gorcum).

KLEINKNECHT, A., 1987a, *Innovation Patterns in Crisis and Prosperity. Schumpeter's Long Cycle Reconsidered* (London: Macmillan and New York: St. Martin's Press).

THE JOURNAL OF INDUSTRIAL ECONOMICS

Published first in October 1952, the *Journal* has a very wide international circulation, and has established itself as the leading journal in the field of industrial economics. It was founded to promote the analysis of modern industry, particularly the behaviour of firms, and the functioning of markets. More specifically it seeks to bring the tools of modern economic analysis to bear on the analysis of real problems of industrial economies.

Contributions are welcomed covering all the major areas of industrial economics. One such area is the relationship between market structure and market behaviour in the areas of pricing, product differentiation, advertising and the dissemination of information and R&D. Another area focuses more directly on the firm, its objectives, finance, investment and growth. A third area comprises the background environment within which industrial firms operate: the changing structure of industry, public policy on monopoly and restrictive trade practices, regulation, fiscal and monetary policies as they affect firms, and underlying changes in productivity and international competitiveness.

The *Journal* has a tradition of publishing a blend of theory and evidence. Theoretical discussion is welcomed provided that the more abstract theory includes sufficient introduction and other explanation to convey the significance of the material to the general reader who wants to decide whether to follow the analysis through. Empirical analysis, and especially econometric analysis, should include an explanation of the data sources used, of the methods applied and of the underlying theoretical basis of the study. The *Journal* has a particular tradition of case studies of firms and industries, which the Editors would wish to continue. However, contributors of such studies are asked to remember that a study will be of interest to the international readership of the *Journal* only if it makes a particular contribution to the methodology of such studies, or if the empirical results are exceptionally interesting.

Alongside articles of more normal length, the Editors are ready to publish shorter notes, especially where these give interim results of important research studies, or where they report significant new empirical results. Books are not reviewed, but substantial review articles will be considered for publication.

Information for Contributors

Submissions (*three* copies are required) should be well written, clearly typed and carefully prepared for the printer in accordance with the *Journal*'s 'Notes for Contributors' (*Journal of Industrial Economics*, 35 (March 1987), pp. 359–363), copies of which may be obtained from the General Editor. An Abstract, conforming to the requirements of *The Journal of Economic Literature* and not exceeding 100 words, must accompany each submission.

Typescripts from North America should be sent to the North American Editor, Journal of Industrial Economics, Department of Public Policy and Management, The Wharton School, University of Pennsylvania, Philadelphia 19104, USA.

Typescripts from *all* other countries should be sent to the General Editor, Journal of Industrial Economics, Institute of Economics and Statistics, University of Oxford, St Cross Building, Manor Road, Oxford OX1 3UL, UK.

Information for Subscribers

The *Journal* is published four times a year, in September, December, March and June, by Basil Blackwell Ltd., 108 Cowley Road, Oxford OX4 1JF, UK, *or* PO Box 1320, Murray Hill Station, NY 10156, USA.

	UK	Overseas	USA
Institutions	£34.00	£43.00	$76.00
Individuals	£17.00	£22.00	$35.00
Students	£8.00	£10.00	$15.00

The reduced rates will be allowed to any individual student for a maximum period of three years.

CONTRIBUTORS TO THE ISSUE

J. A. KAY: Centre for Business Strategy, London Business School, UK, and Associate Editor of this *Journal*.
C. N. MORRIS: London Economics, UK.
AVNER SHAKED: London School of Economics and Political Science, UK.
JOHN SUTTON: London School of Economics and Political Science, UK.
DAVID J. RAVENSCRAFT: School of Business Administration, University of North Carolina, USA.
F. M. SCHERER: Swarthmore College, USA, and Editor of this *Journal*.
STEVEN G. LANNING: Bell Laboratories, New Jersey, USA.
MARVIN B. LIEBERMAN: Graduate School of Business, Stanford University, USA.
JOHN T. SCOTT: Dartmouth College, USA, and Associate Editor of this *Journal*.
GEORGE PASCOE: US Federal Trade Commission, Washington, USA.
SWATI BHATT: Federal Reserve Bank of New York, USA.
MARCEL BOYER: University of Montreal, Canada.
MICHEL MOREAUX: GREMAQ, Université des Sciences Sociales de Toulouse, France.
JONG SEOK KIM: Dartmouth College, USA.
ANDRÉ DE PALMA: Université Libre de Bruxelles, Belgium.
VICTOR GINSBURGH: Université Libre de Bruxelles, Belgium *and* CORE.
JACQUES-FRANÇOIS THISSE: CORE, Université Catholique de Louvain, Belgium.
ALFRED KLEINKNECHT: Rijksuniversiteit Limburg, The Netherlands.

US Mailing: Second class postage paid at New York. Postmaster: Send address corrections to: Journal of Industrial Economics, c/o Expediters of the Printed Word Ltd., 515 Madison Avenue, New York, NY 10022 (US Mailing Agent).

Reprints of Back Volumes: Volumes 1–28 of the *Journal* are available (in complete volumes only) from the Kraus Reprint Corporation, Route 100, Millwood, New York 10546, USA. More recent back issues are available from the publisher at the current single issue price.

Microfilm: An agreement for the supply of microfilm copies from Volume 1 onwards has been made with University Microfilms International, Department PR, 30–32 Mortimer Street, London W1N 7RA, England, or 300 North Zeeb Road, Ann Arbor, Michigan 48106, USA.

Set in Monophoto Times by Advanced Filmsetters (Glasgow) Ltd
Printed and Bound in Great Britain by Whitstable Litho, Kent

THE JOURNAL OF INDUSTRIAL ECONOMICS

Volume XXXVI MARCH 1988 No. 3

GIACOMO BONANNO and JOHN VICKERS
Vertical Separation 257

FREDERICK HARRIS
Testable Competing Hypotheses from Structure-Performance Theory: Efficient Structure Versus Market Power 267

ERIC RASMUSEN
Entry for Buyout 281

THOMAS W. ROSS
Brand Information and Price 301

MASAHIRO ABIRU
Vertical Integration, Variable Proportions and Successive Oligopolies 315

RALPH D. SANDLER
Market Share Instability in Commercial Airline Markets and the Impact of Deregulation 327

ANNE E. PRESTON
The Effects of Property Rights on Labor Costs of Nonprofit Firms: an Application to the Day Care Industry 337

Short Notes and Articles

THOMAS VON UNGERN-STERNBERG
Cartel Stability in Sealed Bid Second Price Auctions 351

THOMAS G. PARRY
The Multinational Enterprise and Restrictive Conditions in International Technology Transfer: Some New Australian Evidence 359

ISSN 0022-1821
BASIL BLACKWELL OXFORD ENGLAND

THE JOURNAL OF INDUSTRIAL ECONOMICS 0022-1821 $2.00
Volume XXXVI March 1988 No. 3

VERTICAL SEPARATION*

GIACOMO BONANNO AND JOHN VICKERS

A simple duopoly model is used to show the advantage to a manufacturer of selling his product through an independent retailer (vertical separation) rather than directly to consumers (vertical integration). Vertical separation is profitable insofar as it induces more friendly behaviour from the rival manufacturer. We consider the case where franchise fees can be used to extract retailers' surplus. We show that vertical separation is in the collective, as well as individual, interest of manufacturers, and hence facilitates some collusion in the simple setting that we examine.

I. INTRODUCTION

THE THEME of much work on vertical integration is that "integration harmonizes interests" (Williamson [1971, p. 117]). For example, if a manufacturer acts as retailer of his own products, he does not have to bother with arrangements to deal with the conflicting incentives that an independent retailer (or retailers) would have. However, in an oligopolistic market, the disharmony of interests between manufacturer and retailer entailed by vertical *separation* (as opposed to integration) may be turned to the manufacturer's advantage. In this paper we examine the strategic motive for vertical separation.[1]

In the model below there are two single-product firms manufacturing differentiated goods. Each firm decides whether to be the retailer of its own product (vertical integration) or to sell through an independent retailer (vertical separation). In the latter event, the manufacturer chooses the wholesale price at which he will supply his retailer. Retailers achieve Nash equilibrium in prices. We consider the case where the manufacturer can charge a franchise fee to the retailer (which in principle could be negative). With perfect competition between potential retailers, this fee transfers all the retailer's surplus to the manufacturer. In these circumstances we show that it is always in the individual interest of a manufacturer to choose vertical separation and to set a wholesale price which is higher than unit manufacturing costs (assumed to be constant). Moreover, we show that vertical separation is in the collective interest of the manufacturers inasmuch as their profits at equilibrium with vertical separation exceed their profits at equilibrium with vertical integration. Thus there is a sense in which vertical

* We are grateful to two anonymous referees for helpful comments. Responsibility for any errors is ours.

[1] See Vickers [1985, especially page 146].

separation facilitates some collusion, though it does not permit perfect collusion. Our results generalise to n-firm oligopoly, but we confine attention to duopoly for the sake of simplicity and to use illustrative diagrams.

It must be noted that our analysis applies only to cases where a retailer sells the product of just one manufacturer. It is of course essential to many retailing operations that the products of a wide variety of manufacturers are sold (see Stahl [1982], Bliss [1986]), but there are important instances of our assumption, including cars and hamburgers. Our analysis is also confined to the case where each manufacturer uses just one retailer. By contrast, the recent literature on vertical restraints (see Mathewson and Winter [1984] and Rey and Tirole [1986a, 1986b]) looks at the problem facing a single manufacturer who uses several retailers. Among other things, that literature explores externalities between the manufacturer's several retailers, which we ignore, since our purpose is to look at strategic interaction between manufacturers and the resulting benefits of vertical separation.

In the next section we describe the model and prove our results, while section III contains some concluding remarks.

II. VERTICAL SEPARATION WITH FRANCHISE FEES

As said in the Introduction, we shall confine attention to the case of duopoly, in order to make use of simple geometric arguments. We consider the case in which each manufacturer can charge a franchise fee to his retailer so as fully to extract the retailer's surplus. In that event, each manufacturer is concerned to maximise the final price of his product (net of production costs) multiplied by the quantity sold.

Let p^i be the price of good i ($i = 1, 2$), net of unit cost of supply, which we assume to be constant. Let $p = (p^1, p^2)$. The demand function for good i is denoted by $D^i(p)$. While superscripts are used to distinguish between goods, subscripts will be used to denote partial derivatives with respect to prices. Thus, for example, $D^2_{12} = \partial D^2/\partial p_1 \partial p_2$. We make standard (mild) assumptions about the demand functions:

Assumption 1. Demand for good i is decreasing and concave in the price of good i:

$$(1) \qquad D^i_i(p) < 0 \quad \text{and} \quad D^i_{ii}(p) \leqslant 0, \qquad \text{for all } p \text{ and } i = 1, 2$$

Assumption 2. Goods are substitutes[2]:

$$(2) \qquad D^i_j(p) > 0, \qquad \text{for all } p \text{ and } i, j = 1, 2$$

Let

$$(3) \qquad \Pi^i(p) = p^i D^i(p)$$

[2] If the goods are independent, because of the double marginalisation problem (Spengler [1950]) vertical integration (weakly) dominates vertical separation for both manufacturers (the two are equivalent if and only if there is a fully extracting franchise fee).

Then if each manufacturer is vertically integrated, $\Pi^i(p)$ will be manufacturer i's payoff function. We take Nash equilibrium in prices as our solution concept.[3] That is to say, each firm chooses its price optimally, given the price chosen by its rival. The Nash equilibrium (which under additional very mild assumptions exists and is unique)[4] will be given by the solution to $\Pi^i_i(p) = 0$ $(i = 1, 2)$. Let it be denoted by

(4) $$p^* = (p^{*1}, p^{*2})$$

On the other hand, if manufacturers are *not* vertically integrated, final product prices will depend on the arrangements that they have with their retailers. We shall suppose that manufacturers set wholesale prices, and that retailers can buy as much as they want at those prices, which effectively become the retailers' unit costs.[5] Let w^i be the wholesale price set by manufacturer i to his own retailer and let $w = (w^1, w^2)$. Then the payoff function of retailer i will be given by

(5) $$R^i(p; w^i) = (p^i - w^i)D^i(p)$$

By our assumptions, for each w there will be a unique Nash equilibrium of the game between retailers (with payoff functions given by (5)).[6] Let it be denoted by

(6) $$p(w) = (p^1(w), p^2(w))$$

It is worth noting that $R^i(p; 0) \equiv \Pi^i(p)$ and therefore $p(0) = p^*$. We assume that for each w the Nash equilibrium between retailers is stable:

Assumption 3 (stability). For all w and for each $i = 1, 2$

(7) $$R^i_{ii}(p(w); w^i) + R^i_{ji}(p(w); w^i) < 0$$

Finally, we assume that the variables in the game between retailers are strategic complements[7]:

Assumption 4. Retailers' prices are strategic complements:

(8) $$R^i_{ji}(p; w^i) \equiv D^i_j(p) + (p^i - w^i)D^i_{ji}(p) > 0$$

for all p with $p^i \geqslant w^i$.

[3] See the remarks concerning Cournot competition in section III.

[4] Assumptions 1 and 2 are sufficient to ensure existence and uniqueness if we add the following very mild assumptions: $D^i(0) > 0$ and, for each p^j, D^i becomes zero (and has a negative slope) at some finite price p^i which depends continuously on p^j and is bounded away from infinity. These two assumptions guarantee the existence of a positive price vector p such that $\Pi^i_i(p) = 0$ for each $i = 1, 2$ (see Bonanno and Zeeman [1985]). Strict concavity of Π^i implied by assumption 1 then ensures that such a p is unique and is a Nash equilibrium.

[5] Since we have defined the prices p^1 and p^2 net of unit supply costs, we have already taken other retailing expenses (which are part of supply costs) into account.

[6] As in footnote 4, existence and uniqueness of an equilibrium with retail prices in excess of wholesale prices are guaranteed for all w such that $D^i(w) > 0$ $(i = 1, 2)$.

[7] See Bulow *et al.* [1985]. In view of assumption 2, a sufficient (but not necessary) condition for this is that $D^i_{ji}(p) \geqslant 0$ for all p.

Assumptions 3 and 4 imply that in (p^1, p^2)-space the slope of the reaction curve of retailer 1 (with respect to the p^1-axis) is positive and greater than the positive slope of the reaction curve of retailer 2. This means that if retailer 2 increased his price by Δp, then retailer 1 would find it optimal to increase his price in response, although not by as much as Δp. Furthermore, assumptions 3 and 4 together imply that $\partial p^2/\partial w^1 > 0$ and therefore if manufacturer 1 increases his wholesale price, *both* retailers' prices will go up. These facts are used in the proof of proposition 1, which establishes the individual incentive for vertical separation.

Let $\pi^i(w)$ be the profit of manufacturer i at the Nash equilibrium between retailers, when franchise fees can be used to extract retailers' profits. That is,

$$\pi^i(w) = \Pi^i(p(w)) \tag{9}$$

Proposition 1. If franchise fees can be used to extract the retailers' profits, it is in the individual interest of each manufacturer to choose vertical separation and charge his retailer a wholesale price in excess of unit production cost, no matter whether the other manufacturer is vertically integrated or separated.

Proof. Let $\hat{w}^2$ be the wholesale price charged by manufacturer 2 to his own retailer (if $\hat{w}^2 = 0$, manufacturer 2 is vertically integrated; note that we do not rule out the possibility that $\hat{w}^2$ is negative). We shall first show that $w^1 = 0$ (that is, vertical integration) is not manufacturer 1's optimal response to $\hat{w}^2$. By the implicit function theorem applied to $R_i^i = 0$ $(i = 1, 2)$ at the Nash equilibrium corresponding to $w^1 = 0$ and $w^2 = \hat{w}^2$, we have

$$\frac{\partial p^2(0, \hat{w}^2)}{\partial w^1} = \frac{R_{12}^2(p(0, \hat{w}^2); \hat{w}^2)}{\Omega} \frac{\partial R_1^1(p(0, \hat{w}^2); 0)}{\partial w^1} \tag{10}$$

where $\Omega = R_{11}^1 R_{22}^2 - R_{21}^1 R_{12}^2$ (with all partial derivatives evaluated at the point (p, w) given by $p = p(0, \hat{w}^2)$ and $w = (0, \hat{w}^2)$), which is positive by assumptions 1, 3 and 4. Thus $\partial p^2/\partial w^1 > 0$. Now, differentiating (9) with respect to w^1 we obtain

$$\begin{aligned} \frac{\partial \pi^1(0, \hat{w}^2)}{\partial w^1} &= \Pi_1^1(p(0, \hat{w}^2)) \frac{\partial p^1(0, \hat{w}^2)}{\partial w^1} + \Pi_2^1(p(0, \hat{w}^2)) \frac{\partial p^2(0, \hat{w}^2)}{\partial w^1} \\ &= \Pi_2^1(p(0, \hat{w}^2)) \frac{\partial p^2(0, \hat{w}^2)}{\partial w^1} > 0 \end{aligned} \tag{11}$$

since $\Pi_1^1(p(0, \hat{w}^2)) = R_1^1(p(0, \hat{w}^2); 0) = 0$, because $p(0, \hat{w}^2)$ is the Nash equilibrium corresponding to $w^1 = 0$ and $w^2 = \hat{w}^2$ (and $\Pi_2^1 > 0$ by assumption 2). We now show that the best response to $\hat{w}^2$ is a *positive* w^1. Suppose not, and let $\hat{w}^1 < 0$ be the best response. At the Nash equilibrium corresponding to $(\hat{w}^1, \hat{w}^2)$ we have $R_1^1 = \Pi_1^1 - \hat{w}^1 D_1^1 = 0$ and therefore $\Pi_1^1 > 0$ (since $\hat{w}^1 < 0$, by our supposition, and $D_1^1 < 0$). Thus

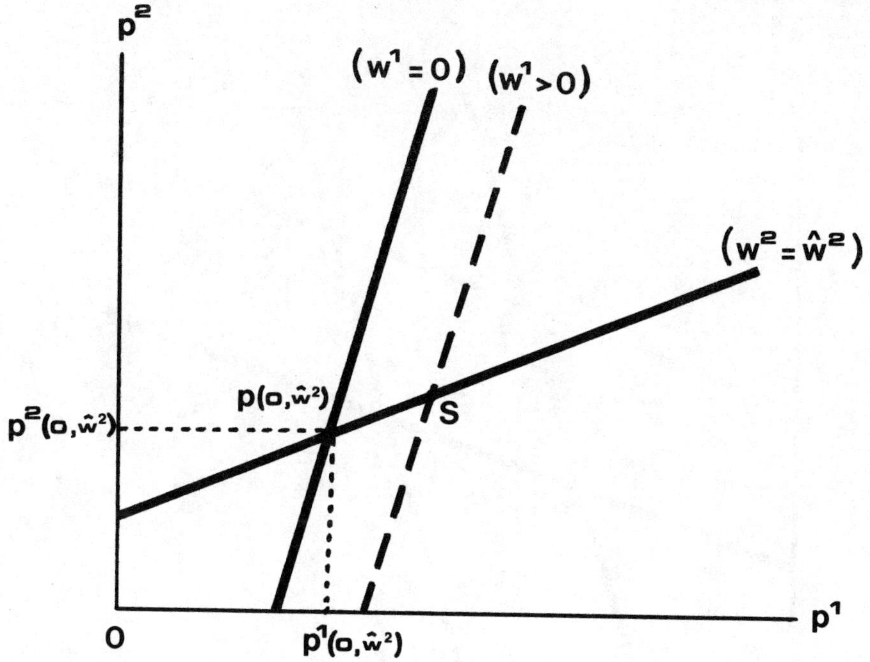

Figure 1

$\partial\pi^1/\partial w^1 = \Pi_1^1(\partial p^1/\partial w^1)+\Pi_2^1(\partial p^2/\partial w^1) > 0$, since—by the implicit function theorem and assumptions 1–4—also the remaining terms are positive. Q.E.D.

Proposition 1 becomes obvious if one looks at Figure 1.

The steeper of the two continuous lines represents the reaction curve of the vertically integrated manufacturer 1, while the other continuous line represents the reaction curve of retailer 2 given the wholesale price $\hat{w}^2$ (or the reaction curve of the vertically integrated manufacturer 2 if $\hat{w}^2 = 0$). The dashed line represents the reaction curve of *retailer* 1 when manufacturer 1 chooses vertical separation and charges a positive wholesale price $w^1 > 0$. If manufacturer 1 chooses vertical integration, the Nash equilibrium is given by $p(0, \hat{w}^2)$. On the other hand, given the relative slopes of the reaction curves, if manufacturer 1 chooses vertical separation, the Nash equilibrium (between retailer 1 and retailer 2) will be along retailer 2's reaction curve at a point where both final prices have gone up (point *S*). Since at $p(0, \hat{w}^2)$, Π^1 is at a maximum with respect to p^1 (the point $p(0, \hat{w}^2)$ lies on the reaction curve given by $\Pi_1^1 = 0$), the first-order effect on Π^1 of the increase in p^1 is zero, while the first-order effect of the increase in p^2 is positive. Thus it pays manufacturer 1 to choose vertical separation and charge a wholesale price in excess of production cost. In other words, by increasing w^1, manufacturer 1

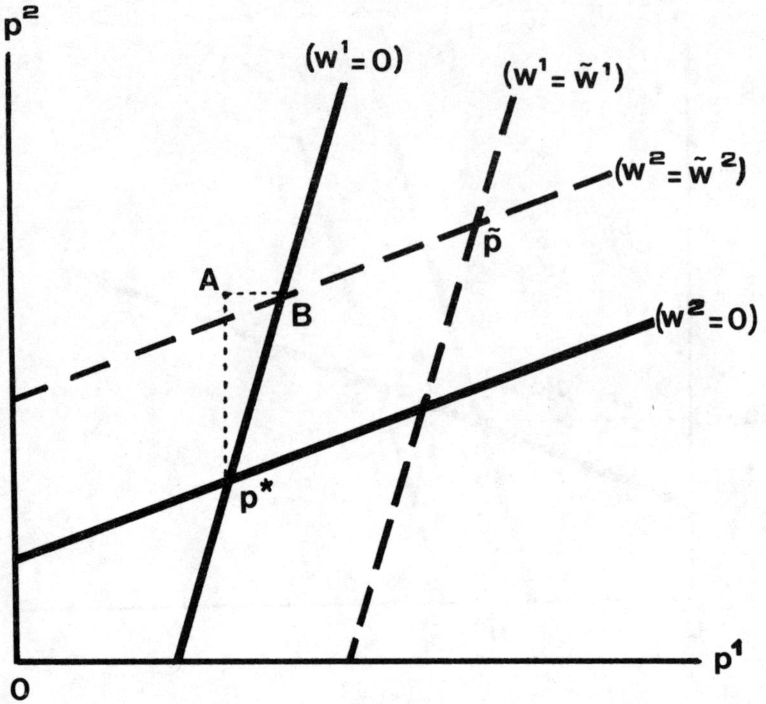

Figure 2

shifts his retailer's reaction curve outwards and can choose the best point on retailer 2's reaction curve.

It is not only in the *individual* interest of a manufacturer to separate vertically. Next we show that both manufacturers will be better off if they both choose vertical separation and charge wholesale prices in excess of production costs (and can collect their retailer's profits by means of a franchise fee) than if they remain integrated. Let

(12) $\tilde{w} = (\tilde{w}^1, \tilde{w}^2)$

be the Nash equilibrium of the game between manufacturers where the payoff functions are given by (9), and let

(13) $\tilde{p} = (p^1(\tilde{w}), p^2(\tilde{w}))$

be the corresponding equilibrium retail prices. (In other words, $(\tilde{w}, \tilde{p})$ is the perfect equilibrium of the two-stage game in which first manufacturers choose wholesale prices and then retailers compete in retail prices.)

Proposition 2. For each $i = 1, 2$,

(14) $\pi^i(\tilde{w}) > \pi^i(0) \equiv \Pi^i(p^*)$

We shall give a simple geometric proof of the above proposition by referring to Figure 2.

First of all, by proposition 1 we have that $\tilde{w}^i > 0$ for each $i = 1, 2$. In Figure 2 the continuous lines represent the reaction curves of the vertically integrated manufacturers and the dashed lines the reaction curves of the retailers given $w^1 = \tilde{w}^1$ and $w^2 = \tilde{w}^2$. Consider manufacturer 1. At point A we have that

$$\Pi^1(A) > \Pi^1(p^*) \tag{15}$$

by assumption 2, since at A, p^1 has remained constant, while p^2 has increased. Furthermore,

$$\Pi^1(B) \geqslant \Pi^1(A) \tag{16}$$

by definition of reaction curve (in the movement from A to B, p^2 remains constant). Finally, it must be that

$$\pi^1(\tilde{w}) \equiv \Pi^1(\tilde{p}) \geqslant \Pi^1(B) \tag{17}$$

by definition of $\tilde{w}$. In fact, given $\tilde{w}^2$, manufacturer 1 could choose $w^1 = 0$ (i.e. vertical integration) and the corresponding equilibrium would be point B. The same argument obviously applies to manufacturer 2. Q.E.D.

Propositions 1 and 2 imply that the two-stage game in which first manufacturers choose wholesale prices (a zero wholesale price being interpreted as the decision to be vertically integrated) and then retailers compete in retail prices, has a unique perfect equilibrium at which both manufacturers choose vertical separation and charge wholesale prices in excess of production costs, provided franchise fees can be used to extract retailers' surplus.

III. CONCLUDING REMARKS

Vertical separation with wholesale prices in excess of production costs is profitable when there are fully extracting franchise fees for the following reason. By raising his wholesale price, manufacturer 1 causes the price charged by retailer 1 to rise. Given our (rather mild) assumptions on demand, the reaction function of seller 2 in price space is upward sloping and, therefore, the price of retailer 2 rises too, which benefits manufacturer 1. Starting from a position where wholesale price equals production cost, the effect upon profits of a small increase in wholesale price due to the change in p^1 is negligible, whereas that due to the induced change in p^2 is distinctly positive. Hence the overall effect is beneficial. Vertical separation permits the increase in wholesale price, whereas in-house retailing effectively constrains the whole price to equal production cost.

Reaction functions slope up when the variables in the game between retailers are strategic complements (see Bulow *et al.* [1985]), but if those variables are strategic substitutes—as is often the case if quantities are the strategic variables—very different results hold. In the Cournot example in Vickers [1985], vertical separation is in the individual (but not the collective) interest of manufacturers, and it involves a wholesale price *less* than unit production cost, accompanied by a negative franchise fee, i.e. a fee paid *to* the retailer. Although the strategic advantage of vertical separation remains, its nature is therefore quite different when the strategic variables in the game between retailers are altered.

In this paper we have looked at the case of two manufacturers each of whom has one retailer. Let this be called the (2, 1) case. The extension of the analysis to the (m, 1) case is straightforward, though somewhat tedious. In section I we noted that other authors have investigated the (1, n) case (i.e. one manufacturer with several retailing agents), which involves problems of *intra*-brand competition quite distinct from the questions of *inter*-brand competition examined here. Perhaps the next step is to attempt to combine both issues in a study of the general (m, n) case.

We have shown that vertical separation, in conjunction with an appropriate contract between manufacturer and retailer, can be a profitable strategic move, which works by inducing the rival firm to act in a more friendly manner. The well-known literature on strategic commitment examines several other ways of seeking to achieve the same end (including, for example, strategic investment in capacity or R & D to alter costs), and an important question for future research concerns the relative merits of these various instruments. In reality, vertical separation does not operate costlessly (as we assumed for the purposes of our simple model). There may be costs of information and coordination, and franchise fees cannot always be used to extract retailers' profits fully. However, vertical separation has some advantages as a method of commitment. Compared with internal incentives and organisation designed to achieve the same strategic goals, separation makes the commitment more observable and harder to reverse. Compared with strategic investment to alter costs, separation does not distort factor choice and worsen internal efficiency. We therefore believe that vertical separation—and vertical arrangements between manufacturers and retailers more generally—deserve some consideration from a strategic viewpoint.

GIACOMO BONANNO AND JOHN VICKERS,
Nuffield College,
Oxford OX1 1NF,
UK.

ACCEPTED JUNE 1987

REFERENCES

BLISS, C., 1986, 'The Economic Theory of Retailing', Discussion Paper No. 3, Nuffield College, Oxford.

BONANNO, G. and ZEEMAN, E. C., 1985, 'Limited Knowledge of Demand and Oligopoly Equilibria', *Journal of Economic Theory*, 35, pp. 276–283.

BULOW, J. I., GEANAKOPLOS, J. D. and KLEMPERER, P. D., 1985, 'Multiproduct Oligopoly: Strategic Substitutes and Complements', *Journal of Political Economy*, 93, pp. 488–511.

MATHEWSON, G. F. and WINTER, R. A., 1984, 'An Economic Theory of Vertical Restraints', *Rand Journal of Economics*, 15, pp. 27–38.

REY, P. and TIROLE, J., 1986a, 'Vertical Restraints from a Principal-Agent Viewpoint', in PELLEGRINI, L. and REDDY, S. (eds.), *Marketing Channels: Relationships and Performance* (Lexington: Lexington Books, New York).

REY, P. and TIROLE, J., 1986b, 'The Logic of Vertical Restraints', *American Economic Review*, 76, pp. 923–939.

SPENGLER, J., 1950, 'Vertical Integration and Anti-Trust Policy', *Journal of Political Economy*, 58, pp. 347–352.

STAHL, K., 1982, 'Differentiated Products, Consumer Search and Locational Oligopoly', *Journal of Industrial Economics*, 31, pp. 97–113.

VICKERS, J., 1985, 'Delegation and the Theory of the Firm', *Economic Journal*, Conference Supplement, pp. 138–147.

THE JOURNAL OF INDUSTRIAL ECONOMICS 0022-1821 $2.00
Volume XXXVI March 1988 No. 3

TESTABLE COMPETING HYPOTHESES FROM STRUCTURE-PERFORMANCE THEORY: EFFICIENT STRUCTURE VERSUS MARKET POWER*

FREDERICK HARRIS

This paper provides a structure-performance theory that can accommodate leading firm efficiency as well as several competing market power hypotheses. We derive testable implications distinguishing the simple collusion, product differentiation, and scale economy hypotheses from the innovative leading firm alternative. It is shown that recent evidence of a positive market share-price-cost margin (*PCM*) relationship and a non-positive concentration-*PCM* relationship can reject the scale economy and simple collusion hypotheses in homogeneous product markets. Unfortunately, this same evidence cannot reject the product differentiation hypothesis in favor of leading firm efficiency.

I. INTRODUCTION

AN EMERGING tenet of structure-performance research holds that a positive share-performance relationship combined with a non-positive concentration performance relationship provides evidence of leading firm efficiency (see Demsetz [1974] and Smirlock, Gilligan and Marshall [1984]). Although Clarke, Davies, and Waterson [1984] recently rejected this "efficient structure" hypothesis for a subsample of UK manufacturing industries, some supportive evidence appears in the traditional empirical literature (e.g., Shepherd [1982]), in the PIMS and FTC LB studies (Gale and Branch [1982], Martin [1983], Ravenscraft [1983]), in Mueller's [1987] persistent profit projections, in Leamer specification searches (Bothwell, Cooley and Hall [1984]), and in my recent paper on price-cost margins under risk (Harris [1986]). Moreover, nearly all the attempts to employ capitalized value measures of performance—i.e., Tobin's q or relative excess value—have also reported positive market share but insignificant concentration effects.[1]

Before the efficient structure hypothesis becomes manifest in a doctrinaire pro-merger policy, it is crucial to assess whether this recent groundswell of empirical evidence does in fact support leading firm efficiency. This paper provides a representative agent theory of the structure-performance relationship that can accommodate leading firm efficiency as well as several

* I wish to thank two anonymous referees and Larry White for several very constructive criticisms and suggested revisions. Eirik Furubotn, Stephen Martin, Dennis Mueller, Roger Sherman and John Trapani also provided helpful advice. This research was supported by a University of Texas ORF grant.

[1] See Hirschey [1982], [1985], Harris [1984], and the references cited therein.

competing market power hypotheses. We seek to distinguish a simple collusion hypothesis, a product differentiation hypothesis, and a scale economy hypothesis from the innovative leading firm alternative. By reformulating and extending the Stigler–Cowling–Waterson oligopoly model, we elucidate testable implications capable of distinguishing among the competing hypotheses.

II. CONCENTRATION AND MARKET SHARE IN HOMOGENEOUS PRODUCT OLIGOPOLY

Cowling and Waterson [1976] first formalized the structure-performance implications of profit-maximizing output choice in homogeneous product oligopoly. For price-takers, profits may be written

$$\pi_j = [P_0(q^m) - MC_j(q_j)]q_j - FC_j \tag{1}$$

where P_0, price, is a function of market output (q^m), marginal cost (MC) is a function of firm output (q_j), and FC is fixed cost. Eqn. (1) allows for asymmetrical oligopoly attributable to differing MC_j across firms within the same relevant market, even under constant cost conditions. And, in addition, we have allowed for production scale economies.

Differentiating (1) with respect to q_j, rearranging and manipulating yields

$$\frac{(P_0 - MC)^*}{P_0} = -\frac{S_j}{\eta_p^m}\frac{\partial q^m}{\partial q_j} + \frac{q_j}{P_0}\frac{\partial MC_j}{\partial q_j} \tag{2}$$

where S_j is the firm's market share and η_p^m is the price elasticity of market demand. To interpret (2) further, we employ the concept of a function coefficient ($\varepsilon_j = ATC/MC > 0$) to capture the firm's returns to scale at equilibrium q_j. For homogeneous production functions the output elasticity of MC is $(1/\varepsilon - 1)$ (see Ferguson [1971]), so (2) may be written

$$\frac{(P_0 - MC_j)^*}{P_0} = -\frac{S_j}{\eta_p^m}\frac{\partial q^m}{\partial q_j} + \left(\frac{1}{\varepsilon_j} - 1\right)\frac{MC_j}{P_0} \tag{3}$$

where the firm's mark-up and margin will rise, fall, or remain unchanged depending on whether production exhibits decreasing ($\varepsilon_j < 1$), increasing ($\varepsilon_j > 1$), or constant ($\varepsilon_j = 1$) returns to scale.[2] Finally, following Cowling and Waterson, we expand $\partial q^m/\partial q_j = (\partial q_j/\partial q_j) + (\partial q^r/\partial q_j) \equiv (1 + \lambda_j)$ to obtain

$$\frac{(P_0 - MC_j)^*}{P_0} = \frac{S_j}{-\eta_p^m}(1 + \lambda_j) + \left(\frac{1}{\varepsilon_j} - 1\right)\frac{MC_j}{P_0} \tag{4}$$

where $\partial q^r/\partial q_j$ (hereafter λ_j) is the rival response expectation in outputs. In general, a "conjectural variation" for the summed output of rivals like λ_j may be positive, negative, or zero and may differ across firms within the same relevant market (see Kwoka and Ravenscraft [1986]).

[2] Martin [1987] derives a similar expression for the more observable average cost margin in which case MC_j/P_0 on the r.h.s. of (3) becomes AVC_j/P_0.

Oligopolistic interdependence can take on many forms in this model. Under Cournot rival response expectations, $\lambda_j = 0$ and (4) reduces immediately to the familiar Lerner index of monopoly power $-1/\eta_P^m$ as $S_j \to 1$ with constant returns to scale, or to the natural monopoly equilibrium as $S_j \to 1$ with $\varepsilon > 1$. Alternatively, with N equal size firms and implicitly no leading firm efficiencies (that is, $MC_j = MC_k$), $S_j = 1/N$, and consequently, (4) reduces to the competitive equilibrium: $\lim_{N \to \infty} (P - MC)/P = 0$ under constant cost conditions (that is, $\varepsilon = 1$). Waterson [1984, p. 23] and Kurz [1985] describe another limiting case of tacit collusion in which $\lambda_j = (1 - S_j)/S_j > 0$,—that is, firms anticipate proportional and lockstep rival output responses just maintaining the current share distribution. Not surprisingly, this "Nash implementable" collusive oligopoly equilibrium,[3] yielding in the present model

$$\text{(5)} \qquad \frac{(P_0 - MC_j)^*}{P_0} = -\frac{1}{\eta_P^m} + \left(\frac{1}{\varepsilon_j} - 1\right)\frac{MC_j}{P_0}$$

would be preferred by small share firms over the non-cooperative Cournot equilibrium,

$$\text{(6)} \qquad \frac{(P_0 - MC_j)^*}{P_0} = -\frac{S_j}{\eta_P^m} + \left(\frac{1}{\varepsilon_j} - 1\right)\frac{MC_j}{P_0}$$

To derive the relationship between concentration and price-cost performance for this homogeneous products regime, some of the asymmetric oligopoly features in (4)–(6) must be abandoned. Cowling and Waterson [1976] impose the restriction $\varepsilon_j = 1$, and then multiplying that special case of (4) by q_j, dividing by q^m, and summing across all firms, they obtain

$$\text{(7)} \qquad \frac{(P_0 - AVC)^*}{P_0} = \frac{\sum S_j}{-\eta_P^m}\frac{q_j}{q^m}(1 + \lambda_j) = \frac{\sum S_j^2}{-\eta_P^m}\left(1 + \frac{\sum S_j^2 \lambda_j}{\sum S_j^2}\right)$$
$$= \frac{H}{-\eta_P^m}\left(1 + \frac{\sum S_j^2 \lambda_j}{H}\right)$$

where $(P - AVC)/P$ is industry operating profit as a ratio of sales and H is the Herfindahl concentration index. Under Cournot assumptions, $\lambda_j = 0$ and optimal price-cost margins (PCM^*) equal $H/-\eta_p^m$ implying $\partial PCM^*/\partial H > 0$. Moreover, since $0 < H < 1$, positive margins and the collusive oligopoly equilibrium in (5) restrict the rival response parameters to $-H < \sum S_j^2 \lambda_j < (1 - H)$. Consequently, concentration and price-cost performance are positively related in the Cowling and Waterson model even if $\lambda_j \neq 0$.

Although Eqn. (7) allows the rival response expectations (the λ_j) to differ across firms within the relevant market, there is no additional scope for

[3] Kurz [1985] has shown that this share maintenance mechanism can emerge from the feasibly unanimous procedural agreements in a cooperative oligopoly game if blocking *coalitions* are disallowed.

oligopolistic asymmetries. In particular, Demsetz [1974] and Peltzman [1977] argue that models like (7) fail to reflect either innovative firms or scale economies, both sources of leading firm efficiency. Indeed, the positive inter-industry relationship between PCM and H in (7) arises *because of* intra-industry cost differentials and the ensuing output expansions by low-cost producers of these homogeneous products (Clarke and Davies [1982]); yet, (7) suppresses the cost differences. In contrast, we *expect* MC_j to differ across firms in accordance with their tangible, albeit temporary, success in the risky innovation game (Reinganum [1985]). All firms attempt to innovate (i.e., to discover cost-reducing new technology and adapt it to their own use); some succeed in attaining high S_j and PCM_j, and others fail.[4] Whether leading firms are then imitated until another draw from the innovation urn depends upon the feasibility of preemptive patents and upon rival price response behavior. Vickers [1986] has shown that with Bertrand price competition and incremental technological change, a high-cost duopolist will not adopt the new technology, since start-up costs would be unrecoverable.[5]

Although the analysis of dynamic oligopoly games is far from complete, several conclusions have emerged. (i) Innovation takes time, and, during the uncertain period between innovations, the low-cost incumbent will earn efficiency rents. (ii) In the absence of preemptive patents, absolute cost differentials need not imply the emergence of monopoly. (iii) Yet, asymmetric oligopoly equilibrium favorable to the "efficient structure" hypothesis may persist until the next "drastic" technological change. In our single-period context, this means that MC_j may differ even if $\varepsilon_j = 1$. At a minimum, the l.h.s. of (7) must then be written $(P_0 \sum q_j - \sum MC_j q_j)/P_0 q^m$, though the aggregation continues to suppress the intraindustry cost differentials.

To allow for production scale economies, we reintroduce the function coefficient into (7):

$$(8) \qquad \frac{(P_0 \sum q_j - \sum MC_j q_j)^*}{P_0 q^m} = \frac{H}{-\eta_P^m}\left(1+\frac{\sum S_j^2 \lambda_j}{H}\right)+\sum\left(\frac{1}{\varepsilon_j}-1\right)S_j\frac{MC_j}{P_0}$$

Here, otherwise identical firms can have different mark-ups and margins because of scale effects. And since across observations from several industries H and ε_j should be positively correlated *a priori*, one must exclude the possibility of scale economies before one concludes that a positive concentration-performance relationship at the industry level is attributable to leading firm efficiency.

To distinguish both innovative firms and scale effects from the collusive

[4] Such an argument was first introduced in Mancke [1974].

[5] More generally, in a dynamic sequence of such games, whether the incumbent's cost advantage will persist and lead to an increasingly dominant market structure depends upon the size of the initial cost differential, the size of the next cost reduction (ΔC), the endogenous probability of invention by the low-cost firm as $\Delta C \to 0$, and the rival response expectations (Fudenberg and Tirole [1986]).

potential in highly concentrated oligopoly groups, we must return to the firm-level analysis in (4). Writing λ_j as a function of the rival output response elasticity (α_j) and the firm's market share,

$$\lambda_j = \left(\frac{\partial q^r}{\partial q_j}\frac{q_j}{q^r}\right)\frac{q^r}{q^m}\frac{q^m}{q_j} = \alpha_j\left(\frac{1-S_j}{S_j}\right)$$

and substituting into (4), we obtain

$$\frac{(P_0 - MC_j)^*}{P_0} = \frac{S_j + \alpha_j(1-S_j)}{-\eta_P^m} + \left(\frac{1}{\varepsilon_j} - 1\right)\frac{MC_j}{P_0} \tag{9}$$

Then, parameterizing α_j as a measure of collusive potential throughout the relevant market and hypothesizing that $\alpha_j \gtreqless 0$ is a monotonically increasing function of H yields an estimable general model for homogeneous products:[6]

$$\frac{(P_0 - MC_j)^*}{P_0} = 1 - \varepsilon_j + \varepsilon_j \frac{(S_j + \alpha_j(H)(1-S_j))}{-\eta_P^m} \tag{9'}$$

Differentiating (9′) with respect to H and S_j, we can derive the effect of market share and concentration on firm-specific PCM^*:

$$\frac{\partial PCM_j^*}{\partial H} = \varepsilon_j \frac{(1-S_j)}{-\eta_P^m}\frac{\partial \alpha_j}{\partial H} > 0 \quad \text{for} \quad \frac{\partial \alpha_j}{\partial H} > 0 \tag{10}$$

$$\frac{\partial PCM_j^*}{\partial S_j} = \varepsilon_j \frac{(1-\alpha_j)}{-\eta_P^m} + \frac{[(S_j + \alpha_j(1-S_j)) - 1]}{-\eta_P^m}\frac{\partial \varepsilon_j}{\partial q_j} q^m \tag{11}$$

Since $0 < \varepsilon_j \gtreqless 1$ and $\alpha_j \gtreqless 0$ is bounded from above by the collusive oligopoly equilibrium in (5) where $\alpha = 1$, the first term on the r.h.s. of (11) is positive. To evaluate the second term, collect ε_j terms in (9′) which yields $PCM_j^* = 1 + \varepsilon_j[\Phi]$ where $[\Phi]$ is the bracketed term in (11). Recognizing that $1 > PCM_j^* > 0$ and $\varepsilon_j > 0$ implies $0 > [\Phi] > -1/\varepsilon$—i.e., that $[\Phi]$ is negative. Finally, using $\partial q_j/\partial S_j = q^m$ and $\partial \varepsilon_j/\partial q_j \leqslant 0$ for *IRS*, *CRS*, or *DRS* production,[7] we conclude that the second term on the r.h.s. of (11) is also positive and therefore that $\partial PCM_j^*/\partial S_j > 0$.

Competing hypotheses with homogeneous products

Leading firm efficiency entails either scale effects or absolute cost advantages attributable to successful innovation. It is important to separate these two arguments both in theory and in empirical testing. Innovative firms experience higher shares, lower costs, and higher PCM^*s. In Eqn. (9), this means that even if scale effects were non-existent (i.e., $\varepsilon = 1$), MC_j on the l.h.s. would decline as share rises, thereby generating Ricardian rent. Although the

[6] Kwoka and Ravenscraft [1986] pursue an interesting sophistication of this simple collusion hypothesis by having α_j depend on S_j and ε_j as well as H.

[7] Consider the ratio ATC/MC as q_j increases for $\varepsilon \gtreqless 1$, and see Ferguson [1971, p. 162].

market power effects in (11)—i.e., $\partial PCM^*/\partial S = (1-\alpha)/-\eta_p^m > 0$—would be indistinguishable from the innovation effects, which also of course raise PCM^*s, this proves to be no problem within the context of the present model. For with homogeneous products and $\varepsilon = 1$, persistently high shares and any attendant "market power" arises only through innovative cost reductions. Apart from white noise randomness (and possible Gibrat effects), innovative leading firms is a tautologically true hypothesis when there can be no asymmetry on the demand side on an oligopolistic market. In homogeneous product markets under constant returns to scale, persistently high share firms must be innovative price cutters; there is no other way to capture and retain market share.[8]

In contrast, the simple collusion and scale economy hypotheses are both rejectable, given homogeneous products. The limiting case of a collusive oligopoly equilibrium in (5) implies $\alpha = 1$. Following Stigler [1964] in hypothesizing that collusive potential $(0 < \alpha \leqslant 1)$ is positively related to H, Eqn. (9′) implies a positive partial correlation between firm-specific PCM^* and H. This implication disaggregates Cowling and Waterson's result in (7) and allows the simple collusion hypothesis to be distinguished from the innovative leading firm hypothesis. However, the recent evidence of a positive share-performance relationship and no significant concentration-performance relationship, *ceteris paribus*, rejects this simple collusion hypothesis (e.g., Gale and Branch [1982], Bothwell, Cooley, and Hall [1984], Harris [1986], and Mueller [1987]).

Of course, it is crucial to control for scale economies in attempting to test the simple collusion hypothesis. Since $\partial H/\partial\varepsilon > 0$, by assumption, an insignificant empirical relationship between H and PCM^* might be attributable to the output increases, price reductions, and *declining* margins associated with scale economies in production. Strictly speaking, we can seldom specify whether a firm's $\varepsilon \gtrless 1$ without actually estimating the production function. What we can observe, however, is an apparent increase in ε_j *across firms* when the minimum efficient scale (e.g., the midpoint plant size value of shipments/ industry value of shipments) rises. Differentiating (9′) with respect to ε_j yields,

$$\text{(12)} \qquad \frac{\partial PCM_j^*}{\partial \varepsilon_j} = \frac{[S_j + \alpha_j(H)(1-S_j) - 1]}{-\eta_P^m} + \frac{\varepsilon_j(1-S_j)}{-\eta_P^m}\frac{\partial \alpha_j}{\partial H}\frac{\partial H}{\partial \varepsilon_j}$$

By previous argument, the bracketed term reflects a negative effect highlighted by Martin [1987, pp. 13–15]—namely, that optimal margins *decline* as prices are cut to realize scale economies, *ceteris paribus*. Offsetting this factor is the concentration effect in the second term—i.e., higher scale economies imply more concentration which (under the simple collusion hypothesis, $\partial\alpha_j/\partial H > 0$) implies higher margins.

[8] As we shall soon see, however, this result does not carry over to the differentiated products world.

Separating the direct and indirect effects of scale economies by including measures of both ε_j and H among the regressors in an estimation of (9′), the scale economy hypothesis for established competitors can be rejected by a *non-negative* relationship between PCM^* and ε_j. Of course, scale economies may have an additional, barrier to entry effect on *potential* competitors, thereby raising price-cost margins. Testing the relationship in (9′) therefore requires control variables accounting for barriers to entry (e.g., cost advantage ratios and absolute capital requirements) in addition to measures of ε_j. Even then, one may still observe the competing effects of scale economies on established versus potential entrant firms. Harris [1986, pp. 48–49] found the negative effect on established firm margins predominant for consumer convenience manufacturers (e.g., cosmetics, cereal and beer), but the barrier to entry effect predominant for consumer non-convenience manufacturers (e.g., tires, televisions, and clothing).

A few additional comments on specification in this homogeneous products model are warranted. Martin [1987] and Harris [1986], [1987] have argued (i) that $(P_0-MC)^*/P_0$ may be replaced by the observable $(P-AVC)^*/P_0$ in (9) and (9′) since the output elasticity of MC and AVC are identical (i.e., $1/\varepsilon-1$) for homogeneous productions functions,[9] and (ii) that an empirical model of (9′) must control for differences in the firm-specific cost of capital (COC_j) and the capital intensity $(\text{asset/sales})_j$ ratio. In addition, (9′) clearly leads to regression relations that are non-linear in the parameters, so it is not possible simply to rename variables and emerge with the usual linear or loglinear estimating equation. A flexible functional form for entering the control variables (like COC_j) should be investigated, but an empirical model testing the theoretical relationships between PCM^* and S_j, H_j, and ε_j should be true to the inherently nonlinear character of (9′).

III. CONCENTRATION AND MARKET SHARE IN DIFFERENTIATED PRODUCT OLIGOPOLY

To allow for differentiated products and the resultant demand asymmetries, consider the profit-maximizing pricing decision of a dominant firm engaged in competition among the few (i.e., a member of a dominant oligopoly group). To simplify, decompose the firm's perceived demand, q^1, into the effects on market demand, rival supply, and pricing by the rest of the oligopoly group: $q^1 \equiv q[q^m(p^1,\ldots), q^r(p^1,\ldots), p^r(p^1,\ldots)]$ where q^m = market demand, P^1 = price, q^r = rivals' summed supply, and $p^r(p^1)$ = a rival (price) response function.[10] Differentiating q^1 with respect to p^1 and manipulating (see Harris

[9] MC/P_0 on the r.h.s. of (9) also becomes the observable AVC/P.

[10] For simplicity, we narrow the rivalrous reaction problem of $n(n-1)$ firm interactions by assuming that the $n-1$ rival firms adopt identical prices based on identical demand, cost, and rival reaction functions. However, $p^r \gtreqless p^1$ given differentiated products. A similar model was first explored formally in Stigler [1940].

Implicit in this framework is the identification of a "relevant market" for the oligopoly's

[1986]), we obtain an expression for the dominant firm's own-price elasticity of demand, η^1,

$$(13) \qquad \eta^1 = \eta_p^m \frac{q^m}{q^1} - \theta^s \frac{q^r}{q^1} + \eta^c \eta^r$$

where $\eta^m < 0$ is the price elasticity of market demand, $\theta^s \gtreqless 0$ is the conjectural own-price elasticity of rival supply, $\eta^c \geqslant 0$ is the cross-price elasticity of firm 1 demand, and $\eta^r \gtreqless 0$ is the conjectural rival price response elasticity. Recognizing that q^m/q^1 is the inverse of firm 1's market share $(1/S_1)$ and that $q^r/q^m \equiv (1-S_1)$, and taking the simplest case of identical MC across firms with CRS production technology, the profit maximizing price-cost margin may be written

$$(14) \qquad \frac{(p^1 - MC)^*}{p^1} = \frac{S_1}{-\eta_p^m + \theta^s(1-S_1) - \eta^c \eta^r S_1}$$

Differentiating (14) with respect to S_1 and using (13) yields $-(\eta^1)^{-2}(\eta_p^m - \theta^s)S_1^{-2} > 0$ if $\theta^s \geqslant 0$ or $\eta^m < \theta^s < 0$. That is, increases in market share imply higher profit margins, *ceteris paribus*, except for the perverse case in which rivals raise production by more than the increase in market demand attributable to firm 1's price cut (i.e., $\theta^s < \eta_p^m < 0$). In general, of course, we expect rivals to *reduce* production in the above situation. With homogeneous products, a decreased (increased) price by firm 1 will cause fewer (greater) anticipated sales by the rival producers, *ceteris paribus*; consequently, only reduced (expanded) production—i.e., $\theta^s > 0$—can maintain an optimal inventory at the rival firms.[11] Given differentiated products, increasing sub-market segmentation (i.e., $\eta^c \to 0$) implies $\theta^s \to 0$ *from above* since at worsened (improved) relative prices rival sellers cannot expect to attract (lose) customers precipitated to enter (exit) the market by firm 1's price cut (rise). In light of these anticipated alterations in the pre-existing distribution of buyers across products (cf. Kumar and Satterthwaite [1985]), optimal inventory considerations dictate $\theta^s \geqslant 0$ which implies $\partial PCM_j^*/\partial S_j^* > 0$, *ceteris paribus*.

To be validated, the above rival response conjectures should be derived from equilibrium behavior in a dynamic oligopoly game (e.g., Riordan [1985]). While this paper is not intended to embed the static structure-performance relationship in a dynamic game, it is important to note that in our context subgame perfect trigger strategies could well include inventory disequilibria. Note that the unambiguous share-performance result continues to hold despite strategic behavior leading to $\theta^s < 0$, as long as the resulting rival inventory disequilibrium is either temporary or bounded (i.e.,

differentiated products (e.g., a city-pair airline market). Waterson [1984, pp. 2 and 26–28] defends such market definitions for the purpose of extending classic oligopoly models to handle differentiated products.

[11] At the competitive extreme, ultra-free entry and constant costs imply a perceived $\theta^s \to \infty$, $\eta^1 \to -\infty$, and $p^1 \to MC$ due to potential entry and rival supply.

$\eta_p^m < \theta^s < 0$). In addition, notice the sign of $\partial PCM_j^*/\partial S_j^*$ in (14) does not depend upon η^r (since η^1 is squared), and it is therefore robust across all rival price response conjectures (i.e., $\eta^r \gtreqless 0$). Consequently, in a differentiated products setting, a positive empirical association between market share and profit performance can be explained *a priori* by the exercise of leading firm market power over price.

While this analytical link between shares and margins is quite general, just the opposite is true of the relationship between concentration and margins. In (13) and (14), concentration affects both the intraindustry pricing differential and the oligopoly group's supply through the conjectural rival response elasticities η^r and θ^s. In the spirit of Stigler's [1964] model of the heightened collusive potential in concentrated oligopoly groups, more effective monitoring, detection, and enforcement of quotas in concentrated markets secure Cournot-type rival supply responses to renegade discounting (i.e., $\theta^s \rightarrow 0$).[12] By (14), this effect of higher H, taken alone, implies higher PCMs. In addition, however, renegade discounting by firm 1 causes cartel price erosion, $\eta^r > 0$, which is *retarded* by better monitoring, detection, and enforcement the higher the concentration (i.e., $\partial \eta^r/\partial H < 0$). This second effect, taken alone, implies higher H will *reduce* PCMs because, when higher concentration retards rivalrous price competition, the firm's perceived own-price elasticity of demand *increases.*

The intuitive logic of this second, competing, influence of concentration is analogous to the effect on margins of increasing $|\eta^m|$—e.g., as a result of more or closer substitutes outside the relevant market. If rivalrous price cutting declines with higher concentration, then for any given degree of substitutability between rival products within the relevant market (i.e., for any given η^c), own-price reductions induce more current customers to switch from rival firms. When combined with any given effect on new customers (through η^m), own-price changes therefore have larger net effects on firm 1 demand. As argued by Cubbin [1983], the greater the likelihood of moving down Chamberlain's dd′ schedule rather than down the less elastic share-of-the market DD′ schedule, the smaller the retaliation for a price cut and the lower the oligopolist's equilibrium price. We have hypothesized that higher concentration may actually reduce the chance of widespread price erosion in response to renegade discounting. At the extreme, cartels can perhaps orchestrate pricing punishment schemes of limited duration, but tacitly collusive oligopolies must approach punishment more obliquely.[13]

[12] It may be objected that these are differentiated, not homogeneous, product models. Stigler [1964], however, highlights the role of buyer heterogeneity even with "homogeneous products". And Wernerfelt's [1985] recent investigation of optimal punishment schemes for oligopoly supergames demonstrates that product differentiation can enhance collusion about output.

[13] For example, Kreps and Scheinkman [1983] have shown that under certain conditions (e.g., two periods, no demand uncertainty, and *ex ante* capacity choice) duopolists nominally engaged in Bertrand price competition will choose Cournot outputs and prices, appearing to play a quantity-setting game. Also see Wernerfelt [1985] and footnote 12.

Rewriting (14) with $\theta^s(H)$ and $\eta^r(H)$ and differentiating with respect to H yields,

$$\text{(15)} \qquad \partial PCM/\partial H = -\frac{1}{\eta_j^2}\left[\frac{(1-S)}{S}\frac{\partial\theta^s}{\partial H} - \eta^c\frac{\partial\eta^r}{\partial H}\right] \gtreqless 0$$

since $\partial\theta^s/\partial H < 0$, $\partial\eta^r/\partial H < 0$ by assumption, and $\eta^c \geqslant 0$ within the relevant market. As long as product differentiation and market segmentation are incomplete (i.e., $\eta^c \neq 0$) and monitoring mechanisms fail to eliminate quota violations by rival firms (i.e., $\theta^s \neq 0$), higher concentration generates two opposing influences on price-cost margins. As in Clarke, Davies and Waterson [1984], the unambiguous concentration results of the homogeneous products model do not carry over. Consequently, in differentiated product markets, empirical evidence of no systematic relationship between concentration and price-cost performance can be consistent with higher collusive potential in concentrated oligopoly groups.

Competing hypotheses with differentiated products

To readdress the alternative hypotheses of innovative leading firms and scale economies, we rewrite (1) as $\pi_j = [P_j - MC_j(q_j)]q_j - FC_j$ where MC_j can differ across firms even if scale effects are non-existent. Differentiating with respect to P_j and substituting from (13), we obtain

$$\text{(14')} \qquad \frac{(P_j - MC_j)^*}{P_j} = 1 + \left(\frac{S_j}{-\eta_p^m + \theta^s(1-S_j) - \eta^c\eta^r S_j} - 1\right)\varepsilon_j$$

which in generalizing (14) provides a differentiated products version of (4). The influence of shares on margins in (14′) entails three conceptually distinct mechanisms:

$$\text{(16)} \qquad \frac{\partial(P_j - MC_j)^*}{\partial S_j} = -\frac{1}{\eta_j^2}(\eta_p^m - \theta^s)\frac{\varepsilon_j}{S_j^2} + [\Psi]\frac{\partial\varepsilon_j}{\partial q_j}q^m > 0$$

because $1 > PCM_j^* > 0$ and $\varepsilon_j > 0$ imply $[\Psi]$, the bracketed term in (14′), is negative. As in the homogeneous products model of the previous section, higher shares may lead to the cost reductions associated with scale effects (i.e., the second term in (16)) or reflect cost-reducing innovations (i.e., $\partial MC_j < 0$ on the l.h.s. of (14′)) both of which raise PCM^*s. In addition, however, with differentiated products, higher shares and PCM^*s may simply reflect market power over price (i.e., the first term on the r.h.s. of (14′)).

Although the scale effects can be estimated independently and confirmed or rejected, unfortunately the market power hypothesis and the innovative leading firm hypothesis are indistinguishable. Both imply a positive correlation between market share and measures of price-cost performance, *ceteris paribus*. And unlike the homogeneous products case (where high margin firms were of necessity innovative cost cutters), here the market power and innovation hypotheses do not collapse into one another. Instead, each stands as a theoretically distinct explanation for high differentiated product prices, mark-ups, or profit margins. Innovative leading firms and differentiated product market power are at present empirically indistinguishable hypotheses.[14]

Similarly, we can extend the analysis of concentration and scale effects by differentiating (14′) with respect to H and ε_j which yields ε_j times the r.h.s. of (15) $\gtreqless 0$, and

$$(17) \qquad \frac{\partial PCM^*}{\partial \varepsilon_j} = [\Psi] - \frac{\varepsilon_j}{\eta_j^2}\left[\frac{(1-S)}{S}\frac{\partial \theta^s}{\partial H} - \eta^c \frac{\partial \eta^r}{\partial H}\right]\frac{\partial H}{\partial \varepsilon_j}$$

As in the previous section, scale economies are confirmed by a negative correlation between PCM_j^* and measures of ε_j in estimating equations based on (14′)—i.e., the bracketed term in (14′), $[\Psi]$, is negative by previous argument. In addition, of course, we have argued that $\partial H/\partial \varepsilon_j > 0$ and this indirect effect of scale economies appears in the second term of (17). Although clearly scale effects *can* be separated from the collusion hypothesis that $\partial \theta^s/\partial H < 0$ and $\partial \eta^r/\partial H < 0$, these latter two implications of the heightened collusive potential in more concentrated differentiated product markets oppose one another in (15) and (17). Consequently, while the scale economy hypothesis is rejectable, the effect of concentration on differentiated product PCM^*s is indeterminate *a priori*. This indeterminancy contrasts with the situation for homogeneous products where the simple collusion hypothesis was rejectable based on a non-positive relationship between H and PCM^*. Again, the presence of differentiated products confounds hypothesis testing of structure-performance relationships.

IV. CONCLUSION

This paper sets forth a theoretical framework within which currently prominent structure-performance hypotheses can be analyzed. In modeling the differentiated products market power, scale economy, simple collusion, and innovative leading firm hypotheses, we have focused particular attention on testable implications carefully derived from formal theories. Success in distinguishing among these competing alternatives hinges, we find, on the presence of homogeneous versus differentiated products.

For products like steel I-beams and cement, we have shown that the scale economy and simple collusion hypotheses may be tested directly and rejected (in the latter case by an insignificant concentration-margin relationship). On the other hand, we have demonstrated that the innovative leading firm hypothesis is tautologically true for such products. For *differentiated*

[14] In principle, direct measures of technological innovations within an industry could distinguish Ricardian rent from market power over price, but needless to say, such data are unavailable for the large cross-sections employed in structure-performance empirical work.

products like cereals, cosmetics, and soft drinks, however, neither the simple collusion hypothesis nor the innovative leading firm efficiency hypothesis is rejectable. In the former case, we have demonstrated two opposing effects on price-cost margins attributable to the heightened collusive potential in highly concentrated oligopoly groups. Secondly, we have shown that innovative leading firm cost reduction must compete with a conceptually independent but observationally equivalent alternative hypothesis—that of differentiated product market power over price by high share firms.

Unfortunately, only direct measures of technological innovations within numerous industries can distinguish empirically between innovative leading firm cost reductions and differentiated product market power (see footnote 14). A positive cross-sectional correlation between market share and profit margins, and no relationship between concentration and profit margins, *ceteris paribus*, is consistent with both hypotheses, rejecting neither alternative. On a positive note, leading firm efficiency attributable not to cost-reducing innovations but rather to scale effects remains a testable and rejectable third alternative even with differentiated products.

In conclusion, let me suggest that the struggle to distinguish between innovative leading firms and those dominant firms merely exercising market power over price is no idle gesture. Success in this effort provides a pivot point for well-informed merger policy. And perhaps more importantly, the careful derivation of testable competing hypotheses must be placed high on the agenda of structure-performance research. In the case at hand, our theoretical analysis highlights the need (especially in differentiated product markets) for direct measures of Ricardian rent if one hopes to distinguish the imprint of an efficient market structure from that left behind by single firm market power.

FREDERICK H. deB. HARRIS,
Department of Economics,
College of Business Administration,
University of Texas at Arlington,
P.O. Box 19479,
Arlington, TX 76019,
USA.

ACCEPTED APRIL 1987

REFERENCES

Bothwell, J., Cooley, T. and Hall, T., 1984, 'A New View of the Structure-Performance Debate', *Journal of Industrial Economics*, 32 (June), pp. 397–417.

Clarke, R. and Davies, S., 1982, 'Market Structure and Price-Cost Margins', *Economica*, 49 (August), pp. 277–287.

Clarke, R. and Waterson, M., 1984, 'The Profitability-Concentration Relation: Market Power or Efficiency', *Journal of Industrial Economics*, 32 (June), pp. 435–450.

COWLING, K. and WATERSON, M., 1976, 'Price-Cost Margins and Market Structure', *Economica*, 43 (August), pp. 267–274.

CUBBIN, J., 1983, 'Apparent Collusion and Conjectural Variations in Differentiated Oligopoly', *International Journal of Industrial Organization*, 1 (June), pp. 155–163.

DEMSETZ, H., 1974, 'Two Systems of Belief About Monopoly', in H. J. GOLDSCHMID, H. M. MANN and J. F. WESTON (eds.), *Industrial Concentration: The New Learning* (Little, Brown and Company, Boston).

FERGUSON, C., 1971, *The Neoclassical Theory of Production and Distribution* (Cambridge University Press, Cambridge).

FUDENBERG, D. and TIROLE, J., 1986, *Dynamic Models of Oligopoly* (Harwood Academic, Chur, Switzerland).

GALE, B. and BRANCH, B., 1982, 'Concentration versus Market Share: Which Determines Performance and Why Does It Matter?', *Antitrust Bulletin*, 27 (Spring), pp. 83–105.

HARRIS, F., 1984, 'Growth Expectations, Excess Value, and the Risk-Adjusted Return to Market Power', *Southern Economic Journal*, 51 (July), pp. 166–179.

HARRIS, F., 1986, 'Market Structure and Price-Cost Performance Under Endogenous Profit Risk', *Journal of Industrial Economics*, 35 (September), pp. 35–59.

HARRIS, F., 1987, 'Capital Intensity and the Firm's Cost of Capital', *Review of Economics and Statistics*, forthcoming.

HIRSCHEY, M., 1982, 'Intangible Capital Aspects of Advertising and R & D Expenditures', *Journal of Industrial Economics*, 30 (June), pp. 375–390.

HIRSCHEY, M., 1985, 'Market Structure and Market Value', *Journal of Business*, 58 (October), pp. 89–98.

KREPS, D. and SCHEINKMAN, 1983, 'Quantity Precommitment and Bertrand Competition Yield Cournot Outcomes', *Bell Journal of Economics*, 14 (Spring), pp. 326–337.

KUMAR, K. and SATTERTHWAITE, 1985, 'Monopolistic Competition, Aggregation of Competitive Information, and the Amount of Product Differentiation', *Journal of Economic Theory*, 37, pp. 32–54.

KURZ, M., 1985, 'Cooperative Oligopoly Equilibrium', *European Economic Review*, 27, pp. 3–24.

KWOKA, J. and RAVENSCRAFT, D., 1986, 'Cooperation v. Rivalry: Price-Cost Margins by Line of Business', *Economica*, 53 (August), pp. 351–363.

MANCKE, R., 1974, 'Causes of Interfirm Profitability Differences: A new Interpretation', *Quarterly Journal of Economics*, 88 (May), pp. 181–193.

MARTIN, S., 1983, *Market, Firm, and Economic Performance*, Salomon Brothers Monograph Series in Finance and Economics (N.Y.U. Graduate School of Business).

MARTIN, S., 1987, 'The Measurement of Profitability and the Diagnosis of Market Power', *International Journal of Industrial Organization*, forthcoming.

MUELLER, D., 1987, 'The Determinants of Persistent Profits', Consultant's Report, Federal Trade Commission, June 1983 and *Profits in the Long Run* (Cambridge University Press), forthcoming.

PELTZMAN, S., 1977, 'The Gains and Losses from Industrial Concentration', *Journal of Law and Economics*, 20 (October), pp. 229–263.

RAVENSCRAFT, D., 1983, 'Structure-Profit Relationships at the Line of Business and Industry Levels', *Review of Economics and Statistics*, 65 (February), pp. 25–37.

REINGANUM, J., 1985, 'Innovation and Industry Evolution', *Quarterly Journal of Economics*, 100 (February), pp. 81–99.

RIORDAN, M., 1985, 'Imperfect Information and Dynamic Conjectural Variations', *Rand Journal of Economics*, 16 (Spring), pp. 41–50.

SHEPHERD, W., 1982, 'The Elements of Market Structure', *Review of Economics and Statistics*, 54 (February), pp. 25–37.

SMIRLOCK, M., GILLIGAN, T. and MARSHALL, W., 1984, 'Tobin's q and the Structure-Performance Relationship', *American Economic Review*, 74 (December), pp. 1051–1060.

STIGLER, G., 1940, 'Notes on the Theory of Duopoly', *Journal of Political Economy*, 48 (June), pp. 521–541.

STIGLER, G., 1964, 'A Theory of Oligopoly', *Journal of Political Economy*, 72 (February), pp. 44–61.

VICKERS, J., 1986, 'The Evolution of Market Structure When There is a Sequence of Innovations', *Journal of Industrial Economics*, 35 (September), pp. 1–12.

WATERSON, M., 1984, *Economic Theory of Industry* (Cambridge University Press, Cambridge).

WERNERFELT, B., 1985, 'Tacit Collusion and Product Differentiation', Kellogg School Discussion Paper No. 693, Northwestern University (July).

THE JOURNAL OF INDUSTRIAL ECONOMICS 0022–1821 $2.00
Volume XXXVI March 1988 No. 3

ENTRY FOR BUYOUT

ERIC RASMUSEN*

The possibility of buying out an entrant has an important effect on entry deterrence. Entrants can blackmail the incumbent by threatening to keep prices low, and buyout can make entry profitable which otherwise would not be. In particular, the entry deterrence policy of excess capacity to reduce the post-entry price can not only fail, but work against the incumbent. The presence of multiple oligopolistic incumbents or multiple potential entrants, however, can discourage entry for buyout.

I. INTRODUCTION

THE LONG literature on entry deterrence has always assumed that if entry is made unprofitable, no entry will occur. But as followers of professional football may have suspected, a clearly unprofitable competitor might rationally enter a market in the hopes of selling out to the incumbent. I will model such a situation, and try to show what conditions facilitate entry for buyout.

In the simplest entry deterrence model, the incumbent successfully maintains monopoly by threatening to expand output and cut price after other firms enter, but he succeeds only because potential entrants believe the threat. If entrants are rational this strategy fails: price warfare hurts the incumbent as well as the entrant, so the monopolist would let the entrant have a share of profits after entry; potential entrants, foreseeing the accommodating response, ignore the threat.

Deterred entry is a Nash equilibrium, but not a "perfect" Nash equilibrium. It is Nash because the entrant chooses to stay out, given the incumbent's strategy of cutting prices after entry, and the incumbent does not mind committing himself to cutting prices, given that entry never occurs. A perfect Nash equilibrium is a set of strategies that is a Nash equilibrium for every proper subgame: if the game is started at any of the nodes of the game tree, including those off the equilibrium path, the strategies the agents pick to maximize their objective function from that node onwards must be part of the equilibrium strategy for the entire game. In the subgame which begins after entry has already occurred, the incumbent would not choose to cut prices, so cutting prices after entry is not part of a perfect equilibrium. In the perfect equilibrium, entry occurs and is accommodated.

* I would like to thank Joseph Farrell, Franklin Fisher, Ivan P'ng, Jean Tirole, Sheridan Titman, and two anonymous referees for helpful comments on various drafts of this paper. The National Science Foundation and the Sloan Foundation provided financial support.

The point is older than the concept of perfect equilibrium and has been made, for example, by McGee [1958] in the context of predatory pricing, which he argues is not a credible threat because it hurts the predator as well as the preyed upon. McGee concludes that Standard Oil's episodes of price warfare in the nineteenth century and its ultimate buyout of small refineries are examples not of predatory behaviour, but simply merger to increase market power.

Many economists feel that the layman's widespread belief that entry deterrence does occur is justified by something missing from a model like McGee's, and have searched for the misssing element. Entry deterrence requires some way for the incumbent to commit himself to unprofitable post-entry pricing. The incumbent cannot sign a contract requiring himself to lower the price after entry, but he can perhaps change his investment policy to make such behaviour optimal. Spence [1977] shows how the incumbent would build capacity in excess of normal use, if he could credibly threaten to use it after entry. Dixit [1980] constructs a similar model in which firms follow Cournot behaviour and incur fixed as well as variable operating costs. After entry occurs output can be so great that both firms' profits net of capacity costs are negative. Having already sunk the capacity cost, the incumbent fights entry without further expense. The entrant's capacity cost is not yet sunk, so he refrains from entry.[1]

An outcome not modelled by Spence and Dixit is that the incumbent buys out the entrant. An incumbent who fights entry bears two costs: the loss from selling at a price below average total cost, and the opportunity cost of not earning monopoly profits. He can make the first a sunk cost, but not the second. The entrant, foreseeing that the incumbent will buy him out, will enter despite knowing that the duopoly price will be less than his average total cost. The incumbent faces a second perfectness problem, for while he may try to deter entry by threatening not to buy out entrants, the threat is not credible, and as a rational agent he will indeed buy them out once they have entered.

The possibility of buyout changes the direction of credible threats. In the Spence and Dixit models the incumbent threatens the entrant with low prices; with buyout, the entrant threatens the incumbent with low prices. For the threat to be credible the entrant's optimal behaviour if he is not bought out must be to stay in the market and continue to depress the price (an exception, explained below, being when the entrant might drive the incumbent from the market). To fulfill this condition, once the entrant has entered, his capacity cost sunk, the duopoly price must at least equal average variable cost.

Section II sets up a buyout game with one potential entrant and solves for the equilibrium of a numerical example. Section III is a more general analysis

[1] In Dixit [1980], the incumbent never holds unused capacity as he does in Spence [1977], although he might hold more capacity than without the threat of entry. Bulow, Geanakoplos, and Klemperer [1985] show that with a slight change of Dixit's assumptions the incumbent does hold unused capacity.

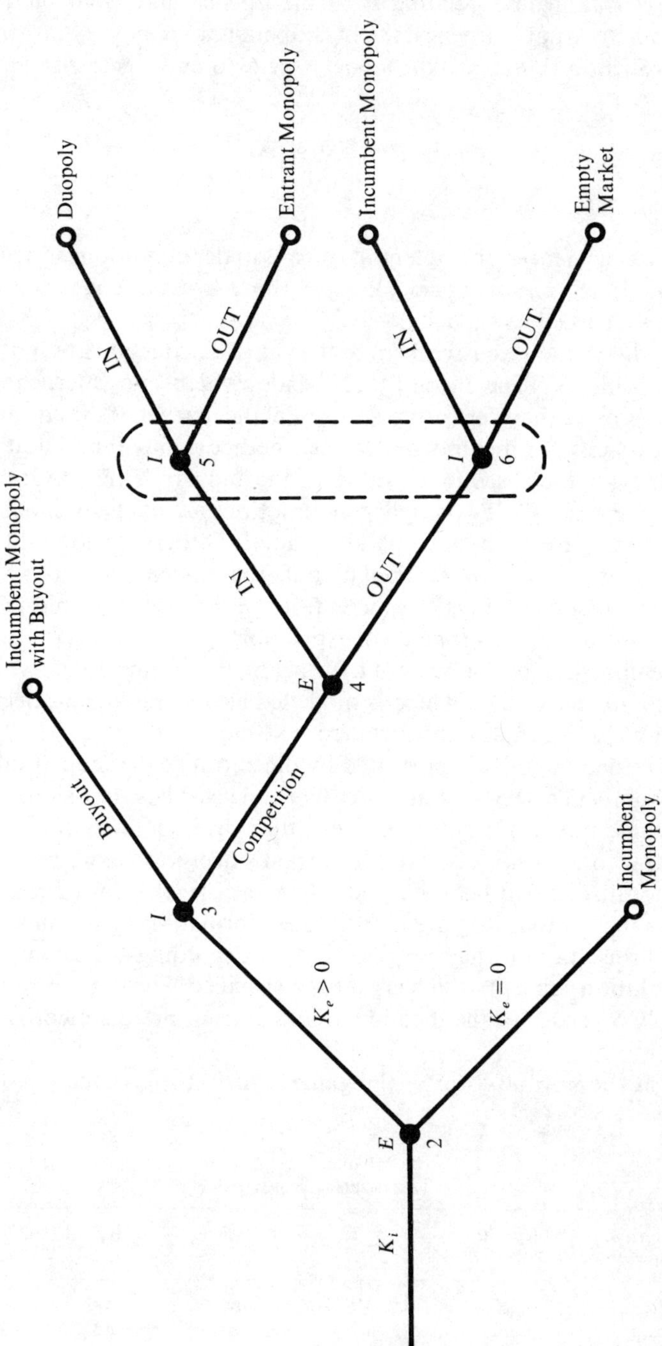
I
1
K_i
E
2
$K_e > 0$
$K_e = 0$
Incumbent Monopoly
I
3
Buyout
Incumbent Monopoly with Buyout
Competition
E
4
IN
OUT
I
5
I
6
IN
OUT
IN
OUT
Duopoly
Entrant Monopoly
Incumbent Monopoly
Empty Market

Figure 1.

of the one-entrant game, relating it to the Spence and Dixit models and discussing briefly what happens if the incumbent is an oligopoly rather than a single firm. Section IV extends the model to two potential entrants.

II. ONE ENTRANT

II(i). *The model*

An incumbent firm faces one potential entrant under conditions of symmetric information. Each unit of capacity costs a, the interest rate is r, and a firm's output cannot exceed its capacity.

Figure 1 shows the extensive form of the game. The incumbent moves first, selecting capacity K_i. The entrant then decides whether to enter, choosing a capacity K_e greater than zero, or to stay out of the market. If the entrant picks a positive capacity the incumbent decides whether to buy him out at price B and be left with the discounted value of the industry's net revenues as a monopoly, the value R^*. Two implicit assumptions are made by choosing this extensive form: The entrant must build a plant (for otherwise he could be paid not to enter at all); and once bought out, the entrant does not re-enter. Whether the incumbent buys out the entrant or vice versa is unimportant; I adopt this convention only for ease of exposition.

If the incumbent does not buy out the entrant, both firms decide whether to stay in the industry or exit, which is modelled as a simultaneous decision to avoid giving either firm an unwarranted first-mover advantage. In Figure 1 the IN/OUT decisions are represented by the entrant's decision at node four and the incumbent's decisions at nodes five and six. These decisions are non-trivial because the price might be less than average variable cost. The incumbent, who does not observe the entrant's decision before he makes his own, cannot distinguish between nodes five and six; the dotted line around the nodes indicates that they are in the same information set for him.

If both firms stay in, they produce output according to the appropriate duopoly solution concept, which is yet to be specified. The present value of the net duopoly revenues of the incumbent and entrant are denoted by R_i^d and R_e^d.

Table I is the normal form of the game, which displays the payoffs from

TABLE I
THE NORMAL FORM

Entrant: / *Incumbent:*	$K_e = 0$		$K_e > 0, IN$		$K_e > 0, OUT$	
Buyout, IN	$R^*-aK_i,$	0	$R^*-aK_i-B,$	$B-aK_e$	$R^*-aK_i-B,$	$B-aK_e$
No buyout, IN	$R^*-aK_i,$	0	$R_i^d-aK_i,$	$R_e^d-aK_e$	$R^*-aK_i,$	$-aK_e$
No buyout, OUT	$R^*-aK_i,$	0	$-aK_i,$	R^*-aK_e	$-aK_i,$	$-aK_e$

different strategy combinations. The incumbent chooses the capacity K_i, whether to buy out the entrant, and whether to stay in after deciding not to buy him out. The entrant chooses the capacity K_e and whether to stay in if not bought out.

The payoffs depend on the discounted value of the net monopoly revenue R^*, the discounted values of net duopoly revenues R_e^d and R_i^d, the capacity cost a, and the buyout price B. To find the equilibrium strategies we need to make two stronger assumptions about firm behaviour. First, we need a duopoly solution concept to determine the duopoly net revenues as a function of the two firms' capacities. Second, we need a bargaining solution to determine the buyout price as a function of the monopoly and duopoly revenues. Duopoly and bargaining are the subjects of large and continuing literatures, but they are of subsidiary importance in this model, which only tries to say what the equilibrium of the dynamic game will be for given solution concepts.

II(ii). *A numerical example*

Before going on to solve for the equilibrium of the general game, let us analyze an example, loosely based on Dixit [1980], which uses a particular duopoly concept and bargaining solution. The market lasts one period and has the demand curve

(1) $$P = 100 - Q_i - Q_e$$

where Q_i and Q_e are the outputs of the two firms. The cost per unit of capacity is $a = 10$, the marginal cost of output is 10, and the fixed cost is $F = 601$. Output follows Cournot behaviour and the bargaining solution splits the surplus equally.[2] Figure 1 shows the extensive form.

If the incumbent faced no threat of entry, it would behave as a simple monopolist, choosing a capacity equal to the output which solves

(2) $$\max_{Q_i} (100 - Q_i)Q_i - 10Q_i - 10Q_i$$

which has the first order condition

(3) $$80 - 2Q_i = 0$$

The monopoly capacity is $K_i = 40$ and the monopoly output is $Q_i = 40$, yielding a net operating revenue of $R^*(40) = (60 - 10)40 - 601 = 1399$, where the notation $R^*(40)$ signifies the net operating revenue of a monopolist with a capacity of 40. The return of 1399 is well above the capacity cost of 400.

It turns out that this is the same output and capacity the incumbent

[2] Splitting the surplus evenly between two bargaining players can be justified axiomatically (it is identical to the Nash [1950] bargaining solution here), or as the perfect equilibrium of a dynamic game with a small but positive discount rate (Rubinstein [1982]).

chooses if entry is possible, but buyout is not. If the potential entrant were to enter he could do no better than to choose the capacity $K_e = 30$, which costs 300. If the two firms are in the market with capacities of $K_i = 40$ and $K_e = 30$, following Cournot behaviour they solve

(4) $$\max_{Q_i} (100-Q_i-Q_e)Q_i-10Q_i \quad \text{subject to} \quad Q_i \leqslant 40$$

and

(5) $$\max_{Q_e} (100-Q_i-Q_e)Q_e-10Q_e \quad \text{subject to} \quad Q_e \leqslant 30$$

which have first order conditions

(6) $$90-2Q_i-Q_e = 0$$

and

(7) $$90-Q_i-2Q_e = 0$$

The Cournot outputs are $Q_i = 30$ and $Q_e = 30$, yielding a price of 40 and net revenues of $R_i^d = R_e^d = (40-10)30-601 = 299$. The entrant's profit net of capacity cost would be $(299-300) = -1$, which is less than the zero he can obtain by not entering.

The reader familiar with Dixit [1980] will note that the calculation of the Cournot outputs here is different. Here, the implicit assumption is that the choice of capacity is a decision prior to the choice of output, rather than simultaneous with it. The marginal cost of the entrant used in the Cournot calculation is therefore 10, the same as the incumbent's. The entrant's marginal cost viewed from before his plant is built is the higher figure of 20, because he faces the capacity cost as well. In this model the capacity cost is sunk by the time the output decision is made.

Let us next consider the situation when both entry and buyout are possible, but the incumbent still chooses $K_i = 40$. The R_e^d and R_i^d depend on the capacities of the two firms. If the entrant chooses $K_e = 30$ again, then $R_e^d = R_i^d = 299$, just as above. If he buys out the entrant, the incumbent, having increased his capacity to 70, produces a monopoly output of 45. Half of the surplus from buyout is

(8) $$\begin{aligned} B &= 1/2[R^*(70)-(R_e^d+R_i^d)] \\ &= 1/2[45(55-10)-601-(299+299)] = 413 \end{aligned}$$

The entrant is bought out for his Cournot net operating revenue of 299 plus the 413 which is his share of the buyout surplus, a total buyout price of 712. Since 712 exceeds the entrant's capacity cost of 300, allowing buyout leads to entry which would otherwise have been deterred.

The incumbent cannot deter entry by picking a different capacity. Choosing K_i greater than 30 leads to the same Cournot output of 60 and the same buyout price of 712. Choosing K_i less than 30 allows the entrant to make a profit even without being bought out.

Realizing that entry cannot be deterred, the incumbent would not choose an initial capacity of 40. A Cournot player whose capacity is less than or equal to 30 produces a quantity equal to his capacity. Since buyout will occur, if a firm starts with a capacity less than 30 and adds one unit, the marginal cost of capacity is 10 and the marginal benefit is the increase (for the entrant) or decrease (for the incumbent) in the buyout price. If it is the entrant who adds a unit of capacity, R_e^d rises by at least $(40-10)$, the lowest possible Cournot price minus the marginal cost of output. Moreover, R_i^d falls because the entrant's extra output lowers the market price. Under our bargaining solution, the buyout price rises by at least $(40-10)/2$, and since this is greater than the capacity cost of 10, the entrant should add extra capacity up to $K_e = 30$. A parallel argument shows why the incumbent should build a capacity of at least 30. The buyout price is unaffected by increasing the capacities beyond 30, because the duopoly net revenues are unaffected; thus both firms choose capacities of exactly 30.

The industry capacity equals 60 when buyout is allowed, but after the buyout only 45 is used. Monopoly profits in the absence of entry would have been $1399-400 = 999$, while after entry they are $1424-600 = 824$, so buyout has decreased industry profits by 175. Consumer surplus has risen from $0.5(100-60)(40) = 800$ to $0.5(100-55)(45) = 1012.5$, a gain of 212.5, so buyout has raised total welfare in this example. The inefficiency of the entrant's rent-seeking investment in capacity is outbalanced by the increase in output, an outcome, I warn the reader, that is not true in all examples.

III. A MORE GENERAL ANALYSIS OF EQUILIBRIUM WITH ONE ENTRANT

III(i). *The duopoly subgame*

In the numerical example the entrant enters solely to be bought out, but the equilibrium strategies for the game in Figure 1 depend on the exogenous parameters. We will now try to pin down what determines whether entry for buyout succeeds. To solve for the perfect equilibrium of a game we work back from later to earlier subgames, beginning with the subgame in which both firms have entered, buyout has failed to occur, and each firm is considering exiting the market. Afterwards we will consider the buyout decision and the entry decision.

Suppose first that both the entrant and the incumbent are in the market with positive capacities, the game having reached node four of Figure 1. The capacity costs are sunk and irrelevant to current decisions, so the normal form for this subgame is given by Table II.

If R_i^d is positive the dominant strategy for the incumbent is IN, and if R_e^d is positive the dominant strategy for the entrant is also IN. Thus if the duopoly

TABLE II
DUOPOLY SUBGAME

Incumbent: \ Entrant:	$K_e > 0, IN$	$K_e > 0, OUT$
No buyout, IN	R_i^d, R_e^d	$R^*, 0$
No buyout, OUT	$0, R^*$	$0, 0$

price exceeds the average variable cost of each player both stay in if buyout does not occur and node four is reached.

If only R_i^d is positive then IN is still a dominant strategy for the incumbent, and using iterated dominance we can expect the entrant to choose OUT, with its payoff of zero, rather than IN, with its payoff of $R_e^d < 0$ if the incumbent chooses IN. The incumbent has enough of an advantage in variable costs that the entrant's threat to remain in the market is not credible. Similarly, if the entrant has enough of an advantage in variable costs he can force out the incumbent.

If both R_i^d and R_e^d are negative the subgame has no symmetric equilibrium in pure strategies. There are two asymmetric pure strategy equilibria, (IN, OUT) and (OUT, IN), and a mixed strategy equilibrium in which each player chooses both IN and OUT with positive probability. We will use the mixed strategy equilibrium because of the appealing feature that its payoffs are equal for the two firms: each firm's payoff is zero, because in equilibrium each must be indifferent between exiting, which has a payoff of zero, and staying in, which has a payoff that depends on the behaviour of the other firm.

The subgame with negative payoffs if both players remain in the market is an example of the "War of Attrition", a game formulated by Maynard-Smith [1974]. We model the game simply here using one set of simultaneous moves. An alternative is to use a more complicated War of Attrition along the lines of the model in section IV of this paper. Whichever way the subgame is formulated, the expected payoff for each player is zero in the symmetric equilibrium, and for the buyout model it is the value of zero that is important, not why it is zero.

Examples of markets with negative net duopoly revenues are those that are natural monopolies because of declining average operating costs rather than set-up costs. If the duopoly price is close to marginal cost and both firms incur a fixed cost of production each period, the net duopoly revenues are negative, and profits (net duopoly revenues minus capacity costs) are negative *a fortiori*.

III(ii). *The buyout decision*

The entrant is only bought out if he might not exit in the duopoly subgame. If the entrant is known to choose OUT, the incumbent prefers to wait rather than pay him to exit. Similarly, if the incumbent is known to choose OUT, the entrant can wait for the incumbent to exit.

If both the entrant and the incumbent would choose IN as either a pure strategy or part of a mixed strategy, the expected payoffs are either (R_i^d, R_e^d) for pure strategies, or (0, 0) for mixed. Since $(R_i^d + R_e^d)$ and 0 are both less than R^*, there is an industry surplus from buyout. Buyout occurs if we assume that the bargaining solution is such that $(R^* - B) \geqslant R_i^d$ and $B \geqslant R_e^d$, (that is, each player receives at least his threat point payoffs). In a natural monopoly, where the expected duopoly payoffs of both firms are zero, any buyout price such that $0 < B < R^*$ induces buyout. If the game reaches node three, and an entrant not bought out stays in with positive probability, we expect buyout to occur.

In this paper we will not delve into the justifications for different bargaining solutions, but merely note what is important for buyout. A more elaborate model would make the buyout price a function of the structural parameters.

III(iii). *The capacity decisions*

The potential entrant enters if he would be bought out for a price exceeding his capacity cost or if he could make a profit without buyout.

Proposition 1: Entry is deterred if and only if for any capacity the entrant might choose, one of the following sets of conditions holds:

(A) The entrant's duopoly profit is negative and the incumbent's is not:

(i) $R_e^d < 0$ and $R_i^d \geqslant 0$; or

(B) The buyout price and the present value of the entrant's net duopoly revenues are both less than his capacity cost, and the incumbent cannot be driven from the market:

(ii) $B < aK_e$, and
(iii) $R_e^d < aK_e$ and $R_i^d \geqslant 0$.

Proof: If Condition (i) is true, the incumbent refrains from buyout because he knows the entrant would exit with probability one if not bought out. The entrant knows he would not be bought out and his profits without buyout would be negative, so he does not enter. Condition (i) is sufficient to deter entry.

If Conditions (ii) and (iii) are true, the incumbent might choose to buy out the entrant, but for a price less than the entrant's capacity cost. The entrant does not earn enough in a duopoly market to pay for his capacity if he is not bought out, and if there is no buyout the market will be a duopoly. Therefore he does not enter. Conditions (ii) and (iii) are jointly sufficient to deter entry.

If (i) and either (ii) or (iii) is false, then the entrant can enter, credibly threaten to stay in the market, and end up with a positive payoff. For entry to be deterred it is necessary that (i) and either (ii) or (iii) be true. ||

Condition (ii) is true if the buyout price, which depends on the surplus acquired by moving from duopoly to monopoly, is less than the entrant's capacity costs, which may happen for either of two reasons: (a) the surplus to be split is small; or (b) the bargaining solution gives the entrant a small share of the surplus.

The surplus is small if the duopoly price is high and close to the monopoly price, although a high duopoly price also makes it less likely that Condition (iii) is satisfied. If aK_e is large enough, both (ii) and (iii) can be simultaneously true and entry is deterred.

If the surplus is large, the entrant's share might still be small enough for Condition (iii) to be satisfied if the bargaining solution is biased against the entrant or the bargainer with less capacity. Even if the bargaining solution is not biased, the buyout price depends on the duopoly solution, and if the entrant's duopoly revenues are small and the incumbent's are large, the buyout price could be less than the entrant's capacity cost.

The incumbent chooses his capacity depending on whether he can satisfy one of the two sets of conditions for entry deterrence. He chooses the monopoly capacity or some larger capacity if he can deter entry cheaply enough. Otherwise his capacity is less than the monopoly level, unless under the bargaining solution a large K_i helps reduce the buyout price.

The importance of perfectness can be seen at every node of Figure 1. If one of the players was able to commit himself at the start of the game to an action at a future node, then any of the following commitments might be profitable. The entrant might commit to enter at node two. The incumbent might commit not to buy out the entrant at node three. The entrant might commit to staying in at node four, and the incumbent to staying in at nodes five and six. Finally, the incumbent might commit to high output in the duopoly market, to make the entrant's net duopoly revenue negative. Since none of the commitments are optimal if the nodes are actually reached, they are useful only as threats to prevent them from being reached. The possibility of commitment vastly increases the number of equilibria; the many non-perfect Nash equilibria make behaviour unpredictable.

III(iv). *The Spence and Dixit models*

Spence [1977] and Dixit [1980] examine games similar to this one. Spence assumes that the incumbent follows the behavioural rule of using all of his capacity after entry. From this one can calculate the capacity which deters entry by making the entrant's duopoly profit negative. The incumbent chooses that capacity, and the entrant chooses to stay out.

Condition (i) is not satisfied in the Spence model, but Condition (ii) is satisfied. If entry for buyout is to be deterred, it must be because the buyout solution is biased in one direction, or the surplus from buyout is small relative to capacity cost. The difference between duopoly and monopoly revenue is large, so buyout is the likely outcome.

The Spence model represents one extreme of duopoly behaviour: heavy price-cutting after entry, which is the behaviour most vulnerable to entry for buyout. The deeper is the price-cutting, the greater is the surplus from buyout and the greater the buyout price. For the incumbent to commit to price-cutting is counterproductive unless he can also commit to abstain from buyout. This is a phenomenon much like the "judo economics" of Gelman and Salop [1983]. In their model, as in this one, the entrant makes use of the vulnerability of the larger incumbent to lower prices. Their point, that the entrant can enter profitably if he limits his capacity, is different from that of the present paper, but both points are based on the entrant's ability to profit from price warfare.

The Dixit model assumes that marginal cost is constant, that each firm incurs a fixed operating cost, and that duopoly behaviour is Cournot. If the fixed cost is high enough, the entrant's net revenue is less than the sum of his various costs, and entry is deterred even if the Cournot price is also less than the incumbent's average cost. Whether the incumbent decides to deter entry by choosing a large capacity depends on the size of the fixed cost: he may be unable to deter entry, able and willing, or able but unwilling because of the cost. In the numerical example we looked at above, entry-deterring capacity was the same as the monopoly capacity, so the incumbent chose to deter entry.

If buyout is introduced, the same range of possibilities exists, but entry deterrence is less often possible or profitable. The fixed cost has two offsetting effects. Entry is more difficult, because unless the entrant's Cournot revenues cover his fixed cost of production (as distinct from his sunk entry cost), he cannot credibly threaten to remain in the market. If the fixed cost is large, however, the surplus from moving to monopoly from duopoly is greater, which increases the buyout price.

The equilibrium depends on the size of the fixed cost. With Cournot pricing and a fixed cost of zero, the profits per unit sold are positive and identical for the incumbent and the entrant. If the fixed cost is small enough, entry cannot be deterred, because Conditions (i) and (iii) are violated. In the numerical example Conditions (i) and (iii) are violated if F is between 0 and 600, so that even if the entrant is not bought out, he can profit by entering and selling at the duopoly price.

If the fixed cost is larger, Condition (i) is still violated because net duopoly revenues are positive, but Condition (iii) becomes true because the revenues are not great enough to compensate for the capacity cost. The entrant still might enter, but only to be bought out. This happens for F between 600 and 900.

If the fixed cost is greater than 900 and the entrant's capacity and output is smaller than the incumbent's, Condition (i) might become true. It can never be true in the numerical example, because the costs and the net duopoly revenues are the same for both firms, but it would be if the two firms faced different fixed costs, such as $F_i = 800$ and $F_e = 1000$. The entrant's net duopoly revenue then does not exceed the fixed cost, but the incumbent's does. Entry is deterred because the incumbent would simply wait for the entrant to exit.

If the fixed cost is still larger, (i) is false because net duopoly revenue is negative for both firms. In the numerical example this happens over the range $F = 900$ to $F = 1425$, because the gross Cournot revenue is 900 for each firm. Condition (iii) is still true, so for entry to be deterred, Condition (ii), that $B < aK_e$, must be true of every possible K_e. The surplus from buyout is very high, so (ii) can be true only if the bargaining solution is biased against one of the firms or capacity is very expensive, neither of which is the case in the numerical example.

Finally, if the fixed cost is large enough entry is deterred because the entrant cannot obtain a positive payoff even with buyout. If F exceeds 1425 then $R^* < 45(55-10)-1425 = 600$, so half of the monopoly revenues does not compensate the entrant for his capacity cost of 300. An industry with such high fixed costs is a natural monopoly.

III(v). *One entrant and many incumbents*

Oligopolists care as much about entry deterrence as do monopolists, but they face the additional problem that deterred entry is a public good. If deterring entry is costly, as it is when achieved via excess capacity, one might think that each firm would hope to free-ride on the others, and total investment in entry deterrence would be suboptimal from the point of view of the oligopoly.

Bernheim [1984] has shown that this simple argument is flawed. Entry is a discontinuous event—the entrant is either in or out—so a small amount of under-investment in entry deterrence by any one oligopolist results in entry and a large loss in both group and individual profits. Optimal investment in entry deterrence is a Nash equilibrium, since no single firm has incentive to deviate and induce entry.[3]

Waldman [1985] shows that Bernheim's result changes if we add uncertainty over the amount of entry deterrence required to deter entry. Uncertainty smooths out the discontinuity in the payoff function, and an oligopolist can reduce his spending on entry deterrence without being certain that he will provoke entry. Entry may or may not be deterred in equilibrium, but there is always underinvestment in entry deterrence.

[3] Optimal investment in entry deterrence is not the unique Nash equilibrium; there is another in which all firms underinvest and entry occurs. Readers familiar with agency theory will note that the Bernheim problem is analogous to the problem of team members choosing effort under a contract which punishes them if the group output falls below a threshold level (Holmstrom [1982]).

What is the effect of possible buyout? When buyout is involved, the oligopoly is actually better than a monopoly at deterring entry, precisely because of the free rider problem. Once the entrant has entered, buying him out is a public good. The firm that buys him out bears the entire cost, but the benefit is shared by all the oligopolists. The buyout price that any oligopolist is willing to pay is much smaller than the gain in industry profits, so the oligopoly buyout price is more likely to be less than the entrant's capacity cost. Because of the lower buyout price, entry into an oligopoly is less attractive, even if the oligopoly output is the same as the monopoly output.

IV. TWO POTENTIAL ENTRANTS

An incumbent who can keep out a single potential entrant can keep out any number, but when entry cannot be deterred the number of potential entrants is important. In buying out the first entrant, the incumbent takes into account future buyouts, as does the entrant in deciding whether to be bought out immediately or to wait.

The complexity of the game increases rapidly with the number of potential entrants, so we will simplify by abstracting from the choice of capacity and oligopoly output. We will use discrete time, and a discount rate specified to be small enough that the model is genuinely multi-period: $0 < r < 1/3$. Instead of choosing a particular capacity, assume that any entrant must pay an entry fee of K, and that operating revenue is rR if there is one firm in the market, zero otherwise. The present value of monopoly profits starting from any period is thus R.

The two potential entrants simultaneously decide each period whether to enter or wait. After this decision is made, the incumbent can offer to buy out any entrants in the market, and the entrants can agree or not agree to be bought out. The following period these decisions are repeated, except that an entrant cannot re-enter once he has been bought out.

We assume that the outcome of bargaining is that the buyout price for one entrant is half of the incumbent's gross gain from the buyout, and that the buyout price for each of two entrants bought out simultaneously is one third of the incumbent's gross gain from their buyout. If all three firms are in the market, both entrants are bought out immediately and together.

The game's structure is therefore:

0 1 The potential entrants choose Enter or Wait separately and simultaneously.

0 2 The incumbent offers Buyout or Not Buyout to any firms in the market.

0 3 If all three firms are in the market, the entrants are bought out. If only one has entered, he chooses to Agree or Not Agree.

1 1 Potential entrants that have not yet entered choose Enter or Wait.

12 The incumbent offers Buyout or Not Buyout to any firms in the market.

13 If all three firms are in the market, the entrants are bought out. If only one has entered, he chooses to Agree or Not Agree.

Each entrant's strategy must tell him whether to enter and whether to agree to a buyout for each possible history of the game, even though there may be a unique equilibrium history. For example, the strategy I describe below as *Never Enter* specifies that the entrant never enters—but to be a strategy, it must also specify what happens if, off the equilibrium path, the player suddenly finds he has entered and has the option of being bought out. Because the model must specify behaviour at all nodes of the game, expanding the model beyond two entrants is more tedious than productive.

Fortunately, different combinations of the six relatively simple strategies listed below are subgame perfect Nash equilibria. I have given each strategy a descriptive name and starred the parts of the strategies which are never used unless some player deviates from equilibrium.

Entrant strategies

Immediate entry

1. Enter immediately, whatever the past history of the game.
*2. After entry, do not agree to be bought out if the other firm has not yet entered.

Delay entry

1. If the other entrant has not yet entered, enter with probability θ.
2. If the other firm has entered and been bought out, enter with probability 1.
*3. If the other firm has entered and not been bought out, do not enter.
4. After entry, agree to be bought out immediately.

Responsive entry

1. If the other entrant has not yet entered, do not enter.
*2. If the other firm has entered and been bought out, enter.
*3. If the other firm has entered and not been bought out, do not enter.
*4. After entry, be bought out immediately.

Never enter

1. Never enter.
*2. After entry, be bought out immediately.

Incumbent strategies

Buy now

1. Offer to buy out any entrant.

Hold out

1. Do not offer a buyout unless both entrants have entered.

There are two equilibria with the outcome of deterrence, which results when revenue is low relative to the cost of entry:
Equilibrium A. *Never Enter* and *Buy Now*.
Equilibrium B. *Responsive Entry* and *Buy Now*.

There are three equilibria with the outcome of entry, which results when revenue is high relative to the cost of entry:
Equilibrium C. *Immediate Entry* and *Buy Now*.
Equilibrium D. *Immediate Entry* and *Hold Out*.
Equilibrium E. *Delay Entry* and *Hold Out*.

If $R/2 \leqslant K$, the equilibrium is A: (*Never Enter* and *Buy Now*). Entry without buyout is unprofitable because the net operating revenues are zero after entry, and buyout is unprofitable because the buyout price cannot compensate for the cost of entry. If an entrant did enter, however, both he and the incumbent would wish for a buyout to take place immediately.

If $R/3 \leqslant K \leqslant R/2$, the equilibrium is B: (*Responsive Entry* and *Buy Now*). In this parameter range falls the interesting situation in which if there were just one potential entrant, entry would occur, but because there are two, entry is deterred. If both entrants were bought out simultaneously, the buyout price of $R/3$ would be insufficient to compensate for the cost of entry. If one entrant were bought out first, the buyout price of $R/4$ would not compensate for his cost of entry. But if (off the equilibrium path) one entrant entered and was bought out, the sole remaining entrant would find it profitable to enter. Entry is deterred only by the threat of future entry.

If $0 \leqslant K \leqslant R/3$, entry is not deterred, and both C: (*Immediate Entry* and *Buy Now*) and D: (*Immediate Entry* and *Hold Out*) are possible. Given that one entrant is going to enter, the other might as well enter also; no buyout will occur till he enters, so the payoff would just be delayed, which is undesirable because of discounting. No buyout of just one entrant occurs because if (off the equilibrium path) one entrant fails to enter, immediate buyout would give the entrant who did enter $(rR/2+R/4)$ and the incumbent $(rR/2+R/4)$, whereas waiting would give each of them $(1/(1+r))R/3$, a lower amount because we assumed that the discount rate is less than $1/3$. The incumbent has two possible equilibrium strategies here because even if he offers a buyout, a lone entrant would refuse him.

If $0 \leqslant K \leqslant R/4$, Equilibrium E: (*Delay Entry* and *Hold Out*) is also possible, along with Equilibria C and D. In this equilibrium, the entrants would be willing to be bought out by themselves if the alternative were not to enter at all, but they each prefer to be bought out second. As a result, there is no pure strategy equilibrium. Instead, they enter probabilistically, a strategy we will have to consider carefully.

First, consider what happens after entry has occurred. The second entrant is not going to enter until a buyout happens. Off the equilibrium path, if a buyout fails to occur immediately, the second entrant is quite happy to stick with his strategy of delaying entry, because he expects the other entrant to be bought out in the next period. He would consider entering only if he expected a whole series of deviations from equilibrium behaviour, but perfect equilibrium only demands that a strategy be Nash for each subgame. The incumbent will buy out the first entrant, who will agree. The first entrant's payoff will be $(rR/2+R/4)$, the same as the incumbent's, and lower than the $(1/(1+r))R/2$ of the second entrant.

Why does an entrant enter first with any positive probability? Because if he does not, there is some chance that both entrants will stay out so long that the discounted payoffs will be very low. This is the typical problem in a war of attrition.

We can calculate the probability of entry θ as follows. Adopting the perspective of one entrant (Alpha), fix the mixing probability of the other entrant (Beta) at θ. Denote Alpha's expected present value of payoffs as V_{IN} if he enters and V_{OUT} if he waits. These two pure strategy payoffs must be equal in a mixed strategy equilibrium. If Alpha enters, he is bought out at a price of $R/4$ if Beta has not entered (which happens with probability $[1-\theta]$), and a price of $R/3$ if Beta does enter. Thus,

$$(9) \qquad V_{IN}=(1-\theta)(R/4-K)+\theta(R/3-K)$$

If Alpha and Beta both stay out, the expected value of Alpha's payoff is unchanged (except for discounting) the following period. If Beta does enter immediately, then Alpha enters next period and receives the high buyout price of $R/2$. Thus,

$$(10) \qquad V_{OUT}=\left[\frac{1}{1+r}\right][(1-\theta)V_{OUT}+\theta(R/2-K)]$$

and with a little rearranging we obtain

$$(11) \qquad V_{OUT}=\left(\frac{\theta}{r+\theta}\right)(R/2-K)$$

To find the mixing probability, equations (9) and (11) could be set equal to each other, and solved for θ using the quadratic formula, but the details of this computation are not interesting enough to occupy us here. What is important to note, however, is that for the range of discount rates we are considering, θ is small, because the difference between the buyout price $R/2$ (obtainable by waiting) and $R/3$ or $R/4$ is large relative to the discounting loss from waiting. If, for example, the parameters have the values $K = 1$, $R = 5$, and $r = 0.10$, the equilibrium value of θ obtained from equations (9) and (10) is only about 0.021. Thus, this equilibrium can be almost equivalent observationally to equilibria A and B, in which entry is deterred.

The model could be generalized to n potential entrants, but because the strategies must specify behavior for every possible combination of moves off the equilibrium path, the mechanics would be so complicated as to be unenlightening.

What we have seen in this section is that adding a second potential entrant can either reduce the incumbent's payoff or increase it. The incumbent's payoff is reduced if both potential entrants do enter, whether they enter together or at different times; it is increased if adding a second potential entrant deters entry altogether by making it credible that the incumbent would not buy out the first entrant at a satisfactory price. In either case the first entrant is hurt by the presence of a second entrant.

V. FURTHER IMPLICATIONS

The possibility of buying out entrants makes it more difficult for a monopolist to use excess capacity to deter entry. The entrant, hoping to be bought out, may enter even if expected revenues are less than costs, if having entered he is as credibly willing to remain as the incumbent. Otherwise the incumbent refuses to buy him out, and the entrant, foreseeing this, does not enter.

Although the incumbent may not be able to fully protect his profits, entry does not make the output market competitive, because the incumbent charges the monopoly price except during the brief intervals between entry and buyout. Entry undertaken solely for buyout helps the consumer only insofar as monopoly output rises as a result of the increase in the monopolist's capacity, but the squandering of monopoly rents on the real costs of entry always decreases industry profits.

Antitrust laws prevent us from observing blatant examples of entry for buyout today, but in the nineteenth century the great trusts invariably faced the problem of entry, whether motivated by direct profits from undercutting prices or by the prospect of buyout. In some cases entrants re-entered and were bought out a second time, suggesting that buyout was their motive. A certain Mr. Kellog left his job at the Gunpowder Trust to manage a new gunpowder firm, which he quickly sold to the Trust. Soon afterwards, he founded a second gunpowder firm which he also sold, after a period of fierce price competition. Some years later, Indian Powder was founded by another ex-employee. After driving the price down to near or below cost, he sold out to the Trust, which included in the buyout contract a provision that he stay out of the powder business for twenty years (Elzinga [1970]).

The Sugar Trust faced similar problems. The American Sugar Refining

Company was formed in 1888 by merging firms owning a total of twenty plants, of which ten were shut down within a year. In the 1980s other firms frequently entered and were bought out by American. At least one of these entrants could not have operated at a profit, and we are told that

> "A contractor, Adolph Segal, apparently made a regular business of building refineries to sell to the trust. With the backing of Frederick Hipple, Segal in 1895 built the United States Sugar Refinery at Camden, New Jersey, with authorized capitalization of $2,000,000. This was sold to the trust and later events showed that it must have been built for this purpose since lack of a proper water supply rendered it inoperative."—Zerbe (1969).

Entry in these circumstances is rent-seeking behaviour, of which the dissipation of monopoly rents is the typical result (Posner [1975]). In deciding whether to allow buyout, the government must balance the possible increase in output against the certain increase in industry costs. The increase in costs is especially likely to dominate if there is more than one potential entrant, since after the first is bought out, subsequent buyouts are less likely to increase the amount of capacity the incumbent uses.

Even an incumbent with lower production costs than the entrant is not necessarily safe from entry. A firm which is a natural monopoly because of a set-up cost independent of output is still vulnerable to entry for buyout since the set-up cost has no effect on pricing. Nor is entry necessarily deterred if the incumbent's variable costs are lower than the entrant's, since the duopoly net revenue of each firm could still be positive.

Whatever the relative costs of the firms may be, outside observers might interpret these episodes using the classic story that a small firm enters the market, the incumbent monopolist lowers his price to below cost, and the unfortunate entrant is forced to sell out, a victim of predatory pricing. Appearances are deceiving; the unfortunate entrant is the one not bought out. In this model, incumbents favor laws banning buyouts, entrants oppose them, and consumers are commonly indifferent. The model excludes the many other reasons entrants might be bought out—to combine strengths of different firms, or to liquidate high-cost firms which entered mistakenly—so any policy implications should be regarded carefully, but it serves as a reminder that buyout is one motivation for entry and can influence a firm's entry deterrence policy.

ERIC RASMUSEN,
Anderson Graduate School of Management,
University of California,
Los Angeles,
CA 90024,
USA.

ACCEPTED APRIL 1987

REFERENCES

BERNHEIM, D., 1984, 'Strategic Deterrence of Sequential Entry into an Industry', *Rand Journal of Economics*, Vol. 15, pp. 1–11.

BULOW, J., GEANAKOPLOS, J. and KLEMPERER, P., 1985, 'Holding Idle Capacity to Deter Entry', *Economic Journal*, Vol. 95, pp. 178–182.

DIXIT, A., 1980, 'The Role of Investment in Entry Deterrence', *Economic Journal*, Vol. 90, pp. 95–106.

ELZINGA, K., 1970, 'Predatory Pricing: The Case of the Gunpowder Trust', *Journal of Law and Economics*, Vol. 13, pp. 273–290.

GELMAN, J. and SALOP, S., 1983, 'Judo Economics: Capacity Limitation and Coupon Competition', *Bell Journal of Economics*, Vol. 14, pp. 315–325.

HOLMSTROM, B., 1982, 'Moral Hazard in Teams', *Bell Journal of Economics*, Vol. 13, pp. 324–340.

MAYNARD SMITH, J., 1974, 'The Theory of Games and the Evolution of Animal Conflicts', *The Journal of Theoretical Biology*, Vol. 47, pp. 209–221.

MCGEE, J., 1958, 'Predatory Price Cutting: The Standard Oil (N.J.) Case', *Journal of Law and Economics*, Vol. 1, pp. 137–169.

NASH, J., 1950, 'The Bargaining Problem', *Econometrica*, Vol. 18, pp. 155–162.

POSNER, R., 1975, 'The Social Costs of Monopoly and Regulation', *Journal of Political Economy*, Vol. 83, pp. 807–827.

RUBINSTEIN, A., 1982, 'Perfect Equilibrium In A Bargaining Model', *Econometrica*, Vol. 50, pp. 1–9.

SPENCE, A. M., 1977, 'Entry, Capacity, Investment, and Oligopolistic Pricing', *Bell Journal of Economics*, Vol. 8, pp. 534–544.

WALDMAN, M., 1987, 'Noncooperative Entry Deterrence, Uncertainty, and the Free Rider Problem', *Review of Economic Studies*, 54, pp. 301–310.

ZERBE, R., 1969, 'The American Sugar Refining Company 1887–1914: The Story of a Monopoly', *Journal of Law and Economics*, Vol. 12, pp. 339–376.

THE JOURNAL OF INDUSTRIAL ECONOMICS 0022-1821 $2.00
Volume XXXVI March 1988 No. 3

BRAND INFORMATION AND PRICE*

THOMAS W. ROSS

While it is generally agreed that markets perform better when information is more complete, little has been said about how the added benefits are distributed. This essay explores this question in a model of brand selection. Buyers select from among that subset of available brands of which they are aware. When this subset grows, there are social surplus gains, but the distribution of these gains between firms and consumers is shown to be sensitive to the structure of the market. It is possible for either the sellers or the buyers to be worse off in the better informed environment.

I. INTRODUCTION

MOST OF the literature on consumer search has focused on consumers' search for the lowest price available on a homogeneous good. For consumer durables and even semi-durables this probably is the most common form of search. Non-durables are a different matter, however. Because they are purchased relatively frequently and a typical retailer may carry several brands of a single good, price information is not necessarily scarce. Here a different sort of search behaviour, brand search, may be observed. Brand search is the search over a subset of the available brands of a class of products, for the brand that best suits the searcher's tastes. There is an obvious and important qualitative difference between price search and brand search: given identical search histories two price searchers will make the same final selection[1] while two brand searchers may not.

In this essay I consider aspects of the brand search problem using a very simple model of brand selection. The principal interest is in the effect of improved brand information on equilibrium price in both competitive and monopolistic markets. Added information can be seen to have two opposing influences on price. First, more information means better consumer-brand matching and therefore a higher average willingness-to-pay. Under some market conditions this effect may push price upward. On the other hand, with more brand information, a buyer is better informed about substitutes. This tends to raise demand elasticities and push price downward.

* The author is grateful to Tom Nagle for some early discussions and to B. Hanessian, B. Hayes, J. McMillan, P. Pashigian, M. Riordan, P. Spiller, the N. American editor and an anonymous referee for helpful comments. Remaining errors are his alone. Research support from the Center for the Study of the Economy and the State at the University of Chicago, and the Carleton Industrial Organization Research Unit is also gratefully acknowledged.

[1] Or they will be indifferent between each other's selections.

The deeper purpose of this essay is to develop a simple model to show who benefits when there is more information in a market. It is demonstrated that, while more information always increases *total* welfare, the distribution of the benefits is very sensitive to the structure of the market. It is indeed possible for consumers or firms to be worse off in the better informed world.

Those familiar with modern search theory will recognize that developing a fully general model in which (i) consumers adopt optimal sequential search strategies and (ii) firms (taking (i) into account) freely choose price and product characteristics, is very difficult.[2] For this reason, I employ a simple model that leans on strong assumptions. The next section outlines this model, while that following describes the equilibria and how equilibrium price is affected by increased search activity. The fourth section offers some brief concluding remarks.

II. THE MODEL

The model of brand preference used here is Salop's [1979] model of product variety. Product variety space is described by a circle with individual brands located around the circle according to their particular characteristics. The closer two brands are to each other along the circumference of the circle, the more similar consumers see them to be. Let there be N brands in the market now, and let them be equally spaced around the circle. Their locations are assumed to be fixed. The case in which $N = 4$ is illustrated in Figure 1. We

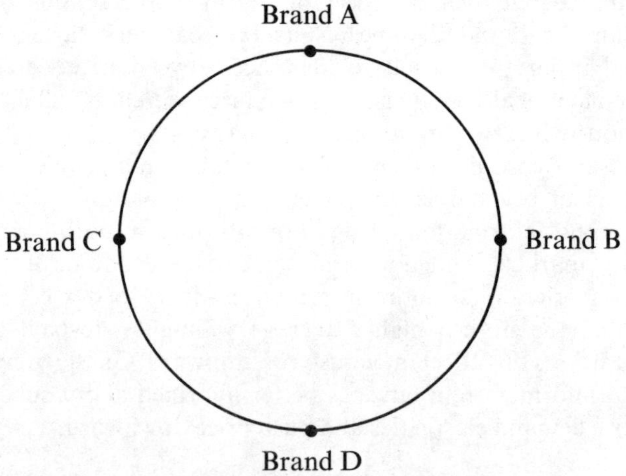

Figure 1

[2] See, for example, Rothschild [1973]. Peter Morgan [1983] has recently shown that fixed sample and sequential search are really both special cases of a more general search strategy in which buyers choose the number of observations to draw each period as well as the number of periods to search. He also derives conditions under which each strategy will be optimal.

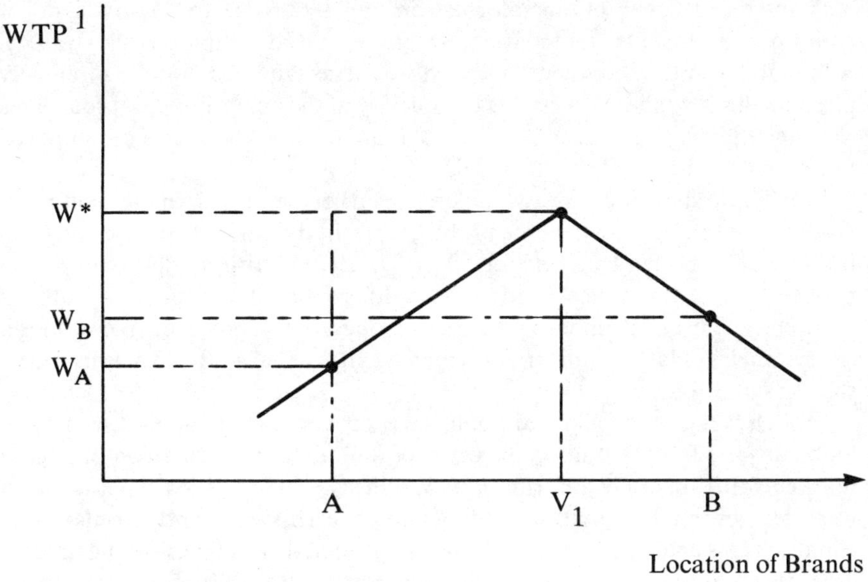

Figure 2

assume that all brands are equally costly to produce and that marginal costs are constant and equal to *c*.

There are *X* buyers and their tastes differ. Each consumer has a favorite point in product space; that is, a place where he would most like to have a brand located. We assume, for convenience, that buyers' favorite points are uniformly distributed around the circle with density *m*. Consumers, who buy one or zero units per period, are willing to pay W^* for a brand located on their favorite point but only $W^* - b \cdot d$ for a brand located *d* units from that point. The parameters W^* and *b* are assumed the same for all buyers.[3]

Let v_i represent the locations of buyers around the circle. As an example, we put consumer 1's favorite point, v_1, between brands *A* and *B*. This portion of the circle is represented on the horizontal axis of Figure 2. From the figure we can read buyer 1's willingness-to-pay (WTP^1) for the two brands as W_A and W_B.

To this point, the model is virtually identical to Salop's. It is the imperfect information that turns it into a model of brand search. Each buyer will only know the prices and characteristics of *S* of the *N* brands and will therefore choose from among those *S* one brand to buy. The brand that a customer liked most, if he knew about all *N* brands, and all *N* prices were the same, is called his "favorite" brand. The brand he likes most of the *S* on which he has information is his "preferred" brand.

[3] In the spatial competition literature *b* is interpreted as a transportation cost parameter.

While I shall speak of this information on S brands as an "endowment", it could be viewed as the outcome of an optimal fixed sample search strategy. Allowing for optimal sequential search would certainly be more theoretically pleasing but it would increase the complexity of the analysis several-fold. This simplification is justified, as the principal interest is in the effects of improved brand information and not in explaining the level of search.

Finally, we shall consider two different market structures. In the monopoly version one firm will own *all* the brands, while in the competitive version each brand will be owned by a different firm. The competitive model is not one of perfect competition since products are differentiated and no new entry is allowed. The firms do choose prices noncooperatively, however. We will look for symmetric Nash equilibria in which all firms charge the same price and sell the same quantity.

Models very much like this one have proven useful in related studies. Satterthwaite [1979] studied the effect of the number of sellers on price in a market with imperfect information. Wolinsky [1984] asked whether such imperfect brand information might lead to excessive brand proliferation. Finally, Grossman and Shapiro [1984] considered the effects of informative advertising in this type of model, though their analysis is quite different from that contained here.

III. EQUILIBRIA AND THE EFFECTS OF ADDED INFORMATION

To make the most clear exposition I shall work with a special case in which $N = 4$ and $S = 2$ or 3. This is the simplest example which allows us to consider two levels of search which both (i) leave the buyers with some choice (i.e., $S > 1$) and yet, (ii) involve less than full information (i.e., $S < N$). Generalizing to any N and any intermediate S would be notationally messy, but would not affect the general results.

After drawing information on two brands chosen at random from among the four (A, B, C, D) available, we will observe six different information sets based on draws of (A, B), (A, C), (A, D), (B, C), (B, D) and (C, D). Because the selections are random, the $X/6$ customers who have any particular set will be uniformly distributed around the circle. Note that there are only two *qualitatively* distinct types of information sets here. Two-thirds of the buyers will draw adjacent brands. These buyers, drawing (A, B), (A, C), (C, D) or (B, D), will be said to have drawn "near-brands". Buyers who draw (A, D) or (B, C) will be said to have drawn "far-brands".

The $S = 2$ symmetric monopoly equilibrium is described first. Provided that the monopolist charges the same price for all brands, his demand is determined by the number of buyers for whom $W^* - b \cdot d \geqslant p$ for at least one of the two brands they know about. Consider the buyers with information set (A, B) illustrated in Figure 3. The straight line cuts the circle in half; buyers located above the line will (for equal prices) prefer brand A while those below

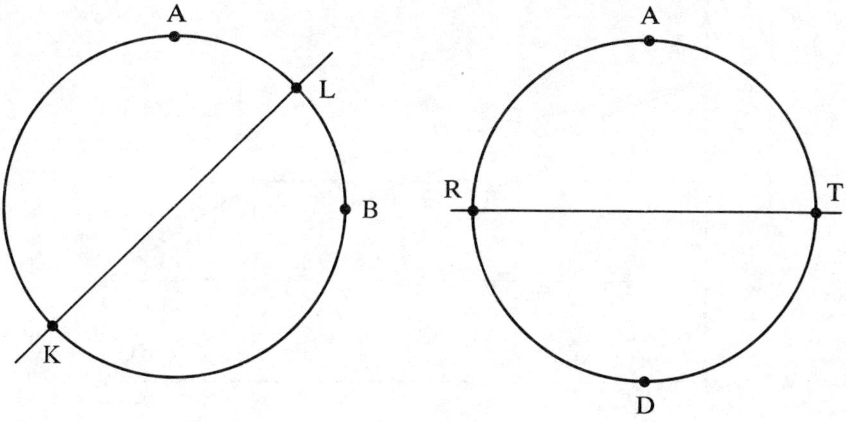

Near brands

Far brands

Figure 3

will prefer B. If we arbitrarily define the circumference of the circle to be 4 (so that $X = 4\,\mathrm{m}$), brands are one unit of distance apart and the furthest a customer can be from one of the two brands drawn is 3/2—in this case at point K in the figure.

If the monopolist sets a price $p_H = W^*$ he will clearly sell nothing, while if he charges $p_L = W^* - 3b/2$ or less, everyone will buy. It is a simple matter to trace the demand function between these two prices, Beginning at p_L we consider raising price a little, say by Δp. This will induce some of those who drew near-brands to drop out. The marginal buyer is defined by $W^* - bd_m = p$ where d_m is the distance of the marginal buyer from his preferred of the two brands. For the near-brand case in Figure 3, it is clear that as price rises above p_L some customers just above and below point K will refuse to buy. The sales lost (Δq) from this positive Δp will then be $2m \cdot \Delta d_m \cdot (2/3)$. In this expression the 2 refers to the two margins at which the market area is shrinking and the 2/3 adjusts for the fact that only those who drew near-brands are marginal. Since $\Delta d_m = -\Delta p/b$, $\Delta q = -(4m/3b)\Delta p$. Thus, quantity demanded falls linearly with increases in price above p_L.

Once price equals p_M, where $p_M = W^* - b$, some of those who drew far-brands will start to drop out, so demand becomes more elastic. These buyers drop out at a faster rate than the others as p rises above p_M since the market for these customers shrinks on four margins. For example, in the far-brand case in Figure 3, customers will begin to drop out above and below R and

$$\Delta q = 2m \cdot \Delta d_m \cdot (2/3) + 4m \cdot \Delta d_m \cdot (1/3)$$

or

$$\Delta q = -(8m/3b)\Delta p$$

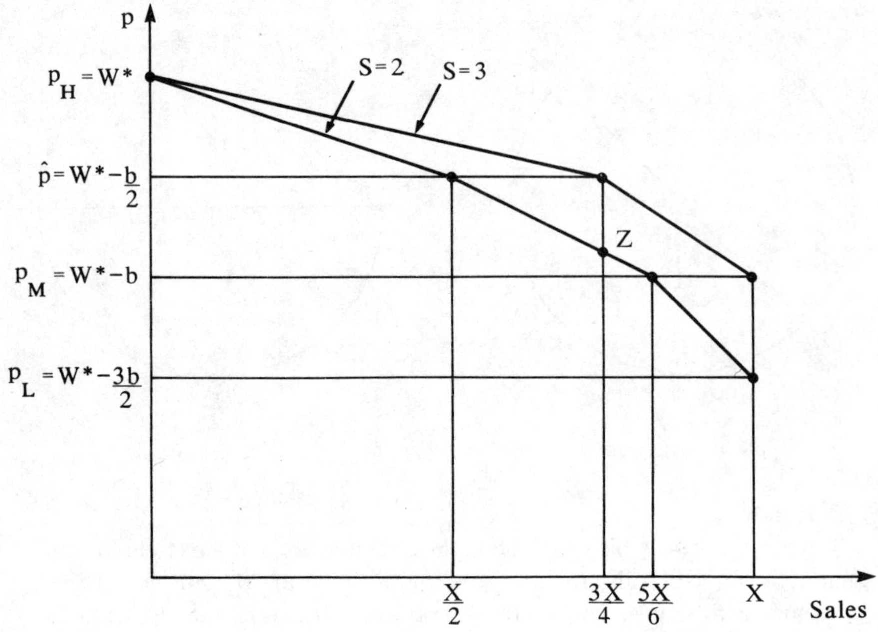

Figure 4

This linear relation continues until a price of $\hat{p} = W^* - b/2$ is reached. At this point buyers like those at point L in Figure 3 drop out and there are now four margins for those who drew near-brands. Demand becomes still more elastic and now we have:

$$\Delta q = 4m \cdot \Delta d_m$$

or

$$\Delta q = -(4m/b)\Delta p$$

At a price equal to $\hat{p}$, precisely one half of the potential customers will actually purchase. This demand curve is illustrated in Figure 4.

Depending upon the marginal costs of production, a variety of equilibria are possible. For low enough c it may be profitable for the monopolist to price at p_L and serve everyone. For a somewhat higher level of c it becomes profitable for the monopolist to permit the dropping out of buyers who draw brands far from their preferred points. In this range, between p_L and $\hat{p}$, all the buyers who draw their favorite brand continue to buy. For prices higher than $\hat{p}$, possible with very high c, this is no longer true.

Now consider the demand curve when $S = 3$. In this case four different search histories are possible: (A, B, C), (A, B, D), (A, C, D) and (B, C, D). Notice that there is no longer any near-brand vs far-brand distinction; these different information sets will be qualitatively identical for our purposes. The furthest that the best brand of the three can be from any buyer's favorite point is now only one unit. This means that with a price as high as $p_M = W^* - b$ the seller can get everyone to buy. Raising p above this minimum price will lose customers at the rate $\Delta q = -(2m/b)\Delta p$. Again there will be a kink at $\hat{p} = W^* - b/2$ as some buyers who had drawn their favorite brand choose to drop out. Gaps, areas of unserved buyers, open up between close brands such as A and C, and A and B. With three gaps in the circle rather than just the one, the slope of the demand curve is just 1/3 what it was below $\hat{p}$. $P_H = W^*$ is, of course, still the price that chokes off all demand.

This three-brand demand curve is also drawn in Figure 4. It is everywhere above the $S = 2$ demand, reflecting the better matching of consumers to brands. One can see from looking at the two piece-wise linear demand curves what will happen to equilibrium price. If we restrict our attention to the reasonable case in which consumers do buy if they find their favorite brand, that is $p < \hat{p}$, it is clear that equilibrium price will rise. Initial prices at or above $\hat{p}$ will not change as long as c is constant.[4]

This new endowment of brand information has interesting effects upon welfare. Since the new demand curve is everywhere outside the old and since the quantity sold will in general go up when the new information is introduced, it must be the case that total surplus has increased.[5] Obviously, the monopolist's profits have increased as well but have consumers shared in these new benefits? The answer is that they may indeed be *worse* off after receiving the extra information. They may also be better off.

If the initial price (p_1) was at or above $\hat{p}$ we know that price will not change. In this case there must be more consumers' surplus with the added information. Similarly if p_1 is only a little below $\hat{p}$ the price will only rise up to $\hat{p}$ and the consumers can still be better off. For still lower initial prices, however, it can be shown that the increase in price more than makes up for the better matching buyers with brands. This is easiest to see in the case where the initial price equals p_L so that everyone is in the market.

Proposition. If the initial monopoly price in this market equals p_L, the added brand information will result in a new equilibrium price $p_L + b/2$ and a lower level of consumers' surplus.

Proof. See the Appendix.

We then have the somewhat surprising result that while the (costlessly) added information will lead to superior matching and hence to greater total surplus, under certain conditions it will leave buyers, as a class, worse off.[6]

[4] With rising marginal costs, initial prices above p would increase as well.

[5] In fact, it is possible for output to go down if the initial price lies between p_M and the price at the point Z in Figure 4. Output would never fall below $3X/4$ in this case, however, and it is easy to prove that total surplus must still be higher when $S = 3$.

[6] Some buyers will be made better off, of course; for example those who find that the third brand they draw sits exactly on their favorite point.

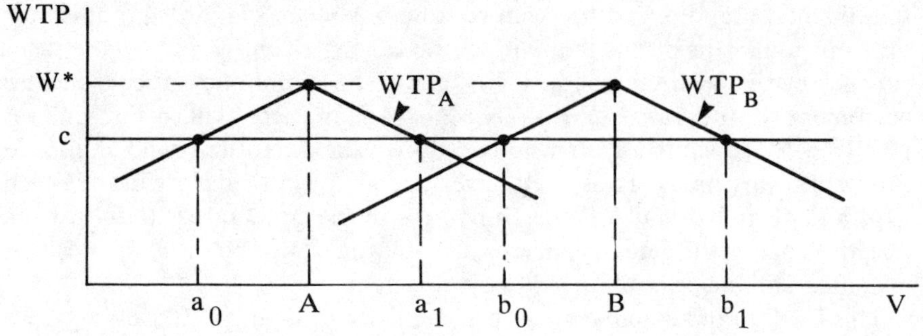

Figure 5

We turn now to a "competitive" version of this model. Again, more brand information will lead to better matching and upward pressure on price. However, in this case more brand information also means that price cutters can expect bigger sales gains and this would tend to depress equilibrium price. Which effect will dominate?

To explore this question we look for Nash (in price) symmetric equilibria for the four different firms owning the four brands of our model. We begin by finding equilibrium in the two-brand information set case.

As with the monopoly model, a variety of types of equilibria are possible. Most simply, if marginal costs are high enough and b is large enough each brand will function as a localized monopoly unaffected by the other brands. Such a case is illustrated in Figure 5. Note carefully the difference between the *WTP* curves in Figure 5 (and all later figures) and that in Figure 2. In the earlier case, the curve illustrated the *WTP* of one particular buyer for brands located at the various points along the horizontal axis. In Figure 5, it is the identity of the consumers that varies along the axis; the curves then tell us the *WTP* of these different buyers for the two given brands, *A* and *B*.

Even with a price as low as marginal cost these brands are not competitive and only customers who find their favorite brand (and not all of them) will be able to buy. With information on two brands, this represents $m/2$ buyers per unit distance, while with three it is $3m/4$. The two demand curves for brand *A* in this case are illustrated in Figure 6. Both are linear with slopes equal $b/2m$ times the reciprocal of the proportion of buyers aware of the brand. In this case, the added information rotates the demand curve outward, leaving equilibrium price unaffected. Here, both the firms and the customers benefit.

Such a market can hardly be called competitive, however, so we turn to a different situation. To compare results here with those for its monopoly equilibrium counterpart described in the Appendix, we consider the effect of further search on a symmetric equilibrium in which everyone buys. To find such an equilibrium we look for a price p^* that, when charged by all four firms, solves each individual firm's first order condition for profit maximiza-

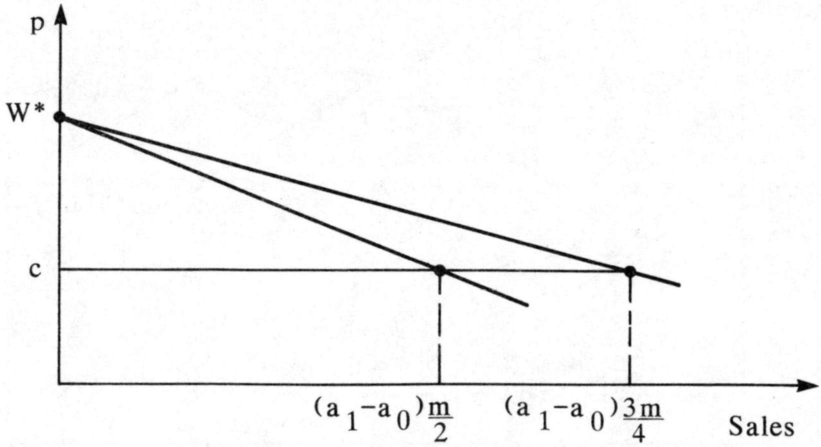

Figure 6

tion. Profit for one firm, A for example, can be written

$$\pi^A = (p_A - c)\cdot q_A(p)$$

where $q_A(p)$ is the demand for brand A given the vector of prices charged by all brands $p = (p_A, p_B, p_C, p_D)$. The first order condition is:

$$\partial\pi^A/\partial p_A = (p_A - c)\cdot\partial q_A/\partial p_A + q_A(p) = 0$$

or

$$-(p_A - c)\cdot\partial q_A/\partial p_A = q_A(p)$$

Since we are looking for a symmetric equilibrium in which everyone buys, $q_A(p)$ will simply be 1/4 of all sales or $X/4$. To solve for p_A we must now evaluate $\partial q_A/\partial p_A$ where $p_A = p_B = p_C = p_D$. This is straightforward in this simple model. Consider, for example, the buyers who drew (A, B). Their *WTP*s for these two brands are illustrated in Figure 7.

The fattened part of the WTP_A curve indicates that, among these buyers, A's market area extends from midway between C and D to midway between A and B when they charge identical prices. To see the effect on A's sales of an increase in price Δp_A (holding p_B constant) we need only shift WTP_A down by Δp_A. Brand A will clearly lose sales at both ends of its market and at the same rate at each end. The size of A's market area will shrink at *each* end by: $\Delta d_m = -\Delta p_A/2b$. The sales lost from (A, B) buyers will then equal $2\cdot\Delta d_m\cdot m/6 = \Delta d_m\cdot m/3$ since only one sixth of all buyers will be of the (A, B) type. Identical sales losses will come from (A, C) and (A, D) buyers too, so the total sales loss will be

$$\Delta q_A = \Delta d_m\cdot m = -(m/2b)\Delta p_A$$

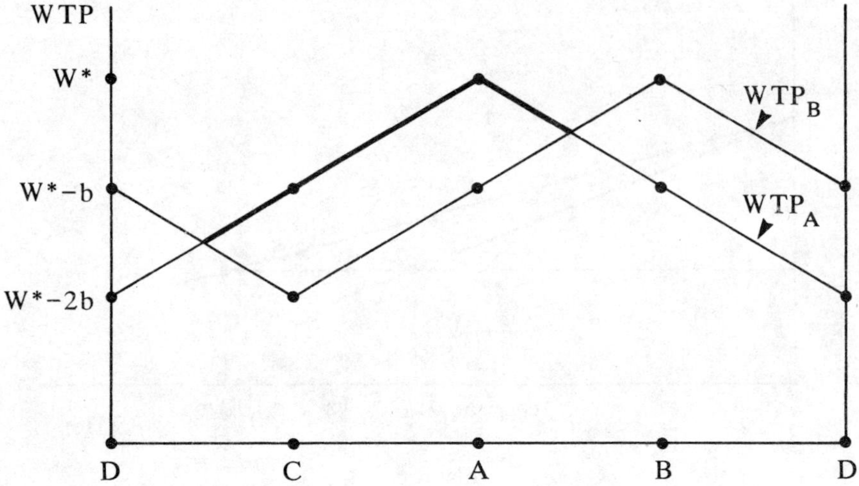

Figure 7

and the slope of A's demand curve when $p_A = p_B = p_C = p_D$ and everyone is buying is:

$$\partial q_A/\partial p_A = -m/2b$$

Substituting this into the first order condition together with $q_A = X/4$ we get

$$(p_2^* - c)m/2b = X/4$$

or

$$p_2^* = c + Xb/2m = c + 2b$$

where p_2^* represents equilibrium price when $S = 2$.

In solving for the equilibrium price when $S = 3$, we know that q_A in the first order condition will again equal $X/4$, so the only unknown is the value $\partial q_A/\partial p_A$. Consider the set of $X/4$ buyers who draw (A, B, C). We could draw in WTP_C in Figure 7 but we hardly need to. At equal prices A's portion of the (A, B, C) market will extend from midway between A and C to midway between A and B. An increase in price Δp_A will have the same effect on each margin here as it did in the two-brand information case, namely

$$\Delta d_m = -\Delta p_A/2b$$

Total sales lost from these consumers will then equal $2 \cdot \Delta d_m \cdot m/4 = \Delta d_m \cdot m/2$. Identical losses will be suffered from the (A, C, D) and (A, B, D) consumers as well, however, so these losses must be tripled leaving

$$\Delta q_A = \Delta d_m \cdot 3m/2 = -(3m/4b)\Delta p_A$$

Now A's demand curve has slope $\partial q_A / \partial p_A = -3m/4b$ so the three-brand information equilibrium price will be

$$p_3^* = c + Xb/3m = c + 4b/3$$

and, importantly,

$$p_3^* < p_2^*$$

The welfare comparisons are quite simple in this case. Since the price is lower and their sales no greater, the firms are clearly worse off. With the better matching, consumers' average *WTP*s must be higher.[7] As they also paid a lower price they are clearly better off and with no change in costs, the net effect on *total* surplus must be positive as well.

Thus, we have seen that, although the added information has raised consumers' *WTP*, the pro-competitive effects of greater brand choice is more influential, resulting in lower equilibrium prices.[8]

While entry is not explicitly considered here, the model does have some implications regarding the number of firms that can exist in a free entry equilibrium. If $N = 4$ when $S = 2$ was just such a monopolistically competitive equilibrium, the lower levels of profits obtained when S increases to 3 may force some firm(s) out of the market. Such a rationalization may have further beneficial welfare effects: Wolinsky [1984] has noted a tendency for there to be too many brands in equilibrium in a model like this one.

IV. SUMMARY AND CONCLUSIONS

My interest in this line of research began as part of some work on coupons. One use for coupons, marketers tell us, is as a subsidy to search, to encourage consumers to try new (new to the consumers, not necessarily to the market) brands.[9] The question then arises: when consumers have more brand information can we expect higher or lower prices to obtain? The better consumers are matched to products the greater their demand will be and this should have a positive effect on price. Brand information obtained from further search, however, means that each buyer faces more potential sellers, stimulating competition, tending to lower price.

The results derived here indicate that when there is only one firm so that

[7] Those unclear about this point will find some treatment of the change in average *WTP* in the Appendix.

[8] The astute reader will recognize that there is another type of competitive equilibrium not examined here, namely a type in which there are some buyers who do not buy because they have drawn badly given their tastes. Thus there will be gaps but not between all brands. For example, consumers located midway between C and D who draw (A, B) may choose not to buy. The results for such cases are qualitatively similar to those for the case with no gaps derived here. Nevertheless, as a referee has pointed out, it is not difficult to believe that a slightly different model might permit competitive firms to gain if the added information brings many more buyers into the market.

[9] I am grateful to Tom Nagle for discussions on this point.

this second effect is absent, prices *will* in general rise. A further result demonstrates that the price increase could be so large that it would leave consumers worse off despite the fact that they will be better matched with brands. In contrast, total surplus and the firm's profits both necessarily rise.

When there is competition, however, the extra information always helps consumers, through better matching *and* (in some cases, at least) lower prices.

It is very difficult to say whether these results will stand up to generalizations of the model, but including larger numbers of brands and different values of S will not yield qualitative differences. It is less clear, however, what would happen if we were able to incorporate sequential, costly search and to study non-symmetric equilibria.

The most important point goes beyond the specifics of the model. While markets will, in general, perform better when agents have more information, it is possible that not everyone will get a bigger slice of the pie. The structure of the market is seen to play an important role in determining which parties benefit from any added information, and which (if any) are hurt.

THOMAS W. ROSS,
Hoover Institution,
Stanford, CA 94305,
USA.

and

Department of Economics,
Carleton University,
Ottawa,
Canada, K1S 5B6.

ACCEPTED MAY 1987

APPENDIX

Proof of Proposition

Consider the situation of consumers who draw (A, B) initially. What follows applies equally well to those with different information sets. Now in Figure A-1 we illustrate consumers' WTP for the two brands. There, the circumference of the circle is laid along the horizontal axis. The vertical values give the willingness-to-pay for each brand for consumers located at every point around the circle. The fat upper (envelope) curve represents the willingness-to-pay for the preferred brand. The highest price that keeps everyone buying is that at the minimum of this curve, i.e., $W^* - 3b/2$. We can now determine the average willingness-to-pay for the preferred brand. The average WTP for consumers from A to B is $(W^* - b/4)$, from B to D $(W^* - b/2)$ etc. Putting these pieces together we find the overall WTP for the preferred brand with information (A, B)

$$AvWTP_2(AB) = W^* - 5b/8$$

Since the price paid is $W^* - 3b/2$ the average consumer's surplus will be

$$AvCS_2(AB) = (W^* - 5b/8) - (W^* - 3b/2) = (7/8)b$$

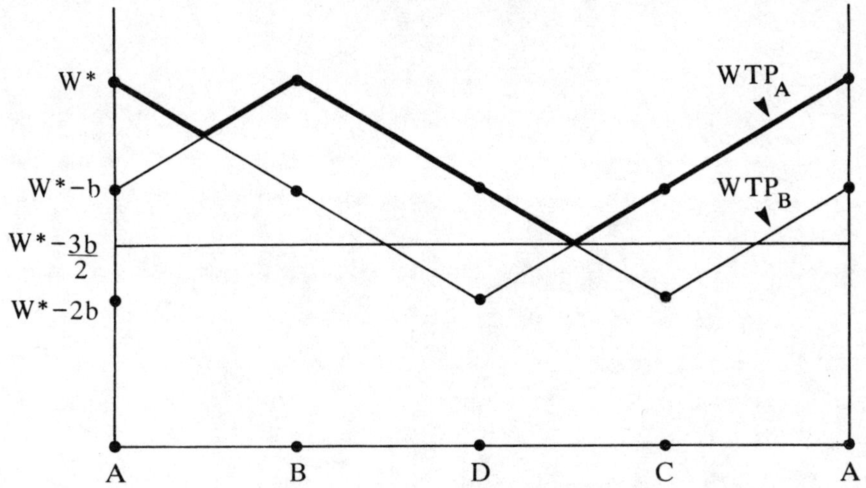

Figure A-1

While this surplus was calculated for buyers with (A, B) information, it should be clear that it applies to all buyers who draw close brands, i.e. (A, C), (B, D), (C, D) as well. In fact, two-thirds of all consumers will draw close brands. One third, however, the (A, D) and (B, C) groups, will have drawn distant brands and their average WTP will be a little different. We can show, using the same technique, that it is a little higher

$$AvWTP_2(AD) = W^* - b/2$$

and therefore, so is their average surplus

$$AvCS_2(AD) = b$$

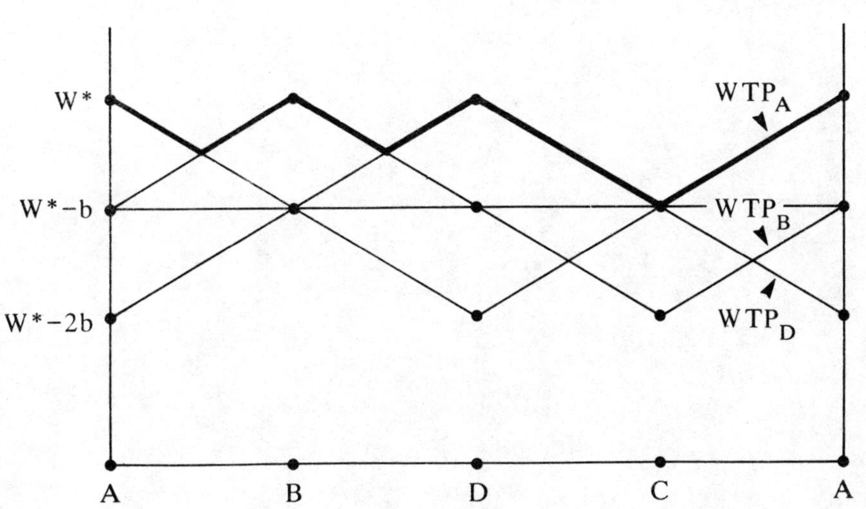

Figure A-2

THE JOURNAL OF INDUSTRIAL ECONOMICS 0022-1821 $2.00
Volume XXXVI March 1988 No. 3

VERTICAL INTEGRATION, VARIABLE PROPORTIONS AND SUCCESSIVE OLIGOPOLIES

MASAHIRO ABIRU*

This paper investigates the problem of how the effect of vertical integration upon the final product price is related to the production and/or the market structures. Some ambiguous results of the previous models are shown to involve the compound effect of vertical and horizontal merger. Our model considers purely vertical integration and shows that the (Lerner) index of monopoly remains unaffected before and after merger. Vertical integration is shown accordingly to yield an unambiguous decrease in the final product price—an increase in consumer welfare. Also discussed are implications for antitrust laws.

I. INTRODUCTION

THE THEORY of vertical integration can be divided into two main streams in terms of the assumptions employed and the welfare implications derived.[1]

One is the stream initiated by Warren-Boulton [1974] which, allowing for substitution between inputs, shows by computer simulation that the integration of a monopolistic input supplier and a perfectly competitive final good producer will result in an increase in the final product price (welfare loss). Mallela and Nahata [1980] improve the analysis in the same framework, and show at the fully analytical level that a merger of this sort may yield a decrease in the final product price when the elasticity of substitution is less than one; otherwise, it results in an increase. From this result alone, however, we cannot deduce many relevant policy implications since the models do not consider market structures, such as oligopolies, which are empirically more likely.

The other approach represented by Greenhut–Ohta [for brevity GO, 1976, 1979] takes market imperfection into account, and advances the powerful policy implication that merger or collusion between an input supplier and a final good producer brings about lower prices, greater output and sales, and greater profits to a merged or colluding firm (welfare gain to both producers and consumers). This approach, however, is criticized in that the assumptions

* The author is deeply indebted to Yasuhiro Sakai, Hiroshi Ohta and Yoshiyasu Ono for their valuable discussions and to Babu Nahata for his encouragement through personal correspondence. The author would like to acknowledge special thanks to Martin Bronfenbrenner for his helpful suggestions. Comments by an anonymous referee have also been incisively constructive. They are, however, not responsible for any errors that may remain in the paper.

[1] Concerning the profitability of vertical integration, see Vernon and Graham [1971] and Mallela–Nahata [1980, theorem 4, p. 1022].

TABLE I
ALTERNATIVE MODELS OF VERTICAL MERGER

	Production Structure	*Preference Structure*	*Market Structure*	*Merger Effect*
Warren-Boulton [1974]	Variable Proportions C.E.S. Production	Constant-Elasticity Demand	Monopolist vs Competitors	+, − (Indeterminate)
Greenhut–Ohta [1976]	Fixed Proportions	Linear Demand Nonlinear-Demand	Monopolist vs Competitors	0 (No Impact)
			Monopolist vs Monopolist	+ (Lower Price)
			Monopolist vs Oligopolists	+
Greenhut–Ohta [1979]	Fixed Proportions	General Demand Form	Oligopolists vs Oligopolists	+
Mallela–Nahata [1980]	Variable Proportions C.E.S. Production	Constant-Elasticity Demand	Monopolist vs Competitors	+, −
Waterson [1982]	Variable Proportions C.E.S. Production	Constant-Elasticity Demand	Monopolist vs Oligopolists	+, −
Quirmbach [1986A]	General Production Function Form	General Demand Form	Monopolist vs Contestable Market	+, −
Quirmbach [1986B]	General Production Function Form	General Demand Form	Monopolist vs Competitors	+, −
The Present Paper	Variable Proportions C.E.S. Production	Constant-Elasticity Demand	Oligopolists vs Oligopolists	+

GO employed are too restrictive.[2] They assume a production function with fixed input proportions, which eliminates any possibility of substitution between inputs. (The opposing stream assumes conventional variable proportions production functions.)

Does it follow therefore that these distinctively different sets of assumptions are indeed responsible for the mutually opposing results of the two contrasting models? Which one of the two conflicting assumptions, i.e., the market-structure assumption or the technology-choice assumption, is crucial in determining the direction of change in the final product price? And which is more relevant in formulating policy implications?

The purpose of this paper is to answer these and other related questions. By so doing, we follow the Warren-Boulton model as to production technology and demand conditions, but analyze the Warren-Boulton case in more general market structures in line with GO. Similar work has been presented by Waterson [1982], who analyzes the effect of vertical integration between an input monopolist and an oligopolist by using a C.E.S. production function, and shows by computer simulation that the final product price declines as long as the elasticity of substitution is fairly low; otherwise it often rises.

It may seem from this result that the welfare effect of vertical integration depends on the substitution parameter. This is not the case, however. In fact, under certain particular assumptions we can show that regardless of the elasticity of substitution or the market structure under consideration, the effect of vertical integration is to decrease the price of the final product.

The reason for the dichotomy between this and Waterson's result can be found in the interpretation of vertical integration. Waterson takes *vertical* to mean in effect both *horizontal* and *vertical.* What he analyzes is a compound effect of vertical and horizontal integration. It is generally accepted that the horizontal merger increases the price of a final good.[3] It follows that Waterson's result is *not* dependent on the degree of substitution but rather on *horizontal* effects.

Our model may be related to and contrasted with the existing literature as shown in Table I. They are classified in terms of underlying assumptions regarding market structures, production technologies, demand conditions and welfare implications. Table I shows on one hand that our model is not sufficiently general in terms of the demand conditions, but the demand conditions seem not to play a decisive role in determining the welfare implications. On the other hand, our model is quite general in terms of both technology and market structure assumptions and these two assumptions appear to be more crucial for the welfare results than are the demand conditions.

[2] See Haring and Kaserman [1978].
[3] See e.g., Greenhut and Ohta [1976].

Our findings concerning the pure effects of "vertical" integration will be presented in the following manner. In the next section, we will set forth the basic framework. Section III establishes two related propositions (in the form of lemma and theorem) to prove our case. The final section will present some policy implications.

II. THE BASIC FRAMEWORK: PRICE BEFORE INTEGRATION

As we noted in the introduction, while the model presented by Warren-Boulton assumes production technology which appears quite general, their assumptions regarding market structure are rather restrictive. In this section, we will construct an alternative model of vertical integration, i.e., a case of successive Cournot oligopolies, on the basis of final market demand with constant demand elasticity and a C.E.S. production function.

Consider m identical downstream firms and n identical upstream firms. Assume that each downstream firm produces the final good under conditions of constant elasticity of substitution and constant returns to scale. Thus:

$$(1)\qquad x_i = Y[\delta A_i^{(\sigma-1)/\sigma}+(1-\delta)B_i^{(\sigma-1)/\sigma}]^{\sigma/(\sigma-1)}, \qquad i = 1,\ldots m$$

where x_i is the ith downstream firm's output, $\sigma(>0)$ the elasticity of substitution, $Y(>0)$ the efficiency parameter and $\delta(1>\delta>0)$ the distributive parameter. Input A_i is supplied to the ith downstream firm by n upstream firms at the market price of P_a and is produced with constant marginal cost M_a.[4] The other input B_i is supplied in the competitive market at a given price P_b.

Each downstream firm is assumed to behave as a competitive buyer of inputs, and therefore considers input prices to be given as it tries to minimize the cost of production, $P_aA_i+P_bB_i$, subject to Eq. (1). The first order conditions for cost minimization accordingly are:

$$(2)\qquad \frac{B_i}{A_i} = \left(\frac{(1-\delta)P_a}{\delta P_b}\right)^{\sigma}, \qquad i = 1,2,\ldots m$$

Solving Eqs. (1) and (2) for A_i and B_i readily yields each downstream firm's cost function:

$$(3)\qquad C_i^b = P_aA_i+P_bB_i = \frac{1}{Y}(\delta^\sigma P_a^{1-\sigma}+(1-\delta)^\sigma P_b^{1-\sigma})^{1/(1-\sigma)}x_i, \qquad i = 1,2,\ldots m$$

where the superscript "b" denotes "before integration".

The final market demand is assumed to be of constant elasticity:

$$(4)\qquad X = ZP_x^{-\eta}$$

[4] The assumption of constant marginal cost is not needed for our results to hold.

where $Z > 0$, $\eta > 1$ and P_x is the unit price of the final product X. In equilibrium the market demand equals the aggregate supply x_i by m downstream oligopolists:

$$(5) \qquad X = \sum_{i=1}^{m} x_i$$

Since each Cournot downstream firm considers its rivals' supply as fixed, the first order profit maximization conditions subject to (3), (4) and (5) yield the reaction functions:

$$(6) \qquad P_x - \frac{x_i}{\eta X} P_x = c^b, \qquad i = 1, 2, \ldots m$$

where c^b stands for the marginal (and average) cost of producing x_i. Since (6) applies equally to all i, it follows that $X = \sum_{i=1}^{m} x_i = mx_i$. Therefore Eq. (6) becomes:

$$(7) \qquad P_x\left(1 - \frac{1}{m\eta}\right) = c^b$$

where c^b, from Eq. (3), is given by:[5]

$$(8) \qquad c^b = \frac{1}{Y}(\delta^\sigma P_a^{1-\sigma} + (1-\delta)^\sigma P_b^{1-\sigma})^{1/(1-\sigma)}$$

Thus, the product price is clearly seen to depend upon, among other parameters, the input price P_a. Before vertical merger, this input price is given to the m downstream firms in the market in which n upstream firms compete with one another as Cournot oligopolists. The input price, while given to the downstream firms, itself depends upon the Cournot behavior of the upstream sellers. Each upstream Cournot oligopolist will sell inputs so as to maximize profit. The first order conditions for profit maximization in the Cournot upstream market require:

$$(9) \qquad P_a\left(1 - \frac{1}{nE}\right) = M_a$$

where M_a stands for the marginal cost of producing A, n for the number of upstream Cournot oligopolists, and E for the elasticity of derived demand for A, which must be greater than unity since we assume positive marginal cost. The elasticity E is further specifiable as:[6]

$$(10) \qquad E = k_a\eta + (1-k_a)\sigma, \qquad 0 \leqslant k_a \leqslant 1$$

[5] There is a typographical error in Eq. (6) of Waterson [1982, p. 132]; the correct expression for c^b is given by our Eq. (8).

[6] Waterson [1980] proves that this formula [Hicks, 1963], derived under conditions of perfect competition, also holds in the case of oligopoly.

where k_a is the share of the cost of A in the total cost of producing X. (The parameter k_a is not a constant; it can be shown to be a unique function of P_a: $k_a = (1+((1-\delta)/\delta)^{\sigma}(P_a/P_b)^{\sigma-1})^{-1}$. See e.g. Waterson [1982].)

The product price before merger is thus uniquely determined by solving equations (7), (8), (9) and (10) for P_x. This P_x, henceforth, will be referred to as P_x^b, the superscript "b" standing for "before merger".

III. THE WELFARE EFFECTS OF VERTICAL INTEGRATION

III(i). *Price after vertical integration*

Before we proceed to examine the impacts of vertical integration, we stress that our basic model is fully general as set out above: it contains each of the previous models as a special case. When the number of upstream firms falls to one ($n = 1$), the model becomes identical with Waterson's [1982]. When the elasticity of substitution is equal to zero ($\sigma = 0$), this model approximates the GO model [1979].[7] Further, if the number of upstream firms is one and the number of downstream firms tends to infinity ($n = 1$ and $m \to \infty$), our model reduces to the models of Warren-Boulton [1974] and Mallela–Nahata [1980]. However, we do not intend to generalize the model for the sake of generality; instead we provide a possible framework to settle the controversy about the effect of vertical integration on the final product price. In this context, the interpretation of "vertical" integration plays the crucial role.

The cost function of a downstream firm after merger with an upstream firm is obtained directly by replacing P_a with M_a in Eq. (3):

$$(11) \qquad C_i^a = \frac{1}{Y}(\delta^{\sigma} M_a^{1-\sigma} + (1-\delta)^{\sigma} P_b^{1-\sigma})^{1/(1-\sigma)} x_i, \qquad i = 1, 2, \ldots \mu$$

where the superscript "a" denotes "after integration" and μ "number of firms participating in vertical integration". Taking the same procedures above, we obtain each integrated firm's reaction function after merger:

$$(12) \qquad P_x^a\left(1 - \frac{1}{\mu\eta}\right) = c^a = \frac{1}{Y}(\delta^{\sigma} M_a^{1-\sigma} + (1-\delta)^{\sigma} P_b^{1-\sigma})^{1/(1-\sigma)}$$

where P_x^a and c^a stand respectively for the final price and the marginal cost of producing X after integration. This gives, in general, the final product price when each firm attempts to integrate vertically with a downstream or upstream firm. Moreover, this can readily be compared with the treatment of "vertical" integration in the previous models. (The analysis by Waterson [1982], for example, limited itself to the case in which $\mu = 1$ in the above

[7] Our model with $\sigma = 0$ is not exactly the same as GO's since GO [1979] assumes the demand function which is less restrictive than our constant elasticity demand.

equation. However, this in effect involves the compound effect of vertical and horizontal integration because m downstream firms initially assumed to exist *horizontally* before integration are required to be merged into one and only one firm after *vertical* integration. Since we are interested only in the effect of vertical integration by itself, any horizontal effect has to be eliminated.)

One way to pursue the pure theory is simply to consider the case of $\mu = m = n$. When $m \neq n$, the vertical merger could involve musical chairs and resultant elimination or horizontal take-over of some slow firms which fail to integrate vertically. Avoiding such complication, we will initially consider the special case with $m = n$, to be followed by a more general case where $m \neq n$.

III(ii). *The pure effect of complete vertical integration: The case $\mu = m = n$*

We are now in position to prove our fundamental proposition set forth at the outset as we consider the case $\mu = m = n$. Initially the following conditions are derived from Eqs. (7) and (12):

$$(13) \qquad \frac{P_x^b - c^b}{P_x^b} = \frac{P_x^a - c^a}{P_x^d} = \frac{1}{\mu\eta}$$

where the left end and middle part of Eq. (13) represents the so-called Lerner index of monopoly, before integration and after integration, respectively. Since both are equal to $1/\mu\eta$ we see that the Lerner index of monopoly is left unchanged by vertical integration. This proves the following LEMMA.

Lemma. Suppose that m homogeneous Cournot firms in the downstream industry are faced by market demand with constant elasticity. Then the Lerner index of monopoly remains unchanged if these downstream firms integrate one-to-one vertically with homogeneous upstream firms.

Our fundamental proposition is now immediately derivable from this Lemma and the following observation. A comparison of the final product prices before and after integration is reduced to the comparison of the marginal costs through Eqs. (8) and (12), which comparison in turn depends on that of P_a and M_a. Namely,

$$(14) \qquad P_x^a \leqslant P_x^b, \quad \text{if and only if} \quad M_a \leqslant P_a$$

which will be true if and only if $nE > 1$ from Eq. (9). Since $n \geqslant 1$ and E is required to be greater than unity under a positive marginal cost, it follows that $P_x^a < P_x^b$, thus establishing the following THEOREM.

Theorem. Suppose that the downstream industry is characterized by the constant elasticity of substitution in production besides the conditions of the Lemma. Then the effect of vertical integration of downstream firms with upstream firms is to lower the final product price.

It goes without saying that the reduction in the final good price due to a vertical merger causes an increase in the equilibrium quantity according to the demand function as shown in Eq. (4).

III(iii). *The pure effects of partial vertical integration: The case $\mu \leqslant m < n$*

As we noted above, not all firms can effect one-to-one vertical integration when $m \neq n$. Nevertheless, we note that insofar as the downstream firms are fewer in number than the upstream firms, the Lerner index of monopoly remains unaltered before and after complete vertical merger, being given by $1/m\eta$ via Eq. (7) and $1/\mu\eta$ via Eq. (12), where $\mu = m$.[8] Thus, because marginal cost after vertical integration can be shown to be strictly lower, the welfare effect of vertical integration remains strictly positive, and moreover dominates the negative horizontal effects, if any, of liquidated upstream firms.

Our Lemma does not apply, however, to the case in which the smaller number μ of firms is in the upstream industry, that is, $\mu = n < m$. The Lerner index of monopoly after complete vertical merger is clearly higher than before since $1/m\eta < 1/n\eta$ insofar as $n < m$. It is worthy of note here that our proposition no longer holds in this case $n < m$ due to the unavoidable horizontal effect that arises even under conditions of partial integration, that is, $\mu < n < m$.[9]

Let us consider a case in which at least one firm remains unintegrated in each of the vertically related industries and keeps behaving as a Cournot successive oligopolist so that $\mu < m < n$. This is the case considered, although not definitively, by GO [1979]. We consider the GO results, and moreover go beyond them by relaxing their assumption of $\sigma = 0$. (Our demand function is more restrictive than GO's, however.)

At the upstream stage μ input oligopolists are eliminated from the market because of the vertical integration. Therefore, $(n-\mu)$ nonintegrated upstream firms now supply the input to the $(m-\mu)$ nonintegrated downstream oligopolists. The optimization conditions for the $(n-\mu)$ upstream nonintegrated firms are then given:

$$(9)' \qquad P_a^n\left(1-\frac{1}{(n-\mu)E}\right) = M_a$$

where P_a^n stands for input price for the nonintegrated firms. Immediately from the comparison of this equation and Eq. (9), we see that the input price for nonintegrated downstream firms is not equal to the price before integra-

[8] In contrast to Waterson [1982, section III], we assume that, after merger, the integrated firms do not trade with nonintegrated firms.

[9] Quirmbach [1986A, 1986B] also refers to partial integration. However, Quirmbach's partial integration is not exactly the same as ours. In our model it is not possible, after merger, for the upstream monopolist to sell the input to the independent downstream competitors as we assumed above.

tion as long as $\mu > 0$. More precisely, depending upon the parameter value, $P_a^n \gtreqless P_a$.

The first-order profit-maximization conditions for these μ integrated firms are:

$$(15) \qquad P_x^a - \frac{x_i}{\eta X} P_x^a = c^a, \qquad i = 1, 2, \dots \mu$$

The optimization conditions for the remaining $(m-\mu)$ nonintegrated firms are subject to Eq. (6) over $j = \mu+1, \dots m$, to obtain:

$$(16) \qquad P_x^a - \frac{x_j}{\eta X} P_x^a = c^n, \qquad j = \mu+1, \mu+2, \dots m$$

where c^n stands for marginal cost of the nonintegrated firms. Note c^n is now distinguished from c^b in Eq. (6) as seen below:

$$(17) \qquad c^n = (\delta^\sigma P_a^{n\,1-\sigma} + (1-\delta)^\sigma P_b^{1-\sigma})^{1/(1-\sigma)}$$

Aggregating Eqs. (15) and (16), respectively, over $i = 1, \dots \mu$ and $j = \mu+1, \dots m$, then yields:

$$(18) \qquad \mu P_x^a - \frac{\mu x_i}{\eta X} P_x^a = \mu c^a$$

and

$$(19) \qquad (m-\mu) P_x^a - \frac{(m-\mu) x_j}{\eta X} P_x^a = (m-\mu) c^n$$

These two equations provide, respectively, the aggregate inputs of the μ integrated and $(m-\mu)$ nonintegrated firms. Since market equilibrium requires $X = \mu x_i + (m-\mu) x_j$, adding Eq. (18) to Eq. (19) and dividing both sides by m yields:[10]

$$(20) \qquad P_x^a \left(1 - \frac{1}{m\eta}\right) = c^n - \frac{\mu}{m}(c^n - c^a)$$

[10] The nonintegrated firms may not be able to survive due to their inability to cover the average costs. In order to cover the costs, the final market price must exceed the nonintegrated firms' marginal cost; $P_x^a > c^n$. This condition can be written via Eq. (8), Eq. (9)', Eq. (12) and Eq. (19) as: When $0 < \sigma < 1$,

$$\delta^\sigma P_a^{1-\sigma} \left\{ \left(1 - \frac{1}{(n-\mu)E}\right)^{1-\sigma} - \left(1 - \frac{1}{\mu\eta}\right)^{1-\sigma} \right\} + (1-\delta)^\sigma P_b^{1-\sigma} \left\{ 1 - \left(1 - \frac{1}{\mu\eta}\right)^{1-\sigma} \right\} > 0$$

And when $\sigma > 1$,

$$\delta^\sigma P_a^{1-\sigma} \left\{ \left(1 - \frac{1}{(n-\mu)E}\right)^{1-\sigma} - \left(1 - \frac{1}{\mu\eta}\right)^{1-\sigma} \right\} + (1-\delta)^\sigma P_b^{1-\sigma} \left\{ 1 - \left(1 - \frac{1}{\mu\eta}\right)^{1-\sigma} \right\} < 0$$

A sufficient condition for these inequalities to hold is given by: $\mu\eta < (n-\mu)E$. Partial integration will be feasible in this case. Otherwise, i.e., when $P_x^a < c^n$, nonintegrated firms have no choice but take part in the vertical integration.

Thus the marginal cost after merger is expressed as the weighted average of marginal costs for both integrated and nonintegrated firms. The left hand sides of Eq. (7) and Eq. (20) are the same form, so we have only to compare the right hand sides of these equations to prove the theorem. The right hand side of Eq. (20) can be shown to be strictly less than that of Eq. (7) or c^b when $\sigma = 0$. The same relation holds generally even when $\sigma > 0$ insofar as both n and E are sufficiently large, or one of $1/nE$, $1/(n-\mu)E$ nearly zero.[11] This condition, however, is put only to facilitate the analytical proof. In fact we have also run a computer simulation with m, n, μ, δ, σ and P_b as parameters. We obtain the result that the above relation holds even when both n and E are as small as $n = 2$ and $E = 1.5$. Provided these conditions are acceptable, we finally have:

$$(21) \qquad P_x^a\left(1-\frac{1}{m\eta}\right) < c^b$$

Note that Eq. (20) gives the final good price when only μ firms integrate vertically while the remaining firms behave independently as before. The Lerner indices before and after merger in the light of Eqs. (7) and (20) are both seen to be $1/m\mu$ (LEMMA). It then follows from Eqs. (7) and (21) that the final market prices after vertical integration are strictly lower than those before merger (THEOREM).

IV. *Policy implications*

Throughout the discussion of this paper, we have generalized selected models of vertical integration which have appeared since the 1970s in an attempt to answer the question whether the effect of vertical integration on the final product price is sensitive to the degree of substitution and/or the market structures as suggested in the controversy. Remarkably the result is not what has been believed: Greenhut and Ohta's conclusion on welfare may be extended to cover *not only* cases involving moderate substitution [Waterson 1982] *but also* the cases far beyond. We also show that previous vertical integration models involve both vertical effects and horizontal effects. However, these two effects are offsetting each other; e.g. see Mallela–Nahata [1980].

The propositions proved in this paper are worth repeating because of the robustness of their implications for antitrust regulation. Under Cournot assumptions with constant elasticity of final product demand and a smaller number of firms in the downstream industry:

(i) the Lerner index of monopoly remains unaffected by purely vertical integration;

(ii) Vertical integration decreases the price of the final product.

[11] Details of the proof can be obtained from the author upon request.

Antitrust authorities have led the battle against conglomerate takeovers on grounds that vertical integration would actually (or even potentially, prior to 1973) reduce competition, restrict output and raise the final output prices.[12] Our theorems show, however, that these views are not quite valid. It is true, as we noted above, that antitrust authorities' assumptions hold for the case of horizontal integration. Therefore, we propose that antitrust authorities should first make a clear distinction between "vertical" and "horizontal" integration, and then focus their attention on ways to eliminate the "horizontal" effect.

MASAHIRO ABIRU,
Faculty of Economics,
Fukuoka University,
8-19-1 Nanakuma Jyonan-ku,
Fukuoka 814-01,
Japan.

ACCEPTED APRIL 1987

REFERENCES

GREENHUT, M. L. and OHTA, H., 1976, 'Related Market Conditions and Interindustrial Merger', *American Economic Review*, 66 (June), pp. 267–277.

GREENHUT, M. L. and OHTA, H., 1979, 'Vertical Integration of Successive Oligopolists', *American Economic Review*, 69 (March), pp. 137–141.

HARING, J. R. and KASERMAN, D. L., 1978, 'Related Market Conditions and Interindustrial Mergers: Comment', *American Economic Review*, 68, No. 1, pp. 225–227.

HICKS, J. R., 1963, *The Theory of Wages*, 2nd ed. (Macmillan).

LERNER, A. P., 1934, 'The Concept of Monopoly and Measurement of Monopoly Power', *The Review of Economic Studies*, 1, pp. 157–175.

MALLELA, P. and NAHATA, B., 1980, 'Theory of Vertical Control with Variable Proportions', *Journal of Political Economy*, 88 (August), pp. 1009–1025.

QUIRMBACH, C. H., 1986A, 'Vertical Integration: Scale Distortions, Partial Integration and the Direction of Price Change', *Quarterly Journal of Economics*, 101 (February), pp. 131–147.

QUIRMBACH, C. H., 1986B, 'The Path of Price Changes in Vertical Integration', *Journal of Political Economy*, 94 (October), pp. 1110–1119.

SPENGLER, J. J., 1950, 'Vertical Integration and Antitrust Policy', *Journal of Political Economy*, 58 (February–December), pp. 347–352.

VERNON, J. M. and GRAHAM, D. A., 1971, 'Profitability of Monopolization by Vertical Integration', *Journal of Political Economy*, 79 (July/August), pp. 924–925.

WARREN-BOULTON, F. R., 1974, 'Vertical Control with Variable Proportions', *Journal of Political Economy*, 82 (July/August), pp. 783–802.

WATERSON, M., 1980, 'Oligopoly and Derived Demand', *Economics Letters*, 5, No. 2, pp. 115–118.

WATERSON, M., 1982, 'Vertical Integration, Variable Proportions and Oligopoly', *The Economic Journal*, 92 (March), pp. 129–144.

[12] See e.g., Spengler [1950, p. 347] and Mallela and Nahata [1980, p. 1024].

THE JOURNAL OF INDUSTRIAL ECONOMICS 0022-1821 $2.00
Volume XXXVI March 1988 No. 3

MARKET SHARE INSTABILITY IN COMMERCIAL AIRLINE MARKETS AND THE IMPACT OF DEREGULATION

RALPH D. SANDLER*

While the degree of rivalry in a market is often concealed and therefore difficult to observe directly, various measures of market share variation have been used in the literature as an indicator of behavior. Using a similar measure, the primary task of the study was to estimate the degree to which rivalry (both price and non-price) had actually increased during the first two years of deregulation. The paper also provides an analytical framework which may be used to assess the impact of regulatory reform on rivalry in other industries.

I. INTRODUCTION

THE Airline Deregulation Act (ADA) of 1978 represented a major change in national aviation policy. Even today this watershed event and its consequences are a topic of debate and a basis of increasing concern as the industry becomes more concentrated.[1] To economists this change in policy presents a unique opportunity to compare the behavior of firms in an industry before and after economic regulation. While behavior or the degree of rivalry in a market is often concealed and therefore difficult to observe directly, various measures of market share variation have been used in the literature as an indicator of behavior. By using a similar measure that captures both price and non-price rivalry, the behavior of regulated carriers primarily engaging in service rivalry can be compared to the behavior of carriers now free to compete on the basis of price as well as service.

The purpose of this paper is to measure empirically the determinants of market rivalry in city-pair airline markets and then to estimate the degree to which rivalry (both price and non-price) actually increased during the first two years of deregulation. A sample of 123 large city-pair airline markets were selected for analysis. While separate regression estimates were made for the periods before (1974–76) and after (1978–80) deregulation, this paper only reports on the results of a pooled regression equation using data for both

* This paper was taken from my doctoral dissertation, Florida State University. I am grateful to Fred Bell, Charlie Conn, Gary Fournier and Gregory Miller for their helpful comments on previous drafts of this paper. I also want to acknowledge the important suggestions of Lawrence White and two anonymous referees.

[1] Recent articles in the business press reflect the public policy concern with increasing concentration in airline markets. For an example, see Welles [1986].

periods.[2] The central question to be explored is whether the ADA really did "shake things up" and thereby increase the degree of rivalry in airline markets.

II. METHODOLOGY

Market share instability

Although it has never been applied to aviation markets, there is an extensive literature on the degree of rivalry in other industries as measured by market share variation.[3] More recent studies have provided a thorough discussion of the conceptual foundation of market share instability, which is now viewed as a proxy for the overall behavior of firms in a market.[4] Generally, one would expect that the greater the stability, the higher the probability that cooperative behavior would exist among rivals in a particular market. By contrast, a churning among competing firms, as reflected by market share instability, may suggest an active rivalry.

Scope of analysis

The years 1974–76 and 1978–80 were selected for comparative analysis. During 1974–76, the Civil Aeronautics Board (CAB) continued to exercise rigid control over virtually every aspect of interstate commercial aviation; hence the period should be fairly representative of industry behavior under regulatory conditions.[5] Selecting an appropriate deregulated period, however, was much more difficult. The transition from regulation was a gradual one, taking place over several years and consisting of both legislative and regulatory initiatives. However, in the spring of 1978 the CAB embarked on a major drive to weaken many anticompetitive aspects of regulation, a move which involved an abrupt departure from legal precedent.[6] Measures were adopted to both streamline route award procedures and allow airlines pricing flexibility. Therefore, even though the ADA was not enacted until October, all of 1978 can be safely viewed as the first year of deregulation. While the ADA provided for the gradual elimination of statutory authority over pricing, routes, and entry, the CAB phased out regulation in these areas long before the sunset provisions of the Act. Carriers were able to exercise pricing flexibility throughout the period and from the beginning of 1979 were virtually free to operate in any markets they wished. Thus, 1978–80 represents

[2] See Sandler [1984, pp. 163–166] for separate regression estimates.

[3] See Gort [1963], Hymer and Pashigian [1962], Jacoby [1964], Joskow [1960], and Ogur [1976].

[4] See Haggestad and Rhoades [1976] and Caves and Porter [1978].

[5] See Behrman [1980, pp. 114–120].

[6] See Behrman [1980, pp. 114–120].

a period during which carriers were operating under conditions of considerable freedom and should therefore provide a striking comparison with 1974–76.[7]

Data and sampling procedures

In day-to-day competition for customers the relevant market, and the one upon which this paper is based, is that comprised of persons desiring to travel between a particular pair of cities. The primary data source used was the 10 percent sample of passenger traffic collected each year by the CAB.[8] A cross-section of 123 airline markets was selected from a list of the most heavily traveled domestic markets.[9] Since the number of carriers actually serving any particular market depends upon the density of market demand, heavily traveled markets were selected for analysis because they were more likely to have at least two active rivals providing service throughout the period of investigation (1974–76 and 1978–80).[10]

III. MODEL

Measure of market share instability

A measure of relative instability (I), based on the index originally constructed by Hymer and Pashigian [1962], will serve as the dependent variable in the paper. Other measures of instability, such as turnover, were considered but found to be inappropriate given the airline industry's structure.[11] Relative market share instability was calculated as the percentage point change of share for each carrier in a market for the year-pairs 1974–75, 1975–76, 1978–79 and 1979–80. These changes were divided by their respective shares and then summed for each period of analysis (1974–76 and then 1978–80).[12]

[7] Sampling from a later period was ruled out. By the summer of 1981, the Patco strike and subsequent firing of air traffic controllers led to restricted operations at twenty-two major airports and most likely distorted traffic over the period 1981–82.

[8] CAB, *Origin-Destination Survey of Airline Passenger Traffic, Domestic*, Table 10. Various years.

[9] CAB, *Origin-Destination Survey of Airline Passenger Traffic, Domestic*, Table 6, for the twelve month period ending September 30, 1981.

[10] Also, sampling error is small in heavily traveled markets.

[11] See Cook [1975] for a discussion of various market share measures of rivalry.

[12] $$I = \sum_{i=1}^{N} \left| \frac{MS_{i,t} - MS_{i,t-1}}{MS_{i,t-1}} \right|$$

Where I = relative market share instability, N = number of air carriers in the market, $MS_{i,t}$ = market share of the ith carrier at time t as calculated from the CAB's 10 percent sample of passenger traffic. Thus, the smaller I, the greater the level of stability in a market.

Determinants of market share instability

There are a number of major factors that should either facilitate or limit the effectiveness of cooperative behavior and hence the degree of rivalry in city-pair airline markets. First, the relationship between seller concentration and instability has been a recurring theme in the literature. Because of the structural characteristics of the airline industry, a Herfindahl index (*HERF*) was calculated for each market and then also averaged for the year pairs 1975–76 and 1979–80.[13] One would expect that highly concentrated markets should be characterized by relatively stable market shares, a reflection of passive rivalry. Consequently, *HERF* should be negatively related to the degree of stability, a statistical relationship that has been upheld in the literature.[14]

Secondly, because of scarce airport access, slots (take-offs and landings per hour) are allocated by scheduling committees at four highly congested airports: National in Washington, D.C. (*WASH*), O'Hare in Chicago (*CHI*), Kennedy and LaGuardia (*NY*) in New York City. These committees are authorized by the Federal Aviation Administration and are exempt from antitrust laws.[15] While rivals are explicitly prohibited from discussing any aspect of competition in city-pair markets, there is concern that such an arrangement may have anticompetitive implications.[16] Research has already demonstrated that markets serving the constrained airports of New York and Chicago had higher fares.[17] The higher fares, however, do not necessarily reflect the presence of market power and may indicate the higher opportunity cost associated with scarce airport resources. While that research was not capable of distinguishing between the two, a comparative examination of market share variation in all those markets that involved one of the four slot-constrained airports may reveal a systematic tendency toward greater stability. A dichotomous variable was used to test this hypothesis where markets subject to scheduling committees (*WASH*, *CHI*, *NY*) were assigned a value of one and all other markets were assigned a value of zero.[18]

[13] Very few airline markets have more than a limited number of carriers actually providing service, so that even a two-firm concentration ratio would take on a uniformly high value in every sampled market. Consequently, a Herfindahl index was used where

$$HERF = \sum_{i=1}^{N} S_i^2$$

S_i is the market share of the ith carrier.

[14] See Gort [1963], Ogur [1976], Caves and Porter [1978], Haggestad and Rhoades [1976, 1978].

[15] See Grether, Isaac and Plott [1981] for a discussion and analysis of the dynamics of slot allocations.

[16] In addition to Grether *et al.* [1981], Cohen [1983], Eads [1983], Koran and Ogur [1983, p. 16] have all expressed concern about scheduling committees.

[17] Graham, Kaplan and Sibley [1983, pp. 132–133].

[18] New York City markets include service to Kennedy and LaGuardia airports which are slot-constrained and Newark Airport which is not. The CAB data, however, do not distinguish among these New York City airports and thus neither does this research.

Third, traditional economic analysis has emphasized the relationship between the structure of a particular market and the behavior of firms actually operating in that market. Others have suggested that traditional analysis be broadened to consider the possibility of multiple market contact.[19] A large proportion of an airline's capital cost (i.e., its aircraft) is highly mobile and can be easily shifted from one market to another. Factor mobility makes retaliation a potentially more effective threat since a rival, if provoked, can quickly shift its assets. Firms that meet in many markets may develop a "live and let live" philosophy since action in any one market may induce retaliation in other markets. Conversely, it has been suggested that a positive relationship is also possible where multiple market contact may heighten competitive interaction if rivalry initially is intense.[20]

In order to test for this relationship, a measure of linkage was developed based on the work of Haggestad and Rhoades [1978]. To calculate the number of multiple contacts between major rivals, a matrix was constructed for each of the 123 airline markets in the sample for each period of analysis. What follows is an example of a matrix constructed to identify the number of multiple contacts among rivals of a three carrier market:

Three Carrier Market

$$LK = \begin{bmatrix} l_{11} & l_{12} & l_{13} \\ l_{21} & l_{22} & l_{23} \\ l_{31} & l_{32} & l_{33} \end{bmatrix}$$

where l_{rs} $(r \neq s)$ is the number of times that the rth largest carrier in the market meets the sth largest carrier. The matrix is symmetric ($l_{rs} = l_{sr}$), so the measure of contact—LK^*—is the sum of the off-diagonal terms l_{12}, l_{13} and l_{23}.

If LK^* is zero, major carriers in the market do not meet elsewhere in the sample. The greater LK^*, the greater the number of contacts among major rivals. In order to account for the fact that some carriers only compete in a relatively small number of markets, the measure (LK^*) was divided by the total number of markets in the sample in which the three carriers operated:

$$\overline{LK} = \frac{LK^*}{\sum_{i=1}^{3} m_i}$$

where $\overline{LK}$ is the adjusted measure of linkage and m_i is the number of markets in the sample in which the ith carrier operates.

Two additional variables were included in the analysis. First, during the period 1978–80 a number of markets experienced entry by a new carrier(s)

[19] See Haggestad and Rhoades [1978] for an excellent discussion and Scherer [1980, pp. 340–342] for a survey of conflicting evidence.

[20] This was first suggested as a possibility by Solomon [1970].

that subsequently seized a share of the market.[21] In order to control for the instability caused by entry, a dichotomous variable (*ENTR*) was used whereby markets in which at least one competitor entered and claimed 10 percent or more of the market's passengers were assigned a value of one. All other markets were assigned a value of zero. The coefficient of this variable should be seen, at least partially, as an indicator of the arithmetic adjustments that must follow from an entrant's capturing 10 percent of the market. Finally, labor strikes have contributed to a loss of market share and therefore general instability in a number of markets.[22] A dichotomous variable (*STRIKE*) was used to account for this disturbance.

The impact of deregulation

A pooled regression equation was estimated using data for both the 1974–76 and 1978–80 period. In order to determine whether market share instability had actually increased because of deregulation, a dichotomous variable (*DEREG*) was included to capture those aspects of deregulation such as pricing flexibility and the threat of potential competition that could not be attributed to other variables in the model. Observations covering the 1978–80 period were assigned a value of one and those covering the 1974–76 period a value of zero.

Structural changes may have also taken place within the model indirectly, causing a change in instability. For example, the behavioral relationship between instability and the three slot-constrained airports has certainly changed because of deregulation. In an attempt to control for these parametric changes, a dichotomous variable ($D = 1$ for the 1978–80 period) was used to create a set of six additional interactive variables.

IV. EMPIRICAL RESULTS

The results of the pooled regression are shown in Table I. Because the regression was specified in semilog form, the coefficients measure the proportional change in instability. The dichotomous variable *DEREG* was positive and significant, indicating that a 57 percent increase in relative instability can be directly attributed to deregulation.[23] These results provide strong support for the conventional view that regulatory reform did change the nature of rivalry in commercial airline markets.

[21] While a decision by a major competitor to withdraw from a market would have had an equally disruptive effect, no such occurrence was recorded.

[22] Information on airline strikes is found in the technical notes, CAB, *Air Carrier Financial Statistics*, various issues.

[23] The coefficient was adjusted in accordance with Halvorsen and Palmquist [1980, pp. 474–475].

TABLE I
THE IMPACT OF AIRLINE DEREGULATION ON INSTABILITY USING POOLED DATA FOR BOTH 1976–78 AND 1978–80 SEMILOG SPECIFICATION, DEPENDENT VARIABLE = LOG(I)

Regressors	*Estimated Coefficients**	*Regressors*	*Estimated Coefficients**
HERF	-0.51^b	$HERF \times D$	-0.62^c
	(-1.70)		(-1.34)
CHI	-0.09	$CHI \times D$	0.13
	(-1.14)		(1.20)
NY	-0.22^a	$NY \times D$	0.27^a
	(-2.88)		(2.44)
WASH	-0.17^c	$WASH \times D$	0.08
	(-1.50)		(0.51)
$\overline{LK}$	0.78^a	$\overline{LK} \times D$	-0.55
	(4.05)		(-1.19)
ENTR	0.17^b	$STRIKE \times D$	-0.14
	(2.05)		(-0.97)
STRIKE	0.26^b	*INTERCEPT*	1.79^a
	(2.65)		(9.80)
DEREG	0.45^b	Adj R^2	0.26
	(1.68)		

* t values are given in parentheses.
Significance levels are: a = 1%; b = 5%; c = 10%.

In general, the model's other variables conformed to expectations. While all slot-constrained airports had the predicted direction of influence, both *NY* and *WASH* exhibited a statistically significant tendency toward greater stability. Conversely, labor strikes (*STRIKE*) and new carrier entry (*ENTR*) tended to destabilize market shares. As anticipated, the concentration variable *HERF* was significant and had the hypothesized direction of influence. The variable $\overline{LK}$ was positive and significant, a reasonable expectation in an industry where rivalry is often intense to begin with and where it is easy for a carrier to retaliate and engage the same rival in another market.

With one exception, the results indicate that very little additional instability comes from the interactive variables. The greater instability displayed by the variable $NY \times D$ may be explained by separate regression estimates that suggested that the ability of airport scheduling committees to exercise market power during the 1978–80 period was considerably reduced.[24] Even though the coefficient for $HERF \times D$ is negative, the sum of the coefficients for *DEREG* (0.45) and $HERF \times D\,(-0.62)$ remain positive up to the point where *HERF* exceeds 0.726.[25] Therefore, deregulation had a greater positive effect in less concentrated markets and a lesser (but still positive) effect in all but the extremely concentrated markets.

[24] For a discussion of these separate regression results, see Sandler [1984, pp. 140–166].
[25] A Herfindahl index of 0.726 is only reached in a two carrier market where the leading firm has approximately 83 percent of the market.

V. CONCLUSIONS

Recent changes in national aviation policy have provided an excellent opportunity to explore the changing nature of rivalry in the airline industry. It was clearly demonstrated that instability, and hence the degree of rivalry, was significantly greater during a period in which carriers were allowed to operate under conditions of considerable freedom. In addition, deregulation had a positive affect in all but the extremely concentrated airline markets.

It is possible to use the same analytical framework to assess the impact of regulatory reform on other industries. Limitations on price competition are frequently imposed on many regulated industries so that it is often difficult to compare the behavior of rivals before and after regulatory reform. Using market share instability allows one to compare the changing relationship between behavior and important structural factors.

RALPH D. SANDLER,
Business and Management Department,
Spring Hill College,
Mobile, Ala. 36608,
USA.

ACCEPTED JANUARY 1987

REFERENCES

BEHRMAN, B., 1980, 'Civil Aeronautics Board', In *The Politics of Regulation*, edited by James Q. Wilson (Basic Books, Inc., New York), pp. 91–120.

CAVES, R. E. and PORTER, M. E., 1978, 'Market Structure, Oligopoly and Stability of Market Shares', *The Journal of Industrial Economics* (June), pp. 289–313.

COHEN, M. S., 1983, 'The Antitrust Implications of Airline Deregulation', *The Antitrust Bulletin* (Spring), pp. 172–173.

COOK, E. F., 1975, 'Market Share Measures of Rivalry', unpublished dissertation, Case Western Reserve University.

EADS, G. C., 1983, 'Airline Competitive Conduct', *The Antitrust Bulletin* (Spring), pp. 164–165.

GORT, M., 1963, 'Analysis of Stability and Change in Market Structure', *Journal of Political Economy* (February), pp. 51–63.

GRAHAM, D. R., KAPLAN, D. P. and SIBLEY, D. S., 1983, 'Efficiency and Competition in the Airline Industry', *Bell Journal of Economics* (Spring), pp. 118–138.

GRETHER, D. M., ISAAC, R. M. and PLOTT, C. R., 1981, 'The Allocation of Landing Rights by Unanimity Among Competitors', *American Economic Review* (May), pp. 166–171.

HAGGESTAD, A. and RHOADES, S. A., 1976, 'Concentration and Firm Stability in Commercial Banking', *Review of Economics and Statistics* (November), pp. 443–452.

HAGGESTAD, A. and RHOADES, S. A., 1978, 'Multi-Market Interdependence and Local Market Competition in Banking', *Review of Economics and Statistics* (November), pp. 523–532.

HALVORSEN, R. and PALMQUIST, R., 1980, 'The Interpretation of Dummy Variables', *American Economic Review* (June), pp. 474–475.

HYMER, S. and PASHIGIAN, P., 1962, 'Turnover of Firms as a Measure of Market Behavior', *Review of Economics and Statistics* (February), pp. 82–87.

JACOBY, N. H., 1964, 'The Relative Stability of Market Shares, A Theory and Evidence from Several Industries', *Journal of Industrial Economics* (March), pp. 83–107.

JOSKOW, J., 1960, 'Structural Indicia: Rank-Shift Analysis as a Supplement to Concentration Ratios', *Review of Economics and Statistics* (February), pp. 113–116.

KORAN, D. W. and OGUR, J. D., 1983, U.S. Federal Trade Commission, Bureau of Economics, *Airport Access Problems: Lessons Learned from Slot Regulation by the FAA*, Washington, D.C.

OGUR, J. D., 1976, U.S. Federal Trade Commission, Bureau of Economics, *Staff Report on Competition and Market Share Instability*, Washington, D.C.

SANDLER, R. D., 1984, 'Market-Share Stability in Commercial Airline Markets and the Impact of Deregulation', unpublished Ph.D. dissertation, Florida State University.

SCHERER, R. M., 1980, *Industrial Market Structure and Economic Performance*, 2nd ed. (Rand McNally, Chicago), pp. 340–342.

SOLOMON, E. H., 1970, 'Bank Merger Policy and Problems: A Linkage Theory of Oligopoly', *Journal of Money, Banking and Credit* (August), pp. 323–326.

WELLES, C., 1986, 'Is Deregulation Working?' *Business Week*, December 22, 1986, pp. 50–55.

THE JOURNAL OF INDUSTRIAL ECONOMICS 0022-1821 $2.00
Volume XXXVI March 1988 No. 3

THE EFFECTS OF PROPERTY RIGHTS ON LABOR COSTS OF NONPROFIT FIRMS: AN APPLICATION TO THE DAY CARE INDUSTRY*

ANNE E. PRESTON

This paper estimates differences in labor costs between nonprofit and for-profit firms in the day care industry. A theoretical model which draws on the property rights literature as well as recent theories of nonprofit labor markets predicts that the magnitude and sign of the nonprofit salary differential will depend on specific characteristics of the samples analyzed. Empirical results reveal that in the most competitive segment of the day care industry, the nonprofit salary differential is insignificant. However, in the less competitive, government subsidized segment of the industry, the nonprofit differential is significantly positive; it ranges from 5 to 10 percent.

I. INTRODUCTION

THE ECONOMIC theory of property rights predicts that, once ownership and control are separated within an organization, managers will not necessarily minimize costs. While this theory is often used to explain differences in behavior between owner-controlled and manager-controlled firms, it can also be used to explain differences in the behavior of nonprofit and profit-making firms. Because there is no owner to which the nonprofit manager is held accountable, there are even fewer constraints on his behavior than would be found in a manager-controlled, for-profit firm. Therefore, input costs of manager-controlled non-profit firms may be higher than those of manager-controlled for-profit firms. While there is considerable empirical support for the property rights hypothesis,[1] recent empirical studies documenting low economy-wide nonprofit wages[2] seem to negate the theory's importance in explaining differences in labor costs between nonprofit and for-profit firms.

Theoretical explanations for this negative nonprofit wage differential in economy-wide samples have not been fully developed or tested. Some explanations attribute the observed nonprofit differential to imperfect industry or occupational controls.[3] Other researchers claim that the differential has a

* The author would like to thank Susan Rose-Ackerman for her thoughtful comments on an earlier draft.

[1] See Furobotn and Pejovich [1972] for a survey of this literature.

[2] Both Mervis and Hackett [1983] and Preston [1987] find that, when comparing otherwise identical individuals, wages of the nonprofit worker are insignificantly lower than those of the for-profit worker.

[3] There is little evidence to support this hypothesis. Inclusion of occupational controls in wage equations causes the nonprofit differential to become more negative (see Preston [1987]) rather

theoretical basis: relatively low nonprofit wages are a result of socially conscious workers willing to supply labor at lower than market wages to institutions which generate social benefits.[4]

This study develops a model of relative labor costs of for-profit and nonprofit firms which explains both a negative economy-wide nonprofit wage differential and a positive intraindustry nonprofit wage differential. The model incorporates two theoretical forces proposed in previous studies: the property rights hypothesis, which argues that the nonprofit manager may pay higher wages than his for-profit counterpart, and the hypothesis that nonprofit workers may supply their labor at lower than market wage rates to firms producing social benefits. These theoretical forces would produce a non-negative nonprofit differential within a narrowly defined industry where the services provided by nonprofit and for-profit firms and the social benefits of these services are very similar. In addition, if the industry is not perfectly competitive, the differential may be positive as nonprofit managers pursue utility maximization.

Empirical tests use data on caregivers in the day care industry. The sample is well suited for empirical analysis of these theoretical predictions: first, there should be little difference in social benefits provided by nonprofit and for-profit day care centers; second, there are identifiable subsections of the day care industry in which firms operate under different degrees of competition.

II. DISCRETION OF MANAGERS AND DONATIONS BY WORKERS

Differences between nonprofit and for-profit firms can be traced to differences in legal treatment.[5] For example, by state law, only those nonprofit firms whose services generate social benefits will be awarded preferential tax treatment and the privilege to solicit tax deductible donations. As a result, there is a difference in the nature of goods in the two sectors: nonprofit goods and services should generate a higher level of social benefits than do for-profit goods and services. In addition, because of the difference in tax status, nonprofit firms earn a greater amount of donative revenue than do similar for-profit organizations, all else equal. Furthermore, federal law prohibits the nonprofit firm from distributing profits to those individuals in control of the organization. Therefore in imperfect markets, nonprofit firms may be operating under strategies different than profit maximization. These legal restrictions may alter outcomes observed in labor markets through their

---

than move towards zero. Intra-industry studies are difficult to perform because of data limitations. However the two studies which do exist, Weisbrod's study of lawyers [1983] and Borjas *et al.*'s study of nursing homes [1983], both document a negative nonprofit differential. The Borjas *et al.* study finds that this negative differential is significant only in the case of a comparison of religious nonprofit and for-profit nursing homes.

[4] Weisbrod [1983] and Preston [1987] both present this hypothesis of worker behavior as a potential explanation for the low nonprofit wages.

[5] For a more complete treatment of the legal issues surrounding nonprofit incorporation, see Hansmann [1980].

effects on the demand for labor by the nonprofit firm and the supply of labor by the nonprofit worker.

With respect to worker supply decisions, the stipulation in state laws that the nonprofit firm must provide social benefits becomes important. Following previous theoretical developments, the model here assumes that a worker's utility is a function of both the wage and the perceived social benefits generated by the firm.[6] Any worker, who places a positive utility on contributing to social welfare and who perceives the social benefit of a product to be positive, will be willing to donate or forgo a portion of the wages he earns in the nonprofit firm producing that good. This loss in wages amounts to a "labor donation". As long as social benefits generated by a nonprofit firm are greater than those of a for-profit firm and the demand for nonprofit workers is less than or equal to the supply of socially conscious workers, the equilibrium labor donation will be positive. Therefore, supply forces put downward pressure on nonprofit wages.[7]

The demand for labor is derived from the process in which the firm maximizes its objective function. Because federal law forbids nonprofit firms from distributing profits to managers, the nonprofit manager may have discretion to maximize personal utility at the expense of profits in imperfectly competitive markets. If nonprofit managers value a highly paid or qualified work force, it is conceivable that utility maximization may result in elevated wages and overly qualified personnel. These inefficiencies should be more pronounced in a nonprofit firm than in a for-profit firm because there is no market for corporate control in the nonprofit sector. Therefore legal restrictions affecting the demand for labor may result in upward pressure on nonprofit wages.

Differences in the demand for labor by nonprofit and for-profit firms must also take into account that, because of differential tax treatment, nonprofit firms will receive more donative income than will for-profit firms. The amount of donations received by a firm is modeled as a positive function of the social benefits generated by the firm's good and the efficiency of the firm. As a result, while additional donative revenue can be used by nonprofit managers to buy increased levels of utility, this inefficient behavior will be tempered, the more sensitive donations are to firm efficiency.[8]

[6] Social benefits of a particular good are subject to extreme measurement difficulties both because they are not easily translated into dollars and because their magnitudes vary according to the interpretation of the analyst. For the purposes of the model, a worker's utility need only be dependent on perceived social benefits, the benefits to society which the worker himself perceives to be tied to the good produced by the nonprofit firm.

[7] Donating money to a socially beneficial organization and donating labor to the organization are probably imperfect substitutes since donating labor allows more control over provision of the service.

[8] One can extend the argument here to include the cost of in-kind donations (such as volunteer labor and donated capital equipment) in the donations function. This additional type of donation further decreases the costs to nonprofit firms allowing non-profit managers the discretion to funnel more revenue into salaries without increasing the price of the service.

Two conflicting theoretical forces determine the size and the magnitude of the nonprofit wage differential. On the demand side of the labor market, managerial discretion in imperfect markets may allow the nonprofit manager to funnel excess profits back to workers in the form of increased wages. On the other side of the transaction, socially conscious workers may be willing to supply labor at lower than market wages to institutions which generate social benefits. The strength of these competing forces and the resulting sign of the nonprofit wage differential depends on the industry market structure, the social benefit differentials between the nonprofit and for-profit firms within the sample, and the degree of competition in the market for donations.

Within a narrowly defined industry such as day care, the social benefits associated with the service may be high, but the social benefit differentials between nonprofit and for-profit firms is likely to be small. Thus the supply forces putting downward pressure on wages should be similar for nonprofit and for-profit firms. The size of the demand force within the industry depends on the degree of product market competition and the goals of the nonprofit day care center.

III. INDUSTRY CHARACTERISTICS

The day care center industry is one of the few four-digit industries which houses large for-profit and nonprofit sectors: according to Rudney and Weitzman [1983], approximately 60 percent of the industry's workers were employed by nonprofit centers in 1980. Similar to most nonprofit services, the day care service is privately consumed yet it has positive social externalities. Society benefits from the education of its youth and the labor productivity of its young women. These general social benefits may be heightened when child care is consumed by underprivileged and minority families.[9]

In general the industry structure can be characterized as monopolistic competition. According to the census definition, establishments must provide child care and supervision as a primary service and may provide educational programs as an additional service. Therefore services may be differentiated along a variety of different dimensions including location, clientele characteristics, and quality characteristics. Products have a small fixed cost component both in absolute cost terms and in relation to total costs; therefore barriers to entry due to economies of scale or high absolute costs are minimal.[10] The only other potential obstacles to entry are the licensing requirements instituted by state and local day care agencies. State and local day care codes vary

[9] For a more complete discussion of the private and public benefits of day care provision, see Young and Nelson [1973].

[10] Thompson [1972] estimates that labor costs represent roughly 75% of total costs in the industry in 1971, while the data used in the current analysis shows that labor costs account for approximately 63.3% of costs. In addition many day care supplies, such as books and toys, are variable costs.

greatly, but they usually control program characteristics, enrolment policies, staff qualifications, group size, and staff-to-child ratios. Most researchers have found that these regulations are so lenient that compliance is almost automatic.[11]

In 1976–1977, the years in which this study's data were collected, federal regulations applied to centers which served federally funded children. These regulations, the Federal Interagency Day Care Requirements (FIDCR), were adopted in 1968 and used as standards for centers receiving federal funds under Titles IV-a and IV-b of the Social Security Act, certain provisions of the Equal Opportunity Act, and other federal legislation.[12] Federal regulations generally required higher quality levels than did state regulations. FIDCR established standards for group sizes, child-to-staff ratios, nutrition, medical examinations, social services for families, child development counseling, and parental participation. In 1976 the regulations were written into law with the Title XX Amendments to the Social Security Act, and strict penalties were instituted for non-compliance. However, controversy over this strict enforcement procedure led Congress to put a moratorium on the federal enforcement of the child-to-staff ratio standards in 1976 while the FIDCR regulations were reconsidered. Enforcement was not suspended for centers receiving federal reimbursement under Title IV and the Child Care Food Program of the Department of Agriculture (CCFP), and Title XX centers were not allowed to increase their child-to-staff ratios above 1975 levels. In 1980 the FIDCR regulations were abolished, and federally funded centers were required to follow state and local regulations exclusively.

The complexity of the requirements for federal funding and the actual regulations themselves probably resulted in an elevation of entry barriers into the federally funded branch of the industry. Jackson [1973] finds evidence that the fragmented nature of the federal grant programs provided such a confusing array of funding sources, specifications, and matching requirements that there was a large fixed cost of information gathering involved in starting a federally funded center. In addition compliance with the higher quality standards in the federal regulations increased both marginal costs and fixed costs of provision.[13] There is some question as to whether federal quality standards were met since the federal regulations were never strictly enforced, and the moratorium was in place at the time of this study. However, Coelen *et al.*'s initial analysis of these data [1979] finds that federally funded centers were much more likely to comply with FIDCR than were non-federally funded centers. (67% of the federally funded centers and 38% of the non-federally funded centers complied with the federal child-to-staff requirements.)

[11] See Coelen, Glantz and Calore [1979] and Kushman [1979].

[12] All federal aid to day care is channelled through the state. Title IV-a and IV-b of the Social Security Act correspond to AFDC and child welfare service programs respectively.

[13] See Rose-Ackerman [1983] for a discussion of the effects of compliance with federal regulations on costs.

In addition the moratorium and its varied requirements on different types of federally funded centers probably created new complexities, further increasing the information costs facing centers entering the federally financed portion of the industry. The high fixed costs created by federal regulation elevated entry barriers, potentially allowing equilibrium profits to exist. Because nonprofit centers are not legally allowed to distribute profits, any surplus in these centers might have been used to finance non-cost minimizing activities, such as higher levels of pay and worker quality.

Therefore firms within the market may have been operating under differing degrees of competition. Specifically, those firms subject only to state and local regulations acted as monopolistically competitive firms where the resulting equilibrium was an allotment of market space such that each center maximized profits to survive.[14] However, centers in the federally funded and regulated segment of the industry may have had a certain amount of monopoly power allowing non-cost minimizing activities and profits to persist. As a result, the property rights prediction of higher salaries in nonprofit firms should exist in the less competitive, federally financed portion of the industry. Therefore centers will be divided according to whether they were subject to FIDCR regulations.[15] The nonprofit salary differential will be calculated for each of the two subsamples.

IV. THE DATA AND ECONOMETRIC SPECIFICATIONS

To study salary differences of nonprofit and for-profit day care centers, I use data collected by Abt Associates for the 1976–77 National Day Care Center Supply Study.[16] The questionnaire asks about a variety of center character-

[14] Rose-Ackerman [1986] investigates market responses to interstate differences in demand. She finds that the presence of nonprofit and government subsidized centers may affect inframarginal prices, but on the margin, the industry behaves like a monopolistically competitive industry containing only profit maximizing firms.

[15] The data used in this study identify centers which receive government subsidization. Federal law allows state agencies to waive federal child-to-staff ratios in centers which serve no more than 5 subsidized children (or 20% of enrolment whichever is lower). The study also identifies centers which are eligible for this waiver. Because the impeded competition of the federally financed sector results from both the information costs involved with entry and the fixed costs associated with the federal standards, the less competitive subsample includes only those federally financed centers subject to the FIDCR regulations. The second subsample consists of centers that are not subject to FIDCR regulations (i.e. those centers which receive no federal subsidization plus those federally financed centers which are eligible for a waiver of the regulations).

[16] From lists of licensed centers collected by state day care offices, a state-by-state random sample was created such that one of every 7.2 centers in a state was drawn from the original sample to participate in the subsample. In order to be included in the Abt study a center was required to meet several requirements: the center provides non-live-in day care services, is open at least 25 hours per week, has the capacity to care for at least 13 children, operates at least nine months per year, and enrolls predominantly non-handicapped children. Centers which did not meet these requirements were dropped from the population. The final sample included 3167 centers. Abt surveyed each of the centers by telephone, and the results of the study are presented in Coelen, Glantz and Calore [1979].

istics including staffing, financing, quality levels, and nonprofit status. Since the focus here is the labor force of nonprofit and for-profit day care centers, all government run centers (including centers run by public schools and head start programs) are excluded from the sample. In order to analyze the effects of different degrees of competition within the industry, the total sample is divided into the FIDCR and the non-FIDCR subsamples as described in section III. All analysis is done separately on these two subsamples.

An empirical model of salary determination for caregivers in the day care industry is used to estimate nonprofit salary differentials and the effects of monetary donations on salaries within different sectors of the industry. The following reduced form log salary equation is estimated using human capital, demographic, regional and institutional controls.

$$\ln(SALARY_i) = a_1 + b_1\vec{X}_i + c_1\vec{Y}_i + d_1\vec{R}_i + f_1 NP_i + \varepsilon_i$$

where $SALARY_i$ = weekly caregiver salary in firm i;
$\vec{X}_i$ = vector of human capital and demographic controls;
$\vec{Y}_i$ = vector of center-specific controls;
$\vec{R}_i$ = vector of region controls;
NP_i = dummy variable determining nonprofit status;
ε_i = residual assumed $N(0, \sigma^2)$

The unit of observation is the center. Because information is only available on the range of salaries in each center, the equations are estimated separately for the minimum weekly salary and the maximum weekly salary.

The labor demand equation contributing to this reduced form equation models the demand for labor as a function of the wage, the quality of the personnel, and the demographic characteristics of the personnel. Because individual characteristics are not available, group characteristics at each center are used to control for labor quality. Mean, minimum, and maximum education and experience levels for caregivers are included in each log salary equation. Other labor quality controls include the percentage of workers in the firm who have received special child care training, and dummy variables representing the employment of a social worker, a nurse, a child development specialist, a hearing, speech, or vision specialist, or a psychologist. Demographic controls, the percentage of the staff who are male, black, or other minority, account for any discriminatory differences in pay.

Labor supplied is a function of the wage, the social benefits associated with work, and the difficulty of the work. Center-specific characteristics used as proxies for the difficulty of the job are the percentage of children who are mentally retarded, physically handicapped, or emotionally disturbed, child-to-staff ratios, and staff-to-director ratios. Because increases in each of these variables signal increased levels of responsibility, positive relationships between these variables and salaries are expected.

The theoretical model of section II predicts that increased levels of social benefits shift the supply of labor out putting downward pressure on wages. Unfortunately controls for social benefit provision are at best imperfect. Because it is assumed that day care provision to the underprivileged generates greater social benefits, the percentage of enrolled children who are black, other minority, or from single-parent families are added to the regression. If these variables are correlated with differences in social benefit provision, the theoretical model predicts negative coefficients in salary equations. Unfortunately a conflicting hypothesis argues for the opposite correlation: children from single parent homes or low income households may be less disciplined, thus increasing the difficulty of the caregiver's job.

Two variables representing parental participation may indirectly exert pressure on wages. Involvement of parents in staff selection may result in higher quality personnel being hired. In addition parental involvement in budget review may minimize the independence of managers who try to use excess profits to pad the wage bill.

In order to estimate the nonprofit salary differential, a nonprofit dummy variable is included in the equation. As noted in section II, nonprofit status may affect both the supply and the demand of labor, putting conflicting forces on the salary. In the supply equation the nonprofit variable may be a proxy for a higher level of social benefits, and in the demand equation it may indicate looser control over a manager's discretionary use of funds.

Finally the impact of donative revenue on salaries must also be taken into account since the level of donations received by day care centers varies by nonprofit status. Here donations are defined as revenue originating from sources other than the recipient of the service; therefore donations include government subsidies, revenue from welfare departments, and cash received from private individuals or institutions.[17] The theory described in section II models donations received by a firm as a positive function of social benefits produced by the firm and the efficiency of the firm. Because the level of wages may signal the degree of efficiency of a firm, donations are not exogenous to the model. Therefore, a two equation system is estimated using two-stage least squares. The two structural equations are the salary equation outlined above with a donations variable included and the following donations equation:

$$DON_i = a_2 + b_2 SIZE_i + c_2 CC_i + d_2 SALARY_i + f_2 NP_i + g_2 P_i + \varepsilon_i$$

where DON_i = monthly donations received by center i measured in thousands of dollars;

$SIZE_i$ = the number of children enrolled in center i;

CC_i = clientele and program characteristics of center i;

P_i = dummy variable determining whether parents help raise funds.

[17] The monetary donations variable gives all donations received in an average month and is measured in thousands of dollars.

The sign on the predicted donations variable in the salary equation is ambiguous. If donations are highly sensitive to inefficiency, donations will be given to the most efficient firms, and extra profits will be channelled into social benefit provision, which in turn leads to higher labor donations. Here the behavior of monetary donors monitors firm behavior. However, if donations are insensitive to inefficiency, they become an extra revenue source which managers can channel into perquisites, such as high quality personnel or above-market wages. An interaction between the donations variable and nonprofit status will also be added to the equation. This interaction term determines whether donations are funnelled into higher than market wages to different degrees in the nonprofit and for-profit firms.

V. RESULTS

Table I presents the nonprofit and donations coefficients from salary equations estimated separately for the non-FIDCR and the FIDCR centers.[18] (The complete set of coefficient estimates are presented in Appendix A.) In the

TABLE I
CROSS-SECTION ESTIMATES OF NONPROFIT SALARY DIFFERENTIALS FOR FULL-TIME CAREGIVERS

Dependent Variable	*(1) Maximum Salary*[a]	*(2) Maximum Salary*	*(3) Maximum Salary*	*(4) Minimum Salary*	*(5) Minimum Salary*	*(6) Minimum Salary*
	Panel a: Non-FIDCR Centers [n = 1210]					
Nonprofit	0.030	0.012	0.003	−0.007	−0.018	−0.026
	(0.019)	(0.218)	(0.002)	(0.017)	(0.018)	(0.019)
Donations[b]	—	0.115**	0.069	—	0.070	0.026
		(0.052)	(0.070)		(0.043)	(0.057)
Donations × Nonprofit	—	—	0.068	—	—	0.064
			(0.066)			(0.054)
	Panel b: FIDCR Centers [n = 695]					
Nonprofit	0.102***	0.115***	0.099***	0.050**	0.058***	0.050***
	(0.030)	(0.022)	(0.043)	(0.023)	(0.023)	(0.022)
Donations	—	0.016***	0.012	—	0.009**	0.008
		(0.006)	(0.009)		(0.004)	(0.007)
Donations × Nonprofit	—	—	0.005	—	—	0.002
			(0.010)			(0.007)

[a] All dependent variables have been transformed into natural logarithms.
[b] Donations are measured in thousands of dollars. The donations variable entered into the equation is the predicted value derived from the reduced form donations equation.
* Significant at the 0.10 level using a two-tailed test.
** Significant at the 0.05 level using a two-tailed test.
*** Significant at the 0.01 level using a two-tailed test.

[18] An F-test was performed to test the hypothesis that the coefficients in the FIDCR equations and the non-FIDCR equations were identical. The hypothesis was rejected at the 0.01 significance level for the maximum salary equation and only at the 0.25 significance level for the minimum salary equation.

non-FIDCR centers in panel a, the nonprofit differential is insignificant for both the maximum salary equation (column 1) and the minimum salary equation (column 4). Adding the predicted donations variable to the equations decreases the estimates of the differentials, and they are still insignificantly different from zero. The coefficients on the donations variable are positive and significantly different from zero at the 0.025 and 0.11 levels for the maximum and minimum salaries respectively. Adding the interaction between donations and nonprofit status has little effect on the estimated coefficients.[19] While point estimates signal that donations are channelled into salaries to a greater extent in the nonprofit centers than in the for-profit centers, the coefficients on the interaction variables are insignificantly different from zero. Evaluating the effect of donations at the average salary levels, a one standard deviation increase in donations ($\sigma = 98$ dollars) from the average level of 178 dollars, increases maximum and minimum weekly salaries by 1.4 dollars and 0.65 dollars respectively in the non-FIDCR centers. In an average center with eight caregivers, roughly one third of donations go into caregiver salaries;[20] the remainder may be used to cover other types of costs, increase directors' salaries, increase quality levels, or, in for-profit centers, increase profits.

The results in panel a of Table I reveal that in non-FIDCR centers, the branch of the industry most closely characterized by the monopolistically competitive model, nonprofit centers behave similarly to for-profit centers and salaries are comparable across the two sectors. Even though donations tend to increase salaries in all centers and nonprofit centers tend to have higher levels of donations,[21] the effect of donations on salaries is small enough that the nonprofit salary differential in the non-FIDCR sector is insignificant even in models which exclude the donations variable.

Panel b of Table I presents results for the FIDCR centers, the less competitive sector of the industry. The coefficients in columns 1 and 4 of panel b reveal that maximum salaries and minimum salaries are approximately 10 percent and 5 percent higher respectively in nonprofit centers than in for-profit centers. Inclusion of the predicted donations variable (columns 2 and 5) causes only slight changes in the magnitudes of the nonprofit coefficients. The donations variable has a small positive, significant effect on

[19] F-tests reveal that, while the coefficients on the two donations variables are insignificant in both the maximum and minimum salary equations, the two variables together have a significant effect at the 0.01 level in the maximum salary equation and at the 0.10 level in the minimum salary equation.

[20] Here, I assume that the average weekly increase for each worker in a center is the average of the increases for the maximum and minimum salaries, or 1.025 dollars. Therefore each workers' monthly increase is just 4.1 dollars. In an average center of 8 workers the increase in the monthly wage bill would be 32.8 dollars.

[21] In this sector of the industry, the average nonprofit center receives 300 dollars of monthly monetary donations, while the average for-profit center receives only 80 dollars of monthly monetary donations.

both maximum and minimum salaries. A one standard deviation increase in donations ($\sigma = 5827$ dollars) from the average level of 3947 dollars increases maximum and minimum weekly salaries by 11.7 and 5.8 dollars respectively. Addition of the interaction term between donations and nonprofit status has little effect on the nonprofit coefficients, and there is no evidence that non-profit centers channel donations into salaries to a greater degree than do for-profit centers.[22]

These results give increased support for an extension of the property rights hypothesis: because the ties between owner and manager are even less clearly defined in nonprofit firms than in manager-controlled, for-profit firms, there is more room for inefficient behavior in nonprofit firms than in for-profit firms.[23] In narrowly defined markets where nonprofit and for-profit firms compete, the nonprofit pay differential will be either zero or positive depending on the degree of competition in the industry. In a competitive product market similar to the non-FIDCR sector of the day care industry, nonprofit firms must remain competitive with for-profit firms, regardless of the relationship between owner and manager. As revealed in this study the nonprofit salary differential will not be positive. Once institutional or governmental barriers impede competition, as is the case in FIDCR centers, property rights considerations lead to possible differences in efficiency levels between the competing firms. Nonprofit centers pay significantly higher salaries than for-profit centers in the less competitive sector of the day care industry.

VI. CONCLUSION

The model of section II suggests that the negative nonprofit pay differentials observed in previous studies may not be consistent across all samples of workers studied. The negative differentials previously observed are the result of dominant worker supply forces where socially conscious workers donate a portion of their wages to socially worthwhile organizations. However opposing this downward pressure on wages is a demand force in which managers use excess profits to finance higher salaries and labor costs. This demand force which puts upward pressure on wages may be dominant in industries or segments of industries where social benefit differentials between nonprofit and for-profit firms are small and where institutional or natural barriers impede competition.

The day care industry provides a useful setting in which to test these predictions. The industry is composed of nonprofit and for-profit centers

[22] Again F-tests reveal that the two donations variables jointly have a significant effect on salaries at the 0.025 level and just under the 0.10 level for maximum and minimum salaries respectively.

[23] The high pay of the nonprofit firms may also serve to increase quality in cases where increased pay reduces turnover and the quality of care is inversely related to turnover.

competing against each other. Furthermore, the degree of competition varies across certain sectors within the day care industry. The non-federally regulated branch of the industry is characterized by free entry and small firms with low fixed costs and zero profits. In the federally regulated sector, large information costs involved with obtaining federal support as well as elevated quality standards impede entry and competition; thus the opportunity for managers to channel excess profits into higher wages may exist. As a result the theoretical model predicts that due to stronger demand-side forces (i.e., the property rights effect) in federally regulated day care centers, the nonprofit wage differential will be greater in this branch of the industry.

Results from salary equations from a cross-section of day care centers support the predictions of the model. In the sample of non-federally financed centers, salary differentials between nonprofit and for-profit centers are not significantly different from zero. On the other hand, in the federally financed and regulated branch of the industry, nonprofit salaries are approximately 5 percent to 10 percent higher than for-profit salaries. In both sectors of the industry increased levels of donations feed into increased salary levels; however this effect is small and has no appreciable effect on the estimates of non-profit salary differentials.

The results are especially important in relation to previous and future research on the nonprofit sector. The positive nonprofit salary differential of the federally financed sector of the day care industry stands in contrast to the negative nonprofit salary differential found in previous studies. These results support the hypothesis that property rights are an important determinant of an organization's efficiency and should be included in a more complete model of wage determination in the nonprofit sector. However, because the theoretical model in this study predicts different nonprofit labor cost differentials in different samples, further empirical studies of the relative salaries in nonprofit organizations are needed. Finally, the pattern, in which nonprofit wages are higher than for-profit wages only in the less competitive sector of the industry, gives empirical evidence that market forces are important determinants of the behavior of nonprofit organizations.

ANNE E. PRESTON,
W. Averell Harriman College,
303 Harriman Hall,
SUNY at Stony Brook,
Stony Brook, NY 11794-3775,
USA.

ACCEPTED APRIL 1987

REFERENCES

BORJAS, G. J., FRECH, III, H. E. and GINSBERG, P., 1983, 'Property Rights and Wages: The Case of Nursing Homes', *Journal of Human Resources*, 18, 2 (Spring), pp. 231–246.

COELEN, C., GLANTZ, F. and CALORE, D., 1979, *Day Care Centers in the U.S., A National Profile, 1976–1977* (Abt Books, Cambridge, Mass.).

FAMA, E. and JENSEN, M., 1983, 'Agency Problems and Residual Claims', *Journal of Law and Economics*, 26, 2 (June), pp. 327–350.

FUROBOTN, E. and PEJOVICH, S., 1972, "Property Rights and Economic Theory: A Survey of Recent Literature', *Journal of Economic Literature*, 10, 4 (December), pp. 1137–1162.

HANSMANN, H., 1980, 'The Role of Non-Profit Enterprise', *The Yale Law Journal*, 39, 5 (April), pp. 835–898.

JACKSON, E., 1973, 'The Present System of Publicly Supported Day Care', in DENNIS R. YOUNG and RICHARD R. NELSON (eds.), *Public Policy for Day Care of Young Children* (Lexington Books, Lexington, Mass.).

JAMES, E. and ROSE-ACKERMAN, S., 1986, The Nonprofit Enterprise in Market Economies, a monograph in J. LESBOURNE and H. SONNENSHEIN (eds.), *Fundamentals of Pure and Applied Economies* (Harwood Academic Publishing, London).

KUSHMAN, J. E., 1979, 'A Three-Sector Model of Day Care Center Services', *Journal of Human Resources*, 14, 4 (Fall), pp. 543–562.

MERVIS, P. H. and HACKETT, E. J., 1983, 'Work and Work Force Characteristics in the Nonprofit Sector', *Monthly Labor Review*, 106 (April), pp. 3–12.

PRESTON, A. E., 1987, 'The Non-Profit Worker in a For-Profit World', unpublished working paper.

ROSE-ACKERMAN, S., 1986, 'Altruistic Non-Profit Firms in Competitive Markets: The Case of Day Care Centers in the United States', *Journal of Consumer Policy*, 3.

ROSE-ACKERMAN, S., 1983, 'Unintended Consequences: Regulating the Quality of Subsidized Day Care', *Journal of Policy and Management*, 3, 1, pp. 14–30.

RUDNEY, G. and WEITZMAN, M., 1983, 'Significance of Employment and Earnings in the Philanthropic Sector, 1972–1982', Program on Nonprofit Organizations Working Paper No. 77, Yale University, New Haven.

THOMPSON, L. C., 1972, 'A Study in Child Care, 1970–71', Vol. 3, *Costs and Quality Issues for Operators*, National Technical Information Service, Document BP-20-63.

WEISBROD, B., 1983, 'Non-Profit and Proprietary Sector Behavior: Wage Differentials among Lawyers', *Journal of Labor Economics*, 1, 3 (July), pp. 246–263.

YOUNG, D. and NELSON, R. R. (eds.), 1973, *Public Policy for Day Care of Young Children* (Lexington Books, Lexington, Mass.).

APPENDIX A

Coefficients from Maximum Salary Equations

	FIDCR		Non-FIDCR	
	Coefficient	Standard Error	Coefficient	Standard Error
1. Intercept	3.646***	0.145	3.923***	0.103
Center Employs:				
2. Hearing, speech, or vision specialist	0.018***	0.041	−0.013	0.041
3. Child development specialist	−0.006	0.023	0.063***	0.021
4. Psychologist	−0.006	0.040	0.021	0.044
5. Nurse	0.012	0.028	0.030	0.024
6. Social worker	0.039	0.026	0.003	0.031
Education:				
7. Maximum	0.037***	0.010	0.021***	0.008
8. Minimum	0.007	0.010	−0.011	0.009
9. Mean	0.028	0.018	0.046***	0.015
Experience:				
10. Maximum	0.006**	0.003	0.0002	0.002
11. Minimum	−0.012	0.011	0.007	0.006
12. Mean	−0.002	0.010	−0.010*	0.006
Percent of Staff:				
13. Male[24]	0.281**	0.122	0.141	0.088
14. Black	−0.065	0.072	−0.158**	0.064
15. Other non-white	0.138	0.115	−0.100*	0.084
16. Extra child care training	0.066	0.041	0.049*	0.282
Percent of Children:				
17. Black	0.107*	0.059	0.104*	0.056
18. Non-white other	0.037	0.082	0.118	0.071
19. From single parent family	0.054	0.042	0.119***	0.040
20. Physically handicapped	0.012	0.022	0.051**	0.024
21. Mentally retarded	0.015	0.021	−0.079*	0.046
22. Emotionally disturbed	−0.006	0.007	0.002	0.016
Region:				
23. Northeast	0.061*	0.033	0.016	0.030
24. Southeast	−0.014	0.043	−0.079***	0.027
25. Midwest	−0.002	0.031	−0.101***	0.025
Other:				
26. Child-to staff ratio	−0.002	0.002	−0.0003	0.001
27. Director-to-staff hours	−0.221*	0.124	−0.045	0.033
28. Parents staff	0.039	0.028	0.004	0.033
29. Parents review budget	0.035	0.028	0.024	0.024
30. Enrolment	−0.00003	0.0003	0.001**	0.0003
R^2	0.295		0.251	

* Significant at the 0.10 level using a two-tailed test. ** Significant at the 0.05 level using a two-tailed test.
*** Significant at the 0.01 level using a two-tailed test.

[24] The percent of the staff that are male has a large, significant, positive effect on maximum salaries in FIDCR centers. However the addition of this variable to the model causes explained variation in maximum salaries to increase by only 2 percent. While this coefficient may be signaling discriminatory pay practices, further analysis would be necessary to prove this hypothesis.

THE JOURNAL OF INDUSTRIAL ECONOMICS 0022-1821 $2.00
Volume XXXVI March 1988 No. 3

CARTEL STABILITY IN SEALED BID SECOND PRICE AUCTIONS

THOMAS VON UNGERN-STERNBERG

One of the great advantages of sealed bid second price auctions is that they lead to very simple bidding strategies. This paper shows that they also suffer from a major inconvenience: They greatly facilitate collusion among the participants, even if the cartel's designated winner is *not* the one with the highest valuation.

I. INTRODUCTION

THERE is a substantial theoretical literature on the properties of different types of auctions. The most widely studied are the English auction (where the price is increased till there is only one bidder left); the Dutch auction (where the price is decreased till a bidder claims the object), the *first-price* sealed bid auction (where the bidder placing the highest bid obtains the object at a price equal to his bid); and the *second*-price sealed bid auction (where the highest bidder obtains the object at a price equal to the second highest bid). A model of particular interest for studying these various forms of auctions is the *independent private values model.* In that model a number of risk neutral bidders bid for a single indivisible object, of which they know the value it has for themselves but not for the other bidders. Within the framework of this model a number of equivalence results about the four auction forms briefly described above have been proven:

(a) the Dutch auction and the first price sealed bid auction (henceforth first price auction) are strategically equivalent;
(b) the English auction and the second price sealed bid auction (henceforth second price auction) are strategically equivalent;

and, most strikingly,

(c) all four auction forms lead to identical expected revenues for the seller.

These results would seem to indicate that sellers should be indifferent as to the form of auction that is chosen. Furthermore, in both the English auction and the second price auction, the bidders have a very simple *dominant* bidding strategy. In the English auction each bidder continues bidding until his own valuation of the object is reached. In the second price auction each bidder places a bid equal to his own valuation.[1]

In view of these equivalence results and the simplicity of the dominant strategies it is somewhat surprising that second price auctions are practically

[1] For a more detailed description of the various forms of auctions and a summary of the results c.f. Milgrom and Weber [1985].

never held in real world situations. When sealed bid auctions are used in the allocation of construction contracts, for example, it is usually the first price auction that is chosen and never (to my knowledge) the second price variety.

One potential explanation for this observation is, of course, that the sellers have not really understood how auctions work. They believe they will get a better deal if they take the price of the highest bid rather than the second highest bid. While there is probably some justification to this line of argument, it is certainly not particularly satisfactory from a theoretical point of view, and unlikely to be the whole story.

An interesting alternative explanation was recently suggested by Robinson [1985]. In a most stimulating paper he argues that second price (and English) auctions are more likely to facilitate *collusive behaviour* on the part of the bidders than first price (and Dutch) auctions. In view of the fact that collusion is widely believed to play a considerable role in real world auctions this is, of course, a strong reason *not* to employ the second pricc variety.[2]

Robinson limits his analysis to the case of one shot auctions. He proves that adhering to the cartel rules is an *incentive compatible* strategy for the case of second price (or English) auctions but not for first price (or Dutch) auctions. In proving these results he considers *only* the case where the designated winner is also the one with the highest valuation of the object, i.e. the one who would win the object even in the absence of a cartel (though he would then, of course, pay a higher price). This last limitation is quite significant. While in a one shot auction it is certainly the case that the cartel can maximize its aggregate profits by having as designated winner the member with the highest valuation, there are a number of important reasons why this strategy will not usually be observed in real world situations. To understand this, note first of all that most real world cartels take the form of *repeated games.* Rather than making direct side-payments the designated winner can then reward his colleagues by abiding with the cartel rules when their turn as designated winner comes along. Deviant behaviour is thus discouraged by the threat of retaliation in some subsequent stage of the game. While this way of organizing a cartel does lead to lower aggregate profits as compared to a strategy where the designated winner is always the one with the highest valuation, it does have significant advantages: First, agreements of this kind are usually harder to prove than agreements involving direct side-payments. In countries where cartels are illegal this is an important consideration. Second, the fear of losing contact with the customers will usually constitute a compelling reason for the less efficient producers (the bidders with lower valuations) to prefer actively participating in production rather than living off the side payments they receive from the more efficient cartel members, even if this does lead to lower *short run* profits. As Scherer notes: A high cost firm "would surely not consent to such a drastic step" (shutting down its own

[2] C.f. Finsinger [1986] for some Swiss data on cartellization in the case of government construction contracts.

production plant) "unless an ironclad agreement were reached assuring that it would receive a substantial share of the enhanced industry profits".[3] The empirical evidence available from Switzerland (where cartels are by and large legal) indicates that, as a rule, the inefficient cartel members receive very little income in the form of side payments and produce most of their sales volume themselves. Indeed, it may well be the case that the most important welfare losses caused by the Swiss cartels arise from the continued operation of inefficient producers and not from the much vaunted dead weight triangles.[4]

II. INEFFICIENT DESIGNATED WINNERS

In view of these observations it seems of some interest to study the extent to which different auction forms facilitate collusion when the designated winner is *not* also the bidder with the highest valuation of the object. It turns out that the second price auction is still the one most apt to facilitate collusion. The interactions leading to this result are, however, rather different to those occurring when the designated winner is the one with the highest valuation.

To show this, let us first introduce the following notation: Assume there are H bidders $i = 1 \ldots H$, whose valuations of the objects are given by v_i, $i = 1 \ldots H$. Without loss of generality assume we have ordered the bidders in such a way that we have $v_{i-1} < v_i$, $i = 2 \ldots H$. The bidder with the highest valuation is thus bidder H. The *bid* of bidder i (with valuation v_i) is denoted b_i, and the bid of the designated winner w (with valuation v_w) is denoted b_w. Finally, the reservation price of the seller, i.e. the price at which he will keep the object rather than sell, is equal to R.

When the designated winner is also the one with the highest valuation (the case analyzed by Robinson) all the designated winner has to do to stabilize the cartel is to pursue his own dominant strategy. Place a bid b_H equal to his own valuation v_H. The other cartel members then realize that they cannot make any profits by deviating from the cartel strategy: The only way for the other cartel members to win the object is to place a bid $b_i > b_H$. This would allow them to win the object but only at the price b_H offered by the designated winner, i.e. a price exceeding their own valuation. (Because $v_i < v_H$, and $b_H = v_H$ we must have $v_i < b_H$.) Any cartel strategy where the designated winner asks the other cartel members to bid some price arbitrarily close to the seller's reservation R (or not bid at all) is thus incentive compatible.

When the designated winner w is *not* also the one with the highest valuation (that is, $v_w < v_H$) this argument no longer works. All those cartel members with a higher valuation than the designated winner (i.e. all those for whom $v_i > v_w$) can make a positive profit by outbidding the designated winner if he plays his dominant strategy (bid $b_w = v_w$). However, the designated winner can pursue an alternative more successful strategy. *He deviates from his*

[3] C.f. Scherer [1980, p. 159].
[4] C.f. the reports of the Swiss Cartelcommission.

dominant strategy, and places a bid that exceeds his own valuation (that is $b_w > v_w$). By *committing* himself to placing a bid exceeding the highest valuation of all other cartel members, i.e. placing a bid such that

$$(1) \qquad v_i - b_w < 0, \qquad i = 1 \ldots H$$

he can once again create a situation where no one has any incentive to deviate from the cartel agreement.

The essential difference between first and second price auctions for the purposes of cartel stabilization is thus as follows: In a first price auction, the cartel members can control only one economically relevant parameter, the price bid by the designated winner. As soon as this price is below the valuation of any cartel member, there is the possibility of profitable deviation from the cartel strategy by those members with higher valuations. In a second price auction, the situation is different. The cartel has *two* economically relevant parameters at its disposal: the price bid by the designated winner and the highest price bid by the other cartel members. In the case of a stable cartel, the designated winner obtains the contract at the price of the second highest bid. This opens the following possibility: First the cartel determines the highest price to be bid by the other cartel members, i.e. the price to be paid by the designated winner. The designated winner then *commits* himself to place a bid which is so high that no cartel member can expect to make any profit by overbidding him. This high bid by the designated winner robs the other cartel participants of any incentive to deviate from the cartel agreement. The cartel can effectively use the designated winner's bid to *preempt* any of the other cartel participants from cheating.

The commitment by the designated winner to place a very high bid is easiest to make in the case of sealed bid second price auctions. All he has to do is publicly post the envelope containing his bid. Commitment is less easy in the case of English auctions. In these auctions there is always the possibility of the designated winner changing his strategy as the auction proceeds (the price gets too high). The conclusion is thus that second-price auctions are most open to collusive agreements.

III. THE ROLE OF OUTSIDERS

The logic of the argument of the previous section indicates that the designated winner in a second price auction does not even have to know the highest valuation v_H. All he has to do is commit himself to an arbitrarily high "fantasy bid" in order to ensure cartel stability. In practice he would be very unwise to pursue a policy of this kind. To understand this one must increase the realism of the model of the previous section by introducing the possibility that cartel outsiders may also participate in the auction. The presence of cartel outsiders complicates the designated winner's problem in the following way: The higher he places his own bid b_w above his own true valuation v_w, the lower is the probability of a cartel member deviating. For $b_w > v_H$ the probability of deviation is 0. On the other hand, if the designated winner places a bid $b_w > v_w$ there is the possibility of an outsider placing a bid b_0 that lies somewhere between b_w and v_w. The designated winner would then incur a loss equal to $b_0 - v_w$. The designated winner will have to take this into account when formulating his own optimal bid. To formally derive the designated winner's optimal bidding strategy, let us start off with the assumption that all the other cartel members have agreed to place bids of R (the seller's reservation price) and that there is only *one* outsider. The designated winner does not know this outsider's bid b_0.[5] His subjective belief is that it is distributed according to the frequency distribution $f(b_0)$ with cumulative density function $F(b_0)$. The designated winner's subjective probability that one of the cartel members will cheat on the agreement and overbid him if he places a bid of b_w is given by the cumulative density function $[1-G(v_w)]$ with frequency distribution $g(v_w)$.

The designated winner's expected profits can now be determined as follows: If he is overbid by one of the cartel members his profits are zero. This event occurs with probability $(1-G(b_w))$. If the designated winner is not overbid by a cartel member, four types of situations can arise: The outsider places a bid in excess of b_w the designated winner's profits are then zero; the outsider places a bid between b_w and v_w; the designated winner then makes a loss of $(v_w - b_0)$; the outsider places a bid b_0 between v_w and R; the designated winner then makes a profit of $(v_w - b_0)$; the outsider places a bid lower than R; the designated winner then makes a profit of $v_w - R$. Weighing these various events by their probabilities, we see that the expected profits of the designated winner are equal to

$$\Pi_w = [1-G(b_w)]0 + G(b_w)[A] \tag{2}$$

with

$$A = 0\int_{b_w}^{\infty} f(b_0)db_0 + \int_{v_w}^{b_w} f(b_0)(v_w - b_0)db_0 + \int_{R}^{v_w} f(b_0)(v_w - b_0)db_0 + F(v_w)[v_w - R]$$

If the designated winner is risk neutral, he will set b_w so as to maximize his expected profits. Deriving (2) with respect to b_w we obtain that the designated winner's optimal bidding strategy b_w^* is given by

$$\frac{\delta \Pi_w}{\delta b_w} = 0 \rightarrow G(b_w^*)f(b_w^*)(b_w^* - v_w) = g(b_w^*)[A] \tag{3}$$

Equation (3) is easy to interpret. The LHS gives us the increase in expected losses of the designated winner resulting from the fact that by placing a bid of

[5] As we are talking about second price auctions, the outsider's bid b_0 will, of course, be equal to his valuation v_0.

v_w he increases the probability of overbidding the outsider who may himself have placed a bid marginally lower than b_w. The designated winner will balance this against the increase in expected profits which results from the fact that his higher bid reduces the cartel members' incentives to deviate.

Note that one would expect to have $g(b_w) = 0$ for all $b_w > v_H$, as no cartel member has any incentive to deviate, if the designated winner's bid is greater than the highest evaluation of any cartel member. Equation (2) thus also tells us that we will always have $b_w^* < v_H$ provided only that $v_w < v_H$ and $f(v_H) > 0$. Unless the designated winner is himself the cartel member with the highest valuation, the fear of being outbid by an outsider will always cause him to reduce his own bid below v_H. There is then always some incentive for the most efficient cartel member(s) to break the cartel rules. An important further insight can be obtained by differentiating Π_w with respect to b_w at the point $b_w = v_w$. We obtain

$$\text{(4)} \qquad \frac{\delta \Pi_w}{\delta b_w | b_w = v_w} = g(b_w) \cdot A > 0 \quad \text{if} \quad A > 0 \quad \text{and} \quad g(b_w) > 0$$

Equation (4) tells us that the designated winner always has an incentive to increase his bid above his own valuation if two conditions are satisfied:

(a) he can thereby reduce the probability of cartel member deviation;

and

(b) he makes positive profits if the other cartel members adhere to the cartel rules ($A > 0$).

The existence of cartel outsiders may reduce but cannot eliminate the designated winner's incentive to increase his bid above his own valuation in order to encourage cartel discipline.

Extending the analysis to the case of more than one cartel outsider is straightforward. All one has to do is to change the interpretation of the function $f(b_0)$. Rather than being the density function of the bid of the one outsider, one has to reinterpret it as being the density function of the *highest* outsider bid. The rest of the analysis then goes through exactly as before.

IV. REPEATED AUCTIONS

The formal analysis remains essentially the same if one allows for the repeated game nature of many cartel agreements. The essential modification brought about by the possibility of future retaliation is that potential deviants must now trade-off the profits to be made by cheating on the cartel in the current period, against the costs of retaliation (e.g. exclusion) in future periods. Denote by r_i the expected costs the cartel can cause member i if he deviates from the cartel agreement in the current period. Deviation will then be profitable for member i in the current period only if the current profits he thus generates exceed these future costs, that is $(v_i - b_w) > r_i$. Similarly the designated winner can stabilize the cartel if he places a bid b_w such that

(5) $v_i - b_w < r_i, \quad i = 1 \ldots H$

Comparing (5) and (1) we see that the need to employ the designated winner's current bid as a tool to prevent deviation decreases as the possibilities of future retaliation increase.

The importance of this result emerges when seen in the context of the analysis of the previous section. It was shown there that the danger of being overbid by outsiders will prevent the designated winner from placing a bid too far in excess of his own valuation. The analysis here indicates that it is by no means necessary for the designated winner to place a bid equal to the highest valuation in order to ensure cartel stability. The repeated game nature of many cartel agreements will provide a first (important) incentive to adhere to the cartel agreement. A relatively modest difference between the designated winner's bid and own valuation (that is, $b_w - v_w$) may then be sufficient to ensure cartel stability.

V. CONCLUSION

Cartels are stabilized by two kinds of forces. The fear of future retaliations and the lack of incentives to break the cartel rules even in the current period. This paper has shown that sealed bid second price auctions greatly facilitate the stabilization of collusive agreements for the second reason even if the designated winner is not himself the cartel member with the highest valuation. This is because the designated winner can commit himself to a high price and thus dissuade chiselling by the other cartel members. The designated winner's incentives to pursue such a strategy are to some extent limited by the fear of outsiders also participating in the auction. Nevertheless, policy makers are well advised to think twice about the use of sealed bid second price auctions if there is a danger of collusion among a large fraction of potential bidders. The same conclusions hold, to a lesser extent, for English auctions.

The analysis presented here was performed within the framework of the independent private values model. One would, however, expect similar results to emerge in other, more complicated auction models as well. The main force driving the results was the fact that a high bid by the designated winner reduces a potential chiseller's expected profits. This should have a dampening effect on the incentives to deviate from cartel agreements in most kinds of auctions.

THOMAS VON UNGERN-STERNBERG,
DEEP,
Université de Lausanne,
Ecole des H.E.C.,
CH-1015 Lausanne,
Switzerland.

ACCEPTED MAY 1987

REFERENCES

FINSINGER, J., 1986, *Der Submissionswettbewerb* (Haupt Verlag, Bern).

MILGROM, P. R. and WEBER, R. J., 1982, 'A Theory of Auctions and Competitive Bidding', *Econometrica*, 50, 5, pp. 1089–1122.

Reports of the Swiss Cartelcommission (various years).

ROBINSON, M. S., 1985, 'Collusion and the Choice of Auction', *Rand Journal of Economics*, 16, 1, pp. 141–145.

SCHERER, F. M., 1980, *Industrial Market Structure and Economic Performance* (Rand McNally, Chicago).

THE JOURNAL OF INDUSTRIAL ECONOMICS 0022-1821 $2.00
Volume XXXVI March 1988 No. 3

THE MULTINATIONAL ENTERPRISE AND RESTRICTIVE CONDITIONS IN INTERNATIONAL TECHNOLOGY TRANSFER: SOME NEW AUSTRALIAN EVIDENCE

THOMAS G. PARRY*

The paper reports the results of a survey of 393 Australian firms regarding their access to overseas-sourced technology and the extent and nature of restrictions attached to technology transfer. The results suggest that Australian firms are not generally subject to *widespread* binding restrictions attached to technology sourced from overseas. Furthermore, with the exception of restrictions on technology re-licensing, there is no significant difference between foreign- and domestically-owned firms in the incidence of restrictions.

THIS NOTE reports the results of a survey of 393 Australian firms, both domestic and foreign-owned enterprises in the manufacturing, mining and construction sectors, regarding their access to overseas technology and the extent and nature of restrictions attached to technology transfer.

Information was obtained on the access to overseas technology by a sample of "innovating" companies in Australian industry. The information covers the extent of general access to overseas-sourced know-how and the importance of restrictions attached to overseas-sourced know-how. The sample includes subsidiaries of foreign firms (based on a specified definition of an overseas "controlling interest") as well as domestically-owned firms. Details of the sample are set out in the Appendix.

I. ACCESS TO OVERSEAS KNOW-HOW

FIRMS were asked whether they generally have access to the results of the R & D carried out by overseas firms and whether or not a direct charge was levied. As seen in Table I, 75 foreign-owned firms (59 per cent of all foreign-owned firms) generally have access to overseas know-how from all sources (primarily from their foreign affiliates). These results are very similar to those for an earlier survey of foreign-owned firms in Australian manufacturing by Parry and Watson [1979]. In that study of 196 foreign-owned enterprises operating in the Australian manufacturing sector (no domestically-owned

* This paper is based on a major study of R & D and innovation in Australian industry undertaken for the Department of Industry, Technology and Commerce by Price Waterhouse Government Liaison (Price Waterhouse [1985]). The comments of two referees on an earlier draft of this paper are gratefully acknowledged.

TABLE I
GENERAL ACCESS TO OVERSEAS KNOW-HOW* (No. of Firms)

	Foreign-owned	*Domestically-owned*
Yes	75	62
No	52	204
Total	127	266

* From parent or affiliate or other foreign enterprise.

firms were included in the survey), 63 per cent had access to overseas know-how from overseas affiliate firms.

In the current survey, only 62 domestically-owned firms (23 per cent) have access to overseas know-how from all sources, primarily from unaffiliated foreign enterprises. Hence, foreign-owned firms have relatively greater access than domestically-owned firms to overseas know-how, primarily (though not exclusively) through their overseas parent or affiliate. This suggests either that MNEs tend to rely on intra-firm technology transfer more than on market transactions or that indigenous firms compared with foreign subsidiaries are less concerned with securing access to overseas technology. In fact other evidence from the main survey suggests that domestic firms have relatively limited access to outside (to the enterprise) technology from all sources.

II. USE-RESTRICTIONS ON OVERSEAS KNOW-HOW

Table II presents data regarding the existence of use-restrictions *which have some impact on the enterprise* attached to the use of overseas know-how. A distinction needs to be drawn between a formal restriction which has no relevance to an individual firm—a nominal restriction—and one which is "binding". A licensee may identify a formal use-restriction which has no practical effect on its operations. For example, a firm may be subject to formal territorial or blanket export restrictions which have no effect because the firm, for various reasons, would not be able to compete in export markets. The use-restriction would still be identified, but it would be of no importance to the

TABLE II
PROPORTION OF FIRMS WITH GENERAL ACCESS TO OVERSEAS KNOW-HOW SUBJECT TO USE-RESTRICTIONS

Restriction	*Foreign-owned*	*Domestically-owned*
Export restrictions	16%	19%
Licensing restrictions	25%	14%
Purchasing requirements	16%	19%

technology-receiving enterprise. A binding export restriction, on the other hand, will limit the technology recipient's ability to export goods or services to one or more markets and, thus, have an important effect on its operations.

Three common types of use-restrictions associated with overseas know-how were included:

- restrictions on the export of products or processes which embody the know-how obtained from the overseas source;
- restrictions on the re-licensing of technology which embodies the know-how obtained from the overseas source;
- requirements to purchase designated raw materials, capital equipment or other inputs.

As shown in Table II, for both foreign- and domestically-owned firms with general access to know-how from overseas sources (137 enterprises in total), use-restrictions with some impact on the enterprise's operations were generally of limited importance.

The most commonly identified use-restriction is that on the licensing of the technology which embodies the overseas know-how. Further, the only significant difference between the incidence of use-restrictions experienced by foreign-owned and domestically-owned firms is in the case of restrictions on technology licensing [Z-test significant at 10%].

For foreign-owned firms, restrictions on licensing were the most commonly identified restriction, with a quarter of these firms with general access to overseas know-how identifying some restriction having an effect on enterprise operations. However, as seen below, such restrictions had relatively little importance in terms of hampering the activities of the technology-receiving enterprise—the "binding" restriction. Only 14.5% of domestically-owned firms with general access to overseas know-how identified licensing restrictions as having any effect at all.

Restrictions on exports and purchasing requirements were identified as having some restrictive effect by only a small proportion of both foreign- and domestically-owned enterprises. There is no significant difference between the responses of foreign- and domestically-owned firms in the other two categories of use-restriction.

Use-restrictions with *some* impact are not widespread for either foreign- or domestically-owned firms, though they are more common in the case of licensing restrictions facing foreign-owned firms. Of considerable interest, there is not a marked difference between foreign- and domestically-owned firms with respect to the incidence of restrictions, with the possible exception of licensing restrictions, where foreign-owned firms are faced with a higher incidence of restrictions. It needs to be remembered, of course, that domestically-owned firms have far less access to overseas-sourced technology in general.

TABLE III
IMPORTANCE OF EXPORT RESTRICTIONS

Level of importance	*Foreign-owned*	*Domestically-owned*
Slight/some	58%	42%
Moderate/high	42%	58%

TABLE IV
IMPORTANCE OF RESTRICTIONS ON LICENSING

Level of importance	*Foreign-owned*	*Domestically-owned*
Slight/some	63%	56%
Moderate/high	37%	44%

TABLE V
IMPORTANCE OF PURCHASING REQUIREMENTS

Level of importance	*Foreign-owned*	*Domestically-owned*
Slight/some	58%	50%
Moderate/high	42%	50%

The incidence of restrictions with an *important* impact in limiting the enterprise's operations in some way is even lower, as seen in Tables III, IV and V. Firms identified the level of importance of the restriction in terms of its effect on enterprise activities. The effect of restrictions was identified as being "slight or of some importance" or "moderate or highly important". There is little difference between the relative importance of these more important binding use-restrictions as between foreign- and domestically-owned firms. There is only a slightly greater impact on the operations of domestically-owned firms associated with all three categories of use restriction.

The proportion of binding restrictions which appear to have an important impact for both foreign- and domestically-owned technology recipients is high, though the absolute number of firms involved in both categories is small. Of course, the real significance of binding restrictions will depend on the nature of the technology involved and the actual value of the lost opportunities to the technology recipient. In this context, then, binding use restrictions with an important effect, associated with both intra-firm and market-based technology transfer, may be significant in parts of Australian industry. Of course, any overall assessment of such restrictions must take into account the legitimate interests of the technology supplier in protecting its proprietary rights in and maximising its returns from the technology.

III. COMPARISONS WITH OTHER STUDIES

Few studies in fact have identified use-restrictions associated with access to overseas know-how which are "binding" as distinct from nominal, nor have other studies attempted to identify "important" effects on the technology-recipient's activities. Most studies of use-restrictions have simply identified the existence of a use-restriction, which may or may not be binding. There are several recent studies which examine the existence of use-restrictions. It is likely that the differences between the findings reported here and those of some other studies lie in the distinction between nominal and binding restrictions.

An earlier study of foreign-owned firms in Australian manufacturing by Parry and Watson [1979] identified restrictions associated with access to overseas know-how from parents or affiliates and other overseas firms. Export restrictions were identified by 37 per cent of firms obtaining know-how from an overseas parent or affiliate, and 60 per cent of (foreign-owned) firms obtaining know-how from an unrelated overseas enterprise. These figures are significantly higher than those for foreign-owned firms reported in this study, though the inclusion of non-binding restrictions in the earlier study undoubtedly accounts for much of this difference.

A survey of licensee companies in the United Kingdom and Canada by Caves *et al.*[1983] found that 34 per cent of licensing agreements were subject to a marketing restriction of some type which may limit the ability of the licensee to export. The study does not distinguish between licensing agreements between related and unrelated firms, nor does the study examine the relative importance of the restrictions in terms of the effect on the licensee's ability to export.

Finally, Contractor's [1981] detailed study of technology licensing suggests a much higher incidence of restrictions on exporting (in the form of territorial restrictions) imposed on licensees than in our own study, but less evidence of purchasing restrictions. Once again, it is likely that Contractor's higher figures include non-binding export restrictions attached to licensing agreements.

It appears, then, that Australian firms obtaining technology from overseas are not generally subject to widespread *binding* use-restrictions. Furthermore, with the exception of restrictions on re-licensing technology, there is no significant difference between foreign- and domestically-owned firms in the incidence of use-restrictions. This finding needs to be interpreted against the relatively limited reliance of domestically-owned firms on overseas-sourced technology in general. In addition, the importance of individual cases of technology transfer which are subject to use-restrictions needs to be taken into account in determining the overall impact of such restrictions on the technology-importing economy. Nevertheless, the findings do suggest that policies which attempt to encourage "unbundling" of the foreign direct investment package in order to minimise the incidence and effects of restrictive conditions in intra-MNE technology transfer need more careful consideration.

THOMAS G. PARRY,
School of Economics,
The University of New South Wales,
Kensington P.O. Box 1,
NSW,
Australia 2033

ACCEPTED JUNE 1987

APPENDIX: THE SAMPLE

The sampling procedure was based on the requirements of the major study of R&D and innovation in Australian industry carried out by Price Waterhouse, Australia [1985] for the Australian Department of Industry, Technology and Commerce. This involved a two-phase sampling approach. The first phase comprised a short mail-out questionnaire sent by the Australian Bureau of Statistics to 3,077 enterprises in the Australian manufacturing, mining and construction sectors. The coverage was designed to include all enterprises previously identified by the Australian Bureau of Statistics as involved in R&D plus a 10 per cent sample of all other enterprises classified to the mining, manufacturing and construction sectors.

The overall sample was stratified to meet the requirements of the main study and covered firm size—small, medium and large—by employee numbers; receipt of Commonwealth Government Australian Industrial Research and Development Incentive Grants; and, within manufacturing, the level of protection of the industry to which the firm was assigned—high, average and low tariff-equivalent assistance.

It was anticipated (correctly) that the proportion of foreign-owned and domestically-owned firms in the final sample would broadly correspond with the proportions existing in the relevant industry sectors in Australia.

From the phase-one mail-out, 1640 firms responded, of which 1066 firms identified themselves as "innovators"—

- as a result of the enterprise's own technical or industrial activity, having introduced a new or improved product or a new production process, or an improved production process designed to increase efficiency or reduce production costs between 1980 and November, 1984.

From these 1066 innovators, a stratified sample of 393 firms was selected for detailed interview regarding a range of issues, of which access to overseas know-how was one. The stratification of this final interview sample was based on the same criteria as used for phase one plus an additional classification of enterprises according to the technological environment—high, medium or low—of the industry to which they were classified.

The final sample of 393 firms comprised 127 foreign-owned firms (32.3 per cent) and 266 domestically-owned firms (67.7 per cent).

REFERENCES

Caves, R. E., Crookell, H. and Killing, P. C., 1983, 'The Imperfect Market for Technology Licenses', *Oxford Bulletin of Economics and Statistics*, 45, pp. 249–267.

CONTRACTOR, F. J., 1981, *International Technology Licensing: Compensation, Costs and Negotiation* (Lexington, New York).

PARRY, T. G. and WATSON, J. F., 1979, 'Technology Flows and Foreign Investment in the Australian Manufacturing Sector', *Australian Economic Papers*, 18, pp. 103–118.

PRICE WATERHOUSE, 1985, *The Promotion of Indigenous IR&D in Australia and the Effectiveness of the Australian Industrial Research and Development Incentives Scheme* (Department of Industry, Technology and Commerce, Canberra).

We are very grateful to the following, in addition to our Associate Editors, for acting as referees over the past year:

F. Gerard Adams
University of Pennsylvania
Wm. James Adams
University of Michigan
H. Franklin Allen
University of Pennsylvania
Erin M. Anderson
University of Pennsylvania
Albert Ando
University of Pennsylvania
R. W. Bacon
University of Oxford
Stanley M. Besen
Rand Corporation
Roger D. Blair
University of Florida
Marshall E. Blume
University of Pennsylvania
A. Boltho
University of Oxford
G. Bonanno
University of Oxford
Kenneth D. Boyer
Michigan State University
Ralph M. Bradburd
Williams College
Timothy J. Brennan
George Washington University
Eugene F. Brigham
University of Florida
Jeremy Bulow
University of Chicago
Dennis Bushe
Marine Midland Bank, N.A.
M. Casson
University of Reading
Stephen G. Cecchetti
New York University
D. Cracknell
British Telecom Centre
David L. Crawford
University of Pennsylvania
James A. Dalton
Putnam, Hayes & Bartlett, Inc.
Patricia M. Danzon
University of Pennsylvania
E. de Ghellinck
CRIDE
Patrick J. DeGraba
Cornell University
Avinash K. Dixit
Princeton University
R. Dixon
University of Melbourne
S. Domberger
University of Sydney
Espen B. Eckbo
University of British Columbia
J. Edwards
University of Cambridge
Robert A. Eisenbeis
University of North Carolina at Chapel Hill
Gerald R. Faulhaber
University of Pennsylvania
Robert M. Feinberg
Pennsylvania State University
C. C. Findlay
University of Adelaide
Alan A. Fisher
Federal Trade Commission
P. Forsyth
Australian National University
J. R. Franks
London Business School/University of California
Ann F. Friedlaender
Massachusetts Institute of Technology
James W. Friedman
University of North Carolina at Chapel Hill
P. Geroski
Centre for Business Strategy
S. Glaister
London School of Economics and Political Science
Amihai Glazer
University of California
Devra L. Golbe
Rutgers University
Victor P. Goldberg
Northwestern University
Edward L. Golding
University of Florida
Frank M. Gollop
Boston College
Michael Gort
SUNY Buffalo
R. Goss
UWIST

Henry G. Grabowski
Duke University
C. Greenhalgh
University of Oxford
Curtis M. Grimm
University of Maryland
George R. Hall
Putnam, Hayes & Bartlett, Inc.
William F. Hamilton
University of Pennsylvania
Frederick H. deB. Harris
University of Texas at Arlington
Robert S. Harris
University of North Carolina at Chapel Hill
P. Hart
University of Reading
K. Hartley
University of York
Robert G. Hawkins
Rensselaer Poly Institute
Timothy John Hazeldine
University of British Columbia
Wallace E. Hendricks
University of Illinois at Urbana-Champaign
C. Hill
Michigan State University
Barry T. Hirsch
University of North Carolina at Greensboro
Jack Hirshleifer
University of California at Los Angeles
Benjamin Hobbs
Case Western University
P. Holl
City University
Glenn Hubbard
Northwestern University
K. Hughes
University of Manchester
Daniel E. Ingberman
University of Pennsylvania
N. Ireland
University of Warwick
M. Irish
University of Bristol
F. Owen Irvine, Jr.
Michigan State University
William R. Johnson
University of Virginia
Boyan Jovanovic
New York University
David R. Kamerschen
University of Georgia
David L. Kaserman
Auburn University
Barbara G. Katz
New York University
Arnold Kling
Federal Home Loan Mortgage Corp.
John E. Kwoka, Jr.
George Washington University
James Langenfeld
General Motors Corp.
Li Way Lee
Wayne State University
Richard C. Levin
Yale University
Arthur Lewbel
Brandeis University
Frank Lichtenberg
Columbia University
Marvin B. Lieberman
Stanford University
Stan J. Liebowitz
University of Chicago
Peter D. Linneman
University of Pennsylvania
Samuel E. Loescher
Indiana University
C. A. Knox Lovell
University of North Carolina at Chapel Hill
Edwin Mansfield
University of Pennsylvania
R. Marris
University of London
Robert E. Martin
Louisiana State University
Stephen Martin
Michigan State University
Alison Masson
Federal Trade Commission
Steven A. Matthews
Northwestern University
Joseph W. McAnneny
Economists, Inc.
A. J. McGuinness
University of Sheffield
G. Meeks
University of Cambridge
Peter Mieszkowski
Rice University
Richard A. Miller
Wesleyan University

M. Moreaux
Universite des Sciences Sociales de Toulouse
Philip B. Nelson
Economists, Inc.
Richard R. Nelson
Columbia University
Roger G. Noll
Stanford University
G. Norman
University of Leicester
Walter Y. Oi
University of Rochester
Stanley I. Ornstein
University of California at Los Angeles
F. Dale Orr
Bell Canada
Sharon M. Oster
Yale School of Organization & Management
A. Oswald
London School of Economics and Political Science
John C. Panzar
Northwestern University
James L. Pappas
University of Wisconsin
B. Peter Pashigian
University of Chicago
K. Pavitt
University of Sussex
W. Peterson
University of Cambridge
Charles E. Phelps
University of Rochester
Owen R. Phillips
University of Wyoming
J. Pickering
UMIST
Russell W. Pittman
United States Department of Justice
Robert H. Porter
State University of New York at Stony Brook
Andrew W. Postlewaite
University of Pennsylvania
Richard E. Quandt
Princeton University
John Rapoport
Mt. Holyoke College
David J. Ravenscraft
Federal Trade Commission
Jennifer F. Reinganum
California Institute of Technology
Peter C. Reiss
Stanford University
Stanley Reynolds
University of Arizona
Stephen A. Rhoades
Board of Governors of the Federal Reserve System
Jay R. Ritter
University of Michigan
Rafael Rob
University of Pennsylvania
Gary L. Roberts
Federal Trade Commission
A. Romeo
Unilever plc
Thomas W. Ross
Hoover Institution
Geoffrey S. Rothwell
Stanford University
David E. M. Sappington
Bell Communications Research
Mark A. Satterthwaite
Northwestern University
Marius Schwartz
Georgetown University
Roger Sherman
University of Virginia
Hyun S. Shin
Nuffield College
Robin C. Sickles
Rice University
M. Slater
University of Oxford
Richard Spady
Bell Communications Research
Chester S. Spatt
Carnegie-Mellon University
Barbara J. Spencer
University of British Columbia
Pablo T. Spiller
University of Illinois
R. C. Stapleton
University of Cambridge
Hans Stohl
Vanderbilt University
P. Stoneman
University of Warwick
Pankaj Tandon
Boston University
R. Tarling
University of Cambridge

George Tauchen
University of Chicago
Lacy Glenn Thomas
Columbia University
Thomas H. Tietenberg
Colby College
M. Utton
University of Reading
James VanderWeide
Duke University
Philip A. Viton
Ohio State University
Xavier Vives
University of Pennsylvania
Ingo Vogelsang
Boston University
Douglas W. Webbink
Federal Trade Commission
Leonard W. Weiss
University of Wisconsin
Steven S. Wildman
Economists, Inc.
Ralph A. Winter
University of Toronto
A. Wolinsky
University of Pennsylvania
Dennis A. Yao
University of Pennsylvania

CALL FOR PAPERS

ASSOCIATION OF MANAGERIAL ECONOMISTS
SIXTH ANNUAL MEETING

New York, New York
December 28–30, 1988

Three sessions of competitively selected papers will be featured in conjunction with the Allied Social Science Associations (ASSA) Annual Meeting. Theoretical, empirical and policy analyses across a broad spectrum of topics will be featured, including: advertising, competitive strategy, financial decisions, forecasting, innovation, and regulation. Especially encouraged are papers integrating the theory of accounting, finance and industrial organization in topic areas such as: the *market for corporate control* (buyouts, mergers, share repurchases, spinoffs), *managerial labor markets*, *measuring monopoly profits*, and the *information content of accounting data.* Both members and nonmembers are invited to submit papers, offer their services as session chairs and discussants, and/or make program suggestions to:

Professor Mark HIRSCHEY,
AME Program Chair,
Jones Graduate School, Rice University,
P.O. Box 1892, Houston, TX 77251–1892,
Phone: (713) 527–8101, x. 2549.

Submission Deadline: *July 15, 1988.*

P. W. S. ANDREWS MEMORIAL ESSAY PRIZE—£300

The PWSA Memorial Prize of £300 is awarded annually. Competitors for the prize are asked to submit an essay on a subject of their own choice within the general field of Industrial Economics and Theory of the Firm, broadly interpreted. Entry to the competition is open to anyone under 30 years of age (or over 30, if not more than eight years have elapsed since taking a first degree). The essay, written in English, and not exceeding 10 000 words in length, should be a work of original research by the candidate only, not previously published and not previously awarded any other prize.

The winning essay must be submitted to *The Journal of Industrial Economics*, though the decision whether or not to publish it rests with the Editors.

The closing date for entries is 31st December.

Further details are available from:

Miss B. Cox,
University House,
The University of Lancaster,
Bailrigg, Lancaster, LA1 4YX, UK.

The General Editor,
Journal of Industrial Economics,
The Institute of Economics and Statistics,
The University of Oxford,
St Cross Building, Manor Road,
Oxford, OX1 3UL, UK.

The North American Editor,
Journal of Industrial Economics,
Department of Public Policy and Management,
The Wharton School,
University of Pennsylvania,
Philadelphia, PA 19104–6372,
USA.

THE JOURNAL OF INDUSTRIAL ECONOMICS

Published first in October 1952, the *Journal* has a very wide international circulation, and has established itself as the leading journal in the field of industrial economics. It was founded to promote the analysis of modern industry, particularly the behaviour of firms, and the functioning of markets. More specifically it seeks to bring the tools of modern economic analysis to bear on the analysis of real problems of industrial economies.

Contributions are welcomed covering all the major areas of industrial economics. One such area is the relationship between market structure and market behaviour in the areas of pricing, product differentiation, advertising and the dissemination of information and R&D. Another area focuses more directly on the firm, its objectives, finance, investment and growth. A third area comprises the background environment within which industrial firms operate: the changing structure of industry, public policy on monopoly and restrictive trade practices, regulation, fiscal and monetary policies as they affect firms, and underlying changes in productivity and international competitiveness.

The *Journal* has a tradition of publishing a blend of theory and evidence. Theoretical discussion is welcomed provided that the more abstract theory includes sufficient introduction and other explanation to convey the significance of the material to the general reader who wants to decide whether to follow the analysis through. Empirical analysis, and especially econometric analysis, should include an explanation of the data sources used, of the methods applied and of the underlying theoretical basis of the study. The *Journal* has a particular tradition of case studies of firms and industries, which the Editors would wish to continue. However, contributors of such studies are asked to remember that a study will be of interest to the international readership of the *Journal* only if it makes a particular contribution to the methodology of such studies, or if the empirical results are exceptionally interesting.

Alongside articles of more normal length, the Editors are ready to publish shorter notes, especially where these give interim results of important research studies, or where they report significant new empirical results. Books are not reviewed, but substantial review articles will be considered for publication.

Information for Contributors

Submissions (*three* copies are required) should be well written, clearly typed and carefully prepared for the printer in accordance with the *Journal*'s 'Notes for Contributors' (*Journal of Industrial Economics*, 35 (March 1987), pp. 359–363), copies of which may be obtained from the General Editor. An Abstract, conforming to the requirements of *The Journal of Economic Literature* and not exceeding 100 words, must accompany each submission.

Typescripts from North America should be sent to the North American Editor, Journal of Industrial Economics, Department of Public Policy and Management, The Wharton School, University of Pennsylvania, Philadelphia 19104, USA.

Typescripts from *all* other countries should be sent to the General Editor, Journal of Industrial Economics, Institute of Economics and Statistics, University of Oxford, St Cross Building, Manor Road, Oxford OX1 3UL, UK.

Information for Subscribers

The *Journal* is published four times a year, in September, December, March and June, by Basil Blackwell Ltd., 108 Cowley Road, Oxford OX4 1JF, UK, *or* PO Box 1320, Murray Hill Station, NY 10156, USA.

	UK	Overseas	USA
Institutions	£34.00	£43.00	$76.00
Individuals	£17.00	£22.00	$35.00
Students	£8.00	£10.00	$15.00

The reduced rates will be allowed to any individual student for a maximum period of three years.

CONTRIBUTORS TO THE ISSUE

GIACOMO BONANNO: Nuffield College, University of Oxford, UK.
JOHN VICKERS: Nuffield College, University of Oxford, UK, and Editor of this *Journal*.
FREDERICK HARRIS: University of Texas at Arlington, USA.
ERIC RASMUSEN: Anderson Graduate School of Management, University of California, USA.
THOMAS W. ROSS: Hoover Institution, USA, and Carleton University, Ottawa, Canada.
MASAHIRO ABIRU: Fukuoka University, Japan.
RALPH D. SANDLER: Spring Hill College, USA.
ANNE E. PRESTON: W. Averell Harriman College, USA.
THOMAS VON UNGERN-STERNBERG: DEEP, Université de Lausanne, Switzerland, and Associate Editor of this *Journal*.
THOMAS G. PARRY: University of New South Wales, Australia.

US Mailing: Second class postage paid at New York. Postmaster: Send address corrections to: Journal of Industrial Economics, c/o Expediters of the Printed Word Ltd., 515 Madison Avenue, New York, NY 10022 (US Mailing Agent).

Reprints of Back Volumes: Volumes 1–28 of the *Journal* are available (in complete volumes only) from the Kraus Reprint Corporation, Route 100, Millwood, New York 10546, USA. More recent back issues are available from the publisher at the current single issue price.

Microfilm: An agreement for the supply of microfilm copies from Volume 1 onwards has been made with University Microfilms International, Department PR, 30–32 Mortimer Street, London W1N 7RA, England, or 300 North Zeeb Road, Ann Arbor, Michigan 48106, USA.

Set in Monophoto Times by Advanced Filmsetters (Glasgow) Ltd
Printed and Bound in Great Britain by Whitstable Litho, Kent

THE JOURNAL OF INDUSTRIAL ECONOMICS

Volume XXXVI JUNE 1988 No. 4

CHRISTOPHER BLISS
A Theory of Retail Pricing 375

RONALD BEWLEY and DENZIL G. FIEBIG
Estimation of Price Elasticities for an International Telephone Demand Model 393

DAVID BESANKO, SHABTAI DONNENFELD and LAWRENCE J. WHITE
The Multiproduct Firm, Quality Choice, and Regulation 411

X. MARTINEZ-GIRALT and D. J. NEVEN
Can Price Competition Dominate Market Segmentation? 431

J. C. H. JONES and D. G. FERGUSON
Location and Survival in the National Hockey League 443

ARAKEL BEDROSSIAN and DEMETRIOS MOSCHOS
Industrial Structure, Concentration and the Speed of Price Adjustment 459

Short Articles and Notes

VICTOR GINSBURGH and PHILIPPE MICHEL
Adjustment Costs, Concentration and Price Behaviour 477

ISSN 0022-1821
BASIL BLACKWELL OXFORD ENGLAND

GENERAL EDITOR

On 1 July 1988 the General Editorship will pass to Stephen W. Davies of the University of East Anglia. His work on the diffusion of innovations, international comparisons of productivity, determinants of industrial structure, and the relationship of market structure and performance will be well known to our readers. Bruce Lyons, also of the University of East Anglia, will share the editorial responsibility. Dr Lyons has worked on international trade and industrial organisation, product differentiation, and entry barriers.

From 1 July 1988 all submissions, except for those originating in North America, should be sent to the following address:

General Editor,
The Journal of Industrial Economics,
Economics Research Centre,
School of Economic and Social Studies,
University of East Anglia,
Norwich NR4 7TJ

P. W. S. ANDREWS MEMORIAL ESSAY PRIZE—£300

The PWSA Memorial Prize of £300 is awarded annually. Competitors for the prize are asked to submit an essay on a subject of their own choice within the general field of Industrial Economics and Theory of the Firm, broadly interpreted. Entry to the competition is open to anyone under 30 years of age (or over 30, if not more than eight years have elapsed since taking a first degree). The essay, written in English, and not exceeding 10 000 words in length, should be a work of original research by the candidate only, not previously published and not previously awarded any other prize.

The winning essay must be submitted to *The Journal of Industrial Economics*, though the decision whether or not to publish it rests with the Editors.

The closing date for entries is 31st December.

Further details are available from:

Miss B. Cox,
University House,
The University of Lancaster,
Bailrigg, Lancaster, LA1 4YX, UK.

General Editor,
Journal of Industrial Economics,
Economics Research Centre,
School of Economic and Social Studies,
University of East Anglia,
Norwich NR4 7TJ.

North American Editor,
Journal of Industrial Economics,
Department of Public Policy and Management,
The Wharton School,
University of Pennsylvania,
Philadelphia, PA 19104–6372,
USA.

THE JOURNAL OF INDUSTRIAL ECONOMICS 0022-1821 $2.00
Volume XXXVI June 1988 No. 4

A THEORY OF RETAIL PRICING*

CHRISTOPHER BLISS

Until recently the retail enterprise (the shop) has been comparatively neglected by economic theorists, partly because they assigned little role to retailing. The growth of interest in the problem in recent years reflects the development of models of imperfect information and the revival of interest in location theory. Pricing theory for the retail enterprise, however, remains a neglected area.

After surveying existing models of retailing, the paper concentrates on the idea that the shop saves its customers costs by assembling goods in one place. This introduces an essential non-convexity and importantly affects the conditions under which shops compete with each other and the constraints on their price setting. Under the admittedly unrealistic assumption of full buyer information, a theory of retail pricing is developed.

"Retail prices are frequently regarded as exceptions both to the law of costs and generally to every rational process of price formation, which is all the more remarkable since these prices are the only ones which are of direct interest to the consumer and which are directly influenced by consumption." (*Knut Wicksell*)

I. INTRODUCTION

UNTIL FAIRLY recently, economic theory has had extraordinarily little to say about the retail enterprise. The theory of production and pricing has been mainly addressed to the manufacturing firm and does not readily translate to the case of a shop. With a manufacturer it is usually fairly clear what it is that is being sold, a certain good for which consumers have demands. What is the good which a shop sells? Although shops sometimes make things, as when a supermarket bakes its own bread, this is incidental to the essential function of a shop. The characteristic activity of a retailer is to retail, which is to sell to final consumers what someone else has made. Shops exist and operate profitably because they perform a service which their customers value. The nature of that service might seem obvious. However, there is more than one aspect to it, and according to which aspect is important, the form of retail competition varies.

Tucker and Yamey [1973] reprints short passages in which Mill, Marshall and Wicksell discuss retailing. They indicate that the great economists of the

* Helpful comments on an early draft from Angus Deaton, Peter Diamond, Rudolpho De La Torre Garcia, Andrew Oswald, Hugo Sonnenschein, Konrad Stahl, John Vickers and members of seminars at MIT, Oxford and Princeton, are gratefully acknowledged.

past did not attach much importance to the theory of retail pricing. Nevertheless, Wicksell (in Tucker and Yamey [1973], pp. 24–26) picked out as two points which distinguish the retail enterprise (i) joint supply and (ii) expert knowledge, and much of the later literature elaborates ideas which fall under these headings. The imperfect competition models of the 1930s tended to concentrate attention on the manufacturer. However Lewis [1945] and Hood and Yamey [1951] applied these ideas to retailing. Yet the result was not a completed theory of retail pricing. To this day the great majority of textbooks on microeconomic theory do not treat retailing at all.

We shall ignore in what follows shops' own brands and associated advertising and consider different shops as essentially selling the same goods to a public which, while its preferences may have been influenced by manufacturers' advertising, is nonetheless informed as to what it is buying and what it would pay elsewhere. This is reminiscent of Kaldor [1960] who argued that the establishment of manufacturers' brands had been an important source of economies of scale in manufacturing.

Two recent developments have directed more attention to retailing. First, the revival of location theory, which was pioneered by Hotelling [1929], has naturally pointed attention to retailing, where location is clearly important. Thus Heal [1980] examines the equilibrium and socially optimal patterns of locations for retail outlets for a single product provided to consumers arranged around the perimeter of a circle, with the producer at the centre. Note that in Heal's model retailing is explained by the increasing returns to scale in transportation. The same idea underlies the location model of Stahl [1982a] which, however, includes more than one product. Stahl's observation that transactions costs when overcoming space create relations between markets for physically different commodities makes the same point as underlies our model of retail pricing.

The second development which has focused attention on retailing is the modelling of information, particularly less than perfect information. Salop and Stiglitz [1977] present a model in which informed and uninformed consumers are catered for by different shops. The uninformed choose a shop at random, the informed always go to the cheaper variety. Price dispersion can be an equilibrium so long as the difference in information persists. Varian [1980] models price dispersion through time in his model of sales. These are illuminating models but it is curious that we have sophisticated models of retail pricing under less than perfect information while we lack a model of the retail pricing of many goods under full information.

In fact some past writers saw the need for a model of retail pricing, or of the determination of mark-ups, for the seller of many goods. However the mathematical complexity of the problem defeated them. Nyström [1970] emphasizes the psychological aspects of buyer behaviour more than the economic. Even so, he treats what he calls "assortment price levels" which is close to the shopper's indirect utility function of our model.

In a remarkable paper, Holton [1957] proposed a model of price discrimination, as he called it, in supermarkets by analogy to price discrimination by a public utility. He saw the significance of the shop's overhead costs and of "one-stop shopping", identified variable mark-ups as something to be explained and considered the possibility that so-called "loss-leading" might be economically rational. Holton, however, like others who tackled our problem, lacked the analytical tools to solve it. He failed to provide a completed theory of retail pricing and made some mistakes. Thus, for example, while rightly identifying the importance of cross elasticities of demand, Holton wrongly concluded

> "Because of the much-advertised convenience of 'one-stop' shopping the cross elasticities of demand are negative among countless combinations of goods in the supermarket."

Probably what Holton intended here is that an increase in any price might drive the shopper to another shop taking all her custom with her. But the cross elasticities are not negative in that case, they are undefined. Loosely speaking one might say that they all equal minus infinity. This, however, should remind us that the retailer must respect the constraint that his shop should offer the customer good value. Respecting that constraint, the cross elasticities of demand are those of a normal demand structure. If a shop charges more for coffee, in which case other prices must be reduced to hold the shopper's custom, the demand for tea will rise.

Further problems with Holton's analysis concern his discussion of competition from specialist shops, which is vitiated by the lack of a well-specified shop production function, and his conclusion that the shop will discriminate "in favour of staples". As will be seen, the likely tendency is the opposite, staples will probably be discriminated against. It is unfortunate that so many criticisms must be addressed to Holton's work, for he comprehended a problem which many others failed even to formulate correctly.

II. PLAN OF THE PAPER

We shall concentrate on the determination of retail prices under full information. By itself this gives a misleading picture but even so the analysis fills an important gap in received theory. Various special features of retailing are not independent of one another. Thus transport costs not only help to explain, as we shall argue, the existence of the multi-product shop but also imperfect information. With transport costs one does not visit all shops to discover which offers the best value.

The key to our view of the shop is contained in one word: overheads. The shop itself incurs overhead costs which must be recovered by marking-up the goods that it buys in. The customers also incur overhead costs in coming to the shop and would incur additional costs if they had to visit more than one shop. This is the rationale of the one-stop (or supermarket) shopping to which the model mainly applies.

Our basic assumptions are discussed in section III. The shop cost function is considered in section IV. Imperfect competition is natural to the economics of the shop. However one can consider a case in which the shop must meet a standard of value for money set by its competitors. This case, with some simplifying assumptions, is the subject of section V. The question whether this type of model can explain so-called "loss-leading" is discussed in section VI. Section VII compares the pricing of a profit maximizing capitalist shop with the policy of a cooperative shop operated for the benefit of its members and considers the efficiency of competitive pricing. In section VIII the model is extended to include the influence of turnover on the overhead costs of the shop. The issue of the specialist shop and its competition with the general shop is discussed in section IX. In section X the model is extended to include differences between consumers, specifically their transport costs, and equilibrium conditions for the individual seller in imperfect competition are derived. Section XI offers conclusions and some further interpretations of the model.

III. WHAT SHOPS DO

One of Wicksell's key concepts for retailing was "joint supply". Joint supply is not the same as in the mutton/wool type of example of the theory of the firm. It is jointness of *sale* that provides the distinctive feature of the shop, not jointness of *production*. Conditions of competition underlie the distinction. A monopolistic producer of sheep must take into account the cross price elasticities of demand for mutton and wool but a competitive sheep farmer need only respond to the prices. Where a shop is concerned, however, there is no analogue to the perfectly competitive case of production theory. A shop enjoys a limited but significant natural monopoly of the demand of the shopper who has incurred the costs of coming to the shop. The shopper will not go to another shop to buy her milk because it is a little cheaper there. Rather she will take account of the price of milk, together with all other prices and the costs of going to various shops, in deciding where to shop.

The function of the shop will now be clear. A shop assembles a collection of goods in one place and enables the shopper to select what she wishes at known prices. This saves the expenditure of time which goes with traditional shopping in which the buyer buys from many sellers, each selling a limited range of goods. It also saves the costs associated with "shopping around" in order to obtain each purchase at the lowest price. This concentrated pattern of shopping, characteristic of food purchase in rich societies, is not universal. A very poor buyer will walk a mile to buy cheaper bread, and in rich countries people will shop around if they are buying something expensive.

In the case with which this paper is concerned a shop offers its customers a price list. Suppose for the time being that the cost of visiting two shops is prohibitive. The consumer is assumed to be fully informed of all the prices charged by all the shops. She will therefore choose to go to that shop which, taking account of the cost of getting there, offers the best value. What a shop provides to its customers is a package, defined by a price list (real or notional). The idea of a notional price list is important. Some things "sold" by shops are free: delightful layouts, fawning assistants, etc. Others are priced at infinity, which is only to say that the shop does not sell that item.

In microeconomic theory there is a device for measuring the value of a price list to a buyer—the indirect utility function (see Varian [1984], p. 116). Let p^0 be the vector of wholesale prices, assumed the same for all shops, and let shop s add mark-ups m^s. Assume that the consumer incurs transport costs in going to shop s equivalent to a reduction in money income of T^s.[1] Let her money income before incurring travel expenses be I. Then the value of shopping in shop s is given by the indirect utility function:

(3.1) $$V\{p^0+m^s, I-T^s\}$$

This indirect utility function is not quite the same as appears in standard expositions, although it may be derived from that case. The difference is that only retail prices appear in the function. This is natural as they are the only variables of our theory, but note that the prices of things not purchased in shops, such as the cost of housing, vacations and financial assets, are implicit in the function. It follows that the function of (3.1), unlike the standard indirect utility function, will not be homogeneous of degree zero in prices and income. Clearly what the shopper will do is to choose a value of s for which (3.1) is maximal. This simple maximization fully specifies the consumer side of equilibrium in a simple case of the model.

IV. THE SHOP COST FUNCTION

The specification of the shop cost function is central to a theory of retailing and the failure to realize this is a major deficiency of previous work. There are two elements to the costs of a retail unit: overhead costs and buying-in costs. We assume that goods are bought in wholesale at prices which the shop cannot influence, and that these prices are the same for all shops. This simplification isolates the analysis from the economies of large scale buying. In fact such economies are important. However they lead the analysis to problems of general equilibrium with imperfect competition and these are best postponed.

The overheads of the shop will be represented by the following function:

(4.1) $$\text{Overhead costs} = C(N, x)$$

[1] The assumption that transport costs are equivalent to a reduction in money income is clearly restrictive as in general it might depend upon the prices in the shop. Suppose, for example, that the shop sells petroleum or repairs shoes. However this restriction simplifies the exposition.

where N is the number of customers using the shop and x is the vector of turnover, or sales. The reason why turnover affects overhead costs will be clear, as floor space, display equipment, wastage and the interest cost of holding stock are all included in costs. It is through the $C(\cdot)$ function that the important consideration of rapidity of turnover will be represented. Obviously the number of customers generating a given volume of turnover has a somewhat independent influence on overhead costs.

Although for expository reasons we shall consider a case in which the $C(\cdot)$ function is homogeneous of degree 1 in N and x, this is not a natural or reasonable assumption. Increasing returns to scale are powerfully in evidence in retailing. However these returns to scale in the production of the retail service must be balanced by increasing costs to the marginal customer as the number attracted to a particular shop increases. The balance can only be analysed when we relax the assumption that consumers are identical in tastes, incomes and transport costs.

We may ignore the direct consideration of buying-in costs if we note that a shop's profit on turnover is the inner product of its vector of margins, m and its turnover, x. Hence the shop's operating profit is the difference between profit on turnover and overhead costs; i.e.:

$$\text{(4.2)} \qquad \text{Profit} = m \cdot x - C(N, x)$$

The maximization of (4.2) will be the objective of the shop but there is a constraint which the shop must respect. Its margins, from which follow its retail prices, must be such that it can attract N customers whose summed demands at those prices will be x.

V. THE PRICING POLICY OF A COMPETITIVE RETAILER

We consider the position of an individual shop in a global long-run equilibrium in which all the customers are the same, all could visit any shop at the same cost, and the number of shops and their capacities are such that there is just enough space for all customers. If we assume the $C(\cdot)$ function to be homogeneous of degree 1, then the size of individual shop is of no consequence and we can assume without loss of generality that each shop caters for one customer. The same assumption will guarantee that no shop makes a pure profit, as this would lead to entry. Profit on turnover will exactly equal overhead costs.

An obvious condition of equilibrium is that all shops should offer equally good value for money as measured by the indirect utility function common to all consumers. A shop offering less good value than others would lose custom, while a shop offering an excess of value could raise some prices and increase its profit. Call the equilibrium level of indirect utility that all shops must offer V_0. The most profitable margins that a shop can charge will solve the following constrained maximization problem:

(5.1) $$\max_m m \cdot x(p^0+m) - C\{1, x(p^0+m)\}$$

subject to:

$$V(p^0+m, I-T) \geqslant V_0$$

where $x(p^0+m)$ is the consumer's demand when she faces prices p^0+m, having already paid transport costs T. Before analysing the solution to (5.1), it is interesting to look at a special case which allows an immediate comparison with another branch of theory. Assume therefore that $C(\cdot)$ is independent of x, so that what a shop sells does not affect its overheads. This is equivalent to assuming that the shop has fixed overheads denoted C_0, and (5.1) reduces to:

(5.2) $$\max_m m \cdot x(p^0+m) - C_0$$

subject to:

$$V(p^0+m, I-T) \geqslant V_0$$

The problem (5.2) is most easily interpreted as the decision process of a competitive retailer for whom V_0 is a given value. However, even an oligopolistic retailer who has decided to offer value V_0 would do well to check that his margins solve (5.2). A model in which V_0 is not fixed for the shop is analysed in section X below. If the shop is a monopolist—the only store in town—then the constraint of (5.2) does not apply and the problem reduces to the profit maximization of a multi-product monopolistic firm.

Before solving (5.2), consider an even more special case. Suppose that the shopper enters the shop committed to spending a fixed sum of money independent of the prices that she will find in the shop. Let her budget be B. The shop must collect C_0 for its overheads, so we assume $B > C_0$. All parties will benefit if the welfare that the consumer obtains from spending the remaining $B - C_0$ is maximized.[2] This would be achieved by having the consumer purchase at wholesale prices with the residual income $B - C_0$, which could be realized by having an entry charge of C_0 to use the shop (this is always an optimal arrangement if feasible) and charging wholesale prices inside the shop. However, if entry is free but all prices are marked up at a rate C_0/B the same result will obtain. This is our first result.

R.1 *If the shopper has a fixed budget, margins will be a constant percentage across all goods. Prices in the shop will be* $p_0(B+C_0)/B$.

The result is only applicable as it stands if all mark-ups can be set at will by the shop. Sometimes, however, the shop is restricted by the nature of the case.

[2] This is not to suggest that the shop only wishes to collect its overheads or that it cares about the shopper's welfare. It would obviously like to make as much a profit as possible. In equilibrium, however, the level of V_0 that it must match will be such that it only recovers its overheads.

Thus chandeliers on the ceiling are either free or not provided. They and similar goods are the public goods of retailing. Assuming that such goods have been provided in optimal quantity, and their costs included in C_0, R.1 applies.

If the fixed budget case were typical, the theory of retail pricing would not be interesting. Unfortunately we cannot turn it into an approximate result. If the budget is approximately constant it does not follow that margins will be approximately equal. We now turn to the general case.

Let the Lagrange multiplier attaching to the constraint in (5.2) be λ. Then the necessary condition for a maximum is:

$$(5.3) \qquad x + m \cdot \mathbf{X} - \lambda V_I x = 0$$

where $\mathbf{X}$ is the matrix of partial derivatives of the demand function $x(p^0 + m)$ and V_I is the partial derivative of V with respect to I, both evaluated at the solution. (5.3) incorporates the identity:

$$(5.4) \qquad V_m = -V_I x$$

The condition (5.3) is equivalent to the Ramsey condition for optimal indirect taxation (see Atkinson and Stiglitz [1980], pp. 370–5). Thus (5.3) may be transformed using the Slutsky equations to show that margins reduce all compensated demands in approximately the same proportion. This conclusion is unsurprising because the shop's problem is essentially the same as a problem of optimal indirect taxation. Margins are the equivalent of indirect taxes on purchases and it is in the shop's interest, as a profit maximizer, to collect whatever it collects from the shopper so as to minimally reduce her welfare.

Now the fixed budget case falls into place. With a fixed budget, non-shop expenditure is irrelevant, all shop expenditure can be taxed, taxation is proportional to expenditure on all items. In taxation theory this is equivalent to an income tax. We have now arrived at our second result.

R.2 *Where consumers are not fixed-budget shoppers, margins are set according to Ramsey Tax Rules.*

From (5.3) we obtain a formula for the optimal margins of the following form:

$$(5.5) \qquad m = (\lambda V_I - 1) x \cdot \mathbf{X}^{-1}$$

Unfortunately this formula is hard to interpret intuitively and difficult to apply empirically. If $\mathbf{X}$ has small off-diagonal terms, we can say that goods in inelastic demand attract high margins.[3] However, assuming $\mathbf{X}$ nearly diagonal is known to be a highly restrictive assumption. We can say that if one good is purchased in fixed quantity regardless of prices (which could only be over a

[3] This conclusion runs against Holton's claim that discrimination will be in favour of staples.

certain range of prices) then only that good need attract a margin. This is obvious, as the margin is equivalent to an entrance fee.

One must regret that R.2 as it stands is not easy to apply; however the framework from which it was derived is not as restrictive as may appear. Although simplifying assumptions were employed, the essence of the model is that the consumer has incurred a cost to come to the shop and would have to incur a further cost to go elsewhere. To this extent she is a captive buyer. However, had the shop not offered good value for money she would not have come. Thus the framework is rather general. It covers in particular the non-competitive case. The value offered by a shop is in a sense its "price" and whatever "price" the shop is charging it will set the optimal margins derived from (5.1).

VI. LOSS-LEADING

It is interesting to see whether our model can throw light on "loss-leading". With loss-leading the shop sells one or more items at less than cost. In terms of the model, m has negative components. The terminology carries the suggestion that the shopper is enticed into the shop by the lure of a bargain and once inside will buy other items. This may describe the behaviour of some shoppers but to include it in our account would go against the rational full-information choice on which the model is based. The present analysis, however, opens up the possibility that loss-leading, that is negative elements of m, might be explained as a consequence of optimal shop pricing. Taking into consideration that $\mathbf{X}^{-1}$ is unsigned, we note that a negative element of m cannot be excluded. If $\mathbf{X}$ were implausibly assumed to be diagonal, this would involve a positive element on the diagonal of the uncompensated demand matrix, i.e. a Giffen good, but taking off-diagonal elements into account, not even that is required.

It is not obvious however that loss leading is a phenomenon that needs to be explained. Most examples are probably spurious. The shop may be selling at a sale price to clear excess stock and the price is not below opportunity cost; or the price is low but not below the wholesale price. If the view is maintained that every sale owes the shop a standard rate of mark-up to cover overheads, a view which our theory cannot allow to pass without challenge, then goods with low rates of mark-up are losing. Customers are attracted to the shop and buy goods with high rates of mark-up. The careless observer may conclude that loss-leading has induced the customer to overpay for other items. The fallacy of this conclusion has been thoroughly exposed by our model.

VII. THE PRICING POLICY OF A CO-OPERATIVE SHOP

The problem which the cooperative shop faces is dual to (5.1) and (5.2). Whereas those programmes concern the maximization of profit subject to a welfare constraint, the cooperative shop is concerned with the maximization of welfare subject to the constraint that its profit on turnover shall cover its overhead costs. We continue for the time being with the assumption that overhead costs are constant (this assumption is relaxed in section VIII) together with the other special assumptions of section V, so that we consider a cooperative model dual to (5.2). This takes the form:

(7.1)[4] $$\underset{m}{\text{Max}}\; V(p^0+m, I-T)$$

subject to:

$$m\cdot x(p^0+m) \geqslant C_0$$

This may be compared with (5.2), now denoted (7.2):

(7.2) $$\underset{m}{\text{Max}}\; m\cdot x(p^0+m)-C_0$$

subject to:

$$V(p^0+m, I-T) \geqslant V_0$$

and the duality is apparent. Clearly (7.2) and (7.1) will not generally lead to the same solution for m. If, however, the value of V_0 in (7.2) is the same as the solution for $V(\cdot)$ in (7.1), then m will be the same. Denoting by μ the Lagrange multiplier attaching to the constraint of (7.1), the first-order conditions for a maximum are:

(7.3) $$-V_I x+\mu[x+m\cdot \mathbf{X}] = 0$$

which may be compared with (5.3), now denoted (7.4):

(7.4) $$x+m\cdot \mathbf{X}-\lambda V_I x = 0$$

the necessary condition for the profit maximizing shop. Clearly when V_0 takes the value of the solution to (7.1), all the variables in (7.3) take the same values as in (7.4) and $\mu = 1/\lambda$.

The comparison with a cooperative shop allows an evaluation of the welfare optimality of the profit maximizing equilibrium. If we assume that the shop cannot charge an entrance fee, then Ramsey pricing is the welfare cost minimizing way of collecting from the consumer the overhead expenses necessary to run the shop. Under free entry conditions in which the profit maximizing shop makes no pure surplus of profit over overhead costs, the private shop is indistinguishable from the cooperative, and it solves the same constrained problem. This is an example of the conclusion that a welfare maximizing utility should depart from marginal cost pricing, see Baumol and Bradford [1970]. If it were indeed the case that all consumers were identical on every visit to the shop, shops would surely charge entrance fees and offer

[4] Spence [1980] considers a problem equivalent to this and shows that if consumers differ the cooperative will use quantity dependent prices.

the customer better value. The problem with entrance fees arises when all consumers do not have the same incomes and tastes.

VIII. THE EFFECT OF TURNOVER ON OVERHEADS

We now consider the solution to the more general case of the profit maximizing shop in which turnover affects the overhead component of costs. We hold to the assumptions of constant returns and the uniformity of consumers, so that we may still consider a shop which caters for one customer. We therefore solve (5.1), now denoted (8.1):

$$(8.1) \qquad \max_{m} m \cdot x(p^0+m) - C\{1, x(p^0+m)\}$$

subject to:

$$V(p^0+m, I-T) \geqslant V_0$$

Again denoting the Lagrange multiplier for the constraint by λ, the necessary condition for a maximum is:

$$(8.2) \qquad x + m \cdot \mathbf{X} - C_x \cdot \mathbf{X} - \lambda V_I x = 0$$

which may be compared with the necessary condition for the solution to (5.2), now denoted (8.3).

$$(8.3) \qquad x + m \cdot \mathbf{X} - \lambda V_I x = 0$$

Taking into account the effects of turnover on overhead costs has resulted in an arithmetic addition to the influences already considered. The analogue in (8.2) to m in (8.3) is $m - C_x$. Here C_x is the vector of marginal carrying costs of the various goods. Thus (8.2) tells us that the margins which are subject to the Ramsey pricing principle are margins over and above marginal carrying costs. This finding is summarized in R.3.

R.3 *Under competition with identical consumers and no economies of scale, goods are sold in the shop at prices which are the sum of wholesale prices, marginal carrying costs, and additional margins which go towards paying that part of overhead costs not covered by marginal carrying costs. The level of the third component of the margin on any particular good will be determined by the Ramsey taxation rules.*

Our model is now seen to be in harmony with the view from which many people would start, that margins will be highest on goods with a low rate of turnover or a high wastage rate.

IX. COMPETITION FROM SPECIALIST SHOPS

Will the tendency of shops to price discriminate under one stop shopping give rise to competition from second call shops specializing in the sale of those goods which the general shop prices highly? The possibility of such competition is something which the general shop must take into account as it may limit its ability to price discriminate according to the Ramsey tax rules. The question also arises of whether, when margins contribute towards overheads, competition is beneficial. These issues are the subject of the present section.

First note that competition from second-call shops is not necessarily a development which the first-call shop will wish to counteract.[5] The cost function of a shop may be such that a large scale of operation carries with it diseconomies of scale. In that case, the first-call shop might even benefit if a second-call shop takes part of the job of providing for the customer's needs away from it.

We consider whether competition from second-call shops can be effective. Assume that all shops have the same cost function and that the consumer's cost of visiting any shop is the same cost T. Therefore the cost of visiting two shops will be $2T$. As the consumer may now face two price lists we need a notation for the result of shopping carefully in two shops. We work in terms of the marked-up prices in two shops, p_1 and p_2. Thus $p_i = p_0 + m_i$. We denote by $\downarrow(p_1, p_2)$ the vector formed by taking the minimum of each component of p_1 and p_2, and by $x^i(p_1, p_2)$ the demand vector for goods in shop i $(i = 1, 2)$ when prices in shop 1 and shop 2 are respectively p_1 and p_2.

Let shop 1 set its prices and consider whether another (second-call) shop could induce the customer to undertake an extra visit to take advantage of another set of prices. This is equivalent to the condition that p_2 can be chosen such that:

$$V[p_1, I-T] < V[\downarrow(p_1, p_2), I-2T] \tag{9.1}$$

and

$$C[1, x^2(p_1, p_2)] \geqslant (p_2 - p_0)\cdot x^2(p_1, p_2) \tag{9.2}$$

When (9.1) and (9.2) are both satisfied, the second-call shop 2, charging prices p_2, improves the consumer's welfare, despite the cost of an extra visit, and covers its costs. This is not to say that there will be an equilibrium with two-call shopping, but only that the position with only one shop charging prices p_1 will not be an equilibrium.[6]

The possibility that (9.1) and (9.2) might be satisfied must be taken seriously. The second shop might even be a notional seller representing direct

[5] If an equilibrium is going to arise in which the consumer visits two shops it is of course arbitrary which is designated the first-call and which the second-call. However, starting from the consideration of the case in which only one shop is visited, it is natural to imagine that a second-call, having been previously excluded, becomes possible and to analyse the consequences for the equilibrium of one shop.

[6] Cournot behaviour on the part of entrants as second-call shops is being assumed. Hence the entrant does not take into account the fact that by entering and undermining the profitability of the first-call shop, he ensures that the first-call shop will not continue to operate charging prices p_1.

mail order sale from the manufacturer. Then the second T represents the fixed cost of postage and the trouble of ordering and components of p_2 for which mail order is possible will be low, as mail order reduces costs. Consumers may well find that the trouble and expense of mail order is justified by the saving in prices.

There are cases in which a profit maximizing choice of prices ignoring the possibility that a second-call shop will enter, as in section V, would make a second call shop profitable and undermine the profitability of the first-call shop. This is evidently not an equilibrium. We next ask whether there exist equilibria characterized by two-call shopping in which both types of shop cover their costs. This cannot generally be excluded. However one simple assumption rules it out. With two shops to choose from the consumer pays prices $\downarrow(p_1, p_2)$ and her total demands generate enough revenue over buying-in costs to defray the costs of both shops. Suppose that demand in shop i is x^i $(i = 1, 2)$. Then the summed costs of the two shops is:

$$C(1, x^1) + C(1, x^2) \tag{9.3}$$

Now consider one shop charging prices $\downarrow(p_1, p_2)$ and meeting all the consumer's needs in one place, so saving her T, the cost of one journey. The revenue generated by this shop will be the value designated in (9.3), and its costs will be:

$$C(1, x^1 + x^2) \tag{9.4}$$

If $C(1, x)$ is convex $[-C(1, x)$ is concave$]$ in x and homogeneous of degree 1 in x, we have

$$C[1, 0.5x^1 + 0.5x^2] \leqslant 0.5C(1, x^1) + 0.5C(1, x^2) \tag{9.5}$$

by concavity, and hence:

$$C[1, x^1 + x^2] \leqslant C(1, x^1) + C(1, x^2) \tag{9.6}$$

by homogeneity.

It follows from (9.6) that the two shop state was not an equilibrium. A shop charging suitable prices, which will not perhaps maximize profit assuming no competition from second-call shops, would incur no more costs than the two shops together and would save the consumer expense. We thus arrive at R.4.

R.4 *If the cost function of the shop is convex and homogeneous of degree 1 in x, the only possible type of equilibrium involves one kind of shop.*

This is a special case, but it makes a general point clear. If the eventual outcome is that one type of shop serves the public, but because of potential competition from specialist shops this shop cannot charge the Ramsey prices of section V, then the consumer is worse off as a result of the competition. For we have seen that Ramsey pricing is optimal given the constraint that the shop cannot charge an entrance fee. Competition from specialist shops might interfere with optimality. Of course that harmful form of competition should not be confused with the competition from other first-call shops which ensures that the shop will raise only enough revenue to cover its overhead costs. This is entirely in the consumer's interest.

X. CONSUMERS WITH DIFFERENT TRANSPORT COSTS

Although we have covered a lot of ground, our model is still restricted by the artificial assumptions that all consumers are the same and that the cost function is homogeneous of degree 1 in the number of customers served. When these assumptions are relaxed, the model is greatly complicated, and we make no attempt to provide a general treatment. Rather we consider a simple model in which consumers differ only by their costs of travelling to the shop. The same method may be applicable to differences of taste or income. So the model, although special, illustrates what kinds of result are available. The model treats a problem similar to that treated by Stahl [1982b] although the approach is different.

We change the model so that the number of customers for which the shop caters is determined as part of the solution. We assume that consumers differ only in the distance that they have to travel to reach the nearest shop. Let the cost function $C(N, x)$ not be homogeneous of degree 1 in N. Suppose instead that costs increase less than proportionately to the number of customers served. This tendency to increasing returns will be offset by the increasing cost which the marginal customer will have to incur to travel to the shop. In this way we obtain a simple generalization of the model of section V. Overhead costs will now vary with N and so will the indirect utility which the shop's price list must provide.

Imagine that shops are equidistant from each other around the circumference of a circle, along which consumers are spaced out uniformly. Suppose an equilibrium which apportions consumers equally between shops.[7] Each shop must offer such value that the marginal consumer, the one equidistant from two shops, will be indifferent between shopping in one shop or the other. Again there is a value of V_0 which a shop must offer but now it is the marginal consumer whose custom must be retained. However N is not fixed. Let each shop assume that other shops will not alter their prices in response to a change in its own prices. In equilibrium it must be that no shop will wish to increase or reduce the number of customers attracted by varying V.

Measure distance in units such that adding one unit of distance corresponds to adding consumers at rate 1, and let the cost to a consumer of travelling a unit of distance be γ. Let each shop serve N^* consumers and charge margins m^*. Then the distance which the marginal consumer travels in equilibrium will be $N^*/2$. Were a shop to choose a value of N other than N^*, the value

[7] This may not be the only kind of equilibrium possible.

which the marginal consumer would obtain by going to her alternative shop would be:

$$(10.1) \qquad V[p_0 + m^*, I + \gamma(N^* - N/2)]$$

where m^* denotes the equilibrium value of m. The profit maximization problem (5.1) now generalizes to:

$$(10.2) \qquad \operatorname*{Max}_{m,N} m \cdot \int_0^{N/2} x(p^0 + m, I - \gamma M)dM - C\left\{N, \int_0^{N/2} x(p^0 + m, I - \gamma M)dM\right\}$$

subject to:

$$(10.3) \qquad V[p_0 + m, I - \gamma N/2] \geqslant V[p_0 + m^*, I - \gamma(N^* - N/2)]$$

Here the variable of integration, denoted M, is the distance to the marginal consumer. Denote by Sx the sum of demands given by the integral:

$$(10.4) \qquad \int_0^{N/2} x(p^0 + m, I - \gamma M)dM$$

and let $\mathbf{SX}$ similarly denote the integral of the demand matrices. Let λ be the Lagrange multiplier attaching to (10.3).

The necessary conditions for the solution of (10.2) and (10.3) are,

$$(10.5) \qquad m\colon\ Sx + m \cdot \mathbf{SX} - C_{\mathbf{SX}} \cdot \mathbf{SX} - \lambda V_I x = 0$$

$$(10.6) \qquad N\colon\ m \cdot x - C_N - C_{\mathbf{SX}} \cdot x - \lambda\gamma V_I = 0$$

where $C_{\mathbf{SX}}$ denotes the vector of partial derivatives of overhead costs with respect to the integrals of demands, and V_I and x refer to the marginal utility of income and the demands of the marginal consumer. Here (10.6) takes into account that the derivative of the constraint (10.3) with respect to N, viz.

$$(10.7) \qquad -\gamma V_I[p_0 + m, I - \gamma N/2]/2 - \gamma V_I[p_0 + m^*, I + \gamma(N^* - N/2)]/2$$

is equal in equilibrium, when $N = N^*$, to $-\gamma V_I$.

First compare (10.5) with (8.2), the first-order conditions for a shop with overheads affected by turnover, which is repeated for convenience as (10.8).

$$(10.8) \qquad x + m \cdot \mathbf{X} - C_x \cdot \mathbf{X} - \lambda V_I x = 0$$

At a glance it appears that they are the same condition, except that the sum of demands and of the demand matrices has replaced the demand and the demand matrix of the single consumer. We seem to have Ramsey pricing added to marginal turnover costs again. However closer inspection reveals that (10.5) is not the integral of conditions of the form of (10.8), because the final term, $-V_I x$, is not obtained by integrating over all consumers but is derived from the demand and marginal utility of income of the marginal consumer. Hence, even assuming margins small, we cannot say that margins net of marginal turnover costs approximately reduce all demands proportionately. The term for the reduction of demands in (10.5) is integrated over all consumers, as is the first term involving levels of demands. However the final term, in levels of demand, refers only to the marginal consumer. The condition resembles Ramsey pricing but the marginal consumer is given an additional, negative, weight. Thus we have:

R.5 *With many consumers with different transport costs, the shop will again price discriminate. Margins over marginal turnover costs will reduce all compensated demands proportionately to a weighted difference between total demands and the demand of the marginal consumer.*

Fortunately, there is no difficulty in interpreting (10.6). The Lagrange multiplier λ measures the cost to the programme of having to meet a marginally higher level of value for money for the marginal consumer. γV_I measures the cost to a consumer in utility terms of travelling a little further. Hence $\lambda\gamma V_I$ is the cost to the shop of lowering its prices optimally to attract an extra consumer. Now the meanings of the terms of (10.6), interpreted as gains or losses consequent upon attracting an extra consumer, are detailed in (10.9), which is seen to be a natural marginal condition for optimum shop size:

(10.9) $$m \cdot x - C_N - C_{\mathbf{SX}} \cdot x - \lambda\gamma V_I = 0$$

[*Additional revenue from margins* minus *Additional cost due an extra customer* minus *Additional cost due to extra demand* minus *Cost of being more competitive* = 0.]

We have concentrated on distance from the shop as the factor differentiating one consumer from another. One should also consider differences in tastes and income. It is clear that similar results will be obtainable whenever consumers may be represented by a single parameter such as distance. Hence, if consumers A and B prefer to shop in a certain shop, then all consumers "lying between" A and B, must prefer to shop in the same shop. This property is evident with distance and is not obvious where consumers are arranged along a line by income. With tastes it is not even clear that a one-dimensional representation is adequate. We do not pursue these issues because they lead into a refined location theory that is beyond the scope of the present paper.

XI. CONCLUSIONS

The argument has ranged widely and a summary would be out of place. However one result, that the shop will choose margins according to the Ramsey minimum-welfare-loss rule recurs in some form in all versions of the model. This is fairly obvious when consumers are the same and the value for money which the shop must provide is set by competition. However, Ramsey pricing carries over to other cases, although when the shop is an imperfect competitor the pricing formula is changed and the marginal consumer plays a special role.

There is much that the model leaves out. We have deliberately excluded imperfect information. However, no model of retailing is complete which neglects the issue of information. People trust certain shops. Sometimes this is a question of quality, but sometimes what is trusted is a pricing policy. The consumer lacks information concerning prices in all shops but trusts a certain shop to give good value.

The model was suggested by shopping in the supermarket. However, as the analysis has a simple structure, other interpretations suggest themselves. The essence of the model is that the consumer buys a package and that the costs buying bits and pieces of that package from different sources are high, even prohibitive. Further examples include restaurants, hotels, and such integrated product packages as computer and camera systems. In these examples the consumer commits himself to one price list rather than another, and the model applies.

CHRISTOPHER BLISS,
Nuffield College,
Oxford,
UK.

ACCEPTED SEPTEMBER 1987

REFERENCES

ATKINSON, A. B. and STIGLITZ, J. E., 1980, *Lectures on Public Economics* (McGraw-Hill Inc.).

BAUMOL, W. J. and BRADFORD, D. F., 1970, 'Optimal Departures from Marginal Cost Pricing', *American Economic Review*, LX, pp. 265–283.

HEAL, G., 1980, 'Spatial Structure in the Retail Trade: a Study in Product Differentiation with Increasing Returns', *Bell Journal of Economics*, Vol. 11, No. 2, pp. 565–583.

HOLTON, R. H., 1957, 'Price Discrimination in Supermarkets', *Journal of Industrial Economics*, Vol. 6, pp. 13–32.

HOOD, S. J. and YAMEY, B. S., 1951, 'Imperfect Competition in Retail Trade', *Economica*, NS, 18, pp. 119–137.

HOTELLING, H., 1929, 'Stability in Competition', *Economic Journal*, 39, pp. 41–57.

KALDOR, N., 1960, 'The Economic Aspects of Advertising' in N. KALDOR (ed.), *Essays on Value and Distribution* (The Free Press of Glencoe, Illinois).

LEWIS, W. A., 1945, 'Competition in Retail Trade', *Economica*, 12, pp. 202–234.

NYSTRÖM, H., 1970, Retail Pricing: an Integrated Economic and Psychological Approach, Economic Research Institute, Stockholm.

SALOP, S. and STIGLITZ, J. E., 1977, 'Bargains and Ripoffs: a Model of Monopolistically Competitive Price Dispersion', *Review of Economic Studies*, 44, pp. 493–510.

SPENCE, A. M., 1980, 'Multi-product Quantity Dependent Prices and Profitability Constraints', *Review of Economic Studies*, XLVII, pp. 821–841.

STAHL, K., 1982a, 'Location and Spatial Pricing Theory with Non-convex Transportation Cost Schedules', *Bell Journal of Economics*, 13, No. 2, pp. 575–582.

STAHL, K., 1982b, 'Differentiated Products, Consumer Search and Locational Oligopoly', *Journal of Industrial Economics*, XXXI, pp. 97–113.

TUCKER, K. A. and YAMEY, B. S., 1973, Economics of Retailing (Penguin Modern Economics Readings).

VARIAN, H. R., 1984, *Microeconomic Analysis*, 2nd ed., W. W. Norton & Co. Inc.

VARIAN, H. R., 1980, 'A Model of Sales', *American Economic Review*, Vol. 70, No. 4.

THE JOURNAL OF INDUSTRIAL ECONOMICS 0022-1821 $2.00
Volume XXXVI June 1988 No. 4

ESTIMATION OF PRICE ELASTICITIES FOR AN INTERNATIONAL TELEPHONE DEMAND MODEL*

RONALD BEWLEY AND DENZIL G. FIEBIG

The demand for international telephone calls in Australia is comprised of three components: the operator-connected services; station-to-station and person-to-person and the direct dialling service; ISD. Associated with these individual services are three distinct prices: the ISD tariff, operator-connected tariff and person-to-person surcharge. In order to estimate elasticities for both tariffs and the surcharge an econometric model is developed that has two sub-models, each of which consists of an aggregate equation and an allocation system. One model determines how the total number of calls is allocated among the three services while the second allocates the total number of minutes called between ISD and operator-connected services. The model is estimated using aggregate data for telephone traffic emanating from Australia.

I. INTRODUCTION

INITIALLY all international calls placed in Australia were on a person-to-person basis. Beginning in 1968 a station-to-station service was added and by 1974 all major countries were linked to Australia by this new service. Calls made on a person-to-person or station-to-station basis require operator assistance. In 1976 a further new service that allows for direct dialling, International Subscriber Dialling (ISD), was added. Associated with these individual services are three distinct prices: the ISD tariff, the operator-connected tariff and the person-to-person surcharge. The aim of this paper is to develop econometric models of the demand for each of these services. Specifically, estimates are provided and analyzed for the own and cross-price elasticities of each of the price variables.

The analysis extends the work of existing published studies in a number of aspects. Importantly, previous studies of overseas telecommunications demand (Lago [1970], Yatrakis [1972], Craver [1976], Rea and Lage [1978], Craver and Neckowitz [1980] and Schultz and Triantis [1982]) concentrate only on an aggregate telephone service. Any substitutability that may exist between the constituent services is ignored.

Another deficiency of these studies is that they do not make a distinction

* The authors are indebted to OTC Australia for supplying the data and to the members of the Demand Forecasting Section for their encouragement and assistance. The views expressed are not necessarily shared by the management of OTC. The helpful comments of two anonymous referees and the editor are also gratefully acknowledged. A preliminary version of this paper was presented at the 14th Conference of Economists, Sydney, May 1985.

between the initial decision to make a telephone call and the decision concerning the length of the call. Invariably such studies have either used the total number of calls or the total number of minutes as the dependent variable. Both of these, together with the implicit notion of call duration, are important components of the demand for telephone services and need to be accounted for in the modelling process. It should be noted that this is the approach taken in the recent work of Pacey [1983] and Park *et al.* [1983], but both are only concerned with a single, local telephone service.

It is these neglected aspects of international telephone demand that will be our major concern. The paper continues with a brief overview of the theory of telephone demand. This is followed by a description of the data available for this study. Section IV discusses the econometric model used; while the estimates it generates are given in Section V. A complete discussion of elasticity estimates together with a comparison of results from other studies appears as Section VI. The paper ends with some brief conclusions.

II. TELEPHONE DEMAND

A coherent theory of telephone demand has developed from the contributions of Squire [1973], Rohlfs [1974], Mitchell [1978] and Taylor [1980]. This work distinguishes between the demand for access to the telephone system and the demand for use of the system. A potential consumer decides on how many calls they would make given current prices and income, then compares the expected benefit with the access price in order to decide whether to subscribe or not.

Given the consumer has access to the system, several dimensions of usage demand need to be isolated. Making a telephone call involves several decisions including:

(i) the type of call; collect, person, station, etc.;
(ii) the duration of the call;
(iii) time of day to make the call.

Attention will be focused on some, but not all of these important dimensions of telephone demand.

Since our concern is with international calls, the demand for access is given much less prominence than the demand for use. A consumer contemplating making overseas calls is likely to have access to the telephone system and be making local calls. Also, Australia at present does not have a permanent system of time differentiated prices for overseas calls. The consumer will still need to decide on the particular time to make an overseas call but the decision will not be affected by price differences.

The problem then is to model the number of calls made, total paid minutes and the choice of service. Following Taylor [1980], the distinction between calls and minutes is taken to be similar to that between access and use.

Consumers decide whether to make a call just as they decide whether to subscribe to the system. Then they decide on the level of usage that is represented by the length of the call. Both aspects of demand will often have separate prices. There may be an initial surcharge or a minimum call duration; this is the "access" price of making a call. The price of extra minutes is then the "usage" price. Importantly, the demand for calls and for minutes will both depend on the two prices; access and usage. A decrease in the access price will lead to more calls being made and in turn more minutes of conversation. The effect on average duration of calls will be uncertain, depending on the average length of the stimulated calls. A decrease in the usage price will increase minutes and more calls are likely to be made. Here one would expect average call duration to increase.

In making a call the consumer has a choice between dialling the call directly or using an operator-connected service. Because of the additional costs in the latter, the consumer will generally be charged more than when the call is dialled directly. Obviously this additional cost needs to be compared with the increased service associated with using the operator. Substitution between telephone and other telecommunications services, such as telex and telegram have previously been considered in Lago [1970], Yatrakis [1972] and Rea and Lage [1978]. However, the cross-price effects for telephone have tended to be small. Our analysis will concentrate on the more neglected area of substitution; that between the individual telephone services.

III. DATA

The basic data to be analyzed are quarterly, extending from 1976.III to 1983.I, yielding a total of 27 observations. This covers the period since the introduction of ISD, which represents a time of extremely rapid growth in overseas telephone demand. Naturally, the period has also been characterized by the rapid diffusion of the ISD service. By the end of our sample period this service accounted for over 60% of total traffic. In revising this work, an attempt was made to gain access to the most recent telephone data. Unfortunately, this attempt was unsuccessful.

Ideally one would like to explain movements in calls and minutes for each of the individual services that comprise overseas telephone demand for Australia. However, this is not possible. It should be noted that the number of collect calls have not been recorded separately until recently. Furthermore, the tariff and surcharge for collect calls are historically identical to the person equivalents. There is no alternative but to aggregate the person and collect services into one service which, for convenience, will be referred to as person.

The three services to be analyzed are ISD, person and station. Let N_1, N_2 and N_3 be the number of calls made for these services and define, $N = \sum_{i=1}^{3} N_i$

to be the total number of calls. For minutes we will only distinguish between those associated with ISD, M_1, and operator-connected, M_2. Total minutes is denoted by $M = M_1 + M_2$.

OTC Australia has at its disposal 3 instruments to alter demand patterns: the ISD tariff, P_1, the operator-connected tariff, P_2, and the surcharge on person calls, S. Each tariff represents a per minute charge but there is a 3 minute minimum charge on operator-connected calls. In addition there is a difference between the prices of a few nearby countries, referred to as short haul, and those of the rest of the world, or long haul.

Traffic to short haul countries is dominated by New Zealand and Papua New Guinea. If these two countries are taken to define the short haul with the long haul being defined as the remainder, the short haul accounted for 19% of total outgoing telephone traffic in 1982. Amongst the long haul countries the major streams are Great Britain, USA, Canada, Italy, Greece, West Germany, Japan and Hong Kong. In 1982 these eight countries accounted for a further 55% of total outgoing telephone traffic.

IV. ECONOMETRIC MODEL

The econometric model to be utilized has two major sub-models each of which consists of an aggregate equation and an allocation system. One sub-model explains the total number of calls and determines how they are allocated among the three services: ISD, person and station; while the second sub-model explains the total number of minutes called and their allocation, conditional on the first model. In the choice-of-service sub-model it is assumed that the allocation of calls is made between the services on the basis of the cost associated with a call of minimum duration. In other words the fixed cost of a call is defined to include any surcharge, together with minimum duration requirements.

Having decided on how many calls to make and how to allocate them between the individual services, a decision needs to be made regarding call duration. Because of the existence of minimum call periods, we have decided to model excess minutes rather than total paid minutes. When making an operator-connected call, the consumer immediately incurs a charge that is at least equal to the minimum period. The additional decision to be made is how many minutes in excess of this minimum will be demanded. Although ISD is not subject to a minimum period, other than that determined by the measuring device, it is reasonable to assume that the consumer perceives some minimum period which is necessary to transmit some simple message.

Once a call is placed, a certain number of minutes is charged and the second sub-model jointly determines the excess minutes for ISD and operator-connected calls and hence total excess minutes. The "price" of person and station differ only in the surcharge and as such no distinction is made between these services in the excess minutes sub-model. Because of the identity linking total excess minutes and its two components, only two equations need to be considered. We have chosen to model the aggregate equation and the ratio of operator-connected excess minutes to that aggregate. The choice of service is assumed to have been made prior to the decision that determines call duration.

Let us now define explicitly the fixed costs associated with the individual services and the resultant notion of excess minutes. Since there is a 3 minute minimum charge on operator-connected calls, the fixed costs for person and station calls are

(1) $$F_2 = 3P_2 + S$$

and

(2) $$F_3 = 3P_2$$

respectively. The fixed cost of an ISD call is taken to be

(3) $$F_1 = \delta P_1$$

where δ is a parameter to be specified.

A priori δ was thought to be small. This view was supported by some limited experimentation. The model was estimated over a grid of values for δ ranging from 0.1 to 4.0 minutes. Being a perceived minimum call duration, δ needs to be strictly greater than zero. Moreover, we shall observe below that our model is not defined for δ equal to zero. The particular choice of six seconds as the minimum value corresponds to the basic recording unit or pulse associated with ISD calls. Over the grid chosen, $\delta = 0.1$ proved to be superior in terms of minimizing error sums of squares and as such the analysis proceeded conditional on this particular value.

Using 3 and 0.1 minutes as the minimum call durations for operator-connected and ISD calls, the excess paid minutes for ISD are

(4) $$E_1 = M_1 - 0.1N_1$$

and for operator-connected calls

(5) $$E_2 = M_2 - 3(N_2 + N_3)$$

Total excess paid minutes are defined as $E = E_1 + E_2$.

The choice of service allocation model comprises a system of dynamic share equations. For ease of exposition let us delay discussion of the dynamics and consider initially the equilibrium version of these share equations. Specifically, they are given by

(6) $$w_{it} = \exp[f_{it}] \Big/ \sum_{j=1}^{3} \exp[f_{jt}], \qquad i = 1, 2, 3$$

where $w_i = N_i/N$ defines the share of total calls of the ith service,

$$f_{it} = \beta_{io} + \beta_{i1} \ln (F_2/F_1)_t + \beta_{i2} \ln (F_3/F_1)_t + \beta_{i3} \ln Z_t$$

Z = number of subscribers connected by ISD; (as distinct from N_1 which is the number of calls made by these subscribers).

Thus the availability of the ISD service affects the allocation together with relative fixed costs. The particular functional form chosen is the homogeneous version of the generalized addilog, introduced by Bewley [1982]. It has the desirable feature of ensuring additivity and non-negativity of the estimated shares.

Although highly non-linear, (6) can readily be transformed into an equation more suitable for estimation. The method used here is based on Bewley [1982] and yields

$$\text{(7)} \qquad \ln (w_i/\tilde{w})_t = \bar{\beta}_{io} + \bar{\beta}_{i1} \ln (F_2/F_1)_t + \bar{\beta}_{i2} \ln (F_3/F_1)_t + \bar{\beta}_{i3} \ln Z_t, \qquad i = 1, 2, 3$$

where the tilde denotes a geometric mean. Also the parameters of (6) and (7) are related by

$$\text{(8)} \qquad \bar{\beta}_{ij} = \beta_{ij} - \sum_{k=1}^{3} \beta_{kj}/3, \qquad i = 1, 2, 3; \quad j = 0, 1, 2, 3$$

In specifying an aggregate equation for calls one needs to recognize that there has been a rapid growth in international telecommunications services over the past 20 years, apart from any growth that could be associated with the introduction of ISD. With such a rapidly changing environment it is necessary to allow for an adjustment in consumer behaviour to a variable desired demand. The actual specification chosen is based on Chow's [1967] attempt to model the life-cycle pattern of a product. Consider the differential form of the Gompertz curve

$$\text{(9)} \qquad \partial \ln N/\partial t = \alpha(\ln N^* - \ln N)$$

where N^* is the desired or equilibrium level of calls. In order to convert this to an estimatable form, approximate the derivative of $\ln N$ by its first difference $\Delta \ln N_t$, and the existing number of calls by its lagged value, and assume that the desired value is determined by a set of price and income variables.

Although the separate inclusion of the individual prices in the determination of $\ln N^*$ is desirable, it is not practical because of severe multicollinearity problems. As an alternative the following specification is used:

$$\text{(10)} \qquad \ln N_t^* = \phi_0 + \phi_1 \ln (F/C)_t + \phi_2 \ln G_t$$

where F, G and C are, respectively, average fixed cost of making an overseas call, real Australian GDP and the Australian consumer price index. F is found by averaging the individual fixed costs associated with the three individual services according to $F = \sum_{i=1}^{3} w_i F_i$.

Equation (9) becomes

$$\Delta \ln N_t = \alpha\phi_0 + \alpha\phi_1 \ln (F/C)_t + \alpha\phi_2 \ln G_t - \alpha \ln N_{t-1} \tag{11}$$

Homogeneity of degree zero in prices has been imposed by using the ratio of F to C. Interest will center on estimates of α which relates to the speed of adjustment, the impact multipliers ($\alpha\phi_i$), and the equilibrium parameters (ϕ_i).

Proceeding in a similar fashion, the aggregate excess minutes equation is given by

$$\Delta \ln E_t = \theta\lambda_0 + \theta\lambda_1 \ln (P/C)_t + \theta\lambda_2 \ln G_t - \theta \ln E_{t-1} \tag{12}$$

where P is the average tariff, θ is the adjustment coefficient and the λ_i are the equilibrium coefficients. Define the shares of total excess minutes associated with each service by $q_i = E_i/E, \quad i = 1, 2$; hence $P = q_1 P_1 + q_2 P_2$.

One possible alternative to these aggregate equations would be to use the number of telephone connections as an explanatory variable. Unfortunately, the unavailability of quarterly data precluded this possibility. Also, a migration variable was initially included in the specification of the aggregate equations but it proved to have little explanatory power and was subsequently omitted.

Equation (12) determines the total number of minutes over and above the minimum charge period. This total needs to be allocated between ISD and operator-connected calls. The equilibrium share equations are given by

$$q_{it} = \exp[g_{it}] \Big/ \sum_{j=1}^{2} \exp[g_{jt}], \qquad i = 1, 2 \tag{13}$$

where $g_{it} = \gamma_{i0} + \gamma_{i1} \ln (P_2/P_1)_t + \gamma_{i2} \ln E_t$

The transformed versions are

$$\ln (q_i/\tilde{q})_t = \bar{\gamma}_{i0} + \bar{\gamma}_{i1} \ln (P_2/P_1)_t + \bar{\gamma}_{i2} \ln E_t \tag{14}$$

where the parameters of (13) are related to those of (14) by

$$\bar{\gamma}_{ij} = \gamma_{ij} - \sum_{k=1}^{2} \gamma_{kj}/2, \qquad i = 1, 2; \quad j = 0, 1, 2 \tag{15}$$

Let us now consider the dynamics of the allocation models. Because they are systems of equations a generalized partial adjustment framework is appropriate. The nature of the transformation which linearizes the share equations implies the dependent variables, and hence their lags, sum identically to zero. One lagged dependent variable needs to be deleted from each equation to avoid perfect collinearity: Hunt [1981] shows that this does not alter the model's properties. Furthermore, the same singularity problem implies one equation needs to be deleted and hence the adjustment matrix degenerates to a 2 by 2 in the choice-of-service model and a scalar in the excess minutes models. (Further discussion of these issues can be found in Bewley [1986].)

Estimation of the choice-of-service model under these conditions proved to be somewhat unsatisfactory because of instability problems. An alternative to be adopted here is to use a restricted dynamic framework. Each share is taken to be a function of its own lagged value but not lagged values of the remaining shares. Operationally this only affects the choice-of-service model: because of the dimensionality of the excess minutes model its restricted version is observationally equivalent to the unrestricted version.

Now the adding-up properties imply that the coefficients on the lagged dependent variables will be equal across share equations. In other words, the basic equations are

$$\ln(w_i/\tilde{w})_t = \bar{\beta}_{io} + \bar{\beta}_{i1}\ln(F_2/F_1)_t + \bar{\beta}_{i2}\ln(F_3/F_1)_t + \bar{\beta}_{i3}\ln Z_t + \bar{\beta}_4\ln(w_i/\tilde{w})_{t-1}, \qquad i = 1,2,3 \tag{16}$$

and

$$\ln(q_i/\tilde{q})_t = \bar{\gamma}_{io} + \bar{\gamma}_{i1}\ln(P_2/P_1)_t + \bar{\gamma}_{i2}\ln E_t + \bar{\gamma}_3\ln(q_i/\tilde{q})_{t-1}, \qquad i = 1,2 \tag{17}$$

where the coefficients on the lagged dependent variables are not subscripted by i.

V. ESTIMATION RESULTS

The basic model comprises equations (11), (12), (16) and (17), each of which could refer to an individual stream of traffic or possibly aggregate world traffic. Our analysis proceeds with an intermediate level of aggregation. In line with the two-tier price system mentioned previously, demand for long and short haul countries is considered separately. This treatment of total demand allows differences in responses between the two types of countries to emerge. Further, disaggregation to the individual stream level is not feasible given the large number of streams involved.

With regard to the price responses, the view is taken, at least in the long run, that differences between the two types of countries are likely to be small. This notion is formalized by assuming the equilibrium price coefficients to be equal for the long and short haul in each of the basic equations. In other words, speed of adjustment, or short run price coefficients and all other responses for any particular equation are allowed to vary but not the equilibrium price response.

Estimation of the equations in their present form would require the imposition of non-linear cross-equation restrictions. Alternatively, use of

Bewley's [1979] pseudo-structural form provides a useful simplification. It facilitates the direct estimation of equilibrium coefficients and in turn the required cross-equation restrictions become linear.

In particular consider the aggregate calls equation given by (11). This can now be written as

$$\Delta \ln N_{ht} = \pi_{h0} + \pi_{h1} \ln (F/C)_{ht} + \pi_{h2} \ln G_t + \pi_{h3} \ln N_{h,t-1} + \varepsilon^*_{ht} \tag{18}$$

where the subscript $h = L$ or S is used to denote long or short haul. Recall that $\pi_{h1} = \alpha_h \phi_{h1}$ and $\pi_{h3} = -\alpha_h$. Consequently the equality of equilibrium price responses implies a non-linear restriction of the form, $\pi_{L1}/\pi_{L3} = \pi_{S1}/\pi_{S3}$. However, it is a simple matter to reparameterize (18) by dividing through π_{h3}, then rewriting as

$$\ln N_{ht} = \phi_{h0} + \phi_{h1} \ln (F/C)_{ht} + \phi_{h2} \ln G_t + \phi_{h3} \Delta \ln N_{ht} + \varepsilon_{ht} \tag{19}$$

where $\varepsilon_{ht} = \varepsilon^*_{ht}/\pi_{h3}$. This is referred to by Bewley [1979] as the pseudo-structural form. The obvious advantage is that the equilibrium coefficients, ϕ_{hi}'s, now appear directly. As such the restriction of interest is now linear, $\phi_{L1} = \phi_{S1}$. It is also the case that the negative of the coefficient on $\Delta \ln N$ is given by $-\phi_{h3} = (1-\alpha_h)/\alpha_h$ which is the mean response.

The added complication that this formulation does present is that OLS is not an appropriate estimation procedure because of the presence of $\Delta \ln N_{ht}$ on the right-hand side of (19). Without the cross-equation restriction, (19) can be efficiently estimated by *2SLS* using (18) as the first stage. There is an exact correspondence between the resultant estimates and standard errors and those implied by OLS estimation of (18). When the cross-equation restrictions are imposed, FIML is appropriate and normality of ε_{ht} is assured given normality of ε^*_{ht}.

Similar transformations are applied to equations (12), (16) and (17) to provide the appropriate pseudo-structural forms. It is clearly overly optimistic to estimate the entire system by FIML given the relatively short period of data that was available. Indeed even after separating equations into the calls and excess minutes sub-models convergence problems were present. As a consequence the model was estimated in three blocks, namely: the entire excess minutes sub-model, the aggregate calls equations and the choice-of-service system. Since the complete model is block diagonal, a similar assumption about the error covariance matrix implies that our estimator is efficient.

Each of the basic equations were augmented by seasonal dummy variables. All of these, with the exception of the fourth quarter seasonal dummy proved to have little explanatory power. In all specifications reported, only the single seasonal dummy, denoted by *D*, is included.

All estimation was carried out using TSP. Coefficient estimates, together with their asymptotic t ratios are provided in Tables I to IV. Also included are the standard error of the estimate (SEE) and the Durbin Watson (DW) statistics for each individual equation. The system R^2 based on a likelihood ratio test and defined in Bewley [1985] is 0.91. Correlation matrices for the explanatory variables in the different equations were also calculated. These provided simple correlation coefficients that are not atypical of economic time-series data and as such have not been reported.

A Wald test was constructed to test the equality of the equilibrium price coefficients for the long and short haul. This statistic was 15.2 which should be compared to a χ^2 variable with 7 degrees of freedom; for example the 1% and 5% critical values are respectively 18.5 and 14.1. Although the evidence in support of the null hypothesis is seemingly weak, one must recall the well documented failure of such asymptotic tests in small systems of equations. In particular these tests tend to be severely biased towards rejection of the null hypothesis; see Bewley [1986] for details. At present, appropriate adjustments to correct for this bias in our particular case have not been developed. As such we proceed by reporting results that incorporate the equality restrictions.

Notice that for the excess minutes allocation model it is only necessary to report the results from one equation. Here the operator equation is reported. For the ISD equation, the estimated coefficient of the lagged dependent variable will be the same as that in the operator equation while remaining coefficient estimates are equal in magnitude but opposite in sign as are the t ratios. With the choice of service model there is also a redundant equation whose coefficients can be deduced from those of the remaining two equations. Here, though, the correspondence is not as direct as for the excess minutes model and as such the results for all three services are reported.

Results for the aggregate calls and excess minutes models are presented in Table I. All of the coefficients are correctly signed and most are highly

TABLE I
AGGREGATE EQUATIONS: PSEUDO-STRUCTURAL FORM[a]

	Calls		*Excess Minutes*	
Variable	*Long Haul*	*Short Haul*	*Long Haul*	*Short Haul*
Price	−0.469		−2.484	
	(−3.548)		(−9.088)	
ln *G*	7.475	5.448	1.781	4.641
	(7.372)	(4.755)	(1.909)	(3.097)
First difference of dependent variable	−2.499	−2.348	−0.355	−1.550
	(−4.863)	(−3.787)	(−1.005)	(−2.409)
D	0.304	0.188	0.112	0.246
	(3.565)	(2.309)	(1.650)	(1.110)
Constant	−58.596	−41.002	−15.920	−45.810
	(−6.501)	(−3.961)	(−2.217)	(−3.637)
SEE	0.1405	0.1486	0.0456	0.1303
DW	2.24	2.68	1.84	2.40

[a] Asymptotic t ratios are given in parenthesis.

TABLE II
SHORT-RUN AGGREGATE PRICE ELASTICITIES[a]

	Calls	*Excess Minutes*
Long Haul	−0.134	−1.833
	(−3.067)	(−2.900)
Short Haul	−0.140	−0.974
	(−3.868)	(−3.611)

[a] Asymptotic t ratios are given in parenthesis.

significant. In particular the two price coefficients are very well determined. Because of the double-log specification utilized, these coefficients can be interpreted as elasticities. With respect to the respective price indices utilized, calls are inelastic while excess minutes are very elastic. This is what could be expected. Faced with high telecommunications costs, the consumer is more likely to reduce the length of a call rather than not make the call at all.

Recall that these are equilibrium responses. Also of interest are the impact multipliers or short run responses which will vary between the long and short hauls. The estimates for prices are provided in Table II and again are highly significant. Importantly, there are some, but not marked differences between the long and short haul. Excess minutes are marginally inelastic for short haul and elastic for long haul, while calls are extremely inelastic in both cases.

The excess minutes equation for operator-connected calls is presented in Table III. Once again, coefficients have expected signs, although several have small t ratios. This is not the case for the price coefficient which is reasonably well determined. Notice that the estimated coefficients cannot be interpreted

TABLE III
OPERATOR-CONNECTED SHARE OF EXCESS MINUTES: PSEUDO-STRUCTURAL FORM[a]

Variable	*Long Haul*	*Short Haul*
$\ln(P_2/P_1)$	−1.735	
	(−2.507)	
$\ln E$	−0.509	−0.217
	(−12.751)	(−1.147)
$\Delta \ln(q_2/\tilde{q})$	−0.899	−3.619
	(−2.085)	(−2.850)
D	−0.071	−0.143
	(−0.770)	(−1.466)
Constant	8.483	3.103
	(13.237)	(1.135)
SEE	0.0570	0.1909
DW	2.14	2.10

[a] Asymptotic t ratios are given in parenthesis.

TABLE IV
CHOICE-OF-SERVICE MODEL: PSEUDO-STRUCTURAL FORM[a]

Variable	ISD Long Haul	ISD Short Haul	Person Long Haul	Person Short Haul	Station Long Haul	Station Short Haul
$\ln(F_2/F_1)$	2.243		−1.583		−0.660	
	(1.833)		−(0.845)		(−0.424)	
$\ln(F_3/F_1)$	−0.697		3.431		−2.734	
	(−0.211)		(0.527)		(−0.390)	
$\ln Z$	0.188	0.081	−0.187	−0.175	−0.000	0.094
	(1.208)	(0.710)	(−1.022)	(−2.003)	(−0.003)	(1.189)
$\Delta\ln(w_1/\tilde{w})$	−4.450	−2.400				
	(−6.497)	(−4.017)				
$\Delta\ln(w_2/\tilde{w})$			−4.450	−2.400		
			(−6.497)	(−4.017)		
$\Delta\ln(w_3/\tilde{w})$					−4.450	−2.400
					(−6.497)	(−4.017)
D	0.625	0.146	−0.733	−0.218	0.108	0.072
	(2.215)	(0.962)	(−1.338)	(−1.390)	(0.205)	(0.295)
Constant	−8.432	−7.208	−3.569	−3.798	12.001	11.006
	(−1.000)	(−0.880)	(−0.209)	(−0.234)	(0.629)	(0.592)
SEE	[b]	[b]	0.4779	0.1566	0.3143	0.1526
DW	[b]	[b]	2.23	2.69	2.79	2.39

[a] Asymptotic t ratios are given in parenthesis.
[b] Not available for the redundant equation.

as elasticities because of the presence of $\ln E$ as an explanatory variable. A complete discussion of elasticities is presented in the next section.

The negative coefficients associated with $\ln E$ reflect the greater growth in ISD excess minutes relative to the operator-connected excess minutes. This implies a declining operator-connected excess minutes share as aggregate excess minutes increase. In the long haul this decline is noticeable over the entire sample period while for short haul the share initially increases until 1978 where it remains stable around 0.5 until 1981. Only then does it exhibit a decline in share similar to that in the long haul. These factors explain the marked differences in the importance of aggregate excess minutes in each of the equations.

Results for the choice of service model, as presented in Table IV, are mixed with many coefficients being insignificant and some signs are contrary to expectations. In particular only one of the fixed cost coefficients is important; $\ln(F_2/F_1)$ in the ISD equation. Increasing F_2 has a strong positive impact on the share of ISD calls while increasing F_1 has just the opposite effect. The station and person calls shares are not overly responsive to any of the fixed costs.

With the exception of short haul station, the coefficients for $\ln Z$ are correctly signed. Increased ISD availability implies an increased ISD share of calls at the expense of operator-connected calls. However several of these responses are insignificant.

The coefficients on the first differenced dependent variables are highly significant. Importantly, there is a marked difference between the long and short haul responses. For the former the mean response is 4.45 quarters while for the latter it is only 2.40 quarters.

VI. FURTHER DISCUSSION

In the previous section price effects were discussed and, where possible, interpreted as elasticities. However, these responses are with respect to price indices, whereas one is probably more interested in the impact of the individual price instruments; P_1, P_2 and S. Our estimation results can be utilized to provide such price elasticities for calls and excess minutes. In addition the relationships between paid minutes, the number of calls and excess minutes allow the calculation of elasticities for paid minutes. All elasticity calculations utilize the mean values of any variables involved.

Tables V, VI and VII summarize our calculations. As could be expected the differences between the long and short haul equilibrium elasticities are small. They only differ to the extent of variation in mean values of long and short haul variables used in the elasticity calculations. On the other hand large differences often occur for the impact elasticities.

The effect of price and surcharge changes on the number of calls for the three services are presented in Table V. With respect to P_1 the own-price effect is inelastic in the short run but quite elastic in the long run. There is a strong substitution effect between ISD and station calls for changes in P_1. Also for changes in P_2 there is a substitution effect into ISD calls but this is not as strong. Somewhat surprisingly person calls behave as complements for

TABLE V
IMPLIED PRICE ELASTICITIES FROM THE CHOICE-OF-SERVICE MODEL

	Impact Elasticities			*Equilibrium Elasticities*		
Price	*ISD*	*Person*	*Station*	*ISD*	*Person*	*Station*
			Long Haul			
P_1	−0.30	−0.35	0.61	−1.62	−1.92	3.32
P_2	0.15	0.48	−0.55	0.84	2.59	−3.00
S	0.14	−0.12	−0.06	0.78	−0.67	−0.32
			Short Haul			
P_1	−0.57	−0.66	0.88	−1.94	−2.24	3.00
P_2	0.32	0.86	−0.79	1.10	2.92	−2.69
S	0.25	−0.20	−0.09	0.84	−0.68	−0.31

TABLE VI
IMPLIED PRICE ELASTICITIES FROM EXCESS MINUTES ALLOCATION MODEL

	Impact Elasticities		*Equilibrium Elasticities*	
Price	*ISD*	*Operator-Connected*	*ISD*	*Operator-Connected*
		Long Haul		
P_1	−1.71	0.51	−3.01	1.47
P_2	−0.37	−1.61	−0.35	−2.29
		Short Haul		
P_1	−0.98	−0.11	−3.83	0.99
P_2	−0.15	−0.80	−0.10	−2.39

ISD calls; they respond directly rather than inversely to changes in both prices.

For increases in the surcharge the main response is, as expected, a movement from person to ISD calls. However, all effects are relatively small.

The elasticities associated with operator-connected and ISD excess minutes are summarized in Table VI. All of the own-price effects are elastic, or close to being elastic. This is especially evident for the equilibrium coefficients. Another notable feature of the own-price effects is the difference between the impact elasticities for long and short haul. The latter are markedly smaller in magnitude.

The pattern of cross-price effects is interesting. Typically one might expect these elasticities to be positive, which is the case for changes in P_1 with the exception of the short haul impact elasticity. In other words increasing the price of an extra ISD minute implies an increase in the operator-connected

TABLE VII
IMPLIED PRICE ELASTICITIES FROM AGGREGATE MODELS

	Impact Elasticities			*Equilibrium Elasticities*		
Price	*Calls*	*Excess Minutes*	*Paid Minutes*	*Calls*	*Excess Minutes*	*Paid Minutes*
			Long Haul			
P_1	−0.00	−0.75	−0.41	−0.01	−1.02	−0.41
P_2	−0.10	−1.08	−0.81	−0.36	−1.47	−1.13
S	−0.04	—	−0.01	−0.10	—	−0.06
π	−0.10	−1.83	−1.22	−0.37	−2.48	−1.54
			Short Haul			
P_1	−0.00	−0.52	−0.35	−0.01	−1.34	−0.96
P_2	−0.11	−0.45	−0.34	−0.37	−1.14	−0.89
S	−0.03	—	0.00	−0.09	—	0.00
π	−0.11	−0.97	−0.69	−0.38	−2.48	−1.85

excess minutes. However, for P_2 this is not the case: these cross-price effects are negative. Apparently the decrease in overall excess minutes associated with the price increase has a stronger impact than the increase associated with the substitution effect. It is worth noting that the substitution effect is positive relative to the share in these cases. In other words the elasticity of the share of ISD excess minutes relative to a change in P_2 is always positive.

Price elasticities for the aggregate traffic variables are provided in Table VII. All estimates have the expected sign. The most notable feature of these elasticities is that the total number of calls is not overly responsive to any of the instruments. P_2 is important in the long-run but even here the equilibrium responses are inelastic. Although P_2, and to a lesser extent P_1, contribute to the fixed cost of making a telephone call, changes in either of these two prices are reflected more in the duration of a call than in the decision to make it. Nevertheless, excess and paid minutes are often inelastic with respect to P_1 and P_2, while excess minutes is more responsive with respect to both prices. Notice that S has almost no impact on all of the variables. Together with our previous results it seems reasonable to conclude that changes in the surcharge have little impact on overseas telephone demand in Australia.

A comparison of our results with those obtained in other studies of international telephone demand would now seem appropriate. Unfortunately, we know of no other study that investigates the substitution effects between individual services. In addition, existing studies model either calls or minutes but not both. For example, Rea and Lage [1978] argue that because the two are highly correlated, results are not materially affected by the choice of one in favour of the other. Unfortunately this does not follow. As our analysis has emphasized, calls and minutes are both important aspects of telephone demand. Moreover, they react quite differently to price changes. Our results suggest that minutes are much more responsive to price changes than calls.

This leaves the comparison of price elasticities for the aggregate variables. The studies of Craver and Neckowitz [1980] and Schultz and Triantis [1982] are probably closest to ours in terms of the data period and frequency, and the level of aggregation. Both report equilibrium elasticities for calls; -0.67 in the case of Craver and Neckowitz and -0.419 for Schultz and Triantis. These are qualitatively similar to our equilibrium call elasticity relative to the average price, P. Our estimate was found to be -0.489 with a standard error of 0.132.

Notice that comparisons with our elasticities associated with P_1 and P_2 are not appropriate here. These other studies invariably use a price that is a weighted average of similar individual prices. A more appropriate comparison could be with an elasticity resulting from both ISD and operator tariffs being increased by the same proportion. Such elasticities have been calculated and are associated with the π variable in Table VII. The effect on calls is always inelastic but the effect on paid minutes is elastic except in the short run, short haul case.

VII. CONCLUSION

The demand for international telephone calls in Australia has been modelled using a system of two sub-models. One sub-model determines the total number of calls and how they are allocated among the three services; ISD, person and station. The second determines total number of minutes called and its allocation to ISD and the operator-connected services. This dichotomy allows insights into the effects of changes in the ISD and operator tariffs and the person surcharge that have not previously been available in studies of international telephone demand. The main implications of our results from Australia are as follows:

(i) the surcharge has little or no impact on telephone demand;
(ii) generally, the substitution effects between services are strong, both in terms of calls and minutes;
(iii) total calls are not overly responsive to any of the price instruments;
(iv) total minutes are more responsive than calls.

Of wider interest is the modelling approach used here. Hopefully this will represent a useful basis for further research in international telecommunications demand.

ACCEPTED JULY 1987

RONALD BEWLEY,
The University of New South Wales,
Kensington,
New South Wales 2034,
Australia.

DENZIL G. FIEBIG,
University of Sydney,
Sydney,
New South Wales 2060,
Australia.

REFERENCES

BEWLEY, R. A., 1979, 'The Direct Estimation of the Equilibrium Response in a Linear Dynamic Model', *Economics Letters,* 3, pp. 357–361.

BEWLEY, R. A., 1982, 'The Generalized Addilog Demand System Applied to Australian Time Series and Cross Section Data', *Australian Economic Papers,* 21, pp. 177–192.

BEWLEY, R. A., 1985, 'Goodness of Fit for Allocation Models', *Economics Letters,* 17, pp. 227–229.

BEWLEY, R. A., 1986, *Allocation Models: Specification, Estimation and Applications* (Ballinger Publishing Co., Cambridge, MA).

CHOW, G. C., 1967, 'Technical Change and the Demand for Computers', *American Economic Review,* 57, pp. 1117–1130.

Craver, R. F., 1976, 'An Estimate of the Price Elasticity of Demand for International Telecommunications', *Telecommunication Journal*, 43, pp. 671–675.

Craver, R. F. and Neckowitz, H., 1980, 'International Telecommunications: the Evolution of Demand Analysis', *Telecommunication Journal*, 47, pp. 217–223.

Hunt, B. F., 1981, 'Estimation of a System of Linear Dynamic Asset Demand Equations: Computational Considerations', *Economics Letters*, 8, pp. 355–360.

Lago, A. M., 1970, 'Demand Forecasting Model of International Telecommunications and Their Policy Implications', *Journal of Industrial Economics*, 19, pp. 6–21.

Mitchell, B. M., 1978, 'Optimal Pricing of Local Telephone Service', *American Economic Review*, 68, pp. 517–537.

Pacey, P. L., 1983, 'Long Distance Demand: a Point-to-point Model', *Southern Economic Journal*, 49, pp. 1094–1107.

Park, R. E., Wetzel, B. M. and Mitchell, B. M., 1983, 'Price Elasticities for Local Telephone Calls', *Econometrica*, 51, pp. 1699–1730.

Rea, J. D. and Lage, G. M., 1978, 'Estimates of Demand Elasticities for International Telecommunications Services', *Journal of Industrial Economics*, 26, pp. 363–381.

Rohlfs, J., 1974, 'A Theory of Interdependent Demand for a Communications Service', *Bell Journal of Economics and Management Science*, 5, pp. 16–37.

Schultz, W. R. and Triantis, J. E., 1982, 'An International Telephone Demand Study Using Pooled Estimation Techniques', *Proceedings, American Statistical Association, Business and Economic Statistics Section*, pp. 537–542.

Squire, L., 1973, 'Some Aspects of Optimal Pricing for Telecommunications', *Bell Journal of Economics and Management Science*, 4, pp. 515–525.

Taylor, L. D., 1980, *Telephone Demand: a Survey and Critique* (Ballinger Publishing Co., Cambridge, MA).

Yatrakis, P. G., 1972, 'Determinants of the Demand for International Telecommunications', *Telecommunication Journal*, 39, pp. 732–746.

THE JOURNAL OF INDUSTRIAL ECONOMICS 0022-1821/$2.00
Volume XXXVI June 1988 No. 4

THE MULTIPRODUCT FIRM, QUALITY CHOICE, AND REGULATION*

DAVID BESANKO, SHABTAI DONNENFELD AND LAWRENCE J. WHITE

A monopolist facing a market of heterogeneous consumers will distort the quality array. This paper explores three regulatory remedies—minimum quality standards (MQS), maximum price regulation (MPR), and rate of return regulation (RORR)—that counteract this distortion. MQS and MPR raise the quality offered to consumers with a low willingness-to-pay for quality. While MQS have no effect on the quality offered to consumers with a high willingness-to-pay, MPR decreases the quality offered to this group. If production of high- (low-)quality goods is capital-intensive, RORR increases (decreases) the quality offered to both groups.

I. INTRODUCTION

AN IMPORTANT objective of economic regulation is correcting allocative distortions that arise in imperfectly competitive markets. For a simple monopolist, the nature of these distortions is straightforward, and the effects of corrective regulatory remedies (e.g., a price ceiling or a rate of return constraint) are easy to predict. However, for a monopolist facing heterogeneous consumers with varying tastes for quality, the nature of the allocative distortions is more complex. As numerous authors have shown (e.g., White [1977], Mussa and Rosen [1978], Maskin and Riley [1984] and Besanko, Donnenfeld and White [1987]), the array of prices and qualities offered by a monopolist unable to practice perfect price discrimination will differ from the array that would arise in a perfectly competitive equilibrium. Given the complexity of the distortions, it is not obvious what the effects of simple regulatory remedies might be.

The objective of this paper is to examine the positive and normative effects of three widely-used regulatory policies—minimum quality standards, maximum price regulation, and rate of return regulation—with a model in which a monopolist faces consumers whose heterogeneous preferences for product quality cannot be directly observed. In the unregulated equilibrium, the monopolist deteriorates the quality offered to the groups with the lower willingness-to-pay for quality. The "obvious" remedy for this distortion

* The authors would like to acknowledge the helpful comments of F. M. Scherer and two anonymous referees. Part of this research was performed when White was financed by a Jules Backman Faculty Fellowship at New York University. Besanko gratefully acknowledges the financial support of the National Science Foundation, Grant No. SES-8408335. Responsibility for all errors is our own.

would be a minimum quality standard. However, we show that this distortion can also be counteracted by maximum price regulation and—under some plausible circumstances—by rate of return regulation as well. This theoretical insight suggests that if direct regulation of product or service quality is unfeasible (perhaps because quality is difficult for a regulator to monitor), other regulatory arrangements may result in quality improvements as an important side effect.

This paper is organized as follows. Section II presents the basic model used throughout the paper and contains an analysis of the unregulated monopoly equilibrium. Section III analyzes three regulatory regimes and their impact on the monopolist's quality decisions. Section III(i) discusses minimum quality standards (MQS); section III(ii) analyzes maximum price regulation (MPR); and section III(iii) studies rate of return regulation (RORR). Section IV compares the welfare properties of those remedies. Section V summarizes and concludes.

II. THE MODEL

Assume that a particular good or service can be produced in a wide variety of qualities indexed by $q \geqslant 0$, with larger values of q corresponding to higher quality. Following Mussa and Rosen [1978] and Maskin and Riley [1984], we assume that a consumer buys only one unit of the product but may choose among the variety array.[1]

One example to which this model would apply is cable television. The product is a subscription to cable television service, and quality would be the number of channels provided under a particular service option. The lowest quality offered by the firm would correspond to "basic" service, while higher qualities would correspond to "premium" service offerings. This example is pertinent to our analysis because cable television in the United States has had a history of extensive quality and price regulation, and there is still much debate about the wisdom of efforts to relax these regulations.[2]

A type-i consumer has a utility function:

$$(1) \qquad u_i = x_i + v_i(q)$$

where x_i represents all other goods and $v_i(q)$ represents total willingness-to-pay for quality, where $v_i(0) = 0$, $v_i'(q) > 0$ and $v_i''(q) \leqslant 0$.[3] The consumer's

[1] The assumption that a consumer purchases one unit is not crucial to the analysis. In their 1984 paper, Maskin and Riley show that monopolistic quality distortions when consumers can purchase more than one unit are very similar to the distortions arising in a model where consumers purchase but one unit.

[2] Until 1986, cable rates (except for "specialty services" such as HBO) were regulated by local governments. Service quality in cable television is regulated by the Federal Communications Commission (FCC). An example of a service quality regulation is the FCC's requirement that local cable systems carry any local broadcast signal as part of its basic service offering. Quality standards of this type are now being phased out, however.

[3] The functional form in (1) allows us to ignore income effects.

surplus is:

(2) $$CS_i = v_i(q) - p$$

where p is the price of the product.

We assume that there are two groups of consumers: n_I consumers of type I and n_{II} consumers of type II. The two groups have different total and marginal willingness-to-pay curves. Specifically, $v_I(q) > v_{II}(q)$, for every $q > 0$, and $v'_I(q) > v'_{II}(q)$. That is, group I consumers have a higher total and marginal willingness-to-pay for quality than do group II consumers.

The monopolist firm can produce any or all of the quality levels by means of a technology exhibiting constant returns to scale and scope.[4] Hence, for a fixed quality, there is a constant unit cost, $c(q)$. We assume that $c(0) = 0$, $c'(q) > 0$, and $c''(q) > 0$; i.e., unit costs increase at an increasing rate in quality.[5]

Facing only two types of consumers, the monopolist will produce at most two different qualities. The price and quality the monopolist would offer each type of buyer under perfect discrimination is determined by:

(3) $$\max_{\substack{q_i \geqslant 0 \\ p_i \geqslant 0}} \pi = \sum_{i=I}^{II} n_i[p_i - c(q_i)]$$

subject to:

(4) $$v_I(q_I) - p_I \geqslant 0$$

(5) $$v_{II}(q_{II}) - p_{II} \geqslant 0$$

Constraints (4) and (5) are the market participation constraints. Under perfect discrimination, the monopolist extracts the entire surplus from each group of buyers, so (4) and (5) hold as equalities. The qualities offered are determined by the condition:[6]

$$v'_i(q_i^*) = c'(q_i^*) \qquad \text{for } i = I, II$$

Hence, the perfect discrimination solution entails socially optimal qualities that equate the marginal benefit with marginal cost of quality.

When a buyer's type is not observable, perfect discrimination is not feasible. The price-quality pairs offered to both groups of buyers must satisfy the self-selection constraints given by:

(6) $$v_I(q_I) - p_I \geqslant v_I(q_{II}) - p_{II}$$

[4] The insights of our model also hold under specifications with non-constant returns to scale in output. See Besanko and Donnenfeld [1986].

[5] Throughout the analysis we will also maintain the following regularity assumptions: (i) $v(\cdot)$ and $c(\cdot)$ have first and second derivatives which are continuous almost everywhere on $[0, \infty)$; (ii) $\lim_{q \to \infty} c'(q) = \infty$; (iii) $v'_i(0) > c'(0)$ for $i = I, II$; (iv) $v'_i(\cdot)$ is bounded from above.

[6] The regularity assumptions stated in the previous footnote ensure the existence of an interior solution to the monopolist's problem under perfect discrimination.

(7) $v_{II}(q_{II}) - p_{II} \geqslant v_{II}(q_I) - p_I$

These constraints ensure that group i buyers will choose the price-quality combination (p_i, q_i) the monopolist "designs" for that group.

The problem of a monopolist unable to observe buyer types is to maximize (3) subject to (4)–(7) and $q_i \geqslant 0$, $p_i \geqslant 0$ for $i = I, II$. The profit-maximizing qualities and prices are derived in the Appendix and are given by:[7]

(8) $v_I'(q_I^M) = c'(q_I^M)$

(9) $v_{II}'(q_{II}^M) = c'(q_{II}^M) + n_I n_{II}^{-1}[v_I'(q_{II}^M) - v_{II}'(q_{II}^M)]$

(10) $p_I^M = v_I(q_I^M) - [v_I(q_{II}^M) - v_{II}(q_{II}^M)]$

(11) $p_{II}^M = v_{II}(q_{II}^M)$

(The superscript M denotes profit-maximizing values.)

The optimal solution to the monopolist's problem is a separating equilibrium in which each group is offered a distinct price-quality pair. Equation (8) indicates that group I receives the socially optimal quality. Equation (9) indicates that group II receives a less than socially optimal quality. The magnitude of the distortion depends on the size of each group of consumers and the difference in each group's marginal willingness-to-pay for quality.[8]

The intuition for this result can be illustrated by a diagram. In Figure 1, the curves u_I and u_{II} depict the zero-surplus curves for group I and group II consumers respectively. The shapes of these curves are determined by the assumptions made about preferences. Note that the zero-surplus curve of group I is strictly above that of group II. Points A^* and B^* depict the perfect discrimination solution, while A^M and B^M depict the solution under imperfect discrimination. With imperfect observability of buyer types, the perfect discrimination solution is not feasible. If the monopolist offered the price-quality pairs A^* and B^*, group I consumers would choose B^* because this pair entails positive rather than zero surplus. To counteract this incentive, the monopolist must lower group I's price from p_I^* to $\tilde{p}_I$. However, the monopolist can increase profits by reducing the quality offered to group II from q_{II}^* to q_{II}^M. This makes the price-quality pair offered to group II less attractive to group I consumers and allows the monopolist to raise the price of quality q_I^* from $\tilde{p}_I$ to p_I^M. The quality distortion reduces the profits extracted from group II, but in a neighborhood of B^* this profit reduction is of a second-order of smallness in relation to the increase in profits extracted

[7] These conditions pertain to the case in which the monopolist sells to both groups (equivalently, sets $q_{II} > 0$). The case in which the monopolist sells only to group I consumers is discussed below.

[8] Under alternative assumptions about the relationship between total and marginal willingness-to-pay, the quality distortions can occur at the high end of the market. See Donnenfeld and White [1984].

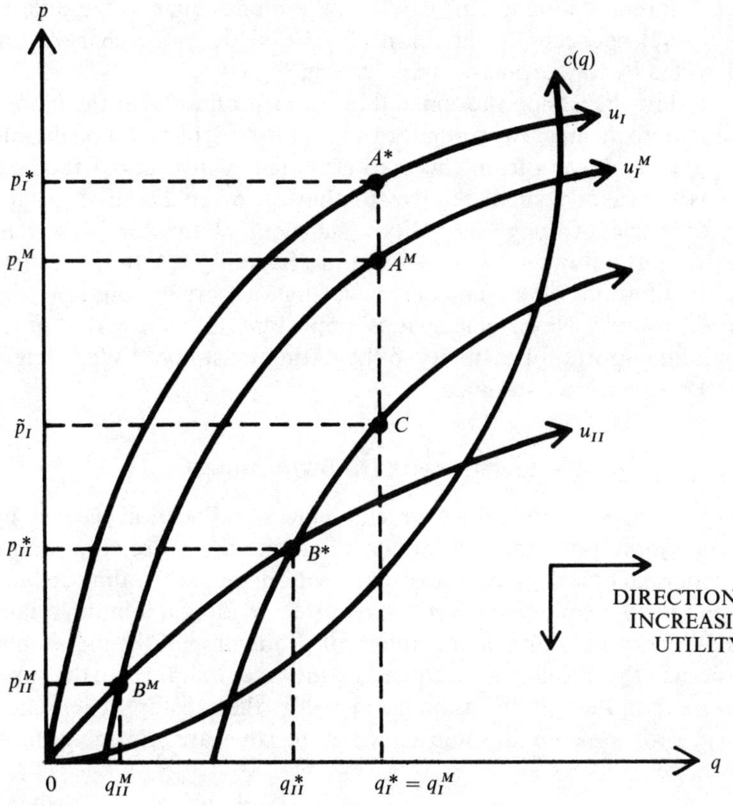

Figure 1
Unregulated Monopoly Equilibrium

from group I.[9] Hence group II buyers end up with a less than socially optimal quality level.

As can be seen from (10) and (11), the pricing strategy of the monopolist is modified under imperfect observability. The monopolist extracts the entire surplus of group II consumers, but because the quality level is lower, the price p_{II}^M is lower than under perfect discrimination. Condition (10) indicates that the monopolist does not extract the full surplus from group I consumers (otherwise they would switch to (q_{II}^M, p_{II}^M)). The price charged must be lower

[9] Formally, at B^* the reduction in profits from group II due to a small decrease δ in the quality offered to group II is approximately

$$n_{II}\delta(v'_{II}(q_{II}^*) - c'(q_{II}^*)) = 0$$

while the increase in profits extracted from group I is approximately

$$n_I\delta(v'_I(q_{II}^*) - v'_{II}(q_{II}^*)) > 0.$$

than I's maximum willingness-to-pay by an amount equal to the difference $v_I(q_{II}^M) - v_{II}(q_{II}^M)$ between I's valuation of q_{II}^M and the price charged for it. This is depicted by the surplus curve $u_I^M > 0$ in Figure 1.

The preceding discussion presumed that it was profitable for the monopolist to sell to both groups. However, the monopolist might find it profitable to exclude group II buyers from the market.[10] This will occur if the size of group II is sufficiently small relative to that of group I and if group I's marginal willingness-to-pay for quality is sufficiently large relative to that of group II. In what follows we will assume that the utility function parameters and the distribution of buyers are such that a corner solution is not profit-maximizing.[11] Nevertheless, it is important to realize that market exclusion is an important possibility in the setting we study.[12] We will return to the market exclusion issue later.

III. REMEDIES FOR THE DISTORTION

The possible remedies to reduce or eliminate misallocation caused by a conventional monopoly are well known: eliminate the source of monopoly power; encourage first-degree price discrimination; place a binding ceiling on price or on the allowable rate of return; require a binding minimum quantity to be produced; or subsidize consumption or production of the monopolized good (assuming the misallocation caused by the taxes that finance the subsidy is less severe than the misallocation corrected by the subsidy). The remedies for quality distortion contain some analogies, but they are more complicated.

III(i). *Minimum quality standards* (*MQS*)

Suppose that regulation prohibits the sale of products with quality less than $\underline{q}$, where $q_I^M > \underline{q} > q_{II}^M$. Under MQS, the monopolist maximizes (3) subject to (4)–(7) and the minimum quality constraints, $q_i \geqslant \underline{q}, \quad i = I, II$. Using the approach for the solution of the unregulated problem outlined in the Appendix, it is straightforward to demonstrate that the solution to the monopolist's problem under MQS (denoted by a superscript S) has the following features:

(i) Constraints (5) and (6) are binding while (4) and (7) are slack;
(ii) $q_I^S = q_I^M$; i.e., MQS do not affect the quality provided to group I;

[10] Because $v_i(0) = 0$ and $c(0) = 0$, the exclusion of group II from the market is equivalent to offering group II a price-quality pair in which $p_{II}^M = 0$ and $q_{II}^M = 0$.

[11] As noted in the Appendix, a corner solution can be ruled out in our model by assuming

$$v_{II}'(0) - c'(0) - n_I n_{II}^{-1}[v_I'(0) - v_{II}'(0)] \geqslant 0.$$

This assumption will be maintained throughout our analysis.

[12] A complete analysis of the market exclusion issue in a model with a continuum of consumer groups is available in Besanko, Donnenfeld and White [1987].

(iii) $q_{II}^S = \underline{q}$; i.e. the minimum quality constraint is binding for group II;
(iv) $p_{II}^S > p_{II}^M$;
(v) $p_I^S < p_I^M$.

To examine the welfare properties of MQS, we define social welfare as the sum of producer's and consumers' surpluses:

$$W = \sum_{i=I}^{II} n_i[v_i(q_i) - c(q_i)]$$

We now evaluate the derivative of W with respect to $\underline{q}$ at the unregulated equilibrium (i.e., where $\underline{q} = q_{II}^M$). If this derivative is positive, then "slight" MQS would have positive welfare effects. Carrying this out, we find:

$$\text{(12)} \qquad \left.\frac{dW}{d\underline{q}}\right|_{\underline{q} = q_{II}^M} = \sum_{i=I}^{II} n_i[v_i'(q_i) - c'(q_i)]\,\partial q_i/\partial \underline{q}$$

The expression in the square brackets in (12) is zero for $i = I$ by (8) and is positive for $i = II$ by (9). Hence, "slight" MQS must improve welfare. This occurs because the quality level provided to group II, which is distorted by the monopolist, is pushed in a less-distorting direction, while the quality provided to group I is left unchanged. This result provides another instance, like that of Leland [1979] and Shapiro [1983], in which *MQS* can remedy the effects of market failure—incomplete information by buyers about product quality in the Leland and Shapiro models, monopoly power and the monopolist's inability to discriminate perfectly in our model.

It is clear that MQS can be pushed too far—past the point of efficiency for group II—and thus reduce welfare. It is also possible that, short of this point, the monopolist might decide to exclude group II from the market by producing q_I^M solely and selling it at $p_I^M = v(q_I^M)$, thus extracting the maximum surplus from group I.[13] This outcome entails even greater inefficiency than the unregulated equilibrium, since by excluding group II, positive social surplus is foregone.[14]

The effects of the MQS could also be achieved by *minimum* price regulation. Let a minimum price $\underline{p}$ be imposed, such that $p_{II}^M < \underline{p} < p_I^M$. The first-order conditions for profit maximization simplify to:

$$\text{(13)} \qquad v_I'(q_I) = c'(q_I)$$

[13] This outcome is possible even in the absence of a corner solution in the unregulated case. Intuitively, this outcome is more likely to occur the less profitable are sales to group II in the unregulated equilibrium. More specifically, MQS will induce exclusion of group II when the size n_{II} of group II is sufficiently small relative to the size n_I of group I and if group I's total willingness-to-pay $v_I(\underline{q})$ for the minimum allowable quality is sufficiently large relative to group II's total willingness-to-pay $v_{II}(\underline{q})$.

[14] This would not be true in the case in which the unregulated monopolist excludes group II customers from the market. In this case, MQS has no impact—positive or negative—on social welfare.

(14) $v'_{II}(q_{II}) = c'(q_{II}) + n_I n_{II}^{-1}[v'_I(q_{II}) - v'_{II}(q_{II})] - \lambda v'_{II}(q_{II})$

(15) $v_{II}(q_{II}) - \underline{p} = 0$

where $\lambda > 0$ is the Lagrange multiplier associated with the minimum price constraint.

The effects of a change in the minimum price are given by:

(16) $\partial q_I / \partial \underline{p} = 0$

(17) $\partial q_{II} / \partial \underline{p} = [v'_{II}(q_{II})]^{-1} > 0$

Because the positive effects of minimum price regulation are the same as for MQS, the welfare consequences of an initial level of binding regulation must also be the same.

The last result may appear surprising, since minimum price regulation has a history of being used to thwart the effects of competition and in that context causes a welfare reduction. But in our model, the profit-maximizing monopolist distorts quality downwards, so an offsetting distortion (minimum price regulation) can improve welfare.

A third (and equivalent) policy operating directly on the distortion would be a subsidy for the consumption or production of higher-quality goods in the relevant range for group *II*.[15] The subsidy rate would have to be inversely related to quality (i.e., higher-quality goods would receive a lower subsidy), so as to alter the marginal calculus of the monopolist and offset the distortion.

III(ii). *Maximum price regulation* (*MPR*)

Suppose that a ceiling, $\bar{p}$, is placed on the price a monopolist can charge, such that $p_I^M > \bar{p} > p_{II}^M$. Assuming that constraint (7) is slack, the first-order conditions for profit maximization simplify to:[16]

(18) $v'_I(q_I^C) = c'(q_I^C) + \phi n_I^{-1} v'_I(q_I^C)$

(19) $v'_{II}(q_{II}^C) = c'(q_{II}^C) + [n_I - \phi] n_{II}^{-1}[v'_I(q_{II}^C) - v'_{II}(q_{II}^C)]$

(20) $\bar{p} = v_I(q_I^C) - [v_I(q_{II}^C) - v_{II}(q_{II}^C)]$

[15] This assumes, of course, that the deadweight loss caused by taxation to support the subsidy is less than the distortion that is remedied.

[16] In contrast to the unregulated equilibrium in which constraint (6) was binding and constraint (7) was slack at the optimal solution, constraints (6) and (7) may both be binding under MPR, depending on parameter values. When both (6) and (7) are binding the monopolist "pools"—i.e., offers the same price-quality pair $(p^C. q^C)$ to each group. It is straightforward to show that $q_{II}^M < q^C < q_I^M$. Thus, the pooling solution has the same qualitative properties as the solution characterized in (18)–(20). If the ceiling price is sufficiently close to the monopoly price for group *I*, (7) will be slack and conditions (18)–(20) will characterize the optimal solution. A full characterization of the equilibrium under price regulation including the pooling solution is available on request from the authors.

where $\phi > 0$ is the Lagrange multiplier for the constraint $p_I \leqslant \bar{p}$, and the superscript C denotes profit-maximizing values under a price ceiling.[17]

The effect of MPR can be seen by comparing (18) and (19) with conditions (8) and (9), describing the unregulated equilibrium. A comparison of (8) and (18) implies that $q_I^C < q_I^M$—MPR induces a quality deterioration for group I. By contrast, a comparison of (9) and (19) reveals that $q_{II}^C > q_{II}^M$—MPR results in a quality improvement for group II.

The intuition behind these results is straightforward. The unregulated monopolist reduces group II's quality in order to increase the price it can charge group I. Imposition of the price ceiling forces the monopolist to lower group I's price, which limits the benefit to the monopolist from deteriorating group II's quality. Hence, $q_{II}^C > q_{II}^M$. At the same time, the price ceiling limits the surplus the monopolist can extract from group I. Hence, increments to q_I are not as valuable as they otherwise would be. Consequently, $q_I^C < q_I^M$.

To examine the welfare properties of "slight" MPR, we will evaluate the derivative of the welfare function W with respect to $\bar{p}$ at the unregulated equilibrium. Carrying this out, we find:

$$(21) \qquad \left.\frac{dW}{d\bar{p}}\right|_{\bar{p} = p_I^M} = \sum_{i=I}^{II} n_i[v_i'(q_i) - c'(q_i)]\,\partial q_i/\partial \bar{p} < 0$$

From (8) and (9), we know that at the initial equilibrium, the bracketed term is zero for $i = I$ and positive for $i = II$. We also know from the previous discussion that $\partial q_{II}/\partial \bar{p} < 0$; hence the result in (21), which implies that "slight" MPR improves welfare. Note that in this case as well as with MQS, only group I benefits from the regulation; the monopolist continues to extract the full surplus from group II.

As in the case of MQS, MPR can be pushed too far. If $\bar{p} < p_{II}^M < p_I^M$, the solution described in (18)–(20) is not feasible because $p_{II}^C > \bar{p}$.[18] When $\bar{p} < p_{II}^M$, one can show that the monopolist's optimal policy is to offer a single price-quality pair $(\bar{p}, q^C)$ such that $q^C < q_{II}^M < q_I^M$. In this case MPR unambiguously deteriorates product quality and causes social welfare to decrease.

[17] In writing (19) we have assumed that a corner solution is not optimal (i.e., $q_{II}^C > 0$). To justify that assumption note that under a corner solution the first-order condition for q_{II} corresponding to (19) would take the form

$$v_{II}'(0) - c'(0) - [n_I - \phi]n_{II}^{-1}[v_I'(0) - v_{II}'(0)] \leqslant 0$$

However, the above expression contradicts our assumption that

$$v_{II}'(0) - c'(0) - n_I n_{II}^{-1}[v_I'(0) - v_{II}'(0)] \geqslant 0$$

Hence, in contrast to MQS, the imposition of a price ceiling that is sufficiently close to p_I^M does not increase the likelihood that group II is excluded from the market.

The contrasting effects of MQS and MPR on market exclusion have been demonstrated by Besanko, Donnenfeld and White [1987] in a model consisting of a continuum of consumer groups.

[18] This is because $p_{II}^C = v(q_{II}^C) > v(q_{II}^M) = p_{II}^M > \bar{p}$.

It is worth noting that unlike the policy tools operating directly on q_{II}, the price ceiling on p_I does not have an equally effective counterpart in the form of a maximum quality standard for q_I. Such a standard would only lower q_I, causing inefficiency, while not affecting q_{II}.

III(iii). *Rate of return regulation (RORR)*

To examine how RORR affects the firm's quality decision as well as its choice of inputs, we consider the following technology:

$$l = L(k, q)$$

where k is capital and l is labor. $L(k, q)$ denotes the amount of labor required to produce one unit of the good of quality q, given the quantity k of capital per unit of output.[19] The properties of $L(k, q)$ are: (i) $L_k < 0$; (ii) $L_q > 0$; (iii) $L_{kk} > 0$; (iv) $L_{qq} > 0$; and (v) $L_{qk} \lesseqgtr 0$. Property (i) indicates that, for a given q, less labor is required when more capital is used. Property (ii) indicates that for a fixed amount of capital, higher quality requires more labor. Properties (iii) and (iv) reflect the diminishing marginal productivity of labor and capital. Finally, property (v) indicates whether the *marginal* labor requirement L_q for extra quality increases or decreases when more capital is present. Equivalently, this condition indicates whether the marginal rate of substitution L_k of labor for capital increases or decreases as quality increases. When $L_{qk} < (>) 0$, the cost-minimizing quantity of capital increases (decreases) in quality, and capital is a normal (inferior) input with respect to quality.

Let w represent the wage rate and r the cost of capital. The unit production cost $c(q)$ is given by:

$$c(q) = \min_{k \geqslant 0} [wL(q, k) + rk] \tag{22}$$

The profit-maximization problem for the unregulated monopolist yields the following first-order conditions for q_i and k_i:

$$v_I'(q_I^M) = wL_q(q_I^M, k_I^M) \tag{23}$$

$$-wL_k(q_I^M, k_I^M) = r \tag{24}$$

$$v_{II}'(q_{II}^M) = wL_q(q_{II}^M, k_{II}^M) + n_I n_{II}^{-1} [v_I'(q_{II}^M) - v_{II}'(q_{II}^M)] \tag{25}$$

$$-wL_k(q_{II}^M, k_{II}^M) = r \tag{26}$$

(As before, the superscript M denotes profit-maximizing values.) Equations (23) and (25) determine the optimal qualities and are analogous to conditions (8) and (9). Equations (24) and (26) determine the cost-minimizing levels of capital and labor employed to produce goods of quality q_i^M, $i = I, II$.

[19] Recall we are assuming no economies of scale or scope. Thus there is no loss of generality in representing the monopolist's technology in terms of the per unit labor requirement.

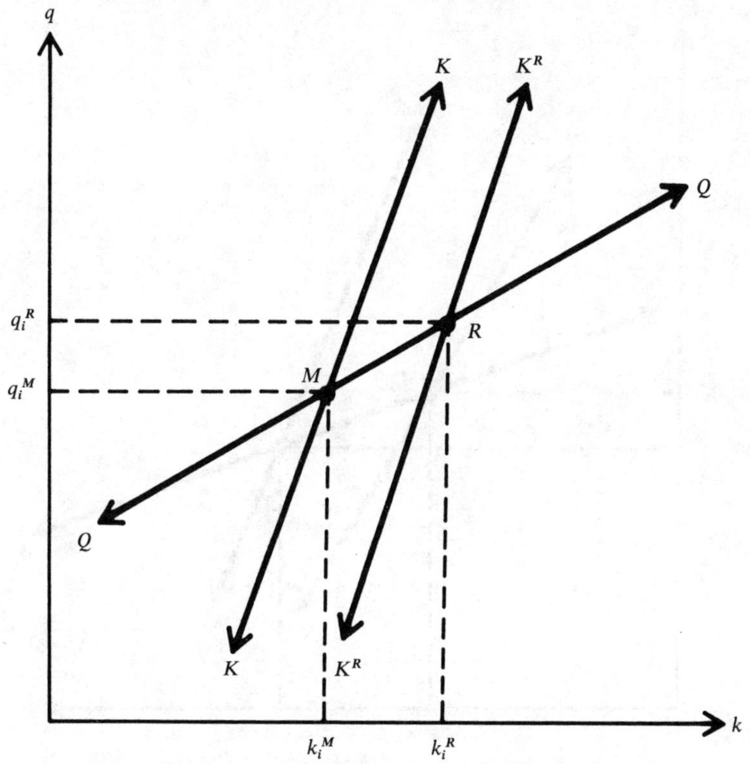

Figure 2
Unregulated and RORR Equilibria: $L_{qk} < 0$

It will prove useful to present the solution to (23)–(26) diagrammatically. The QQ schedule in Figure 2 depicts the profit-maximizing quality q_i for group i as a function of a fixed quantity k_i of capital. For $i = I$, the QQ schedule is derived from (23), and for $i = II$ the QQ schedule is derived from (25). Totally differentiating (23) and (25) with respect to k_i reveals that the QQ schedule is upward (downward) sloping as $L_{qk} < (>) 0$.[20] Figure 2 depicts

[20] Total differentiation of (23) (or (25)) with respect to k_i yields:

$$\left.\frac{dq_i}{dk_i}\right|_{QQ} = \frac{wL_{qk}(q_i, k_i)}{\pi_{q_i q_i}(q_i, k_i)}, \qquad i = I, II, \text{ where } \pi_{q_I q_I}(q_I, k_I) = v_I''(q_I) - wL_{qq}(q_I, k_I),$$

and

$$\pi_{q_{II} q_{II}}(q_{II}, k_{II}) = v_{II}''(q_{II}) - n_I n_{II}^{-1}[v_I''(q_{II}) - v_{II}''(q_{II})] - wL_{qq}(q_{II}, k_{II}).$$

Because $\pi_{q_i q_i} < 0$ for $i = I, II$,

$$\left.\frac{dq_i}{dk_i}\right|_{QQ} \gtrless 0 \quad \text{as} \quad L_{qk} \lesseqgtr 0.$$

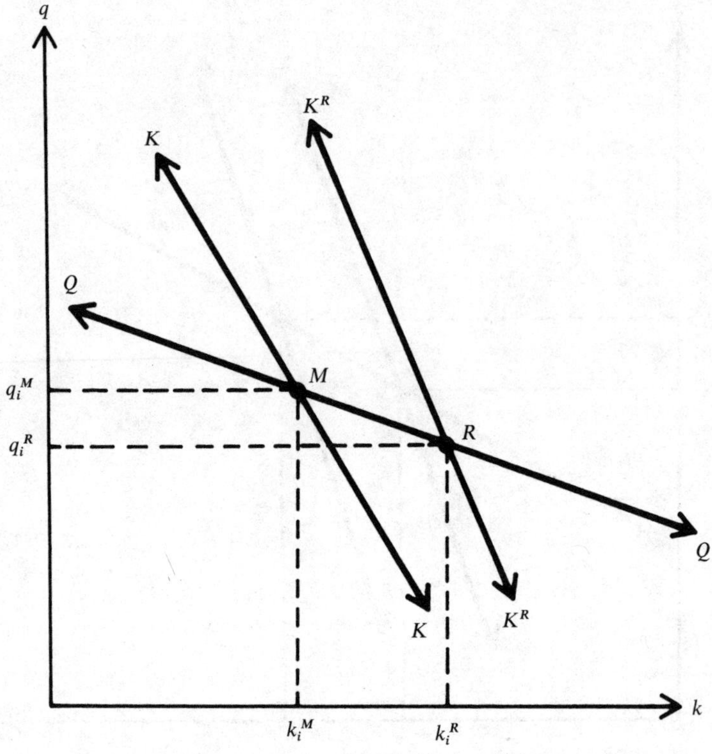

Figure 3
Unregulated and RORR Equilibria: $L_{qk} > 0$

the QQ schedule when $L_{qk} < 0$, and Figure 3 depicts the QQ schedule when $L_{qk} > 0$.

The KK schedule in Figure 2 depicts the cost-minimizing quantity k_i of capital for any fixed quality q_i. This schedule is obtained by solving either (24) or (26) for k_i in terms of q_i. Totally differentiating (24) and (26) with respect to q_i reveals that the KK schedule is upward (downward) sloping as $L_{qk} < (>) 0$.[21] Figure 2 depicts the KK schedule when $L_{qk} < 0$, and Figure 3 depicts the KK schedule when $L_{qk} > 0$.

The profit-maximizing quality q_i^M and capital k_i^M for group i occur at the intersection of the KK and QQ schedules, which is depicted as point M in

[21] Total differentiation of (24) (or (26)) with respect to q_i yields:

$$\left.\frac{dq_i}{dk_i}\right|_{KK} = \frac{-L_{kk}(q_i, k_i)}{L_{qk}(q_i, k_i)} \gtrless 0 \quad \text{as} \quad L_{qk}(q_i, k_i) \lessgtr 0, \quad i = I, II.$$

Figures 2 and 3. The second-order conditions for the profit-maximization problem imply that at point M the KK schedule is steeper than the QQ schedule.[22]

We now examine the impact of RORR. Let s^M denote the unregulated rate of return. Suppose that the allowed rate of return is s, where $r < s < s^M$. This regulatory constraint can be written as:

$$\sum_{i=I}^{II} n_i[p_i - wL(q_i, k_i)] \leqslant s \sum_{i=I}^{II} n_i k_i \tag{27}$$

The regulated firm's profit-maximization problem yields the following first-order conditions:

$$v_I'(q_I^R) = wL_q(q_I^R, k_I^R) \tag{23'}$$

$$-wL_k(q_I^R, k_I^R) = \frac{r - \psi s}{1 - \psi} \tag{24'}$$

$$v_{II}'(q_{II}^R) = wL_q(q_{II}^R, k_{II}^R) + n_I n_{II}^{-1}[v_I'(q_{II}^R) - v_{II}'(q_{II}^R)] \tag{25'}$$

$$-wL_k(q_{II}^R, k_{II}^R) = \frac{r - \psi s}{1 - \psi} \tag{26'}$$

where $0 < \psi < 1$ is the Lagrange multiplier associated with (27). The superscript R denotes the maximizing values under RORR.

The principal implications of our analysis are: (i) RORR induces the firm to increase its employment of capital; (ii) the monopolist will increase (decrease) the quality offered to each group if $L_{qk} < (>) 0$.[23]

We prove these results as follows. First, note that (23′) and (25′) are identical to (23) and (25); i.e., in both cases the quality schedule is depicted by the same QQ schedule. However, (24′) and (26′) differ from (24) and (26), since

[22] The second-order conditions for the profit-maximization problem imply:

$$\Delta_i = (\pi_{k_i k_i} \pi_{q_i q_i} - \pi_{q_i k_i}^2)|_M > 0, \quad i = I, II, \text{ where } \pi_{q_i k_i} = -wL_{qk}(q_i, k_i),$$

and

$$\pi_{k_i k_i} = -wL_{kk}(q_i, k_i), \quad i = I, II.$$

Rearranging the expression for Δ_i yields:

$$\left.\frac{dq_i}{dk_i}\right|_{KK}^{M} = \frac{-L_{kk}(q_i^M, k_i^M)}{L_{qk}(q_i^M, k_i^M)} \gtrless \frac{wL_{qk}(q_i^M, k_i^M)}{\pi_{q_i q_i}(q_i^M, k_i^M)} = \left.\frac{dq_i}{dk_i}\right|_{QQ}^{M}, \qquad \text{as } L_{qk} \lesseqgtr 0, \qquad i = I, II.$$

When $L_{qk} < 0$ the QQ and KK schedules slope upward, and the KK schedule is steeper at M. When $L_{qk} > 0$ the QQ and KK schedules slope downward, and the KK schedule has a more negative slope at M.

[23] Spence [1975] obtains a similar result in the context of a model in which the regulated monopolist is assumed to produce a single quality. Sheshinski [1976] also presents a model of RORR similar to that of Spence.

the effective cost of capital under RORR is $\hat{r} \equiv \dfrac{r - \psi s}{1 - \psi}$. Since $0 < \psi < 1$, $\hat{r} < r$. Consequently, the capital schedule $K^R K^R$ corresponding to (24′) (or (26′)) lies to the right of KK. From Figure 2, $L_{qk} < 0$ implies $k_i^R > k_i^M$ and $q_i^R > q_i^M$ for $i = I, II$. From Figure 3, $L_{qk} > 0$ implies $k_i^R > k_i^M$ and $q_i^R < q_i^M$ for $i = I, II$.

Intuitively, RORR reduces the firm's effective cost of capital, which induces the firm to increase its capital stock. If $L_{qk} < 0$, the higher-quality good (q_I) is more capital-intensive. Thus, expansion of the capital stock takes place most readily by increasing the quality of the high-quality good. This in turn slackens the self-selection constraint and leads to an increase in quality for the low-quality good as well. Hence, the firm reacts to RORR by upgrading the entire quality schedule.

By contrast, when $L_{qk} > 0$, lower-quality goods are more capital-intensive. Hence, the monopolist expands its use of capital by *decreasing* the quality levels of both the high-quality and the low-quality goods.

Thus, depending on the nature of technology, the positive effects of RORR are mixed. The regulated monopolist always uses too much capital. But if $L_{qk} < 0$, the monopolist upgrades the qualities provided to both consumer types. This diminishes the distortion faced by consumers who prefer low-quality goods but introduces a new distortion for those who prefer high-quality goods. By contrast, if $L_{qk} > 0$, the monopolist decreases the quality provided to both types and unequivocally increases the distortion.

The normative effects of RORR are similarly mixed. To address the welfare question, we examine the case of "slight" RORR—i.e., a level of s sufficiently close to s^M.[24] Social welfare is given by:

$$W = \sum_{i=I}^{II} n_i[v_i(q_i) - wL(q_i, k_i) - rk_i]$$

Differentiating W with respect to s and evaluating at $s = s^M$ yields:

$$(28)\qquad \left.\frac{dW}{ds}\right|_{s = s^M} = \sum_{i=I}^{II} n_i[v_i'(q_i^M) - wL_q(q_i^M, k_i^M)]\, \partial q_i^M/\partial s - \sum_{i=I}^{II} n_i[wL_k(q_i^M, k_i^M) + r]\, \partial k_i^M/\partial s \lesseqgtr 0, \qquad \text{as } L_{qk} \lesseqgtr 0$$

From (23) and (25), the expression in the first square brackets in (28) is zero for $i = I$ and positive for $i = II$. The term $\partial q_i^M/\partial s$ is negative (positive) if

[24] This analysis is similar to Sheshinski's [1971] welfare analysis of RORR of a single-product monopolist. Callen, Mathewson and Mohring [1976] present an alternative welfare analysis of RORR in the single-product context.

$L_{qk} < (>) 0$. Hence, when $L_{qk} < (>) 0$ the first term in (28) is strictly negative (positive). From (24) and (26), the expression in the second square brackets in (28) is zero for $i = I, II$. Thus, the overall effect of "slight" RORR is to increase welfare when $L_{qk} < 0$ and decrease welfare when $L_{qk} > 0$.

Our analysis shows that an additional distortion can accompany RORR when the regulated firm produces a good or service with a quality dimension. Averch and Johnson [1962] demonstrated that a two-product regulated monopolist would distort prices to encourage sales of the more capital-intensive product. But their model did not encompass any notion of quality. In our analysis the regulated monopolist produces the two products (two quality levels) and is induced to distort the quality levels themselves.

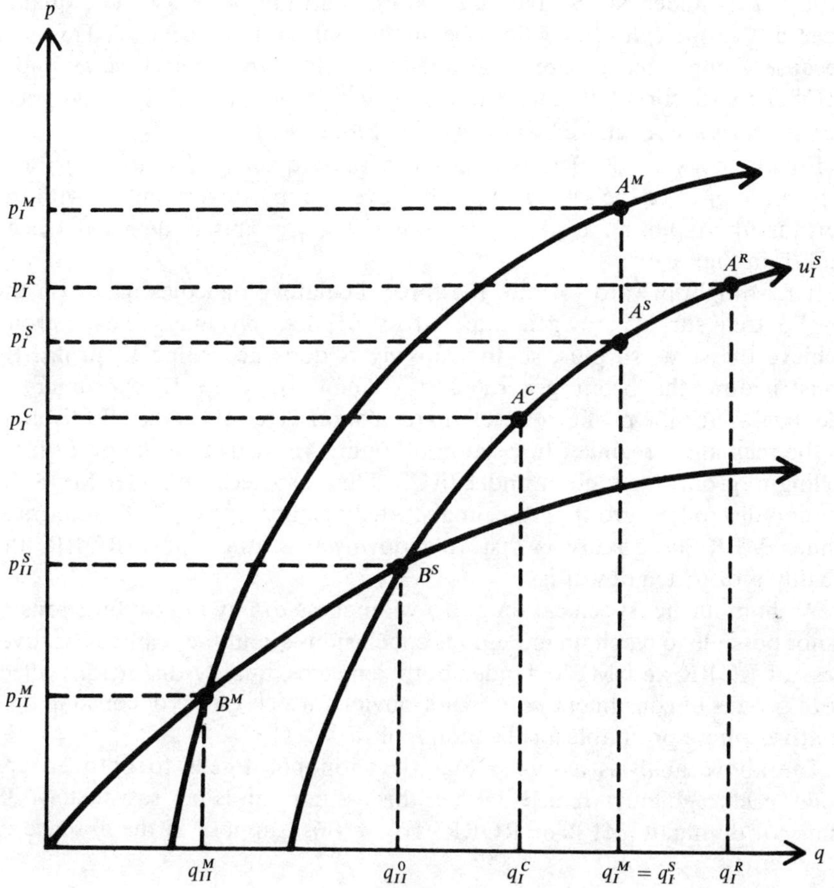

Figure 4
Comparison of Regulatory Remedies

IV. A COMPARISON OF REGULATORY REMEDIES

We have seen that MQS, MPR and RORR counteract monopolistic distortions in different ways. However, it is not obvious which remedy is most effective. To compare their effectiveness, we choose the following benchmark: the regulator structures a regulatory policy to induce the monopolist to offer group *II* buyers a "target" quality q_{II}^0 which exceeds q_{II}^M.[25] Such a target could be reached by imposing MQS, $\underline{q} = q_{II}^0$. From our discussion in section III(i), we know that $p_{II}^S > p_{II}^M$, $q_I^S = q_I^M$ and $p_I^S < p_I^M$. Thus group *I* buyers end up with a surplus u_I^S that is higher than the surplus obtained without MQS. This is depicted by the price-quality pairs A^S and B^S in Figure 4.

Consider now MPR that induces the monopolist to offer the same pair to group *II* as under MQS, that is, $q_{II}^C = q_{II}^S = q_{II}^0$ and $p_{II}^C = p_{II}^S$. The quality offered to group *I* at $p_I^C = \bar{p}$ must be on the same surplus curve u_I^S. This is so because group *I* buyers are confronted with the same alternative as under MQS. From section III(ii), we know $q_I^C < q_I^M$. Hence, under MPR the price-quality pairs are A^C and B^S, as depicted in Figure 4.

Finally, consider RORR that leads to same quality $q_{II}^R = q_{II}^S = q_{II}^0$ and thus $p_{II}^R = p_{II}^S$. For the same reason as above, group *I* buyers end up with the surplus u_I^S. Assuming $L_{qk} < 0$, we know $q_I^R > q_I^M$. This is depicted by A^R and B^S in Figure 4.

It is straightforward to rank the three regulatory remedies based on the level of total surplus they generate. Across regimes, consumers in each group achieve the same surplus, so the ranking is done according to profit. By construction, the profit generated by selling to group *II* consumers is identical. Thus the profit from selling to group *I* determines the effectiveness of the regulatory regimes. Inspection of Figure 4 reveals that the profit from selling to group *I* is highest under MQS. This is so because under MQS the monopolist offers group *I* the undistorted quality $q_I^S = q_I^M$. By contrast, under MPR the quality is distorted downwards, and under RORR, the quality is distorted upwards.

Without further specification of the willingness-to-pay or cost functions, it is not possible to reach unambiguous conclusions about the relative effectiveness of RORR and MPR. Under both remedies, quality distortions affect both groups of consumers, so it is not obvious which group of consumers is relatively more profitable for the monopolist.

The above analysis assumed that the monopolist sells to both groups under each regulatory remedy. When this assumption is not satisfied, MQS may not dominate MPR or RORR. To see this, suppose in the absence of

[25] Clearly the target q_{II}^0 must be *feasible*. That is, under the proposed regulatory remedies it must be rational for the monopolist to offer quality q_{II}^0 to group *II*. Throughout this discussion we therefore assume that under any regulatory remedy the monopolist serves both groups.

regulation the monopolist is indifferent between serving and not serving group *II*. Under MQS for any arbitrary $\underline{q}$ the monopolist would sell only to group *I*, and MQS would not increase social welfare. By contrast, under "slight" MPR the monopolist would continue to sell to both groups and would increase the quality offered to group *II*.[26] As the analysis of "slight" MPR indicates, social welfare would increase.

Thus, the welfare ranking of the regulatory remedies depends in part on the relative profitability of the low willingness-to-pay group. If this group is highly profitable for the monopolist in the unregulated equilibrium, then the preferred regulatory remedy would be MQS. If, however, this group is only marginally profitable in the unregulated equilibrium, either MPR or RORR may be preferable to MQS, with the choice between MPR and RORR depending on the parameters of the utility and cost functions and the relative number of consumers in groups *I* and *II*.

An alternative method for analyzing comparative welfare effects would be to first determine the quality standard, price ceiling, and rate of return that maximize total surplus. These maximization problems would take into account the monopolist's response to a remedy. Then one would compare maximum total surpluses across optimal regulatory regimes. A comparison of welfare effects along these lines will be the topic of future research.

V. CONCLUSION

A monopolist will use its market power to distort the quality choices offered to consumers, thereby inducing social inefficiency. We have explored the properties of three regulatory remedies—MQS, MPR, and RORR—that can counteract this distortion. All three can improve social welfare. They operate in different ways, however. MQS and MPR both raise the quality offered to consumers who prefer low-quality goods, thereby reducing the distortion faced by these consumers. By contrast, RORR has mixed effects. If higher-quality goods are relatively capital-intensive, RORR increases the qualities offered to *both* consumer groups, which reduces the distortion faced by the consumers who prefer low-quality goods but distorts the quality offered to consumers who prefer high-quality goods. On the other hand, if lower-quality goods are relatively capital-intensive, RORR causes quality to be distorted downward to both consumer types. In either case, RORR causes too much capital to be used.

We also examined the relative effectiveness of the above regulatory instruments and found that MQS dominates other types of regulation as long as the firm continues to serve all consumers after the standards have been

[26] See footnote 17 above.

imposed. If this assumption does not hold, however, then either MPR or RORR may dominate MQS.

DAVID BESANKO,
School of Business,
Indiana University,
Bloomington, IN 47401,
USA.

ACCEPTED JUNE 1987

SHABTAI DONNENFELD,
Recanati Graduate School of Business,
Tel-Aviv University,
Tel-Aviv 69978,
Israel.

LAWRENCE J. WHITE,
Graduate School of Business Administration,
New York University,
New York, NY 10006,
USA.

APPENDIX

In this Appendix we characterize the profit-maximizing prices and qualities (p_i^M, q_i^M), $i = I, II$. To characterize the solution to the profit-maximization problem, we will assume that (4) and (7) are slack and characterize the solution to the less-constrained problem: maximize (3) subject to (5), (6) and $q_i \geqslant 0$, $p_i \geqslant 0$ for $i = I, II$. We then demonstrate that that solution satisfies (4) and (7), which implies that the optimal solution to the less-constrained problem is the optimal solution to the profit-maximization problem.

As a first step in the characterization of the less-constrained problem, note that (6) must be a binding constraint. Otherwise, the monopolist could increase p_I slightly and increase profits. Thus

(A.1) $$p_I = v_I(q_I) - v_I(q_{II}) + p_{II}$$

Note, too, that (5) must be a binding constraint. Otherwise, the monopolist could increase p_{II} and increase profits. Thus

(A.2) $$p_{II} = v_{II}(q_{II})$$

Substituting (A.1) and (A.2) into (3) we can restate the less-constrained problem as

(A.3) $$\max_{q_i \geqslant 0} n_I\{v_I(q_I) - c(q_I)\} + n_{II}\{v_{II}(q_{II}) - n_I n_{II}^{-1}[v_I(q_{II}) - v_{II}(q_{II})] - c(q_{II})\}$$

(The non-negativity constraints on p_i have been dropped; as will become evident below, they will always be satisfied by the solution to the problem in (A.3).)

To ensure the existence of a unique interior solution to the less-constrained problem we shall assume that

$$v_{II}(q) - n_I n_{II}^{-1}[v_I(q) - v_{II}(q)] - c(q)$$

is strictly pseudo-concave in q and

$$v_{II}'(0) - n_I n_{II}^{-1}[v_I'(0) - v_{II}'(0)] - c'(0) \geqslant 0$$

The necessary and sufficient conditions for the less-constrained problem are:

(A.4) $v_I'(q_I^M) = c'(q_I^M)$

(A.5) $v_{II}'(q_{II}^M) - n_I n_{II}^{-1}[v_I'(q_{II}^M) - v_{II}'(q_{II}^M)] - c'(q_{II}^M) = 0$

Conditions (A.4) and (A.5) together with our assumptions on $v_i(\cdot)$ and $v_i'(\cdot)$ imply:

$$q_I^M = q_I^* > q_{II}^* > q_{II}^M$$

The corresponding prices are derived from (A.1) and (A.2) and are given by:

(A.6) $p_I^M = v_I(q_I^M) - [v_I(q_{II}^M) - v_{II}(q_{II}^M)] > 0$

(A.7) $p_{II}^M = v_{II}(q_{II}^M)$

To verify that the solution to the less-constrained problem satisfies (7), note that (A.6) and (A.7) imply:

(A.8) $v_{II}(q_{II}^M) - p_{II}^M - \{v_{II}(q_I^M) - p_I^M\} = \{v_I(q_I^M) - v_{II}(q_I^M)\} - \{v_I(q_{II}^M) - v_{II}(q_{II}^M)\} > 0$

The inequality in (A.8) follows because we have assumed that $v_I(q) - v_{II}(q)$ is increasing in q and $q_I^M > q_{II}^M$.

To verify that (4) is satisfied, note:

$$v_I(q_I^M) - p_I^M = v_I(q_{II}^M) - v_{II}(q_{II}^M) > 0$$

Hence the optimal solution to the less-constrained problem satisfies (4) and (7), and therefore represents the solution to the monopolist's profit-maximization problem.

REFERENCES

AVERCH, H. and JOHNSON, L. L., 1962, 'Behavior of the Firm Under Regulatory Constraint', *American Economic Review*, 52, pp. 1053–1069.

BESANKO, D. and DONNENFELD, S., 1986, 'Monopoly, Product Variety, and Regulation', unpublished manuscript.

BESANKO, D., DONNENFELD, S. and WHITE, L. J., 1987, 'Monopoly and Quality Distortion: Effects and Remedies', *Quarterly Journal of Economics* (forthcoming).

CALLEN, J., MATHEWSON, G. F. and MOHRING, H., 1976, "The Benefits and Costs of Rate of Return Regulation', *American Economic Review*, 66, pp. 290–297.

DONNENFELD, S. and WHITE, L. J., 1984, "Product Variety and the Inefficiency of Monopoly', New York University Working Paper.

LELAND, H. E., 1979, "Quacks, Lemons, and Licensing: A Theory of Minimum Quality Standards', *Journal of Political Economy*, 86, pp. 1328–1346.

MASKIN, E. and RILEY, J., 1984, 'Monopoly with Incomplete Information', *Rand Journal of Economics*, 15, pp. 171–196.

MUSSA, M. and ROSEN, S., 1978, 'Monopoly and Product Quality', *Journal of Economic Theory*, 18, pp. 301–317.

SHAPIRO, C., 1983, 'Premiums for High Quality Products as Returns to Reputations', *Quarterly Journal of Economics*, 98, pp. 659–679.

SHESHINSKI, E., 1971, 'Welfare Aspects of a Regulatory Constraint: Note', *American Economic Review*, 61, pp. 175–178.

SHESHINSKI, E., 1976, 'Quality and Quantity Regulation in Monopoly Situations', *Economica*, 43, pp. 127–137.

SPENCE, A. M., 1975, 'Monopoly, Quality and Regulation', *Bell Journal of Economics*, 6, pp. 417–429.

WHITE, L. J., 1977, 'Market Structure and Product Varieties', *American Economic Review*, 67, pp. 179–182.

THE JOURNAL OF INDUSTRIAL ECONOMICS 0022-1821 $2.00
Volume XXXVI June 1988 No. 4

CAN PRICE COMPETITION DOMINATE MARKET SEGMENTATION?

X. Martinez-Giralt and D. J. Neven*

This note analyses duopoly competition in a two stage (location-price) game, while allowing each firm to establish a couple of outlets. Both the circle and the line model of spatial competition are considered. Our main result is clear-cut: in equilibrium neither firm will take up the opportunity of opening two stores. This is a warning that market segmentation, i.e. competition from multiple outlets, might not be attractive at all, because it entails more intense price competition.

I. INTRODUCTION

It is often argued that the theory of spatial competition would gain in relevance by allowing firms to establish several outlets. Indeed, to open several retail shops in a given neighbourhood (e.g. food stores or petrol stations) is common practice for a firm in the real world. Thinking in terms of differentiated products, it is not unusual either to observe large corporations selling several products in the same market. By doing so, firms can tailor products for different (horizontal) market segments and accordingly charge higher prices.

Brander and Eaton [1984] first analysed competition between multi-product firms. They examined a constellation of four possible products and assumed that both duopolists will sell a pair of products. By contrast, we shall assume that there is a continuum of possible product "locations". We consider two popular paradigms of spatial competition, namely the bounded line and the unit circle. We assume that two firms operate, each of them being allowed to set up a couple of outlets. We seek a perfect equilibrium in a two stage game such that firms decide on the locations of their outlets in the first stage and subsequently compete in prices.

In this context, the outlets opened by the firms could be of two types: on the one hand, firms' outlets could be intertwined ("interlaced"), so that any outlet of a firm is surrounded by the outlets of its competitor. On the other hand, firms could select neighbouring positions for their outlets. When the set of possible locations is represented by a bounded line, it is well known that (with quadratic transport costs) duopolists with a single outlet will locate at opposite ends of the market (d'Aspremont *et al.* [1979]). In addition, a monopolist will usually find it profitable to open several stores (Bonnano

* CORE (Louvain-la-Neuve, Belgium) and INSEAD (Fontainebleau, France). We would like to thank J.-F. Thisse for very useful comments.

[1987]). It would thus accord with intuition that duopolists with a couple of stores each should take up the opportunity of segmenting the market, presumably with neighbouring positions.

When the set of possible products is represented by a circle, intuition would call for an equilibrium in which firms open intertwined outlets, at opposite points of a diameter. Indeed, we know that duopolists with a single retail point would choose that configuration. Besides, symmetric locations would also accord with intuition, so that firms would select orthogonal diameters. Hence, we would expect to obtain a store at each quarter, opposite stores being managed by the same firm.

However, none of these intuitions proves correct in our models because they underestimate the impact of price competition. For both the circle and the line models, we find that in equilibrium each firm will bunch its two stores at the same point! Hence, the incentive to relax price competition dominates the incentive to segment the market. This is also to say that Brander and Eaton's [1984] assumption that both firms select two products is not innocuous. When the number of products is endogenised, it turns out (at least in these models) that product line rivalry will never occur. Section II deals with the circle model of spatial competition while section III will be devoted to the line model.

II. THE CIRCLE MODEL OF SPATIAL COMPETITION

The model is of two firms locating in the unit circle, each one running two outlets and selling an homogeneous commodity. Production takes place at constant marginal costs (zero, without loss of generality). Consumers are uniformly distributed over the circle and have a rectangular demand, with the same reservation price. This reservation price will be arbitrarily large so that each consumer will buy one unit from the outlet for which delivered price is lowest. Consumers thus bear the transportation cost which we assume will be quadratic in the distance. Before looking at location tendencies (B), we seek (A) a price equilibrium, locations being fixed.

A—*Price Equilibrium*

We shall take in turn the two cases distinguished above, with on the one hand intertwined outlets and on the other hand neighbouring retail points.

(i) Intertwined outlets. Assume firm $T(S)$ has opened two stores at locations $T_1, T_2)((S_1, S_2))$ as pictured in Figure 1. The marginal consumer $\bar{X}_{ij}$, indifferent between buying from T_i at price P_{Ti} and S_j at price P_{Sj} is defined as:

$$\bar{X}_{ij} = \frac{P_{Ti} - P_{Sj}}{2(T_i - S_j)} + \frac{T_i + S_j}{2}$$

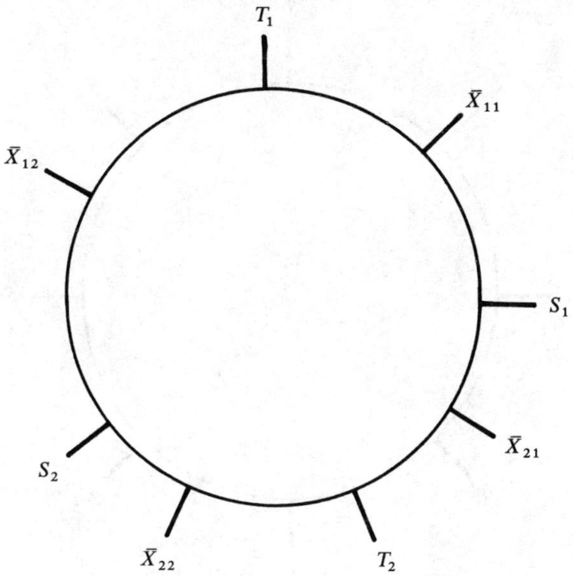

Figure 1

Picking an origin for normalisation ($S_1 = 0$), the aggregate demand curves $D(.)$ can be written:

$$D(S_1) = \bar{X}_{11} + (1 - \bar{X}_{21})$$

$$D(S_2) = \bar{X}_{22} - \bar{X}_{12}$$

$$D(T_1) = \bar{X}_{12} - \bar{X}_{11}$$

$$D(T_2) = \bar{X}_{21} - \bar{X}_{22}$$

These demand functions are linear in prices, hence concave. Profits will thus be quasi-concave and existence of equilibrium follows from standard arguments (see e.g. Friedmann [1977]).[1] As shown in Martinez-Giralt [1985] this equilibrium is also unique.

(ii) Neighbouring outlets. A configuration with neighbouring outlets is represented in Figure 2. We need to define additional marginal consumers, indifferent between buying two products of the same firm, say $\bar{X}_K$, with $K = S, T$:

$$\bar{X}_K = \frac{P_{K_2} - P_{K_1}}{2(K_2 - K_1)} + \frac{K_2 - K_1}{2}$$

[1] Explicit equilibrium prices are available upon request from the authors.

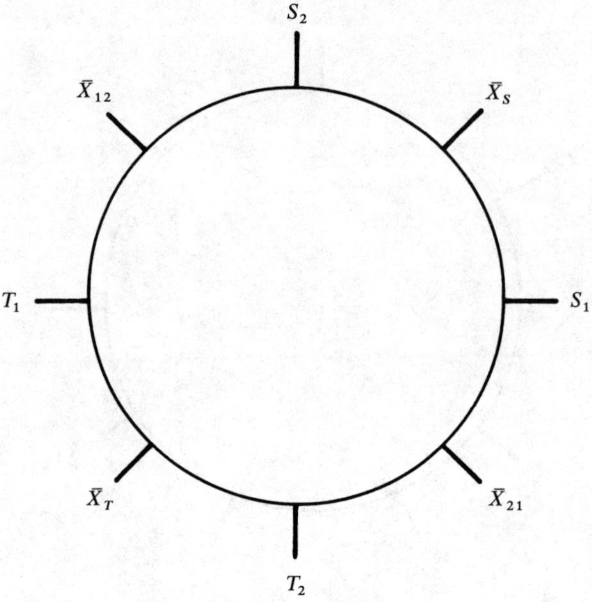

Figure 2

The aggregate demand functions are then written:

$$D(S_1) = \bar{X}_S + (1 - \bar{X}_{21})$$

$$D(S_2) = \bar{X}_{12} - \bar{X}_S$$

$$D(T_1) = \bar{X}_T - \bar{X}_{12}$$

$$D(T_2) = \bar{X}_{21} - \bar{X}_T$$

Again demand is concave. So is profit and hence, equilibrium exists.[2] A proof for uniqueness of this equilibrium is provided in Martinez-Giralt [1985].

B—*Locations*

Our main result is summarised as follows:

Proposition 1. Consider a two-stage game in which firms position their outlets in the first stage and subsequently compete in prices. There is a perfect equilibrium in this game such that each firm positions its two outlets at the same point. In equilibrium, firms locate (their two outlets) at opposite ends of a diameter.

[2] Again, equilibrium prices can be provided upon request.

The proof of this proposition is developed in the appendix and goes along the following lines: first, it is shown that, if one firm locates its two outlets at a single point, the second firm will position its two outlets symmetrically around that point. Second, we investigate this set of symmetric locations and show that in equilibrium this second firm will also collapse its two outlets into a single point. It follows that a location pattern in which firms collapse their outlets at opposite points of a diameter is in equilibrium.

Next, in order to qualify uniqueness of the equilibrium just derived, we will focus on quasi-symmetric location patterns: these are location patterns such that outlets (whoever owns them) are positioned at opposite ends of two diameters. We obtain the following result:

Proposition 2. (i) The equilibrium described in Proposition 1 is unique among quasi-symmetric patterns involving neighbouring outlets. (ii) In addition, there is no quasi-symmetric equilibrium such that firms' outlets are intertwined.

The first part of this proposition, which deals with quasi-symmetric patterns involving neighbouring positions, is shown in Martinez-Giralt [1985]. The proof, which will not be reproduced here, is based on the observation that a firm will always have an incentive to locate its two outlets as close as possible, whatever the quasi-symmetric locations of the other firm. Hence, the only equilibrium with neighbouring patterns is such that firms collapse their outlets. With respect to the second part of Proposition 2, dealing with intertwined patterns, a proof is provided in the Appendix. It proceeds by elimination: first we show that only the symmetric pattern could be in equilibrium (among intertwined positions). Second, we find that departing from symmetric intertwined positions would be optimal because firms would have an incentive to switch towards a neighbouring pattern.

Hence, even though intuition would *a priori* call for a location equilibrium in which firms segment the market with intertwined positions, we find that neighbouring positions will always be preferred. Moreover, there is an equilibrium, unique among quasi-symmetric patterns such that firms collapse their outlets. This result stems from the strength of price competition; by choosing neighbouring positions, firms avoid price competition since their outlets will then face competition (in total) on two sides only (instead of four with intertwined patterns). Similarly, collapsing the outlets will relax price competition best, since the distance between competitors will then be maximised.

With respect to the uniqueness of equilibrium, we cannot rule out the existence of asymmetric equilibria. However, asymmetric equilibria seem highly unlikely, given the symmetry of the model.

Next, one can wonder whether the results obtained are not specific to the circle model of spatial competition. Indeed, while locating on a circle, firms cannot avoid competing on both sides of their market. By contrast, on a line, if firms choose neighbouring positions, they will compete on one side only. Firms might thus have a stronger incentive to open two outlets, in order to raise price in their submarket. We shall now turn to this second model.

III. THE LINE MODEL OF SPATIAL COMPETITION

In this section we assume that the set of products can be represented as a bounded line of length L. All the other assumptions of the previous model are kept. It is well known (see d'Aspremont *et al.* [1979]) that, with quadratic transport cost, a price equilibrium exists in duopoly and is unique. As shown by Bonanno [1987], allowing firms to establish a second outlet does not jeopardise the concavity of profits, and, hence, equilibrium. With respect to locations, we obtain the following result:

Proposition 3. Assume that two firms, allowed to establish a couple of outlets, locate on a line and subsequently compete in price. There is a perfect equilibrium in this game such that both firms collapse their outlets and locate at opposite ends of the line.

The proof of this proposition can be found in the Appendix. For the sake of brevity, we shall not be concerned in this section with uniqueness of the equilibrium. It can, however, be discussed along the same line as above.

To conclude, it does not seem that the lack of incentive to set up a product "line", is peculiar to the circle model. A similar behaviour of collapsing the outlets into a single point is portrayed in the line model. As before, the incentive to relax price competition drives the result.

CONCLUSION

In this note, we have developed the two simple models allowing for competition from multiple outlets. For the circle model of spatial competition, we conclude that firms will always prefer to compete from a connected segment of the market. Hence, it is not optimal for firms to split the market into several disconnected segments (thus involving intertwined outlets). Firms will prefer to select neighbouring positions for their stores and will optimally collapse them into a single point. Consequently, neither firm takes up the opportunity of opening two stores. They do so because the resulting location pattern best internalises price competition. Accordingly, the incentive to relax price competition dominates the incentive to segment the market.

The same result holds in Hotelling's model (linear bounded market, instead of a circle). There is an equilibrium such that firms collapse their outlets at opposite ends of the line.

The assumption of a quadratic transportation cost might, however, be crucial for these results, since this function is known to generate most intense price competition (see d'Aspremont *et al.* [1979], or Neven [1985]). All in all, this note issues a warning that the question of multi-outlets competition might be void if price competition were intense. This problem should thus be carefully modelled by allowing for additional ingredients such as elastic demand, economics of scope or the threat of entry.

X. MARTINEZ-GIRALT,
CORE,
34 Voie du Roman Pays,
1348 Louvain-la-Neuve,
Belgium.

ACCEPTED JULY 1987

D. J. NEVEN,
INSEAD,
Boulevard de Constance,
77305 Fontainebleau,
France.

APPENDIX

A—*Proof of Proposition 1*

Assume that firm S positions its two stores at the same spot. The profit of firm T can then be expressed as a function of the distance β_2, β_3 (with $S_1 = 1-\beta_2+\beta_3$), (see Figure 3).

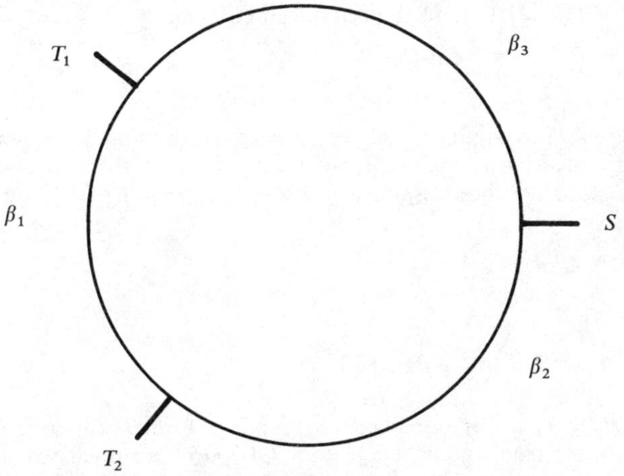

Figure 3

Having substituted for equilibrium prices, the profit of firm T is written:

$$\Pi_T(\beta_2, \beta_3) = \frac{A}{72(\beta_2+\beta_3)(1-\beta_2-\beta_3)}$$

where

$$\begin{aligned}A = {} & 9(\beta_3)^5+9(\beta_2)^5-18(\beta_3)^4-18(\beta_2)^5+9(\beta_3)^3+9(\beta_2)^3\\ & +\beta_3[-4(\beta_2)^5+45(\beta_2)^4-96(\beta_2)^3+55(\beta_2)^2]\\ & +(\beta_3)^2[55\beta_2-156(\beta_2)^2+90(\beta_2)^3-16(\beta_2)^4]\\ & +(\beta_3)^3[-96\beta_2+90(\beta_2)^2-24(\beta_2)^3]\\ & +(\beta_3)^4[45\beta_2-16(\beta_2)^2]-4(\beta_3)^5\beta_2\end{aligned}$$

Note that at $\beta_3 = 1-\beta_2$, the profit function is not defined ($\Pi_T(S) = 0/0$). First, we show that the critical points of this function occur for symmetric locations around S (this is $\beta_3 = \beta_2$).

Transform the profit function, using the following change of variable: $\beta_3 = z-\beta_2$, with $z \in [0, 1]$. One obtains:

$$\Pi_T(z-B_2, \beta_2) = \Pi_T(z, \beta_2) = \frac{A'}{72z^2(1-z)} \qquad \text{in which } A' = A'(z, \beta_2)$$

Clearly,

$$\frac{\partial \Pi_T(z, \beta_2)}{\partial(\beta_2)} = 0, \qquad \text{if} \quad \frac{\partial A'(z, \beta_2)}{\partial(\beta_2)} = 0$$

and

$$\frac{\partial A'(z, \beta_2)}{\partial(\beta_2)} = 4z(2\beta_2(z^3+6z-7)-z(z^3+6z-7))$$

which is equal to zero if $\beta_2 = z/2$. It follows that critical points of the profit function will only occur if $\beta_2 = \beta_3$. Next, we concentrate on these locations (such that $\beta_2 = \beta_3$). As mentioned above, the profit function is not defined for $\beta_2 = 1-\beta_3$, (which in this case implies $\beta_2 = \beta_3 = \frac{1}{2}$). Using l'Hopital rule, we obtain:

$$\lim_{\beta_3 \to 1-\beta_2} \Pi_T(\beta_3, \beta_2) = \frac{\beta_2(1-\beta_2)}{2}$$

This expression has a maximum for $\beta_2 = \frac{1}{2}$. Hence, positioning its two outlets at the same point (opposite S) is an optimal reply (locally) for firm T. Finally, we check that this strategy is globally a best response; when $\beta_2 = \beta_3 = \beta$, $\beta \in [0, \frac{1}{2}]$, profits can be written as:

$$\Pi_T(\beta) = \tfrac{1}{9}\beta(\beta-2)^2$$

and

$$\frac{\partial \Pi_T(\beta)}{\partial(\beta)} > 0, \qquad \text{for all } \beta \in [0, \tfrac{1}{2}]$$

Consequently, $\beta_2 = \beta_3 = \frac{1}{2}$, is globally a best response. Firm T will optimally collapse its two outlets into a single point, opposite S. Of course, a similar reasoning can be held for firm S, so that there is a perfect equilibrium such that each firm opens one store at opposite ends of a diameter.

B—*Proof of Proposition 2*

We show first (1) that only the symmetric pattern could be in equilibrium. We subsequently (2) rule it out as well.

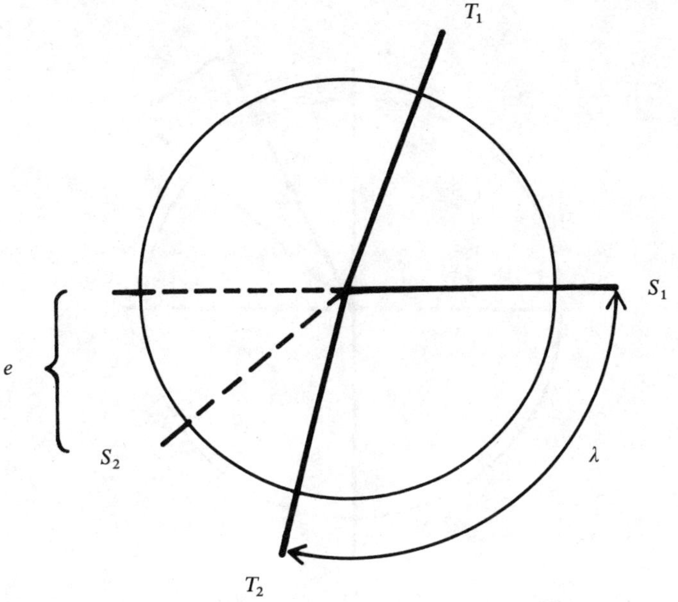

Figure 4

(1) We concentrate on firm S (a similar reasoning can be held for firm T and will be omitted). We look at the situation described in Figure 3, in which firm S contemplates moving its second store S_2, at some distance e, away from a quasi-symmetric pattern. Its profit can then be expressed as a function of λ and e only (see Figure 4), in which λ characterises the set of quasi-symmetric locations:

$$\Pi_S(e, \lambda) = \overset{*}{P}{}^2_{S_1}[4\lambda(\tfrac{1}{2}-\lambda)]^{-1} + \overset{*}{P}{}^2_{S_2}[4(\tfrac{1}{2}-\lambda+e)(\lambda-e)]^{-1}$$

in which $\overset{*}{P}_{S_1}$, $\overset{*}{P}_{S_2}$ denote equilibrium prices for S_1 and S_2, respectively (from the second stage). We evaluate the first derivative of this profit function with respect to e at $e = 0$, in order to find out whether firm S has an incentive to depart from a quasi-symmetric pattern:

$$\frac{\partial \Pi_S(e, \lambda)}{\partial e}\Big|_{e=0} =$$

$$\frac{P_{S_1|e=0}}{2\lambda(\frac{1}{2}-\lambda)}\left[\frac{-(27/8)\lambda+(27/4)\lambda^2+72\lambda^3-216\lambda^4+144\lambda^5}{4((9/16)+(3/2)\lambda-3\lambda^2)^2}\right]$$

$$+\frac{P_{S_2|e=0}}{4\lambda(\frac{1}{2}-\lambda)}\left[\frac{\frac{1}{2}-2\lambda}{\lambda(\frac{1}{2}-\lambda)T}P_{S_2|e=0}+M\right]$$

where

$$P_{S_1|e=0} = \frac{(9/8)\lambda+(3/4)\lambda^2-12\lambda^3+12\lambda^4}{4((9/16)+(3/2)\lambda-3\lambda^2)} = P_{S_2|e=0}$$

$$M = \frac{-(81/128)+(207/16)\lambda^2-(9/4)\lambda^3-45\lambda^4+36\lambda^5}{2((9/16)+(3/2)\lambda-3\lambda^2)^2}$$

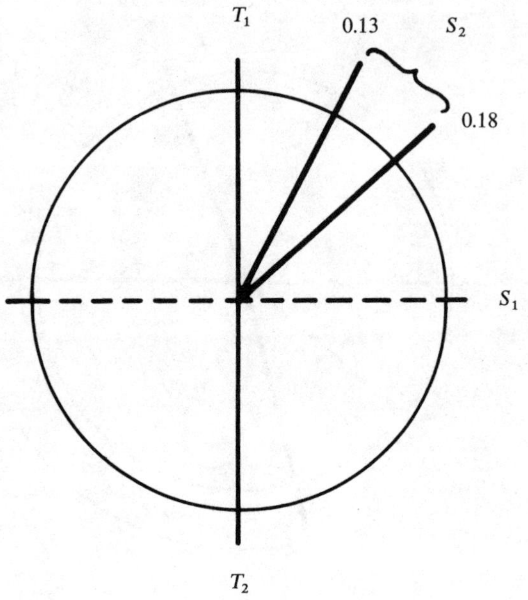

Figure 5

Finally we look whether this partial derivative cancels out for some value of λ (which describes the set of quasi-symmetric patterns). It turns out that this derivative goes to zero, only for $\lambda = \frac{1}{4}$. (For details, see Martinez-Giralt [1985]). Hence, only the symmetric pattern can possibly lie in equilibrium. One can also check that for $\lambda = \frac{1}{4}$, $e = 0$, the second order condition is satisfied.

(2) Even though it can be shown that the symmetric pattern is a local equilibrium (details available from the authors), it is not a global equilibrium. This follows from the fact that firms have an incentive to depart from this position, switching towards a neighbouring pattern.

Assume that firm T has opened two stores, at $T_1 = 0$, $T_2 = \frac{1}{2}$, and firm S has one store at $S_1 = \frac{1}{4}$. We simulate the profits accruing to both firms, when S_2 is located between T_1 and S_1 with $S_2 - T_1 = \delta$. (Details of the computations will be provided upon request, see Figure 5.)

The following table gives the profits of both firms for $\delta \in [0.12, 0.20]$:

δ	Π_S	Π_T
0.12	0.0307265911	0.0507544602
0.13	0.0316903192	0.0529506022
0.14	0.0325036024	0.0551013931
0.15	0.0331170644	0.0572109333
0.16	0.0334342535	0.0592837109
0.17	0.0332563149	0.0613250091
0.18	0.0321385824	0.0633413417
0.19	0.0289621627	0.0653404215
0.20	0.0203561812	0.0673282963

Since the profit earned by firm S while locating S_2 symmetrically at $S_2 = \frac{3}{4}$, is equal

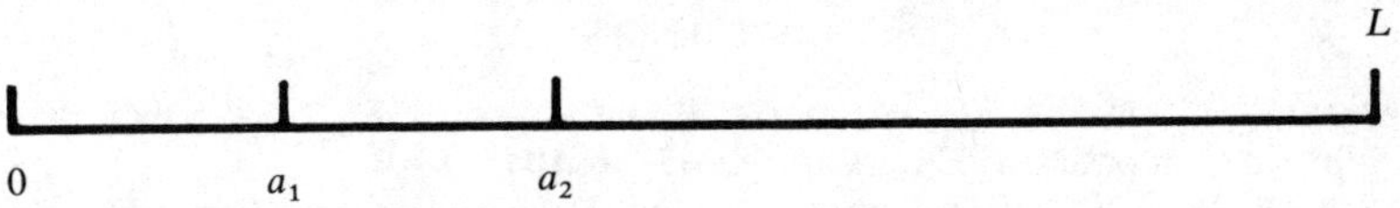

Figure 6

to ± 0.031, it is clear from this table that a location $S_2 \in [0.13, 0.18]$ yields more profit than the symmetric pattern. This pattern is thus not a global Nash equilibrium.

C—*Proof of Proposition 3*

In what follows, we concentrate on the following situation (see Figure 6): firm 1 locates two outlets at distances a_1, a_2, respectively, from the origin. Firm 2 has one outlet (b) at the opposite end of the market (L). We will show that firm 1 will optimally locate both outlets at 0 (i.e. $a_1 = a_2 = 0$). Since a similar reasoning could be held for firm 2, this completes the proof.

First, (i), we deal with the price equilibrium and subsequently (ii) turn to locations.

(i) *Price Equilibrium.* Let $x(y)$ denote the marginal consumer between a_1 and a_2 (a_2 and b). With

$$x = \frac{Pa_2 - Pa_1}{2(a_2 - a_1)} + \frac{a_1 + a_2}{2}$$

$$y = \frac{Pb - Pa_2}{2(L - a_2)} + \frac{L + a_2}{2}$$

the profit functions are then written:

$$\Pi_1 = Pa_1(x) + Pa_2(y - x)$$

$$\Pi_2 = Pb(L - y)$$

As mentioned above, these functions are concave in own prices. The equilibrium prices corresponding to this case can be found in Bonanno [1987].

(ii) *Locations.* We now maximise the profit of firm 1 in the first stage, with respect to a_1, a_2.

First-order derivatives are written:

$$\frac{\partial \Pi_1}{\partial a_1} = \frac{1}{8}(a_2 + a_1)(a_2 - 3a_1)$$

$$\frac{\partial \Pi_1}{\partial a_2} = \frac{1}{72}(-12L^2 - 40La_2 + 15a_2^2 - 9a_1^2 + 18a_1 a_2)$$

Second-order derivatives are given by:

$$\frac{\partial^2 \Pi_1}{\partial a_1^2} = \frac{-1}{4}(a_2 + 3a_1) \qquad (< 0, \quad \text{for all } a_1, a_2)$$

$$\frac{\partial^2 \Pi_1}{\partial a_2^2} = \frac{1}{36}(-20L + 15a_2 + 9a_1)$$

Taking into account the constraint ($a_1, a_2 \geqslant 0$), first-order conditions will be met only for $a_1 = a_2 = 0$. At this point second-order conditions are also verified.

REFERENCES

D'ASPREMONT, C., JASKOLD-GABSZEWICZ, J. and THISSE, J.-F., 1979, 'On Hotelling's Stability in Competition', *Econometrica*, 47, pp. 1045–1050.

BONANNO, J., 1987, 'Location Choice, Product Proliferation and Entry Deterrence', *The Review of Economic Studies*, 54, pp. 37–45.

BRANDER, J. and EATON, J., 1984, 'Product Line Rivalry', *American Economic Review*, 74(3), pp. 323–333.

FRIEDMAN, J., 1977, *Oligopoly and the Theory of Games* (Amsterdam, North Holland).

MARTINEZ-GIRALT, X., 1985, 'Perfect Equilibrium, Spatial Competition and Multiple Outlets', ICERD DP 85/120, London School of Economics.

NEVEN, D., 1985, 'Two-Stage (Perfect) Equilibrium in Hotelling's Model', *The Journal of Industrial Economics*, 33, pp. 317–325.

THE JOURNAL OF INDUSTRIAL ECONOMICS 0022–1821 $2.00
Volume XXXVI June 1988 No. 4

LOCATION AND SURVIVAL IN THE NATIONAL HOCKEY LEAGUE*

J. C. H. JONES AND D. G. FERGUSON

A model of professional sport franchises is introduced and used to explore the locational and other determinants of profitability. Particular attention is paid to the effect of location on attendance, market power and long run team quality. When estimated using data for the NHL in 1977–78 the model indicates that location has an effect on each of these and that their combined effect on profitability is effective in explaining prior and subsequent decisions concerning League expansion and franchise relocation. A number of other matters are also addressed, including League arguments for antitrust exemption and League policies to restrict expansion.

Hockey is the Canadian metaphor...some people call it our national religion.

[Kidd and MacFarlane: *The Death of Hockey*]

IN THE literature on professional team sport there has been a persistent dispute over team and league viability. More specifically, the questions usually raised concern: why teams survive in a particular location, why the better quality locations appear to produce the better quality teams, why teams of a given quality relocate, why leagues expand to one city rather than another and whether expansions exhaust the set of viable locations or still restrict league size.[1]

The standard explanation of viability focuses on the revenue determinants of profits. One view is that some combination of team performance (winning–losing) and the effects of restrictive league wide rules (drafts, reserve clauses, etc.) promote "uncertainty of game outcome" and hence attendance. This, in turn, increases revenue and profits. Most recently, however, the demise of many intra-league rules, coupled with the lack of statistical support for the rules-uncertainty-revenue mechanism, has shifted emphasis to locational attributes: each location, having different attributes (population, income, etc.), and thus different revenue generating ability, presumably has different profit potential.[2]

* We would like to thank L. Laudadio, J. A. Schofield, Peter Kennedy, M. Crapelle, S. Nadeau and K. Stewart for helpful comments; and M. Crapelle and Betty J. Jones for research assistance.

[1] For the most complete view of the issues see Noll [1974 and 1982]. For the specific issues of, team movements, better quality locations producing better quality teams, and leagues having too few teams, see Quirk [1973], Quirk and El Hodiri [1974], and Noll [1982], respectively.

[2] See Quirk and El Hodiri [1974], Noll [1974 and 1982], Jones [1984] and the references cited therein.

These arguments are not mutually exclusive and, ultimately, the importance of each for profitability and team viability is an empirical matter. Therefore, the object of this paper is two-fold. First, to construct short and long run models of team demand, which will allow us to consider the importance of location and other attributes for revenue generation in existing or potential locations. Specifically, we consider teams as local monopolists and set up a simple two equation model of demand with price and attendance as the endogenous variables. This format repairs a specification problem associated with single equation models of the demand for league sport, and also lets us focus explicitly on profitability which we treat as endogenous.[3] From the model we obtain composite measures of locational quality and team quality which are used to assess the effect of the former on the latter. Second, to estimate this model for one particular sports league. These estimates, combined with other revenue sources and costs, determine team profit which then permits us to examine survival, and the effects of potential relocation and expansion in both the short run and long run with endogenous team quality.

Our sports league is the National Hockey League (NHL) as represented by data—a single observation of locational attributes and multiple game observations (632 games for 16 teams)[4] proxying other attributes (uncertainty, the effects of various league rules, team performance, etc.)—for the 1977/78 season. This has two advantages. One, in contrast to most other sports leagues, the NHL does not have a national US television contract and its members do not share gate-receipts. This simplifies matters and makes the locational effects on revenue clearer. Two, the 1977/78 season predated the last NHL expansion (to Edmonton, Hartford, Quebec City, and Winnipeg in 1979). In addition, the league has permitted some teams to shift (Atlanta to Calgary in 1980, and Denver to New Jersey in 1982) but rejected other proposed relocations (St. Louis to Saskatoon in 1983).[5] Therefore, it will be instructive to determine which locational factors may have led to the acceptance of some new sites but rejection of others.

The major general conclusion from our analysis is that the model is particularly effective in explaining what has happened in the short run and the long run with the location of expansion teams and the relocation of existing teams. More specifically, we also note: the importance of a Canadian

[3] Demand studies of league sports conventionally consider attendance as endogenous and price as exogenous. For a review see Noll [1974], Schofield [1983] and Jones [1984]. But prices are set at the beginning of the season by individual teams presumably to maximize team profits. Therefore, a correct specification requires both price and attendance be endogenous. From our estimated price and attendance equations it is possible to identify the coefficients of the demand functions which underly both. For more on this matter see footnote 8 and the discussion to which it is appended.

[4] The data necessary to calculate the price variable was only available for 16 of the 18 teams (see note 6 below).

[5] The NHL by-laws state that all owners must agree to a franchise shift and that any owner has complete territorial monopoly within a radius of 50 miles of the present location.

location for team attendance and market power; a positive association between team quality and the quality of location; and the existence of a number of viable locations which currently do not have teams.

The remainder of this paper provides the rationale underlying these conclusions. It is organized into three parts: I, the short run and long run models and their empirical content are outlined; II, the empirical results and simulations are reported; and III, conclusions are drawn.

I. THE MODELS

I(i). *Location, price and attendance in the short run*

It is assumed that the demand for attendance at a particular game is a linear function of the price charged by the home team, with both the position and slope of the demand curve depending on the locational attributes of the home franchise and the attributes of the game which, as described below, reflect the standings of the teams, the effect of league rules, and the proximity of the playoffs. Formally, we assume that,

$$A_{gt} = c_{gt}(a_t - b_t p_t) \tag{1}$$

where g denotes the game, t the home franchise, A_{gt} the attendance at game g of team t, and p_t the price charged by team t. The terms c_{gt}, a_t, b_t are explained by other variables, with c_{gt} depending on the attributes of the teams playing in game g of home team t, and a_t, b_t depending only on the locational attributes of the home franchise.

Although the particular form in (1) was chosen for its tractability, it does have an intrinsic appeal and allows us to consider in some detail how the specific features of teams and their locations affect demand. In examining (1), the term in parenthesis $(a_t - b_t p_t)$ may be interpreted as the underlying demand in a particular location as it depends on such factors as the income, nationality, and population of the home city. The c_{gt} term captures the variation in demand from game to game in response to the standings of teams, the proximity of the playoffs, the playing style of the teams, etc.

As noted in the introduction, one of the principal points of departure from previous studies is the explicit recognition of the endogeneity of the prices charged by teams. In this respect we assume that the teams seek to maximize season profits and that, for a given season, the marginal costs of extra attendance are negligible, so that all costs associated with attendance are fixed. The profit maximizing price is then simply the revenue maximizing price, where attendance revenue for team t,

$$R_t = p_t\left(\sum_g A_{gt}\right) \tag{2}$$

is obtained by summing attendance over all games. From (1) and (2) it follows that the revenue (profit) maximizing price is,

$$(3) \qquad p_t^* = \tfrac{1}{2}a_t/b_t$$

which is the price at which the elasticity of demand,

$$(4) \qquad E_t = \frac{p_t}{a_t/b_t - p_t}$$

is unity. Substituting the chosen price into (1) yields the attendance equation,

$$(5) \qquad A_{gt}^* = c_{gt}\left(\frac{a_t}{2}\right)$$

which, together with the price equation (3), summarizes behaviour in the model as it depends on team and locational attributes. Further, from (2), (3) and (5) we also obtain the revenue function for the teams in their existing locations,

$$(6) \qquad R_t^* = \frac{1}{4}\left(\frac{a_t^2}{b_t}\right)\left(\sum_g c_{gt}\right)$$

To consider the implications of placing teams in alternative cities we need only note that, by construction, the first term in (6) is locationally dependent, but the second term depends on the characteristics of the teams playing which presumably would be invariant under a change in the team's location. Thus, we may define the revenue of team t (indexed by its current location) in alternate site τ as,

$$(7) \qquad R_{t\tau}^* = \frac{1}{4}\left(\frac{a_\tau^2}{b_\tau}\right)\left(\sum_g c_{gt}\right) = H_\tau Q_t$$

where, by construction, $R_t^* = R_{tt}^*$ (i.e. R_t^* is the attendance revenue of the team in its current location).

For want of a better expression, the first term in (7),

$$H_\tau = \frac{1}{4}\left(\frac{a_\tau^2}{b_\tau}\right)$$

which depends only on locational variables, will be referred to as the "locational quality" of a franchise. It represents the combined revenue effect of a location on market power in (3) and on attendance in (5). The relative size of the H_τ provides the basis on which to rank the revenue generating ability of all actual or potential locations for a franchise.

Each entry c_{gt} in the second term,

$$Q_t = \sum_g c_{gt}$$

depends on the characteristics of both the home and visiting teams at a particular point in the season. However, because of the interlocking schedule, the variation in Q_t across teams will depend primarily on the characteristics of the home team. As a result we will refer to Q_t as representing "team quality". It is to be understood that Q_t refers, not only to the team's won–loss record (the standard usage), but also to any other attribute of the team which enables it to generate revenue. Together, H_τ and Q_t allow us to consider the implications of placing a team with varying "quality" in alternative locations of varying "quality".

To complete the description of the model, we assume that a_t, b_t and c_{gt} are log linear functions of location and game attributes. Hence,

$$\log a_t = \alpha_0 + \alpha_1 CAN + \alpha_2 LPOP + \alpha_3 LINC \tag{8}$$

$$\log b_t = \beta_0 + \beta_1 CAN + \beta_2 LPOP + \beta_3 LINC \tag{9}$$

$$\begin{aligned} \log c_{gt} = {} & \gamma_0 + \gamma_1 LHTRL + \gamma_2 LVTRL + \gamma_3 UT3 + \gamma_4 UT3B3 \\ & + \gamma_5 PLD4Q + \gamma_6 STFF + \gamma_7 STFS + \gamma_8 STSS + \gamma_9 LSTAR \\ & + \gamma_{10} DAY \end{aligned} \tag{10}$$

where the L prefix denotes a logarithm and the variable definitions are as follows.

For the locational attributes, CAN is a dummy variable with a value of 1 if the game is played in a Canadian city, POP is city population, and INC is *per capita* income. For game attributes, $HTRL$ and $VTRL$ represent the ranking of the home and visiting teams (1 to 16) prior to the game; $UT3$ and $UT3B3$ are dummy variables with a value of 1 representing respectively, a situation when teams ranked in the top three play each other, and a circumstance when a team ranked in the top three plays a team ranked in the bottom three; $PLD4Q$ proxies "playoff drive" and is a dummy variable of 1 based on the point spread between teams in the fourth quarter of the season; the ST variables are style dummies taking a value of 1 when games involve either fighting (FF), skating (SS) or fighting-skating (FS) teams, defined as plus (FF) and minus (SS) 1/2 standard deviation from the mean of the previous season's penalty minutes; $STAR$ denotes the number (plus 1) of "superstars" in any given game; and DAY is a dummy variable with a value of 1 for a game played on the weekend.[6] The general rationale for the inclusion of these locational

[6] Briefly, POP and INC are derived from: *Statistical Abstract of the US*, 1979; *Census of Canada*, 1976; US Dept. of Commerce, *Survey of Current Business*, April 1979, Vol. 59; Statistics Canada, *Income Estimates for Sub-Provincial Areas*, 1982. The variables A_{gt}, $HTRL$, $VTRL$, $UT3$, $UT3B3$, $PLD4Q$, and DAY, are from the *Victoria Daily Times*, Sept. 1977–May 1978. The ST variables are from the *NHL Press Guide* 1977/78. $STAR$ is based on a "qualitative" assessment. A complete listing of definitions, sources, and ST and $STAR$ attributes by team will be provided on request. The variable pt is defined as: average seat price per team 1977/78 equals average seat price per team 1975/76 extrapolated at the CPI rate in 16 franchise cities (see col. (1) Table I in the text). The sources are: US Congress, House Select Committee on Professional Sport, *Final Report*, 1977, Appendix III, C-9; US Dept. of Commerce, Statistical Abstract of the United States, "Consumer Price Indices, Selected Cities or SMSA", 1980; Statistics Canada, *Consumer Prices and Price Indexes for Regional Cities*, Nov. 1977, May 1979.

and game attributes is fairly well established in the literature,[7] but the relationship of the latter to league-wide rules will be more precisely specified below.

Given the content of (8), (9), and (10), equations (3) and (5) may be written as,

$$\text{(11)} \qquad \log A_{gt} = (\log \tfrac{1}{2} + \alpha_0 + \gamma_0) + \alpha_1 CAN + \alpha_2 LPOP + \alpha_3 LINC + \gamma_1 LHTRL + \gamma_2 LVTRL + \gamma_3 UT3 + \gamma_4 UT3B3 + \gamma_5 PLD4Q + \gamma_6 STFF + \gamma_7 STFS + \gamma_8 STSS + \gamma_9 LSTAR + \gamma_{10} DAY$$

$$\text{(12)} \qquad \log p_t = (\log \tfrac{1}{2} + \alpha_0 - \beta_0) + (\alpha_1 - \beta_1) CAN + (\alpha_2 - \beta_2) LPOP + (\alpha_3 - \beta_3) LINC$$

As a result of the functional forms adopted above, there are no binding cross equation restrictions on the coefficients of these reduced form equations. However, since both are derived from the demand function, the possibility arises that the disturbance terms may not be independent (as would be the case, for example, if there are omitted variables). Consequently, in arriving at the results reported below, we employed Zellner's [1962] method of seemingly unrelated regressions. For the same reason, we chose to estimate the reduced form equations since this allows us to avoid the simultaneous equation bias (due to the non-zero covariance in the error teams) that would arise in estimating the structural form equations.[8] In addition, there are three other points worth noting.

First, from (11) and (12) it is possible to identify all of the structural coefficients in (8), (9) and (10) with the exception of the intercepts. The restrictions imposed by the estimates in (11) and (12) leave one degree of freedom in choosing α_0, β_0, γ_0 which, given the log linear form of (8), (9) and (10), acts to scale both H_t and Q_t simultaneously. However, because revenue is obtained directly from the product of the antilogs of the dependent variables in (11) and (12), such scaling does not affect the revenue estimates. In addition, of course, it affects neither the ranking of H_t nor Q_t nor the correlation

[7] See, for example, No. 11 [1974, pp. 115–157], Schofield [1983], and Jones [1984]. In the specification of our model it should be noted that no recognition is given to the fact that Montreal and Toronto regularly sell out and, hence, that attendance is constrained by the capacity of their arenas. Inclusion of a variable representing arena capacity does not properly recognize this constraint and we could not think of an operative alternative way of doing so. The consequence is that the results reported below most likely underestimate the importance of a Canadian location for demand and franchise revenue. However, this only serves to strengthen our conclusions.

[8] Moreover, cross equation restrictions will necessarily exist between any monopoly price equation and the (structural form) demand function from which it is derived. As a result, previous studies which have used OLS to estimate structural form demand functions will generate estimators that are less efficient and, if the covariance is nonzero, the estimators will also be asymptotically biased.

between them. Consequently, none of the uses to which we put the estimated equations is affected.

For the sake of convenience in presenting Table I we have chosen a particular scaling that yields estimates for both team and locational quality which are of the same order of magnitude. But, it should be kept in mind that these numbers are unique only up to scalar multiplication and that, to retain consistency with the estimated restrictions, scaling Q_t by a factor λ requires that H_t be scaled by a factor λ^{-1}.

Second, the coefficients in (11) can be interpreted directly in terms of their effect on demand, a positive (negative) value indicating that increases in that variable increases (decreases) demand. In terms of specific content, the variables with coefficients α_1 through α_3 represent the locational attributes. The existing literature generally assumes that α_1 and α_2 are positive ($\alpha_1, \alpha_2, > 0$), although the expectations for α_3 are ambiguous depending on whether attendance at hockey games is viewed as a normal or inferior good ($\alpha_3 \gtreqless 0$).

The remaining variables represent the characteristics of particular games and of the teams playing in them. The anticipated signs for the γ coefficients are based on the assumptions that people prefer to attend games involving winning teams ($\gamma_1 < 0, \gamma_2 < 0$), teams that are closely matched ($\gamma_3 > 0, \gamma_4 < 0$), games that are closer to the playoffs ($\gamma_5 > 0$), games that involve fights ($\gamma_6 > 0, \gamma_7 > 0, \gamma_8 < 0$) and superstars ($\gamma_9 > 0$), and games on weekends ($\gamma_{10} > 0$). These assumptions provide the rationale for a number of the policies and rules adopted by the league.[9] This is true, in particular, of actions which promote: greater competitive equality and uncertainty of game outcome through drafts, reserve clauses, roster limits; certain styles of play through rules governing player conduct; greater interest by increasing the number of teams in the playoffs; greater accessibility by scheduling games on weekends. Whether these policies are actually effective can be inferred from the sign and statistical significance of the corresponding coefficients in (11).

Third, as far as the price equation is concerned, from (4) it follows that the estimates $(\alpha_i - \beta_i)$ in (12) represent the inverse effect of the locational variables on the elasticity of demand. Thus, a positive (negative) value indicates that, as that variable is increased, the elasticity of demand falls (rises). Since, *ceteris paribus*, an increase in a_t/b_t increases demand, we expect the signs of the coefficients in (12) to be the same as the equivalent coefficients in (11): $\alpha_1 - \beta_1$, $\alpha_2 - \beta_2, > 0$; and $\alpha_3 - \beta_3 \gtreqless 0$.

I(ii). *Location and team quality in the long run*

Quirk and El Hodiri [1974] presented a model in which teams were able to vary their stock of playing skills through the sale and purchase of player

[9] In Jones [1969 and 1984] league behaviour is explained using a variation of the quasi joint profit maximizing model.

contracts. Their principal conclusion was that, the greater the revenue generating ability of a team's location, the greater will be its long-run stock of skills. Expanding their argument to cover not only playing skills but also any other player attributes which contribute to the team's profitability, leads to the conclusion that the quality of a team, as we have defined it, will itself depend on its location's quality.[10]

For any single season the attributes which underlie a team's quality are predetermined and the model in (I(i)) above can be used to assess the immediate alternatives facing a team. However, the long-run implications of selecting a particular location should recognize the potential effect of the location's quality on the team's quality. A proper treatment of this would require data extending over many seasons with the time period being one during which the league structure (the number and location of teams) was stable. The magnitude of this task and the disruptions which most sports leagues (including the NHL) have undergone in the last twenty years put such a treatment beyond our abilities.

In its place we propose to simply examine the relationship between team quality and location as it existed in the season we are considering. In effect we will assume that, for any single season, the departures from long-run team quality are random so that the estimation of,

$$(13) \qquad Q_t^L = \delta_0 + \delta_1 H_t$$

yields an estimate of the expected long-run team quality. To the extent that the effects of the entry of new teams in the 1970s had worked themselves out, this equation can provide some basis on which to assess the effect of location on team quality and hence the long-run effect of location on franchise profitability. Specifically, substituting (13) into (7), the long-run revenue of a team in location t will be,

$$(14) \qquad R_t^L = \delta_0 H_t + \delta_1 H_t^2$$

I(iii). *Summary*

Using the models developed above as a basis for empirically resolving the issues surrounding franchise viability we can proceed sequentially as follows: (a) the importance of locational attributes and other factors for attendance can be determined from estimating (11); (b) those locational features which increase market power can be identified from estimating (12); (c) the significance of locational quality (H_t) for current and prospective locations can be calculated by applying the appropriate coefficients of (11) and (12) to

[10] A relatively simple derivation of the relationship between Q_t and H_t for the case in which there are multiple attributes underlying team quality may be obtained from the authors on request.

(8) and (9), and team quality (Q_t) can be calculated by applying the appropriate coefficients of (11) and (12) to (10); (d), given (c), short-run revenue in any location can be simulated as the product of H_τ and Q_t, and long-run revenue R_t^L can be computed by estimating (13) and applying the coefficients to (14); (e), given (d), and estimates of other revenue (playoff and broadcasting) and costs, we can determine short-run and long-run profitability, and hence assess franchise viability in the short and long run.

It is to the empirical results we now turn.

II. THE EMPIRICAL RESULTS

II(i). *Locational attributes and attendance*

The results for (11) are shown in (15) below, with the asymptotic *t* statistics in parenthesis.

$$(15)\qquad \begin{aligned} LA_{gt} = {} & \underset{(9.3177)}{0.2205CAN} + \underset{(4.7947)}{0.0910LPOP} - \underset{(2.4139)}{0.3766LINC} - \underset{(5.5197)}{0.0847LHTRL} \\ & - \underset{(2.6319)}{0.0377LVRL} - \underset{(2.4385)}{0.1201UT3} - \underset{(0.3303)}{0.0108UT3B3} \\ & + \underset{(2.4401)}{0.0921PLD4Q} + \underset{(2.2579)}{0.2137STFF} + \underset{(1.6269)}{0.0664STFS} \\ & - \underset{(2.3501)}{0.1226STSS} + \underset{(5.8375)}{0.1535LSTAR} + \underset{(4.0298)}{0.0607DAY} + \underset{(8.3075)}{12.148CON} \\ & \bar{R}^2 = 0.4412 \quad n = 632 \end{aligned}$$

Three conclusions are appropriate.[11] First, the locational attributes are strong, the *CAN* coefficient particularly so. The signs of *CAN* and *POP* are as anticipated, but *LINC* is negative. This suggests that attendance at hockey games is an inferior good for the population as a whole.[12] Second, the effects of some of the league rules are also important: fighting (*STFF* and *STFS*), rather than skating (*STSS*) is demand increasing, as is scheduling (*DAY*) and making the playoffs (*PLD4Q*). But there is nothing in the results to suggest

[11] Although the *t* statistics in (15) are asymptotic values, the sample is large enough ($n = 632$) to avoid the inference problems usually associated with small sample estimators in systems of equations.

[12] It is also possible that *LINC* is acting as a proxy for the availability of sporting substitutes. We attempted to partially solve this problem by introducing a variable, the number of major league sports teams in the city, to measure sporting competition. This turned out to be highly collinear with *POP* (a correlation of over +0.8) so it was dropped. The same problem arose with attempts to introduce ethnicity (black population, the correlation with *CAN* being over −0.9), so this variable was also dropped.

that the rules responsible for creating uncertainty ($UT3$ and $UT3B3$) are important.[13] Only if the distribution of superstars ($STAR$) is a unique function of drafts, reserve clauses, etc.—which is far from certain—can these rules be considered anything but rent seeking instruments. Third, team standing ($LHTRL$ and $LVTRL$) is obviously important.

II(ii). *Locational attributes and market power*

The results for the price equation (12) are shown in (16) with the asymptotic t statistic in parenthesis.

$$(16) \qquad \underset{}{Lp_t} = \underset{(3.7803)}{0.1905CAN} + \underset{(1.8724)}{0.0630LPOP} - \underset{(0.7170)}{0.1887LINC} + \underset{(1.4542)}{3.3642CON}$$

$$\bar{R}^2 = 0.5692 \quad n = 16$$

As anticipated, the signs of the coefficients are the same as those of the corresponding variables in the attendance equation. With respect to both attendance and market power, a large Canadian city with a relatively low per-capita income is optimal.

II(iii). *Locational quality and team quality*

Using the estimates of the structural parameters obtained from (15) and (16), the measures of locational and team quality were constructed and are reported in cols. (2) and (3) of Table I.

With respect to locational quality, the "hoser" effect, as represented by the CAN variable in (15) and (16), is quite evident. If existing teams are ranked according to the size of H_τ in col. (2), then Montreal, Toronto and Vancouver are the top ranked teams; and, if all cities (franchise and non-franchise) are ranked according to H_τ, the only US city ranked in the top ten overall is New York. Thus, if locational factors are predominantly important in determining survival, the NHL decisions to "expand" by adding Winnipeg, Quebec City, and Edmonton, and allowing Atlanta to relocate in Calgary are perfectly logical. All Canadian cities are ranked ahead of any non-franchise American city in the sample, and ahead of a number of currently franchised American locations.

Of course it is possible that, in the short run, team quality would offset locational quality. Thus, a good team may offset a relatively poor location or a poor team may fail to exploit the potential of a good location. It depends on the degree to which H_t and Q_t are related. From Table I it is evident that the correspondence between locational quality (H_τ) and team quality (Q_t) is not

[13] The sign of $UT3$ is incorrect and $UT3B3$ is statistically insignificant. This could be due to multicollinearity, and indeed, if the A_{gt} equation is estimated alone using OLS techniques and subjected to the ridge procedure, the signs of the variables become as anticipated *a priori*.

TABLE I
LOCATION, TEAM QUALITY, REVENUE AND PROFITABILITY

Team/ Location (1)	Locational Quality H_τ (2)	Short Run Team Quality Q_t (3)	Long Run Team Quality Q_t^L (4)	REVENUE (000) Short Run EXISTING TEAMS Attendance (5)	Season (6)	Long Run ALL TEAMS Attendance (7)	Season (8)
Atlanta	2074	1884	1937	3908	4329	4017	4516
Boston	2181	2287	1964	4989	6585	4284	4835
Buffalo	2029	2156	1925	4376	5463	3907	4385
Chicago	2346	2020	2006	4740	5375	4708	5345
Detroit	2182	1894	1964	4133	4896	4286	4838
Los Angeles	2361	2046	2010	4831	5351	4746	5393
Minnesota	2008	1748	1920	3512	3792*	3855	4324
Montreal	3489	2447	2298	8539	11 526	8018	9490
NY Islanders	2524	2274	2052	5739	6799	5179	5920
NY Rangers	2524	1996	2052	5040	5790	5179	5920
Philadelphia	2389	2242	2017	5357	6900	4819	5482
Pittsburgh	2126	1841	1950	3914	4227	4146	4670
St. Louis	2132	1776	1952	3787	4090*	4161	4688
Toronto	3234	2086	2233	6747	8879	7222	8470
Vancouver	2793	1806	2120	5046	5450	5922	6837
Washington	1961	1800	1908	3531	3814*	3742	4189
				MINNESOTA QUALITY			
Calgary	2462		2036	4305	4650	5012	5717
Cincinnati	1996		1917	3491	3770*	3826	4289
Edmonton	2538		2055	4438	4793	5216	5966
Hamilton	2702		2097	4725	5103	5667	6520
Houston	2040		1928	3567	3853*	3933	4417
Indianapolis	1898		1892	3319	3584*	3591	4010*
Milwaukee	1915		1896	3348	3616*	3631	4058*
Ottawa	2534		2054	4431	4786	5206	5953
Quebec	2760		2112	4826	5212	5829	6721
Saskatoon	2211		1972	3867	4176	4360	4926
Seattle	1844		1878	3223	3481*	3463	3860*
Winnipeg	2783		2118	4866	5255	5894	6802

* Indicates that season revenue is less than estimates of operating costs of $4 153 065.

exact (compare cols. (2) and (3)).[14] Nevertheless, the estimation of (13) yields the following results (t statistics in parenthesis),

$$Q_t = \underset{(5.2339)}{1407.3} + \underset{(2.317)}{0.25532} H_t \qquad (17)$$

$$\bar{R}^2 = 0.2246 \quad F = 5.344$$

[14] As an example, the quality rankings of Boston and Buffalo (2 and 5 respectively) clearly exceed their locational rankings (10 and 14 respectively); while the converse is true for Vancouver (Q_t, 13 and H_τ, 3) and Toronto (Q_t, 6 and H_τ, 2).

which do not allow us to reject the Quirk–El Hodiri hypothesis that team quality is dependent on locational quality.[15] This being the case, long run team quality (Q_t^L) can be determined by applying the coefficients of (17) to (13). These results are reported in col. (4) of Table I.

II(iv). *Location and attendance revenue*

Given cols. (2), (3) and (4) of Table I we can simulate short and long run attendance revenue. Of the many possible short run simulations we present only the results for teams in their existing locations, and for teams of Minnesota quality placed in each of the alternative non-franchise cities. These results are reported in col. (5). Minnesota was chosen for special illustrative treatment because it is the lowest quality existing team (col. (3))—and hence represents the worst case scenario—and, given the way the NHL has stocked its expansion franchises, it could serve to indicate the short run consequences of league expansion. The long run attendance revenue for all sites (H_t multiplied by Q_t^L) is shown in col. (7).

II(v). *Revenue, costs, and survival*

While attendance revenue gives some indication of whether new or relocated franchises could survive, ultimately, survival depends on total costs and revenues. Unfortunately, there is only a limited amount of information on costs and non-attendance revenue. Despite these difficulties we have attempted to construct as complete and accurate estimates as possible. We define total revenue as the sum of attendance, playoff, and broadcast revenue for a given season. Short and long run season revenue estimates are reported in cols. (6) and (8) respectively.[16] While the revenue estimates differ between teams, because of data difficulties, we had no option but to produce a common estimate of total operating costs.[17] This totalled $4 153 065 for a

[15] It is also worthwhile pointing that although we deliberately sought to adopt a broad definition of team quality, the rank correlation between A_t and the team's final standings in 1977/78 is 0.9529. This supports the narrow view of team quality adopted in Quirk–El Hodiri and elsewhere.

[16] Short run playoff revenue is estimated as average revenue per regular season game × number of home playoff games in 1978 (zero for Minnesota). Short run broadcast revenue is a variable percentage of the sum of attendance plus playoff revenue depending on different levels of regular season attendance, see Noll [1974:25]. Long run playoff revenue is regular season game revenue × estimated number of playoff games for a team with long-run quality corresponding to the quality of its location. Long run broadcast revenue is estimated as 10 per cent of the sum of attendance and playoff revenue. Precise detail on estimation procedures will be supplied by the authors on request.

[17] Total operating cost 1977/78, is *TOC* 1972/73, *less* player depreciation and salary cost 1972/73, extrapolated to 1977/78 (at the rate of price inflation by *CPI* in the franchise cities), plus player salary cost 1977/78. See, Noll [1974:25], Jones and Davies [1978:723], *Toronto Globe and Mail* [March 14, 1978, 37]. Precise detail on estimation procedure will be supplied by the authors on request.

NHL team in 1977/78, and the entries marked with an asterisk in cols. (6) and (8) indicate those teams for which cost exceeds revenue.

Two conclusions seem appropriate. First, as noted earlier, the model works well in explaining the expansion of the NHL into Edmonton, Quebec City and Winnipeg and the relocation of Atlanta's team to Calgary. In addition, because of their long-run profit (col. (8)), it provides one explanation of why teams continued to exist in Minnesota, St. Louis and Washington despite their simulated short-run losses (col. (6)).[18]

Second, the results support the view that the league has not exhausted the set of profitable locations. In particular this raises the issue of why the NHL has not expanded to the Canadian cities Hamilton, Ottawa and Saskatoon which are preferable to all potential, and at least 8 existing, US locations (col. (8)). We offer two explanations.

One, the Canadian cities are not necessary for a US national TV network contract (the apparent reason for expansion in the 1960s and early 1970s), and could only reduce TV revenue for existing Canadian teams.[19] This rationale should also apply to Edmonton, Quebec City and Winnipeg, but these cities were admitted as part of the pact ending the war with the World Hockey Association,[20] and, indeed, they do share unequally in Canadian TV revenue.[21]

Two, if expansion fees, player depreciation, and costs associated with stadia construction are added to the above operating costs, short-run book losses are guaranteed.[22] Thus, the franchise holder must be in a position to use a tax loss (or write it off as advertising expenses), and, if US tax laws are more advantageous than Canadian (there is no public information on this subject in Canada), the demand for franchises may be greater in the US (and so expansion fees would be higher) even though H_τ is smaller.

There may be other explanations but the point is—H_τ not withstanding—Canadian cities may not automatically be a locational nirvana.

III. CONCLUSION

From the foregoing analysis the following conclusions seem *a propos.*

[18] Incidentally, these figures lend merit to the practice of some sports leagues redistributing revenue. If the NHL were to expand to include *all* teams in our sample (the worst quality case scenario), all short run losses (col. (6)) could be eliminated by redistributing the short run profits of *either* Montreal or Toronto.

[19] For an analysis of expansion in 1960s and 1970s see Jones [1976]. Vancouver was excluded for years because Montreal and Toronto did not want to share TV revenue (Jones [1969, 19]).

[20] Jones and Walsh [1987].

[21] The range is from $900 000 to $5 million, *Toronto Globe and Mail*, July 25, 1984, p. 54.

[22] Expansion fees vary as to time and location. Entrants in 1979 paid $4–6 million. In 1983 Detroit changed hands for $4 million but in 1983 Denver shifted to New Jersey and, with indemnity payments, paid $29.5 million, see *Toronto Globe and Mail*, Nov. 20, 1979, 301, and Feb. 5, 1985, 16; Kurlantzick [1983, p. 203]. With indemnity payments Hamilton is the most vulnerable, falling within both the Toronto and Buffalo 50 mile limit. Player depreciation is roughly a third of *TOC*.

In general, the model, which emphasizes locational profitability, works well in explaining what has happened in the NHL in terms of the location of expansion teams, franchise relocation, and why teams survive in their current locations in the long run despite short-run losses.

More specifically, we can conclude:

First, locational attributes, certain league rules, and team success, are important elements determining attendance. Second, the major elements in creating locational market power and so increasing the chances of franchise survival, are population and location in Canada. Third, the corollary of these two conclusions is that locational quality is the key element in franchise revenue determination. Although team quality may offset poor locational quality in the short run, in the long run there is evidence to support the argument that better quality teams tend to emerge in better quality locations. Four, simulations of attendance revenue combined with estimates of other revenue sources and estimates of costs indicate that there are a number of viable locations which do not have teams.

Finally, the one pervasive element in the empirical analysis is the significance of a Canadian location. The "hoser" variable is simultaneously a proxy for Canadian sporting culture and a talisman for franchise survival. It is probably no accident that, at the entrance to the Canadian Pavilion at the World Fair of 1986, there is a single ikon which presumably described Canada to the world—the largest hockey stick and puck in the world.[23] Seemingly, everyone recognizes that in Canada, "Hockey is King".

J. C. H. JONES AND D. G. FERGUSON,
Department of Economics,
University of Victoria,
P.O. Box 1700,
Victoria, BC V8W,
Canada.

ACCEPTED JUNE 1987

REFERENCES

JONES, J. C. H., 1969, 'The Economics of the National Hockey League', *Canadian Journal of Economics*, 2, pp. 1–20.

JONES, J. C. H., 1976, 'The Economics of the National Hockey League Revisited ...', in R. S. GRUNEAU and J. G. ALBINSON, *Canadian Sport: Sociological Perspectives* (Addison-Wesley, Don Mills).

JONES, J. C. H. and DAVIES, D. K., 1978, 'Not Even Semi-Tough: Professional Sport and Canadian Antitrust', *Antitrust Bulletin*, 23, pp. 713–743.

JONES, J. C. H. and WALSH, W. D., 1987, 'The World Hockey Association and Player Exploitation in the National Hockey League', *Quarterly Review of Economics and Business* 27, pp. 87–101.

[23] The stick is 205 feet in height and 120 000 pounds in weight, and is approximately 40 times the regulation size. It now stands quite literally among the totem poles in the Cowichan Valley on Vancouver Island.

KIDD, B. and MCFARLANE, J., 1972, *The Death of Hockey* (New Press, Toronto).
KURLANTZICK, L. S., 1983, 'Thoughts on Professional Sports and the Antitrust Laws: Los Angeles Memorial Coliseum Commission v. NFL', *Connecticut Law Review*, 15, pp. 183–208.
NOLL, R. G., 1974 (ed.), *Government and the Sports Business* (Brookings, Washington, DC).
NOLL, R. G., 1982, 'Major League Sports', in WALTER ADAMS (ed.) *The Structure of American Industry*, 6th Edition (Macmillan, New York).
QUIRK, J., 1973, 'An Economic Analysis of Team Movements in Professional Sports', *Law and Contemporary Problems*, 38, pp. 42–66.
QUIRK, J. and EL HODIRI, M., 1974, 'The Economic Theory of a Sports League', in R. NOLL (ed.), *Government and the Sports Business* (Brookings, Washington, DC), pp. 33–80.
SCHOFIELD, J. A., 1983, 'Performance and Attendance at Professional Team Sports', *Journal of Sports Behaviour*, 6, 4, pp. 196–206.
ZELLNER, A., 1962, 'An Efficient Method of Estimating Seemingly Unrelated Regressions and Tests for Aggregation Bias', *Journal of the American Statistical Association*, 57, pp. 348–368.

THE JOURNAL OF INDUSTRIAL ECONOMICS 0022–1821 $2.00
Volume XXXVI June 1988 No. 4

INDUSTRIAL STRUCTURE, CONCENTRATION AND THE SPEED OF PRICE ADJUSTMENT*

ARAKEL BEDROSSIAN AND DEMETRIOS MOSCHOS

It is argued that the relationship between market structure and the speed of price adjustment involves two distinct forces with opposing directions; "the leadership effect" and the "industry profitability effect". The direction of the relationship will depend on the relative importance of these effects. Estimation of an equation explaining the speed of price adjustment in terms of industrial concentration and the length of the production period provided evidence of negative effects for both the above variables.

I. INTRODUCTION

SINCE THE publication of Means' [1935] seminal article on the mechanism with which market structure affects pricing behaviour, research on the issue has dominated the area of industrial economics. Recently with a number of papers Domberger [1979], [1978], [1982], [1983] seems to confirm that the relationship between the speed at which prices adjust to changes in costs is a positive function of industrial concentration. Nonetheless the evidence is far from being conclusive as yet; see for instance Dixon [1983].

Based on the same theme the present paper focuses on the crucial role of distinguishing between profitability at the firm level and profitability at the industry level in analysing the channels through which concentration exerts an influence on the price adjustment speed. It is suggested in particular that since relative firm profitability within an industry and relative profitability among industries are likely to work in opposite directions, the relationship in question may well be a negative one. The analytical framework is based on the hypothesis that the speed of price adjustment is systematically related to industrial concentration and the length of the production period. The hypothesis is put to the test against the evidence drawn from a sample of twenty Greek manufacturing industries defined at the two-digit SIC level.

The structure of the paper is as follows: Section II deals with the theoretical considerations regarding the determinants of the adjustment speed. Section III describes the methodology of the empirical investigation. Section IV provides for the presentation and discussion of the main results of the paper. Finally, section V gives a summary of the main conclusions.

* We are grateful to T. Hitiris and two anonymous referees for valuable comments and suggestions on an earlier draft. Errors and omissions naturally belong to the authors.

II. THE DETERMINANTS OF THE PRICE ADJUSTMENT SPEED

In a Walrasian world where every firm behaves as a price taker the analysis of price dynamics is based on the theory of excess demand. Nevertheless, as pointed out by Arrow [1959], in industrial markets characterized by the absence of the Walrasian auctioneer, price decisions are actually made by firms. The analysis underlying conventional industrial behaviour suggests that industrial prices are cost dominated in the sense that price levels are determined as a markup upon costs, either direct or full, calculated at the actual or standard level of operation.[1] However, the formation of the equilibrium price level as a markup over costs does not imply that the adjustment of the actual to the equilibrium price level is instantaneous. Indeed there are good reasons for the existence of lags in price adjustment to a perceived change in costs.

At the industry level different firms do not necessarily perceive cost increases at the same time and by the same amount. Differences may arise from firm policies with respect to supply agreements at fixed prices with various durations, practices of holding different stocks of raw materials and semi-finished goods, different credit facilities to customers and suppliers etc. Consequently the industry price will adjust gradually over time.[2]

In addition there are adjustment lags inherent in the decision of the firm to adapt to a change in costs. These lags are traditionally taken to be the lags of informing customers of impending price rises, distributing price lists etc. Moreover, since the industrial productive process requires that some of the productive factors are stocked at least temporarily by the firm, there is a lag between the transformation of the productive inputs into the final product. This lag is the production lag or production period. The problem of attributing value to the final product is of course related to the accounting principles used by the firm. Such principles range between two extremes, depending on whether the firm prices on the basis of historic costs or on the basis of replacement costs. In the first case the firm does not adjust its final price in a period of rising prices until stocks of inputs bought at lower prices are exhausted (First In First Out principle (FIFO)), while in the second case the firm adjusts its price instantaneously to a change in input costs (Last In First Out principle (LIFO)). An intermediate (and rather more realistic) accounting practice between historic and replacement cost is the average cost pricing by which purchases of material and labour are valued at their average

[1] See, for example, papers by Eckstein and Fromm [1968], Godley and Nordhaus [1972], McFetridge [1973], Shahling [1977] and Shinjo [1977] among others.

[2] There is, of course, the aggregation problem with respect to the price index of the industry in the sense that this index is defined as the average of the corresponding micro (firm) price indices. Theil [1954] has shown the conditions under which the aggregate relationships hold at the micro level as well. However, the aggregation problem cannot be overcome in practice since the aggregate price variables are defined as the arithmetic averages of the corresponding micro variables.

cost. Unless the valuation principle used by industrial firms is based on LIFO method, which in any case is rather the exception than the rule (see Okun [1981]), it is obvious that the speed at which prices adjust to changes in costs depends on the length of the production period.

The crucial question which has attracted the main interest of research in the area relates to the direction and extent at which market structure affects the adjustment speed of the industry price level. Considerations with respect to behavioural decision making of firms suggest that the pattern of price adjustment is largely influenced by firms' attitudes and uncertainties about the behaviour of their competitors. Stigler [1964] has argued that in industries with a relatively small number of firms, secret price reductions can be easily monitored, since the smaller the number of firms, the stronger is the effect of a price reduction by a typical firm on the sales of its rivals. If one extends this analysis to dynamic pricing behaviour where secret price cutting can take the form of slow adjustment to cost increases, it can then be argued that the smaller the number of firms in the industry the more parallel will the price adjustment be among firms.

In an uncertain oligopolistic environment, short-run price adjustments at the firm level will generally depend on the firm's conjectures about price changes of its rivals with respect to a change in its own price. Domberger's [1983] analysis of the effect of market structure on the short-run price adjustment process relies on profitability as an element affecting adjustment costs. These costs arise from uncertainties about rivals' behaviour since an industrial firm faces the problem that if it adjusts its prices upwards by more than its rivals then this adjustment will affect negatively its sales and market shares. On the basis that the cost of an upward price adjustment is positively related with the subjective evaluation of the risk of losing sales and market shares, Domberger argues that the higher the profitability the lower is the burden of risk associated with an upward adjustment decision at the firm level. Given the considerable amount of theoretical analysis and empirical evidence indicating the existence of a positive link[3] between profitability and industrial concentration, Domberger [1983] concludes that "firms in concentrated industries with correspondingly higher price cost margins are more likely to behave as price leaders than those of more fragmented industries" (p. 52).

It is important to note, however, that the crucial factor underlying the phenomenon of price leadership in the above analysis is not the industry price-cost margin relative to other industries, but the profitability of individual firms relative to their rivals within the same industry.[4] The role of price leader is firm specific since the risk involved in an upward price

[3] Note, however, that this link is not particularly strong (see Hannah and Kay [1977]).

[4] The relationship between profitability at the firm level and price leadership is analysed in Holthausen [1978] who argues that "the largest firms with the greatest profit cushion against possible loss can best afford the role of price leader" (p. 345).

adjustment is at the firm rather than at the industry level. In a price game characterized by interfirm differences in profitability all the participants are aware that firms with the highest profitability are likely to dominate the game. Thus, it is to the advantage of all firms in the industry to avoid delays in the adjustment of prices to changes in costs. Such an adjustment process is most likely to occur in concentrated industries dominated by a single firm or a collusive group of firms. If, on the other hand, the industry is concentrated, but the oligopolistic nucleus consists of more or less equally dominant and profitable rival firms, competition in the form of delays in adjusting prices is likely to be facilitated by the already existing high profit margins, in contrast with fragmented industries with low profit margins where the room for interfirm price competition is obviously low.

The effect of profitability at the industry level on the speed of price adjustment is quite different in nature from the "leadership effect". Industry profit margins are inversely associated with disequilibrium costs, which represent profits foregone by keeping industry price cost margins below their equilibrium levels. Furthermore, the squeeze of profit margins may represent a serious constraint, since it may lead firms to the threshold of bankruptcy. It follows that, *ceteris paribus*, the lower is the profit margin at the industry level, the higher is likely to be the speed of price adjustment to a rise in costs,[5] hence the relationship between concentration and the speed of price adjustment is likely to be negative.

The discussion so far implies that the "leadership effect" associated with interfirm profitability differentials within the industry and the "industry profitability effect" are likely to exert opposite influences on the speed of price adjustment. Thus if interfirm differences in profitability among leading firms are most prominent in concentrated industries and the positive "leadership effect" dominates the negative "industry profitability effect" or if concentration is characterized by collusive behaviour, the effect of industry concentration on the speed of price adjustment is likely to be positive. Such a positive relationship is likely to occur only in the above, rather specific, descriptions of the state of affairs of industrial market structure. Otherwise the relationship between market concentration and the speed of price adjustment may well be a negative one.[6]

It is worth noting that the relationship between concentration and the speed of price adjustment is likely to be asymmetric with respect to cost increases and decreases. In the event of a decline in costs the price leadership analysis would imply that firms with relatively high profit margins are in a better position to delay the adjustment process, since their high profit

[5] Under the assumption that cost functions are quadratic, the higher are the disequilibrium costs relative to adjustment costs, the faster is the speed of price adjustment (see Griliches [1967]).

[6] The presence of price controls which are directed disproportionately towards large firms and concentrated industries may be an additional factor contributing to the emergence of a negative relationship between concentration and the adjustment speed.

margins allow them to take this risk. On the other hand, in the absence of interfirm differences in profitability, fierce price competition in the form of a relatively fast downward adjustment is most likely to take place in concentrated industries with high profitability. In any event to test for the degree of such an asymmetry the availability of long enough time series on price-cost decreases as well as increases is required. This asymmetry, however, is practically irrelevant for time periods characterized by cost inflation.[7]

The speed of price adjustment as a function of the production period and industrial concentration is given in equation (1).

$$(1) \qquad \lambda = f(PLA, CR)$$

where λ is the speed of price adjustment, PLA is the length of the production period and CR is an index of industrial concentration. The arguments presented so far imply that while $\partial\lambda/PLA$ is expected to have a negative sign, the sign of $\partial\lambda/\partial CR$ cannot be determined *a priori.*

The ambiguity concerning the direction of the effect of industrial concentration on the price adjustment speed is reflected on the existing empirical evidence. While Domberger [1979] in his study of the UK manufacturing found a significant positive relationship between the adjustment speed and concentration, recent similar work by Dixon [1983] on the Australian manufacturing industries indicates the existence of a negative relationship. Dixon's findings seem to provide support to Scherer's [1980] conclusion that "there is a tendency for concentrated industries to pass on, in the year they occurred, a smaller fraction of cost increases... than atomistically structured industries" (p. 356).

Thus, the explanation of this difference in the results can probably be attributed to the fact that in the above two studies concentration indices of similar magnitude are dissimilar with respect to interfirm differences in profitability (leadership effect).

In this respect it should be emphasized that various aspects of industrial behaviour, such as the degree of competition among firms and the possibility of collusive behaviour, represent unobservable elements to the outside analyst. As such the net effect of these elements together with interfirm differences in profitability cannot be captured by relatively simple indicators of industrial structure. Thus, the results obtained from formations based on (1) should be interpreted with relative caution.

III. THE METHODOLOGY OF THE EMPIRICAL INVESTIGATION

The empirical analysis is conducted on the basis of a two-step estimation procedure. The first step is concerned with the fitting of a set of price

[7] The sample period of the time series price equations used in this paper and presented in section IV is clearly dominated by cost increases.

adjustment equations to quarterly time series data and obtaining the speed of price adjustment coefficients for a sample of industries. The second step examines the effects of industrial concentration and the length of the production period on the price adjustment speed by means of a cross-section analysis.

The equilibrium price level is specified in log-linear form as a markup over unit labour and unit material costs. In an oligopoly framework the equilibrium markup is related to industrial concentration positively and to the elasticity of demand negatively.[8] On the assumption that major changes in industrial structure take a considerable time to manifest themselves, only demand conditions, as proxied by the deviation of actual output from its trend, are allowed to have an influence on the markup.[9]

Formally the equilibrium price level is defined as

$$\text{(2)} \qquad \ln P_t^* = \alpha_0 + \alpha_1(\ln y_t - \ln \bar{y}_t) + \beta_1 \ln ULC_t + \beta_2 \ln UMC_t + \eta_t$$

where P_t^* is the desired or equilibrium price level in period t, y is the actual output, $\bar{y}$ is the trend output, ULC is the unit labour cost, UMC is the unit material cost and η_t is a random error which is assumed to account for all the non-systematic and non-measurable influences. It is expected that α_1, β_1, $\beta_2 > 0$.

The derivation of the speed of price adjustment is based on the familiar partial adjustment mechanism according to which the actual proportional change in prices is some fraction of the desired proportional change

$$\text{(3)} \qquad \ln P_t - \ln P_{t-1} = \lambda(\ln P_t^* - \ln P_{t-1}); \qquad 0 \leqslant \lambda < 1$$

where λ is the speed of price adjustment which can be assumed to be constant over a period of cost and price increases.[10] Substitution of (2) into (3) yields the following estimating form[11]

$$\text{(4)} \qquad \ln P_t = \lambda\alpha_0 + \lambda\alpha_1(\ln y_t - \ln \bar{y}_t) + \lambda\beta_1 \ln ULC_t + \lambda\beta_2 \ln UMC_t + (1-\lambda)\ln P_{t-1} + \varepsilon_t$$

where $\varepsilon_t = \lambda\eta_t$ and $\eta_t \sim NID(0, \sigma^2)$.

[8] In this framework the markup over marginal costs at the industry level is equal to H/η, where H is the Herfindhal index of concentration and η is the elasticity of demand (e.g. see Hannah and Kay [1977]). Under the assumption of a Cobb-Douglas production function and upon disaggregation of marginal costs into labour and material costs, the price level can be written as a markup over unit costs. Note that it is the price level which is related to the level of excess demand via the markup and not the rate of change of prices as in the competitive price determination models.

[9] Note, however, that short-run demand fluctuations do not necessarily imply nor are they perceived by firms as elasticity changes.

[10] See section II.

[11] It is also possible to include an error term j_t in (3) in which case the error in (4) would become composite, i.e. $\varepsilon_t = j_t + \lambda\eta_t$. Under the assumption that each of these error terms is uncorrelated with its own past value and with that of the other no estimation problems arise.

Equation (4) is the basic estimating form. In order to allow for the possible delayed effect of unit cost changes on pricing behaviour due to inflexibilities commonly found in the real world, such as large scale purchases of materials and associated large stocks, wage agreements and supply contracts, the price equation was also estimated using lagged values of ULC and UMC. Similarly the excess demand proxy was also used in lagged form.

Equation (4) is estimated for the period 1963.Q1–1977.Q4 for each and every Greek manufacturing sector defined at the two-digit SIC level of aggregation. It should be noted that common practice is to approximate the notion of industrial markets by defining industrial sectors as disaggregately as possible, i.e. on the three-digit SIC sectoral level which broadly corresponds to the UK M.L.H. classification. Although data coverage on the three-digit SIC level is available on Greek manufacturing sectors for concentration indices, it is non-existent as far as the variables entering equation (4) are concerned, i.e. on prices, unit labour and unit material costs. Nonetheless, even if such information were available one would have doubts on the reliability of such disaggregate data since by the structure and size of Greek manufacturing sectors (defined at the three-digit SIC level of aggregation) the notion of the market would be non-existent since in many cases it would be identified with one or two firms.

The second step of the estimation procedure is concerned with the interindustry regression of the values of the adjustment speed coefficient (λ) on an index of industrial concentration and the production lag.

It is important to note that the estimates of λ are average values for the estimation period 1963.Q1–1977.Q4. On the other hand, an average measure of concentration for the period 1963–1977 could not be constructed due to lack of data for each and every year of this period. Hence we were obliged to use concentration indices referring to specific years. Cross-section series of concentration measures from 1969, 1970 and 1971 were alternatively employed in the regressions in the expectation that these single year measures lying in the neighbourhood of the center of the 1963–1977 period are adequate representations of the whole period. Finally, the values of the production lag which are constructed from time series data refer to the year 1970. A description of the data is given in Appendix 1.

A further point relates to the estimation method of the cross-section relationship. The basic equation to be estimated is of the form

$$(5) \qquad \lambda_i = \gamma_0 + \gamma_1 CR_i + \gamma_2 PLA_i + v_i \qquad (i = 1, 2, \ldots, 20)$$

where CR is a measure of industrial concentration, PLA is the length of the production period and v_i is an independent error term which is assumed to have a zero mean and constant variance σ_v^2. However, since λ_i are unobservable, point estimates $\hat{\lambda}_i$ obtained from (4) are used instead. These cross-section observations $\hat{\lambda}_i$ have their own variance $\text{var}(\hat{\lambda}_i)$ which are not identical across the sample of industries. Hence the estimating equation

TABLE I
TIME SERIES ESTIMATES OF PRICE EQUATIONS

Sector	*CONSTANT*	*ED* × 100	*ULC*	*UMC*	P_{t-1}	ρ	λ	*SE/SSR*	*METHOD*	R^2/h
20	0.3872	0.0496*	0.1507	0.2992	0.4658	0.3586	0.5342	0.0238	*CORC*	0.9928
	(3.03)	(2.00)	(6.15)	(5.07)	(4.80)	(2.93)	(5.50)	0.0299		2.14
21	0.0046	0.0650*	0.0843	0.2061	0.7084	—	0.2916	0.0218	OLS	0.9938
	(0.06)	(2.95)	(3.02)	(4.49)	(8.55)		(3.52)	0.0258		1.56
22	0.2058	0.0267*	0.0370	0.1024	0.8169	—	0.1831	0.0337	OLS	0.9786
	(1.78)	(1.64)	(2.56)	(4.35)	(16.09)		(3.61)	0.6122		−0.55
23	−0.0785	0.1404*	0.0492	0.1195	0.8510	0.6073	0.1490	0.0197	*CORC*	0.6073
	(0.80)	(2.87)	(0.86)	(1.81)	(8.18)	(5.82)	(1.43)	0.0206		5.82
24	−0.2019	−0.0224	−0.0460	0.0654	1.0270	—	−0.0270	0.0175	OLS	0.9970
	(4.00)	(0.83)	(1.38)	(1.31)	(21.55)		(0.57)	0.0165		0.75
25	−0.2329	0.1687	0.0194	0.1547	0.8754	—	0.1246	0.0390	OLS	0.9896
	(2.18)	(2.96)	(0.26)	(2.26)	(9.24)		(1.31)	0.0821		1.06
26	0.2857	−0.0201*	0.0731	0.2132	0.6521	—	0.3479	0.0284	OLS	0.9893
	(2.41)	(0.39)	(1.97)	(4.20)	(8.71)		(4.65)	0.0434		−0.61
27	−0.0708	0.905	0.1322	0.3060	0.5796	0.8108	0.4204	0.0380	*CORC*	0.9914
	(0.25)	(0.280)	(2.030)	(3.270)	(5.63)	(10.55)	(4.09)	0.0763		3.18
28	−0.1535	0.1301*	0.2264	0.5048	0.2794	0.6746	0.7206	0.0414	*CORC*	0.9922
	(0.84)	(1.60)	(2.610)	(7.000)	(2.95)	(6.96)	(7.62)	0.0911		2.25
29	−0.0150	0.0731*	0.0205*	0.5468	0.4345	0.6603	0.5655	0.0334	*CORC*	0.9909
	(0.08)	(1.16)	(0.380)	(7.340)	(5.77)	(6.70)	(7.51)	0.0592		3.22
30	−0.238	0.0239*	0.0954	0.1295	0.7824	0.7215	0.2176	0.0185	*CORC*	0.9959
	(0.17)	(1.10)	(2.58)	(3.42)	(10.53)	(7.94)	(2.93)	0.0181		5.88
31	0.0698	0.0465*	0.0651	0.2209	0.6974	0.7146	0.3026	0.0161	*CORC*	0.9965
	(0.54)	(1.47)	(1.68)	(4.91)	(0.952)	(7.78)	(4.13)	0.0138		2.52
32	−1.0541	0.02803	0.3895	0.3937	0.4437	0.3900	0.5564	0.1026	*CORC*	0.9836
	(3.25)	(3.90)	(3.46)	(2.14)	(2.39)	(3.12)	(3.00)	0.5575		—

Sector	CONSTANT	ED × 100	ULC	UMC	P_{t-1}	ρ	λ	SE/SSR	METHOD	R^2/h
33	−0.0883	0.0668*	0.1228*	0.1098	0.7851	0.7340	0.2149	0.0165	CORC	0.9968
	(0.62)	(1.83)	(2.26)	(3.19)	(11.78)	(8.230)	(3.220)	0.0144		3.65
34	−0.3392	0.0765*	0.0521	0.1620	0.8528	0.5550	0.1472	0.0336	CORC	0.9921
	(1.62)	(2.540)	(1.03)	(2.69)	(12.64)	(5.09)	(2.18)	0.0600		4.69
35	−0.0725	0.0383*	0.0796	0.4264	0.5114	0.8725	0.4886	0.0225	CORC	0.9971
	(0.31)	(1.16)	(2.06)	(4.68)	(4.83)	(13.60)	(4.61)	0.0268		6.72
36	−0.1854	−0.1019	0.0241	0.3071	0.7093	0.5957	0.2907	0.0232	CORC	0.9968
	(1.60)	(1.42)	(0.45)	(3.30)	(6.38)	(5.65)	(2.61)	0.0284		3.42
37	0.2228	0.0467*	0.0863*	0.2138*	0.6526	0.5075	0.3474	1.0272	CORC	0.9911
	(1.32)	(1.04)	(1.91)	(2.33)	(4.69)	(4.49)	(2.50)	0.0391		7.72
38	−0.909	0.0658*	0.10389*	0.0684	0.8485	—	0.1515	0.03341	OLS	0.9917
	(1.29)	(1.38)	(2.10)	(1.41)	(14.35)		(2.56)	0.06026		−0.68
39	0.3839	0.0163	0.0299	0.404	0.8481	—	0.1519	0.0168	OLS	0.9757
	(1.61)	(0.62)	(1.35)	(2.08)	(11.22)		(2.01)	0.0153		0.84

Notes: An asterix refers to the coefficient estimate of the lagged variable. Figures in parentheses are t-statistics, *SE* is the standard error of the regression, *SSR* is the sum of squared residuals, ρ is the first order autoregressive coefficient in *CORC* and *h* is Durbin's statistic for first order autoregressive errors obtained from the OLS estimates.

becomes

(6) $\hat{\lambda}_i = \gamma_0 + \gamma_1 CR_i + {}_2 PLA_i + w_i \qquad (i = 1, 2, \ldots, 20)$

where w_i is a composite error term with variance $\sigma^2_{w_i} = \sigma_v^2 + \text{var}(\hat{\lambda}_i)$ on the assumption that the two components of w_i are independent. Clearly the errors of (6) are heteroscedastic and the extent of heteroscedasticity depends on the relative importance of σ_v^2 and $\text{var}(\hat{\lambda}_i)$. Since OLS estimates of (6) are inefficient the cross-section relationship was estimated by the weighted least squares method (see Saxonhouse [1977]).[12]

IV. RESULTS

Equation (4) as well as its variants containing lagged values of *ULC*, *UMC* and $ED = (\ln y_t - \ln \bar{y}_t)$ were initially estimated by OLS. The results suggested the presence of serially uncorrelated error terms in only seven out of the twenty sectors. In the remaining thirteen sectors Durbin's h statistic revealed first order autocorrelation in the residuals. One possible source of misspecification may arise from the exclusion of unit capital cost in the estimating equation (4). In the absence of available data, unit capital cost has been assumed to be constant throughout the period of examination. Serially correlated errors may be the result of autocorrelation in unit capital cost. The dynamics of the price equations are another possible cause of misspecification. It is possible that equations with a more complicated dynamic structure provide a better explanation of the data generation process at least for some sectors. After all, the requirement that the same specification yields equally satisfactory results across twenty industries with a variety of characteristics is rather stringent. It must be pointed out, however, that the purpose of the first stage estimation is not the specification of the "true" model, but of a model that explains adequately the available data. In view of these considerations we proceeded by estimating the equations with serially correlated errors by using *CORC* as a convenient method, without any further search for misspecification, on the assumption that it eliminates serial correlation and at the same time provides relatively reliable estimates of the speed of price adjustment. In some equations the use of one or more lagged cost or excess demand variables improved the overall estimate of the equation. The results for the 20 two-digit SIC sectors are reported in Table I.

[12] This is equivalent to the GLS estimation of equation (6) which exploits the information contained in the variance–covariance matrix $(\sigma_v^2 + \text{var}(\hat{\lambda}_i) I_{20}$. However, it does not exploit the covariance of the coefficient estimates of the time series regressions. Domberger [1979] used the OLS method to estimate the effect of CR_i on λ_i. Winters [1981] criticized Domberger for not taking into account the heteroscedasticity in the errors. Domberger [1983] showed that the use of the appropriate weighted least squares method provided regression estimates which were very close to his OLS estimates. Dixon [1983] obtained his results by the weighted least squares method, but instead of using $(\sigma_v^2 + \text{var}(\hat{\lambda}_i))^{1/2}$ as weights he used $(\text{var}(\hat{\lambda}_i))^{1/2}$.

TABLE II

WEIGHTED LEAST SQUARES ESTIMATES OF EQUATIONS EXPLAINING THE PARTIAL ADJUSTMENT COEFFICIENT (NINETEEN INDUSTRIES SAMPLE)

Eq.	*Weight*	$CR2_{69}$	$CR4_{69}$	$CR2_{70}$	$CR4_{70}$	$CR2_{71}$	$CR4_{71}$	*PLA*	*SE*	*SSR*	*K*
E1	0.5741	−0.0040						−0.0678	0.9074	13.1733	7.15
	(5.42)	(1.63)						(1.74)			
E2	0.5736		−0.0027					−0.0692	0.9117	13.2997	6.56
	(5.28)		(1.47)					(1.76)			
E3	0.5691			−0.0049				−0.0590	0.9102	13.2537	7.99
	(5.59)			(1.83)				(1.51)			
E4	0.583692				−0.0037			−0.0601	0.9056	13.1212	8.57
	(5.69)				(1.96)			(1.57)			
E5	0.5874					−0.0043		−0.0721	0.9104	13.2628	6.93
	(5.31)					(1.57)		(1.87)			
E6	0.5953						−0.0031	−0.0734	0.9103	13.2576	6.82
	(5.23)						(1.54)	(1.90)			

Notes: See notes to Table I. K is the Wald test of H_0 that the coefficients of CR and PLA are jointly zero ($R\beta - r = 0$) against H_1 that they are different from zero ($R\beta - r \neq 0$)

$$K = (Rb-r)'R(X'\Omega X)^{-1}(Rb-r)/s^2 \sim \chi_2^2 \quad \text{approximately,}$$

where Ω is a diagonal $N \times N$ matrix with typical ii element $\hat{\sigma}_v^2 + \text{var}(\hat{\lambda}_i)$ and $\hat{\sigma}_v^2$ is $e'eN^{-1}$ where e is the vector of OLS residuals of a typical cross-section equation and X the matrix of observations of the explanatory variables. The critical value of χ_2^2 at the 0.05 level is 5.99.

In all equations the coefficient estimates of the cost variables have the correct sign. The unit material cost variable seems to perform better than the unit labour cost variable in terms of the precision of the estimates. The excess demand proxy performs well in a limited number of equations only. However, in those equations where the coefficient estimate has a wrong sign it is insignificant at the 0.1 level.[13] The estimates of λ display considerable variability. In all equations they are significantly less than unity. The value of λ for sector 24 is negative but not significantly different from zero. The overall performance of the price equations is reasonably good with the exception of sector 24. In fact none of the coefficient estimates in the price equation for sector 24 is well defined and the matrices of simple and multiple correlation coefficients of the explanatory variables indicate signs of serious multicollinearity. In view of this, the price equation for sector 24 was considered unacceptable and was excluded from the cross-section sample. For sectors 23 and 25 the estimate of λ is greater than zero at the 0.1 significance level only. Given that a zero value of λ implies the implausible property of a complete price rigidity, it was decided to run the regressions of λ on *PLA* and *CR* using both the nineteen (i.e. excluding sector 23) and the seventeen (i.e. excluding sectors 23, 24 and 25) industry samples.

With respect to the performance of the price equations it should be pointed out that the hypothesis of the equilibrium price level, being a markup over unit labour and unit material costs, implies the restriction $\beta_1 + \beta_2 = 1$ on the coefficients of equation (2). The cost elasticities of the equilibrium price level $\hat{\beta}(= \hat{\beta}_1 + \hat{\beta}_2)$ implied by the estimates of Table I together with their asymptotic standard errors are given in Appendix 2. For all the nineteen industries the implied cost elasticities are not significantly different from unity at the 0.1 level.

The weighted least squares estimates of the equations relating the speed of price adjustment to concentration and the length of the production period over the nineteen industry sample are presented in Table II. Two alternative measures of concentration were used: the 4-firm concentration ratio, *CR*4, and the 2-firm concentration ratio, *CR*2. The regressions were estimated using the 1969, 1970 and 1971 values of the concentration measures.[14] In

[13] In view of the poor performance of the excess demand variable, a dummy variable taking the value of 1 in periods of demand expansion and a value of 0 in periods of contraction was also experimented with as an alternative measure of demand conditions. This procedure did not alter the conclusions about the performance of the demand variable and had very little effect on coefficients of the cost variables presented in Table I. Thus, the estimates suggest that for the great majority of the industries, short-run demand fluctuations have no effect on prices.

[14] Since concentration measures refer to domestic production, an examination of the possible role of foreign suppliers in domestic markets and of exportation of domestic production was attempted in equation (5) by means of including two further explanatory variables: *IMP* defined as imports by sector over sales and *EXP* defined as exports by sector over sales. However, the inclusion of the above variables yielded highly insignificant estimates contrary to Dixon's [1983] findings. Moreover, the coefficient estimates of *PLA* and *CR* and the constant term took values almost identical to those presented in Tables II and III.

TABLE III

WEIGHTED LEAST SQUARES ESTIMATES OF EQUATIONS EXPLAINING THE PARTIAL ADJUSTMENT COEFFICIENT (SEVENTEEN INDUSTRIES SAMPLE)

Eq.	*Weight*	$CR2_{69}$	$CR4_{69}$	$CR2_{70}$	$CR4_{70}$	$CR2_{71}$	$CR4_{71}$	*PLA*	*SE*	*SSE*	*K*
E1	0.6301	−0.0046						−0.0749	0.9043	11.4477	10.99
	(6.38)	(2.04)						(2.11)			
E2	0.6356		−0.0033					−0.0760	0.9073	11.5245	10.50
	(6.26)		(1.95)					(2.19)			
E3	0.6253			−0.0056				−0.0657	0.9572	11.5230	11.44
	(6.62)			(2.30)				(1.86)			
E4	0.6429				−0.0043			−0.0668	0.8997	11.3314	13.70
	(6.81)				(2.50)			(1.94)			
E5	0.6492					−0.0051		−0.0800	0.9061	11.4954	10.87
	(6.28)					(2.02)		(2.27)			
E6	0.6635						−0.0038	−0.0812	0.9040	11.4431	11.13
	(6.27)						(2.07)	(2.32)			

Notes: See notes to Table II. The critical value of a χ_2^2 variate at the 0.01 level is 9.21.

equations E1, E2, E5 and E6 of Table II the effects of *PLA* are significantly less than zero at the 0.05 level, but the effects of concentration are not significantly different from zero. In equations E3 and E4 of Table II, however, one-tail t-tests for negative effects of *PLA* are significant at the 0.1 level only. Furthermore, since two-tail t-tests for the significance of the coefficients of concentration are also significant at the 0.1 level, with the t-test in E4 bordering on the 0.05 level, it would seem inappropriate to exclude the concentration variables which in any case are those with the relatively more "significant" coefficients. In addition, Wald tests (*K*) of the null hypothesis that *CR* and *PLA* are jointly zero against the alternative that they are different from zero, which are approximately distributed as χ_2^2 in small samples, are significant at the 0.05 level and this is also the case with equations E1, E2, E5 and E6.

The cross-section results for the seventeen industry sample are given in Table III. The coefficient estimates of Table III have the same signs as those of Table II but are larger in magnitude. In all equations of Table III the coefficients of *PLA* are significantly less than zero at the 0.05 level. Two-tail t-tests for the significance of the coefficients of *CR* are also significant at the 0.05 in all equations with the exception of E2 where the t-statistic is bordering on significance. Wald tests (*K*) indicate that in all six equations of Table III the estimates of *CR* and *PLA* are now jointly significant at the 0.01 level.

It is possible that the omission of sectors 23 and 25 from the sample biases the results thus giving rise to stronger negative effects and especially for *CR*. This would be particularly the case if weighted λ and *CR* had both low values in relation to their sample means. Yet this does not appear to be the case in our sample, since for sector 23 both the variables lie below their sample means, whereas for sector 24 weighted λ and *CR* lie above and below their sample means respectively.

V. CONCLUSIONS

This paper has argued that the influence of industrial structure upon the speed at which prices adjust to changes in costs can be decomposed into two opposing in nature effects; the leadership effect and the industry profitability effect. Unless one can determine the relative significance of these factors, the size of the coefficient of a concentration index in an equation explaining price adjustment speed is not *a priori* predictable. Furthermore, such a decomposition of the notion of concentration that encompasses both the above factors can provide an explanation of the conflicting empirical evidence that exists on the subject. Application of the relationship under examination to the data drawn from the two-digit SIC sectors of Greece suggests that both the length of the production period and industrial concentration exert negative effects on the adjustment speed. Evidently short-run price rigidities are prolonged in sectors with high industrial concentration and longer production processes.

ACCEPTED SEPTEMBER 1987

ARAKEL BEDROSSIAN,
University of York,
Department of Economics,
Heslington,
York YO1 5DD
UK.

DEMETRIOS MOSCHOS,
Bank of Greece,
Economic Research Department,
Athens 102 50,
Greece.

APPENDIX 1

The data required for the generation of the variables used in this study are obtained from quite a number of published sources. Moreover the construction of variables like *ULC*, *UMC* and *PLA* involves an elaborate generation procedure, the description of which is beyond the scope of this paper. An extensive summary of this procedure can be found in Bedrossian [1986].

Time series variables referring to equation (4) are approximated as follows:

P_t: Wholesale price indices are used; see *Monthly Statistical Bulletin*, various issues, published by the National Statistical Service of Greece (NSSG).

ULC_t: Unit labour cost is defined as

$$ULC = P_W \cdot L \cdot \frac{1}{y}$$

where P_W is the wage rate, L is employment and y is output. P_W is a composite index including data on wages and salaries obtained from *Labour Statistics*, published quarterly by NSSG. Employment is measured by man-hours; data on employment and hours are obtained from *Labour Statistics*. Output data are available from the *Annual Industrial Surveys*. The generation of quarterly output figures is described in Bedrossian [1986].

UMC_t: Unit material cost is defined as

$$UMC = P_M \cdot M \cdot \frac{1}{y}$$

where P_M is a material price index and M is the volume of materials. Both variables are approximated by using information from *Input–Output Tables of the Greek Economy 1958–1971*, published by the Center of Planning and Economic Research.

For the interested reader, the above time series data are available from the authors upon request.

Cross-section variables referring to equation (5) are approximated as follows:

CR_i: is the two or four firm concentration ratio based on employment data. Firm employment data for the two and four larger companies are obtained from ICAP publications for the years 1969, 1970, 1971. Total sectoral employment data for those years are obtained from the *Annual Industrial Surveys*.

PLA_i: A methodology for the construction of PLA can be found in Carlson [1973] and Coutts *et al.* [1978]. The generation of data required for the calculation of PLA is described in Bedrossian [1986]. The data on PLA (referring to quarters) and data on $CR_2(\times 100)$ and $CR_4(\times 100)$ for the two-digit SIC Manufacturing Industries of Greece are available from the authors on request.

APPENDIX 2

The derivation of the asymptotic standard errors of the cost elasticities of the equilibrium price levels can be briefly described as follows. Let $\delta_1 = \lambda\beta_1, \delta_2 = \lambda\beta_2$ and $\delta_3 = 1-\lambda$ be the coefficients of $\ln ULC$, $\ln UMC$ and $\ln P_{t-1}$ in equation (4). The cost elasticity of the equilibrium price level is given by $\beta = (\delta_1+\delta_2)/(1-\delta_3) = g(\delta_1, \delta_2, \delta_3)$. An estimate of β can be obtained as $\hat{\beta} = (\hat{\delta}_1+\hat{\delta}_2)/(1-\hat{\delta}_3)$. The asymptotic variance of $\hat{\beta}$ can be approximated by $\sigma_{v\beta^2} = \Phi' V \Phi$ where

$$\Phi' = \left(\frac{\partial g}{\partial \delta_1}, \frac{\partial g}{\partial \delta_2}, \frac{\partial g}{\partial \delta_3}\right) = (1/(1-\delta_3), 1/(1-\delta_3), -(\delta_1+\delta_2)/(1-\delta_3)^2)$$

and V is the asymptotic variance–covariance matrix of the vector $(\hat{\delta}_1, \hat{\delta}_2, \hat{\delta}_3)$. By replacing the unknowns $\delta_1, \delta_2, \delta_3$ by their estimates $\hat{\delta}_1$, $\hat{\delta}_2$ and $\hat{\delta}_3$ we obtain an estimate of Φ'. The estimate of V is given by the regression results of equation (4). We can therefore obtain estimates of $\Phi' V \Phi$, $\hat{\sigma}_{v\beta^2}$. The test statistic for testing $H_0: \beta_1+\beta_2 = 1$ against $H_1: \beta_1+\beta_2 \neq 1$ is $(\hat{\beta}-1)/\hat{\sigma}_\beta$ which is asymptotically distributed on $N(0, 1)$ on H_0. The implied cost elasticities ($\hat{\beta}$), together with their asymptotic standard errors, are given in Table A.1.

TABLE A.1
IMPLIED COST ELASTICITIES ($\hat{\beta}$) OF TIME SERIES PRICE EQUATIONS

	Industrial Sector	$\hat{\beta}$*(asym.S.E.)*	*t-stat of* $1-\hat{\beta}$
20	Food preparation industries	0.84(0.292)	0.548
21	Beverage industries	1.00(0.519)	0.000
22	Tobacco manufactures	0.76(0.379)	0.633
23	Textiles	1.13(2.239)	0.058
24	Footwear and clothing	—	—
25	Wood and cork industries	1.40(1.925)	0.208
26	Furniture and fixture	0.83(0.330)	0.515
27	Paper and pulp industries	1.04(0.513)	0.078
28	Printing and publishing	1.01(0.263)	0.038
29	Leather and fur industries	1.00(0.260)	0.000
30	Rubber and plastics	1.03(0.656)	0.046
31	Chemical industries	0.95(0.465)	0.108
32	Petroleum and coal refining	1.41(0.869)	0.472
33	Non-metallic mineral products	1.08(0.645)	0.124
34	Basic metal industries	1.45(1.230)	0.366
35	Fabricated metals except machinery	1.04(0.454)	0.088
36	Machinery except electrical	1.14(0.857)	0.163
37	Electrical machinery	0.86(0.667)	0.210
38	Transport equipment industries	1.14(0.772)	0.181
39	Miscellaneous industries	0.46(0.400)	1.350

REFERENCES

ARROW, K., 1959, 'Towards a Theory of Price Adjustment' in Abramovitz, M. (ed.), *The Allocation of Economic Resources* (Stanford University Press, Stanford).

BEDROSSIAN, A., 1986, *An Econometric Analysis of the Price Determination Process in the Greek Manufacturing Industries, 1963–1977*, unpublished Ph.D. thesis, University of York.

CARLSON, J. A., 1973, 'The Production Lag', *American Economic Review*, 63, pp. 73–86.

COUTTS, K., GODLEY, W. and NORDHAUS, W., 1978, *Industrial Pricing in the United Kingdom* (Cambridge University Press, London).

DIXON, R., 1983, 'Industry Structure and the Speed of Price-Adjustment', *Journal of Industrial Economics*, 31, pp. 25–37.

DOMBERGER, S., 1979, 'Price Adjustment and Market Structure', *Economic Journal*, 89, March 1979, pp. 96–108.

DOMBERGER, S., 1980, 'Price Dynamics and Industrial Structure in the U.K.: An Input–Output Analysis', *Manchester School*, 48, pp. 284–306.

DOMBERGER, S., 1982, 'Industrial Structure and the Inflationary Process', in M. S. ARTIS, C. S. GREEN, D. LESLIE and G. W. SMITH (eds.), *Demand Management, Supply Constraints and Inflation* (Manchester University Press, Manchester).

DOMBERGER, S., 1983, *Industrial Structure, Pricing and Inflation* (Martin Robertson, Oxford).

ECKSTEIN, O. and FROMM, G., 1968, 'The Price Equation', *American Economic Review*, 58, pp. 1159–1183.

GODLEY, W. and NORDHAUS, W., 1972, 'Pricing in the Trade Cycle', *Economic Journal*, 82, pp. 853–882.

GRILICHES, Z., 1967, 'Distributed Lags: A Survey', *Econometrica*, 35, pp. 16–49.

HANNAH, L. and KAY, S. A., 1977, *Concentration in Modern Industry: Theory Measurement and the U.K. Experience* (The Macmillan Press, London).

HOLTHAUSEN, D. M., 1978, 'Kinky Demand, Risk Aversion and Price Leadership', *International Economic Review*, 20, pp. 341–348.

MEANS, G. C., 1935, *Industrial Prices and their Relative Inflexibility*, US Senate Document 13, 74th Congress, 1st Session, Washington.

MCFETRIDGE, D. C., 1973, 'The Determinants of Pricing Behaviour: A study of the Canadian Cotton Textile Industry', *Journal of Industrial Economics*, 21, pp. 141–151.

OKUN, A., 1981, *Prices and Quantities: A Macroeconomic Analysis* (Basil Blackwell, Oxford).

SAXONHOUSE, G. R., 1977, 'Regressions from Samples Having Different Characteristics', *Review of Economics and Statistics*, 59, pp. 234–237.

SCHERER, F. M., 1980, *Industrial Market Structure and Economic Performance* (Rand McNally, Chicago, Second Edition).

SHAHLING, L., 1977, 'Price Behaviour in U.S. Manufacturing: An Empirical Analysis of the Speed of Adjustment', *American Economic Review*, 67, pp. 911–924.

SHINJO, K., 1977, 'Business Pricing Policies and Inflation: The Japanese Case', *Review of Economics and Statistics*, 59, pp. 447–455.

STIGLER, G. S., 1964, 'A Theory of Oligopoly', *Journal of Political Economy*, 72, pp. 44–61.

THEIL, H., 1954, *Linear Aggregation of Economic Relations* (North-Holland, Amsterdam).

WINTERS, A. L., 1981, 'Price Adjustment and Market Structure: A Comment', *Economic Journal*, 91, pp. 1026–1030.

THE JOURNAL OF INDUSTRIAL ECONOMICS 0022-1821 $2.00
Volume XXXVI June 1988 No. 4

ADJUSTMENT COSTS, CONCENTRATION AND PRICE BEHAVIOUR*

VICTOR GINSBURGH AND PHILIPPE MICHEL

The effect of concentration on price stickiness is studied, by assuming quadratic and more general forms of adjustment costs. We analyze and characterize the two contradictory conclusions which emerge from empirical studies.

THE ASSUMPTION that there exists a relation between the degree of concentration in an industry and the speed at which prices adjust to production costs has been the topic of a large number of (mainly empirical) papers. The various (contradictory) results can be summarized as follows:

(a) The more concentrated the industry, the *more* rapidly will cost variations be transmitted into prices. The rationale for this, as argued by Stigler [1964] is that secret cutting of prices is easier to detect by others when there are few firms, and will thus be avoided; for the same reason, in concentrated industries, firms will avoid lagging prices behind costs. Empirical evidence of this link between price sluggishness and concentration is given by Domberger [1981], [1983].

(b) The more concentrated the industry, the *less* rapidly will cost variations be transmitted into prices. Reasons for this behaviour have been given (i) by Sweezy [1939]—an oligopolist expects his competitors to react differently to a decrease and to an increase of his price; while a decrease will be followed, an increase will not; this leads to a discontinuity in the marginal revenue curve and variations in the cost curve will not be passed onto prices; (ii) by Eichner [1973]—concentrated industries are often associated with increasing returns to scale and hence large irreversible investments, which induce firms to peg their prices on long run objectives rather than follow short run cost fluctuations; (iii) by Phlips [1980], [1983]—intertemporal price discrimination leads to markup pricing, but the markup is smaller in concentrated industries than in others; and (iv) by Ross and Wachter [1975]—in oligopolistic industries, prices do not react to costs continuously, but in discrete steps. Empirical evidence can be found e.g. in Phlips [1973], Dixon [1983], Encaoua [1983], Encaoua and Geroski [1984].

In this paper, we consider an oligopolistic industry in which firms bear

* We are largely indebted to S. Domberger who has pointed out to us the particularity of the assumption of quadratic adjustment costs. The first author acknowledges support from the Centre National de la Recherche Scientifique, Paris and Action de Recherches Concertées of the Belgian Government under contract 84-89/65.

adjustment costs on output changes.[1] We first study the simple case of quadratic adjustment costs which leads to conclusion (b) that concentration decreases the speed of adjustment of prices. We next consider more general forms of adjustment costs and show that, under reasonable assumptions, both empirical observations (a) and (b) can be sustained.

A simple linear quadratic model

There are n firms in the industry and, at time t, each firm chooses its output q_{it} in order to maximize[2] its profit π_{it}, with

$$\pi_{it} = q_{it}p_t(q_t) - \gamma_i q_{it} - c_i(q_{it}, q_{i,t-1})$$

In this expression, $p_t(q_t)$ is the industry demand curve with

$$q_t = \sum_i q_{it},$$

γ_i is the marginal production cost and $c_i(q_{it}, q_{i,t-1})$ is a cost which originates from changes in the output level.

Let us approximate the industry demand curve by:

$$p_t(q_t) = \alpha - \beta q_t; \qquad \beta > 0$$

and assume that adjustment costs are quadratic and identical for all firms:

$$c_i(q_{it}, q_{i,t-1}) = \frac{c}{2}(q_{it} - q_{i,t-1})^2$$

In the Cournot approach, each firm i is a quantity setter; the first order condition leads to

$$\frac{\partial \pi_{it}}{\partial q_{it}} = \alpha - \beta q_t - 2\beta q_{it} - \gamma_i - c(q_{it} - q_{i,t-1}) = 0$$

Aggregating over firms and solving for q_t leads to

$$q_t = \lambda q_{t-1} + \mu\left(\alpha - \frac{\sum \gamma_i}{n}\right)$$

where $\lambda = c/((n+2)\beta + c)$ and $\mu = n/((n+2)\beta + c)$.

Alternatively, in terms of the industry price level, we have:

$$p_t = \lambda p_{t-1} + \xi(2\alpha + \sum \gamma_i) \qquad (1)$$

where $\xi = \beta/((n+2)\beta + c)$.

[1] This leads to the same conclusion as the usual assumption of adjustment costs on prices, but seems a more reasonable formulation, since it can be interpreted in terms of capacity adjustment costs.

[2] To keep things simple, we maximize the static profit function. Intertemporal optimization of profits leads to the same conclusions. See Ginsburgh, Michel and Moes [1987].

In (1), costs are transmitted into prices ($\xi > 0$) but there is a lag as long as $\lambda > 0$. Clearly, a positive adjustment cost c implies $0 < \lambda < 1$ for finite n. Notice also that $\partial\lambda/\partial n < 0$ which shows that adjustment of prices to costs will be faster the larger the number of firms in the industry. If the industry is competitive, even in the presence of output adjustment costs, λ tends to 0 when n becomes large and prices will instantaneously react to the average marginal cost (the limit of $\xi \sum \gamma_i$ tends to $\bar{\gamma} = \sum \gamma_i/n$).

Another assumption on adjustment costs

Quadratic costs are largely responsible for the previous conclusion. To see this, we consider a cost function $c(q_{it}, q_{i,t-1})$ which is convex and homogeneous of degree θ.

In order to aggregate over firms the first order conditions, we assume that firms are identical, so that $q_{it} = q_t/n$ and $\gamma_i = \gamma$. Then,

$$\alpha - \beta q_t - 2\beta \frac{q_t}{n} - \gamma - c_1\left(\frac{q_t}{n}, \frac{q_{t-1}}{n}\right) = 0$$

where c_1 is the derivative of $c(.,.)$ with respect to the first argument. Since c is homogeneous of degree θ, c_1 is homogeneous of degree $\theta - 1$, and

$$c_1\left(\frac{q_t}{n}, \frac{q_{t-1}}{n}\right) = n^{1-\theta} c_1(q_t, q_{t-1})$$

Substituting $(\alpha - p_t)/\beta$ for q_t, we get

$$F(p_t, p_{t-1}) = -\frac{2\alpha}{n} + \frac{n+2}{n} p_t - \gamma - c_1\left(\frac{\alpha - p_t}{\beta}, \frac{\alpha - p_{t-1}}{\beta}\right) = 0$$

Hence,

$$\lambda = \frac{dp_t}{dp_{t-1}} = -\frac{\partial F}{\partial p_{t-1}} \bigg/ \frac{\partial F}{\partial p_t}$$

will give us an expression for inertia:

$$\lambda = \frac{-c_{12}}{\beta(n+2)n^{\theta-2} + c_{11}}$$

where c_{11} and c_{12} are the partial derivatives of c_1. Convexity of c and the assumption that $c_{12} < 0$ ensure $\lambda > 0$.

The marginal effect

$$\frac{d\lambda}{dn} = \frac{-\beta c_{12}}{[\beta(n+2)n^{\theta-2} + c_{11}]^2} [(1-\theta)n^{\theta-2} + 2(2-\theta)n^{\theta-3}]$$

may be positive or negative. It is always positive if $\theta \leqslant 1$, i.e. if there are economies of scale in adjustment costs. It is always negative if $\theta \geqslant 2$, i.e. in the case of large diseconomies of scale. For $1 < \theta < 2$,

$$\frac{d\lambda}{dn} \lesseqgtr 0 \Leftrightarrow n \lesseqgtr \frac{2(2-\theta)}{\theta-1}$$

When the number of firms goes to infinity, three cases have to be distinguished:
(1) Economies of scale in adjustment costs ($\theta \leqslant 1$) imply

$$\lim_{n \to \infty} \lambda = \frac{-c_{12}}{c_{11}} > 0 \quad \text{and} \quad \frac{d\lambda}{dn} > 0$$

so that even under perfect competition, prices do not adjust instantaneously to costs and there is a negative effect of concentration on price inertia.
(2) Large diseconomies of scale in adjustment costs ($\theta \geqslant 2$) imply

$$\lim_{n \to \infty} \lambda = 0 \quad \text{and} \quad \frac{d\lambda}{dn} < 0$$

There is no price stickiness if markets are perfect, and a positive effect of concentration on price inertia.
(3) Small diseconomies of scale ($1 < \theta < 2$) lead to

$$\lim_{n \to \infty} \lambda = 0$$

while the effect of concentration on inertia changes with the number of firms n; the effect is negative for small n and positive for large n.

Very little, if anything, is known about the costs which firms bear when they adjust their output. The assumption of quadratic costs is probably the most common. It leads, as we have seen, to rather specific results. However, for functions close to the quadratic (i.e. θ close to 2) it is interesting to note that the conclusions are not only theoretically satisfactory (since prices will instantaneously adjust to costs in a competitive environment) but, also, that they are consistent with apparently contradictory empirical findings. They show that the effects depend on the number of firms in an industry, suggesting the possibility of a test using cross country industry data.

VICTOR GINSBURGH,
CEME,
University of Brussels,
50 Avenue F. Roosevelt,
1050 Brussels,
Belgium; [and *CORE*].

ACCEPTED JULY 1987

PHILIPPE MICHEL,
University of Paris I,
12 Place du Panthéon,
75231 Paris Cedex 01,
France.

REFERENCES

DIXON, R., 1983, 'Industry Structure and the Speed of Price Adjustment', *The Journal of Industrial Economics*, 32, pp. 25–37.

DOMBERGER, S., 1981, 'Price Adjustment and Market Structure: A Reply', *The Economic Journal*, 89, pp. 96–108.

DOMBERGER, S., 1983, *Industrial Structure, Pricing and Inflation* (M. Robertson, Oxford).

EICHNER, A. S., 1973, 'A Theory of the Markup Under Oligopoly', *The Economic Journal*, 83, pp. 1184–1200.

ENCAOUA, D., 1983, 'Dynamique des Prix et Structure Industrielle: Une Analyse Théorique et Econométrique', Document de Travail OECD.

ENCAOUA, D. and GEROSKI, P., 1984, 'Price Dynamics and Competition in Five OECD Countries', Université de Paris I.

GINSBURGH, V., MICHEL, PH. and MOES, PH., 1987, 'Quantity Dynamics vs. Price Dynamics', manuscript.

PHLIPS, L., 1973, 'Illusions in Testing for Administered Prices: a Reply', *The Journal of Industrial Economics*, 21, pp. 196–199.

PHLIPS, L., 1980, 'Intertemporal Price Discrimination and Sticky Prices', *Quarterly Journal of Economics*, 94, pp. 525–542.

PHLIPS, L., 1983, *The Economics of Price Discrimination* (Cambridge University Press, Cambridge).

ROSS, S. A. and WACHTER, M. L., 1975, 'Pricing and Timing Decisions in Oligopoly Industries', *Quarterly Journal of Economics*, 89, pp. 115–137.

STIGLER, G. J., 1964, 'A Theory of Oligopoly', *Journal of Political Economy*, 72, pp. 44–61.

SWEEZY, P., 1939, 'Demand Under Conditions of Oligopoly', *Journal of Political Economy*, 47, 568–573.

EUROPEAN ASSOCIATION
FOR
RESEARCH IN INDUSTRIAL ECONOMICS

15th Annual Conference
August 31–September 2, 1988

ANNOUNCEMENT

The fifteenth Annual Conference of EARIE, the European Association for Research in Industrial Economics, will be held on 31 August–2 September 1988 at the Woudestein Campus, Erasmus University, Rotterdam, The Netherlands.

All mail and enquiries should be directed to:

Hans Schenk,
GRASP/Rotterdam School of Management,
Erasmus University Rotterdam,
PO Box 1738,
3000 DR Rotterdam,
The Netherlands.
Tel. (0)10.4082005/4081386; Fax (0)10.4520204

THE JOURNAL OF INDUSTRIAL ECONOMICS

Published first in October 1952, the *Journal* has a very wide international circulation, and has established itself as the leading journal in the field of industrial economics. It was founded to promote the analysis of modern industry, particularly the behaviour of firms, and the functioning of markets. More specifically it seeks to bring the tools of modern economic analysis to bear on the analysis of real problems of industrial economies.

Contributions are welcomed covering all the major areas of industrial economics. One such area is the relationship between market structure and market behaviour in the areas of pricing, product differentiation, advertising and the dissemination of information and R&D. Another area focuses more directly on the firm, its objectives, finance, investment and growth. A third area comprises the background environment within which industrial firms operate: the changing structure of industry, public policy on monopoly and restrictive trade practices, regulation, fiscal and monetary policies as they affect firms, and underlying changes in productivity and international competitiveness.

The *Journal* has a tradition of publishing a blend of theory and evidence. Theoretical discussion is welcomed provided that the more abstract theory includes sufficient introduction and other explanation to convey the significance of the material to the general reader who wants to decide whether to follow the analysis through. Empirical analysis, and especially econometric analysis, should include an explanation of the data sources used, of the methods applied and of the underlying theoretical basis of the study. The *Journal* has a particular tradition of case studies of firms and industries, which the Editors would wish to continue. However, contributors of such studies are asked to remember that a study will be of interest to the international readership of the *Journal* only if it makes a particular contribution to the methodology of such studies, or if the empirical results are exceptionally interesting.

Alongside articles of more normal length, the Editors are ready to publish shorter notes, especially where these give interim results of important research studies, or where they report significant new empirical results. Books are not reviewed, but substantial review articles will be considered for publication.

Information for Contributors

Submissions (*three* copies are required) should be well written, clearly typed and carefully prepared for the printer in accordance with the *Journal*'s 'Notes for Contributors' (*Journal of Industrial Economics*, 35 (March 1987), pp. 359–363), copies of which may be obtained from the General Editor. An Abstract, conforming to the requirements of *The Journal of Economic Literature* and not exceeding 100 words, must accompany each submission.

Typescripts from North America should be sent to the North American Editor, Journal of Industrial Economics, Department of Public Policy and Management, The Wharton School, University of Pennsylvania, Philadelphia 19104, USA.

Typescripts from *all* other countries should be sent to the General Editor, Journal of Industrial Economics, Economics Research Centre, School of Economic and Social Studies, University of East Anglia, Norwich NR4 7TJ, UK.

Information for Subscribers

The *Journal* is published four times a year, in September, December, March and June, by Basil Blackwell Ltd., 108 Cowley Road, Oxford OX4 1JF, UK, *or* PO Box 1320, Murray Hill Station, NY 10156, USA.

	UK	Overseas	USA
Institutions	£34.00	£43.00	$76.00
Individuals	£17.00	£22.00	$35.00
Students	£8.00	£10.00	$15.00

The reduced rates will be allowed to any individual student for a maximum period of three years.

CONTRIBUTORS TO THE ISSUE

CHRISTOPHER BLISS: Nuffield College, University of Oxford, UK.
RONALD BEWLEY: University of New South Wales, Australia.
DENZIL G. FIEBIG: University of Sydney, Australia.
DAVID BESANKO: Indiana University, USA.
SHABTAI DONNENFELD: Tel-Aviv University, Israel.
LAWRENCE J. WHITE: New York University, USA.
X. MARTINEZ-GIRALT: CORE, Louvain-la-Neuve, Belgium.
D. J. NEVEN: INSEAD, Fontainebleau, France, and Associate Editor of this *Journal*.
J. C. H. JONES: University of Victoria, Canada.
D. G. FERGUSON: University of Victoria, Canada.
ARAKEL BEDROSSIAN: University of York, UK.
DEMETRIOS MOSCHOS: Bank of Greece, Athens, Greece.
VICTOR GINSBURGH: CEME, University of Brussels, Belgium.
PHILIPPE MICHEL: University of Paris, France.

US Mailing: Second class postage paid at New York. Postmaster: Send address corrections to: Journal of Industrial Economics, c/o Expediters of the Printed Word Ltd., 515 Madison Avenue, New York, NY 10022 (US Mailing Agent).

Reprints of Back Volumes: Volumes 1–28 of the *Journal* are available (in complete volumes only) from the Kraus Reprint Corporation, Route 100, Millwood, New York 10546, USA. More recent back issues are available from the publisher at the current single issue price.

Microfilm: An agreement for the supply of microfilm copies from Volume 1 onwards has been made with University Microfilms International, Department PR, 30–32 Mortimer Street, London W1N 7RA, England, or 300 North Zeeb Road, Ann Arbor, Michigan 48106, USA.

Set in Monophoto Times by Advanced Filmsetters (Glasgow) Ltd
Printed and Bound in Great Britain by Whitstable Litho, Kent